The Black-Tailed
Prairie Dog

Wildlife Behavior and Ecology
George B. Schaller, Editor

John L. Hoogland

The Black-Tailed
Prairie Dog

Social Life of a Burrowing Mammal

The University of Chicago Press
Chicago and London

John L. Hoogland is associate professor of biology at the
University of Maryland's Appalachian Environmental Laboratory.

The University of Chicago Press, Chicago 60637
The University of Chicago Press, Ltd., London
© 1995 by The University of Chicago
All rights reserved. Published 1995
Printed in the United States of America
04 03 02 01 00 99 98 97 96 95   1 2 3 4 5
ISBN: 0-226-35117-3 (cloth)
0-226-35118-1 (paper)

Library of Congress Cataloging-in-Publication Data

Hoogland, John L.
    The black-tailed prairie dog : social life of a burrowing mammal /
John L. Hoogland
        p.   cm. — (Wildlife behavior and ecology)
    Includes bibliographical references (p.   ) and index.
    1. Cynomys ludovicianus—Behavior. 2. Social behavior in animals.
3. Cynomys ludovicianus—Reproduction. I. Title. II. Series.
QL737.R68H65   1995
599.32'32—dc20   94–13900
                                                                    CIP

The paper used in this publication meets the minimum requirements of the
American National Standard for Information Sciences—Permanence of Paper
for Printed Library Materials, ANSI Z39.48-1984.
This book is printed on acid-free paper.

I dedicate this book to

Richard D. Alexander, whose standard of
excellence I am always pursuing

and to

My wife (Judy) and my children (Mark, Simon,
Margaret, and Alexander), who help with every
step of the pursuit

Photo by Leonard Rue Enterprises

Contents

Preface   xiii

Chapter 1. Prairie Dogs and Coloniality   **1**

Prairie Dogs as Social Animals   1
The Evolution of Coloniality   2

Chapter 2. Taxonomy and Natural History   **7**

Taxonomy   7
Natural History   13
Prairie Dogs and People   20

Chapter 3. Burrows   **26**

General Description of Prairie Dog Burrows   26
Multiple Entrances to the Same Burrow   28
Plugging of Burrow Entrances   29
Burrow Mounds and Types of Burrow Entrances   30
Functions of Burrow Mounds   31
Do Prairie Dogs Switch Burrows during the Night?   31
Sharing of Burrows   34
Mortality within Burrows   35
Burrow Density versus Colony Size and Colony Density   36

Chapter 4. Study Sites and Methods   **37**

Study Sites   37
Methods for Capturing, Marking, and Observing Prairie Dogs   42
Possible Problems with the Study Colony   68

Chapter 5. Costs and Benefits of Coloniality   72

Why Do Animals Live in Colonies?   72
The Costs of Prairie Dog Coloniality   76
Possible Reasons for Prairie Dog Coloniality   87
Comparative Data from White-Tailed Prairie Dogs   96

Chapter 6. The Coterie   102

Number, Composition, Size, and Longevity of Coteries   103
Male Coalitions within Multi-Male Coteries   108
Parental Care within Coteries   115
The Home Coterie Territory   115
Fission and Fusion of Coteries   121
Why Do Prairie Dogs Live in Coteries?   123

Chapter 7. Infanticide, the Major
Cause of Juvenile Mortality   125

Type I: Infanticide by Lactating Females   125
Type II: Infanticide by Female Immigrants   150
Type III: Killing of Abandoned Litters   151
Type IV: Infanticide by Invading Males   153

Chapter 8. The Antipredator Call   163

Description of the Antipredator Call   163
Experiments with the Stuffed American Badger   170
Individual Variation in Antipredator Calls   170
Are Antipredator Calls Costly?   171
Nepotism and Antipredator Calls   172
Are Antipredator Calls Merely an Expression
    of Parental Care?   172
Antipredator Calling versus Vulnerability
    of Listening Conspecifics   175
Changes in Antipredator Calling versus Changes
    in the Presence of Nearby Kin   176
Do Antipredator Calls Show Differential Nepotism?   177
Antipredator Calling When Other Individuals Are Calling   178
Antipredator Calling versus Coterie Size   178
Antipredator Calling versus Age   179
The Importance of Antipredator Calls
    in Other Coterie Territories   179
Do Prairie Dogs Have an "All Clear" Call?   181
Do Antipredator Calls Enhance Self-Preservation?   183

Chapter 9. Communal Nursing   187

Types of Communal Nursing   187
Behavioral Observations That Suggest Communal Nursing   188
Frequency of Communal Nursing   191
Is Communal Nursing Merely an Unnatural Response
    to Livetrapping?   194
How Costly Is Communal Nursing?   194
Are Foster Mothers Willing Participants
    in Communal Nursing?   195
Genetic Relationship of Foster Mother to Foster Offspring   195
Do Infanticidal Females Become Foster Mothers?   196
Possible Payoffs from Communal Nursing   196
Does Communal Nursing Occur in Other Species
    of Squirrels?   199

Chapter 10. Kin Recognition, Social
Learning, and Eusociality   201

Factors That Affect Alloparenting   201
Definitions   202
Nepotism in Behavioral Interactions   202
Nepotism versus Competition   205
Do Prairie Dogs Have Dominance Hierarchies?   206
Do Males Discriminate between Their Own
    and Other Males' Offspring?   207
Do Prairie Dogs Interact More Amicably with
    Close Kin Than with More Distant Kin?   208
Nepotism versus Kinship in Other Contexts   210
Kin Recognition and Direct Social Learning   210
Why Don't Prairie Dogs Discriminate between
    Close Kin and More Distant Kin?   214
Cooperative Breeding and Eusociality   217

Chapter 11. Behavioral Observations
of Estrus and Copulations   221

Discovery That Copulations Occur Underground   221
Diagnostic Behaviors Associated with
    Underground Copulations   222
Evidence for the Accuracy of Behavioral
    Observations of Estrus and Copulations   248
Inclement Weather: The Worst Enemy
    of Behavioral Observations   257
Why Do Black-Tailed Prairie Dogs Copulate Underground?   258

Chapter 12. Annual and Lifetime Reproductive Success   260

Ways to Determine Maternity and Paternity
   in Natural Populations   260
Assignment of Paternity   261
Ways to Estimate Reproductive Success   262
Annual Reproductive Success   263
Lifetime Reproductive Success   270
What about Prairie Dogs That Never Copulate?   272
Multiple Paternity   273
Paternity in Multi-Male Coteries   274
Cuckoldry   275
Evidence of Female Choice   276
Do the Different Estimates of ARS
   and LRS Correlate for Females?   277
Do the Different Estimates of ARS
   and LRS Correlate for Males?   279

Chapter 13. Factors That Affect Annual and Lifetime Reproductive Success   287

Age versus ARS   287
Order of Copulations versus Male ARS   292
Litter Size and Juvenile Body Mass
   at First Emergence versus ARS   294
Parental Body Mass and Dominance versus ARS   298
Weather and Precipitation versus ARS   305
Costs Associated with Previous Reproduction versus ARS   309
Reproductive Synchrony versus ARS   313
Coterie Size versus ARS   320
Type of Coterie versus ARS   329
Longevity versus LRS   334

Chapter 14. Levels of Inbreeding   337

Costs and Benefits of Inbreeding and Outbreeding   337
Four Mechanisms for Avoiding Extreme Inbreeding   339
The Regular Occurrence of Moderate Inbreeding   351
Measuring Costs and Benefits of Inbreeding and Outbreeding   355

**Chapter 15. Do Mothers Manipulate
the Sex Ratio of Their Litters?**   **360**

Fisher's Theory of Juvenile Sex Ratios   360
Sex Ratio of Litters at First Emergence
versus Parental Investment   361
Sex Ratio of Litters at First Emergence versus
Sex Ratio of Adults and Yearlings   365
Sex Ratio of Litters at First Emergence versus
Maternal Age, Rank, and Body Mass   365
Sex Ratio of Litters at First Emergence versus Paternal
Reproductive Success   370
Sex Ratio of Litters at First Emergence versus Local Mate
Competition   371
Sex Ratio of Litters at First Emergence versus Local Resource
Competition and Local Resource Enhancement   371

Chapter 16. Demography and Population Dynamics   **376**

Variations in Colony Size and Colony Composition   376
Annual Variation in Demographic Measures   378
Disappearance versus Dispersal and Mortality   378
Immigration   382
Litter Size and Juvenile Body Mass at First Emergence   384
Conception, Abortion, Gestation, Parturition, and Lactation   384
Survivorship, Fecundity, and Life Tables   393
Age of Sexual Maturity   397
Sexual Dimorphism in Body Mass   397

Chapter 17. Behavioral Ecology of Prairie Dogs   **402**

Appendix A. Common and Scientific Names
of Organisms Mentioned in This Book   413
Appendix B. Descriptions of Infanticides
by Marauding Females   423
Bibliography   427
Index   521

Preface

This is a book about prairie dogs, of course. I wish the subtitle could be "All that you ever wanted to know about prairie dogs." A more appropriate subtitle might be "All that John Hoogland has been fortunate enough to learn about prairie dogs." As you will see, the informational gap between the two is enormous.

Who should read this book? I cannot answer this question, but I can identify those persons I have had in mind while writing. Naturally, I have aimed for the hundreds of professional biologists who study various species of tree squirrels, ground squirrels, chipmunks, and marmots under natural or laboratory conditions. More importantly, however, I have also aimed for students at all levels who are interested in behavioral ecology and sociobiology. By making comparisons with more than 300 animal species, I have tried to show that prairie dogs offer new and provocative insights into just about every major issue in these disciplines. Finally, I have also considered those amateur biologists and tourists who enjoy watching wildlife. By including more than 100 photographs, I have attempted to portray the charming, fascinating, and puzzling life of the prairie dog.

John R. Young introduced me to scientific research when I was in high school, and my parents (Florence and Frederick Hoogland) and seven siblings (Elizabeth, Frederick, Anne, Mary, Jane, Katherine, and Margaret) nurtured my growing interest.

Over the years, 112 field assistants have helped with all aspects of the fieldwork. I am grateful to all of them, and I especially thank Tod Anderson, Diane Angell, Linda Baron, Jim Daley, Chris Fiorello, Craig Flory, Joel Gaynier, Martin Gaynier, Mary Beth Gaynier, Preston Hardison, Alexander J. Hoogland, Judy G. Hoogland, Mark V. Hoogland, Simon T. Hoogland, Margaret A. Hoogland, Vicky Kraupa, Michael Killebrew, Jim Loughry, Antony Marjaras, George Marzonie, Peter McDonald, Regina Mulcahy, Mark Mulhollam, Sarah Partan, Page Pierce, Louis Plummer, Matt Radcliffe, and Peter Walsh.

The staff at Wind Cave National Park assisted my research in myriad ways. I especially thank Lowell Butts, Jean Donnell, Richard Klukas,

Lester McClanahan, Al Lovaas, Ernest Ortega, Sam Pierce, James Randall, and Steve White.

For financial assistance for my research, I thank The National Science Foundation, The National Geographic Society, The American Philosophical Society, The Center for Field Research, Earthwatch, The Max McGraw Wildlife Foundation, The Whitehall Foundation, The American Society of Mammalogists, The American Museum of Natural History, Sigma Xi, The Eppley Foundation for Research, The Universities of Maryland, Michigan, and Minnesota, Princeton University, The Harry Frank Guggenheim Foundation, Frederick W. T. Hoogland, Mr. and Mrs. Roy L. Gaynier, and Mr. and Mrs. Frederick V. Hoogland. For financial assistance for the color photograph on the cover, I thank The Petrified Forest Museum Association and The University of Maryland's Appalachian Environmental Laboratory.

For help with figures and photographs, I thank Greg Beaumont, Patricia Caulfield, Timothy W. Clark, David R. Duncan, J. Perley Fitzgerald, Monte Garrett, Judy Hoogland, Terry Moore, Raymond P. Morgan, Bob Rozinski, Leonard Rue Enterprises, Wendy Shattil, W. John Smith, Gary Turbak, and Wind Cave National Park.

For help with library research, I thank Carole B. Bodnar and Betty Delores Miller of Frostburg State University.

From the moment I initiated research with prairie dogs in 1974, John A. King has been a constant source of inspiration and encouragement. His pioneering research with prairie dogs in the late 1940s laid the foundation for all additional research that I report in this book.

For help with individual chapters, I thank the following: Kenneth B. Armitage, F. Stephen Dobson, Steven A. Frank, J. Edward Gates, Warren G. Holmes, Judy G. Hoogland, Mark V. Hoogland, W. James Loughry, Kenneth R. McKaye, Raymond P. Morgan, Donald H. Owings, Harry W. Power, Thomas Risch, Frank C. Rohwer, Bridget J. Stutchbury, Eric van den Berghe, and Gerald S. Wilkinson.

Susan E. Abrams, Richard D. Alexander, Charles R. Brown, Gail R. Michener, George B. Schaller, and Paul W. Sherman read the entire manuscript and provided copious, detailed, and astute suggestions for improvement. For expert assistance, I thank the following, all of the University of Chicago Press: Joseph Alderfer, Joseph Claude, David Corona, Jennie Lightner, Alex Philipson, Christie Rabke, Carol Saller, and, especially, Susan E. Abrams and Norma Roche.

I also thank Kent B. Fuller of The University of Maryland's Appalachian Environmental Laboratory. Kent has allowed me to pursue my research with prairie dogs in South Dakota and to analyze my results when I am on campus in Maryland.

I am most indebted to my wife (Judy) and my four children (Mark, Simon, Margaret, and Alexander). Without their assistance, patience, and encouragement during the research and the writing, I never could have completed this story about prairie dogs.

1 Prairie Dogs and Coloniality

Prairie Dogs as Social Animals

Black-tailed prairie dogs are diurnal, burrowing rodents that live in prairies of western North America. Coloniality is perhaps the most striking feature of these plump, brown, nonhibernating, herbivorous squirrels that stand about 30 centimeters tall, weigh about 700 grams, and forage from dawn until dusk. Undisturbed colonies contain thousands of residents and extend for kilometers in all directions. Colonies are conspicuous because prairie dogs systematically clip down any grasses and other herbs that grow taller than about 30 centimeters.

Within colonies, prairie dogs live in contiguous, territorial family groups called *coteries*. A coterie's territory covers about one-third of a hectare, and contains about seventy burrow entrances. As many as twenty-six prairie dogs sometimes live in one coterie territory, but most coteries contain a single breeding adult male, three or four adult females, and several nonbreeding yearlings and juveniles. Large coteries sometimes contain two breeding males, commonly brothers. Conversely, one male sometimes controls two adjacent, small coteries. Unlike the more nomadic males, mothers and their daughters usually spend their entire lives within the natal coterie territory. Both sexes usually defer copulation until the second year, and the most common litter size is three or four. Males, who are about 10%–15% heavier than females, never live longer than 5 years. Some females, however, live for 8 years.

Perhaps the most ostentatious prairie dog behavior is the territorial call, or "jump-yip display." While stretching the length of the body nearly vertical, an individual throws the forefeet high into the air as it calls. A single jump-yip usually starts a chain reaction among prairie dogs of the home and adjacent coteries. Amusing and remarkable is the sight of forty or fifty jump-yipping prairie dogs. Other salient behaviors include scratching to remove fleas; pushing, kicking, and pounding dirt to enhance burrow mounds; and collecting mouthfuls of dry grass for underground nests.

Prairie dogs commonly use burrow mounds as vantage points, and spend about one-third of their time scanning for predators. Upon detecting a coyote, bobcat, golden eagle, prairie falcon, or human, a prairie dog commonly warns nearby kin with a loud, repetitious antipredator call. This first call initiates a chorus that consistently frustrates hungry attackers.

Behavioral interactions among prairie dogs are conspicuous and frequent. Within coteries, interactions are amicable and include play, allogrooming, and mouth-to-mouth contacts that resemble kisses. Amicability gives way to hostility in February through April, however, when pregnant and lactating females defend their nursery burrows. Amicability returns in May when juveniles first emerge from their natal burrows and appear aboveground.

When prairie dogs from different coteries meet, they engage in a flagrant territorial dispute that involves staring, tooth chattering, flaring of the tail, bluff charges, and reciprocal anal sniffing. Territorial disputes commonly persist for more than 30 minutes, and sometimes include fights and chases as well.

Less than 100 years ago, black-tailed prairie dogs saturated the prairies of western North America with an estimated population of over 5 billion. Unfortunately and unfairly, prairie dogs fell into disfavor in the late 1800s and early 1900s. Ranchers have viewed them as pests that compete with their livestock for food. Shooting, poisoning, and destruction of habitat reduced populations so drastically that black-tailed prairie dogs were in danger of extinction by the early 1970s. Though no longer in immediate danger of extinction today, prairie dogs are still rare, confined mainly to national wildlife refuges and national parks. I hope that this book will lead to better understanding, appreciation, and conservation of these maligned animals that once played such a major role in the ecosystem of western North America.

The Evolution of Coloniality

Ever since I chuckled upon seeing my first "jump-yip display" in April 1974, Charles Darwin's (1859) theory of natural selection has explicitly guided my research on prairie dogs. *Natural selection*—or differential reproduction, the process by which some parents produce more reproductive offspring than other parents—leads directly to both evolution and adaptation (Williams 1966a; Alexander 1971; Wilson 1975). *Evolution* is a change in the frequency of alleles—variations of the same gene—over time (Maynard Smith 1966; Futuyma 1979). An *adaptation* is "some sort of biological machinery or process shaped by natural selection to help solve one or more problems faced by the organism" (Williams and Nesse 1991; see also Williams 1966a, 1992).

The most common way to transmit alleles to the next generation is via offspring, and natural selection favors those individuals that produce the largest number of reproductive offspring. However, an individual's nondescendant genetic relatives also share many alleles identical by descent, and close kin share more alleles than more distant kin. Consequently, natural selection also might favor individuals that help kin such as siblings, parents, and nieces and nephews to survive and reproduce (Fisher 1958; Hamilton 1964; Maynard Smith 1964; Williams 1966a; West-Eberhard 1975). Reproductive success via offspring is called *direct fitness,* and reproductive success via nondescendant kin is called *indirect fitness* (Brown 1987). Hamilton's (1964) *inclusive fitness* measures an individual's reproductive success via both offspring and nondescendant kin, and thus is a sum of direct and indirect fitness.

Colonies are omnipresent in the animal kingdom—from protozoa through humans. Terms such as "coloniality," "group," and "group-living" are nonetheless slippery (Bertram 1978; Coulson and Dixon 1979; Wittenberger and Hunt 1985). Here I recognize three levels of group-living. The first level is a group of conspecifics and their offspring that live together throughout the year, from generation to generation, in the same well-defined area, with limited immigration and emigration. Some animals that show this first level of group-living have small home territories that span less than a hectare or so, such as prairie dogs, hoary marmots, American pikas, and bush and rock hyraxes (Smith 1987, 1993; Hoeck 1982, 1989; Barash 1989). However, other animals that show the first level of group-living are more mobile, with large home territories that sometimes span several square kilometers, such as wildebeests, African lions, African wild dogs, spotted hyenas, and hanuman langurs (Estes 1966, 1976; Lawick and Lawick-Goodall 1971; Kruuk 1972; Schaller 1972; Hrdy 1977b). The second level is a group of conspecifics that live in the same well-defined area for only part of the year, usually during the reproductive season, with limited immigration or emigration. Examples of this second level include breeding groups of red-winged blackbirds, kittiwakes, cliff swallows, and northern and southern elephant seals (Coulson 1966; Holm 1973; Le Boeuf 1974; McCann 1981; Brown and Brown 1987). The third level of group-living is merely the temporary spatial clumping of individuals of the same or different species. Examples of this third level include most schools of fish, bevies (or coveys) of bobwhites, roosting flocks of starlings, flocks of migrating Canada geese, and overwintering flocks of shorebirds. In this book I consider the first two levels of group-living to be examples of "coloniality," but not the third level.

Coloniality promotes competition for key resources such as food, nest materials, and mates for animals such as Adélie penguins, cattle egrets, and prairie dogs (Tenaza 1971; Siegfried 1972). Coloniality also promotes the transmission of diseases and parasites, sometimes with disastrous consequences, for animals such as sooty terns, harbor seals, and prairie dogs (Feare 1976; Harwood and Hall 1990). Further, young from different families commonly get mixed up within colonies, so that misdirected parental care is a potential problem for colonial animals such as bank swallows, royal and crested terns, and prairie dogs (Davies and Carrick 1962; Buckley and Buckley 1972; Hoogland and Sherman 1976).

With so many costs, why do animals ever form colonies? Alexander (1974) suggested three evolutionary reasons. First, for animals such as barn swallows and northern elephant seals, a severe shortage of suitable habitat might coerce individuals to live in colonies (Bartholomew 1952; Snapp 1976). Second, coloniality for animals such as African wild dogs and cliff swallows might evolve because groups can somehow secure more or better food per individual than can solitary foragers (Lawick and Lawick-Goodall 1971; Brown 1986, 1988). Finally, animals such as prairie dogs, black-headed gulls, and laughing doves might form colonies to defend against predators (Kruuk 1964; Siegfried and Underhill 1975).

In theory, animals might live together in colonies with few accompanying social behaviors. In practice, however, the most interesting social behaviors in the animal kingdom occur within colonial species. Why do social behaviors evolve within colonies? One reason is that they commonly enhance the original benefit of coloniality (Alexander 1974). After detecting a predator, for example, a Belding's ground squirrel, hoary marmot, or prairie dog runs to a burrow mound and thus gives a visual alarm to observant colony members. But the detecting individual commonly gives an antipredator call as well, thereby warning additional colony members (Sherman 1977, 1985; Barash 1989). The antipredator call thus augments the ultimate benefit of coloniality: increased safety from predators.

Social behaviors also evolve to offset the costs of coloniality. For example, allogrooming removes the ectoparasites that are so common for colonial animals such as common vampire bats, Thomson's gazelles, and prairie dogs (Wilkinson 1986; Hart 1990). To counter the cost of increased aggression within colonies, prairie dogs resort to elaborate territorial disputes that commonly yield resolutions without the dangers of physical combat. "Roaring contests" perform a similar function for groups of red deer, red howler monkeys, and mantled howler monkeys (Chivers 1969; Clutton-Brock and Albon 1979; Sekulic 1982; Crockett and Eisenberg 1987).

Finally, social behaviors evolve when they enable individuals to increase their reproductive success in response to special opportunities within colonies. Consider the sterile castes and division of labor within eusocial insects such as mound-building termites, fungus ants, and honeybees (Wilson 1971; Alexander 1974; Hölldobler and Wilson 1991). Such sterility could never evolve without the supreme opportunities within huge colonies for helping genetic relatives (Wilson 1971; Alexander, Noonan, and Crespi 1991).

How should animals sort themselves within colonies? Mated pairs defend territories centered on the home nest in colonial animals such as wandering albatrosses, gray and little blue herons, and herring and laughing gulls (Meanly 1955; Tinbergen 1960; Tickell 1968; Milstein, Prestt, and Bell 1970; Burger and Beer 1976). In other colonial animals, such as red-winged blackbirds, greater spearnose bats, and California sea lions, males defend harems of genetically unrelated females (Holm 1973; Le Boeuf and Reiter 1988; McCracken and Bradbury 1977, 1981). And in still other colonial animals, such as African lions, hanuman langurs, and prairie dogs, males defend harems of female kin (Schaller 1972; Bertram 1975, 1976; Hrdy 1977b).

A male's control of a harem is no guarantee that he will copulate with all the females in that harem. For some animals such as red deer and northern elephant seals, harem masters sometimes lose copulations—or must share copulations with a second male—when females leave the harem (Le Boeuf, Whiting, and Gantt 1972; Clutton-Brock, Guinness, and Albon 1982; Mesnick and Le Boeuf 1991). In other animals such as wild horses and African lions, harem masters sometimes lose copulations to trespassing males (Schaller 1972; Berger 1986). Prairie dog harem masters resemble southern elephant seal harem masters (McCann 1981) in losing copulations for both reasons.

Like other polygynous animals such as red deer and northern elephant seals (Clutton-Brock, Albon, and Guinness 1988; Le Boeuf and Reiter 1988), individual prairie dogs vary enormously in annual and lifetime reproductive success, with variance greater for males than for females. Factors that affect this variation include age, body mass, dominance, reproductive synchrony, coterie size, and longevity.

Inbreeding among animals commonly yields inferior offspring (Ford 1971; Williams 1975; Falconer 1981; Shields 1982). When colonies are isolated and individuals tend to mature and breed near the natal site, the avoidance of inbreeding might be difficult, as for animals such as American pikas and yellow-bellied and hoary marmots (Armitage 1984; Smith 1987; Barash 1989). Such avoidance is also a potential problem for prairie dogs, but four different mechanisms deter copulations with close kin such as parents, offspring, and full and half siblings.

Prairie dogs have much in common with other colonial animals, but often they go one unique, fascinating step further. For example, burrows are commonplace, but only prairie dogs ingeniously fashion mounds at burrow entrances to facilitate underground ventilation. Antipredator calls that benefit *offspring* are ubiquitous among colonial animals, but nonparental prairie dogs also call to warn *more distant kin* such as half siblings, nieces and nephews, and cousins. Infanticide is also widespread among colonial animals, but usually occurs at low frequencies and involves nonkin. However, lactating prairie dog females regularly kill the offspring of close kin, and this type of infanticide is the major source of juvenile mortality. But after juveniles first appear aboveground, mothers suckle not only their own offspring, but the offspring of female kin as well—the same offspring they tried to kill only a few weeks earlier! Levels of inbreeding among prairie dogs are also unusual. They avoid copulating with close kin, but regularly copulate with more distant kin such as half nieces, half nephews, and full first cousins.

Even though prairie dogs are so colonial and social, the rules of prairie dog society are often surprisingly simple. For example, females evidently do not adjust the sex ratios of their litters in response to environmental, physiological, or social cues. Unlike other ground-dwelling squirrels that have distinct antipredator calls for avian and terrestrial predators, prairie dogs use only one call for both. And the kin recognition that is so striking among prairie dogs seems to depend entirely on direct social learning within the home coterie territory.

Coloniality is the obvious and most important theme of this book. Another theme is that important trends in behavioral ecology sometimes do not emerge without longterm research. For example, I did not even suspect infanticide among prairie dogs until 1980, after I had been studying them for 7 years. And I never imagined that females would kill the juvenile offspring of their daughters and sisters.

A third theme is that even longterm research does not always produce clear answers about the behavioral ecology of animals as social and complicated as prairie dogs. Although I have witnessed 770 sexual consortships, for example, I still do not understand why male prairie dogs give a unique mating call after insemination.

A fourth and final theme is that animals do not always evolve a mechanism for doing something that human observers might regard as adaptive (Davies 1992; Williams 1992). For example, cuckolded prairie dog males evidently do not discriminate between their own and another male's offspring. Further, prairie dog mothers do not seem to discriminate between close and more distant kin during behavioral interactions or when committing infanticide. In situations such as these, perhaps behavioral ecologists expect too much of natural selection. More likely is that our imperfect understanding of an animal's ecology and natural history some-times precludes realistic predictions and accurate interpretation of results.

2 Taxonomy and Natural History

Chapter 1 summarizes the lives of prairie dogs as social animals. Here I provide additional background information on prairie dogs that is important for a proper understanding of issues in later chapters.

Taxonomy

Prairie dogs are diurnal, colonial, burrowing rodents of the squirrel family (Sciuridae), and are akin to marmots, tree squirrels, flying squirrels, chipmunks, and ground squirrels (table 2.1). Prairie dogs differ anatomically from their closest relatives, the ground squirrels, by having a larger body size, larger teeth with higher crowns, and broader skulls (Hollister 1916; Drearden 1953; Clark 1973; Hall 1981; Hafner 1984). The paleontological record indicates that prairie dogs diverged from ground squirrels about 2 or 3 million years ago (Wood 1933; Hibbard 1942, 1956; Bryant 1945; Green 1960, 1963; Black 1963; Clark, Hoffmann, and Nadler 1971; Pizzimenti 1975).

Table 2.1. Taxonomy of North American Squirrels

Order Rodentia
  Suborder Protrogomorpha
    Family Sciuridae
      Subfamily Petauristinae
          Glaucomys (flying squirrels)
      Subfamily Sciurinae
        Tribe Tamiini
          Tamias, Eutamias (chipmunks)
        Tribe Sciurini
          Sciurus, Tamiasciurus (tree squirrels)
        Tribe Marmotini
          Subtribe Marmotina
          Marmota (marmots)
          Subtribe Spermophilina
          Spermophilus, Ammospermophilus, Cynomys (ground squirrels
           and prairie dogs)

Source: Modified from Hafner 1984.

So why do we call them prairie dogs? The first part of the common name, of course, refers to their grassland habitat (Hollister 1916; Clark 1977). The second part refers to the antipredator call of the black-tailed prairie dog, which reminded early settlers of a domestic dog's bark (Smith et al. 1977; Clark 1979). Other names for the prairie dog include petit chien, wishtonwish, Louisiana marmot, Louisiana prairie dog, barking squirrel, barking ground squirrel, barking marmot, prairie marmot, prairie squirrel, prairie barker, Missouri barking squirrel, Missouri prairie dog, mound yapper, yaprat, yek-yek, tousa, tillkeha, pispiza, ping-sping-sa, and sod poodle (Coues and Allen 1877; Hollister 1916; Seton 1929; Costello 1970; Halloran 1972; Chace 1976; Smith 1979).

Taxonomists currently recognize five living species of prairie dogs, all in North America: white-tailed prairie dogs, Utah prairie dogs, Gunnison's prairie dogs, Mexican prairie dogs, and black-tailed prairie dogs (Hollister 1916; MacClintock 1970; Clark, Hoffmann, and Nadler 1971; Hall 1981; Pizzimenti 1975) (table 2.2; appendix A). In morphology and appearance, the species are remarkably similar (fig. 2.1). Excluding the tail, adults of all species are 25 to 40 centimeters long. Color of the fur ranges from yellowish to reddish to dark brown (Coues and Allen 1877; Hollister 1916), except for the rare white pelage of certain black-tailed prairie dog mutants (Tate 1947; Costello 1970). Standing adults are distinctly pear-shaped, and adult body mass varies from 300–900 grams in spring to 500–1,500 grams in late summer and early fall (Hollister 1916; Bakko and Brown 1967; Pizzimenti 1975; chap. 16). Prairie dogs thus resemble either small marmots or portly ground squirrels.

Mammalogists currently assign all five of the prairie dog species to the genus *Cynomys* (Pizzimenti 1975). Prior to Hollister's (1916) careful taxonomic revision, different biologists had assigned prairie dogs to the following genera: *Arctomys, Monax, Cynomis, Cynomomus, Mamcynomiscus,* and *Spermophilus* (Coues and Allen 1877; Hollister 1916). Mammalogists have divided the genus *Cynomys* into two subgenera (Hollister 1916; Pizzimenti 1975): *Leucocrossuromys* (consisting of white-tails, gunnisons, and utahs) and *Cynomys* (consisting of mexicans and black-tails). White-tails, utahs, and gunnisons all have short tails—30 to 65 millimeters and less than 20% of the total body length—with a variable amount of white or gray hair. They hibernate for several months of each year, and live in mid- or high-grass meadows at altitudes of 1,700 to 3,000 meters. Mexicans and black-tails have longer tails—60 to ll0 millimeters and more than 20% of the total body length—with a distinct black tip, do not hibernate, and live in low-grass prairies at altitudes of 700 to 1,700 meters. The classification of utahs and mexicans as separate species, rather than as relict populations of white-tails and black-tails respectively, is somewhat arbitrary (Hollister 1916; Pizzimenti 1975).

Fig. 2.1. Two species of prairie dogs. *(a)* White-tailed prairie dog. Note the short, white tail and the black line over the eye. Utah prairie dogs look almost exactly the same. Gunnison's prairie dogs are similar, but without the black line over the eye. (Photo by John L. Hoogland.) *(b)* Black-tailed prairie dog. Note the long, black-tipped tail and the absence of the black line over the eye. Mexican prairie dogs look almost identical, but the tail is slightly longer. (Photo courtesy of Wind Cave National Park.)

Especially for black-tailed prairie dogs, vegetation differentiates colonies from surrounding areas in two ways. First and more conspicuous, the height of vegetation is markedly lower within black-tail colonies (King 1955; Koford 1958; Tileston and Lechleitner 1966; chap. 5). Second, the composition of the plant community is radically different within colonies (Koford 1958; Klatt and Hein 1978; Agnew, Uresk, and Hansen 1986; Whicker and Detling 1988). Indeed, certain plants—such as scarlet globemallow, black nightshade, pigweed, and the appropriately named prairie dog weed—almost never grow outside black-tail colonies (King 1955).

Table 2.2. Descriptions of the Five Species of Prairie Dogs

	Black-tailed prairie dog	Mexican prairie dog	Gunnison's prairie dog	White-tailed prairie dog	Utah prairie dog
Range	Narrow belt from southern Canada to northern Mexico	Central Mexico	Arizona, Colorado, New Mexico, Utah	Colorado, Montana, Utah, Wyoming	Utah
Habitat	Low-grass prairie	Low-grass prairie	High-grass prairie	High-grass prairie	High-grass prairie
Altitude (meters)	700–1,700	700–1,700	1,700–3,000	1,700–3,000	1,700–3,000
Sexual dimorphism (adult male body mass/ adult female body mass)	About 15%	About 15%	>20%	>20%	>20%
Length of tail (mm)	60–100	90–110	30–65	30–65	30–65
Number of teats	8	8	10	10	10
Tail with black tip	Yes	Yes	No	No	No
Black spot above eye	No	No	No	Yes	Yes
Fleas	Common	Common	Common	Common	Common
Lice	Common	?	Rare	Common	Rare
Ticks	Rare	Rare	Rare	Rare	Rare
Typical colony size (adults and yearlings)	>1,000	?	<500	<500	<500
Typical colony density (adults and yearlings per hectare)	>10	<7?	<7	<7	<7

Number of different vocalizations	12	?	9	7	7?
Burrows with "rim craters"	Yes	Yes	No	No	No
Burrow mounds with ≥2 entrances	Rare	Rare	Common	Common	Common
Hibernation	No	No	Yes	Yes	Yes
Number of chromosomes ($2n$)	50	50	40	50	50
Usual place of copulation	Underground	?	Underground	Aboveground	?
Gestation (days)	34 or 35	?	29 or 30	?	?
Lactation (days)	37 to 51	41 to 50?	35 to 44	?	?
Social system	Matrilocality with harem-polygyny	Matrilocality with harem-polygyny	Matrilocality with harem-polygyny	Matrilocality with harem-polygyny	Matrilocality with harem-polygyny
Usual age (years) of first copulation	2	1?	1	1	1
Infanticide	Common	Rare	Rare	Rare	Rare
Status of species	Rare	Endangered	Rare	Rare	Threatened

Sources: Merriam 1892, 1902; Hollister 1916; Burnett and McCampbell 1926; Stockard 1929, 1930, 1934, 1936; Scheffer 1937, 1945; Soper 1938; Longhurst 1944; Dalquest 1953; Wilcomb 1954; King 1955, 1959; Koford 1958; Tileston and Lechleitner 1966; Bakko and Brown 1967; Smith 1967; Erpino 1968; Tipton and Mendez 1968; Tyler 1968; 1970; Lechleitner 1969; Costello 1970; Waring 1970; Clark, Hoffmann, and Nadler 1971; Collier and Spillett 1972a,b, 1973, 1975; Kerwin 1972; Pizzimenti and Nadler 1972; Clark 1973, 1977, 1979; Pizzimenti and Hoffmann 1973; Smith et al. 1973, 1976, 1977; Fitzgerald and Lechleitner 1974; Pizzimenti and McCleneghan 1974; Collier 1975; Pizzimenti 1975; Pizzimenti and Collier 1975; Crocker-Bedford and Spillett 1977, 1981; Hoogland 1977, 1981a,b, 1985, 1986, unpublished data; Wright-Smith 1978; Flath 1979; Slobodchikoff and Coast 1980; Hall 1981; Player and Urness 1982; Slobodchikoff 1984; Ceballos and Wilson 1985; Rayor 1985a,b, 1988; Slobodchikoff, Fischer, and Shapiro 1986; Grossman 1987; Loughry 1987a,b, pers. comm.; Rayor, Brody, and Gilbert 1987; Garrett and Franklin 1988; Shalaway and Slobodchikoff 1988; Slobodchikoff and Schulz 1988; Cully 1989; Robinson and Slobodchikoff 1990; Slobodchikoff, Robinson, and Travis 1990; Trevino-Villarreal 1990; Slobodchikoff et al. 1991; Ceballos, Mellink, and Hanebury 1993; Mellink and Madrigal 1993.

Despite the physical similarities of the various species of prairie dogs, mammalogists can discriminate among specimens. Useful characters for this task include length and color of tail, karyotype, serum proteins, and skeletal measurements (Hollister 1916; Lechleitner 1969; Clark 1973; Pizzimenti and Hoffmann 1973; Pizzimenti and Collier 1975; Pizzimenti 1975).

Can the amateur behavioral ecologist identify prairie dogs living under natural conditions? Yes, fortunately. Because the species' ranges do not overlap (fig. 2.2), locality alone is diagnostic. Prairie dogs living in Kansas, for example, are obviously black-tails, and prairie dogs in western Wyoming must be white-tails. To a lesser degree, vocalizations are also useful to behavioral ecologists. Specifically, antipredator and territorial calls define three distinct groups: (1) gunnisons, (2) white-tails and utahs, and (3) black-tails and mexicans (Tileston and Lechleitner 1966; Waring 1970; Smith et al. 1977; Wright-Smith 1978).

Of the five species, the black-tailed prairie dog is the most common, the most conspicuous, and the one most likely to be found in zoos. When either scientists or nonscientists use the term "prairie dog," they almost invariably mean black-tails. Similarly, I am referring only to black-tails when I use the abbreviated term "prairie dog" in this book.

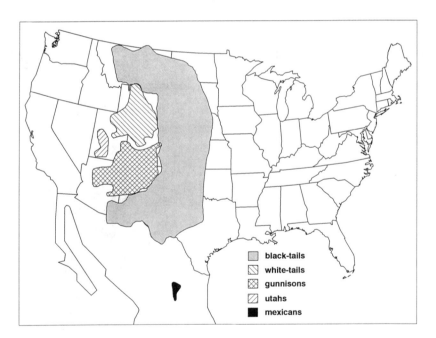

Fig. 2.2. Geographic distribution of the five species of prairie dogs. Because their ranges do not overlap, biologists can determine the species of prairie dog from locality alone.

Natural History

Diurnality

Like most sciurids except northern and southern flying squirrels (Muul 1968, 1969; Dolan and Carter 1977; Sonenshine et al. 1979; Wells-Gosling 1985; Stapp and Mautz 1991), prairie dogs of all species are diurnal and come aboveground only during daylight hours. Consistent with the plethora of cones and paucity of rods in their retinas (Walls 1941, 1942; King 1955; Jacobs and Yolton 1972; Green and Dowling 1975; West and Dowling 1975), individuals released from traps shortly after sunset (i.e., before total darkness) sometimes seem totally disoriented (King 1955; but see chap. 11). In warm weather, individuals first emerge from their burrows at about sunrise and remain aboveground until about sunset (King 1955; Fitzgerald and Lechleitner 1974; Clark 1977). Thus, prairie dogs of all species are radically different from other burrowing rodents such as moles (Hall 1981; Yates and Pedersen 1982), pocket gophers (Williams and Baker 1976; Chase, Howard, and Roseberry 1982), and naked mole rats (Jarvis and Bennett 1991) that spend almost their entire lives underground. Except when hibernating, individuals usually spend more than 95% of their time aboveground in good weather during daylight hours. When temperatures rise above 27°C or so, however, individuals frequently submerge into their burrows, presumably to cool off (Bakko, Porter, and Wunder 1988). Black-tails in South Dakota usually remain underground for only l5 to 20 minutes at a time in hot weather (King 1955; my own unpublished data). White-tails, gunnisons, and mexicans, however, sometimes remain underground for several hours on a hot day before resurfacing in the coolness of late afternoon (Fitzgerald and Lechleitner 1974; Clark 1977; Rayor 1988; Trevino-Villarreal 1990; my own unpublished data).

Even though they spend so much time aboveground during daylight hours, prairie dogs of all species have the exasperating habit of submerging for certain critical behaviors. Black-tailed and Gunnison's prairie dogs, for example, go underground to copulate (chap. 11) and to nurse their own and others' offspring (chap. 9), and black-tails also go underground to kill others' offspring (chap. 7).

Colonies, Wards, and Coteries

Prairie dogs live in aggregations called *colonies, towns,* or *villages* (Coues and Allen 1877; King 1955; Costello 1970). When unsuitable habitat such as a hill, tall vegetation, or a stream divides a prairie dog colony, the resulting subcolonies are called *wards* (King 1955). When such subcolonies are not evident within a colony, I consider that colony to have a single ward; thus, each colony has at least one ward. Residents of one ward can usually see and hear residents of an adjacent ward, but movements and communications between wards are uncommon.

Colonies of black-tailed prairie dogs contain harem-polygynous, territorial family groups called *coteries* (chaps. 1 and 6). Social units similar to coteries also occur within colonies of mexicans (Trevino-Villarreal 1990; W. J. Loughry, pers. comm.) and gunnisons (Fitzgerald and Lechleitner 1974; Rayor 1988; my own unpublished data), and probably also within colonies of white-tails and utahs (Clark 1977; Wright-Smith 1978; my own unpublished data).

The Prairie Dog Diet

Prairie dogs of all species are herbivorous, as shown by observations of foraging individuals and by analyses of feces and stomach contents (Stockard 1930; Kelso 1939; Bonham and Lerwick 1976; Fagerstone 1982; Shalaway and Slobodchikoff 1988; Uresk, Schenbeck, and Cefkin 1988). Exceptions to herbivory include an occasional meal of insects such as cutworms, ground beetles, and short-horned grasshoppers (Whitehead 1927; Kelso 1939; Costello 1970; O'Meilia, Knopf, and Lewis 1982).

Black-tailed prairie dogs are selectively herbivorous, with their preferences at one time of the year differing from preferences at other times (King 1955; Koford 1958; Costello 1970; Rogers-Wydeven and Dahlgren 1982; see table 2.3). Favorite foods in the summer include wheatgrass, grama, buffalo grass, scarlet globemallow, and rabbitbrush (Summers and Linder 1978). Favorites in the winter include prickly pear cactus and thistle; eating of underground roots is also more common in winter (King 1955; Costello 1970; Summers and Linder 1978). Common plants within colonies that prairie dogs usually avoid include sagebrush, threeawn, prairie dog weed, and horseweed (King 1955; Costello 1970; Summers and Linder 1978). Curiously, black-tailed prairie dogs sometimes eat fresh or old American bison scats, which are common within colony sites at Wind Cave National Park.

I did not investigate the diet in detail, but I did discover one important deviation from herbivory for black-tailed prairie dogs: cannibalism. Cannibalism occurs mainly after lactating females kill the unweaned juveniles of other females (chap. 7). I also observed cannibalism in four cases after an adult or yearling died aboveground.

Predators

Numerous animals prey on the various species of prairie dogs (Sperry 1934; Scheffer 1945; Halloran 1972; Olendorff 1976; Campbell et al. 1987; chap. 5). Major mammalian predators include American badgers, bobcats, coyotes, long-tailed weasels, black-footed ferrets, and humans (fig. 2.3); other mammals that occasionally prey on prairie dogs include red foxes, common gray foxes, grizzly bears, and mountain lions. In addition, snakes, especially bull snakes and rattlesnakes, sometimes prey on prairie dogs (Scheffer 1945; Owings and Owings 1979; Halpin 1983; Owings and

Loughry 1985; Loughry 1987a,b). Avian predators include golden eagles, northern harriers, peregrine falcons, prairie falcons, Cooper's hawks, red-tailed hawks, and several other species of buteo and accipiter hawks (fig. 2.4).

Contrary to popular opinion (e.g., Swenk 1915; Hollister 1916; Allen 1967; Costello 1970), burrowing owls usually do not attack prairie dog adults or young. These small, diurnal owls usually live in burrows abandoned by prairie dogs (Scheffer 1937, 1945), and are especially common in prairie dog colonies whose populations have recently crashed—after poisoning or an outbreak of bubonic plague, for example. I have never observed burrowing owls at Wind Cave National Park.

Predators on prairie dogs are more common and important in some areas than in others. The only exception is the black-footed ferret, which is rare everywhere—probably extinct in most prairie dog habitats—and which might be the rarest mammal in all North America (Casey, DuWaldt, and Clark 1986; Richardson 1986; Biggins and Schroeder 1988; Clark 1989; Seal et al. 1989; Oldemeyer et al. 1993).

With so many avian, mammalian, and reptilian enemies, is it any wonder that prairie dogs spend as much as 40% to 50% of their time scanning for predators (chap. 5)?

Molting

At least twice each year, prairie dogs of all species molt the entire pelage (King 1955; Smith 1967). Inexplicably, and incorrectly, Hollister (1916, 9; see also Costello 1970) asserted that prairie dogs molt the fur on the tail only once each year. In the switch from long, thick winter fur to shorter, sparser summer fur, molting starts on the underside and moves to the dorsal side, where it starts near the eyes and progresses posteriorly (fig. 2.5). In the switch from summer fur to winter fur, the progression reverses: from tail to eyes to underside. I could not easily track the ventral fur, but the disappearance of dye markings (chap. 4) indicates that complete molting and replacement of dorsal fur requires about 7 to 14 days for black-tailed prairie dogs.

The initiation and duration of molting vary with latitude, altitude, and other climatic factors (Hollister 1916). At the study colony in South Dakota, black-tail adults and yearlings molt the winter pelage as early as mid-April or as late as June or July. Molting of the summer pelage occurs in August or September. For fast-growing juveniles in their first summer, molting seems to occur almost continuously (Hollister 1916; M. G. Garrett, pers. comm.; W. J. Loughry, pers. comm.).

Molting correlates positively, albeit roughly, with individual condition (Hollister 1916). At my black-tail study colony in South Dakota, for example, the first individuals to molt the winter pelage in mid-April are usually nonbreeding male and female yearlings, which gain body mass

Fig. 2.3. Some mammals that prey on prairie dogs. *(a)* Coyote, which quickly charges into colonies. (Photo courtesy of Wind Cave National Park.) *(b)* American badger, which sometimes enlarges prairie dog burrows in search of prey. (Photo courtesy of Wind Cave National Park.) *(c)* Bobcat, which slowly stalks before pouncing. (Photo by Leonard Rue Enterprises.) *(d)* Black-footed ferret, a slender nocturnal specialist that can easily fit into prairie dog burrows. (Photo courtesy of Wind Cave National Park.)

Fig. 2.4. Some reptiles and birds that prey on prairie dogs. *(a)* rattlesnake; *(b)* golden eagle; *(c)* prairie falcon. (Photos courtesy of Wind Cave National Park.)

rapidly in early spring (chap. 16). Next in early to mid-May come the nonbreeding adults of both sexes, which gain body mass less rapidly. Then in mid- to late May come the breeding males, which gain body mass still less rapidly. And finally in late May—or even June or July—come the lactating females, which frequently *lose* body mass in early spring (chap. 16).

Hibernation

White-tails, gunnisons, and utahs hibernate for several months of each year, whereas black-tails and mexicans do not hibernate. Specifically, individual white-tails, gunnisons, and utahs disappear underground for several consecutive months during late autumn and winter (Fitzgerald and

Fig. 2.5. Initiation of molting. In the spring, dorsal molting begins around the eyes and progresses toward the tail. Before the initiation of molting, this marked prairie dog's head was entirely black. (Photo by John L. Hoogland.)

Lechleitner 1974; Pizzimenti 1975; Clark 1977; Wright-Smith 1978). Black-tails and mexicans, however, come aboveground during all months of the year (King 1955; Pizzimenti and McCleneghan 1974; Harlow and Menkens 1986; Bakko, Porter, and Wunder 1988; Trevino-Villarreal 1990). Among black-tails I have observed two deviations from this pattern (see also Jillson 1871; Anthony 1955; Koford 1958; Thomas and Riedesel 1975; Hamilton and Pfeiffer 1977; Harlow and Menkens 1986). First, during prolonged stretches of severe weather in late autumn and winter, no prairie dogs, or only a small number (fewer than 1% of the colony residents) appear aboveground for several consecutive days. While the brevity of this sort of dormancy precludes the use of the term "hibernation," the resemblance is clear. Second, some individuals remain underground for several weeks in late winter. In 1979, for example, when I began daily behavioral observations on 14 February, six marked yearlings living in one burrow did not first appear aboveground until 12 March. In 1985, when I began daily observations on 16 February, one marked adult male and six marked yearlings living in one burrow did not first appear aboveground until 16 March. And in 1988, when I began daily observations on 21 February, two adult females living in one burrow and one yearling female living in another burrow did not first appear aboveground until 26 March. These sixteen late-emerging individuals, all small and in poor condition, had probably been constantly underground—thus giving the impression of hibernation—since November or December of the previous year.

Population Status

As recently as 100 years ago, western North America was teeming with prairie dogs. The total population was probably over 5 billion, and a single black-tail colony in Texas contained an estimated 400 million residents (Merriam 1902; Clark 1979; Grossman 1987)! However, shooting, poisoning, and destruction of habitat have changed all that (see below). When I started my study of prairie dogs in 1974, four of the five species were on the list of endangered species, with only white-tails exempt. Populations of gunnisons, utahs, and black-tails have all increased in the last 20 years, and only mexicans are still on the list of endangered species; utahs are on the list of threatened species (see table 2.2).

Prairie Dogs and People

Why Do Ranchers Dislike Prairie Dogs?

Ranchers disdain prairie dogs for two reasons (Costello 1970; Jameson 1973; Chace 1976; Petzal 1993). First, they worry that horses and cows will fall into prairie dog burrows and break a leg. Second, they believe that prairie dogs compete with livestock for food. In addition, ranchers complain that prairie dogs are prolific breeders from which they are not safe until every single pest is gone. In response to these complaints, as many as 125,000 people per year sometimes have worked to eliminate prairie dogs via poisoning, drowning, or shooting (Merriam 1902; Swenk 1915; Randall 1976a,b; Clark 1979; Garrett and Franklin 1983)—even though the financial costs of eradication usually exceed the possible benefits (O'Meilia, Knopf, and Lewis 1982; Collins, Workman, and Uresk 1984; Uresk 1985; Knowles 1986a; Radcliffe 1992). In combination with loss of habitat, eradication had brought all the prairie dog species except white-tails to the brink of extinction by the early 1970s (see above).

The ranchers' antagonism toward prairie dogs has secondarily increased their antagonism toward certain predators as well. By eliminating prairie dog populations, for example, ranchers have simultaneously reduced the food supply of coyotes and bobcats. As a result, these deprived predators are more likely to attack cattle and sheep.

None of my research directly concerns the effect of prairie dogs on the raising of livestock. A few comments are nonetheless in order. Consider the possibility of broken legs caused by prairie dog burrows, for which published frequencies do not exist. Over the years I have chatted with more than a hundred ranchers in Wyoming, Colorado, and South Dakota and have asked them about leg fractures. All these ranchers *worry* about broken legs, but only one could pinpoint a possible case. Upon cross-examination, this rancher could only verify that a cow that sometimes foraged in a field with prairie dogs somehow sustained a broken leg. The usual response to my questioning goes something like this: "Well . . . er . . . uh . . . none of my cows has actually broken a leg in a prairie dog burrow. But check with Rancher Jones down the road. Several of his cattle have fallen into prairie dog burrows." A check with Rancher Jones always yields a similar negative response.

Contrary to ranchers' assertions, prairie dogs are not prolific breeders. Both sexes usually defer breeding until the second year, only about 50% of the adult females rear emergent juveniles each year, and litter size is usually only three or four (chap. 16). Further, the physical area occupied by a colony does not automatically increase over time (chaps. 4 and 5). Finally, under natural conditions population crashes commonly follow colony expansions (chaps. 5 and 16).

Mysteriously, Merriam (1902, 258; see also Bailey 1905; Bell 1920; Taylor and Loftfield 1924) somehow calculated that "32 prairie dogs consume as much grass as 1 sheep, and 256 prairie dogs as much as 1 cow." If these calculations are true, then ranchers should indeed detest prairie dogs! *But they are not true,* for at least four reasons. First, despite some overlap and hence competition, prairie dogs avoid numerous plants that livestock prefer and prefer numerous plants that livestock avoid (Coppock, Detling, et al. 1983; Coppock, Ellis, et. al. 1983; O'Meilia, Knopf, and Lewis 1982; Uresk 1984). Second, the presence of prairie dogs improves the quality of certain plants, so that American bison, pronghorn antelope, and livestock commonly *prefer* to forage within colonies (Koford 1958; O'Meilia, Knopf, and Lewis 1982; Coppock, Detling, et al. 1983; Coppock, Ellis, et al. 1983; Knowles 1986b; Krueger 1986). Third, prairie dogs are especially likely to colonize areas *that livestock have already overgrazed* (Bond 1945; Osborn and Allan 1949; Koford 1958; Clark 1968, 1977, 1979; Costello 1970; Snell 1985; Knowles 1986b). Following arrival of the rodents, ranchers grumble: "Look at those prairie dogs. They've eaten all my grass." In reality the prairie dogs are usually the *effect,* rather than the cause, of overgrazing. Finally, consider the scene 200 years ago when millions of American bison lived sympatrically with billions of prairie dogs. Because the habits and dietary requirements of cattle and American bison are so similar, large numbers of cattle and prairie dogs probably should be able to co-exist in the same areas.

I am not arguing here or elsewhere that prairie dogs are always harmless to the livestock rancher. They do sometimes cause financial loss. However, prairie dogs are not the villains that the ranchers allege. Broken legs of livestock caused by prairie dog burrows are rare, competition between livestock and prairie dogs is probably minimal, and sound grazing practices deter colonization by prairie dogs. The inescapable conclusion is that recent attempts to eradicate prairie dogs have been misguided and inappropriate.

Prairie Dogs and the Ecosystem

By their foraging and clipping of tall vegetation, prairie dogs radically alter the plant communities of western North America. Because their colonies attract predators and so many other animals, prairie dogs also have a major impact on wildlife ranging from mites and harvester ants to black-footed ferrets and American bison (table 2.3). For these and other reasons, the extinction of prairie dogs would be a tragedy (Costello 1970; McNulty 1971; Chace 1976; Scott 1977).

Table 2.3. Partial Listing of Plants Eaten or Clipped Down by Prairie Dogs and Animals Attracted to Prairie Dog Colonies

Plants eaten or clipped by prairie dogs
Aster, biscuitroot, black nightshade, brome, buffalo grass, cocklebur, cryptantha, cutleaf nightshade, deathcamus, dropseed, false pennyroyal, fescue, fluffweed, foxtail, glorybind, grama, horseweed, inland saltgrass, knotweed, lambsquarters, mat sandbur, milkvetch, mullein, needle-and-thread, pepperweed, phlox, pigweed, plaintain, prairie dog weed, prickly pear cactus, rabbitbrush, ragweed, ricegrass, Russian thistle, sagebrush, saltbrush, scarlet globemallow, scurfpea, sedge, skeleton weed, snowberry, sorrel, spiny buffalobur nightshade, spurge, stickseed, summer cypress, thistle, threeawn or wire grass, tumblegrass, verbena, wheatgrass, wild onion, winterfat

Animals attracted to prairie dog colonies

Internal parasites
  Protozoa, roundworm, spiny-headed worm, tapeworm
Arachnids
  Black widow spider, mite, pseudoscorpion, tick
Insects
  Bluebottle fly, bombardier beetle, cave cricket, cutworm, darkling beetle, dung beetle, flea, ground beetle, harvester ant, louse, robber fly, short-horned grasshopper
Amphibians
  Tiger salamander, toad
Reptiles
  Bull snake, lesser earless lizard, lined snake, rattlesnake, Texas horned lizard, western box turtle, western hognose snake
Birds
  American robin, black-billed magpie, burrowing owl, Cooper's hawk, ferruginous hawk, golden eagle, goshawk, horned lark, Lapland longspur, lark bunting, McCown's longspur, mountain bluebird, mountain plover, mourning dove, northern harrier, prairie falcon, red-tailed hawk, rough-legged hawk, sharp-shinned hawk, sharp-tailed grouse, Sprague's pipit, Swainson's hawk, western meadowlark
Mammals
  American badger, American bison, black-footed ferret, bobcat, coyote, deer mouse, desert cottontail, long-tailed weasel, mule deer, northern grasshopper mouse, pocket mouse, prairie vole, pronghorn antelope, swift fox, thirteen-lined ground squirrel, wapiti, white-tailed jackrabbit

Sources: Scheffer 1937; King 1955; Koford 1958; Vetterling 1962; Tileston and Lechleitner 1966; Smith 1967; Tyler 1968, 1970; Costello 1970; Buscher and Tyler 1975; Tyler and Buscher 1975; Bonham and Lerwick 1976; Summers and Linder 1978; Fagerstone, Tietjen, and Williams 1981; Uresk 1985; Wilcomb 1954.

Note: Scientific names for organisms listed in this table are in appendix A.

Prairie Dogs as Human Food Items

When they were omnipresent long ago, prairie dogs were important food items for certain Indian tribes and white explorers and settlers (Wedel 1961; Costello 1970). One explorer described the meat as "excellent," another as "well flavoured . . . [resembling] that of the woodchuck" (Scheffer 1945; see also Gorman 1974). More recently, Nordyke and Nordyke (1964, 202) argue that the meat is "tasty" and "superior to wild rabbit or squirrel."

Because they do not hibernate, black-tailed prairie dogs were probably especially valuable to Indians as food during the winter. Perhaps because they are so rare, human consumption of prairie dogs is now trivial.

Prairie Dogs and Medicine

Black-tailed prairie dogs frequently develop gallstones under laboratory conditions. This curiosity has led to a better understanding of gallstones and gall bladder disease among humans (Brenneman et al. 1972; Holzbach et al. 1976; Gurll and DenBesten 1978; Broughton et al. 1991; Roslyn et al. 1991). White-tailed and black-tailed prairie dogs have also been useful in studies of metabolism and hibernation (Bakko 1977; Pfeiffer, Reinking, and Hamilton 1979; Harlow and Menkens 1986; Harlow and Buskirk 1991).

Prairie Dogs as Pets

If captured when young, prairie dogs make excellent, engaging pets (Jillson 1871; Squire 1925; Cates 1927; Dale 1947; Ferrara 1985) (fig. 2.6)—

Fig. 2.6. Prairie dogs as pets. If captured at first juvenile emergence or earlier, prairie dogs make excellent pets. This juvenile pet stays warm in its owner's pocket. (Photo by John L. Hoogland.)

probably because, like young mallards shortly after hatching (Hess 1964, 1973; Lorenz 1970), they seem to "imprint" to their human owners. Prairie dog pets are easily house-trained, and respond with a jump-yip call when the owner returns after a short absence. They like to be groomed by their owners, and try to groom back in return. When a strange human approaches, however, prairie dog pets chatter their teeth and flare their tails—but they almost never bite.

Prairie dogs make good pets only if captured as, or before, they first appear aboveground when about 6 weeks old. Older animals do not tame down enough to make good pets.

If prairie dogs are so charming, then why don't more people have them as pets? One problem is that prairie dogs like to chew on furniture. Another problem is the disagreeable odor sometimes emitted from the perianal scent glands. The most serious problem, however, is that prairie dogs do not breed readily in laboratories or in pet shops. The only way to get more than a few pets, therefore, is to catch them in the wild as they first appear aboveground. This method is difficult and time-consuming, and consequently deters most pet store owners.

Summary

1. Despite their misleading common name, prairie dogs (genus *Cynomys*) are medium-sized (400 to 1,500 grams) rodents of the squirrel family (Sciuridae).

2. Taxonomists currently recognize five species of prairie dogs. White-tailed, Gunnison's, and Utah prairie dogs belong to the subgenus *Leucocrossuromys*. Black-tailed and Mexican prairie dogs belong to the subgenus *Cynomys*.

3. Characters useful for discriminating among specimens of the different prairie dog species include length and color of tail, karyotype, serum proteins, and skeletal measurements. For wild prairie dogs, locality and vocalizations are diagnostic.

4. In good weather prairie dogs first emerge from their burrows at about sunrise, and remain aboveground until about sunset.

5. Physical barriers such as hills or tall vegetation sometimes divide prairie dog colonies into subcolonies called wards. Within colonies, prairie dogs live in territorial, harem-polygynous family groups called coteries.

6. Prairie dogs are herbivorous. Occasional exceptions to herbivory include insectivory and cannibalism.

7. Major predators on prairie dogs include American badgers, bobcats, coyotes, black-footed ferrets, golden eagles, northern harriers, prairie falcons, numerous species of buteo and accipiter hawks, bull snakes, and rattlesnakes.

8. At least twice each year, prairie dogs molt the entire pelage.

9. Although most black-tailed prairie dogs come aboveground during all months of the year, individuals in poor condition sometimes remain underground for several consecutive months and appear to hibernate.

10. Leg fractures due to prairie dog burrows are rare among livestock, and ranchers sometimes misunderstand and exaggerate the competition between prairie dogs and livestock. Further, prairie dogs are more likely to colonize areas that livestock have already overgrazed. Thus, ranchers commonly exterminate prairie dogs for the wrong reasons.

3   Burrows

General Description of Prairie Dog Burrows

Burrows are underground tunnels that have one or more openings to the surface, called burrow entrances. Prairie dog burrows have unique burrow entrances, and are integral to both defense against predators and protection from the weather. Because prairie dogs spend more than half of their lives within their burrows, a chapter describing these burrows seems appropriate.

Prairie dog burrows are typically 10 to 30 centimeters in diameter at the entrances and somewhat narrower underground (Merriam 1902; King 1955; 1984; Sheets, Linder, and Dahlgren 1971; Stromberg 1975; Clark 1977). Usually they are about 5 to 10 meters long and 2 to 3 meters deep, but some burrows are as long as 33 meters and as deep as 5 meters (fig. 3.1; see also King 1955; Sheets, Linder, and Dahlgren 1971; Clark 1977). This variation probably explains why burrows differ in suitability for spending the night (see below), rearing of offspring (chaps. 7 and 11), and refuge from weather and predators (chaps. 5 and 8). The number and positioning of burrow entrances change little over time (King 1955; Clark 1977; chap. 4). Like yellow-bellied, Olympic, and alpine marmots (Couch 1930; Armitage 1962; Barash 1973, 1989), prairie dogs sometimes create trails of worn-down vegetation that connect burrow entrances (King 1955).

Burrows used for rearing of juveniles—i.e., *nursery burrows*—and burrows used for final submergence at sunset contain one or two elliptical nest chambers packed with dry grass; each chamber is approximately 30 centimeters high and 50 centimeters wide (Sheets, Linder, and Dahlgren 1971; Gunderson 1978). I assume, but did not prove, that adults and yearlings use these nest chambers for sleeping and resting. However, I was able to demonstrate, via excavations, that mothers use the nest chambers for rearing their unweaned juveniles (chap. 7). Besides nest chambers, burrows frequently contain smaller enlargements approximately 1 meter below the surface (Merriam 1902; Sheets, Linder, and Dahlgren 1971). These enlargements probably function either as simple turnaround points (Scheffer 1947) or as temporary refuges that allow individuals to listen to aboveground activity.

26

a) simple nursery burrow

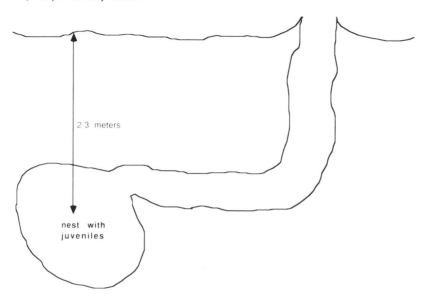

b) complex nursery burrow

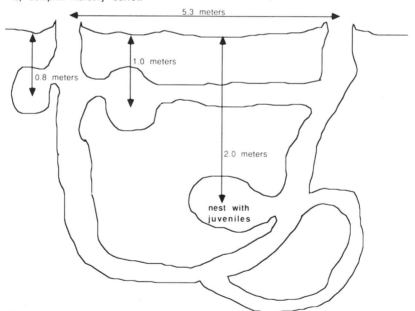

Fig. 3.1. Diagrams of two nursery burrows excavated at the Pringle colony at Wind Cave National Park in April 1984. *(a)* Simple nursery burrow, with single entrance and only one nest chamber. *(b)* Complex nursery burrow, with two entrances, one nest chamber, one chamber without a nest, and internal loop. I have not drawn these two diagrams to exact scale.

Like the burrows of alpine marmots (Arnold et al. 1991), prairie dog burrows probably have temperatures of 5°–10°C in winter and 15°–25°C in summer (Wilcomb 1954; Costello 1970; Gunderson 1978). Burrows thus allow individuals to warm up in winter and cool down in summer. Humidity is always higher within burrows than at the surface, and usually averages about 88% (Wilcomb 1954; Costello 1970; Gunderson 1978).

Four excavations (chap. 7) have revealed a surprising absence of fecal pellets within prairie dog burrows. These results suggest that individuals systematically defecate only when aboveground. They also suggest that, contrary to popular opinion (e.g., Costello 1970; Chace 1976), the typical prairie dog burrow does not have a specific chamber ("toilet" or "latrine") for defecation. However, my results here are at odds with those of other investigators, who found numerous underground scats (Merriam 1902; Whitehead 1927; Wilcomb 1954; King 1955; Sheets, Linder, and Dahlgren 1971). Further, at the entrances of certain burrows I sometimes find hundreds of scats that the prairie dogs evidently have brought aboveground (see also Costello 1970).

Multiple Entrances to the Same Burrow

Like the burrows of thirteen-lined and Belding's ground squirrels and yellow-bellied marmots (Rongstad 1965; Turner 1973; Svendsen 1976; Barash 1989), a prairie dog burrow sometimes has more than one entrance (Scheffer 1937; Wilcomb 1954; Sheets, Linder, and Dahlgren 1971; Stromberg 1978; Vogel, Ellington, and Kilgore 1973). I discover multiple entrances to the same burrow in two ways. Like King (1955), I sometimes see the same marked individual enter at one entrance and then quickly exit at another. More commonly, I learn about multiple entrances during livetrapping. For example, sometimes I chase the only unmarked individual within a coterie territory into a particular entrance and surround that entrance with livetraps (chap. 4)—only to see the unmarked individual emerge at a second, unsurrounded entrance shortly thereafter.

Most burrows have only one or two entrances. However, some burrows have three entrances (Sheets, Linder, and Dahlgren 1971), and a few have as many as five or six (my own unpublished data). Probably to deter invasions, burrow entrances in different coterie territories never connect (fig. 3.2).

For some burrows, the same two or more entrances connect for several consecutive years. For other burrows, two or more entrances connect during certain time intervals but not during others. The latter is especially true of burrows used for rearing juveniles. Specifically, mothers usually select nursery burrows with two or more entrances, but frequently plug one of the entrances—probably to facilitate defense of young against infanticide (King 1955; chap. 7). Such mothers commonly reopen the plugged entrance at about the time when juveniles first appear aboveground.

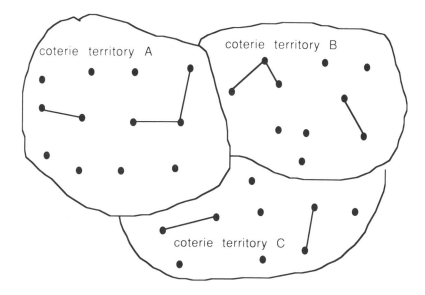

Fig. 3.2. Connection of burrow entrances. A single burrow commonly has multiple entrances within the same coterie territory. However, burrow entrances from different coterie territories never connect.

Plugging of Burrow Entrances

Like Olympic, hoary, and yellow-bellied marmots (Barash 1973, 1989; Armitage 1988), prairie dogs commonly use the same burrow entrances from generation to generation (King 1955; see also chap. 6). Many of the burrow entrances that I first mapped in 1975, for example, were still in use through 1989. At least three factors cause premature deterioration that can be temporary or permanent. First, from lack of use and maintenance, burrow entrances sometimes fill in with dirt and debris. Second, as noted above, a mother sometimes plugs one of the auxiliary entrances to the nursery burrow containing her unweaned offspring. Finally and curiously, prairie dogs sometimes fill in entrances to burrows that contain either black-footed ferrets or snakes (Henderson, Springer, and Adrian 1969; Halpin 1983; Clark, Richardson, et al. 1984; Martin, Schroeder, and Tietjen 1984; Loughry 1987b). In the morning prairie dogs sometimes fill in burrow entrances from which ferrets have taken juveniles, and later in the same day reopen them (Hillman 1968). Does such interment reduce predatory success? An absence of black-footed ferrets (chap. 4) and a paucity of snakes (chap. 5) at the study colony has precluded my investigation of this question.

Burrow Mounds and Types of Burrow Entrances

Like burrows of hoary, Olympic, and yellow-bellied marmots (Barash 1989), a prairie dog burrow often has a conspicuous mound of dirt at its entrance. Regarding these mounds, prairie dog burrow entrances are of three general types.

1. Some entrances, usually found near the colony's periphery, have no conspicuous mound. Individuals do not spend the night or rear offspring in the burrows under these entrances, but do use them for escape during a surprise predatory attack or for short periods of escape during midday heat.

2. Other entrances are surrounded by wide, rounded, unstructured mounds of dirt called *dome craters* (King 1955, 1984; Sheets, Linder, and Dahlgren 1971; Vogel, Ellington, and Kilgore 1973). Dome craters sometimes have a diameter of 2–3 meters, but usually are no higher than 0.2–0.3 meters. Burrows under dome craters are commonly suitable not only for safety from predators, but also for spending the night and rearing offspring.

3. The most conspicuous entrances are surrounded by a high mound of dirt molded into a distinctive rim, called a *rim crater,* and resemble miniature volcanoes (fig. 3.3). Rim craters usually have a diameter of 1.0–1.5 meters and are sometimes as high as 1.0 meters. Burrows under rim craters, like those under dome craters, are commonly suitable for safety from predators, spending the night, and rearing offspring.

Especially when the ground is wet after rain, individuals—usually working alone but sometimes working together on the same mound in small groups of two, three, or even four—reshape the mounds of rim craters by digging, scraping, pushing, and piling the surrounding soil with their front and rear legs (fig. 3.4). With arched backs, they pound the soil into place with the points of their noses, leaving their nose prints in the soil as it bakes and hardens in the sun (Jillson 1871; King 1955, 1984). At a small ward (subcolony) in Colorado, I once observed 22 of the 23 marked adult and yearling residents (96%) working assiduously in small groups on rim craters following a long-overdue rainstorm.

Both dome craters and burrow entrances with no associated mound are commonplace among various species of ground squirrels and marmots (Rongstad 1965; Turner 1973; Svendsen 1976; Barash 1989). Rim craters, however, are unique to black-tailed and Mexican prairie dogs (King 1955; Tileston and Lechleitner 1966; Ceballos-G. and Wilson 1985; Trevino-Villarreal 1990; W. J. Loughry, pers. comm.). Burrows without mounds usually have only one entrance, but burrows with a dome or rim crater usually have at least two entrances.

Fig. 3.3. Rim crater at entrance to burrow. These large mounds, sometimes as high as 1 meter, help prevent flooding, provide a vantage point for scanning as seen here, and improve underground ventilation. (Photo courtesy of Wind Cave National Park.)

Functions of Burrow Mounds

The mounds of dome and rim craters serve the prairie dogs in at least three ways (King 1955, 1984). First, the mounds help prevent flooding after torrential rainstorms (Foster 1924; Whitehead 1927; King 1955; Costello 1970). Second, prairie dogs frequently run to the mounds during times of known or suspected danger, presumably because the elevated mounds facilitate scanning for predators (King 1955, 1959; chap. 5).

A third, and fascinating, function of prairie dog burrow mounds results from the action of Bernoulli's principle on the unique rim crater (Vogel, Ellington, and Kilgore 1973; see also Vogel 1989; King 1984). Specifically, if a burrow has a low dome crater at one end and a higher rim crater at the other end, then the slightest aboveground breeze will create a partial vacuum within the burrow: air enters at the dome crater and exits at the rim crater (fig. 3.5). Such improved ventilation might be important when burrows are especially long and deep or when all the members of a coterie spend the night in the same burrow (see below).

Do Prairie Dogs Switch Burrows during the Night?

Prairie dogs enter burrows at about sunset and remain there until about sunrise the following day. I assume, but have not proved, that the animals

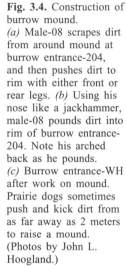

Fig. 3.4. Construction of burrow mound.
(a) Male-08 scrapes dirt from around mound at burrow entrance-204, and then pushes dirt to rim with either front or rear legs. *(b)* Using his nose like a jackhammer, male-08 pounds dirt into rim of burrow entrance-204. Note his arched back as he pounds. *(c)* Burrow entrance-WH after work on mound. Prairie dogs sometimes push and kick dirt from as far away as 2 meters to raise a mound. (Photos by John L. Hoogland.)

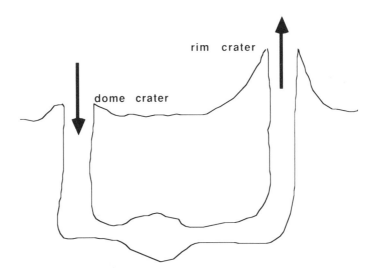

Fig. 3.5. Ventilation within burrows that have two entrances. Even a slight breeze pulls air into the low dome crater and draws it out through the higher rim crater. Such improved ventilation might be important for burrows that harbor as many as fourteen prairie dogs for the night and are as deep as 5 meters and as long as 33 meters.

sleep while they are in their burrows at night. I have, however, used two methods to investigate whether prairie dogs switch burrows during the night.

First, on more than 200 evenings, I have continued to observe at the study colony for 30 minutes or more after all the prairie dogs have apparently submerged for the night. Rarely (fewer than 30 documented cases), a male or female reemerges when all other prairie dogs have been underground for the night for at least 20 minutes, then runs into a different burrow entrance. Invariably, these late movements involve a male or female that has copulated late in the day (chap. 11). On two cloudless nights in different years, both with a full moon and both during the breeding season in early March, a field assistant has watched from sunset until the following sunrise. After the last prairie dog submerged, neither assistant observed prairie dogs aboveground until the following sunrise.

Second, I record first emergences and final submergences of all the marked colony residents each day. I suspect movement during the night when a marked individual submerges into one burrow entrance at the end of one day and then first emerges from a different, unconnected entrance on the following morning. With this method I have scored unequivocal nocturnal movement by fewer than 5 males and fewer than 5 females, all of which had copulated late in the afternoon prior to the movement. In one other case, several individuals moved from the same burrow at night, evidently in response to digging by an American badger. The implication is that prairie dogs do not switch burrows during the night, except under extraordinary circumstances. The exceptions evidently move either some-time in the middle of the night after my departure or sometime early in the morning before my return.

Sharing of Burrows

Questions posed to me about prairie dogs reveal the common belief that each prairie dog within a colony has its own private burrow. Nothing could be further from the truth! For most of the year, all coterie members have equal and unchallenged access to the 60–70 burrow entrances (chap. 6) within the home coterie territory, and sharing of burrows is common. For example, all coterie members usually submerge into the same burrow at night in cold weather and emerge from it in the morning. Similar sharing of burrows during cold weather occurs in Belding's ground squirrels and Alaska, alpine, long-tailed, hoary, and black-capped marmots (Kapitonov 1960; Rausch and Rausch 1971; Morton and Sherman 1978; Barash 1989; Arnold 1990b), and probably conserves body heat (Vickery and Millar 1984; West and Dublin 1984; Canals, Rosenmann, and Bozinovic 1989; Arnold 1988; Bazin and MacArthur 1992).

In large coteries containing more than about seven or eight residents, prairie dogs frequently divide into two or three smaller groups before submerging for the night. Such division is not mandatory, however, and I chuckled each morning in February 1984 when all fourteen members of one coterie first emerged from the same rim crater. Noctural groupings do not always use the same burrow every night, but generally restrict their usage to only three or four different burrows within the home coterie territory.

Sharing of burrows within the home coterie territory is also evident during the day. For example, adults and yearlings of both sexes usually meet no resistance when they choose a burrow to escape either precipi-tation, midday heat, or a predator.

Do coterie members share in the excavation and maintenance of bur-rows within the home coterie territory? Yes, but not equally. For example, all coterie members commonly refurbish burrow mounds and take nest material into burrows where they spend the night. However, these activities are more common among adults than among yearlings. For example, pregnant females sometimes spend as much as 60 consecutive minutes taking mouthfuls of nest material into the home burrow chosen for par-turition and rearing of offspring (chap. 11). Curiously, females that have recently lost their unweaned litters to infanticide (chap. 7) are inordinately attentive to the maintenance of rim craters.

Two circumstances temporarily terminate equal access to all burrows within the home coterie territory. First, in coteries containing two breeding males, each male defends a subset of the burrows within the home coterie territory from the other male (chap. 6). Females in these multi-male coteries, however, still have access to all burrows within the home coterie territory. Second, at some point after copulating, a female begins to defend a territory centered on a particular burrow—i.e., her nursery burrow—to be used for parturition and lactation (chaps. 6 and 11).

Mortality within Burrows

Predation on prairie dogs can occur either aboveground (coyotes, bobcats, aerial predators) or underground (black-footed ferrets, American badgers, snakes) (chap. 5). But where do individuals perish in response to other sources of mortality, such as disease, old age, and poor condition? My information on this point is anecdotal, but five lines of evidence indicate that prairie dogs sometimes die in their burrows.

1. Only rarely do I find aboveground carcasses ($N < 30$).

2. I have observed a small number of individuals in poor condition that have submerged into a burrow at night and have never reappeared aboveground again (chap. 16).

3. I once found an unmaimed yearling prairie dog at a burrow entrance that evidently had died underground before being pushed out of the burrow by other prairie dogs.

4. During an excavation of a burrow (chap. 7) I found an unmaimed dead individual that looked mummified (fig. 3.6).

5. Sometimes on burrow mounds I find prairie dog bones that other prairie dogs have presumably brought to the surface while excavating or refurbishing burrows.

Fig. 3.6. Dead, mummified prairie dog found during excavation of burrow. This carcass indicates that prairie dogs sometimes die underground. (Photo by John L. Hoogland.)

Burrow Density versus Colony Size and Colony Density

Perhaps in response to the ease of excavating in different types of soil, the density of burrow entrances within black-tail colonies shows phenomenal variation: from 10 to 250 per hectare (Martin and Schroeder 1978, 1980; Campbell and Clark 1981; Hoogland 1981a). And perhaps as a function of either the availability of forage or the density of predators, colony density (the number of adults and yearlings per hectare) also varies tremendously: from fewer than 10 to more than 35 (chap. 5). The number of burrow entrances per resident prairie dog also varies greatly (Hoogland 1981a). Consequently, neither the number nor density of burrow entrances accurately predicts prairie dog colony size (i.e., the number of resident adults and yearlings) or colony density (see also King 1955).

Summary

1. Prairie dogs depend on underground burrows for a place to spend the night, protection from extremes in the weather, a place to rear offspring, and refuge from predators. Burrows frequently have two or more entrances.

2. The same burrows are usually functional from generation to generation. Factors that cause premature demise of burrows include lack of use and maintenance; deliberate plugging of secondary burrow entrances by mothers to help deter infanticidal invaders; and deliberate plugging by prairie dogs of burrow entrances containing either black-footed ferrets or snakes.

3. At most burrow entrances is a conspicuous mound of dirt. These mounds reduce flooding, provide high points to facilitate scanning for predators, and promote underground ventilation.

4. Sharing of burrows is common. During pregnancy and lactation, however, females defend a single home nursery burrow from all conspecifics.

5. Neither the number nor the density of burrow entrances accurately predicts the number or density of prairie dogs within colonies.

4 Study Sites and Methods

This chapter describes the study sites and methods that I use to study prairie dogs. Throughout the book I use only common names for plants and animals. Appendix A gives the scientific names for all organisms mentioned in this book. As noted in chapter 2, I usually refer to black-tailed prairie dogs simply as prairie dogs.

Study Sites

In my first year of research, 1974, I worked near Fort Collins, Colorado, where the prairie dogs have no protection from either shooting or poisoning. I soon realized that such conditions are incompatible with longterm research. In 1975 I initiated research at Wind Cave National Park, Hot Springs, South Dakota, where I continued to work until 1989 (fig. 4.1).

Prairie dogs at Wind Cave National Park are theoretically safe from shooting, poisoning, and other types of human disturbance. In 1983 and

Fig. 4.1. Wind Cave National Park, South Dakota, home of the study colony. I worked here from February through June of 1975 through 1989. (Photo by John L. Hoogland.)

1984, however, park rangers reduced several of the colonies at Wind Cave National Park by poisoning and follow-up shooting (Fischer 1982; R. Klukas, pers. comm.). However, the rangers deliberately spared the study colony from such artificial reduction. Further, I have never detected any evidence of unauthorized shooting or poisoning at the study colony.

King (1955), who also studied prairie dogs at Wind Cave National Park, elegantly described the floral, faunal, and climatic conditions there (see also Clark et al. 1982; Agnew, Uresk, and Hansen 1986). In the absence of domestic livestock (cattle, horses, goats, or sheep), ungulates at Wind Cave National Park include American bison (buffalo), pronghorn antelope, wapiti (elk), and mule deer (King 1955; Coppock, Detling, et al. 1983; Coppock, Ellis, et al. 1983; Krueger 1986) (fig. 4.2). Except for the black-footed ferret, almost all the predators known to prey on prairie dogs (chap. 2) live at Wind Cave National Park (but see below).

Fig. 4.2. Two large ungulates that frequently visit prairie dog colonies. *(a)* Pronghorn antelope; *(b)* American bison. (Photos by John L. Hoogland.)

In the mid- and late 1970s, Wind Cave National Park had eleven distinct prairie dog colonies (fig. 4.3). A twelfth colony (Custer) is just outside the park boundary, in Custer State Park. Of these twelve colonies, I have collected data from ten (i.e., all but the Boland and Monte colonies). In the last fifteen years, prairie dogs have colonized several additional areas within Wind Cave National Park (Garrett, Hoogland, and Franklin 1982; Garrett and Franklin 1988; Daley 1989; Radcliffe 1992).

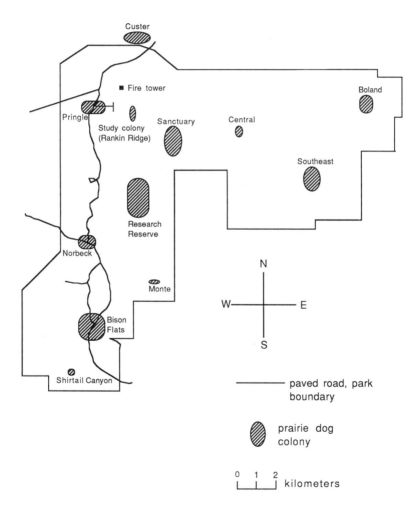

Fig. 4.3. Map showing approximate locations and approximate relative sizes of the eleven prairie dog colonies within Wind Cave National Park in the mid- and late 1970s. A twelfth colony (Custer) is just outside the park boundary, in Custer State Park.

My main study colony is approximately 1 kilometer southwest of Wind Cave National Park's Rankin Ridge fire tower, at an elevation of 1,300 meters (fig. 4.4). The colony is roughly elliptical in shape, with dimensions of approximately 500 meters (north-south) by 130 meters (east-west) (fig. 4.5). The physical area it occupied when I first started in 1975 was 6.60 hectares, and has remained exactly the same through 1989. The number of adults and yearlings at the study colony in May of each year ranges from 92 to 143 (chap. 16). The nearest colony (Pringle) to the study colony is about 1 kilometer away, and another colony (Sanctuary) is about 2 kilometers away (see fig. 4.3). The study colony contains no obvious subdivisions or subcolonies, so that the terms study colony and study ward (chap. 2) are synonymous.

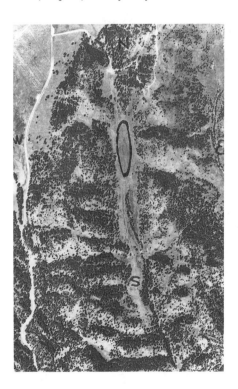 

Fig. 4.4. Two different views of the study colony. *(a)* Aerial photograph. Letters indicate north, south, east, and west. Study colony is outlined in black; roads to north and west appear white. Although the study colony is mostly surrounded by trees, note room for expansion at south end. The colony is only about 1.0 kilometers from a major park road, but is invisible to passing tourists because of trees and hills. Dimensions are approximately 500 meters (north-south) by 130 meters (east-west). (Photo courtesy of Wind Cave National Park.) *(b)* View from area near Rankin Ridge fire tower, looking south. Letters indicate north, south, east, and west. Note corridors for possible expansion on east and west sides of the small island of trees at south end. (Photo by John L. Hoogland.)

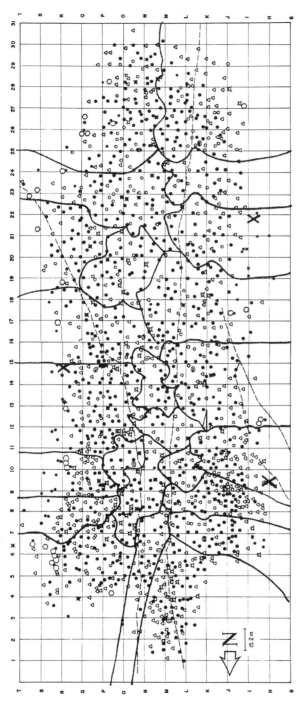

Fig. 4.5. Map of the study colony. Solid black lines indicate the territorial boundaries of the 24 coterie territories in April 1978. I determine the boundaries by mapping sites of territorial disputes. The colony occupies 6.60 hectares and contains 1,591 burrow entrances.

Below is the key for symbols in the map.

● Burrow entrance with dome crater

○ Burrow entrance with rim crater

⊙ Two burrow entrances on the same mound

△ Burrow entrance with no mound

✕ Plugged burrow entrance

✳ Hidden burrow entrance

■ One burrow entrance that branches into two tunnels

▲ One burrow entrance that branches into three tunnels

✕ Observation tower

▽ Shallow burrow, less than 1 meter deep

⬡ Tree

--- Trail of American bison

Though large relative to the study colonies of earlier researchers (King 1955; Tileston and Lechleitner 1966; Garrett and Franklin 1988; Halpin 1987), my study colony is small relative to most other prairie dog colonies, which contain thousands of residents (Merriam 1902; McNulty 1971; Clark 1979; Hoogland 1981a; Halpin 1987; chap. 2).

The number of burrow entrances at the study colony in 1975 was 1,591. A few burrow entrances—perhaps 1% or 2% of the total—fill in each year (chap. 3), but this loss is offset by occasional new excavations. Consequently, the number of burrow entrances remains about 1,600 each year.

From 1974 through 1977, I observed prairie dogs from tents. For 1978 and later years, however, I erected three 5-meter observation towers at the edges of the study colony (fig. 4.6). At the top of each tower is a cubicle (2 meters per side) with one open side that faces the study colony. Two of the towers face east, the other west (see fig. 4.5). Often feeding and interacting directly underneath, the prairie dogs seem oblivious to my presence in the observation tower when I sit quietly.

From a logistical standpoint, the study colony offers three outstanding advantages. First, it is invisible to most tourists. Consequently, wandering hikers only rarely disturb my research—usually about once or twice each year. Second, despite its invisibility, the colony is always accessible because of its proximity to a park road (about 1 kilometer away, behind hills) that Wind Cave National Park personnel quickly plow upon the start of a snowstorm. This accessibility is crucial because one of my objectives each year is to record all copulations, even those that occur during snowstorms in February and March (chaps. 11 and 12). Finally, the colony is small and, because of the surrounding trees, is unlikely to expand. This small, stable size is important because one of my other objectives is to capture and mark all colony residents each year (chap. 16).

Methods for Capturing, Marking, and Observing Prairie Dogs

Field Assistants

One hundred fifteen volunteer field assistants have contributed mightily to my research (table 4.1). Assistants not only help with routine jobs such as livetrapping and marking, but also provide valuable observations and key insights.

Field assistants are of two general types. Approximately half are short-termers who help for 2 weeks or less. Many of these field assistants come via Earthwatch (Watertown, Massachusetts). The other half are long-termers who help for at least 2 months. Most long-termers stay for an entire field season, and a few return for a second season as well.

I monitor the quality of data collected by field assistants in three ways. First, I work closely with all assistants for their first week or so, and then assign tasks according to individual responsibility. Experienced assistants work by themselves or in small groups, but less experienced ones continue

Fig. 4.6. Observation towers. *(a)* East observation tower at the study colony, facing west. Height of the floor is 5 meters. Wire cables stabilize tower against wind and American bison. Cubicle below tower is for handling and marking prairie dogs. *(b)* View from north observation tower, facing east. From this tower I can track about 80 adult and yearling prairie dogs. (Photos by Terry Moore.)

Table 4.1. Time Spent Studying Prairie Dogs

Year	Period(s) of research	Number of days in field	Maximum number of reseachers at one time[a]	Person-hours of research[b]
1974	01 May–31 May, 01 Jul–31 Jul	62	2	1,488
1975	20 Jan–15 Jun, 01 Aug–19 Aug	166	3	4,590
1976	18 Apr–15 Jun, 15 Jul–02 Aug	78	4	2,276
1977	11 Apr–08 Jun, 08 Nov–05 Dec	87	3	2,008
1978	15 Feb–02 Apr, 01 May–03 Jul, 24 Oct–09 Nov	128	6	5,148
1979	14 Feb–21 Jun, 01 Sep–19 Sep	147	3	4,212
1980	17 Feb–12 Jun, 18 Oct–31 Oct	131	6	6,660
1981	15 Feb–09 Jun, 17 Oct–29 Oct	128	3	4,314
1982	16 Feb–19 Jun, 13 Oct–28 Oct	140	6	7,608
1983	13 Feb–13 Jun, 17 Oct–02 Nov	138	6	8,604
1984	09 Feb–22 Jun, 14 Oct–27 Oct	149	5	7,316
1985	16 Feb–18 Jun, 04 Oct–15 Oct	135	4	5,888
1986	17 Feb–04 Jun	108	3	3,450
1987	26 Jan–13 Jun	139	4	5,912
1988	07 Feb–03 Jun	118	2	2,736
1989[c]	01 Apr–15 Aug	137	2	1,000
Totals		1,991	115	73,210

[a]Sometimes I have one crew of field assistants for part of one year (e.g., February through April) and another crew for the other part (e.g., May through June). Consequently, these numbers do not add up properly. The total number of different persons that have helped from 1974 through 1989 is 115. With only rare exceptions (2–3 days per year, always after the last prairie dog copulation but before the first parturition), I am always one of the researchers at the study colony each day.

[b]If three persons each watch prairie dogs for 10 hours on the same day, the number of person-hours of observation for that day is 30.

[c]In 1989, W. J. Loughry and one field assistant conducted all research at the study colony of black-tailed prairie dogs at Wind Cave National Park in South Dakota while I studied Gunnison's prairie dogs at Petrified Forest National Park in Arizona.

to work under my direct supervision. Second, to pose or answer key questions, I stay in communication with assistants in other observation towers via two-way radios. Third, from my observation tower with binoculars, I can see over 75% of the prairie dogs at the study colony. With a 60-power telescope, I can usually find most other prairie dogs as well. Whenever possible, I verify important behaviors—copulations and infanticides, for example—reported to me by field assistants working in other towers.

Time Spent Studying Prairie Dogs

Table 4.1 shows that field assistants and I have spent parts of 16 consecutive years (1974 through 1989) studying prairie dogs. Specifically, we have been in the field for 1,991 days and have logged 73,210 person-hours of research. Approximately 25% of these person-hours are my own. About 70% of the research has centered on watching marked prairie dogs under natural conditions, about 25% on livetrapping and marking, and the remaining 5% on miscellaneous activities such as experimental runs with the stuffed American badger, collection of fleas from burrow entrances, and mapping of burrow entrances.

The time periods shown in Table 4.1 reflect my primary interest in copulations, infanticides, and communal nursings rather than in other behaviors that occur during the nonreproductive season. Specifically, in most years I arrive at Wind Cave National Park in early to mid-February before the first copulation, and keep working until sometime in June when I am certain that the last juvenile has emerged from its natal burrow.

Table 4.1 also shows that I usually return to the study colony for approximately 2 weeks in autumn, when the prairie dogs are *easier* to livetrap than at any other time of the year. The single objective each autumn is to mark all the colony residents just after they have acquired the new winter pelage that they will keep until the following spring (chap. 2). The monumental inconvenience of the short autumn trip is offset by the advantage of having individuals marked and ready for behavioral observations when I arrive in February, when the prairie dogs are *more difficult* to livetrap than at any other time of the year.

In addition to the research with black-tailed prairie dogs, field assistants and I have logged about 5,000 person-hours with white-tailed prairie dogs (1974 through 1976: see Hoogland 1979a, 1981a), about 14,000 person-hours with Gunnison's prairie dogs (1989 through 1994), and about 1,600 person-hours with Utah prairie dogs (1991 through 1994). The Mexican prairie dog is the only prairie dog that I have neither seen nor studied.

Livetrapping

I livetrapped and marked every adult, yearling, and emergent juvenile prairie dog at the study colony at least once every year from 1975 through

1989. The total number of different individuals is 1,483, most of whom I have captured at least twice each year. Of these, 216 were original adult or yearling residents in 1975, 49 were immigrants, and 1,218 were juveniles upon first capture. Seventeen other juveniles emerged but died before I could capture them. In addition, I captured another 200 or so prairie dogs at the colony closest to the study colony (Pringle: see Figure 4.3).

To capture adult and yearling prairie dogs, I follow the example of previous investigators (Fitzgerald and Lechleitner 1974; Clark 1977) and use 15 × 15 × 60-centimeter double-door livetraps (National Livetrap Company or Tomahawk Livetrap Company, both of Tomahawk, Wisconsin) (fig. 4.7). In areas with unmarked prairie dogs, I place livetraps about 1 or 2 meters away from burrow mounds. Prairie dogs prefer whole oats to other types of grain (Pfeiffer 1972), so the choice of bait is easy. Vegetable oil on the treadle deters the blowing away of oats on windy days.

To capture juvenile prairie dogs, I use 13 × 13 × 40-centimeter single-door National or Tomahawk livetraps (fig. 4.8). Because juveniles show little interest in oats, I do not bait the livetraps intended for them; this results in less disruption from oat-happy adults and yearlings. I completely surround each natal burrow entrance with ten to fifteen livetraps on the same day or the day after juveniles first emerge there. The distance from the burrow entrance to the open livetrap doors is usually less than 30 centimeters. I also stuff or surround all burrow entrances known to be

Fig. 4.7. Trapping adults and yearlings. I place double-door livetraps about 2 meters from burrow entrances, and bait them with whole oats. Most prairie dogs are frightened by humans walking within the colony, but not this tame individual at burrow entrance-CN. (Photo by Gary Turbak.)

Fig. 4.8. Trapping juveniles. *(a)* To catch juveniles as they first appear aboveground, I surround the natal burrow entrance with unbaited single-door livetraps. *(b)* Juveniles are reluctant to enter livetraps. Occasionally a juvenile will climb over the surrounding rather than enter a livetrap. *(c)* When litters from two adjacent natal burrows emerge at about the same time, mixing of young from the litters might occur if juveniles crawl over the surroundings. To deter such mixing until all juveniles have been eartagged and marked, I sometimes put an "iron curtain" of traps between the two adjacent natal burrow entrances. At other times I stack traps at the surrounding to discourage climbing over. (Photos by John L. Hoogland.)

connected to the main entrance. The juveniles consequently have no place to go aboveground except into one of the surrounding livetraps. I am thus able to determine precise mother-offspring and sibling-sibling genetic relationships that have been elusive to other prairie dog researchers (King 1955; Tileston and Lechleitner 1966). From 1975 through 1988, for example, I captured, eartagged, and marked over 95% of all emergent juveniles at the study colony before they mixed with juveniles from other litters.

I also resort to surroundings of livetraps to capture trap-shy adults and yearlings. While these surroundings increase the probability of capturing certain uncooperative prairie dogs, they create their own problems. For example, individuals sometimes dig under one of the surrounding livetraps rather than enter. Other times individuals climb over the surrounding. Especially elusive individuals sometimes climb over one layer of additional livetraps—and occasionally even over two layers—rather than be captured.

Maternal efforts to save their offspring from capture within a surrounding are also impressive. Sometimes a mother climbs over a surrounding, grabs her juvenile by the leg or nape of the neck, and then drags it over the surrounding to safety. Occasionally a mother transfers her unmarked juvenile into a burrow containing unmarked juveniles from another litter ($N < 5$ affected litters). When this happens, I am unable to assign the transferred and recipient juveniles to a particular mother and litter.

I make no effort to capture juveniles prior to their first emergence from the natal burrow. I therefore have no information on sex ratio, juvenile body mass, or litter size for pre-emergent juveniles. First juvenile emergence is always the point of reference in discussions of sex ratio, juvenile body mass, and litter size.

I always follow my *cardinal rule of livetrapping:* before picking up or moving a livetrap with a prairie dog inside, I label it with flagging tape that indicates the site of capture (fig. 4.9). This method guarantees the return of each individual to its proper location—an important consideration for animals as sedentary as prairie dogs, which otherwise might not find the way back home. I have another important rule for livetrapping: because prairie dogs in livetraps are vulnerable to attacks by predators such as coyotes, American badgers, and bobcats (Smith 1967), I do not leave the study colony unattended when livetraps are open.

Perhaps because of their frequent exposure to livetraps and handling, most prairie dogs at the study colony are amazingly tolerant of the disturbance caused by livetrapping. To minimize this disturbance, I usually concentrate livetrapping into two periods: in October, 4 months before the breeding season (see below), and in May and June, when juveniles are first emerging from their natal burrows. Livetrapping is nonetheless intrusive in at least four ways. First, while checking livetraps, we scare prairie dogs into their burrows. Many return aboveground almost immediately, but

Fig. 4.9. The cardinal rule of livetrapping prairie dogs: before picking up or moving a trap with a prairie dog inside, I always label it with flagging tape that indicates the site of capture. Here label-A7 agrees with burrow entrance-A7. This method guarantees the return of each prairie dog to its site of capture after the process of eartagging and marking. (Photo by John L. Hoogland.)

others do not reappear until more than 15 minutes after we return to the towers. Second, as noted below, trapped prairie dogs waiting to be marked are sometimes absent from the colony for several hours. Third, marked prairie dogs sometimes spend long periods in livetraps intended for unmarked individuals (see below). Finally, livetrapping imposes certain risks on the prairie dogs. I attribute twelve deaths directly to livetrapping: four juveniles became overheated in traps, each of two adults appeared to suffocate after somehow getting its nose wedged under a trap door, and six other adults and yearlings died in traps from unknown causes. About ten other juvenile deaths resulted indirectly from livetrapping when a prairie dog parent was in a livetrap and unable to defend its offspring against infanticide.

My large sample sizes (e.g., chaps. 15 and 16) might lead the reader to believe that prairie dogs are easy to livetrap. This conclusion is false for several reasons. First, most prairie dogs are easier to livetrap the second or third time, and a few individuals become so fond of oats that they leave the home coterie territory in search of baited livetraps. However, first-time livetrapping of prairie dogs is a different story. For example, I needed over 4 *months* to capture all the prairie dogs at the study colony when I initiated research there in January 1975. In 1987, by contrast, I completed the same task in less than 4 *weeks*. Second, a few individuals become *more difficult* to livetrap over time. If one's objective is to capture an indefinite number of prairie dogs, these few problem individuals go unnoticed. However, because one of my primary objectives each year is to capture *all* colony residents (chap. 16), trap-shy individuals are both conspicuous and exasperating. On numerous occasions I set livetraps every morning for a week or more before finally capturing an elusive individual. All the while, of course, trap-happy individuals repeatedly enter the livetraps. Finally, I expected that naive juvenile prairie dogs would be little deterred by surroundings of livetraps and would therefore be easy to capture. I was the naive one. The usual time between first emergence of a litter and the capture of the last juvenile in that litter is about 4 or 5 days, and uncooperative litters can require more than 14 days!

The best way to overcome the difficulty of livetrapping prairie dogs is to set as many livetraps as possible each morning—not exactly an inexpensive or time-efficient solution. For adults and yearlings, field assistants and I routinely set as many as 200 to 300 of the large, double-door livetraps every morning. Similarly, we set a comparable number of the smaller, single-door livetraps during the peak of first juvenile emergences.

Handling, Sexing, and Eartagging

Before marking, I move flagged livetraps containing prairie dogs into an enclosed wooden cubicle (2 meters per side) at the edge of the study colony (see figs. 4.6 and 4.10c). This cubicle offers three important advantages. First, it allows processing of individuals without disturbing efforts to livetrap additional prairie dogs. Second, the dye used for marking (see below) works only under warm conditions. The protection from the wind afforded by the cubicle is sometimes just enough to make the dye usable. In weather in which the cubicle is inadequate, I mark prairie dogs in a heated room or van. Finally, on rare occasions (fewer than 0.5% of all marking operations), the prairie dog escapes. Within the cubicle, forcing the cornered prairie dog back into a livetrap is a simple procedure, and safe return to the site of capture is therefore guaranteed. Without the cubicle, prairie dogs that escape during handling might not find the way back home.

Within the cubicle, I prod the adult or yearling out of the livetrap and into a conical canvas bag that can be unzipped from either end (fig. 4.10). I handle juveniles directly, with or without gloves depending on their size, and use a plastic sandwich bag for obtaining body mass. Routine measurements for each prairie dog include body mass to the nearest gram with a spring balance, sex, number of observed ectoparasites, percentage of new molt, and number of scars. I make no attempt to measure body size or overall condition directly. However, these variables probably vary directly with body mass for prairie dogs, as they do for Richardson's ground squirrels (Michener 1990).

The external genitalia of male and female prairie dogs, like those of spotted hyenas and naked mole rats (Kruuk 1972; Jarvis 1991), are surprisingly similar. However, the distance between the external genitalia and the anus is sexually asymmetrical. Specifically, the vulva and the anus are contiguous, but the penis and the anus are separated by 2 to 3 centimeters in adults and by 1 to 1.5 centimeters in juveniles (figs. 4.11 and 4.12).

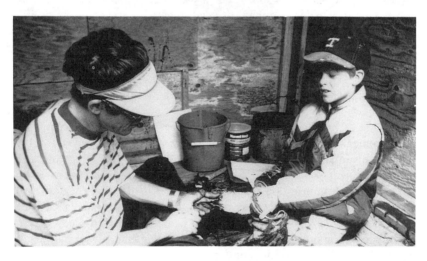

Fig. 4.10. Handling prairie dogs. *(a)* Canvas bag used for handling prairie dogs, custom-designed by Judy G. Hoogland. The bag can be tied at either end, and can be unzipped from either end as well. (Photo by John L. Hoogland.) *(b)* White-tailed prairie dog being held for eartagging. Here I have opened the narrow end of the bag just enough so that the prairie dog's head can protrude. (Photo by John L. Hoogland.) *(c)* Within the cubicle for handling, my son (Mark Hoogland.) holds the front legs of an adult prairie dog through the bag so that I can hold and mark the rear legs. Because the bag works so well for handling adult and yearling prairie dogs, anesthesia is unnecessary. The bag not essential for juveniles, which I handle directly with or without gloves (see fig. 4.12). (Photo by Gary Turbak.)

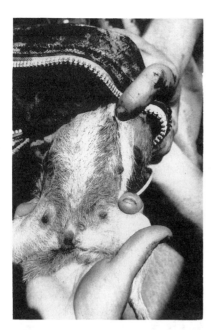

Fig. 4.11. Sexing of adult prairie dogs. *(a)* Adult lactating female. (Photo by Judy G. Hoogland.) *(b)* Adult male with descended testes. (Photo by John L. Hoogland.)

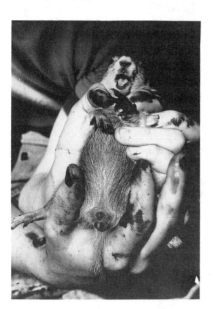

Fig. 4.12. Sexing of juvenile prairie dogs. *(a)* Juvenile female with vulva contiguous to anus. *(b)* Juvenile male with distance of about 1 centimeter between penis and anus. (Photos by Judy G. Hoogland.)

Depending on the stage of the annual cycle, I also record reproductive condition for males (scrotum pigmented or unpigmented; testes descended [scrotal] or undescended) and females (vulva open or closed; lactating or nonlactating). Unfortunately, I have found no quick, reliable method for sexing unmarked prairie dogs from a distance (see also King 1955; Chace 1976).

For eartagging of adults and yearlings, I open the narrow end of the bag just enough for the prairie dog's head to protrude (see figs. 4.10 and 4.13). For other operations involving the bag, a field assistant holds the prairie dog just behind the front legs. I then unzip the wide end of bag and hold the two rear legs with my left hand; my right hand is thus free to comb for ectoparasites and to apply the marking dye. I frequently collect six or seven capillary tubes of blood for later electrophoretic analysis of paternity by clipping the distal end of one or more toenails (chap. 12). After completing all operations, I prod each processed prairie dog back into its flagged livetrap and return it to the site of capture.

In terms of safety, the procedures with the bag work well for both the prairie dogs (only one death during the processing of more than 10,000 adults and yearlings) and the researchers (only two serious bites to the finger). Consequently, I have never seriously considered the use of anesthesias such as ether or nitrous oxide (e.g., see Barash 1973).

For permanent identification, I avoid the toe-clipping used by previous researchers (King 1955; Tileston and Lechleitner 1966; Fitzgerald and Lechleitner 1974; Clark 1977). Instead, I insert a numbered fingerling eartag (National Band and Tag Company, Newport, Kentucky) in each ear (fig. 4.13). Perhaps because their pinnae are tough and leathery, prairie dogs seem oblivious to the eartags, even during insertion. Loss of a single eartag is somewhat common, but only seven prairie dogs at the study colony have lost both eartags before the next recapture. Unlike markers on the pelage, eartags do not disappear with each molting.

Evidently because they mistake white leg bands for fecal sacs, pinyon jay parents sometimes evict banded offspring from the home nest (Marzluff and Balda 1992). For white-footed mice, eartags promote infestation by ticks—probably because the tags interfere with auto- and allogrooming (Ostfeld, Miller, and Schnurr 1993). I have detected no such deleterious effects from the fingerling eartags that I use for the permanent identification of prairie dogs.

Marking of Prairie Dogs

Fingerling eartags enable identification of a prairie dog in the hand. However, unlike certain Olympic and hoary marmots (Barash 1989), prairie dogs do not show sufficient natural variation in the color of pelage to allow identification of individuals from a distance. For long-distance identification I copy previous investigators (King 1955; Tileston and Lechleitner 1966;

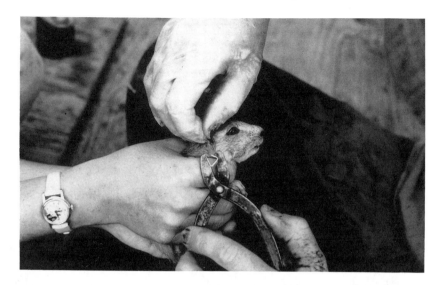

Fig. 4.13. Eartagging prairie dogs.
(a) Eartagging a young prairie dog. I
place a numbered eartag in each ear.
Except when lost in a vicious fight, the
eartags remain with the prairie dog for
life. (Photo by Judy G. Hoogland.)
(b) Adult prairie dog with eartag in
right ear. (Photo by John L. Hoogland.)

Smith 1967; Fitzgerald and Lechleitner 1974) and apply a unique mark
to each individual with Nyanzol-D black fur dye (J. Belmar Incorporated,
North Andover, Massachusetts), which comes as a powder. I make a
saturated dye solution by dissolving the powder in warm distilled water.
Just before applying the marker, I mix a small volume of the dye solution—

2 or 3 milliliters or so, depending on the marker—with an approximately equal volume of 6% hydrogen peroxide.

The Nyanzol-D dye appears rust-colored when first applied, then turns black in about 5 minutes in warm weather (>15°C approximately) (fig. 4.14). In cooler weather the dye requires as much as 20 minutes, and even then the final product is sometimes gray rather than black.

I mark adult males with any number under 50 (one number on each side), and yearling males with black rear legs plus any two-digit number under 50. Adult females have any two-digit number equal to or over 50, and yearling females have black rear legs plus any two-digit number equal

Fig. 4.14. Marking prairie dogs. *(a)* Marking of juvenile prairie dog with Nyanzol-D fur dye. Dye is light brown when first applied. *(b)* After about 5 minutes in warm weather, dyed fur is dark black. Shown here is a 5-stripe juvenile. Dye marks remain until the next molt in either autumn or spring. (Photos by Judy G. Hoogland.)

to or over 50. Some adult females instead receive unique combinations of marks such as blotches, rings, stripes, or rings plus numbers (fig. 4.15). This system allows quick sexing and aging (yearling versus adult) of every prairie dog from a distance. I apply unique eartags to each juvenile, but in most years I only care about identification of *entire litters* rather than *specific juveniles*. I therefore use the same marking pattern for all juveniles of the same litter.

Fig. 4.15. Dye marks used to identify prairie dogs. *(a)* Juvenile-RAC (ring-around-the-collar). *(b)* Yearling female-R51 (rear legs + 51). Notice also how I have marked the burrow entrance-D4 with a jumbo Ritchie cattle eartag mounted on clothesline wire. *(c)* Adult female-HRB (black head + ring-around-the-belly). Amazingly, dye marks such as these do not seem to affect prairie dog behaviors. Note the short vegetation in *(b)* and *(c)*, which facilitates behavioral observations. (Photos by John L. Hoogland.)

The marking process requires about 15 minutes per prairie dog. However, the time between capture of an unmarked individual and later release of that individual after marking is often several hours, especially when I capture several unmarked prairie dogs at the same time. When I catch numerous unmarked prairie dogs late in the day, I usually mark them in a heated room or van and retain them there until the following morning.

Certain marking schemes require more Nyanzol-D dye than others. Male-7, for example, requires little dye, but female-WS (wetsuit) is entirely black from neck to tail. Amazingly, the prairie dogs seem oblivious to their own and others' marks. Specifically, no difference in behavior is evident by, or toward, prairie dogs that I have just marked—even when the mark is as radical as wetsuit. Olfactory cues are evidently more important than visual cues to prairie dogs for the recognition of specific individuals (chap. 10).

Do black marks affect predation? For example, marked prairie dogs are more conspicuous than unmarked ones to humans, and perhaps to natural predators as well. On the other hand, markers might dissuade certain predators who avoid potential prey that are unusual for some reason (Wickler 1968; Owen 1980; Schuler and Hesse 1985; Guilford 1990; Roper 1990). All prairie dogs are marked during my research each year, and predation is rare (chap. 5). Consequently, I cannot say whether black marks make prairie dogs more or less susceptible to predation.

Because they molt the entire pelage both in the spring and again in the autumn (chap. 2), prairie dogs retain their markers only until the next molt. Frustrated by this problem, I considered using permanent long-distance markers. Obvious possibilities are freeze-branding and tattooing (Farrell and Johnson 1973; Lazarus and Rowe 1975; Rood 1980a; Franklin and El-Absy 1985; Sherman, Jarvis, and Alexander 1991). But these methods easily might lead to injury or death. Further, the number of clear, unique, easily applied marks would be low for furry animals as small and light-colored as prairie dogs. In retrospect, I am glad for another reason that I do not use permanent visual markers. Such markers would require fewer recaptures, so that I might not have come to a proper appreciation of the importance of body mass to reproductive success (chap. 16).

Aging of Prairie Dogs

From 1975 through 1989, I captured and processed every adult, yearling, and juvenile prairie dog at the study colony at least once per year. All the original residents in 1975 and all immigrants were of unknown age when first captured. However, all other prairie dogs were juveniles when first captured so that I have known their exact ages thereafter. Consequently, I have had little need to use aging techniques based on either tooth eruption (Stockrahm and Seabloom 1990) or molar attrition (Hoogland and Hutter 1987; Garrett and Franklin 1988; Cox and Franklin 1990).

For certain analyses (e.g., see chapter 13), I use the exact ages (rounded to the nearest year) of prairie dogs first marked as juveniles. More generally, I classify individuals as adults, yearlings, or juveniles. *Juveniles—* also called pups or young—are individuals that first emerged from the natal burrow less than 8 months ago. *Yearlings* have been coming aboveground for 8 months or more, but less than 20 months. *Adults* have been coming aboveground for 20 months or more.

Marking of Burrow Entrances

To mark burrow entrances, I use jumbo, yellow cattle eartags (Ritchie Eartags, Brighton, Colorado) mounted on a 40-centimeter length of clothesline wire (see figs. 4.15b and 4.16). I make no attempt to mark every burrow entrance, but rather concentrate on entrances used for behavioral interactions, final submergence at dusk, or rearing juveniles. Wapiti and pronghorn antelope occasionally remove burrow entrance markers, and American bison sometimes smash them into the ground while wallowing in the dirt. Prairie dogs occasionally chew the burrow entrance markers, but usually for only a few seconds. I mark additional burrow entrances each year, and since 1986 approximately one-half of the burrow entrances at the study colony have had markers.

Daily Routine

My intended daily routine is always the same: to get into the observation tower before the prairie dogs have started to appear aboveground, and to remain there until the last individual has submerged for the night. The time of first emergence in the morning varies with factors such as the severity of the weather, time of sunrise, and stage of the annual reproductive cycle (King 1955; Bakko, Porter, and Wunder 1988; see chaps. 11 and 16), and I attempt to adjust my time of arrival accordingly. On a cold, sunny day in late January or early February, the first prairie dog sometimes does not appear aboveground until as late as 0900 or even 1000 hours, and the last submergence can occur as early as 1530 hours. In the middle of the summer, however, prairie dogs are aboveground from as early as 0530 hours until as late as 2030 hours.

When livetrapping, I arrive at the study colony earlier than usual so that I can set the livetraps before climbing into the tower to record first emergences. Breeding males and estrous females sometimes switch burrows after all other prairie dogs have submerged for the night (chaps. 3 and 11). I therefore continue observations for 30 additional minutes after the last apparent submergence during the breeding season in February and March.

In the early years (1974 through 1979), I worked 7 days per week during the periods of breeding and first juvenile emergences; in April, I sometimes worked only 6 days per week. From 1980 onward, however, at least two observers have been at the study colony from dawn to dusk, 7 days per week, for the entire field season; except for 2 or 3 days after the breeding season but before parturitions, I have always been one of these observers. Being there for more than 99% of the time that they are aboveground, field assistants and I practically *live with* the prairie dogs for 5 months of each year (see table 4.1). This dedication coupled with the longterm nature of the study does not, of course, mean that we see everything that happens or that we discover everything worth learning. It does guarantee, however, that failure to see something does not result from a failure to be there.

Upon my arrival in the morning, I begin to watch the burrow entrances for emerging prairie dogs. Like yellow-bellied marmots (Armitage 1982), prairie dogs usually remain at the burrow entrance for several minutes after first emerging, presumably to scan for predators (King 1955; Hoogland 1979b) (fig. 4.16). This predictable pause greatly enhances the assignment of individuals to their burrow entrances of first emergence. Within a coterie territory, first emergences on a warm morning are highly synchronous, often spanning a period of only 10 to 15 minutes. Researchers working in all three towers are usually able to identify the burrow entrance of first emergence for about 95% of the residents at the study colony each morning.

Fig. 4.16. Scanning for predators early in the morning. Upon first emergence each morning, prairie dogs usually remain at the burrow entrance for several minutes before foraging. Shown here are four marked prairie dogs at burrow entrance-07. (Photo by John L. Hoogland.)

Across the entire study colony, the prairie dogs spread their first emergences over 60 to 120 minutes. In inclement weather (fog, rain, snow, or extreme cold), however, the prairie dogs delay their first emergences and stagger them over as much as several hours.

After all the prairie dogs are aboveground for the day, I turn my attention from first emergences to other behaviors such as copulations, behavioral interactions, and infanticides. As sunset approaches, I begin to watch for final submergences. Final submergences at night are more synchronous than first emergences in the morning, so that the interval between first and last final submergence within the colony is usually only 40 to 60 minutes. Further and more important, prairie dogs usually do not scan from the burrow mound before final submergence—individuals are feeding one minute and gone the next. I therefore feel lucky when field assistants and I are able to record as many as 50% of the burrow entrances of final submergence at the study colony each night.

Curiously, the trees surrounding most of the study colony facilitate the recording of first emergences each morning and final submergences each night. Specifically, shade from the trees delays the sunshine's arrival at the colony's east side in the morning, and hastens the sunshine's departure from the colony's west side in the afternoon. Consequently, the first prairie dogs to emerge each morning are usually on the west side of the colony, and the last prairie dogs to submerge for the night are usually on the east side. In colonies such as Pringle that do not have surrounding trees, first emergences in the morning and final submergences at night are more synchronous because all areas of the colony first recieve, and later lose, sunshine at about the same time.

Why the emphasis on first emergences in the morning and final submergences at night? Knowing where individuals spend the night is important for at least four reasons. First, although watching for amicable interactions is also helpful, the best way to verify that two prairie dogs belong to the same coterie is to show that they use the same burrow at night. Second, the only reliable way to link a mother with her offspring is to verify that she consistently spends the night in a burrow from which juveniles later emerge. Further, an abrupt change in the maternal pattern of burrow usage confirms that the mother has recently lost her litter to infanticide or some other cause. Third, copulations sometimes occur before a male and female first emerge from the same burrow in the morning, or after they have submerged together for the night (chap. 11). The only way to document these copulations, obviously, is to record first emergences and final submergences. Finally, the timing of first emergences and final submergences is also instructive. For example, an unusually early final submergence of a male and female together is a good indicator of a copulation, as is an unusually late first emergence of a male and female together (chap. 11). For females approximately 5 weeks after copulation, an unusually early final submergence is a good indication that parturition is imminent, while an unusually late first emergence is diagnostic of parturition that has already occurred (chap. 16).

Comparisons with Colony Size and Ward Size

When I started in 1974, I predicted that costs and benefits of prairie dog coloniality should vary directly with colony size (i.e., the number of adult and yearling residents). Perhaps some costs and benefits should increase only up to a certain point and then level off.

Entire colonies are amenable to certain analyses regarding the costs and benefits of coloniality: random sampling of fleas per burrow entrance, for example. But other analyses are only feasible within wards (subcolonies; see chap. 2). Tracking aggression per individual, for example, would be practically impossible at large colonies.

From counts of aboveground individuals, ranking the size of wards and colonies is easy. But ranking by density requires estimating the physical area occupied by each ward or colony as well. I therefore base all conclusions on comparisons with ward or colony size rather than ward or colony density.

Measurement of Aggression

Like previous investigators (e.g., Wolfe 1966; Armitage and Downhower 1970; Michener 1973; Thompson 1977; Sherman 1980a), I recognize several types of sciurid aggression. *Fights* involve direct physical contact in the form of biting, kicking, or ramming. A *chase* occurs when one individual actively pursues another fleeing individual. A *runaway* occurs when one prairie dog approaches another, and either runs away or causes the other prairie dog to run away, with no pursuit in either case. *Territorial disputes* at territorial boundaries include staring, bluff charges, flaring of tails, chattering of teeth, and reciprocal sniffing of perianal scent glands (King 1955; Smith 1967) (fig. 4.17).

Rarely, *interment* follows a chase into a burrow entrance. Specifically, the chaser—usually a resident breeding male—sometimes pushes or kicks dirt into the burrow entrance just entered by the fleeing individual—usually another breeding or nonbreeding male of the home coterie territory. Notwithstanding a few notable exceptions that involve hours of hard work to completely close a burrow entrance, interment is usually partial and involves only a minute or two of kicking dirt.

Prairie dogs of both sexes commonly evert their perianal scent glands in the course of territorial disputes (King 1955; Smith 1967) (fig. 4.17). The perianal scent gland has three lobes (Erwin 1971; Jones and Plakke 1981), and is similar to the perianal scent gland of other sciurids, such as Richardson's and Columbian ground squirrels and Olympic and hoary marmots (Sleggs 1926; Kivett, Murie, and Steiner 1976; Kivett 1978;

Fig. 4.17. Juvenile prairie dog showing the three perianal scent glands used in territorial disputes. The volatile secretion from these glands has a strong, skunk-like odor. Similar perianal scent glands occur in other sciurids, such as Richardson's and Columbian ground squirrels and Olympic and hoary marmots (Sleggs 1926; Kivett 1978; Barash 1989). (Photo by John L. Hoogland.)

Barash 1989). Olympic and hoary marmots use cheek glands in certain behavioral interactions (Barash 1989), but I have not observed comparable cheek glands among prairie dogs.

Amicability of Behavioral Interactions

To determine the kinship between two individuals, I have used conventional analysis of pedigrees (Hamilton 1964; Crow and Kimura 1970; Falconer 1981; Shields 1982) to calculate the coefficient of genetic relatedness (r). Coefficients are theoretical, for alleles identical by descent, and thus do not reflect the actual genetic similarity between two individuals (Hamilton 1964; Dawkins 1979).

To examine amicability of behavioral interactions versus kinship (chap. 10), I categorize interactions as either amicable or hostile. Amicable interactions involve a kiss (i.e., oral contact), anal sniff, play, or allogrooming without any subsequent aggression (King 1955; Hoogland 1981b). Hostile interactions usually begin with a kiss or anal sniff that escalates into a fight, chase, or territorial dispute. In looking for possible nepotism, I score combinations of amicable (e.g., kiss + kiss or kiss + allogrooming) or hostile (e.g., fight + chase or chase + territorial dispute) interactions as single interactions.

For each stage of the annual cycle (see chap. 10), I combine all interactions for each dyad and use a single index of amicability. This index—the percentage of interactions that is amicable—is the number of observed amicable interactions divided by the total number of both amicable and hostile interactions multiplied by 100. By this method I weight all dyads equally, regardless of sample size. The mean ± SD number of interactions per dyad per stage is 13.5 ± 4.18 (range = 1–112). When data from the same dyad are available for two or more years, I use data from one year only.

In an earlier analysis (Hoogland 1986), I included data from females that did not rear a litter to first emergence. But unsuccessful females are less aggressive—probably because they have no juveniles to defend (chap. 7)—and thus might be more likely to be nepotistic. In chapter 10 I analyze only female dyads in which both females reared a litter to first juvenile emergence. Similarly, I only analyze male dyads in which both males copulated at least once during the breeding season. Data are available from 9,555 interactions involving 100 male dyads and 11,948 interactions involving 182 female dyads.

Counting of Ectoparasites

Like mammals in general (Kellogg and Ferris 1915; Ewing and Fox 1943; Whitaker and Wilson 1974) and other squirrels in particular (Holdenreid, Evans, and Longanecker 1951; Clark 1959; Hilton and Mahrt 1971; Whitaker and Schmeltz 1973; Michener 1993), prairie dogs frequently harbor fleas, lice, and ticks (Wilcomb 1954; King 1955). The most common flea species are *Opisocrostis hirsutus, O. tuberculatus, O. labis, Pulex simulans, P. irritans,* and *Leptopsylla segnis* (Jellison 1939; Ecke and Johnson 1952; Smit 1958; Costello 1970; Pizzimenti 1975). The most common tick species are *Ixodes kingi* and *Atricholaelaps glasgowi* (King 1955; Pizzimenti 1975; Tyler and Buscher 1975). To my knowledge, nobody has identified the lice that infest prairie dogs.

I count prairie dog ectoparasites by two methods. First, before marking, I comb the sides and back of each individual ten times and then count the number of ectoparasites that fall or jump to the ground (see fig. 5.7b). To prevent counting the same flea, louse, or tick more than once, I put each ectoparasite into ethyl alcohol. The counted ectoparasites probably represent a small percentage of those actually present, and I assume that this percentage is constant. Second, I also count fleas at burrow entrances, by using a 46 × 46-centimeter piece of white flannel attached to flexible cable. Between 1000 and 1800 hours, I submerge the flannel 2 meters into each burrow entrance for 30 seconds (see fig. 5.7a) and then count the fleas that jump onto it (Lechleitner et al. 1968; Barnes, Ogden, and Campos 1972). Unlike the counts from the animals themselves, flea counts from burrow entrances allow quick collection of data from numerous colonies of different sizes. Lice and ticks on the flannel are too rare (<0.3% of all samplings) for any meaningful statistical analysis. I assume for prairie dogs that flea counts from burrow entrances positively correlate with flea counts from the animals themselves—as they do for California ground squirrels (Stewart and Evans 1941)—but I have made no attempt to verify this assumption.

The number of fleas observed at burrow entrances (chap. 5) might seem too small to be of practical significance. However, my technique samples only a small percentage of the fleas living within burrows. Further, individuals submerge into several burrows and visit scores of burrow entrances during the course of a typical day, and thus repeatedly expose themselves to fleas there.

Examination of fresh kills has shown that prairie dogs also harbor numerous endoparasites, including protozoans, tapeworms, roundworms, and spiny-headed worms (Vetterling 1962; Buscher and Tyler 1975). I have made no attempt to quantify endoparasitism among prairie dogs.

Investigation of Vocalizations

Other researchers and I have identified at least twelve distinct prairie dog vocalizations: antipredator call, jump-yip, mating call, defense bark, muffled bark, disputing churr, raspy purr, chuckle, snarl, scream, growl, and tooth chatter (King 1955; Smith 1967; Costello 1970; Waring 1970; Smith, Oppenheimer, and deVilla 1977). Of these, I have investigated only the first four (chaps. 6, 8, and 11).

Experiments with Stuffed American Badgers

To investigate the responses of prairie dogs to a predator, I use stuffed specimens of a natural predator, the American badger (see fig. 5.12). In the descriptions below, notice that the experimental procedure for recording the first visual alarm and first antipredator call (chap. 5) differs slightly from the procedure for recording the identity of antipredator callers (chap. 8).

To determine how quickly prairie dogs give visual alarms and antipredator calls, I use three stuffed American badgers, each mounted on a Plexiglas sled and each presented approximately the same number of times at each ward. I conceal the badger in a black plastic bag just beyond an outermost peripheral burrow mound and then wait in the observation tower for at least 30 minutes until the prairie dogs reappear aboveground and start foraging. Using fishing wire wound around a garden hose reel, a field assistant exposes the badger and slowly pulls it across the colony while I watch the prairie dogs. The assistant pulls the badger at a rate of 11 centimeters per second until 1 minute after the first antipredator call, at a rate of 22 centimeters for the next 5 minutes, and then at a rate of 33 centimeters per second until the badger has passed through the colony (see Hoogland 1977, 1981a for more details). I predicted that individuals in large colonies should detect the predator more quickly than individuals in smaller colonies (chap. 5).

To determine the identity of antipredator callers, I also use the three stuffed American badgers, together presented about seven times per coterie territory per year. I conceal the badger in a brown cloth bag at the edge of a coterie territory and then wait in the observation tower. When all coterie members are foraging aboveground, the field assistant pulls the badger at a constant rate of 22 centimeters per second (see Hoogland 1983b for more details). Meanwhile, I record whether each prairie dog gives or does not give an antipredator call while the badger is crossing the home coterie territory. With only a few exceptions, I perform all experiments shortly after first juvenile emergences (1978 through 1983, and also in 1985). The maximum number of experimental runs in the same coterie territory on the same day is three, all separated by at least 30 minutes. I stop recording data when the badger completes passage through the home territory of the coterie under investigation. For statistical analyses of antipredator calls I have 233 data points from 149 different males and 361 data points from 174 different females. Each of these 594 data points results from approximately seven experimental runs with the stuffed American badgers.

The stuffed badgers offer three advantages for the study of antipredator calls. First, they allow me to concentrate on one coterie at a time so that I can detect the subtle mandibular and abdominal movements of callers (chap. 8). Second, natural predators and live trained predators attack in unpredictable ways. Consequently, the task of trying to determine which individuals are actually threatened and thus more (or less) likely to call is difficult. The stuffed American badgers, however, allow me to expose different prairie dogs to the same level of (simulated) danger. Finally, simulated predators promote large sample sizes. Specifically, I have been able to record 6,000 responses of 323 different prairie dogs to the stuffed American badgers.

One important disadvantage of the stuffed American badgers, of course, is that I do not know whether the prairie dogs respond to them as they would respond to live American badgers. I assume that they do, but cannot rigorously evaluate this assumption because live American badgers at the study colony are rare. Only twice have I been able to identify the source of antipredator calls in response to a live American badger. Both times, as in experiments with the stuffed American badger, certain individuals called while others in the same coterie territory remained silent. I have noticed the same pattern (some calling, others remaining silent) during scores of attacks by live coyotes. Similar patterns of antipredator calling during attacks by live predators occur for Belding's ground squirrels and for yellow-bellied, Olympic, hoary, and alpine marmots (Barash 1975; 1989; Sherman 1977, 1985; Armitage 1982).

Experiments with Radionuclides

Suckling of prairie dog juveniles occurs underground. To investigate the possibility of communal nursing (see chap. 9), Charles Levy, Robert Tamarin, and I use radionuclides to identify the maternal source of milk within juveniles (Tamarin, Sheridan, and Levy 1983; Morimoto, Tamarin, and Levy 1985). Specifically, we inject suspected foster mothers intraperitoneally with 15 microcuries of radionuclide (one radionuclide per prairie dog per coterie), wait 1–3 days, collect samples of blood (6–7 capillary tubes) or scat (1 or 2 pellets, always collected at defecation to guarantee proper identification) from the relevant juveniles, and then check the samples for radionuclide. In 1986, when collecting blood samples, we used the following four radionuclides: ^{60}Co, ^{54}Mn, ^{75}Se, and ^{85}Sr. In 1987, when collecting scat samples, we used ^{85}Sr, ^{113}Sn, ^{75}Se, and ^{65}Zn.

I suspect that a female is a foster mother when her own juvenile offspring have been coming aboveground for 10 days or less and when she spends at least one night in the same burrow with another female's juveniles (i.e., foster offspring) that have also been coming aboveground for 10 days or less.

Levy and Tamarin "blindly" analyzed the samples for radionuclide 2 to 6 weeks after collection. Specifically, they knew nothing about which samples should have shown radionuclides received via communal nursing.

Assignment of Paternity and Determination of Reproductive Success

For most litters, I have behavioral observations of the mother's estrus and copulation(s) as well as blood samples from the mother, all possible sires, and all juveniles. In a minority of cases I have behavioral observations of estrus without blood samples, or vice versa. I made no assignments of paternity before 1978, the year when I learned how to detect copulations (chap. 11) and when I began collecting blood samples. I have been able to determine which juveniles belong to each mother from the outset, so maternal assignments began in 1975.

The seven polymorphic loci used for electrophoretic analyses of paternity are transferrin, esterase-1, esterase-4, nucleoside phosphorylase, 6-phosphogluconate dehydrogenase, phosphoglucomutase-2, and mannose phosphoisomerase (Foltz and Hoogland 1981; Foltz, Hoogland, and Koscielny 1988; Daley 1989, 1992; see also Chesser 1983, 1991a,b). Data from only four or five of these polymorphic loci have been available for certain analyses.

Sometimes coming from the same individual in different years, complete copulatory and electrophoretic data are available from 220 different females ($N = 557$ periods of estrus) and 132 different males ($N = 219$ times that a male copulated at least once during a breeding season). Blood samples for electrophoretic analyses are available from 99% of the emergent litters (291/294) that resulted from these copulations from 1978 through 1988 (N = 898 sampled juveniles).

When a female copulates with a single male, assignment of paternity is easy. Paternities determined from electrophoretic analyses and paternities inferred from behavioral observations are consistent for 99% of litters (168/170) that result when the female evidently copulates with a single male. I could not collect blood samples for two litters whose mothers each copulated with a single male. I assign paternity for both litters to the single male that copulated.

When a female copulates with two or more males and later produces emergent juveniles (N = 92 litters), assignment of paternity depends solely on the electrophoretic analyses as follows:

1. When the blood samples show that a single male has sired all the offspring, then I assign all the offspring to that male (N = 35 litters).

2. When the blood samples show unequivocal multiple paternity, then I assign each offspring to its appropriate sire (N = 13 litters).

3. For 40 litters involving multiple copulations, I can unequivocally assign some, but not all, the offspring to one of the males—i.e., I cannot rule out multiple paternity. In each of these cases, I assign all juveniles to the one male that unequivocally sired at least one or more of them. Surely I have made some errors of assignment in these 40 litters for which electrophoretic data are ambiguous, but errors are probably rare for two reasons. First, multiple paternity is rare (see chap. 12). Second, often I can assign all but one of the juveniles to a single male, and that male has the highest "likelihood of paternity" (see below) for the last juvenile as well.

4. In one case a female copulated with three different males and later reared three emergent juveniles from which I could not collect blood samples due to infanticide. Here I arbitrarily assign single paternity to the first male that copulated because first-copulating males are more likely than later males to sire offspring (chap. 13).

5. In five cases involving multiple copulations, I cannot exclude any of the males from paternity for any of the resulting juveniles. In each case I assign all offspring to the male with the highest "likelihood of paternity" (LOP) (Foltz and Hoogland 1981; Hoogland and Foltz 1982; Foltz and Schwagmeyer 1989). Though the LOP calculations can be tedious, the logic is simple. For example, suppose that a female of genotype AA copulates with two males of genotypes AB and BB and rears five AB offspring. Both males could have fathered all five offspring—i.e., neither can be excluded from paternity for any of the juveniles. However, the

male with genotype *BB* is the more likely sire of each juvenile and therefore of the entire litter—i.e., the male with genotype *BB* has the higher LOP.

For my analyses of annual reproductive success (ARS), I only consider prairie dogs that copulated at least once during the breeding season. I exclude individuals that were sexually inactive for any reason (too young, too old, or condition too poor). For my analyses of lifetime reproductive success (LRS), I only consider individuals that copulated at least once during their lifetimes. In chapter 12 I discuss the effect of these exclusions on my estimates of ARS and LRS. For all analyses of ARS and LRS, I exclude prairie dogs of unknown age that were living at the study colony when I started in 1975. A *breeding individual* is one that copulates—or that is sexually mature and capable of copulating—in the year of investigation.

Only 16 males and 5 females have immigrated into the study colony during my research and later have copulated there (chap. 16). Because male immigrants are almost invariably yearlings that have not yet reproduced, I categorize them as yearlings upon first appearance and use data from them in analyses of LRS (and ARS). However, female immigrants are sometimes older animals that have already reproduced at another colony (chap. 16). I therefore do not use data from female immigrants in analyses of LRS or ARS.

If a prairie dog reproduces at the study colony and then disperses to another colony and reproduces there, my estimate of that individual's LRS will be inaccurately low. This problem is probably trivial, for the reason noted above: most long-distance dispersals occur during the first year (chaps. 14 and 16), before any successful reproduction. Thus, except for a few rare females, prairie dogs usually breed in only one colony over their lifetimes.

Statistical Analyses

Using an IBM-AT minicomputer and a statistical software package called SYSTAT (Wilkinson 1988), I have analyzed all data in this book by nonparametric statistical methods. Though nonparametric tests have less statistical "power" than their parametric equivalents, they often circumvent many of the troublesome parametric assumptions such as equality of variances (Siegel 1956; Conover 1971).

Using a Macintosh-Plus computer, I have drawn all figures with Cricket Graph (Cricket Software) in combination with MacDraw (Apple Computer).

All significance levels (*P*-values) result from two-tailed statistical tests. Means in the text and tables show one standard deviation (SD), but means in figures show one standard error (SE). The number above each SE line indicates the sample size. The term *df* indicates the degrees of freedom for chi-square analyses more complicated than 2×2 (df = 1) or 3×2 (df = 2). When $P > .001$, I have shown the exact P-value. I have shown cases of $P < .001$, even when $P < .0001$, as simply $P < .001$.

For a variety of reasons, sample sizes for seemingly related analyses are not always identical. For example, determining litter size requires only an accurate count of juveniles when they first appear aboveground ($N = 361$ available litters; see chap. 16). However, estimating the frequency of cuckoldry requires blood samples from all juveniles within a litter ($N = 316$ available litters; see chap. 12). Sometimes I explain apparent discrepancies in sample size, but usually I avoid such distractions.

Most parametric and nonparametric statistical tests assume independence of observations (Siegel 1956; Remington and Schork 1970; Conover 1971). However, longterm studies routinely yield multiple observations from the same individuals in the same and different years. How should the behavioral ecologist reconcile these sorts of data with statistical independence? At one extreme, some authors assume independence for multiple observations from the same individual in the same year. At the other extreme, other authors assume dependence of all data from the same individual over several years, and therefore combine these data from the same individual into a single data point. For most analyses, I have used an intermediate approach. Specifically, I assume dependence of data from the same individual in the same year and independence of data from the same individual in different years. In the analysis of litter size versus maternal age (chap. 13), for example, I use data from the same female when she was 2 years old, 3 years old, 4 years old, and so on. For another example, consider antipredator calls in response to the stuffed American badger (chap. 8). Male-19 responded to the badger 9 times in 1978, 5 times in 1979, and 15 times in 1980. I have used one mean calling frequency for male-19 for each year, so that he contributes three data points for statistical analysis.

Results in This Book versus Results in Earlier Publications

Using fewer data, I have previously published several articles that concern many of the same issues addressed in this book. Sometimes I have pointed out major discrepancies between my present and earlier conclusions that result from new analyses with additional data. Where minor or major inconsistencies occur, readers should consider results in this book more accurate and more thorough than results in earlier publications.

Possible Problems with the Study Colony

What are "natural conditions"? This is a difficult question, especially when animals are as social as prairie dogs and when shooting, poisoning, and destruction of habitat have recently reduced populations by over 90% (McNulty 1971; Clark 1979; chap. 2).

Prairie dogs are usually safer and conditions more natural within national parks than elsewhere. But national parks also have problems. Here I summarize some of the obvious conditions at Wind Cave National Park that might have hampered my research.

Let me start with the black-footed ferret, a mustelid predator that specializes on prairie dogs. Black-footed ferrets are on the list of endangered species, and natural populations might already be extinct (Hillman 1968, 1971; Fortenberry 1972; Linder and Hillman 1973; Seal et al. 1989; Reading and Clark 1990; see also chaps. 2 and 5). If the black-footed ferret has played an important role in the evolution of prairie dog sociality, then perhaps *all* today's populations are "unnatural." Attempts to reintroduce laboratory-reared black-footed ferrets into the wild are currently under way (Chadwick 1993; Oldemeyer et al. 1993). If successful, studies of the prairie dogs in recipient sites will be eminently worthwhile.

The fenced area of Wind Cave National Park is only 114 square kilometers. Consequently, the home ranges of most predators include areas outside the park. Though safe from hunters and trappers when inside the park boundaries, predators such as coyotes, bobcats, American badgers, and golden eagles are vulnerable when they wander outside the park. Consequently, the density of predators at the study colony is probably unnaturally low.

Predation at the study colony might be unnaturally low for another reason. While driving past other prairie dog colonies on the route to the study colony each morning, I sometimes spot a coyote or bobcat sitting motionless near a prairie dog burrow mound. The predator's ploy—like the ploy sometimes used by coyotes hunting yellow-bellied marmots (Armitage 1982)—is to catch an unsuspecting prairie dog at first emergence. As noted above, my daily routine is to ascend the observation tower just before the first emergences of the prairie dogs. Although I have observed a bobcat in the colony upon arrival on three occasions, my routine probably deters numerous other predators that otherwise might try the early morning sit-and-wait tactic. The presence of me and my field assistants in the towers probably deters predators at other times of the day as well. Unnaturally low predation rates at the study colony and the total absence of ferrets might affect several conclusions. For example, infanticide (chap. 7) might be rarer if predation on adults and unweaned juveniles were more common (see also chap. 17). Certain demographic measures (chap. 16) and levels of inbreeding (chap. 14) also might be different if predation were more common.

As noted above, I take several precautions to minimize my impact on the social behavior of prairie dogs. I am especially careful—by severely restricting livetrapping, for example—during the critical periods when copulations and infanticides occur.

Shooting and poisoning occurred at Wind Cave National Park in 1983 and 1984, as noted above. Even though park rangers intentionally spared the study colony from such disturbance, the two closest colonies (Pringle and Sanctuary; see fig. 4.3) were not so lucky. Secondary consequences of poisoning at nearby colonies probably have occurred. For example, 43 prairie dogs temporarily or permanently immigrated into the study colony during the 9 years (1975 through 1983) before the shooting and poisoning. In the 6 years following the artificial reduction (1984 through 1989), however, only 6 prairie dogs immigrated into the study colony ($P < .001$, 2×2 chi-square test). Had the higher rate of immigration continued beyond 1983, perhaps infanticide (chap. 7) at the study colony would be more common and moderate inbreeding (chap. 14) would be less common.

Small prairie dog colonies like the study colony do form and persist under natural conditions. However, the majority of prairie dogs live in larger colonies containing thousands of residents. Perhaps many of my results would be different if I had studied prairie dogs in a larger colony.

Hilly habitat with trees surrounds most (>90%) of the study colony's edge. Habitat that appears suitable for expansion occurs only at the north and south ends. With more nearby habitat suitable for expansion, perhaps dispersal (chaps. 14 and 16) and fission of coteries (chap. 6) would be more common and infanticide (chap. 7) would be less common.

Summary

1. My primary study colony is in Wind Cave National Park, South Dakota, and is safe from disturbance caused by shooting, poisoning, and grazing by domestic livestock. I initiated research there in 1975, and continued through 1989.

2. The physical area occupied by the study colony (6.60 hectares) and the number of burrow entrances there (1,591) has remained constant during the entire period of research. Colony size (the number of adult and yearling residents) in May ranges from 92 to 143.

3. To capture adult and yearling prairie dogs, I use double-door livetraps baited with whole oats. To capture juvenile prairie dogs, I use unbaited, smaller, single-door livetraps. To capture juveniles and many trap-shy adults and yearlings, I surround the relevant burrow entrance with livetraps so that the individual cannot emerge without being captured.

4. My daily routine, 7 days a week, is to arrive at the study colony early in the morning before prairie dogs are aboveground and to remain there until all individuals have submerged for the night. Determining which animals spend the night together in the same

burrow is valuable for several reasons. Depending on the stage of the reproductive season, I concentrate my observations on copulations, infanticides, behavioral interactions, or communal nursings.

5. During 1,991 days, 115 field assistants and I have logged 73,210 person-hours of research. Most of these person-hours (about 70%) involve watching marked prairie dogs under natural conditions.

6. I analyze all data by nonparametric statistical methods. Results in this book are more accurate and thorough than results in previous publications.

7. Several conditions at the study colony might be unnatural. Likely possibilities include absence of the black-footed ferret, low density of other predators, reduced immigration due to artificial reduction at nearby colonies, small size of the colony, disturbance from livetrapping, and shortage of adjacent habitat for expansion.

5 Costs and Benefits of Coloniality

Why Do Animals Live in Colonies?

Some animals might live in colonies because of an extreme shortage of suitable habitat, others to obtain more food, and still others to avoid predators (Alexander 1974; Bertram 1978; Wittenberger and Hunt 1985). The first of these possibilities is equivalent to "forced coloniality," in which individuals do not gain from the proximity of conspecifics as they do in the other two types of coloniality (Alexander 1974). Forced coloniality is rare, perhaps being important for animals such as barn swallows, certain seabirds, and northern elephant seals (Bartholomew 1952; Lack 1968; Snapp 1976). However, some colonies where habitat seems to be limiting result because individuals seek out remote places safe from enemies, and thus depend ultimately on attempts to escape predation (Lack 1968; Alexander 1974; Robinson 1985; Wittenberger and Hunt 1985).

Coloniality dependent on the social facilitation of foraging can occur in two ways. The first involves cooperation among conspecifics to capture large or elusive prey that is inaccessible to solitary foragers. Such cooperation probably occurs for predators such as Harris's hawks, killer whales, African wild dogs, and spotted hyenas (Martinez and Klinghammer 1970; Lawick and Lawick-Goodall 1971; Kruuk 1972; Bednarz 1988; Fanshawe and Fitzgibbon 1993). This route to coloniality is uncommon, partly because predators are relatively rare (compared with herbivores, for example) and partly because the teamwork necessary for cooperative hunting does not evolve easily (Alexander 1974).

Coloniality dependent on the social facilitation of foraging also might result when large food supplies—swarming insects, for example—are so ephemeral or unpredictable that solitary foragers can only rarely find them. If so, then communication—whether deliberate or accidental—about the location and quality of food can occur at the colony site, which serves as an "information center" (Ward 1965; Ward and Zahavi 1973; Hoogland and Sherman 1976). Colonies that serve as "information centers" are probably uncommon (Alexander 1974), but perhaps occur for common terns, cliff swallows, ospreys, and evening bats (Erwin 1978, 1979; Waltz 1982, 1987; Brown 1986; Greene 1987; Wilkinson 1992b).

Coloniality is ubiquitous among animals of all taxonomic groups, from protozoans through primates. If coloniality resulting from either shortage of suitable habitat or social foraging is rare, the inescapable conclusion is that coloniality most commonly evolves to reduce predation. Why is this so? One reason is that most animals have one or more predatory species that they must avoid in order to survive and reproduce. By contrast, few animals either experience a severe shortage of suitable habitat or would gain by social foraging.

Coloniality dependent on avoiding predators is common for another reason. Suppose that parents of a solitary avian species always try to chase predators away from the home nest, and that such chasing deters 50% of all attackers. By merely nesting close to another conspecific pair, parents of avian species such as kittiwakes and common, black-headed, and Franklin's gulls instantly increase the probability of successful deterrence of predators because additional parents are now available for cooperative attack ("mobbing") (Kruuk 1964; Burger 1974; Andersson 1976; Gotmark and Andersson 1984). Such increased protection of the home nest need not involve intricate teamwork, but instead results simply because two sets of parents benefit from deterring a predator from the same general area.

Two other benefits are also readily available to prey individuals who initially nest closer than usual for some reason. First, via "protection by dilution" (Hamilton 1971; Bertram 1978; McKaye 1981), the probability that any particular individual will be the predator's victim varies inversely with colony size for animals such as monarch butterflies, common eiders, and black-headed gulls (Patterson 1965; Munro and Bedard 1977; Calvert et al. 1979). Second, via "selfish herd effects" (Hamilton 1971; Vine 1971; Alexander 1974), individuals within groups of animals such as starlings, queleas, and red deer have the opportunity to manipulate other group members into being more conspicuous and vulnerable (Darling 1937; Tinbergen 1951; Crook 1960).

Because of cooperative attack against predators, "protection by dilution," and "selfish herd effects," the initial step toward coloniality is often easy when the ultimate causation is avoidance of predation. However, the initial step is more difficult when coloniality depends on social facilitation of foraging. Reduced predation is thus more likely than social facilitation of foraging to be the founding advantage of coloniality (Alexander 1974; Bayer 1982).

Like coloniality dependent on social facilitation of foraging, coloniality dependent on reduced predation can result from more than one mechanism. I have just discussed the possibilities of cooperative attack, "protection by dilution," and "selfish herd effects," for example. Increased awareness of predators offers another such mechanism. When stalking a solitary individual, a predator must elude only that individual's detection system. When stalking an individual within a colony, however, the predator must elude numerous individuals' detection systems (Bertram 1980; Pulliam and Caraco 1984; Fitzgibbon 1990). If individuals give either an intentional or an unintentional signal after spotting a predator, then colonial animals such as laughing doves, bank swallows, and cliff swallows detect predators more quickly and thus have more time to flee than do solitary individuals (Siegfried and Underhill 1975; Hoogland and Sherman 1976; Brown and Brown 1987).

In colonies that serve as "information centers" (Ward 1965; Ward and Zahavi 1973; Brown 1986), individuals must live close enough so that they can monitor the foraging activities of conspecifics, with or without specific food-finding signals (Alexander 1974; Hoogland and Sherman 1976). Such monitoring does not require dense packing of individuals, and the costs of coloniality will encourage individuals to *minimize* density so long as they can still monitor their conspecifics. In coloniality dependent on reducing predation, however, benefits resulting from "protection by dilution" and "selfish herd effects" are sometimes maximal at the highest possible densities (Hamilton 1971; Alexander 1974; Bertram 1978); an extreme shortage of suitable habitat also might promote high density within colonies. In some extreme cases, nests almost or actually touch, as in colonies of sandwich terns, Adélie penguins, common murres, and northern and Peruvian gannets (Cullen 1960; Tenaza 1971; Birkhead 1977, 1978; Nelson 1978). In other extreme cases, individuals are constantly crawling over or bumping into conspecifics, as in colonies of Mexican free-tailed bats and northern and southern elephant seals (Davis, Herreid, and Short 1962; Le Boeuf 1974, 1981; McCann 1981; McCracken 1984). Colony density thus might help ecologists to distinguish between coloniality dependent on "information centers" and coloniality dependent on either reduced predation or a shortage of suitable habitat.

Regardless of ultimate causation, coloniality is never without certain costs, some of which are automatic and unavoidable (Alexander 1974; Hoogland and Sherman 1976). For example, frequent contacts within colonies inevitably promote the transmission of diseases, ectoparasites, and endoparasites (Schoening, Schwartz, and Lindquist 1956; Simms 1956; Rothschild and Clay 1957; Davis, Herreid, and Short 1962; Kennedy 1975)— sometimes with catastrophic results for animals such as purple martins, sooty terns, brown pelicans, cliff swallows, and harbor and Baikal seals (Camin and Moss 1970; Feare 1976; King, Blankinship, and Paul 1977; Brown and Brown 1986; Harwood and Hall 1990). Bubonic plague commonly eliminates entire colonies of white-tailed, black-tailed, Gunnison's, and Utah prairie dogs (Lechleitner, Tileston, and Kartman 1962; Lechleitner et al. 1968; Barnes, Ogden, and Campos 1972; Collier and Spillett 1975;

Clark 1977; Rayor 1985a; Cully 1989; Fitzgerald 1970, 1993). Infanticide is a major source of mortality for colonial animals such as northern elephant seals, hanuman langurs, and African lions (Hrdy 1974; Bertram 1975; Le Boeuf and Briggs 1977), and is *the* major source of juvenile mortality for Belding's ground squirrels (Sherman 1981b) and prairie dogs (chap. 7).

Colonies also inexorably foster competition for critical resources such as food and mates. Further, the visual and vocal conspicuousness of colonies of animals such as sandwich terns, black-headed gulls, and shelducks commonly attracts the attention of predators (Cullen 1960; Kruuk 1964; Pienkowski and Evans 1982). Finally, even though their usual function is to reduce predation, colonies sometimes offer unique opportunities for certain predatory specialists. Prairie dog coloniality, for example, has probably evolved against diurnal predators such as coyotes, bobcats, golden eagles, and prairie falcons, but has secondarily left prairie dogs exceedingly vulnerable to nocturnal black-footed ferrets (see below).

Both costs and benefits usually increase directly with colony size, but not necessarily in linear fashion. For example, the relationship between ectoparasitism per individual and colony size might be positive only up to a certain asymptotic point—perhaps because an individual can harbor only a finite number of fleas and lice. If the benefits consistently increase more sharply than the costs with colony size, then the upper colony size that is still adaptive might be unlimited. If the costs consistently increase more sharply with colony size, however, then only smaller colony sizes might be adaptive, with one size perhaps being "optimal." Another, albeit remote, possibility is that the ratio of benefits to costs remains constant with colony size; under these "ideal free conditions" (Fretwell and Lucas 1970; Parker and Sutherland 1986), colony size does not affect reproductive success (Pulliam and Caraco 1984; Brown 1985, 1988; Jones 1987).

On the other hand, "optimal" colony size might vary for different individuals (Pulliam and Caraco 1984; Brown, Stutchbury, and Walsh 1990). Individuals that are especially adept at avoiding or removing fleas and lice, for example, can more easily incur the cost of increased ectoparasitism in large colonies—so that "optimal" colony size will be higher for these individuals than for other individuals. Conversely, fast, wary individuals that easily evade predators gain little from the increased vigilance of large colonies—and therefore will have a lower "optimal" colony size than other individuals.

"Optimal" colony size might vary for the same individual over time. When wary, fast, and in good condition, for example, young adults might seek out small colonies and thereby avoid the higher costs of larger colonies. As eyesight and swiftness decline with age, however, individuals probably will be more likely to tolerate the greater costs of larger colonies in order to be safer from predators.

In this chapter I document the increased competition and increased ectoparasitism that result from prairie dog coloniality. I then show that the only offsetting benefit of prairie dog coloniality is probably increased safety from predators. Finally, I assess comparative data from white-tailed prairie dogs.

The Costs of Prairie Dog Coloniality

Increased Aggression

Ecologists measure the intensity of competition in many ways (Tilman 1982). One obvious way is to quantify aggression, with the assumption that aggression results ultimately from competition. I predicted that aggression among prairie dogs would increase directly with ward (subcolony) size (fig. 5.1). But a mere documentation of more fights, chases, runaways, and territorial disputes in larger wards would be trivial. The real issue is whether more aggressive interactions *per individual* occur in larger groups, as they do for animals such as bank swallows and yellow-bellied marmots (Barash 1973; Armitage 1975, 1977; Hoogland and Sherman 1976). Figure 5.2 shows the predicted per individual trends for prairie dogs.

Prairie dogs within an isolated coterie territory—and thus a small ward—obviously cannot interact with prairie dogs from other coterie territories. However, individuals living in a coterie territory surrounded by other territories—i.e., a larger ward—can have both intra- and intercoterie interactions. The positive trends in figure 5.2 probably result primarily from increased intercoterie aggression in the larger wards. However, the prairie dogs in the three wards that I observed were unmarked, so I could not investigate this hypothesis.

Fig. 5.1. Fight involving two prairie dogs. Male-0 is about to attack the unidentified prairie dog on the right. (Photo courtesy of Monte G. Garrett.)

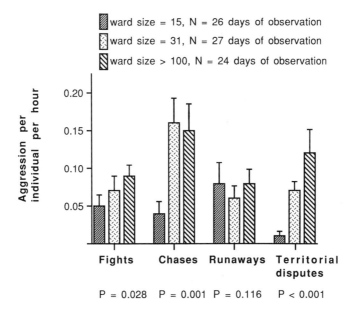

Fig. 5.2. Aggression versus ward size. Two field assistants and I quantified aggression, usually simultaneously, from 1100 hours until 1300 hours, at three wards of different sizes, from 17 February through 25 March 1975. *P*-values are from the Kendall rank correlation test.

Is aggression *costly* to prairie dogs? Three lines of evidence indicate an affirmative answer. First, aggressive interactions among prairie dogs inevitably involve losses of time and energy, as they also do for animals such as acorn woodpeckers, spotted hyenas, and red deer (Kruuk 1972; Koenig 1981b; Clutton-Brock, Guinness, and Albon 1982). The mean ± SD duration of territorial disputes among prairie dogs in February and March of 1978, for example, was 4.76 ± 6.00 minutes ($N = 694$) (fig. 5.3). Two pregnant females in 1980 set the record by having a dispute that began as soon as they first emerged on a cold winter morning and continued until one submerged for the night—over 6 hours with no foraging! Second, winners of aggressive interactions sometimes temporarily or permanently chase losers away from colony sites. Away from burrows and other prairie dogs, evicted losers are easy prey (chap. 16; see also King 1955; Garrett and Franklin 1988). Finally, like other animals in general (Geist 1971; Kruuk 1972; Schaller 1972; Miller 1975; Wilkinson and Shank 1976) and squirrels in particular (Smith 1968; Steiner 1972; Holmes 1977; Sherman and Morton 1984; Michener and Locklear 1990), prairie dogs commonly incur injuries from fights (fig. 5.4). For example, adult males and females have few facial injuries and scars before the frequent, vicious fighting that occurs during the breeding season of February and March (see chap. 11).

By the end of the breeding season, however, facial injuries and scars among breeding individuals are common (fig. 5.5). Further, facial scars are more common among breeding males, who fight more than breeding females and who sometimes incur facial wounds inflicted by their mates during copulation (chap. 11). Injuries include loss of fur and blood, and leg injuries sometimes hobble individuals for several weeks. Two extreme fights led to the loser's death (fig. 5.4b).

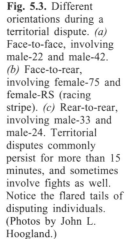

Fig. 5.3. Different orientations during a territorial dispute. *(a)* Face-to-face, involving male-22 and male-42. *(b)* Face-to-rear, involving female-75 and female-RS (racing stripe). *(c)* Rear-to-rear, involving male-33 and male-24. Territorial disputes commonly persist for more than 15 minutes, and sometimes involve fights as well. Notice the flared tails of disputing individuals. (Photos by John L. Hoogland.)

Fig. 5.4. Costly outcomes of aggression among prairie dogs. *(a)* Male-24's head is so scarred that he hardly has any hair left. *(b)* After killing male-00 in a vicious series of fights, male-47 cannibalizes him at burrow entrance-R. (Photos by John L. Hoogland.)

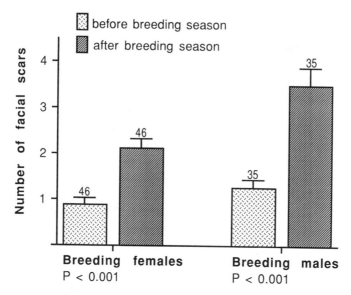

Fig. 5.5. Facial scars before and after the breeding season. In 1984 and 1985, I examined adult prairie dogs for facial scars in February, just before the onset of breeding. I then examined the same individuals for scars in April, shortly after the breeding season was over. The number above each SE line indicates the number of breeding individuals examined. *P*-values are from the Wilcoxon matched-pairs signed-ranks test. Breeding individuals of both sexes have more scars after the breeding season. Further, breeding males have more facial scars than breeding females both before ($P = .044$, Mann-Whitney U test) and after ($P = .008$, Mann-Whitney U test) the breeding season.

Increased Transmission of Diseases and Ectoparasites

Individuals of colonial species probably contract diseases and ectoparasites more often than individuals of closely related solitary species. Further, diseases and ectoparasites probably are more troublesome in large than in smaller colonies (Alexander 1974; Freeland 1976, 1979; Duffy 1983; Brown and Brown 1986). At least two reasons underlie these predictions. First, diseases and ectoparasites spread best during periods of proximity or actual physical contact (Stefferud 1956; Rothschild and Clay 1957; Kennedy 1975). Second, some ectoparasites require repeated contacts with different host individuals for maximal reproductive output (Cheng 1974).

The most devastating disease for prairie dogs is bubonic plague, also called sylvatic plague or wild rodent plague (Eskey and Haas 1940; Miles, Wilcomb, and Irons 1952; Pollitzer and Meyer 1961; Barnes 1982, 1993). Bubonic plague first arrived unnaturally in North America only a few hundred years ago via fleas on animals unloaded from European ships (Pollitzer 1951; Olsen 1981; Barnes 1982, 1993). Fleas are the major vectors, but lice and ticks also might transmit bubonic plague (Hirst 1953; Pollitzer 1952; Barnes 1982, 1993). Entire colonies of prairie dogs quickly disappear after the initial introduction of bubonic plague (Barnes, Ogden, and Campos 1972; Barnes, 1993).

Although bubonic plague devastates other sciurid populations as well, prairie dogs seem to be especially susceptible (Eskey and Haas 1940; Pollitzer and Meyer 1961; Olsen 1981). The logical reason for this difference is that prairie dogs are more densely colonial than other squirrels (Armitage 1981; Hall 1981; Michener 1983). However, their extreme vulnerability might be an artifact that results because prairie dogs are easier to census and track than other, less colonial squirrels (Lechleitner et al. 1968; Miles, Wilcomb, and Irons 1952).

I cannot easily study the transmission of bubonic plague or other prairie dog diseases. I can, however, count ectoparasites, which indirectly influence the transmission of disease. My prediction is that ectoparasitism should increase directly with colony size, as it does for animals such as cliff and barn swallows, Townsend's big-eared bats, and common vampire bats (Kunz 1976; Wilkinson 1985; Brown and Brown 1986; Shields and Crook 1987). Figure 5.6 supports this prediction for flea counts at burrow entrances made in August 1975, June 1977, and April 1978 (fig. 5.7; see chap. 4). However, the variation in fig. 5.6 demonstrates that factors other than colony size also must affect flea infestation of prairie dog burrow entrances.

Do ectoparasites depress individual fitness for prairie dogs, as they do for other colonial animals such as purple martins and cliff swallows (Camin and Moss 1970; Brown and Brown 1986), and for other squirrels such as

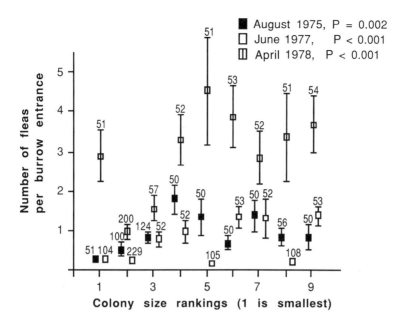

Fig. 5.6. Number of fleas per burrow entrance versus colony size. The number above each SE line indicates the number of burrow entrances sampled. *P*-values are from the Kendall rank correlation test. I could not accurately count all residents at each colony, but could rank colonies by size as shown here.

eastern chipmunks and woodchucks (McKinney and Christian 1970; Ko 1972a,b; Bennett 1973)? Three lines of evidence indicate an affirmative answer. First, although I did not directly observe such transmission, ectoparasites can transmit debilitating or fatal diseases such as bubonic plague (see above). Second, ectoparasites frequently remove blood. Third, their bites, especially those of ticks, sometimes damage the integument and thereby promote infections.

Autogrooming and allogrooming remove ectoparasites for animals such as house mice, common vampire bats, Thomson's and Grant's gazelles, and mantled howler monkeys (Murray 1961, 1987; Bell and Clifford 1964; Wilkinson 1986; Dudley and Milton 1990; Hart 1990). The same is probably true for prairie dogs. If so, then auto- and allogrooming should be more common in large wards, which contain more fleas than smaller wards. These behaviors are costly, not only because they involve time and energy, but also because they reduce individual wariness (Hart et al. 1992; Maestripieri 1993). Curiously, rates of autogrooming and allogrooming in small and large prairie dog wards are almost identical (fig. 5.8).

Fig. 5.7. Two ways to measure ectoparasitism among prairie dogs. *(a)* To measure ectoparasitism at burrow entrances, a researcher counts fleas that jump onto a piece of white flannel that has been submerged 2 meters for 30 seconds. This method only rarely detects lice and ticks. (Photo by John L. Hoogland.) *(b)* To measure ectoparasitism on the prairie dogs, I comb the back and each side 10 times with a fine-toothed comb and then count the fleas, lice, and ticks that fall below. I also count all ectoparasties that I see on the fur or skin. (Photo by Judy G. Hoogland.)

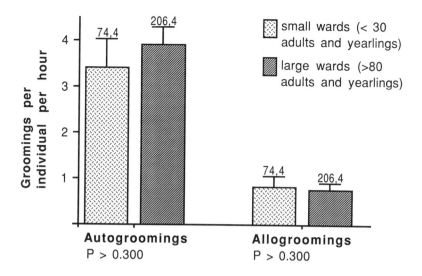

Fig. 5.8. Autogroomings and allogroomings versus ward size. I record groomings during 30-minute periods when I also record individual alertness (see fig. 5.15). The numbers above each SE line indicate the number of 30-minute observation periods and the number of different wards observed. *P*-values are from the Mann-Whitney *U* test.

Increased Probability of Misdirected Parental Care

Parents of solitary animals only rarely mistake another nest for their own, encounter unrelated offspring at the home nest, or have their own offspring wander into strange nests. But these are common problems within colonial animals such as royal and crested terns, common and thick-billed murres, northern elephant seals, and Mexican free-tailed bats (Davies and Carrick 1962; Buckley and Buckley 1972; Le Boeuf, Whiting, and Gantt 1972; McCracken 1984, 1993; Gaston, De Forest, and Noble 1993). One possible consequence is that parents of colonial animals will lose their offspring in a crowd. Another is that parents will accidentally rear others' offspring. Is misdirected parental care another cost of prairie dog coloniality?

Following first juvenile emergences from the natal burrow, quick mixing of young from different litters is ubiquitous for ground squirrels and marmots (McCarley 1966; Michener 1973; Slade and Balph 1974; Leger and Owings 1978; Barash 1989). The same is true for prairie dogs: juveniles from different litters within the home coterie territory begin to interact aboveground within days after first emergence from the natal burrow (fig. 5.9; see also King 1955; Costello 1970). First mixings result primarily from the wanderings of the juveniles themselves. However, first mixings also result when a mother transfers her emergent young from the home nursery burrow to a burrow containing another mother's young. For the latter, the mother uses her mouth to grab her offspring one at a time by the nape of the neck, the belly, or one of the legs (fig. 5.10). Sometimes mothers transfer by slowly "leading" offspring from one burrow entrance to another. Soon after first mixing, juveniles from different litters begin to spend the night together with one or more mothers in the same burrow, where communal nursing occurs (chap. 9). The difficulty of livetrapping entire litters at more than one colony has precluded an investigation of the effect of colony size on juvenile mixing.

When the possibility of misdirected parental care becomes serious, then natural selection sometimes favors either parents that can discriminate between their own and others' offspring, or juveniles that can discriminate between their own and others' parents. Such parent-offspring recognition helps to redirect parental effort, and occurs for colonial animals such as bank and cliff swallows, Mexican free-tailed bats, Galápagos fur seals, and Galápagos sea lions (Trillmich 1981; Beecher, Stoddard, and Loesche 1985; Beecher et al. 1986; Balcombe 1990; Balcombe and McCracken 1992). Curiously, prairie dog mothers do not reject juveniles from other litters of the home coterie territory that wander near the home nursery burrow and mix with their own offspring—even when the invading juveniles have been aboveground for several weeks. Further, emergent juveniles seem unable to discriminate between their own and others' mothers.

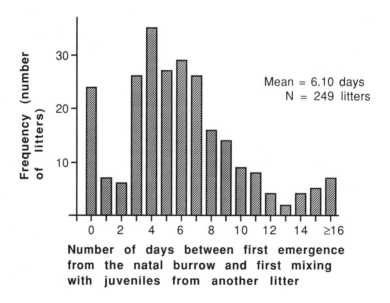

Number of days between first emergence from the natal burrow and first mixing with juveniles from another litter

Fig. 5.9. Number of days between first juvenile emergence and first mixing with young from a different litter. I record mixing when two juveniles interact aboveground or when they appear on the same burrow mound.

Fig. 5.10. Prairie dog mother-H3 transferring juvenile-H3X from the natal burrow to a different burrow. Mothers usually transfer by grabbing the juvenile by one of the legs, as seen here, or by the neck or belly. Sometimes mothers transfer their juveniles to a burrow containing juveniles from another litter. (Photo by John L. Hoogland.)

Evidently the mixing of emergent young from the same coterie territory is not seriously costly to prairie dog mothers, even though communal nursing of foster juveniles is a common result (see also chaps. 9 and 10).

Increased Conspicuousness and Increased Attractiveness to Predators

A colony of animals must almost always be more conspicuous and attractive to predators than is a single animal (Cullen 1960; Sillén-Tullberg 1990; Cooper and Vitt 1991). Increased exposure to predators is therefore a possible cost of coloniality.

A predator might detect a prairie dog colony by seeing mounds at burrow entrances, by seeing the prairie dogs themselves, or by hearing their vocalizations. All three of these potential cues increase directly with ward size ($P < .001$, Kendall rank correlation test; see fig. 5.11 and Hoogland 1979a).

If increased vocal conspicuousness within large wards is costly, then natural selection might favor individuals who are unusually quiet. If so, then territorial (or jump-yip; see chap. 8) calls *per individual* per hour might vary inversely with ward size even though territorial calls per hour vary directly with ward size (fig. 5.11). Contrary to this prediction, the

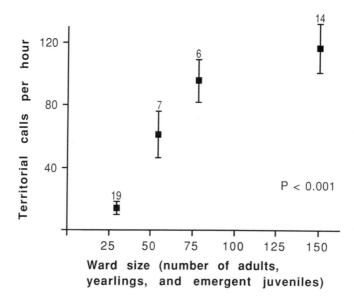

Fig. 5.11. Territorial calls per hour versus ward size. The number above each SE line indicates the number of days on which I counted territorial calls for 30 minutes. The *P*-value is from the Kendall rank correlation test. Ward size for this graph includes emergent juveniles, which sometimes give territorial calls.

number of territorial calls per individual per hour varies directly with ward size ($P < .001$, Kendall rank correlation test; data taken from fig. 5.11, then transformed). Evidently, either increased vocal conspicuousness of colonies to predators is not seriously deleterious, or the importance of territorial calls in aggression outweighs any associated costs. Similarly, prairie dogs evidently do not attempt to reduce the visibility of either themselves or their burrow mounds. Indeed, several of their activities—such as the construction of ostentatious rim craters (chap. 3) and the regular clipping of tall vegetation (chap. 2 and below)—clearly *increase* the visual conspicuousness of colonies.

Miscellaneous Costs

Besides the four costs discussed above, other costs of prairie dog coloniality also might exist. Likely possibilities include increased probability of: deterioration of burrows and their mounds, loss of nest materials to pilfering conspecifics, interference with copulations, misdirected parental care resulting from either intraspecific brood parasitism or cuckoldry, and loss of offspring to marauding conspecifics (Hoogland and Sherman 1976). Because of their rarity (e.g., stealing of nest materials; see below) or difficulty of observation (e.g., infanticide; see chap. 7), I did not compare these miscellaneous costs with prairie dog colony size. Here I will only comment briefly on some of the more interesting miscellaneous costs.

Like Belding's ground squirrels and hoary and Olympic marmots (Sherman and Morton 1979; Barash 1989), prairie dogs—especially pregnant and lactating females—frequently collect nest material for burrows where they spend the night (chap. 3; see also King 1955 and fig. 11.17). I therefore expected regular stealing of nest material similar to what occurs within colonies of birds such as kittiwakes, Adélie penguins, and cattle egrets (Cullen 1957; Tenaza 1971; Siegfried 1972). Incredibly, I observed stealing by only one prairie dog. Female-WA in 1986 repeatedly stole nest material from the burrow where the resident breeding male regularly spent the night and took it into the nursery burrow containing her unweaned offspring.

Interference with copulation—when a male tries to separate a copulatory pair—commonly occurs in colonial animals such as dunnocks, Belding's ground squirrels, yellow-toothed cavies, wild guinea pigs, and stump-tailed macaques (Rood 1972; Hanken and Sherman 1981; Davies 1985; Bruce and Estep 1992). Interference with copulation also occurs among prairie dogs (chaps. 11 and 12).

Intraspecific brood parasitism, common among birds but rare among mammals, occurs when a parent transfers its offspring into another parent's nest for rearing (Yom-Tov 1980; Andersson 1984a; Rohwer and Freeman 1989; Petrie and Møller 1991). Does such parasitism occur within prairie dog colonies? Specifically, do females ever give birth in the nursery burrows of other females? Evidently not. I have never seen a female enter another female's nursery burrow on the same day that the trespassing female also gave birth. Nor have I ever seen a female carry one of her own offspring into another female's nursery burrow, except just before or just after first juvenile emergence (see above and chap. 9).

Misdirected male parental care resulting from cuckoldry is omnipresent among avian species (Wrege and Emlen 1987; Brown and Brown 1988a; Sherman and Morton 1988; Brooker et al. 1990; Møller and Birkhead 1993). The minimal frequency of misdirected paternal care among prairie dogs resulting from cuckoldry is 8% (chap. 12).

The most serious cost of prairie dog coloniality is the increased incidence of infanticide. Because it is so common (affecting 39% of litters born) and so varied (four distinct types), I have devoted an entire chapter to infanticide among prairie dogs (see chap. 7).

Possible Reasons for Prairie Dog Coloniality

Shortage of Suitable Habitat?

Unused Habitat Within or Near Colonies.   Emigration to, and colonization of, new colony sites probably is expensive and dangerous for prairie dogs (chaps. 3 and 16). However, expansion of already existing colonies should be easier and safer. If habitat is limiting, then unused suitable habitat near established colonies should be rare.

Unfortunately, unless prairie dogs are actually living in a particular area, verification of its suitability is practically impossible. With this reservation in mind, I have qualitatively examined nine prairie dog colonies at Wind Cave National Park for evidence of adjacent surplus habitat. Every colony has unused, level prairie habitat adjacent to it that appears suitable for expansion. In other words, prairie dogs seem to be more clumped than necessary.

Evidently in response to adjacent suitable habitat, King's (1955) "ward A" increased from 2.10 hectares in 1948 and 1949 to 2.95 hectares in 1950. Such increases are the rule rather than the exception for prairie dog colonies tracked for more than a year (Lovaas 1973; Knowles 1985; Halpin 1987; Garrett and Franklin 1988). The implication is that prairie dogs typically have unused suitable habitat at their disposal.

Frequency of Isolated Prairie Dogs.   If coloniality results mainly from a shortage of suitable habitat, then prairie dogs should avoid the costs of coloniality by isolating themselves whenever possible. Such isolation could occur either when patches of habitat are large enough for only one individual or when patches are too large to be saturated by the local population. Costello (1970) once found a lone prairie dog living near Nunn, Colorado. Though I have looked, I have never detected an isolated prairie dog. Perhaps this dearth results because isolates are so vulnerable to predation (see below).

Social Facilitation of Foraging?

The usual factors that promote social facilitation of foraging do not apply to prairie dogs. For example, individuals are herbivorous and do not hunt in groups (chap. 2). Further, food supplies are neither large nor unpredictable; rather, individuals feed on herbaceous tidbits growing within the home coterie territory (chap. 6).

One type of social facilitation of foraging might conceivably apply to prairie dogs. Individuals commonly expose subsoil during the excavation and maintenance of burrows. This subsoil promotes the growth of certain plant species uncommon elsewhere (King 1955; Koford 1958). Further, as in human "fallow farming," prairie dogs sometimes avoid foraging in certain areas with undesirable plant species until new, preferred species establish themselves there (King 1955). Finally, individuals sometimes clip down certain undesirable plant species without consuming them, thereby promoting the invasion of new, preferred species (King 1955; Whicker and Detling 1988). Could these fascinating "agricultural" activities—a form of social facilitation of foraging here termed *farming*—be an important benefit of coloniality? Probably not. Prairie dogs restrict all farming and foraging to the home coterie territory. Farming in one coterie territory might affect the growth of plants in adjacent territories, but such incidental effects are probably trivial. Thus, even though farming might theoretically explain the evolution of coteries, it cannot easily explain the clumping of coteries into colonies. Only if prairie dogs fed and farmed throughout the entire area of a colony could the farming hypothesis be relevant to the evolution of large colonies. More likely is that the benefits of farming are secondary consequences of coloniality that has evolved in some other context.

Coloniality might sometimes evolve because groups are better than solitary individuals at defending an important feeding site (Brown and Orians 1970). The conspicuous defense of the home coterie territory by all coterie members suggests that group defense of foraging grounds might be important for prairie dogs. However, recall once again that individuals forage in and defend *only the home coterie territory*, rather than all sections of the home colony. Thus, for reasons that parallel those just presented for farming, group defense of foraging grounds might explain the evolution of coteries, but cannot easily explain the grouping of coteries into colonies (see also chap. 6). Grouping of coteries probably leads to *greater* difficulty in defending a feeding area from conspecifics.

Reduced Predation?

Increased Awareness of Predators.   If coloniality ultimately results from predation pressure, then the rate of predation should vary inversely with colony size, and survivorship and reproductive success should vary directly with colony size. Colonial animals that reap these benefits include black-headed gulls, tricolored and red-winged blackbirds, common eiders, and southern sea lions (Patterson 1965; Payne 1969; Robertson 1973; Munro and Bedard 1977; Campagna et al. 1992).

For prairie dogs, my original hope was to compare predation rates and reproductive success directly with colony size. But two problems quickly surfaced. First, monitoring predation and reproductive success at more than one colony is practically impossible. Second, even though I see numerous apparent attempts by just about all known predators except black-footed ferrets (table 5.1), the prairie dog defense system is consistently successful (see also King 1955; Tileston and Lechleitner 1966; Garrett and Franklin 1988). Incredibly, field assistants and I have observed only 26 predations, 22 of them at the study colony (table 5.2). So few observations might suggest that predation has not been important in the evolution of prairie dog coloniality. Contrarily, so few predations in the face of so many attempts probably result because natural selection has molded an incredibly effective defense against a potentially devastating problem.

My original plan dashed, I have attempted to compare antipredatory defense versus colony size indirectly. Specifically, I perform experiments with a stuffed specimen of an American badger mounted on a plastic sled

Table 5.1. Predators Seen at the Study Colony in 1987 (26 January through 13 June)

Species	Number of sightings
Bald eagle	3
Golden eagle	87
Prairie falcon	12
Northern harrier	6
Cooper's hawk	8
American kestrel	6
Northern goshawk	5
Red-tailed hawk	9
Sharp-shinned hawk	6
Ferruginous hawk	2
Hawk, species unknown	25
Coyote	2
Bobcat	7
American badger	1
Prairie rattlesnake	1
Total	180

Note: I score all sightings, but do not always know whether the predator is actually hunting prairie dogs. These data are from 1987 only, but similar sightings occur at roughly the same frequencies every year.

Table 5.2. Predations Observed at the Study Colony or the Pringle Colony

Colony	Date	Type of predator	Victim	Age of victim	Sex of victim
Pringle	18 May 1979	Prairie falcon	UnX	Weanling	Unknown
Pringle	Apr 1982	Golden eagle	Un	Unknown	Unknown
Pringle	Apr 1983	Golden eagle	Un	Unknown	Unknown
Pringle	07 Apr 1984	Golden eagle	21	1 year	Male
Study colony	11 Jun 1976	Prairie falcon	WAX	Weanling	Male
Study colony	21 Jun 1978	Prairie falcon	WAOX	Weanling	Male
Study colony	06 Jun 1979	Cooper's (?) hawk	HOX	Weanling	Male
Study colony	10 Jun 1979	Prairie falcon	HX	Weanling	Unknown
Study colony	23 Apr 1980	Bobcat	74	3 years	Female
Study colony	21 May 1980	Prairie falcon	WAX	Weanling	Female
Study colony	02 Mar 1981	Bobcat	71	≥ 7 years	Female
Study colony	01 Apr 1981	Bobcat	R81	1 year	Female
Study colony	22 May 1981	Cooper's (?) hawk	TSX	Weanling	Unknown
Study colony	08 Jun 1981	Coyote	RR3	4 years	Female
Study colony	30 Oct 1981	American badger	CR	2.5 years	Female
Study colony	21 Mar 1982	Prairie falcon	RR7	6 years	Female
Study colony	06 May 1984	Coyote	2RS	4 years	Female
Study colony	23 Oct 1984	Coyote	R17	0.5 years	Male
Study colony	26 Oct 1984	Bobcat	R51	0.5 years	Female
Study colony	12 Jun 1985	Coyote	92	3 years	Female
Study colony	21 Mar 1986	Bobcat	WARS	6 years	Female
Study colony	01 May 1986	Bobcat	Un	0.5 years	Male
Study colony	02 Jun 1986	Bobcat	84	4 years	Female
Study colony	13 Jun 1986	Bobcat	WA4	3 years	Female
Study colony	10 Jun 1987	Bobcat	R76	1 year	Female
Study colony	29 Jul 1989	Bobcat	= 4X	Weanling	Male

Fig. 5.12. Three stuffed American badgers on Plexiglas sleds. I used these badgers in more than 1,000 experimental runs to study how quickly prairie dogs detect a predator, and to determine which individuals give antipredator calls. (Photo by John L. Hoogland.)

(fig. 5.12; see chap. 4). My prediction is that individuals in large colonies should detect predators more quickly than individuals in smaller colonies (Galton 1883; Pulliam 1973; Dimond and Lazarus 1974; Treisman 1975a,b).

A prairie dog warns conspecifics of danger in two ways. Sometimes it gives a *visual alarm* by running to a burrow mound or by freezing in one of several alert postures (Clark 1977). Visual alarms are probably secondary consequences of individual efforts to see the predator better, decrease individual conspicuousness, or get closer to an escape burrow. After giving a visual alarm, a prairie dog sometimes gives a *vocal alarm,* or *antipredator call* (chap. 8). Other individuals usually join the first caller, leading to a chorus of antipredator calls during a predatory attack. Antipredator calls probably function primarily, rather than merely second-arily, to warn conspecifics. Perhaps because an alerted prairie dog is practically impossible to capture, both terrestrial and avian predators usually stop hunting following a flurry of visual and vocal alarms. Perhaps the sound of the antipredator call itself also helps to deter predators.

As predicted, prairie dogs detect the American badger and give visual and vocal alarms more quickly in large wards than in smaller wards (fig. 5.13). Earlier alarms in larger wards are probably important for at least two reasons. First, an early signal occurs when the predator is still far enough away so that its success from continued hunting is unlikely. Second and more important, an early alarm gives conspecifics more time to reach safety. The increased ability to detect predators is probably the major benefit of prairie dog coloniality.

The number of visual alarmers during experiments with the stuffed American badger increases directly with ward size (fig. 5.14). The same is probably true for antipredator callers, but I could not investigate this possibility because callers are so numerous and difficult to identify. More visual and vocal alarms in large colonies presumably increase the probability of seeing or hearing an alarm for uninformed individuals. This higher probability might be important under conditions of poor visibility (as on foggy mornings) or poor audibility (as on windy days). Further, the probability of deterring certain predators might vary directly with the number of confusing, distracting, or obnoxious visual and vocal alarm signals.

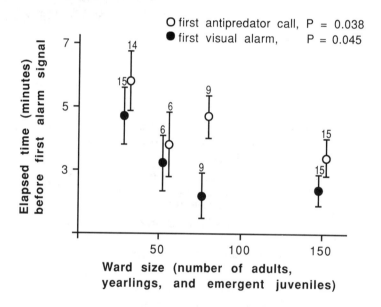

Fig. 5.13. Detection of the stuffed badger versus ward size. The number above each SE line indicates the number of experimental runs with the stuffed American badger. *P*-values are from the Kendall rank correlation test. Ward size for this graph includes emergent juveniles. The vertical axis here shows the elapsed time in *minutes,* and might suggest that the prairie dogs are slow to respond. However, the badger is 30 meters from an outermost peripheral burrow entrance at the start of each experimental run, and sometimes is more than 50 meters from foraging prairie dogs. Further, the field assistant pulls the badger slowly—at a rate of only 11 centimeters per second—so that I can accurately record the first visual alarm and the first antipredator call. For experiments to determine the identity of callers (chap. 8), the field assistant pulls the badger at a faster rate.

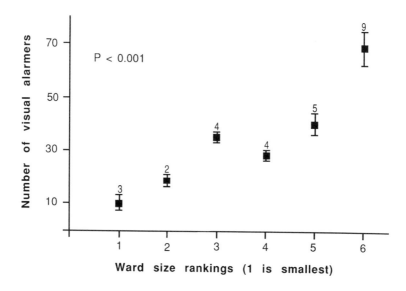

Fig. 5.14. Number of visual alarmers versus ward size. The number above each SE line indicates the number of experimental runs with the stuffed American badger. The *P*-value is from the Kendall rank correlation test. I could not accurately count all residents of each ward, but could rank wards by size, as shown here. A visual alarmer is a prairie dog that stands on or near a burrow mound. Visual alarmers often give antipredator calls as well.

When the potential for detecting predators varies directly with group size, individuals in large groups should be able to scan less often for predators—and thus have more time for feeding (Clark and Mangel 1986; Watts 1985; Elgar 1989; Scheel 1993). Like ostriches (Bertram 1980), several species of geese (Lazarus 1978; Drent and Swierstra 1977; Lazarus and Inglis 1978; Black et al. 1992), white-nosed coatis (Burger and Gochfield 1992), and yellow-bellied and Olympic marmots (Armitage 1962; Barash 1973; Svendsen 1974; Carey and Moore 1986) in larger groups, prairie dogs in large wards spend less time scanning for predators than do prairie dogs in smaller wards (fig. 5.15; see also Kildaw 1991). Such scanning occurs from every imaginable posture (fig. 5.16).

For animals such as Florida scrub jays, Arabian and black-lored babblers, vervet monkeys, dwarf mongooses, and meerkats (Moran 1984; Wickler 1985; Rasa 1986; McGowan and Woolfenden 1989; Baldellou and Henzi 1993), individuals coordinate their vigilance, with certain individuals ("sentinels") scanning for predators more often than others. Prairie dogs do not systematically coordinate their vigilance, but reproductive males do scan for predators slightly more often than females and nonreproductive males (Loughry 1993a,b).

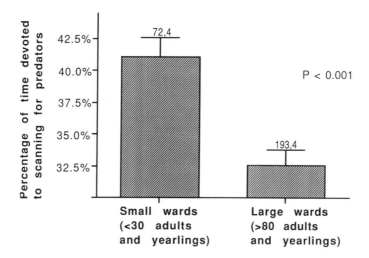

Fig. 5.15. Percentage of time that individual prairie dogs spend scanning for predators (individual alertness) versus ward size. I watch each prairie dog for 30 minutes, and record the number of minutes during which the individual looks around, presumably for predators. The numbers above each SE line indicate the number of 30-minute observation periods and the number of wards observed. The *P*-value is from the Mann-Whitney *U* test.

Increased Ability to Deter Predators.   Prairie dogs do not mob large predators such as coyotes, American badgers, bobcats, or golden eagles. However, like dwarf and banded mongooses (Rood 1975; Rasa 1977), prairie dogs do sometimes physically "mob" certain small predators, as the following examples attest. First, Stromberg (1974) observed two individuals ram into a grounded red-tailed hawk that had just killed a member of the rammers' home coterie. Second, on two occasions I observed three or more prairie dogs cooperatively chasing a long-tailed weasel that had entered the home coterie territory (see also Hillman and Linder 1973). Hillman (1968) observed similar chasing in response to black-footed ferrets, and also observed prairie dogs cooperatively closing burrow entrances entered by black-footed ferrets (chap. 3). Finally, mobbing and harassing by prairie dogs—sometimes accompanied by biting and interment—sometimes occur in response to snakes (King 1955; Owings and Owings 1979; Halpin 1983; Owings and Loughry 1985; Loughry 1987a,b, 1988; see also chaps. 3 and 8). In all these circumstances, prairie dogs ignore small predators in other coterie territories and only attack when the predator enters the home coterie territory.

Adult and yearling prairie dogs are usually too large for predation by long-tailed weasels, snakes, and small aerial predators such as Cooper's and red-tailed hawks. Within only a few weeks after first emergence,

Fig. 5.16. Different levels of individual alertness among prairie dogs. *(a)* Prairie dog stands tall on two legs while scanning for predators from a burrow mound. (Photo by Wendy Shattil/Bob Rozinski, copyright 1992.) *(b)* One prairie dog scans on all fours from a burrow mound, and the other scans while sitting on its rump and rear legs. (Photo by Judy G. Hoogland.) *(c)* Two prairie dogs scan while continuing to feed. (Photo courtesy of J. Perley Fitzgerald.) *(d)* Because its eyes are so high on the head, a prairie dog can scan from a burrow entrance with only the top of its head protruding. During an attack, prairie dogs usually do not completely submerge unless a predator approaches within 5 meters or so. (Photo courtesy of Wind Cave National Park.)

juveniles are also too large. Mortality from small predators is therefore rare, and mobbing of small predators is probably a secondary consequence of the coloniality that has evolved primarily to reduce mortality from larger predators.

Increased "Selfish Herd Effects."   The study colony is small relative to most prairie dog colonies (chap. 4). Most coterie territories abut the colony's edge, so that center-edge comparisons with reproductive success are difficult. I have, however, compared center-edge differences in individual alertness at other, larger colonies. Like peripheral wood pigeons, cliff swallows, and yellow-bellied marmots (Murton 1968; Armitage 1962; Brown and Brown 1987), prairie dogs at colony peripheries spend more time scanning for predators than do more central individuals in 76% of comparisons (16/21; $P = .005$, Wilcoxon matched-pairs signed-ranks test using 21 pairs, each watched for 30 minutes, from 10 wards).

I predicted that prairie dogs would synchronize reproduction within colonies, in order to better capitalize on "selfish herd effects" (Hamilton 1971; Ims 1990a,b). I further predicted that reproductive success would be higher for synchronous breeders than for asynchronous breeders (Patterson 1965; Brown and Brown 1987). Data in chapter 13 support the first prediction, but not the second.

Increased Number and Density of Burrows.   Prairie dogs ultimately depend on their burrows for safety from weather and predators (chap. 3). Suppose that a single prairie dog can excavate and maintain five burrows. Because sharing of burrows occurs (chap. 3), each prairie dog in a colony of two would have access to ten burrows, each prairie dog in a colony of three would have access to fifteen burrows, and so on. Could access to more burrows—and perhaps also a higher density of burrows—explain prairie dog coloniality? If so, then the number and density of burrows should vary directly with colony size. Counting burrow entrances and estimating the density of burrow entrances are easy, but accurate estimates of colony size require livetrapping and therefore are more elusive. Sufficient data to compare prairie dog colony size with the number and density of burrows and burrow entrances are presently unavailable (Hoogland 1981a).

Comparative Data from White-Tailed Prairie Dogs

Costs and Benefits of White-Tail Coloniality

White-tailed prairie dogs also live in colonies. Not surprisingly, white-tails incur many of the same costs of coloniality as do black-tails. For example, aggression, flea infestation, and visual and vocal conspicuousness to predators all vary directly with white-tail colony size (Hoogland 1979a).

Probably in response to the greater ectoparasitism there, white-tails in large wards autogroom more often than white-tails in smaller wards ($P < .010$, Mann-Whitney U test). White-tails also reap many of the same benefits of coloniality as do black-tails. For example, white-tails in large wards detect predators more quickly, see more visual alarms and hear more antipredator calls during a predatory attack, and spend less time scanning for predators than white-tails in smaller wards (Hoogland 1981a).

Black-tail colonies are generally larger and more densely populated than white-tail colonies (fig. 5.17). Consequently, the costs of coloniality should be more extreme for black-tails than for white-tails. Interspecific comparisons support this prediction. For example, competition is probably more extreme among black-tails, as is visual and vocal conspicuousness to predators (Hoogland 1979a). Further, counts from the animals and from their burrow entrances both indicate that black-tails harbor more fleas than white-tails (Hoogland 1979a); as a probable consequence, black-tails auto- and allogroom more than white-tails do ($P < .050$ for both, Mann-Whitney U test).

Interspecific comparisons of benefits also yield the predicted results. Even though they devote less time to individual alertness (35% versus 43%), black-tails detect predators more quickly than white-tails do (Hoogland 1981a). Black-tails also have access to more visual alarms during a predatory attack (Hoogland 1981a). Finally, antipredator calls are louder and more numerous in black-tail colonies (Waring 1970; chap. 8 and unpublished data).

Why Are Black-Tails More Colonial than White-Tails?

Surely no simple reason explains why white-tails live in small, sparsely populated colonies while black-tails live in large, densely populated colonies. Here I will briefly speculate on two likely possibilities (see also Hoogland 1977, 1981a).

Interspecific Differences in Predation. Increased predation might lead to larger, more dense colonies (Alexander 1974; Heard 1992). Specifically, black-tails might be more colonial than white-tails because of higher predation rates over evolutionary time. This possibility seems unlikely in qualitative terms, because known or suspected predators on black-tails and white-tails are identical (Tileston and Lechleitner 1966; Clark 1973, 1977; Campbell and Clark 1981; Hoogland 1981a). In quantitative terms, comparing rates of predation on black-tails and white-tails throughout their ranges would be practically impossible.

But wait, what about black-footed ferrets? Powell (1982) has argued that black-footed ferrets occur only in black-tail habitats. If so, then black-footed ferrets might ultimately explain why black-tails form larger, more

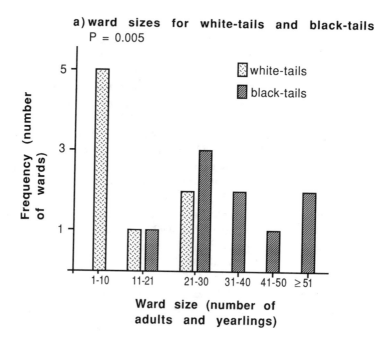

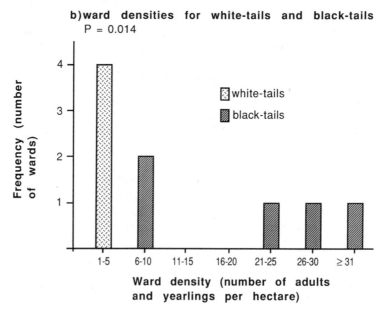

Fig. 5.17. Interspecific comparison of *(a)* ward size and *(b)* ward density for white-tailed and black-tailed prairie dogs. Data are only from wards in which the researcher color-marked every adult and yearling (King 1955; Tileston and Lechleitner 1966; Clark 1977; Garrett and Franklin 1988; Halpin 1987; this study). *P*-values for both graphs are from the Mann-Whitney *U* test.

densely populated colonies than white-tails. However, Powell's argument stems from the black-footed ferret's range map depicted in Hall (1981), which does not include recent findings of live black-footed ferrets and black-footed ferret skulls in white-tail colonies located several hundred kilometers from the nearest black-tail colonies (Martin and Schroeder 1978, 1980; Anderson and Inkley 1985; Clark, Forrest, et al. 1986; Clark, Richardson, et al. 1986; Biggins and Schroeder 1988; Seal et al. 1989). Further, black-footed ferrets are usually active only at night (Hillman 1968; Campbell et al. 1987; Paunovich and Forrest 1987; Richardson et al. 1987; Schroeder 1987). How could nocturnal predation affect the coloniality of animals as diurnal as prairie dogs (chap. 2)? "Selfish herd" effects (Hamilton 1971) offer one possible solution to this problem. More likely, however, is that coloniality of white-tails and black-tails has evolved primarily in response to more diurnal predators such as coyotes, bobcats, and raptors—with the secondary consequence that individuals are especially vulnerable to nocturnal, burrow-entering black-footed ferrets.

Interspecific Differences in Protective Cover.   Some animals depend on hiding from predators to avoid predation, while others depend on detecting predators soon enough to allow time for escape. Despite some marvelous exceptions (e.g., see Wickler 1968; Owen 1980), hiding from predators is usually feasible only for single individuals and small groups that live in habitats with extensive protective cover. Conversely, the potential to detect predators is best for animals that live in large groups and in open habitats, as do various species of ungulates, kangaroos, and primates (Jarman 1974; Kaufmann 1974; Clutton-Brock and Harvey 1977a,b; Alexander et al. 1979). Might interspecific differences in protective cover explain why black-tails are more colonial than white-tails?

Black-tails typically colonize overgrazed habitats with little protective cover (King 1955; Tileston and Lechleitner 1966; Hoogland 1977, 1981a; Coppock, Detling, et al. 1983; Coppock, Ellis, et al. 1983). Black-tails further increase visibility by razing tall plants (fig. 5.18). White-tails, on the other hand, colonize habitats with more, taller plants, which they do not remove or shorten (Tileston and Lechleitner 1966; Clark 1977; Hoogland 1981a). Interspecific differences in protective cover thus might ultimately explain why black-tails form large, densely populated colonies—to maximize quick detection of predators. By contrast, white-tails form small, sparsely populated colonies—to compromise between the benefits of hiding and of quick detection of predators.

Fig. 5.18. Clipping of tall vegetation. *(a)* On 07 June 1976 at 1800 hours, I transplanted tall grasses to an area near the center of a coterie territory. *(b)* By 0900 hours on the following day, prairie dogs had clipped down all the tall vegetation. In 93% of such transplants (13/14) into fourteen different coterie territories of six different wards, prairie dogs removed more than 50% of the tall grasses within a few days. By contrast, all five "control" transplants placed outside ward boundaries were intact after 15 days. (Photos by Judy G. Hoogland.)

Summary

1. Aggressive interactions among prairie dogs that increase directly with ward size include fights, chases, runaways, and territorial disputes. Costs of aggression include lost time and energy, temporary or permanent eviction from the home coterie territory, and bodily injuries.

2. Ectoparasites on prairie dogs include fleas, lice, and ticks. The number of fleas at burrow entrances increases directly with colony size. Costs of ectoparasitism include increased transmission of diseases, loss of blood, and open wounds.

3. Prairie dog juveniles from different litters within the home coterie territory mingle soon after their first emergences from the natal

burrow. Consequently, parents might lose time and energy while trying to locate their own offspring, and mothers sometimes suckle foster offspring. Curiously, parents do not seem to discriminate between their own and others' offspring during the first month that juveniles are aboveground.

4. Miscellaneous costs of prairie dog coloniality include an increased probability of infanticide and of misdirected paternal care resulting from cuckoldry.

5. The availability of seemingly suitable habitat at colony edges and the absence of isolated prairie dogs both suggest that prairie dog coloniality does not result merely from a shortage of habitat.

6. Because individuals are herbivorous and their food supplies are evenly distributed, social facilitation of foraging probably has not been important in the evolution of prairie dog coloniality.

7. Even though they spend less time scanning for predators, prairie dogs in large wards detect predators more quickly than prairie dogs in smaller wards. Reduced predation is probably the primary benefit of prairie dog coloniality.

8. White-tailed prairie dogs live in smaller, less densely populated colonies than do black-tails. Consistent with this interspecific difference, white-tails fight less frequently, are less conspicuous to predators, have fewer ectoparasites, auto- and allogroom less often, and detect predators less quickly than black-tails—even though white-tails spend more time scanning for predators.

9. Unlike white-tail colonies, black-tail colonies contain little protective cover. This interspecific difference might ultimately explain why black-tails form large, densely populated colonies—to maximize quick detection of predators. By contrast, white-tails form small, sparsely populated colonies—to compromise between the benefits of hiding and of quick detection of predators.

6 The Coterie

Within colonies, prairie dogs live in harem-polygynous, territorial, family groups called coteries (fig. 6.1; see also King 1955). Interactions within a coterie are usually amicable, but interactions between coteries are invariably hostile. How large are coteries, and how long do they persist? Why do some coteries have more than one breeding male, and why do two adjacent coteries sometimes share a single breeding male? How does the number of individuals in a coterie vary with the size of the home territory? And why do coteries even exist? Using data from 273 coteries at the study colony (15 to 26 per year), I investigate these and related questions in this chapter. I examine the effect of coterie size and coterie type on male and female reproductive success in chapter 13.

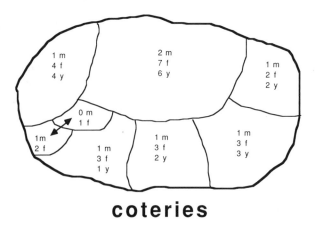

coteries

Fig. 6.1. Composition of coteries within a prairie dog colony. Most coteries contain a single breeding male, but some (multi-male coteries) contain two or more. Occasionally, one large, dominant male controls two separate, adjacent groups of females; I call each such group a half-male coterie. m, breeding males; f, breeding females; y, nonbreeding yearlings of both sexes.

Number, Composition, Size, and Longevity of Coteries

Number of Coteries at the Study Colony

The number of coteries at the study colony ranges from 15 to 26, and varies directly with the number of adults and yearlings in the colony (fig. 6.2). New coteries result either from fission (see below) or from immigration of females from other colonies (chap. 16). Loss of coteries results from extinction (see below).

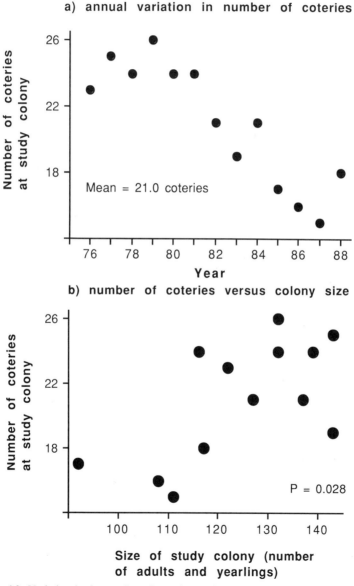

Fig. 6.2. Variation in the number of coteries at the study colony. *(a)* Annual variation in the number of coteries. *(b)* Number of coteries versus colony size. The *P*-value is from the Spearman rank correlation test.

Composition of Coteries

Coteries contain yearlings and breeding adults of both sexes (fig. 6.3). Following reproduction, of course, coteries also contain juveniles.

a) breeding males and adult females

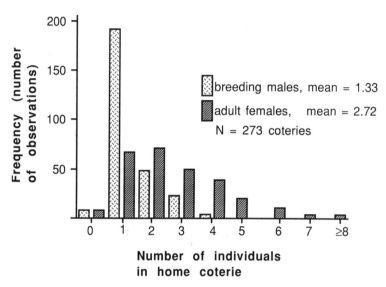

b) yearling males and females

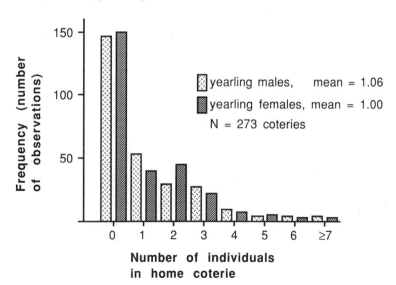

Fig. 6.3. Composition of coteries at the study colony. *(a)* Number of breeding males and adult females in a coterie. *(b)* Number of yearling males and yearling females in a coterie.

Where do coterie members come from? I provide the details in chapter 14, but the answer to this important question is clear and simple. The adult females and yearlings of both sexes in a coterie are the offspring of living or deceased females of that coterie. By contrast, the breeding males within coteries are the offspring of females from other coteries. Consequently, adult females and yearlings of both sexes live with close kin in their home, natal coterie territory. Breeding males, on the other hand, have only nonkin (or distant kin; see chap. 14) in the home breeding coterie territory until they sire offspring there.

Variation in Coterie Size

Coterie size is the number of adults and yearlings within a common territory. Twice a single prairie dog lived alone for several months in a territory at the edge of the study colony. One of these loners was a yearling male, the other a yearling female. At the other extreme, 26 prairie dogs shared the same territory in April 1983! The mean coterie size ($\pm$ SD) at the study colony is 6.13 ± 3.53 (fig. 6.4).

As figure 6.5a shows, 51% of coteries (139/273) contain five or fewer adult and yearling residents. Does this mean that most prairie dogs live in small coteries? No, because 71% of prairie dogs (1190/1673) live in

Fig. 6.4. Members of a coterie feeding together. The average coterie contains about six prairie dogs as shown here. Some coteries have only two residents, and others have as many as twenty-six. Taken during the winter months, this photograph shows the short vegetation within colonies that facilitates behavioral observations. (Photo courtesy of Wind Cave National Park.)

coteries of six or more residents (fig. 6.5b). The typical coterie contains one breeding male, two or three adult females, and one or two yearlings of each sex (figs. 6.3 and 6.4).

a) coterie sizes

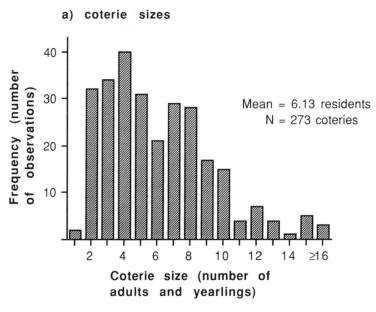

b) prairie dogs in different-sized coteries

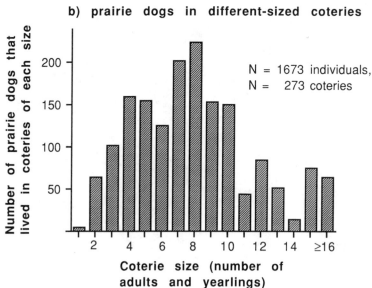

Fig. 6.5. Variation in the size of coteries. *(a)* Variation in coterie size. *(b)* Number of prairie dogs that live in coteries of different sizes.

Some Reasons for Variation in Coterie Size

Coteries differ in size (fig. 6.5). Further, the size of the same coterie varies over time (fig. 6.6). What are some of the reasons for these sorts of variation? Of many possibilities, two come quickly to mind. The first is weather. Knowles (1987) found that prairie dog litter size in Montana correlates positively with precipitation in the previous summer. Because larger litters yield more yearlings in the following year (chap. 13), the link between weather and coterie size is straightforward.

The second factor that correlates with coterie size is the area of the home coterie territory: large territories support more adults and yearlings than do smaller territories (see also below).

Longevity of Coteries

Females, but not males, usually remain in their natal coterie territories for their entire lifetimes (chap. 14). Thus, any discussion of the longevity of coteries only makes sense in terms of females and their daughters. For the reasons described below, all matrilines in the same coterie territory sometimes go extinct. Five of the coteries at the study colony lasted for only a single year, but one or more matrilines in eight other coteries persisted for 14 consecutive years (fig. 6.7).

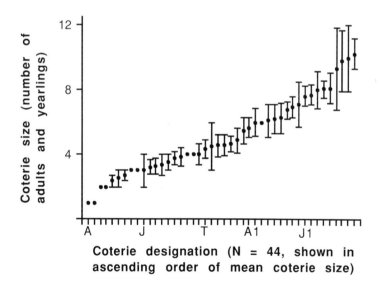

Fig. 6.6. Variation in coterie size for the same coterie in different years. Shown here are means ± one SE, with each dot representing data from a single coterie over its lifetime. The number of years that coterie size is available for each coterie depends on the coterie's lifespan and ranges from 1 to 13 (mean ± SD = 6.43 ± 4.36 years).

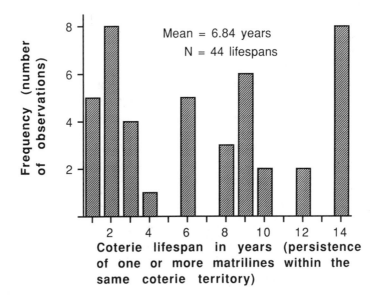

Fig. 6.7. Longevity of coteries (persistence of one or more matrilines within the same coterie territory). These data are from 1975 through 1989, so the maximum observable lifespan is 14 years.

Male Coalitions within Multi-Male Coteries

One-Male and Multi-Male Coteries

Like harems of African lions, wild horses, hanuman langurs, and yellow-bellied, Olympic, and hoary marmots (Packer and Pusey 1982; Berger 1986; Barash 1989; Armitage 1991; Reena and Ram 1992), most prairie dog coteries (192/273 = 70%) contain a single breeding male. But some coteries contain no breeding male, whereas other (multi-male) coteries contain two, three, or even four breeding males (see fig. 6.3). Further, some coteries contain only one breeding male in one year, but two or more in other years. Why such variation within and across years (fig. 6.8)?

Of the eight coteries at the study colony that had no breeding male, three are easy to understand. Two were the solitary prairie dogs living in peripheral territories, and the other was a pair of yearling full brothers whose other close kin had all died. Three other coteries without breeding males contained sexually immature 2-year-old males who had not yet dispersed from, and were still defending, the natal coterie territory. The other two coteries without a resident breeding male each contained a 3-year-old adult male born in a different coterie who was, inexplicably, sexually inactive.

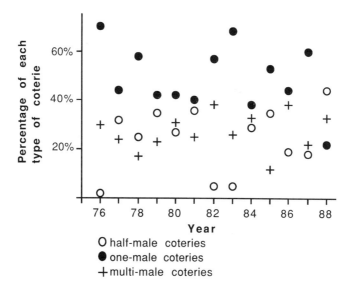

Fig. 6.8. Annual variation in the percentages of half-male, one-male, and multi-male coteries.

Large coteries presumably attract more male attention than smaller ones because they contain more females that will come into estrus (fig. 6.9a) and which cannot easily be monopolized by a single male. If so, then large coteries should contain more breeding males than smaller coteries. Figures 6.9a and 6.9b support this prediction.

The presence of a second or third breeding male has little effect on the interactions among the females within a coterie. Whatever the number of breeding males, the females interact amicably before the breeding season, hostilely during pregnancy and lactation, and amicably again following first juvenile emergences (chap. 10).

Multi-male coteries are of two general types. In the first type, each breeding male defends a specific subsection of the home coterie territory throughout the year. Interactions involving the breeding males are frequent, and always hostile. In the second type of multi-male coterie, the breeding males interact amicably and share the entire home coterie territory before the onset of the breeding season. During the week or so when females come into estrus, however, the breeding males interact hostilely and defend subsections of the home coterie territory. Sometime later the breeding males resume amicable interactions over the entire home coterie territory.

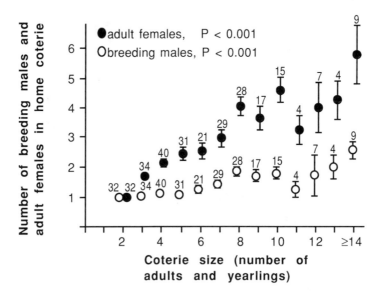

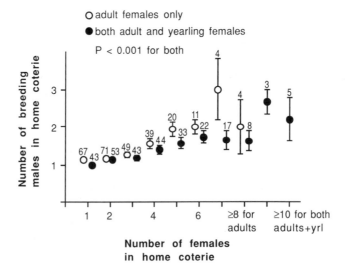

Fig. 6.9. Coterie composition versus coterie size. *(a)* Number of breeding males and adult females in a coterie versus coterie size. *(b)* Number of breeding males in a coterie versus the number of adult and yearling females in the coterie. For these graphs, the number above each SE line indicates the number of coteries, and *P*-values are from the Spearman rank correlation test.

The first type of multi-male coterie is more common than the second type. Specifically, 67% of the multi-male coteries (38/57) show unmitigated hostility, and the other 33% (19/57) show regular amicability, among the breeding males ($N = 57$ multi-male coteries that I could unambiguously categorize from 1978 through 1988).

Not surprisingly, the two types of multi-male coteries correlate with male kinship. Despite some puzzling exceptions, multi-male coteries showing unmitigated male-male hostility usually contain genetically unrelated, or only distantly related, breeding males born in different coteries. By contrast, the breeding males of multi-male coteries showing regular male-male amicability are usually close kin derived from the same coterie (fig. 6.10). Usually such male relatives enter a new breeding coterie territory together, but sometimes a male joins a father, son, or brother who has been living in a different coterie territory for a year or more.

In multi-male coteries showing male-male amicability, the timing of resumption of amicability among the breeding males is variable. At one extreme, amicability does not return until first juvenile emergences. At the other extreme, the breeding males promptly resume congenial interactions on the first day after the last copulation in the home coterie territory (chap. 10).

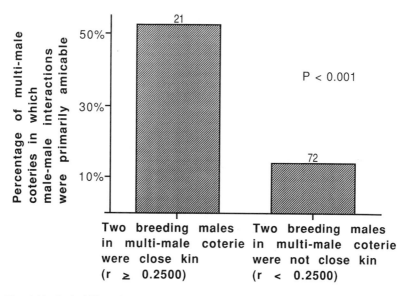

Fig. 6.10. Amicability of male-male interactions versus male kinship in multi-male coteries. For this analysis, I pair each breeding male with every other breeding male within his home multi-male coterie. A two-male coterie has only one dyad (A × B); a three-male coterie has three dyads (A × B, A × C, and B × C), and so on. By "primarily amicable," I mean that more than 75% of intracoterie behavioral interactions among breeding males before and after the breeding season are amicable rather than hostile. The P-value is from the 2 × 2 chi-square test.

Many of the exceptions to the general patterns of male-male amicability versus kinship within multi-male coteries are instructive. For example, of the ten dyads of unrelated males that interacted amicably (fig. 6.10), at least seven have interesting complications. In at least three of the dyads— all observed prior to 1983, when I initiated scrotal examinations to determine sexual activity unambiguously—one of the adult males was probably sexually inactive and thus was not a serious competitor to the single breeding male. In another three dyads, one of the males with descended testes was still in his natal coterie territory with female close kin. Because extreme inbreeding is rare (chap. 14) and because infanticidal males only kill juvenile nonkin (chap. 7), these three males were probably nonthreatening to other breeding males in the home coterie territory. In the seventh dyad, the first male was one of two males that had copulated with the second male's mother in the previous year. This first male might have mistakenly inferred that the second male—a breeding yearling—was his son (chap. 10).

Females usually copulate with both males of a multi-male coterie. Further, although multiple paternity within litters is rare, both males of a multi-male coterie usually sire offspring (chaps. 12 and 13).

For simplicity, and because most multi-male coteries contain only two breeding males (see fig. 6.3a), I have described the two types of multi-male coteries in terms of two breeding males only. Descriptions become more complicated when three or more breeding males live in the same coterie territory. Consider a multi-male coterie containing two full brothers and a third unrelated male, for example. In this case the two brothers usually interact amicably except during the breeding season, but always interact hostilely with the third, unrelated male.

Half-Male Coteries

As just discussed, coteries containing many females commonly attract more than one breeding male. Conversely, like males of other harem-polygynous animals such as African lions and hanuman langurs (Schaller 1972; Hrdy 1977b), a single prairie dog breeding male sometimes dominates two adjacent groups of females. I call each of the latter a *half-male* coterie, because the single breeding male divides his time between the two groups of females. Whereas multi-male coteries are *larger* than one-male coteries, half-male coteries are predictably *smaller* (fig. 6.11).

Ranging from 0% in 1976 to 44% in 1988, half-male coteries have accounted for 25% of the coteries at the study colony (68/273) (see fig. 6.8). In 1977, three "one-third-male coteries" occurred when a single breeding male dominated three distinct groups of females living in three nonoverlapping territories.

Within each half-male coterie, the females interact amicably just as they do in a typical one-male coterie. By contrast, females in a half-male

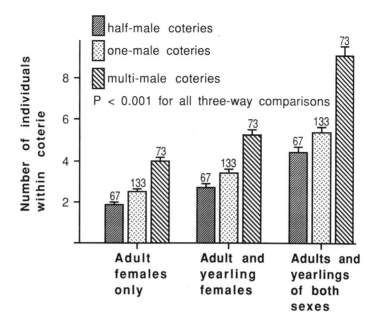

Fig. 6.11. Number of individuals within half-male, one-male, and multi-male coteries. The number above each SE line indicates the number of coteries. *P*-values for three-way comparisons within each index of coterie size (adult females only, adult and yearling females, and adults and yearlings of both sexes) are from the Kruskal-Wallis analysis of variance. All pairwise comparisons for each estimate of coterie size are also significant ($P \leq .024$ for all 9 comparisons, Mann-Whitney *U* test).

coterie invariably interact hostilely with the females of their breeding male's other, adjacent, half-male coterie. Thus, control by the same male of two adjacent coterie territories does not enhance the amicability of intercoterie female interactions.

In some pairs of half-male coteries the single breeding male spends approximately equal time in both coterie territories. In other pairs, however, the male spends over 90% of his time in only one of the territories. The reasons for such variation are not obvious, but probably correlate with factors such as reproductive value of the females, vulnerability of the coterie territories to invasion by strange males, and availability of food.

Because of annual differences in survivorship and reproduction, the number and proportion of breeding males inevitably vary over time for animals such as adders, Florida scrub jays, acorn woodpeckers, Mexican jays, and pied kingfishers (Reyer 1980, 1984; Woolfenden and Fitzpatrick 1984; Brown 1987; Koenig and Mumme 1987; Madsen and Shine 1993). The same is true for prairie dogs (chap. 16). If male-male competition varies directly with the number of breeding males, then the probability that a single breeding male can control two separate coteries should be higher in years when males are relatively scarce. Conversely, the probability that a single breeding male will be forced to share a coterie with another breeding male should be higher in years when males are more numerous. Thus, the frequency of half-male coteries should vary *inversely*, while the frequency of multi-male coteries should vary *directly*, with the number of breeding males at the study colony. Figure 6.12 supports this hypothesis, but the correlation is statistically significant only for half-male coteries.

Although many breeding males live in the same type of coterie (e.g., one-male) for their entire lives, others live in different types in different years. For example, male-22 lived in a multi-male coterie as a 2-year-old, in a one-male coterie as a 3-year-old, and in a multi-male coterie again as a 4-year-old. Only one male lived and copulated in all three types: male-18 controlled a pair of half-male coteries as a 2-year-old, lived in a multi-male coterie as a 3-year-old, and spent his final breeding year in a one-male coterie as a 4-year-old.

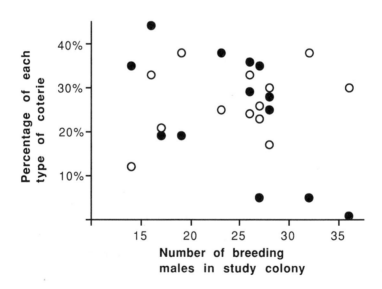

Fig. 6.12. Percentages of half-male and multi-male coteries versus the number of breeding males in the study colony. The correlation with the number of breeding males is negative for half-male coteries and positive for multi-male coteries. *P*-values are from the Spearman rank correlation test.

Parental Care within Coteries

Parental and alloparental (see chap. 10) care within prairie dog coteries takes several forms. For example, both males and females enhance juvenile survivorship with antipredator calling, allogrooming, playing with young, chasing of small predators, maintenance of burrows, harassing of snakes, and nestbuilding. Certain parental behaviors, however, are limited to only one sex. For example, only mothers sleep with unweaned juveniles at night and provide them with milk. And defense of the home coterie territory against invasion by infanticidal males is the sole responsibility of the resident breeding male.

The importance of maternal care to juvenile survivorship in most animals is without question, but paternal care is rarer and more difficult to quantify (Trivers 1972; Wittenberger and Tilson 1980; Kleiman and Malcolm 1981; Elwood 1983; Clutton-Brock 1991). Paternal care is crucial to juvenile survivorship for animals such as western sandpipers, willow ptarmigans, house wrens, owl monkeys, and California mice (Robinson, Wright, and Kinzey 1987; Whitten 1987; Bart and Tornes 1989; Mock and Fujioka 1990; Gubernick, Wright, and Brown 1993). To a lesser extent, paternal care also promotes juvenile survivorship among prairie dogs (chaps. 5, 7, 8, 10, and 13).

The Home Coterie Territory

Coterie members have a well-defined home territory that they defend from prairie dogs of other coteries. Boundaries between coterie territories sometimes coincide with small areas of seemingly unsuitable habitat containing tall vegetation, rocks, or poor drainage. More commonly, though, coterie territories are contiguous, and their boundaries are undetectable to human observers from physical features alone (see also King 1955).

The physical area occupied by coterie territories at the study colony ranges from 0.05 hectares to 1.01 hectares, with a mean ± SD of 0.306 ± 0.167 (fig. 6.13a). The smallest coterie territory was at the periphery of the colony and belonged to the yearling female that lived alone. Curiously, the yearling male that lived alone used the same coterie territory in a different year.

The resident breeding male regularly patrols the boundary of the home coterie territory. Territorial disputes with males from other coteries are common. On a busy day during the breeding season, for example, a resident breeding male sometimes has as many as twenty territorial disputes with other males. Territorial disputes usually last for about 5 minutes, but sometimes persist for hours (chap. 5).

The number of burrow entrances per coterie territory ranges from 5 (for the single prairie dogs) to 214 (fig. 6.13b). Burrow entrances within the same coterie territory often connect by a common underground tunnel, but entrances from different territories never connect. All burrow entrances

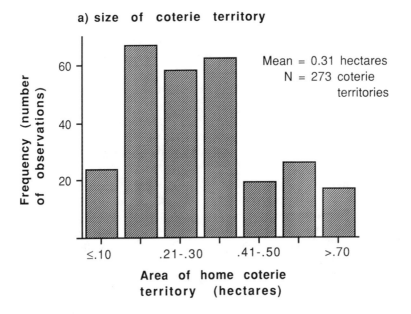

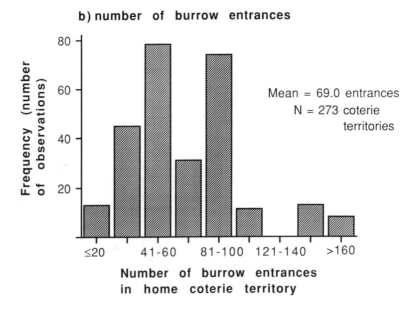

Fig. 6.13. Variation in *(a)* the size of home coterie territories and *(b)* the number of burrow entrances within home coterie territories.

within a coterie territory are probably suitable for refuge during surprise attacks by aerial predators. However, only certain burrows are suitable for other purposes, such as rearing offspring, refuge from digging predators, and spending the night. For example, the coterie territory of the RR2-RSBB-55 coterie contains 83 burrow entrances. However, mothers used only 23% of these entrances (19/83) for rearing juveniles in 1975 through 1988 ($N = 21$ litters; the 19 entrances involve at least 9 separate burrows, most of which have more than one entrance). Probably because of this variation in suitability, mothers compete intensely for access to the best nursery burrows within the home coterie territory (chaps. 7 and 11).

Coterie members defend the home coterie territory vigorously, so that trespassing by prairie dogs from other coteries is rare (King 1955; Tileston and Lechleitner 1966; Halpin 1987). Consequently, individuals obtain over 99% of their food and other resources from the home coterie territory. The presence or absence of certain plant species within the home coterie territory, and the available quantities of these species, significantly limit a prairie dog's selection of forage.

Barring trivial short-term forays of less than 5 minutes, temporary departures from the home coterie territory are of two types. First, on the day of estrus, females sometimes leave the home coterie territory in search of breeding males from other territories (chap. 12). Such females usually return home late on the day of estrus, but sometimes delay return until the following morning. Second, a breeding male sometimes leaves home and invades another coterie territory in search of pre-estrous or estrous females—especially after all the females in his own coterie have copulated (chaps. 11 and 12). Such "gallivanting" (Barash 1981) males usually return within a day or two, but occasionally delay return for as much as a week or more.

The area and configuration of the home coterie territory usually remain constant across generations (King 1955). For example, several of the coterie territories in 1989 were identical to the territories of six generations (14 years) earlier. This constancy can be true despite impressive fluctuations in coterie size. For example, a territory occupied by only two adults in 1980 was identical to the territory occupied in 1986 by six adults and three yearlings.

Despite fluctuations in coterie size, a logical expectation is that larger coterie territories should generally support larger coteries. Figure 6.14a supports this prediction. However, even though larger coteries have larger territories, the area *per prairie dog* varies inversely with coterie size. Consequently, *coterie density*—the number of adults and yearlings living within a coterie divided by that coterie's territory size—increases directly with coterie size (fig. 6.14b). Having made no attempt to disentangle the two variables, I recognize that the effect of coterie size on reproductive success (chap. 13) might be better explained in terms of coterie density.

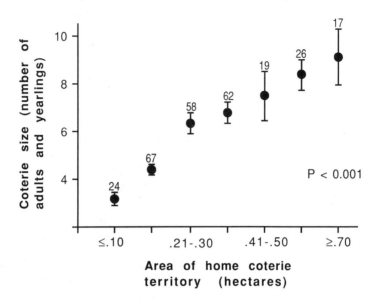

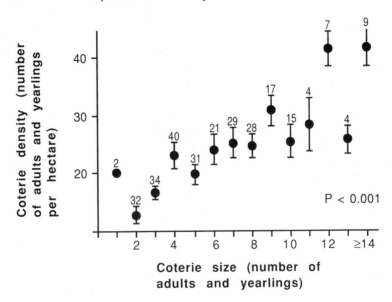

Fig. 6.14. *(a)* Coterie size versus area of the home coterie territory. *(b)* Coterie density versus coterie size. For both graphs, the number above each SE line indicates the number of coteries, and *P*-values are from the Spearman rank correlation test.

What about the number of burrow entrances versus coterie size? Not surprisingly, the larger territories of larger coteries have more burrow entrances (fig. 6.15a), whose number and positioning remain remarkably constant from generation to generation (chaps. 3 and 4). However, the density of burrow entrances does not correlate significantly with coterie size (fig. 6.15b). Consequently, prairie dogs in large coteries have access to more burrow entrances—but fewer entrances *per individual*—than prairie dogs in smaller coteries. Competition for burrows is thus probably more extreme in larger coteries.

The resident breeding male is primarily responsible for the defense of the home coterie territory against intruders, but adult females and yearlings of both sexes also help (King 1955). These latter individuals routinely engage in long territorial disputes when the match-up is approximately even (e.g., breeding female versus breeding female or yearling male versus yearling male). When overmatched, however—for example, when pitted against a larger individual, such as the breeding male of another coterie— an adult female or yearling of either sex usually screams distinctive "defense barks" (King 1955; Smith et al. 1977). Sounding somewhat like antipredator calls, defense barks usually bring the resident breeding male to the caller's side. Upon arriving, the male chases the caller away from the territorial boundary—perhaps to reduce the probability of injury to, or interference from, the caller. The recruited male then confronts the potential interloper.

Territorial disputes involving adult females and yearlings commonly involve a predictable chain reaction. For example, suppose that a large adult female initiates a dispute with a smaller adult female of an adjacent coterie territory. The smaller female usually gives defense barks that attract her resident breeding male, who then chases the caller and challenges the larger female. The larger female, now overmatched, gives defense barks that attract *her* resident breeding male, who then chases her and challenges the breeding male from the other coterie. The two males, both recruited by defense barks from their females, now have a prolonged territorial dispute.

What are the unusual circumstances that lead to changes in the boundaries of coterie territories? Such changes are of four types. The first type occurs when all the members of one coterie disappear for some reason. Each time this happens, I wonder whether adjacent coteries will divide the vacated territory. Curiously, however, a single adjacent coterie always seizes the entire territory, thereby increasing the size of its home coterie territory ($N = 25$). The second type of change occurs when an immigrant female steals part of a peripheral coterie territory and sets up residence there ($N = 3$; see chap. 16). The third type of change occurs during fissions and fusions of coteries (see below). Finally, the established boundary between two adjacent coterie territories sometimes permanently and inexplicably shifts ($N = 3$ shifts).

a) number of burrow entrances

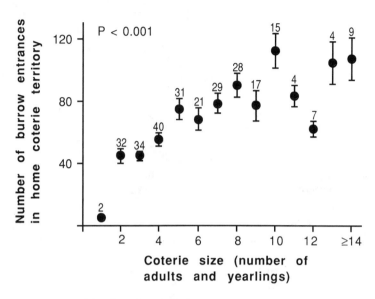

b) density of burrow entrances

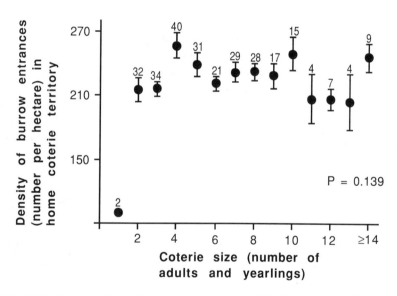

Fig. 6.15. Number and density of burrow entrances within the home coterie territory versus coterie size. *(a)* Number of burrow entrances in the home coterie territory versus coterie size. The *P*-value is from the Spearman rank correlation test. *(b)* Density of burrow entrances in the home coterie territory versus coterie size. The *P*-value is from the Kruskal-Wallis analysis of variance. For both graphs, the number above each SE line indicates the number of coteries.

Fission and Fusion of Coteries

The constancy of the home coterie territory across generations ultimately results because females and their female kin defend a particular territory, their daughters later defend the same territory, and so on. However, like harems of yellow-bellied marmots and African lions (Armitage 1984; Pusey and Packer 1987b), prairie dog coteries sometimes split (fission) (see also Hoogland 1981b; Halpin 1987; Garrett and Franklin 1988). Specifically, 4% of the coteries at the study colony (10/273) split into two smaller coteries in the following year (table 6.1). Two other coteries (1%) split into *three* smaller coteries. In nine of these twelve fissions, the smaller coteries each defended a subsection of the original coterie territory. In the other three fissions, one of the new coteries usurped all or part of an adjacent coterie territory. Following fission, intercoterie interactions involving the

Table 6.1. Fissions of Coteries

Coterie designation before fission	Coterie size in year before fission (adults and yearlings)	Coterie sizes of two resulting coteries (adults and yearlings)	Comments[a]
51-66	15	8, 5	
54-HWA	8	4, 3	The smaller new coterie usurped an adjacent coterie territory after evicting all the residents from that territory.
51-BB5	10	7, 5, 2	This fission yielded three new coteries rather than the usual two.
57	26	16, 4	
80-CBS	10	9, 3	
75-H2	8	12, 3	
88	10	10, 4	
RB3	12	8, 2	
86-RR7	8	9, 3	
BB3	13	12, 6, 3	This fission yielded three new coteries rather than the usual two; the smallest new coterie usurped part of an adjacent coterie territory.
62	12	8, 2	
R65	10	15, 1	The smaller new coterie contained a single yearling female who usurped part of an adjacent coterie territory after she was evicted from her natal coterie territory.

Note: I score juveniles in one year as yearlings in the following year. Consequently, the sum of the two resulting coterie sizes is sometimes greater than the original coterie size.

[a]Unless otherwise noted, the two or three resulting coteries always divide the original coterie territory. Each new coterie then defends a subsection of the original coterie territory.

two new coteries are mostly hostile—and thus resemble intercoterie interactions involving any other pair of adjacent coteries.

Four of the twelve fissions suggest that close kin are more likely than more distant kin to end up in the same new coterie. Following one fission, for example, all four yearling full siblings of one litter formed a new coterie. Following another fission, a mother and her 4-year-old daughter started anew. However, closer kin did not systematically band together in five other fissions. The remaining three fissions involved the movement of only one female. Perhaps fissions do not correlate more closely with kinship because prairie dogs seem unable to discriminate between close and more distant kin within the home coterie (chap. 10). Or perhaps, as for savannah baboon troops (Ron, Henzi, and Motro 1994), factors other than kinship primarily regulate how prairie dog coteries split.

One elementary prediction is that fission should usually involve larger coteries. Figure 6.16 supports this prediction. Other associations with fission are not obvious, however, and the rarity of fission, and the reasons for it, remain puzzling.

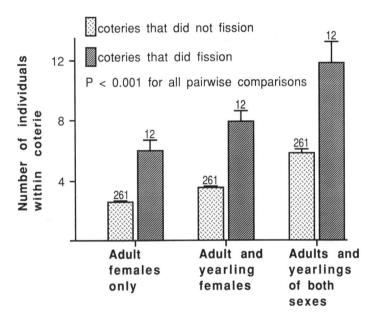

Fig. 6.16. Fission versus coterie size. The number above each SE line indicates the number of coteries. The *P*-value for each pairwise comparison is from the Mann-Whitney *U* test.

Amalgamation (fusion) of females from different matrilocal groups is rare for animals such as African lions, spotted hyenas, and various species of macaques and baboons (Schaller 1972; Kruuk 1972; Pusey and Packer 1987a). The same is true for prairie dogs. Specifically, only four fusions, involving eight coteries (8/273 = 3%), have occurred at the study colony. The scenario is always the same: mortality leads to a coterie containing a single adult female, and adult females from an adjacent coterie territory then invade the lone female's home coterie territory. In 75% of fusions (3/4), the lone female never produces any emergent juveniles following the fusion. Invading females seem merely to tolerate the lone female until she dies ($N = 3$) or until they later evict her ($N = 1$). For these reasons, reference to "fusions" is perhaps misleading. A real fusion—involving longterm amalgamation of unrelated females from different coteries— almost never occurs.

Why Do Prairie Dogs Live in Coteries?

Social organization of individuals within colonies, a secondary consequence of coloniality, can take numerous forms. For example, individuals might wander over the entire colony area during the day and spend the night in any nest or burrow therein. Males might use part of the colony area, while females use another part. Or individuals might form certain groups on some days and other groups on other days. So why do prairie dogs live in stable, harem-polygynous, territorial family groups called coteries?

A good foraging area with burrows is essential for reproduction by prairie dog females. This need probably explains why prairie dog females are territorial. If groups can defend larger, better areas than can individuals, then natural selection might favor cooperating groups within colonies. Despite some intriguing exceptions (Trivers 1971; McCracken and Bradbury 1977, 1981; Axelrod and Hamilton 1981), cooperating groups of conspecifics predictably consist of close kin (Hamilton 1964; Alexander 1974, 1987; Wilson 1975; Brown 1987). Group defense of a foraging area with burrows is thus the probable ultimate explanation for the territorial groupings of female kin within prairie dog colonies.

When groups of females defend territories, natural selection might favor single breeding males who can monopolize such groups. The result is *harem defense polygyny* for animals in general (Alexander 1975; Emlen and Oring 1977), and the coterie system for prairie dogs in particular.

In summary, the evolution of the present-day coterie probably involved the following three stages: first, the formation of unstructured colonies, to increase safety from predators (chap. 5); second, the group defense within colonies of foraging grounds with burrows by female kin, to promote female reproductive success; third, monopolization of territorial female groups by single breeding males, to promote male reproductive success.

Summary

1. A coterie is a territorial, harem-polygynous, family group of prairie dogs within a colony. The typical coterie contains one breeding male, two or three adult females, and one or two yearling offspring of each sex.

2. The number of coteries at the study colony ranges from 15 to 26.

3. Coterie size at the study colony ranges from 1 (a lone individual at the periphery of the colony) to 26, with a mean of 6.13. Even though 51% of the coteries contain five or fewer residents, 71% of the prairie dogs live in coteries of six or more residents.

4. The adult females and yearlings of both sexes within a coterie are almost always the offspring of living or deceased females of the same coterie. By contrast, the breeding males are the offspring of females from other coteries.

5. Thirty percent of coteries contain two or more breeding males. Breeding males in multi-male coteries are commonly close kin.

6. Two adjacent family groups sometimes share the same breeding male. In this arrangement, each family group is called a half-male coterie.

7. Parental care among prairie dogs takes several forms, including antipredator calling, allogrooming, playing with young, chasing of small predators, nestbuilding, nursing, and defense against infanticidal invaders from other coteries.

8. Large coteries have larger territories than smaller coteries. Coterie density also varies directly with coterie size.

9. Fission of coteries is rare, and occurs more commonly in larger coteries. Fusion of coteries is even rarer, and only occurs following reduction of a coterie to a single female.

10. Group defense of foraging grounds with burrows probably accounts for the clumping of female kin within prairie dog colonies. Monopolization of such groups by single males produces the territorial, harem-polygynous units called coteries.

7 Infanticide, the Major Cause of Juvenile Mortality

Infanticide, the killing of conspecific juveniles (Hrdy and Hausfater 1984), occurs among animals in general (Hrdy 1979; Sherman 1981b) and squirrels in particular (McLean 1983; Brody and Melcher 1985; Trulio et al. 1986; Dobson 1990; Vestal 1991). However, the frequency of infanticide is usually low (<10%), and killers are usually genetically unrelated, or only distantly related, to their victims. Not so for prairie dogs. Infanticide accounts for the partial or total demise of 39% of all litters born within prairie dog colonies, and is thus the major cause of juvenile mortality. Further, most of the killers are lactating females who are close kin of the victimized mother; invading males (usually nonkin, but sometimes kin) are also infanticidal.

Because it is the most serious cost of coloniality, with numerous implications for behavioral ecology and sociobiology, I have devoted an entire chapter to the details of prairie dog infanticide. The first part of this chapter deals with infanticide by lactating females, the second part with other types of infanticide.

Type I: Infanticide by Lactating Females

Early Attempts to Document Infanticide by Lactating Females

Most adult prairie dog females, and some yearling females as well, copulate each year (chaps. 12 and 13). However, as for Eurasian badgers (Ahnlund 1980; Cheeseman et al. 1987; Kruuk 1978, 1989; Kruuk and Parish 1987), only about 50% of copulating prairie dog females wean juveniles each year (chaps. 13 and 16). Why so few litters when so many females copulate? Do losses result primarily because females never conceive, because they conceive and then abort their litters before parturition, or because they give birth and then lose their litters during lactation? In 1980 I became serious about finding answers to these troubling questions.

For starters, during the 1980 periods of parturition and lactation I watched carefully all females that had copulated. In previous years I had concentrated observations during the periods of mating and first juvenile emergences. Because all coterie members defend the home coterie territory (chap. 6), trespassers are conspicuous. Further, like maternal Uinta, Belding's, round-tailed, and arctic ground squirrels (Dunford 1977c; Sherman 1980a; Balph 1984; McLean 1982, 1984), each prairie dog mother defends the home nursery burrow containing her offspring from any conspecific that wanders too close (fig. 7.1). I was therefore confident that I would see prairie dogs invading nursery burrows in foreign coterie territories. And I would certainly detect invaders that brought a juvenile aboveground. Although numerous prairie dogs temporarily (<5 minutes) invaded an adjacent coterie territory in 1980, none ever entered a burrow containing pre-emergent juveniles. Nonetheless, several females with young offspring suddenly stopped acting maternally. I noticed that this stoppage sometimes occurred shortly after a lactating female of the home coterie had entered the mother's nursery burrow. Upon exiting, the visiting female sometimes had blood or wet dirt—possibly resulting from the mixture of dirt with blood?—on her face and forefeet. Probably in response to this blood, the visitor then sometimes rubbed her face in the dirt and licked her front claws (fig. 7.2). These observations suggested infanticide. But wait—females of the same coterie are invariably close kin (chaps. 6 and 14)! Could females possibly visit the nursery burrows of their daughters, sisters, and nieces to kill the unweaned offspring there?

A breakthrough came in April 1980 while Monte G. Garrett was working at another colony of marked prairie dogs (the Monte colony; see chap. 4) at Wind Cave National Park. Garrett observed a lactating female running

Fig. 7.1. Female-tic-tac-toe defends burrow entrance-07, which contains her unweaned juveniles. If she is distracted from her defense, female-tic-tac-toe might lose her offspring to infanticide by a lactating female relative of the home coterie. (Photo by John L. Hoogland.)

Fig 7.2. Diagnostic aboveground behaviors that follow underground infanticide by lactating marauders. The probable purpose of these behaviors is to remove blood from the killer's face and claws. *(a)* Female-H4 rubs her face in the dirt at burrow entrance-JC. *(b)* Female-52 carefully licks her front claws at burrow entrance-0. (Photos by John L. Hoogland.)

from the vicinity of her sister's nursery burrow with a live juvenile, which she then quickly killed and cannibalized aboveground. From pointed questioning, I learned that the marauder had licked her front claws extensively and had repeatedly rubbed her face in the dirt after the cannibalism. Lactating females really do sometimes kill the unweaned offspring of close kin! I began to wonder whether such kin-directed infanticide might account for the loss of so many pre-emergent litters each year.

The regular killing of juvenile nondescendant kin was unknown in 1980, except anecdotally for animals such as African wild dogs, dwarf mongooses, and brown hyenas (Lawick 1974; Frame et al. 1979; Rood 1980b, 1990; Packer and Pusey 1984); more recent possible exceptions include plains spadefoot toads and Eurasian badgers (Neal 1986; Kruuk 1989; Lups and Roper 1990; Pfennig, Reeve, and Sherman 1993; Woodroffe 1993). I suspected that I was on to something big, and approached the 1981 field season with great enthusiasm. The limited data base from 1980 indicated that lactating females are the most likely killers, so they became the main targets of observation as soon as females started to give birth in 1981.

Every day from dawn to dusk during the period of lactation, I make a census every 20 minutes of all females that have copulated. If a female is missing at the 20-minute census, she might be foraging in the tall grass or nursing her own young in her home nursery burrow. Or she might be killing the young of another female! Between censuses I watch the females themselves and their nursery burrows for possible marauding, and attempt to locate the females missing at the last census. When a lactating female of the home coterie enters another mother's nursery burrow containing pre-emergent offspring, the victimized mother usually fails to rear a litter to first emergence (fig. 7.3a). The implication is that marauders kill—and then partially or completely cannibalize (see below)—the offspring of other mothers within the home coterie territory. I only score an infanticide when a trespassing female remains for at least 5 minutes in another mother's nursery burrow while the victimized mother is absent.

Diagnostic Behaviors Associated with Infanticide

Female-F stayed underground for only 7 minutes while marauding. At the other extreme, female-RAB marauded female-FR's nursery burrow for 231 minutes on 12 May 1987. The mean ± SD number of minutes that a killer stays underground while marauding is 47.2 ± 36.9 ($N = 61$).

Appendix B documents the incidence of a bloody (BF) or dirty face (DF), rubbing of the face in the dirt (RFD), and licking of the front claws (LFC) in 65 observed cases of presumed infanticide by lactating females. BF or DF occurred at a frequency of 37% (23/63), RFD at a frequency of 48% (31/64), and LFC at a frequency of 57% (36/63).

Infanticidal red-tailed monkeys and Belding's ground squirrels some-times have bloody faces after killing (Struhsaker 1977; Sherman 1981b), but DF, LFC, and RFD are perhaps unique to prairie dogs. I have never seen a mother with a bloody face upon emergence from her own nursery burrow—unless a marauding has already occurred there.

Although RFD sometimes occurs only once for 5 to 10 seconds, more commonly it occurs repeatedly for 30 to 60 seconds per instance. I have seen RFD in only one other context. After a vicious fight, a prairie dog of either sex sometimes rubs its face in the dirt. Facial blood is visible after many of these fights, and the implication is that a prairie dog uses RFD to remove blood (its own or another's) from its face.

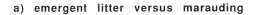

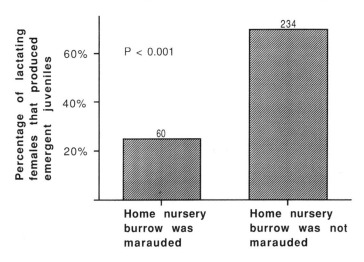

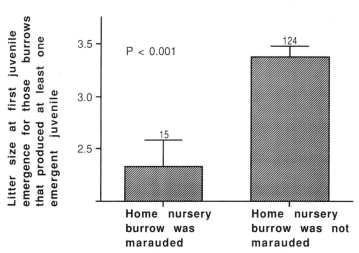

Fig. 7.3. Litter size versus marauding. *(a)* Production of emergent litter versus marauding of the home nursery burrow. I score a marauding whenever a female enters another female's nursery burrow containing pre-emergent offspring and remains there for 5 minutes or longer. The number above each bar indicates the number of nursery burrows under observation; the *P*-value is from the 2×2 chi-square test. *(b)* Litter size at first juvenile emergence versus marauding of the home nursery burrow. Litter sizes shown here are only from 1981 through 1984, 1986, and 1987—the 6 years when marauded nursery burrows yielded emergent juveniles. Data are from only those nursery burrows that produced at least one emergent juvenile. The number above each bar indicates the number of litters examined; the *P*-value is from the Mann-Whitney *U* test.

LFC sometimes lasts for only 5 to 10 seconds, but more commonly lasts for several minutes. LFC involves gentle, careful licking, and is therefore distinct from the rough, jerky cleaning of the claws with the teeth that follows either maintenance of burrow mounds or excavation of burrows. The probable purpose of LFC is to remove blood from the claws. I have never observed LFC in any context other than marauding.

Appendix B shows that some maraudings do not involve BF-DF, RFD, or LFC, others involve one or two of these diagnostic behaviors, and still others involve all three. Further, these behaviors are not necessarily linked to specific killers. For example, female-H4 showed none of the behaviors after killing the offspring of female-2RSA on 07 April 1983. However, female-H4 showed all three behaviors when she killed the offspring of the same female-2RSA a year later on 21 April 1984.

Excavations to Verify Infanticide

Like mothers of other rodents such as golden hamsters, deer mice, and house mice (Day and Galef 1977; Gandelman and Simon 1978; Perrigo 1987; Elwood 1992), perhaps prairie dog mothers sometimes kill their own offspring (e.g., see Type III infanticide described below). If so, then "marauders" might only be eating already dead juveniles that are no longer worth the mother's defense. Garrett's casual observations had revealed one unequivocal case of an aboveground killing in 1980 by a marauding mother. I therefore assumed that my detailed observations would yield numerous aboveground kills to complement and corroborate the cases of presumed underground infanticide. Not so. Although detecting infanticide was my primary objective in both 1980 and 1981, I came up empty both times. I therefore ended the 1981 field season without a single observation of an aboveground kill, and was not convinced that marauders rather than mothers are responsible for infanticides.

Perhaps excavations would settle the question. For example, excavations after cases of presumed infanticide might lead to nests containing recently killed juveniles. I therefore planned excavations for 1982 at the Pringle colony, 1 kilometer from the study colony.

Frequently a victimized mother sees the marauder exiting from her home nursery burrow after committing infanticide there (see below). If so, she usually chases the marauder away, then enters her victimized nursery burrow immediately and remains there for a long time—sometimes for several hours (see below). Further, lactating females usually enter their own nursery burrows during a disturbance, such as when I enter the colony. Therefore, the task of excavating after a case of presumed infanticide *without the victimized mother ending up in her own home nursery burrow* would be formidable. The results would be meaningless if the mother entered her home nursery burrow before the excavation, because I would not know whether the mother or the marauder had killed the juveniles. I therefore devised experiments that involved the trapping and temporary removal of single lactating females. After incarcerating a mother, I carefully watched her undefended nursery burrow for possible marauding. If marauding occurred, my plan was to keep the mother incarcerated, to plug the main entrance and all other entrances to the victimized nursery burrow as soon as the marauder exited so that no other prairie dog could enter, and to begin excavation as soon as possible. Using shovels and hand trowels, field assistants and I excavated one nursery burrow in 1982 after a presumed infanticide there. With the aid of Wind Cave National Park's personnel and heavy machinery, we excavated another victimized nursery burrow in 1983. Both excavations led to empty nests, with no sign of juveniles or blood anywhere in the tunnel system! What could these empty nests possibly mean? Could the marauder have consumed the entire victimized litter? Despite the plugging of entrances, could mice or other animals have eaten the undefended young before we reached the nest? Still baffled, I entered the fifth year of my investigation of infanticide, 1984, with only circumstantial evidence that marauders regularly kill the offspring of close kin.

I planned more excavations for 1984, with two major changes in experimental design. First, I would throw poisonous smoke bombs into the victimized nursery burrow after a case of presumed infanticide and would keep all entrances plugged until the time of excavation. The poisonous gas presumably would kill mice or other animals that otherwise might try to eat the undefended juveniles before excavation. Second, I would dissect both the mother and the presumed killer as soon as possible after the presumed killing. If the stomach of the mother contained only plants while the stomach of the marauder contained flesh and bones, and if the nest was again empty, I would conclude that the marauder had killed and consumed all the young of the victimized litter.

At 1724 on 8 April 1984 at the Pringle colony, female-BS entered an incarcerated female's nursery burrow. Female-BS emerged at 1753 with a distinctly bloody face, then rubbed her face in the dirt before submerging for the night into her own nursery burrow. Excavation of the smoked, plugged nursery burrow began at approximately 1000 on 9 April 1984 (fig. 7.4), and led to a nest containing five juveniles, all approximately 7 days old: two were unmaimed, one had severe wounds on the chest and shoulder, and two were decapitated (fig. 7.5). Because of the poisonous gas, both the maimed and the unmaimed juveniles were dead. Whereas the stomach of the victimized mother contained herbaceous material only, the stomach of female-BS (livetrapped at approximately 0700 on 9 April) contained flesh and bones (fig. 7.6). To verify that the flesh and bones in female-BS's stomach resulted from marauding rather than from the killing of her own litter, we also excavated female-BS's nursery burrow on 10 April. We found a nest containing five, approximately 7-day-old, live juveniles.

Fig. 7.4. Excavation of marauded nursery burrow to verify infanticide. *(a)* The backhoe allowed us to quickly reach the nest of a nursery burrow where marauding had occurred. *(b)* The nest containing young juveniles was 2 meters below the surface. *(c)* By the end, we had excavated more than 100 metric tons of dirt. Figure 3.1b shows a diagram of this excavated nursery burrow. (Photos by John L. Hoogland.)

Fig. 7.5. Victims of infanticide by marauding lactating female-BS (backstripe). The excavation depicted in figure 7.4 finally led to these five juveniles, all about 1 week old. The marauding that produced these victims lasted 29 minutes. (Photo by John L. Hoogland.)

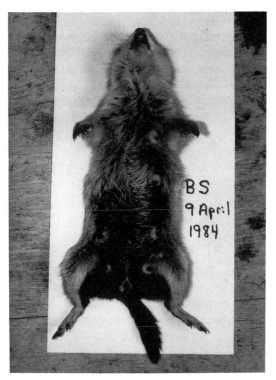

Fig. 7.6. Dissection of marauder. To verify that marauding female-BS cannibalized the victims shown in figure 7.5, I dissected her. In addition to herbaceous material, female-BS's stomach contained flesh and bones. (Photo by John L. Hoogland.)

I would have preferred to excavate more nursery burrows after cases of presumed infanticide. However, officials and personnel at Wind Cave National Park had already gone beyond the call of duty.

The excavations and dissections of 1984 are important for at least three reasons. First, they indicate that marauders sometimes might kill and completely cannibalize all their victims. For example, female-BS on 8 April 1984 consumed over one-half of two juveniles in only 29 minutes. Similarly, the marauder observed by Monte G. Garrett (see above) needed only about 10 minutes to cannibalize approximately 75% of her victim. If the victimized litters that we attempted to excavate in 1982 and 1983 contained only two or three small juveniles, then the killers easily might have killed and completely cannibalized all of them. Such cannibalism would explain the empty nests that we found. Second, the excavations prove that marauders sometimes kill only some, rather than all, juveniles of the victimized litter. Finally, and most importantly, the excavations provide one case of underground infanticide for which the evidence is conclusive that the marauder, rather than the mother, is the culprit.

More Direct Evidence for Infanticide

Perhaps the randomly chosen mother had killed but not consumed her juveniles before I livetrapped her and before the marauder decapitated two of them on 8 April 1984. Or perhaps killing by marauders never occurs when mothers are able to defend their home nursery burrows properly (i.e., when not incarcerated). Seven case histories argue against these remote possibilities, as described below.

1. On 12 May 1984, a female emerged from her full first cousin's nursery burrow with a pre-emergent juvenile that was probably already dead (and therefore is absent from appendix B). The marauder immediately transported the juvenile into a nearby burrow and remained there for 15 minutes. Upon emergence she showed both RFD and LFC. I never saw the juvenile again.

2. On 30 May 1984, a female emerged from her full niece's nursery burrow with a live pre-emergent juvenile, which she quickly killed aboveground. After killing, the marauder showed both RFD and LFC.

3. On 6 June 1984, a female invaded an adjacent coterie territory and entered a burrow containing a recently emerged, healthy juvenile. The marauder emerged 5 minutes later with a distinctly bloody face, and then showed LFC. Several minutes later the disoriented juvenile emerged with fresh, severe wounds on the face and neck. The juvenile disappeared a few days later.

4. On 1 June 1985, a female invaded an adjacent coterie territory and climbed over livetraps to enter a nursery burrow containing two

juveniles that had first appeared aboveground on the previous day. The marauder stayed underground for 80 minutes, and upon emergence showed DF, RFD, and LFC. One of the juveniles emerged while the marauder was in its nursery burrow and entered a livetrap shortly thereafter. The other juvenile never reappeared. This case does not appear in appendix B because the victimized mother was in a livetrap during the marauding.

5. On 12 May 1987, a female emerged two times from her full aunt's nursery burrow with juveniles that were already dead from a previous marauding. After cannibalizing the juveniles aboveground, the female showed BF, RFD, and LFC. A second female that joined in the cannibalism also showed RFD and LFC.

6. On 16 May 1988, I observed a female killing her full sister's pre-emergent juvenile at the entrance to its nursery burrow. I presume that the killer first entered the nursery burrow and pulled out the juvenile, but did not actually see the killer's entry or exit.

7. Field assistants or I observed aboveground kills of recently emergent juveniles by three different males (see below). One of the males showed BF, and two males showed RFD and LFC. A female that partially cannibalized one of the victims also showed RFD.

Ironically, three of these seven cases surfaced in 1984 in the weeks following the crucial excavations. Why did I observe several aboveground cases of infanticide from 1984 through 1988 after seeing nothing from 1980 through 1983? I do not know, but by the end of 1984 I felt certain that my inferences of underground infanticide from behavioral observations are correct.

Genetic Relationship of Killer to Mother of Victims

Marauders are almost always female kin from the victimized mother's home coterie (table 7.1). The most commonly victimized mothers are full and half sisters.

A killer is frequently the daughter of the victimized mother. If the victimized mother has again copulated with the killer's father, then the killer would eliminate full siblings. If the mother has copulated with a different male, however, then the victims would be the killer's half siblings. Males do not usually remain in the same breeding coterie territory for more than two consecutive years, and females usually do not breed or become infanticidal until they are 2 years old (chaps. 13 and 14). Thus, the victims when a female kills her mother's offspring are usually half siblings rather than full siblings—as was true for eight of the nine cases in appendix B and table 7.1. In the ninth case, female-92 killed when she was only a yearling and her father was still in her natal coterie territory.

Table 7.1. Genetic Relationship of Infanticidal Marauders to Mothers of Victims

Relationship	Frequency
Mother	12
Daughter	9
Full sister	13
Half sister	14
Full aunt	4
Half aunt	1
Half great aunt	1
Full niece	5
Half niece	1
Full first cousin	1
Half first cousin once removed	1
No known kinship	3
Total	65

Note: The 65 cases shown here involve 38 different killers and 44 different victimized mothers. Appendix B provides additional information for each case.

Of the four types of infanticide that occur among prairie dogs (see below), marauding by lactating female kin is the most common. The frequency of litters partially eliminated by marauding is 6%, and the frequency of litters totally eliminated by marauding is 16% (table 7.2).

Response of Mother to Marauder

When aboveground, a mother's defense against marauding involves watching the entrance to her home nursery burrow and chasing away all conspecifics that come too close. She quickly evicts any prairie dog that dares to enter. If a marauder can somehow get into another mother's nursery burrow without detection, she remains out of the mother's view and is therefore temporarily safe from retaliation—until she tries to exit. What does the mother do when the killer exits? In 63 of the 65 infanticides observed (appendix B), I was specifically watching the victimized mother at the moment when the killer emerged. In 48% of infanticides (30/63), the mother evidently does not see the killer's exit and thus cannot retaliate. Slightly more frequently, the mother detects the killer's exit (33/63 = 52%), and then viciously attacks or chases her (18/63 = 29%). If she detects the killer's exit, the mother commonly enters her home nursery burrow immediately after detection and remains there for an hour or more (31/63 = 49%).

Sometimes the mother evidently does not know that a marauder is in her nursery burrow but just happens to enter the burrow anyway (11/63 = 17%). Caught red-handed in this way, the marauder sometimes emerges within a few minutes and is unusually dirty—suggesting an underground

Table 7.2. Frequencies of the Four Types of Infanticide

Type of infanticide	Frequencies											
	1978	1979	1980	1981	1982	1983	1984	1985	1986	1987	1988	All years
I. Lactating female killed:												
a) some pre-emergent juveniles in litter	—	—	—	3% (33)	21% (24)	8% (24)	13% (53)	0% (36)	2% (51)	7% (42)	0% (31)	6% (294)
b) all pre-emergent juveniles in litter	—	—	—	24% (33)	21% (24)	13% (24)	19% (53)	11% (36)	12% (51)	5% (42)	26% (31)	16% (294)
II. Invading female immigrant killed some or all emergent juveniles in litter	1% (77)	1% (69)	0% (56)	0% (64)	0% (53)	0% (59)	0% (53)	0% (36)	0% (51)	0% (42)	0% (31)	0% (591)
III. Mother and other coterie members killed all abandoned, pre-emergent juveniles in litter	—	—	—	—	—	15% (40)	17% (53)	11% (36)	0% (51)	0% (42)	16% (31)	9% (253)
IV. Invading yearling male killed:												
a) all pre-emergent juveniles in litter	0% (77)	10% (69)	0% (56)	0% (64)	0% (53)	3% (59)	4% (53)	3% (36)	4% (51)	2% (42)	10% (31)	3% (591)
b) some emergent juveniles in litter	6% (77)	0% (69)	0% (56)	0% (64)	0% (53)	3% (59)	0% (53)	6% (36)	0% (51)	2% (42)	0% (31)	2% (591)
c) all emergent juveniles in litter	3% (77)	0% (69)	0% (56)	8% (64)	0% (53)	2% (59)	0% (53)	0% (36)	4% (51)	2% (42)	0% (31)	2% (591)

Note: Here I show the percentage of litters affected by each type of infanticide. The number in parentheses below each percentage indicates the number of litters monitored for infanticide. In some years I can monitor all litters for certain types of infanticide but only some litters for other types. Dashes indicate no data.

fight with the victimized mother (6/63 = 10%). Rarely the killer remains underground with the mother for as long as several hours (2/63 = 3%). And sometimes (3/63 = 5%) the mother quickly emerges from her nursery burrow—as though she has not detected the killer there.

Except for the fight between killer and victimized mother that commonly occurs during or just after marauding, retaliation by the victimized mother does not occur. On the contrary, the victimized mother loses all aggressiveness within a few days after losing her litter, and starts interacting amicably (kissing and allogrooming, for example; see chap. 10) when the killer allows it. Delayed retaliation also does not seem to occur. Specifically, although mothers that lose a litter to a particular killer in one year sometimes eliminate that killer's litter in a later year, this trend is not rampant. Rather, the opposite is true: killers frequently victimize the same mother in different years (appendix B).

Sometimes a potential marauder enters a nursery burrow when the mother is also in that burrow ($N > 50$ observations). The invader usually stays underground for less than 60 seconds and then quickly returns to the area around her own nursery burrow. Sometimes the defending mother emerges immediately after the invader and chases her away.

Factors Other than Infanticide That Might Eliminate Litters

What about the 71 unmarauded nursery burrows in figure 7.3a that did not yield emergent litters? At least three factors, not necessarily mutually exclusive, might explain these cases. First, noninfanticidal factors such as disease, genetic defects, and predation sometimes might eliminate entire litters. Curiously, I have no direct evidence for any of these mortality factors. Second, some of the 71 nursery burrows belonged to mothers who abandoned and cannibalized their own litters shortly after parturition for one reason or another (Type III infanticide, as described below; see also Dickemann 1975; Sherman 1981b; Hausfater and Hrdy 1984; Fitzgerald 1992; Sargent 1992). Finally, despite persistent tracking of mothers from dawn until dusk during the entire period of lactation, I might fail to detect a few maraudings that are especially subtle. I might miss a few other maraudings because I do not know about a second or third entrance to a female's home nursery burrow. In 1984, for example, I noticed that female-H6 suddenly stopped acting maternally, even though I had seen no marauding of her nursery burrow. Almost immediately I discovered a second entrance to female-H6's nursery burrow. In my ignorance, I had not been closely watching the second entrance for possible marauding.

Partial-Litter versus Whole-Litter Infanticide

What about the 15 marauded nursery burrows in figure 7.3a that still yielded emergent juveniles? Did the marauder fail to kill while in these nursery burrows? Like the killing documented by excavation on 8 April 1984 (see above), perhaps these 15 cases involved the killing of some, but not all, juveniles of the victimized litter. If so, then litter size at first emergence should have been smaller for the 15 marauded nursery burrows than for unmarauded nursery burrows. Figure 7.3b supports this hypothesis of partial-litter infanticide.

Three mothers continued to act maternally following one marauding, but then terminated maternal behaviors shortly after a second marauding (appendix B). The first marauding in these cases presumably involved partial-litter infanticide, and the second marauding evidently finished the job.

Characteristics of Marauders and Victimized Mothers

Appendix B shows the characteristics of marauders and victimized mothers. I have implied that all marauders are lactating, but this is not fully accurate: 78% (51/65) of marauders are lactating at the time of marauding, 12% (8/65) have recently lost their own litters, 5% (3/65) have juveniles that have already emerged from the natal burrow, 3% (2/65) are pregnant, and 2% (1/65) either have not conceived or have aborted shortly after copulation. More precisely, then, most killers are currently lactating, and a few others are in late pregnancy or have just terminated lactation.

The mean $\pm$ SD age of victimized juveniles is 18.1 ± 13.5 days after parturition ($N = 64$), but the range is from 0 to 65 days! The mean $\pm$ SD age of the mother's own offspring (when she still has them) at the time of marauding is 18.4 ± 13.1 days after parturition ($N = 52$), and again the range is extensive (from 2 to 57 days). These similar ages of killers' and victimized mothers' offspring result because females within a coterie breed synchronously (chap. 13). The age of the killer ranges from 1 to 6 years (mean $\pm$ SD $= 3.28 \pm 1.35$, $N = 65$). The age of the victimized mother ranges from 1 to 7 years (mean $\pm$ SD $= 3.06 \pm 1.57$, $N = 65$).

The 65 cases of infanticide described in appendix B involve 38 different killers and 44 different victimized mothers. These numbers emphasize two important points. First, killing clearly involves more than a few idiosyncratic females. Second, individual females differ markedly in both vulnerability to marauding and the tendency to maraud. Whereas numerous females never lose their litters before first emergence, one female (2RSA) lost her litter to marauding in three consecutive years. Similarly, whereas numerous females never maraud, female-H4 marauded eight times and female-92 marauded six times. These latter two females account for 22% of all killings (14/65) performed by lactating females.

Infanticide versus Overcrowding

Infanticide sometimes results directly from overcrowding in laboratory populations of animals such as collared peccaries, European rabbits, house mice, Norway rats, and golden hamsters (Southwick 1955; Myers and Poole 1961; Calhoun 1962; Diamond and Mast 1978; Packard et al. 1990). For free-living populations of animals such as hanuman langurs and numerous invertebrates, overcrowding resulting from unnatural disturbance also might promote infanticide (Fox 1975; Curtin and Dolhinow 1978, 1979; Boggess 1979, 1984; Polis 1981; but see chap. 17).

Suitable habitat for expansion is limited at the study colony (chap. 4). Does this mean that the study colony is overcrowded, and that infanticide there is merely a maladaptive response to such overcrowding? Probably not, for at least three reasons. First, the density of prairie dogs at the study colony is not unusually high. For example, of five ward (subcolony) densities estimated from studies of marked individuals (see fig. 5.17b), the density at the study colony is higher than two but lower than two others; unlike the study colony, the other four colonies all had adjacent habitat that appeared suitable for expansion. Second, Garrett's observation of aboveground infanticide occurred at a young (<10 years old), expanding colony with copious food (Garrett, Hoogland, and Franklin 1982). Further, the Pringle colony, where I observed three maraudings, was also young (<15 years old) and expanding. Finally, in other studies of uncrowded prairie dogs living under natural conditions, many females have failed to wean litters (King 1955; Foreman 1962; Tileston and Lechleitner 1966; Knowles 1985, 1987; Halpin 1987). In summary, infanticide by marauding lactating females seems to be typical and widespread within prairie dog colonies, and independent of overcrowding.

Infanticide versus Coterie Size

Barring the rare killing by a female from a different coterie territory, the probability of losing a litter to a marauder is zero in a coterie territory containing only a single lactating female. At the other extreme, females in large coteries must defend against several possible marauders. Not surprisingly, therefore, the probability of losing a litter to marauding varies directly with the number of females in the home coterie that give birth (fig. 7.7).

Marauders Sometimes Lose Their Own Litters while Marauding

When marauding, a mother leaves her own offspring unguarded. Of the 65 observed cases of infanticide, 4 (6%) occurred while the mother herself was marauding. Two other females (3%) lost their litters to marauders while visiting nursery burrows where infanticide had occurred a few days earlier. Thus, marauding imposes at least one serious cost: an increased probability of losing one's own litter to marauding.

Why Don't Marauders Kill Juvenile Nonkin of Other Coterie Territories?

Natural selection favors individuals who are most successful at transmitting copies of their own alleles to future generations through the reproduction of either themselves or their kin (Fisher 1958; Hamilton 1964;

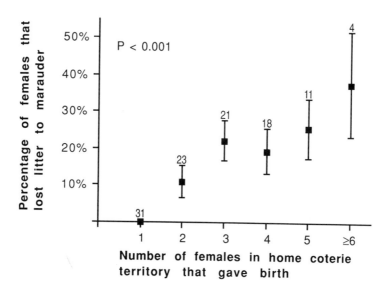

Fig. 7.7. Probability of losing a litter to marauding versus the number of females in the home coterie territory that give birth. The number above each SE line indicates the number of coteries containing each number of parturient females. The *P*-value is from the Spearman rank correlation test.

Williams 1966a; Wilson 1975). In general, individuals should help kin to reproduce when possible (Hamilton 1964; Maynard Smith 1964; Alexander 1974; West-Eberhard 1975; Brown 1987). Within species that practice infanticide, individuals should kill juvenile nonkin rather than juvenile kin when presented with a choice (Rohwer 1978; Nummelin 1989; Elgar and Crespi 1992; Elwood 1992; Fitzgerald and Whoriskey 1992). So why do prairie dog marauders so often kill the offspring of close kin and spare the offspring of nonkin?

The common killing of offspring of close kin by prairie dog marauders is not merely a result of biased observations. As noted above, documenting the killing of nonkin by an invader from a strange coterie territory is much easier than documenting the killing of kin by a member of the home coterie territory.

All coterie members defend the home coterie territory (chap. 6). Within the home territory, however, only the mother defends the nursery burrow containing her pre-emergent young. Consequently, to kill unrelated juveniles in an adjacent coterie territory ($N = 4$ of the cases in appendix B), a marauder must elude the defenses of all members of that coterie *as well as* the mother's defense of her home nursery burrow. To kill related juveniles in the home coterie territory ($N = 61$ of the cases in appendix B), however, a marauder need only elude the mother's defense of her home nursery burrow. This difference in *accessibility* probably explains why marauders regularly kill the offspring of kin rather than the offspring of nonkin.

Are Marauders More Likely to Kill the Offspring of More Distant Kin?

In a coterie territory containing only two lactating mothers, a marauder has no choice of victims. In a coterie territory containing six lactating mothers, on the other hand, a marauder can chose among five potential litters. Natural selection perhaps should favor marauders that preferentially kill offspring of distant kin rather than offspring of closer kin when presented with a choice. Figure 7.8 offers no support for this hypothesis, probably because of limitations in social learning and kin recognition (chap. 10).

Prairie dogs also do not discriminate between close and distant kin in behavioral interactions (chap. 10), in fissions of large coteries (chap. 6), when giving antipredator calls (chap. 8), or during communal nursing

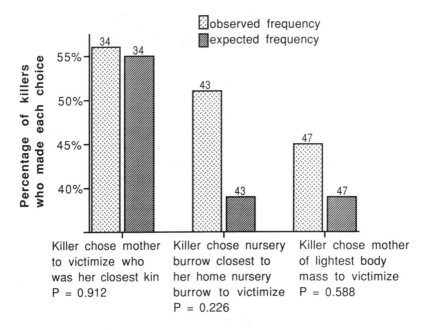

Fig. 7.8. What do marauders do when presented with a choice? Data shown here are only from marauders that had a choice among two or more litters to victimize. The number above each bar indicates the total number of observed maraudings. *P*-values are from the 2 × 2 chi-square test, which compares observed and expected frequencies. Expected values are frequencies that should have resulted if killing is independent of kinship, proximity of the victimized nursery burrow containing pre-emergent juveniles, and body mass of the victimized mother.

(chap. 9). Perhaps the costs and benefits of these latter behaviors are trivial for prairie dogs, and thus too inconsequential for natural selection to favor differential nepotism. The same argument cannot apply to infanticide, for which the stakes are much higher. The failure of infanticidal females to choose between the offspring of close and distant kin is therefore perplexing (see also chap. 10).

In another sense, marauders *do* discriminate between close and distant kin because they regularly kill the offspring of close kin but only rarely kill their own offspring (see below). By a still unknown route (see below), marauding presumably functions to enhance either the marauder's own reproduction or her survivorship. Thus, even though a marauder sometimes might kill the unweaned offspring of close kin—in which case the coefficient of genetic relatedness, r, between herself and the victimized juveniles is always less than .5000, except in the rare case noted above in which a marauder's victims are her own full siblings—the beneficiaries of such killing are either the marauder herself ($r = 1$) or her own offspring ($r \geq$ .5000). Marauders therefore discriminate in favor of themselves and their own juvenile offspring, at the expense of the offspring of close kin. Note that almost all maraudings occur before first juvenile emergences (appendix B), when mothers can easily discriminate between their own and others' offspring (see also chap. 10).

Does Proximity of the Victimized Mother's Home Burrow or the Victimized Mother's Defensive Prowess Affect the Marauder's Choice?

Besides kinship, I have investigated two other factors that might influence a marauder's choice of victims: proximity of the victimized mother's nursery burrow to the marauder's nursery burrow, and defensive prowess of the victimized mother as estimated from her body mass. Killers tend to choose nearby nursery burrows belonging to mothers of low body mass (fig. 7.8). Curiously, however, neither of these trends is statistically significant.

Marauding versus Marauder's Body Mass

Small, light females might be more desperate than heavier females for one of the benefits derived from infanticide, such as increased sustenance or the removal of future competitors. In this scenario, marauders should be *lighter* than nonmarauders. On the other hand, heavy females probably are better able than lighter females to defend their offspring against marauders. This improved defense might allow heavy females more opportunities to maraud with a reduced probability of losing their own litters. In this second scenario, marauders should be *heavier* than nonmarauders. Table 7.3 supports the second scenario.

Table 7.3 shows the mean body masses in October and February for *all* nonmarauding females, including those whose home nursery burrows

Table 7.3. Reproductive Success of Marauders and Nonmarauders

	Marauders	Nonmarauders	Significance of this difference[a]
Probability of weaning a litter[b]	27/46 = 59%	149/245 = 61%	$P = .787$
Probability of mother's survival until following year	9/25 = 36%	62/139 = 45%	$P = .424$
Litter size at first juvenile emergence	3.23 ± 1.11 ($N = 26$)	3.23 ± 1.04 ($N = 151$)	$P = .929$
Juvenile body mass at first emergence (grams)[c]	157 ± 30.7 ($N = 26$)	155 ± 28.4 ($N = 153$)	$P = .740$
Mother's body mass at first juvenile emergence (grams)	695 ± 75.3 ($N = 27$)	701 ± 81.4 ($N = 152$)	$P = .810$
Mother's body mass in previous October (grams)	869 ± 99.8 ($N = 22$)	806 ± 101 ($N = 105$)	$P = .151$
Mother's body mass in previous February (grams)	751 ± 106 ($N = 16$)	698 ± 99.5 ($N = 126$)	$P = .032$

[a]P-values are from either the 2 × 2 chi-square test or the Mann-Whitney U test.

[b]The probability of weaning a litter includes data from all females that copulated and gave birth. All other data in this table are from only those females that produced emergent juveniles.

[c]For juvenile body mass at first emergence, I use a single mean body mass for the entire litter for statistical analyses.

were not marauded. To investigate the importance of body mass further, I have excluded the body masses of unvictimized mothers and have compared only the body masses of marauders and victimized mothers. Killers are heavier than victimized mothers in both October and February (fig. 7.9).

Why Reproduce If Infanticide Is So Likely?

Certain prairie dog females are especially vulnerable to infanticide and live in coteries with known killers (appendix B). Yet such females consistently take on the burden of copulation, pregnancy, and early lactation before losing their litters to killers. Why doesn't natural selection favor earlier cutting of losses for vulnerable females? For example, such females could refrain from coming into estrus, abort their offspring in early pregnancy, or terminate lactation shortly after parturition (Wasser 1983; Wasser and Barash 1983; Bronson 1989; Creel and Creel 1991; Elgar and Crespi 1992; see also below).

The possibility always exists that the heavy, infanticidal female(s) within the home coterie territory will fall victim to a predator during pregnancy or lactation. If so, then the female(s) in that territory susceptible to infanticide might be able to wean a litter after all. As it might for dwarf mongooses (Keane et al. 1994), perhaps this possibility explains why even the most vulnerable prairie dog females predictably copulate and become pregnant each year (see also below).

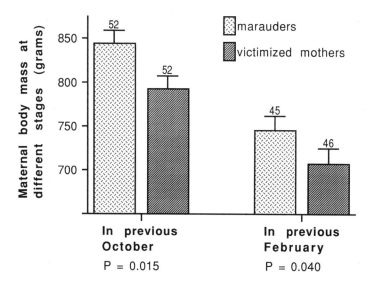

Fig. 7.9. Maternal body mass at two different stages of the annual cycle for marauders and victimized mothers. The number above each SE line indicates the number of females weighed (one killer and one victimized mother for each marauding). *P*-values are from the Wilcoxon matched-pairs signed-ranks test.

Possible Benefits of Marauding

With two such high costs—increased probability of losing one's own litter while marauding and apparent loss in inclusive fitness (Hamilton 1964) associated with eliminating offspring of close kin—why does Type I infanticide persist among prairie dogs? Marauders obtain at least five benefits—not mutually exclusive—that might offset these two costs, as discussed below.

Benefit 1: Removal of Future Competitors. When individuals are philopatric (i.e., unlikely to disperse), infanticide leads to the removal of future competitors (Fox 1975; Hrdy 1979; Sherman 1981b). Killers remove individuals that would compete not only with themselves, but also with their offspring. Such removal might be the primary benefit of infanticide for females of animals such as common muskrats, house mice, white-footed mice, and Belding's ground squirrels (Errington 1963; Sherman 1981b; McCarthy and vom Saal 1985; Wolff and Cicirello 1989).

For animals such as sooty terns, glaucous-winged and herring gulls, and northern elephant seals (Ashmole 1963a; Hunt and Hunt 1976; Pierotti 1987; Le Boeuf and Briggs 1977), mobile juveniles sometimes try to steal food from adults other than their parents. Under these conditions, natural selection might favor infanticide during periods when juveniles are younger and less mobile—i.e., when parents can easily discriminate between nests containing their own offspring and nests containing others' offspring (Sherman 1981b; Pierotti and Murphy 1987; Pierotti 1991; Elwood 1992). Kill them before you adopt them! By removing others' young juveniles, parents become less likely to invest in them later when discrimination between their own and others' offspring is either difficult or unprofitable.

Support for the importance to prairie dogs of removing future competitors comes from the general restriction of infanticide to the home coterie territory (appendix B). On one hand, this is the expected result because competition among females for limited resources is more intense within coteries than between coteries (chap. 6). Further, juveniles that steal milk from females other than their mothers always live in the home coterie territory (chap. 9). On the other hand, restriction of infanticide to the home coterie territory might result merely because juveniles within the home coterie territory are more accessible (see above).

The failure of nonbreeding adult and yearling females to kill argues against the importance of removing future competitors. Nonbreeding females are likely to remain in the natal coterie territory and breed there in subsequent years. Consequently, they would presumably gain all the advantages of removing future competitors without incurring the one indisputable cost: increased probability of losing one's own litter while marauding. However, a nonbreeding female might not survive until the following year. Because of this possible mortality, a nonbreeding female's best, albeit indirect, chance for reproductive success this year is via her breeding female relatives of the home coterie. Perhaps a female does not gain from the removal of future related competitors unless the probability of rearing her own litter—as evidenced by the suckling of her own healthy juveniles, for example—is high. This scenario suggests that, as for animals in general (Hamilton 1964; Alexander 1974; Rubenstein and Wrangham 1980; Armitage 1987a, 1988, 1989), natural selection among prairie dogs is usually more intense for the direct production of offspring than for helping close kin to produce offspring. When the opportunity of direct production of offspring is lost, however, then natural selection favors unsuccessful females that help close kin to rear offspring.

The sex ratio of marauded litters that still produce emergent juveniles also argues against the importance of removing future competitors. Females are more likely than males to remain in the natal coterie territory and compete for resources there (chaps. 6 and 14). If the removal of future competitors is important, then prairie dog marauders—like Belding's ground squirrel marauders (Sherman 1981b)—should preferentially eliminate female juveniles. The result would be a male-biased sex ratio at first juvenile emergence for partially marauded litters. However, of the 35 juveniles that emerged from 15 partially marauded nursery burrows (see fig. 7.3b), the observed sex ratio of 18 males and 17 females is almost identical to the expected sex ratio (chap. 15) of 18.5 males and 16.5 females ($P > .500$, 2×2 chi-square test).

Perhaps killers are unable to discriminate between male and female juveniles living in a dark underground nest. In proximate terms, this might explain why no male-biased sex ratio is evident among partially marauded nursery burrows. In ultimate terms, the failure of killers to discriminate between male and female juveniles remains puzzling if the removal of future competitors is important.

Benefit 2:   Increased Sustenance. If a prairie dog mother's only concern were to remove future competitors, she could kill the offspring of close kin without consuming them. Killing without cannibalism would be faster, so that the marauder could return more quickly to the defense of her own home nursery burrow. However, the behaviors associated with underground infanticides, the aboveground infanticides, and the excavation of 9 April 1984 all indicate that marauders usually cannibalize their victims. Perhaps prairie dog marauders gain additional sustenance from cannibalism—e.g., protein or rare minerals—and thus are better able to nurture themselves and their offspring through the stressful period of lactation. Other animals that might kill and cannibalize primarily to obtain sustenance include white-footed mice, Mongolian gerbils, male Belding's ground squirrels, and chimpanzees (Sherman 1981b; Elwood and Ostermeyer 1984c; Goodall 1986; Wolff and Cicirello 1989; Hiraiwa-Hasegawa 1992).

Benefit 3:   Increased Foraging Area. When a mother is lactating, she defends her home nursery burrow and a territory around that burrow from all conspecifics (chaps. 3, 6, and 11). When all her juveniles die, this maternal defense abruptly ceases. Following infanticide, then, the killer is able to feed in the victimized mother's former territory. With a larger foraging area, the killer more easily obtains the nutrients necessary to complete her own lactation.

Benefit 4:   Victimized Mothers Become Better Helpers. Lactating mothers are busy with maternal duties, such as defense of the home nursery burrow and surrounding territory, collection of additional dry grass for the underground nest, and frequent trips underground to suckle offspring (chaps. 9 and 11). Freed from maternal duties, females that have lost their litters spend more time aboveground scanning for predators. They also spend more time defending the home coterie territory and, especially, refurbishing burrows and burrow mounds. Victimized mothers therefore become more useful to the infanticidal mother. Thus, killers induce victimized mothers to become better helpers (or alloparents; see chap. 10).

Benefit 5:   Victimized Mothers Are Less Likely to Kill. Killers are almost always lactating females (appendix B). After eliminating the offspring of a particular female, a killer is therefore less likely to lose her own offspring to that female, now nonlactating, via marauding at a later date. Thus, a mother lowers the probability of losing her own litter to infanticide if she can first eliminate the offspring of other mothers within the home coterie territory. This benefit is at least partially offset by the increased probability of losing one's own litter *while marauding* (see above).

Once killing has evolved for some other reason, the benefit of eliminating other litters before losing one's own litter might be a secondary advantage that partially explains the evolutionary *maintenance* of killing. However, such a secondary advantage cannot account for the evolutionary *origin* of killing.

Do Marauders Have Higher Reproductive Success than Nonmarauders?

At this point I am unable to evaluate the relative importance of the various benefits gained by lactating females that kill the offspring of close kin. Perhaps different females kill for different reasons, so that several of the five benefits have been important in the evolution of Type I infanticide.

Notice that nonmarauding lactating females of the home coterie share most of the benefits of infanticide that the marauder also receives. For example, when a marauder is suddenly able to forage without retaliation in a victimized mother's territory after infanticide (benefit 3), nonmarauding lactating females of the home coterie can forage there also. Nonmarauding mothers of the home coterie also share benefits 1, 4, and 5. Only for benefit 2, increased sustenance, are marauders the sole beneficiaries. For this reason, perhaps benefit 2 has been more important than the others in the evolution of marauding by lactating prairie dog females. However, nonmarauders sometimes share benefit 2 as well. Specifically, nonmarauding lactating females of the home coterie sometimes obtain additional sustenance via cannibalism if the marauder does not consume all of her dead victims at the time of infanticide. Such cannibalism by nonmarauding mothers usually occurs 1–2 days after infanticide, and is more likely when the juvenile victims are older and larger—and thus more difficult for the marauder to consume completely.

If the benefits of killing are singularly or cumulatively important, then killers should have higher reproductive success than nonkillers. Data through 1984 indicated that marauders fare better in terms of probability of weaning a litter, litter size at first juvenile emergence, and mother's body mass when her juveniles first emerge (Hoogland 1985). Curiously, however, these trends have disappeared with additional data. Specifically, estimates of reproductive success for marauders and nonmarauders through 1988 are practically identical (see table 7.3).

Do the data in table 7.3 mean that infanticide by lactating prairie dog females is maladaptive? Not necessarily, for at least three reasons. First, though large relative to those in previous studies of infanticide (e.g., Hrdy 1974; Sherman 1981b; Packer and Pusey 1984; Trulio et al. 1986; Vestal 1991), the sample sizes in table 7.3 and appendix B are nonetheless small by statistical standards. Perhaps additional data will show that the five benefits of infanticide lead to the predicted greater reproductive success of marauders. Second, marauding involves one unique behavior (careful licking of the front claws) and one almost-unique behavior (rubbing of the face in the dirt). The coupling of complex behaviors such as these with a particular act suggests evolutionary design and adaptation (Williams 1966a, 1992; Dawkins 1986; Emlen et al. 1991). Finally, if infanticide is a maladaptive response to unnatural circumstances, then females should only maraud when such circumstances occur. As noted above, the ubiquity of poor reproduction by prairie dog females at different study colonies suggests that infanticide is a regular and widespread occurrence.

Because the costs of infanticide are more obvious than the benefits, prairie dog mothers probably have more to lose by having their offspring killed than to gain by committing infanticide. If so, then perhaps natural selection should favor mothers who are successful at *preventing* marauding of their own litters rather than at *executing* marauding of others' litters. In any event, I clearly have generated more questions than answers about kin-directed infanticide among prairie dogs. More research is necessary for a better understanding of this puzzling phenomenon.

Is Kin-Directed Infanticide Unique to Prairie Dogs?

At least two avian species show behaviors similar to kin-directed infanticide among prairie dogs. Female acorn woodpeckers commonly destroy fertile eggs laid by their sisters, and male white-fronted bee-eaters frequently disrupt the breeding attempts of their sons (Mumme, Koenig, and Pitelka 1983; Emlen and Wrege 1992). Disrupted bee-eater males, like victimized prairie dog females, abandon their own nests and become helpers (chap. 10) to their infanticidal kin.

Among mammals, only prairie dogs are known to show regular killing of the offspring of close kin by lactating females. However, the social system of prairie dogs is similar to systems of numerous other mammalian species (Eisenberg 1966; Wittenberger 1981; Michener 1983; Smuts et al. 1987; Dunbar 1988). I therefore predict that future research on other matrilocal, harem-polygynous mammals also will reveal regular, subtle killing of the offspring of close kin.

As I have investigated the killing by lactating prairie dog females of the offspring of close kin (Type I infanticide), I have also discovered three other types of infanticide, as described below.

Type II: Infanticide by Female Immigrants

Female immigrants sometimes invade coterie territories and evict the resident adult female(s) there (chaps. 6 and 16). Like female Belding's ground squirrel immigrants (Sherman 1981b), female prairie dog immigrants are infanticidal, as the following two examples attest.

1. On 12 June 1978, immigrant female-61 invaded a coterie territory containing one breeding male, three adult females with emergent juveniles, and yearling female-R66, whose three juveniles had first emerged on 10 June. Female-61 quickly sequestered a part of the coterie territory that included female-R66's nursery burrow. Several hours later I found a dead juvenile with a puncture wound in its neck at the mound of female-R66's nursery burrow. Female-R66's other two juveniles never reappeared aboveground. Female-61 aggressively defended her new territory. All members of the original coterie and their surviving offspring remained exclusively in the spared section of the home coterie territory. Female-61 remained in her territory until March 1979, when female-R66 and her kin evicted female-61 and recaptured the lost turf.

2. In early June 1979, immigrant female-93 moved into a coterie territory that contained one breeding male, one adult female (female-76), and two large juveniles (>200 grams at first emergence on 30 May). On 10 June, female-93 entered the nursery burrow containing female-76 and her two juveniles early in the morning, before they had appeared aboveground, and remained there for 10 minutes. Shortly after female-93's exit, female-76 emerged, completely disoriented. Female-76 then wandered aimlessly into the nearby woods and never returned. When the two juveniles emerged from their natal burrow later in the morning, female-93 viciously attacked them. Had they been smaller, the juveniles almost certainly would have perished. Both juveniles ran to the edge of the coterie territory and hid in the tall vegetation there. One of the juveniles disappeared. The other (female-5str) invaded an adjacent coterie territory where, apparently because of her young age (see chaps. 5 and 10), she met no resistance. Female 5-str was one of only 11 females (out of 523 females first marked as juveniles) that dispersed from the natal coterie territory to another coterie territory within the study colony (chap. 14). She lived in her new coterie territory until she was 3 years old, and there weaned two litters. Although female-93 did not herself kill female-76's two juveniles, her behavior was directly responsible for the disappearance and almost certain death of one of the

juveniles. Except for extraordinary circumstances, female-93's behavior would have led to the demise of the second juvenile as well.

Female immigration—especially into coterie territories containing recently weaned juveniles—is uncommon (chap. 16). Type II infanticide is thus rare, leading to the total ($N = 1$) or partial ($N = 1$) demise of only 0.3% of litters born (2/591) (see table 7.2).

Type III: Killing of Abandoned Litters

Females usually start to show unmistakable maternal behaviors on the day after copulation (chap. 11). However, certain copulating females never show such behaviors. Specifically, these "nonmaternally acting" females do not build underground nests, defend nursery burrows, or sleep alone (chap. 11)—or they show these behaviors only sporadically. Perhaps some of these females fail to conceive. Perhaps others conceive, but then abort and resorb their litters shortly after conception—as prairie dogs sometimes do under both laboratory and natural conditions (Foreman 1962; Knowles 1987). In 1983 and later years, I investigated these possible explanations for "nonmaternally acting" females by livetrapping females approximately 35 days after copulation and looking for signs of parturition (chap. 16).

Curiously, "nonmaternally acting" prairie dog females that have copulated usually *do* give birth, but then abandon their offspring within a day or two after parturition. Sometimes other coterie members—most commonly yearling males and nonlactating females, but sometimes pregnant females, lactating females, or breeding males—are in the mother's burrow at the time of parturition. Evidently the mother and other coterie members kill and cannibalize the newborn young. Whereas mothers actively defend against infanticides of Types I, II, and IV, they do not defend against Type III. Type III infanticide—scored only when a female does not defend, and then abandons, her entire litter within a day or two after parturition—accounts for the total elimination of 9% of litters born (24/253) (see table 7.2).

The clearest example of Type III infanticide involved "nonmaternally acting" female-WA0 on 5 April 1984: she gave birth aboveground and then joined two females of the home coterie in cannibalizing her newborn offspring. Another good example occurred on 8 April 1983, when two "nonmaternally acting" females both gave birth on the same morning in the same burrow. When one of the females first appeared aboveground at 0853 on 8 April, she had a newborn's leg stuck to her fur.

Is Type III infanticide related to female body mass? Specifically, are lighter females more likely than heavy females to abandon their neonates? Figure 7.10 indicates an affirmative answer.

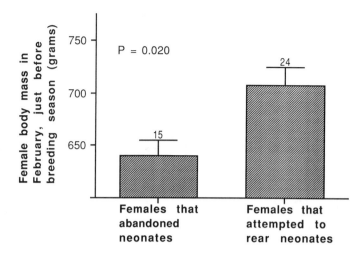

Fig. 7.10. Abandonment of neonates (Type III infanticide) versus adult female body mass. All body masses are from parturient adult females living in coterie territories where at least one female abandoned her neonates. Body masses are unavailable for nine other females that also abandoned their litters. This graph excludes yearling females, which are lighter than adult females. The *P*-value is from the Mann-Whitney *U* test.

Yearling females are lighter than adult females (chap. 16). Does the difference in figure 7.10 result because abandoning females are mostly yearlings? The answer here is negative: only 8% of females that abandon neonates (2/24) are yearlings ($P = .965$ for the 2 × 2 chi-square test that compares observed versus expected number of abandonments by yearling and adult females).

Certain females are especially likely to practice Type I infanticide in the same and different years (appendix B). By contrast, females that practice Type III infanticide in one year are unlikely to abandon their litters again in later years. For example, the 24 observed cases of Type III infanticide involve 24 different females.

Heavier females are more likely than light females to kill the offspring of close kin (see above) via Type I infanticide. However, the heavier female(s) in a coterie territory might fall victim to predation—so that the light female would then be able to rear emergent juveniles (see above). Further, as for mammals in general (Clutton-Brock, Albon, and Guinness 1989) and squirrels in particular (Millar 1977), lactation is probably more costly than pregnancy for prairie dog females. Natural selection might therefore favor light females who are willing to pay the small cost of pregnancy while waiting to see whether the heavier female in the home coterie disappears. But what if the heavier female is still alive when the light female gives birth? Abandonment then might be an adaptation by which the light female avoids the high cost of lactation—i.e., cuts her losses—before inevitably losing the litter to marauding by the heavier female.

Like golden hamster and house mouse mothers (Day and Galef 1977; Gandelman and Simon 1978; Fuchs 1981), prairie dog mothers under laboratory conditions sometimes abandon one or two neonates before trying to rear the others (Anthony and Foreman 1951). Prairie dog mothers might selectively abandon neonates under natural conditions as well, as do mothers in other animals such as crested penguins, African lions, and humans (Mock 1984a; Packer and Pusey 1984; Scrimshaw 1984). For example, once I found two live prairie dog neonates on a burrow mound, and another time I observed a single aboveground neonate. Further, 27% of emergent litters (99/361) contain only one or two juveniles (chap. 16). Partial-litter maraudings account for many of these small litters (see above). Perhaps selective abandonment by the mother accounts for others.

Type IV: Infanticide by Invading Males

Young prairie dog males most commonly disperse away from the natal coterie territory in May and June, when they themselves have been aboveground for approximately a year and when juveniles are once again first appearing aboveground (chaps. 14 and 16). I was able to record the events surrounding eighteen invasions by a yearling male into a coterie territory containing recently emerged juveniles. The inescapable conclusion from the data in table 7.4 and figure 7.11a is that male invaders are commonly infanticidal. Maimed carcasses appeared aboveground following six invasions (fig. 7.12), and field assistants and I witnessed aboveground killings by two different invaders. Sometimes the infanticidal male evicts the resident breeding male upon invasion. Other times he allows him to remain, but aggressively dominates him by restricting his movements to only a small portion of the home coterie territory.

Table 7.4. Fate of Juveniles following Invasion of a Yearling Male into the Home Coterie Territory Shortly after First Juvenile Emergences

Number of invaded coterie territories where 100% of juveniles disappeared	5
Number of invaded coterie territories where ≥ 50%, but < 100%, of juveniles disappeared	5
Number of invaded coterie territories where ≥ 25%, but < 50%, of juveniles disappeared	3
Number of invaded coterie territories where no juveniles disappeared	5
Total	18

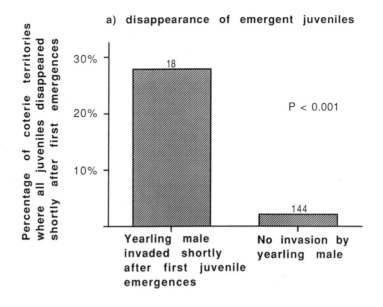

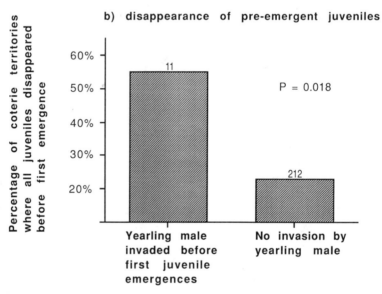

Fig. 7.11. Type IV infanticide. *(a)* Disappearance of all emergent juveniles versus invasion by yearling males. Following invasions by eight other yearling males, more than 25%, but fewer than 100%, of emergent juveniles disappeared (see table 7.4). Twelve different invading males have killed emergent juveniles at the study colony. *(b)* Disappearance of all pre-emergent juveniles versus invasion by yearling males. Nine different invading males have killed pre-emergent juveniles at the study colony. For both graphs, the number above each bar indicates the number of coterie territories, and *P*-values are from the 2 × 2 chi-square test.

Fig. 7.12. Victims of infanticide by invading male. Shortly after male-R22 invaded a new coterie territory in June 1978, I found these two dead, partially cannibalized, marked juveniles aboveground in his new territory. (Photo by John L. Hoogland.)

Twelve invading males were infanticidal after first juvenile emergences. Such killers eliminate some or all juveniles in 4% of litters born (21/591) (see table 7.2). Nine of these twelve males eventually sired offspring in the coterie territory where they killed juveniles. The other three disappeared before the next breeding season.

Yearling males sometimes leave the natal coterie territory and invade a new coterie territory *before* the first emergences of juveniles there. Again infanticide is the common result (fig. 7.11b). Specifically, nine invading males were infanticidal before first juvenile emergences. Such killers eliminate 3% of the litters born (18/591) (see table 7.2). In the next breeding season, four of these nine males sired offspring in the coterie territory where they killed juveniles. Two of the males sired offspring in a coterie territory adjacent to the territory where they killed juveniles, and the other three males disappeared before the next breeding season.

One invader in 1983 eliminated one litter *before* the juveniles had emerged, and another litter *after* the juveniles had emerged. After killing pre-emergent juveniles, males often show the same behaviors diagnostic of infanticidal females (licking of front claws and rubbing of bloody face in the dirt; see above).

I have implied that invading males are always yearlings. More precisely, ten of the twelve invaders that killed emergent juveniles were yearlings and two were 2-year-olds. Five of the nine invaders that killed pre-emergent juveniles were yearlings, two were 2-year-olds, and two were 3-year-olds. One male was infanticidal in two different years—as an invading yearling immigrant in 1981, and as an invading 3-year-old in 1983.

Like males in general (Hrdy 1974, 1984; Bertram 1975; Russell 1981; Freed 1987; Veiga 1993) and male Belding's, arctic, and thirteen-lined ground squirrels in particular (Steiner 1972; Sherman 1981b; McLean 1983; Vestal 1991), infanticidal prairie dog males avoid killing their own juvenile offspring. Such avoidance might result if males can somehow discriminate between offspring and nonoffspring. However, prairie dog males probably resemble males of other animals in having a simpler system (Hrdy 1977a,b; McLean 1983; Labov et al. 1985; Wolff and Cicirello 1989; Whittingham, Taylor, and Robertson 1993; see also chaps. 10 and 12). Specifically, prairie dog males probably discriminate merely between (1) coterie territories where they copulated and thus might have sired offspring—areas in which to avoid infanticide—and (2) coterie territories where they did not copulate—areas in which to kill juveniles.

Rather than discriminating between coterie *territories* where they did or did not copulate for possible infanticide, perhaps prairie dog males resemble males of certain other rodent species and distinguish between *groups of females* with whom they did or did not copulate (Huck, Soltis, and Coopersmith 1982; Elwood 1992). Either system of discrimination would produce approximately equal results for prairie dogs living under natural conditions because females are so tightly linked to their natal coterie territories for their entire lifetimes (chaps. 6 and 16).

Categorizing each infanticide as one of the four types is usually easy for prairie dogs. A few cases, however, are problematic. For example, two females in the same coterie territory abandoned—and evidently killed and cannibalized—their litters shortly after parturition in 1983. However, a 5-year-old male (male-14) had invaded this coterie territory on 2 March 1983, just after the breeding season had ended and when both females were still pregnant. Did the females abandon their offspring because infanticide by the invading male was inevitable anyway? I have classified these abandonments as Type III infanticides, but one could logically argue that they are Type IV infanticides instead.

Do Infanticidal Males Preferentially Kill One Sex?

Females sometimes copulate as yearlings, and almost always copulate as 2-year-olds (chaps. 13 and 16). Invading males therefore might view juvenile females as future mates. Male juveniles, by contrast, would be of no such importance. Perhaps invading males should preferentially kill male juveniles and spare future mates. Curiously, I uncovered no support for this hypothesis. The juvenile carcasses found aboveground, for example, show no male bias. Further, as noted above, male invaders commonly kill *all* juveniles in their new coterie territories (see fig. 7.11).

Reproductive Success of Infanticidal Male Invaders

Infanticide after invasion by a new male is common for other harem-polygynous mammals, such as African lions, purple-faced and hanuman langurs, and mountain gorillas (Rudran 1973; Fossey 1984; Packer and Pusey 1984; Vogel and Lock 1984). The payoff for these males is that victimized mothers come into estrus and conceive more quickly than do mothers that continue lactating. For prairie dogs, however, many of the infanticides occur just before or after the termination of lactation. Further, prairie dog females come into estrus only once each year (chap. 11). Consequently, infanticide by an invading male cannot easily reduce the time until the next estrus.

Why *are* invading prairie dog males infanticidal, then? Juveniles in one year become yearlings the next year. Earlier I argued that invading infanticidal males might gain by reducing the number of competing yearlings present in the following year (Hoogland 1985). Unrelated (or distantly related; see chap. 14) yearlings compete not only with the invading male himself, but also with his mates and his future offspring. Two new trends since 1985, however, cast doubt on my earlier hypothesis. First, the emergence of at least one juvenile within a coterie territory does not significantly correlate with the presence or absence of yearlings in that territory (fig. 7.13). Second, the number of emergent juveniles produced in a coterie territory does not vary systematically with the number of yearlings there ($P = .083$, $N = 218$, Kruskal-Wallis analysis of variance). Further, the correlation that does occur between these two variables is *positive* rather than the expected negative ($P = .096$, Spearman rank correlation test): females reproduce *better* when surrounded by yearlings!

After losing her unweaned young, a female devotes more time to feeding and less time to maternal duties. Consequently, females that fail to produce emergent juveniles gain body mass rapidly and are heavier in May and June than are successful females (chap. 16). This greater body mass of unsuccessful females remains through autumn and into the next breeding season. Like infanticidal male red deer invaders (Bartos and Madlafousek 1994; see also Clutton-Brock, Guinness, and Albon 1982, 1987; Hrdy and Hausfater 1984), do infanticidal male prairie dog invaders gain via the improved condition of the females with whom they will copulate in the next breeding season? Probably not. Specifically, the heavier body mass is seemingly inconsequential because unsuccessful prairie dog females do not survive better than successful females, are no more likely

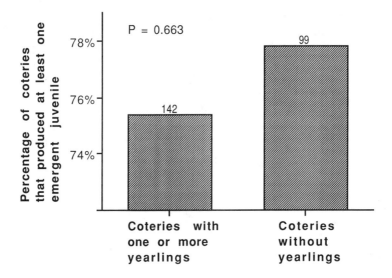

Fig. 7.13. Coterie's production of emergent juveniles versus the presence or absence of yearlings. The number above each bar indicates the number of coterie territories; the *P*-value is from the 2 × 2 chi-square test.

to reproduce in the following year, and do not produce larger litters in the following year (chap. 16).

Increased sustenance via cannibalism is the probable benefit of infanticide for animals such as herring gulls, male Belding's ground squirrels, chimpanzees, and numerous species of fish and insects (Parsons 1971; Fox 1975; Goodall 1977, 1986; Sherman 1981b). Perhaps increased nourishment via cannibalism is also the primary payoff for infanticidal male prairie dog invaders. In support of this hypothesis, several of the aboveground juvenile carcasses found after an invasion by a new male were decapitated and partially eaten (see fig. 7.12). However, I could not consistently verify that the invading male was responsible for the consumption. Further, only one of the invading males that killed aboveground then cannibalized his victim. The adaptive significance of infanticide by invading prairie dog males thus remains unclear.

Pregnancy Block

Via *pregnancy block* (also called the *Bruce effect*), a pregnant female deer mouse, house mouse, or collared lemming under laboratory conditions aborts her unborn offspring after exposure to a strange male with whom she has not copulated (Bruce 1959, 1960; Mallory and Brooks 1978, 1980; Schwagmeyer 1979; Huck 1984; Elwood 1992). Under natural conditions, pregnancy block following invasion of a strange male sometimes occurs for wild horses, African lions, and primates such as hanuman langurs and gelada and savannah baboons (Berger 1983; Pereira 1983; Packer and

Pusey 1984; Mori and Dunbar 1985; Sommer 1987; Agoramoorthy et al. 1988). Among many possibilities (Huck 1984; Elwood 1992), the most likely explanation for pregnancy block is that the strange male would later kill the offspring that he did not sire. The female thus cuts her losses with pregnancy block, and comes into estrus more quickly so that she can begin investing in offspring that are more likely to survive (Bertram 1975; Hrdy 1979; Mallory and Brooks 1980; Labov 1980, 1981a,b; Elwood and Ostermeyer 1984a,b). As noted above, most invasions by prairie dog males occur during late lactation or just after first juvenile emergences. I thus have little opportunity to investigate the possible importance of pregnancy block to prairie dogs.

Infanticidal males sometimes invade a coterie territory where the females still have unweaned offspring (see above). Via a process similar to pregnancy block, perhaps natural selection should favor lactating females that cut their losses by quickly terminating their own litters following the invasion. Why should mothers invest further if the invader inevitably will kill the juveniles later? As suggested by the above anecdote concerning male-14, perhaps some of the abandonments in Type III infanticide represent female responses to real or probable invasion by a strange male.

Male Invaders Sometimes Kill Juvenile Kin

By a strange twist, invading males sometimes kill juvenile kin. Consider the following Type IV infanticide, for example. In 1985, male-24 lived in a coterie territory that contained only one other prairie dog, female-RS. Female-RS copulated exclusively with male-24 and later weaned one male juvenile (male-R12) who survived until the following year. In 1986, male-24 sired five emergent juveniles (from two litters) in a new breeding coterie territory adjacent to female-RS's coterie territory. In early June of 1986, male-R12, then a yearling still in his natal coterie territory, began to invade his father's (male-24's) new coterie territory. Male-24 did not resist his son's invasion. Less than 1 week later, all five of male-24's offspring disappeared. The implication is that male-R12 was infanticidal, and my son (Mark Hoogland) witnessed one of his killings. Because male-R12 was male-24's son, his victims were his half siblings.

Five other young males invaded new coterie territories controlled by their fathers and killed pre-emergent ($N = 3$) or emergent ($N = 2$) juvenile half siblings there. These infanticidal sons account for the partial or total elimination of 2% of all litters born (10/591) (see table 7.2, where I have lumped such killings with other Type IV infanticides). Three of the six invading males that killed juvenile half siblings were still in the invaded coterie territory in the following year, and two sired offspring there.

Why has natural selection favored the killing of half siblings by invading young males? In proximate terms, the probable explanation is that limitations in social learning make it difficult for the invaders to recognize their victims as half siblings (chap. 10).

Breeding males regularly defend the home coterie territory from male invaders (chap. 6), and could easily prevent the invasion of infanticidal yearling sons as well. Why don't they? Could the importance of male coalitions be the ultimate reason? Specifically, perhaps the loss of off-spring to invading sons is a secondary consequence of helping sons to get established in breeding coterie territories. If so, however, why hasn't natural selection worked against such a detrimental secondary consequence?

Infanticide by Sexually Inactive Resident Adult Males

Rarely, the resident adult male in a coterie territory has neither a pigmented scrotum nor descended testes (chaps. 4 and 12). Such males are evidently incapable of insemination—i.e., they are sexually inactive. Females in coterie territories with a sexually inactive resident adult male (SIRAM) usually copulate with either a breeding male from an adjacent territory or a male of the home coterie territory who *is* sexually active (chap. 12). Prairie dog SIRAMs, like silvered-leaf monkey and red colobus SIRAMs (Wolf 1980; Leland, Struhsaker, and Butynski 1984), sometimes became infanticidal. Specifically, I identified one unambiguous killing of pre-emergent juveniles and another unambiguous aboveground killing of emergent juveniles by SIRAMs. The first of these killers (male-4) re-mained in the same coterie territory until the next breeding season and sired offspring there, but the latter (male-R08) had disappeared by the following year. Neither SIRAM was still in his natal coterie territory at the time of infanticide. Both SIRAMs were therefore genetically unrelated to their victims.

Because of my concentration on infanticide by lactating females (see above), I did not become suspicious of infanticide by SIRAMs until 1985. I therefore suspect that SIRAMs eliminate more litters than my sample size of two would suggest.

Is killing by SIRAMs a fifth type of infanticide among prairie dogs? Because they are so similar to killings by invading males, I have considered killings by SIRAMs a subset of Type IV infanticide.

Cumulative Frequency of Infanticide

The four types of infanticide account for the partial or total elimination of 39% of all litters born (see table 7.2). This frequency is lower than the 51% that I reported earlier (Hoogland 1985) because infanticide at the study colony in the later years of my research (1985 through 1988) has been less common, inexplicably, than in earlier years (1978 through 1984).

Eighty-four different prairie dogs killed juveniles from 130 different litters at the study colony from 1978 through 1988: 2 immigrant females, 24 females that abandoned their offspring shortly after parturition, 38 females that killed the offspring of close kin, and 20 invading males.

Summary

1. Almost all adult prairie dog females copulate each year, but only about 50% rear juveniles to first emergence. Infanticide accounts for most of the failures.

2. In the most common type of infanticide which affects 22% of litters born, marauding lactating females kill the unweaned offspring of close kin living in the home coterie territory.

3. Most killings occur underground. However, marauders are identifiable upon emergence from another female's nursery burrow by a bloody or dirty face (BF or DF), careful licking of the front claws (LFC), and rubbing of the face in the dirt (RFD). Aboveground killings show these same diagnostic behaviors.

4. Excavations demonstrate that marauders are responsible for *both* the killing of *and* cannibalism of juveniles. Thus, marauders do not merely cannibalize juveniles already killed or abandoned by the mother.

5. Marauders usually kill all juveniles in a litter, but partial-litter infanticide also occurs.

6. Certain females specialize as killers, and other females are especially likely to lose their litters to infanticide.

7. The probability of losing a litter to marauding varies directly with the number of lactating females in the home coterie.

8. When a lactating female is marauding, her own offspring are vulnerable to infanticide. Nine percent of infanticides occur while the victimized mother herself is marauding.

9. Possible benefits of marauding include the removal of future competitors; increased sustenance; increased foraging area; additional help from victimized mothers who become better helpers; and reduced likelihood of losing one's own litter to infanticide, because victimized mothers are less likely to kill.

10. Marauders are heavier than victimized mothers.

11. Even though certain females are especially vulnerable to infanticide and live in coteries with known killers, such females consistently burden themselves with copulation, pregnancy, and early lactation.

12. Inexplicably, the reproductive success of killers does not differ from that of nonkillers.

13. The prairie dog is the only mammal known to show regular killing of the offspring of close kin by lactating females. Perhaps

future research with other matrilocal, polygynous mammals will reveal similar kin-directed infanticide.

14. Females that immigrate into a coterie territory with emergent juveniles are infanticidal. However, female immigrants are rare. Consequently, Type II infanticide accounts for the partial or total demise of fewer than 1% of litters born.

15. Mothers sometimes abandon their offspring shortly after parturition and allow other individuals from the home coterie to kill and cannibalize them. Light females are more likely than heavier females to abandon. Type III infanticide eliminates 9% of litters born.

16. Dispersal of adult and yearling males usually occurs in May and June, when juveniles are first emerging from their natal burrows. Males that invade a new coterie territory containing young juveniles are commonly infanticidal. Type IV infanticide accounts for the partial or total demise of 7% of litters born.

17. By a strange twist, an invading male sometimes kills juveniles sired by his father (i.e., his half siblings).

18. The four types of infanticide account for the partial or total elimination of 39% of litters born. Infanticide is ubiquitous among other animals, but never in so many contexts and only rarely at such a high frequency.

8 The Antipredator Call

After detecting an enemy and running to a burrow mound, a prairie dog sometimes gives a loud, repetitious antipredator call. This call helps to explain why prairie dogs are so safe within colonies (chap. 5). But why should an individual draw a predator's attention by calling in order to save competing conspecifics? This question of alarm calling has puzzled the most eminent behavioral ecologists, among them Peter Marler (1955, 1959), William Hamilton (1964), John Maynard Smith (1965), George Williams (1966a), Robert Trivers (1971), Richard Alexander (1974), Edward Wilson (1975), Mary Jane West-Eberhard (1975), Eric Charnov and John Krebs (1975), and Richard Dawkins (1976).

Breakthroughs came when Christopher Dunford (1977b) and Paul W. Sherman (1977) independently discovered that antipredator calls of round-tailed and Belding's ground squirrels function primarily to warn offspring (see also chap. 10). Similar results soon appeared for hoary marmots, Sonoma and eastern chipmunks, and thirteen-lined and Richardson's ground squirrels (Smith 1978; Yahner 1978; Noyes and Holmes 1979; Schwagmeyer 1980; Davis 1984a; Owings et al. 1986). As usual, prairie dogs have gone one provocative step further than their sciurid relatives. They not only give antipredator calls to warn offspring, but nonparental prairie dogs also call to warn more distant kin such as nieces, nephews, and cousins.

In this chapter I first describe the prairie dog antipredator call. Using 233 data points from 149 different males and 361 data points from 174 different females—with each data point based on approximately seven experimental runs with stuffed American badgers—I then examine various factors that affect the expression of antipredator calls.

Description of the Antipredator Call

Researchers have given the prairie dog's antipredator call all sorts of interesting names: alarm note (Merriam 1902), squit-tuck (Seton 1926), warning bark (King 1955), alarm bark (Smith 1967), barks (Smith et al. 1977), repetitive barks (Waring 1970), vocal alarm (Hoogland 1981a), and alarm call (Hoogland 1983b). The call is a series of high-pitched "chirk" or "tic-uhl" sounds (King 1955; Smith 1967; Costello 1970; Waring 1970; Smith et al. 1977).

Sonograms show that the chirks of the antipredator calls of different prairie dogs vary in duration, harshness, harmonics, and number of syllables (fig. 8.1; see also Waring 1970; Smith et al. 1977). Calls by the same individual at different times also differ. Some calls contain as few as one or two chirks and last for only a second or two, but others contain thousands of chirks and persist for more than 60 minutes. For antipredator calls that last for more than several minutes, the frequency and intensity of the chirks are usually higher during the first few minutes of calling than in later minutes (Smith 1967).

Not every prairie dog gives an antipredator call when a predator approaches (fig. 8.2). Rather, about 50% of adults and yearlings call during an attack (see below).

Of the prairie dogs that called in response to my experiments with stuffed American badgers, 92% (2074/2256) were either on a burrow mound or only 1 to 2 meters away from a mound. Individuals call from any of the following positions: standing tall on two hind legs, standing on all four legs, or peeking out from a burrow entrance (figs. 8.2 and 8.3).

Antipredator calls by juveniles are common for Sonoma chipmunks and round-tailed, Belding's, and thirteen-lined ground squirrels (Dunford 1977b; Sherman 1977; Smith 1978; Schwagmeyer 1980). However, juvenile prairie

Fig. 8.1. Sonographic variation in the antipredator calls of twelve different prairie dogs. Smith et al. (1977) provide more details for each of these sonograms. (Photo courtesy of W. John Smith.)

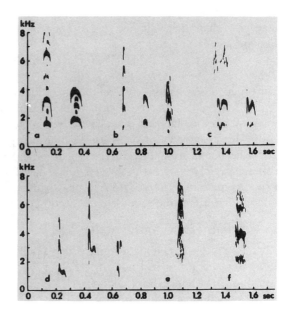

Fig 8.2. Selective antipredator calling. During a predator's attack, about 50% of the prairie dogs—mostly individuals that have either descendant or nondescendant kin within earshot—give antipredator calls. The other 50% watch in silence. (Photo courtesy of Wind Cave National Park.)

Fig. 8.3. Prairie dog giving an antipredator call from burrow entrance. When calling while halfway in a burrow, as seen here, the prairie dog sometimes flicks its tail with each chirk. Calling individuals usually do not completely submerge unless a predator approaches within 5 meters or so. (Photo courtesy of Wind Cave National Park.)

dogs only rarely call during their first few months aboveground. In this chapter, I consider only responses of adult and yearling prairie dogs.

In other species of squirrels, such as white-tailed prairie dogs, round-tailed ground squirrels, and bobak marmots (Clark 1977; Dunford 1977b; Barash 1989), individuals vigorously move the lower jaw when giving an antipredator call. Not so for black-tailed prairie dogs, who move the lower jaw only slightly when calling (Waring 1970). Slight abdominal movements also accompany calling, and individuals occasionally synchronize flicking of the tail with chirking. Prairie dog callers are thus difficult to identify. To categorize individuals as either callers or noncallers, I have resorted to experiments with stuffed American badgers (see below and chap. 4) and a 60-power telescope (fig. 8.4).

Predators such as coyotes, American badgers, bobcats, golden eagles, prairie falcons, and humans inevitably elicit prairie dog antipredator calls. On the other hand, nonpredators such as thirteen-lined ground squirrels, pronghorn antelope, American bison, western meadowlarks, and mountain bluebirds usually do not. Evidently prairie dogs cannot always be certain whether a predator is nearby. When in doubt, they usually call. For example, a pronghorn antelope moving through the woods near the study colony frequently elicits "false" antipredator calls—perhaps because the prairie dogs incorrectly deduce that the moving legs belong to a coyote. Similarly, low-flying American robins often elicit "false" antipredator calls—probably because the prairie dogs cannot instantly discriminate between a small, low-flying robin and a large, high-flying hawk.

For animals in general (Seyfarth, Cheney, and Marler 1980; Pereira and Macedonia 1991) and for alpine and hoary marmots and Uinta, arctic, and Richardson's ground squirrels in particular (Balph and Balph 1966; Melchior 1971; Taulman 1977; Davis 1984a; Hofer and Ingold 1984), dramatically different antipredator calls sometimes indicate different classes of predators; for example, "chatters" might indicate terrestrial predators while "whistles" indicate avian predators. However, for other sciurids such as California and Belding's ground squirrels, three species of Malaysian tree squirrels, and Gunnison's prairie dogs, individuals sometimes give different calls for the same predator, depending on the urgency imposed by that predator (Owings and Leger 1980; Robinson 1981; Owings and Hennessy 1984; Sherman 1985; Slobodchikoff et al. 1991; Tamura and Yong 1993). For example, one call might indicate a *charging* coyote or a *swooping* falcon while another call indicates the lesser risk of a *trotting* coyote or a *perched* falcon. Like yellow-bellied and Olympic marmots and Columbian and thirteen-lined ground squirrels (Waring 1966; Barash 1973, 1989; Betts 1976; Matocha 1977; Schwagmeyer 1980), prairie dogs have only one distinct antipredator call. However, subtle variation in the antipredator calls of prairie dogs—examine figure 8.1, for example—might indicate different types of predators or different levels of urgency (King 1955;

Fig. 8.4. Experiments with stuffed American badger to study antipredator calling. *(a)* Badger concealed in brown cloth bag before experimental run. *(b)* Badger as it emerges from cloth bag. *(c)* Fully exposed badger on Plexiglas sled. As the badger moves across a home coterie territory, I watch through a 60-power telescope and record whether each prairie dog in that territory does or does not give an antipredator call. (Photos by John L. Hoogland.)

Koford 1958; Costello 1970; W. J. Loughry, pers. comm.). For example, individuals seem to call at a faster rate—i.e., more chirks per minute—when danger is especially imminent, but I have not investigated this possibility.

My assertion that prairie dogs have only one distinct antipredator call is not strictly accurate. Like California ground squirrels and three species of Malaysian tree squirrels in response to snakes (Fitch 1948; Owings and Leger 1980; Tamura and Yong 1993), prairie dogs sometimes respond to prairie rattlesnakes and bull snakes with a call that is totally unlike the usual antipredator call (King 1955; Halpin 1983; Owings and Loughry 1985; Loughry 1987a,b, 1988). This antisnake call, sometimes accompanied by foot-thumping (Owings and Owings 1979), superficially resembles a series of jump-yip calls (see below). Because I see so few snakes at the study colony, I have little opportunity to hear or investigate the special call reserved for them.

Upon hearing an antipredator call, a prairie dog stops what it is doing and scans for predators. If no danger is apparent, it resumes its activity. If the listening individual detects a predator, however, it runs to a burrow mound and sometimes initiates its own antipredator call. Only rarely (<1% of observations) does a prairie dog start calling in response to another antipredator call without first detecting the predator itself.

Contrary to popular belief, prairie dogs do *not* automatically submerge into a burrow after hearing or giving an antipredator call. Rather, alerted individuals usually remain on burrow mounds and carefully watch the predator until its departure. Only when the predator comes close—sometimes as close as 5 meters—does a prairie dog usually submerge. This strategy makes good sense. If an individual stays aboveground and sees the predator depart, then it can resume foraging immediately. If forced underground, however, the prairie dog cannot easily know whether the predator is still in the colony—perhaps perched near the burrow entrance into which it has just submerged. Consequently, like Olympic and hoary marmots under similar circumstances (Barash 1989), prairie dogs forced underground by a charging predator sometimes wait for hours before cautiously emerging to forage. For additional safety, prairie dogs chased into one entrance of a burrow by a predator often emerge at another entrance.

The type of refuge burrow used by Belding's ground squirrels depends on the type of predator (Turner 1973; see also Robinson 1980). Specifically, individuals usually jump into the closest burrow in response to diving avian predators or the antipredator calls for such predators, regardless of the number of entrances to the burrow. By contrast, individuals usually jump only into burrows with two or more entrances in response to charging terrestrial predators or calls for such predators. The difference presumably results because avian predators make no attempt to enter or excavate burrows. Terrestrial predators such as American badgers or long-tailed weasels, however, might follow a Belding's ground squirrel into a burrow with only one entrance. My qualitative impression is that prairie dogs are also more choosy about burrows when fleeing from digging predators, but I have not investigated this possibility further.

The probability of an individual prairie dog's giving an antipredator call is inversely proportional to the distance between the prairie dog and the predator. For example, prairie dogs are more likely to call when a stuffed American badger passes through the home coterie territory than when it merely passes through an adjacent coterie territory (fig. 8.5).

The probability of an individual prairie dog's responding to the first antipredator call is inversely proportional to the distance between the caller and the listening conspecific. For example, individuals are more likely to run to a burrow mound or add their own calls in response to calls from within the home coterie territory than in response to calls from adjacent coterie territories (see below). Further, prairie dogs at one end of a large ward (subcolony) usually remain alert only briefly in response to calls at the other end, and are practically oblivious to calls from other wards (see also King 1955).

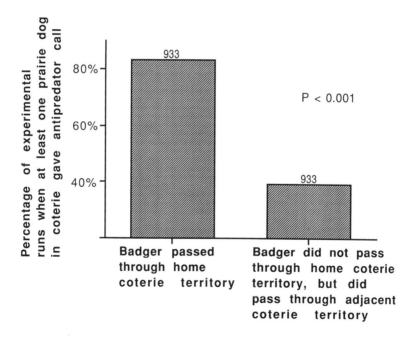

Fig. 8.5. Prairie dogs are more likely to give an antipredator call when a predator passes through the home coterie territory. The number above each bar indicates the number of experimental runs with the stuffed American badger. The *P*-value is from the 2 × 2 chi-square test.

Experiments with the Stuffed American Badger

A predator at a prairie dog colony does not remain there long—usually it has already attacked and is departing before I see it. Consequently, I can almost never accurately record callers and noncallers during a predatory attack—even though I observe scores of predators each year (chap. 5). To record antipredator calls under controlled conditions, I conduct experiments (approximately seven per coterie territory per year) with stuffed specimens of a natural predator, the American badger. Prairie dogs seem to respond to the stuffed badgers as they would to live badgers (chap. 4).

Two lines of evidence indicate that prairie dogs do not habituate to the stuffed American badgers. First, each year I classify the first half of the experimental runs in each coterie territory as early and the second half as late. With habituation, individuals should call less often during the late runs. Table 8.1 indicates no such trend. Second, old prairie dogs, who have seen the stuffed badgers repeatedly for several years, call as often as do younger, more naive prairie dogs (see below).

Individual Variation in Antipredator Calls

Figure 8.6 shows individual variation in the frequency of antipredator calls in response to the stuffed American badgers. The most common calling frequencies are between 0% and 10% and between 91% and 100%, and the two single most common frequencies are 0% and 100%. Consequently, most of the variation in calling frequency results from differences among individuals (e.g., callers versus noncallers) rather than from differences within individuals (e.g., call today but do not call tomorrow).

Table 8.1. Do Prairie Dogs Habituate to the Stuffed American Badgers?

Year	Number of individuals whose calling frequency was the same for early and late experimental runs	Number of individuals that called more often during early experimental runs	Number of individuals that called more often during late experimental runs	Significance of these differences
1978	39	40	29	$P = .189$
1979	59	27	48	$P = .029$
1980	44	35	28	$P = .220$
1981	20	8	13	$P = .366$
1982	49	37	38	$P = .862$
1983	44	10	18	$P = .148$
1985	1	0	1	$P = .317$
Totals	256	157	175	$P = .276$

Note: Each year, I classify the first half of the experimental runs ($N \geq 3$) with the stuffed American badgers as early, and the second half ($N \geq 3$) as late. With habituation, individuals should call less often during late runs. Notice, however, that in 5 of 7 years individuals called *more often* in late runs. P-values are from the Wilcoxon matched-pairs signed-ranks test.

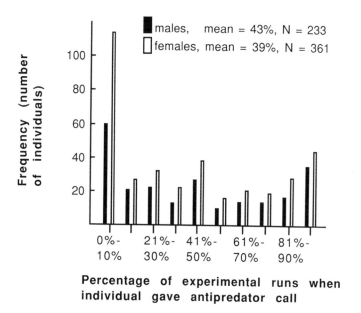

Fig. 8.6. Individual variation in the frequency of antipredator calling. For this and other analyses, I consider data from the same prairie dog in different years as independent (see chap. 4). I observe each individual approximately seven times per year during experimental runs with the stuffed American badger.

Sometimes differences between two seemingly equivalent prairie dogs are dramatic and inexplicable. For example, consider female-81 and female-65, who were same-aged full sisters who lived in the same (natal) coterie territory and who both weaned litters as 2- and 3-year-olds. Female-81 called 100% of the time in response to the stuffed American badgers as a nonbreeding yearling, 67% as a 2-year-old, and 50% as a 3-year-old. By contrast, female-65 called at a frequency of 100% as a nonbreeding yearling, but never again called as either a 2- or a 3-year-old.

Are Antipredator Calls Costly?

Because they are so audibly conspicuous, prairie dog antipredator calls—like those of Belding's ground squirrels (Sherman 1977, 1985)—probably render callers more susceptible to predation. I have obtained no direct evidence on this issue. In all twenty-two predations observed at the study colony (chap. 5), the predator had already succeeded before I could determine whether the victim had called.

Giving the first antipredator call is probably more dangerous than adding a call to an ongoing chorus. Similarly, a 10-minute call is probably more dangerous than a 30-second call. I have not investigated either of these possibilities.

At least three factors might decrease the vulnerability of a calling prairie dog. First, as noted above, the antipredator call requires only slight movement of the mouthparts and abdomen. Individuals thus minimize their visual conspicuousness while giving the call. Second, like callers of animals such as chaffinches, missel thrushes, and Olympic and hoary marmots (Marler 1955, 1957, 1959; Barash 1975, 1989), prairie dog callers are somewhat ventriloquial—at least to humans, and perhaps to other predators as well—and therefore difficult to locate. Third, prairie dogs are among the most colonial of all animals (chaps. 1 and 5). Prairie dog callers are thus perhaps more likely than other animals to "get lost in a crowd" of conspecifics (Hamilton 1971).

Nepotism and Antipredator Calls

Female round-tailed and Belding's ground squirrels are highly matrilocal and live near their mothers, sisters, daughters, nieces, and other female kin. By contrast, males of these species disperse from the natal site when young and disperse again as adults, and thus usually live far away from close kin (Dunford 1977b,c; Sherman and Morton 1984; Holekamp and Sherman 1989). Because female round-tailed and Belding's ground squirrels frequently call while males do not, Dunford (1977b) and Sherman (1977) concluded that their antipredator calls are nepotistic. Two lines of evidence indicate that prairie dog antipredator calls are also nepotistic, as described below.

Male Calling versus Female Calling

Unlike male round-tailed and Belding's ground squirrels, male prairie dogs resemble females in frequently living near close kin. Yearling males, for example, live with parents, siblings, cousins, and other kin in the natal coterie territory, and older males live with offspring in the breeding coterie territory (chaps. 14 and 16). If nepotism is important, then male as well as female prairie dogs commonly should give antipredator calls. Figures 8.7 and 8.8 support this prediction.

Individuals with Nearby Kin versus Individuals of the Same Sex without Nearby Kin

Factors other than the proximity of kin might explain intersexual differences or similarities in antipredator calling (see below; see also Shields 1980; Sherman 1980b, 1985). Consequently, a better test for nepotism is to compare individuals that have nearby kin with individuals *of the same sex* that do not. In support of nepotism, both male and female prairie dogs call often more when surrounded by kin ($r \geq .0625$) (figs. 8.7 and 8.8).

Are Antipredator Calls Merely an Expression of Parental Care?

Shields (1980) correctly emphasized that female round-tailed and Belding's ground squirrels that give antipredator calls usually have living adult or

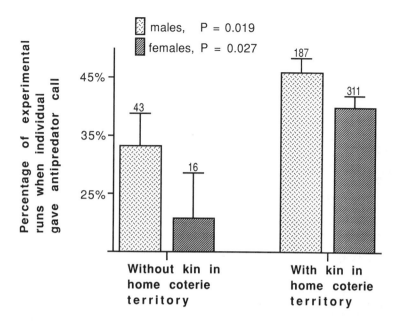

Fig. 8.7. Antipredator calling by prairie dogs with and without genetic relatives in the home coterie territory. For this analysis, *kin* are other prairie dogs sharing a coefficient of genetic relatedness of .0625 or greater. The number above each SE line indicates the number of individuals observed (each approximately seven times per year) during 928 experimental runs with the stuffed American badger. *P*-values are from the Mann-Whitney *U* test. Males and females are equally likely to call (*P* = .178 for comparison involving all data from both sexes, Mann-Whitney *U* test).

juvenile offspring within earshot (Dunford 1975, 1977b,c; Sherman 1981a; Sherman and Morton 1984; see Sherman 1977, 1980b for rare exceptions). Consequently, female antipredator calls in these species probably have evolved primarily in the context of parental care, with nondescendant kin sometimes being secondary beneficiaries. Such maternal calling is still nepotistic, of course (Alexander 1974; Sherman 1980b), but is perhaps less interesting than calling by nonparental kin.

Unlike female round-tailed and Belding's ground squirrels, prairie dogs of both sexes commonly live near kin that do not include offspring (chaps. 6, 14, and 16). Consider the situation in May 1979, for example: only 49% of the adult and yearling females at the study colony (35/72) had offspring in the home coterie, but 81% of these females (58/72) had nondescendant kin in the home coterie; 49% of the females (35/72) had *only* nondescendant kin in the home coterie. Prairie dogs are thus more appropriate than round-tailed and Belding's ground squirrels for studies of the role of parents and other kin in the evolution of antipredator calling.

For my analysis I have categorized individuals with living kin in the home coterie territory as one of three types (fig. 8.8): Type III, with living offspring; Type II, with living parents or full siblings but without living offspring; and Type I, with living kin that do not include offspring, parents, or full siblings. For both sexes, individuals with only nondescendant kin in the home coterie territory (Types I and II) call as often as do individuals with offspring (Type III) (fig. 8.8). Thus, prairie dog antipredator calls commonly warn nondescendant kin, and are not merely an expression of parental care.

One line of evidence, however, *does* suggest the possible importance of parental care in the evolution of the prairie dog's antipredator call. Like hoary marmot females (Barash 1989), prairie dogs of both sexes call more often in years when they produce emergent offspring than in years when they do not (fig. 8.9).

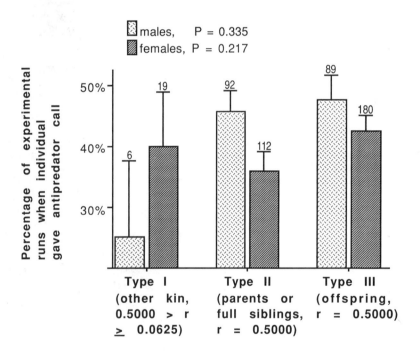

Fig. 8.8. Antipredator calling by individuals with three different types of kin within the home coterie territory. Type III individuals have living offspring (r = .5000) in the home coterie territory. Type II individuals have either living parents or full siblings (r = .5000), but not offspring, in the home coterie territory. Type I individuals have living kin that do not include offspring, parents, or full siblings in the home coterie territory (.5000 > r ≥ .0625). The number above each SE line indicates the number of individuals observed (each approximately seven times per year) during experimental runs with the stuffed American badger. Kin within earshot included adults, yearlings, and juveniles. P-values are from the Kruskal-Wallis analysis of variance. Within each sex, all pairwise comparisons are also insignificant (P > .050 for all, Mann-Whitney U test).

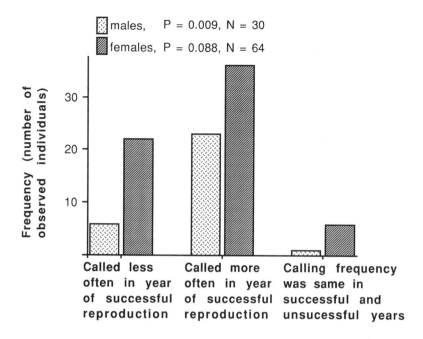

Fig. 8.9. Do prairie dogs give an antipredator call more often in years when they produce emergent juveniles? For this graph I compare the calling frequencies of the same individuals in years when, as adults, they did and did not produce emergent juveniles. When data from three or more years are available for the same individual, I have used data only from the first two consecutive years that show a change in the production of emergent juveniles. Each year, the number of experimental runs with the stuffed American badger for each coterie is approximately seven. *P*-values are from the Wilcoxon matched-pairs signed-ranks test.

The possible importance of parental care to prairie dog antipredator calls is only evident in sensitive pairwise comparisons of the same individuals under different circumstances (fig. 8.9). In less sensitive analyses, these small effects of parental care are diluted and result in calling frequencies that are slightly but insignificantly higher for prairie dog parents (see fig. 8.8).

Antipredator Calling versus Vulnerability of Listening Conspecifics

Young, recently emerged juveniles are more susceptible than older prairie dogs to predation. For example, juveniles are aboveground for only about 25% of my field season each year and constitute only 41% of the total population in May and June (chaps. 15 and 16)—yet they account for 32% of the observed predations (7/22) at the study colony (chap. 5) ($P < .050$

Table 8.2. Antipredator Calling Before and After First Juvenile Emergences from the Natal Burrow

	Number of individuals whose calling frequency did not change after first juvenile emergences	Number of individuals that called less often after first juvenile emergences	Number of individuals that called more often after first juvenile emergences	Significance of these differences
Males that did not produce emergent offspring	2	2	3	$P = .590$
Females that did not produce emergent offspring	9	10	5	$P = .427$
Males that produced emergent offspring	3	3	4	$P = .310$
Females that produced emergent offspring	7	4	11	$P = .009$

Note: In 1979 I recorded antipredator calling in response to the stuffed American badgers during the stages of copulation, pregnancy, and lactation. I then recorded antipredator calling by the same individuals during the several weeks following first juvenile emergences. The individuals that did and did not produce emergent offspring were all from the same fifteen coteries. The productive individuals were all adults, but four of the nonproductive males and four of the nonproductive females were yearlings. The mean ± SD numbers of experimental runs per coterie before and after first juvenile emergences were 9.11 ± 3.93 and 7.69 ± 2.99, respectively. *P*-values are from the Wilcoxon matched-pairs signed-ranks test.

for goodness-of-fit test that compares observed versus expected predations on juveniles and older individuals; see also Loughry 1992). If the antipredator call is nepotistic and sensitive to the vulnerability of listeners, then adult and yearling prairie dogs—like mothers of Sonoma and eastern chipmunks, thirteen-lined and California ground squirrels, and Olympic and hoary marmots (McCarley 1966; Barash 1975, 1989; Smith 1978; Yahner 1978; Schwagmeyer 1980; Owings et al. 1986)—should be especially likely to call shortly after first juvenile emergences. Table 8.2 supports this prediction for prairie dog mothers. Curiously, however, fathers and nonreproductive males and females do *not* call more often after first juvenile emergences.

Changes in Antipredator Calling versus Changes in the Presence of Nearby Kin

If nepotism is important, then individuals should alter their calling frequencies in response to changes in the presence of kin within earshot. Because prairie dogs so consistently live near kin, I have trouble investigating this prediction. Specifically, only five females and only fourteen males have spent a year *without* kin in the home coterie territory followed by, or

Table 8.3. Antipredator Calling by Males That Experienced Two Changes in the Presence of Close Kin ($r \geq .2500$) in the Home Coterie Territory

Individual male	Calling frequency when only nondescendant close kin in home coterie	Calling frequency when no close kin in home coterie	Calling frequency when offspring in home coterie	Calling frequency when no close kin in home coterie
15	67%	0%	100%	—
35	33%	0%	17%	—
19	44%	0%	60%	—
26	100%	17%	100%	—
02	—	0%	71%	35%

Note: For all five males, the absence of close kin in the home coterie occurred after the male had just moved into a new breeding coterie territory. The call frequency indicates the percentage of times that the male called during experimental runs with the stuffed American badgers (approximately seven runs per year per male).

preceded by, a year *with* kin (always offspring, as it turned out) there. Three of the females called more often in years when surrounded by aboveground juvenile offspring, but two did not ($P = .500$, Wilcoxon matched-pairs signed-ranks test). The predicted change is more dramatic for males. Twelve of the males called more often in years when surrounded by juvenile offspring, one did not, and one did not change his calling frequency ($P = .006$, Wilcoxon matched-pairs signed-ranks test).

The preceding discussion concerns males and females that experience a single abrupt change in the presence of kin within the home coterie territory. Five individuals, all males, experienced *two* such abrupt changes in their lifetimes. The obvious prediction is that each of these males should have appropriately altered his calling frequency with each change in the presence of nearby kin. Table 8.3 supports this prediction.

After siring offspring in one coterie territory, a breeding male sometimes disperses to an adjacent coterie territory. Similarly, yearling males sometimes disperse from the natal coterie territory to an adjacent breeding territory (chaps. 14 and 16). Consequently, breeding males sometimes have close kin in an adjacent coterie territory in addition to their offspring in the home coterie territory. Do males adjust their calling frequencies in response to close kin in adjacent coterie territories? My qualitative impression is that they do not, but I did not seriously investigate this possibility (see also below).

Do Antipredator Calls Show Differential Nepotism?

Figure 8.7 shows that prairie dog antipredator calls are nepotistic. Are they also *differentially* nepotistic? Specifically, are individuals with close kin in the home coterie territory more likely to call than individuals with only more distant kin nearby?

Individuals share just as many alleles with their parents and full siblings as with their offspring. Thus, in terms of Hamilton's (1964) coefficient of genetic relatedness (r), prairie dogs with offspring in the home coterie territory are equivalent to individuals with parents or full siblings there. To investigate possible differential nepotism, I have compared the calling frequency of individuals with parents, offspring, or full siblings in the home coterie territory ($r \geq .5000$; Type II and Type III in fig. 8.8) versus the calling frequency of individuals with only more distant kin ($.5000 > r \geq .0625$; Type I in fig. 8.8) nearby. For females, calling frequencies for Type I and Types II–III are the same: 40%. For males, calling frequencies for Type I and Types II–III are 25% and 47%, respectively. For neither sex is the difference significant ($P = .926$ for females, $P = .145$ for males, Mann-Whitney U test). Individuals with only distant kin in the home coterie territory are thus just as likely to give an antipredator call as are individuals with closer kin nearby—i.e., antipredator calls do not show differential nepotism.

Antipredator Calling When Other Individuals Are Calling

Prairie dog antipredator calls are loud and easily heard by any aboveground prairie dog within the home coterie territory. So why should an individual call when another individual in the home coterie is already calling? Two lines of evidence indicate that prairie dogs sometimes do refrain from calling when a coterie member is already calling. First, noncalling individuals sometimes live in coterie territories with another individual that invariably calls. When I deliberately pull a stuffed American badger through the home coterie territory when the unfailing caller is underground for some reason, previously silent prairie dogs sometimes call. Second, a second prairie dog commonly does not begin to call until the first caller has stopped. Despite these two trends, several prairie dogs within a coterie usually call simultaneously during a predatory attack. Adding a second antipredator call might be advantageous for at least two reasons. First, as noted above, prairie dogs sometimes give "false" antipredator calls in response to apparent, but unreal, danger. Individuals sometimes ignore a single coterie member that is calling, but almost always run to a burrow mound and remain alert when two or more coterie members are calling. Thus, a second antipredator call might increase the probability that kin will realize that the danger is real. Second, individuals also might gain by adding a second call if the call somehow enhances self-preservation (see below).

Antipredator Calling versus Coterie Size

For at least two reasons, prairie dogs in large coteries might be more likely to give an antipredator call than prairie dogs in smaller coteries. First, vulnerability of the caller might vary inversely with coterie size due to "selfish herd effects" (Hamilton 1971; chap. 5)—so that prairie dogs in large coteries can call more safely. Second, because the number of kin is usually higher in larger coteries, the benefits of calling might vary directly with coterie size. Contrarily, the presence of numerous other potential callers might render individuals in large coteries *less likely* to call (see above). With these arguments in mind, I have investigated the probability of an individual's giving an antipredator call versus coterie size. Curiously, the probability of calling varies inversely with coterie size for males but not for females (fig. 8.10a).

What about the probability of *hearing* an antipredator call versus coterie size? The probability of at least one antipredator call being given by a coterie member varies directly with coterie size (fig. 8.10b). Similarly, the number of callers regardless of sex varies directly with coterie size ($P <$ .001, Spearman rank correlation test). Thus, one advantage of living in larger coteries is the increased probability of hearing at least one antipredator call during a predatory attack. This advantage is asymptotic: in all coteries containing five or more adult and yearling residents, the guarantee of hearing at least one call is almost 100%.

Antipredator Calling versus Age

Antipredator calling might vary with age for several reasons (Harvey and Greenwood 1978). For example, old individuals of animals such as Belding's ground squirrels and Olympic, hoary, and alpine marmots might call more often than younger individuals because they are more familiar with the best routes for escape and thus can call with less personal risk (Barash 1975, 1989; Sherman 1977). Old individuals also might call more often to assist younger kin of higher reproductive potential. Conversely, natural selection might favor antipredator calling by young individuals of low reproductive value (Fisher 1958; Hamilton 1966) to older kin of higher reproductive value. Despite these intriguing possibilities, antipredator calling in prairie dogs does not vary systematically with age for either sex (fig. 8.11).

The Importance of Antipredator Calls in Other Coterie Territories

The prairie dog antipredator call functions to warn kin living in the home coterie territory (see above). Secondarily, however, the call also warns unrelated (or only distantly related) prairie dogs in other coterie territories. Are these secondary effects important?

A call from an adjacent coterie territory does not necessarily mean immediate danger. This factor probably explains why individuals are less likely to respond—either by running to a burrow mound or by giving additional antipredator calls—to calls from adjacent coterie territories than to calls from the home coterie territory. However, a call from an adjacent

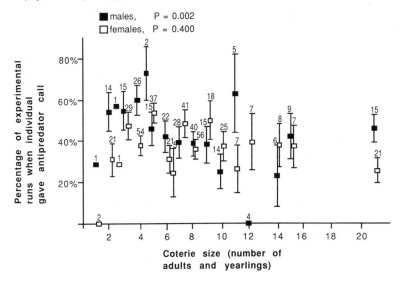

a) probability of giving antipredator call versus coterie size

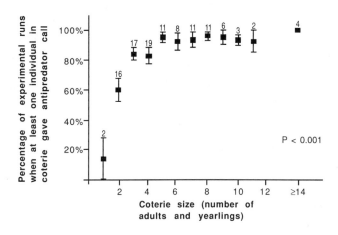

b) probability of hearing antipredator call versus coterie size

Fig. 8.10. Antipredator calling versus coterie size. *(a)* Probability of giving an antipredator call versus coterie size. The number above each SE line indicates the number of individuals observed (each approximately seven times per year) during experimental runs with the stuffed American badger. *P*-values are for Spearman rank correlation coefficients, both negative. *(b)* Probability that at least one prairie dog in the home coterie (male or female) gives an antipredator call versus coterie size. The number above each SE line indicates the number of coteries for which probabilities are available (*N* = approximately seven experimental runs with the stuffed American badger per coterie per year). The *P*-value is from the Spearman rank correlation test. Even with deletion of data from the two coteries of size 1, the positive relationship shown here is still significant (*P* < .001, Spearman rank correlation test).

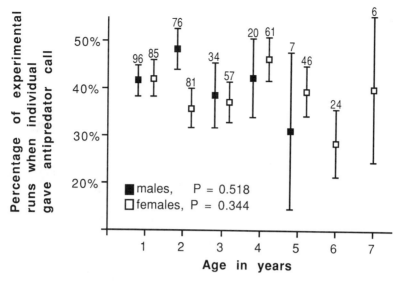

Fig. 8.11. Probability of giving an antipredator call versus age. The number above each SE line indicates the number of individuals observed (each approximately seven times per year) during experimental runs with the stuffed American badger. *P*-values are from the Kruskal-Wallis analysis of variance.

coterie territory alerts a prairie dog to watch for the possible invasion of the predator into its *own* coterie territory. Consequently, individuals in alerted coteries are less likely to be surprised by predators and are more likely to call as soon as the predator enters the home coterie territory. Prairie dogs of one coterie thus "parasitize" and benefit from the antipredator calling in nearby coteries.

Do Prairie Dogs Have an "All Clear" Call?

Earlier in this chapter I listed the myriad names for the prairie dog's antipredator call. A second distinct call also has many names: yelp (Jillson 1871), cry (Wilder 1872), song (Seton 1926), song-bark (Anthony 1955), territorial call (King 1955), all clear call (King 1955; Smith 1967; Costello 1970), wee-oo call (Waring 1970), contagious vocalization (Waring 1970), and jump-yip display (Smith et al. 1976; Halpin 1983; Owings and Loughry 1985). This second call—which I call in this book either the territorial call or the jump-yip—is striking for two reasons. First, while stretching the length of the body nearly vertical, the calling individual throws the forefeet high into the air (fig. 8.12). A loud "Ah-aaah" begins at the peak of the leap and continues into the descent (Smith et al. 1976) (fig. 8.13). Second, a single jump-yip usually starts a chain reaction of other jump-yips among prairie dogs in the home and adjacent coterie territories (Scheffer 1937; King 1955).

Fig. 8.12. Prairie dog giving jump-yip call. Prairie dogs commonly jump-yip, which involves this amusing posture, after a predator has disappeared from view. (Photo courtesy of Wind Cave National Park.)

Fig. 8.13. Sonographic variation in the jump-yip calls of six different prairie dogs. Smith et al. (1976) provide more details for each of these sonograms. (Photo courtesy of W. John Smith.)

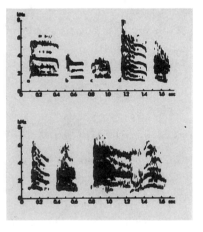

Does the jump-yip serve as an "all clear" call, as first suggested by King (1955)? The answer here is yes and no. During an attack by any predator other than a snake (see above), prairie dogs do not jump-yip while the predator is still threatening. However, they commonly jump-yip shortly after an aerial predator has flown out of sight or a terrestrial predator has trotted away from the colony (King 1955; Smith 1967). By jump-yipping, a prairie dog thus communicates its perception that the danger is over. When other prairie dogs share this perception, a chorus of jump-yips results. Following a predatory attack, then, the jump-yip communicates an important "all clear" message. However, prairie dogs commonly jump-yip throughout the day during territorial disputes and during other behavioral interactions unrelated to predation (Waring 1970; Smith et al. 1976; Loughry 1992; chap. 5). To argue that prairie dogs have a specific "all clear" call thus seems premature and misleading.

Perhaps future research will show that the jump-yips that follow a predatory attack somehow differ from the jump-yips used in behavioral interactions. Such documentation would support the hypothesis of an "all clear" call among prairie dogs.

Do Antipredator Calls Enhance Self-Preservation?

When a prairie dog sounds an antipredator call, scores of other nearby prairie dogs in the home and adjacent coteries run to burrow mounds. These responses to the call might directly benefit the caller for at least three reasons. First, numerous prairie dogs that were previously invisible suddenly become highly conspicuous as they stand on burrow mounds. By bringing other conspecifics to the predator's attention, an antipredator call might encourage the predator to pursue a prairie dog other than the caller (Hamilton 1971; Leger, Owings, and Gelfand 1980; Sherman 1985). Second, perhaps the sudden appearance of numerous running prairie dogs in response to antipredator calls somehow annoys, distracts, or confuses predators (Neill and Cullen 1974; Owens and Goss-Custard 1976; Leger, Owings, and Gelfand 1980). Finally, alerted prairie dogs on mounds can better track the predator and communicate—via visual and vocal signals—changes in the predator's direction of attack. Like calls of Columbian and California ground squirrels (Betts 1976; Owings et al. 1986), prairie dog antipredator calls thus might induce conspecifics to monitor the predator more closely.

Three lines of evidence indicate the possible importance of self-preservation (Cheney and Seyfarth 1981; Sherman 1985) to prairie dog antipredator calls, as outlined below.

First, the prairie dog closest to the stuffed American badger as it first emerges from the brown bag is in more (simulated) danger than are more distant prairie dogs. If antipredator calls promote self-preservation, then the individual closest to the predator should call more often than more distant individuals. Figure 8.14a supports this prediction.

Second, submergence into a burrow—usually one with two or more entrances (see above)—usually occurs only when a stuffed American badger comes within several meters of the burrow mound from which the prairie dog is watching. Thus, submergers are in more (simulated) danger than nonsubmergers and should call more often if antipredator calls promote self-preservation. Figure 8.14b supports this prediction.

Third, suppose that the antipredator call promotes self-preservation because the sound of the call itself is annoying, distracting, or confusing

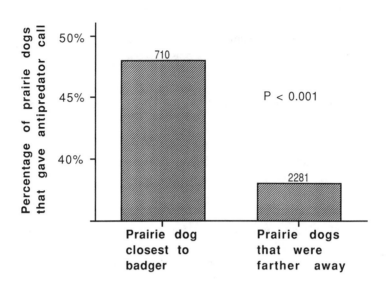

a) calling versus proximity to badger

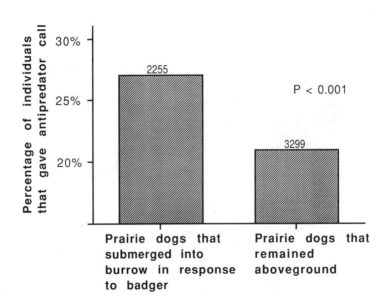

b) calling versus submergence

c) calling versus presence of aboveground conspecifics

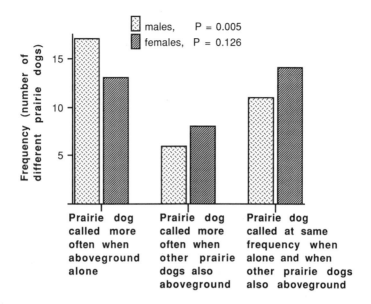

◀ ▲ **Fig. 8.14.** Does antipredator calling promote self-preservation? *(a)* Antipredator calling versus distance from the stuffed American badger. Before each experimental run, I determine which individual is closest to the concealed badger. The number above each bar indicates the number of individuals observed (each approximately seven times per year) during 710 experimental runs. The *P*-value is from the 2 by 2 chi-square test. *(b)* Antipredator calling versus submergence into a burrow. I record antipredator calling by individuals versus whether they submerge into a burrow in response to the stuffed badger. The number above each bar indicates the number of individuals observed (each approximately seven times per year). The *P*-value is from the 2 × 2 chi-square test. *(c)* Antipredator calling versus the presence or absence of other aboveground coterie members. I record antipredator calls in response to the stuffed badger when only one prairie dog within a coterie has appeared aboveground in the morning. I then record antipredator calling by the same prairie dog later in the day when its other coterie members are also aboveground. *P*-values are from the Wilcoxon matched-pairs signed-ranks test.

to predators. If so, then calling would be especially important each morning for the few first emergers who can expect no additional calling from underground coterie members. Figure 8.14c supports this hypothesis. Contrarily, suppose that calling promotes self-preservation because its main effect is the sudden conspicuousness of other prairie dogs running to burrow mounds. If so, then first emergers should remain silent because aboveground conspecifics to manipulate into being conspicuous are so few—and fig. 8.14c would argue *against* the importance of self-preservation.

Like hoary marmots and round-tailed, Belding's, Richardson's, and California ground squirrels without nearby kin (Dunford 1977b; Sherman 1977, 1985; Davis 1984a; Owings and Leger 1980; Barash 1989), prairie dogs without kin in the home coterie territory sometimes give an antipredator call (see fig. 8.7). Many of these individuals are immigrants who do not have any kin anywhere in the study colony. Other possibilities exist (Williams 1966a; Smythe 1970; Trivers 1971; Charnov and Krebs 1975; Sherman 1977), but self-preservation is perhaps the best explanation for calling by prairie dogs without nearby kin.

Summary

1. Adult and yearling prairie dogs of both sexes frequently give an antipredator call in response to predators. Juveniles almost never call.

2. Prairie dogs have only one distinct antipredator call, but variation in the rate of calling might indicate different predators or differences in the imminence of danger.

3. Individual calling rates are bimodal for both sexes: the most common calling frequencies are between 0% and 10% and between 91% and 100%, and the two most common frequencies are 0% and 100%.

4. Both males and females with kin in the home coterie territory are more likely to call than are individuals without nearby kin.

5. Antipredator calls are not merely an expression of parental care. Specifically, individuals with parents and full siblings but no offspring in the home coterie territory call as often as do individuals with offspring there.

6. Antipredator calls do not show differential nepotism. Specifically, individuals with only more distant kin within the home coterie territory ($.5000 > r \geq .0625$) call as often as do individuals with close kin ($r \geq .5000$) there.

7. The probability of giving an antipredator call varies inversely with coterie size for males but not for females. The probability of hearing an antipredator call varies directly with coterie size.

8. Antipredator calling does not vary systematically with age for either sex.

9. The jump-yip call communicates that a predator is no longer menacing. However, individuals utter the same vocalization in scores of other circumstances. To argue that prairie dogs have a specific "all clear" call thus seems premature and misleading.

10. Besides warning kin, antipredator calls might sometimes enhance the survival of the caller.

9 Communal Nursing

Types of Communal Nursing

Communal nursing is the suckling of another female's offspring. Because natural selection favors mothers that are especially attentive to their own offspring, communal nursing should be rare (Wilkinson 1992a). However, mothers of colonial species often cannot easily discriminate between their own and others' offspring (chap. 5). Probably for this reason, communal nursing is surprisingly common among colonial mammals (Packer, Lewis, and Pusey 1992). Despite this ubiquity, the frequency of communal nursing is typically low, usually affecting fewer than 10% of litters.

When a female suckles another female's offspring, I refer to these offspring as *foster offspring,* and to the female as a *foster mother.*

Communal nursing is of two general types. Females without their own nursing young suckle foster offspring in some animals such as African wild dogs, dwarf mongooses, and gray wolves (Lawick 1974; Rood 1980b, 1990; Macdonald and Moehlman 1983; Packard et al. 1985; Creel et al. 1991). However, in other animals, such as house mice, African lions, and African elephants, foster mothers have their own nursing offspring as well (Schaller 1972; Bertram 1976; Dublin 1983; Manning, Wakeland, and Potts 1992). A few animals, such as northern elephant seals and white-nosed coatis, show both types of communal nursing (Le Boeuf, Whiting, and Gantt 1972; Reiter, Stinson, and Le Boeuf 1978; Smith 1980; Russell 1983).

The beneficiaries of communal nursing also vary. For animals such as African lions, African elephants, and dwarf mongooses, foster offspring are usually the offspring of close kin (Bertram 1976; Dublin 1983; Creel et al. 1991). But foster offspring are usually nonkin for animals such as northern elephant seals, evening bats, and Mexican free-tailed bats (Reiter, Panken, and Le Boeuf 1981; Riedman and Le Boeuf 1982; Watkins and Shump 1981; McCracken 1984).

Communal nursing within prairie dog colonies is striking for two reasons. First, it is unusually common, affecting more than 50% of all emergent litters. Second, and more fascinating, mothers sometimes suckle the same juveniles they had tried to kill only 2 to 3 weeks earlier!

Behavioral Observations That Suggest Communal Nursing

For about the first 2 weeks after parturition, prairie dog mothers commonly enter the home nursery burrow once or twice during the day for 30 minutes or more—presumably to suckle their own offspring (chaps. 2 and 16). Additional nursing of offspring probably also occurs at night. Once their pre-emergent offspring are about 2 weeks old, however, prairie dog mothers almost never enter the home nursery burrow during the day until the final submergence at night—except to escape predators or precipitation. Consequently, all suckling of older (>2 weeks), pre-emergent prairie dog juveniles must occur underground between final maternal submergence at night and first maternal emergence in the morning. Similar patterns of nocturnal suckling are probably the rule for all species of ground squirrels and marmots (Ferron 1984; Michener 1983, 1984a; Barash 1989). Following first emergences of prairie dog juveniles, I have observed fewer than five instances of aboveground nursing, all dubious because they lasted for only a few seconds (fig. 9.1).

I was fortunate to discover several diagnostic aboveground behaviors that allow detection of underground copulations (chap. 11) and underground infanticides (chap. 7). I have had no such luck with underground nursing. When a juvenile spends the night in the same burrow with a lactating female, I can only conclude that the juvenile *might* obtain milk from that mother.

Within days after their first emergence from the natal burrow, young prairie dogs from different litters within the home coterie territory begin to interact aboveground (chap. 5). Soon after these first mixings, juveniles from different litters begin to spend the night together in the same burrow with one or more mothers. In the early years of research (e.g., Hoogland 1979a, 1981a), I assumed that weaning in prairie dogs coincides with first juvenile emergence. Researchers working with Olympic marmots and Belding's, arctic, and Richardson's ground squirrels had made the same assumption (e.g., Barash 1973; Holmes and Sherman 1982; Davis 1984c), and I had no reason to believe otherwise. Why would juveniles come aboveground to feed unless they are weaned?

At Wind Cave National Park in May and June, two or three consecutive days of cold, damp weather sometimes occur. Juveniles do not come aboveground to feed during such inclement weather. Several times I have eartagged and color-marked some, but not all, juveniles in a litter before a stretch of bad weather. When I retrap the marked juveniles after the nasty weather in quest of the remaining unmarked ones, they consistently have gained body mass. If juveniles are weaned at first emergence, how can they gain body mass when they do not forage aboveground? I ignored this

Fig. 9.1. Aboveground nursing in prairie dogs. Unfortunately for me, most nursing occurs underground. To investigate communal nursing, I therefore must rely on radionuclides injected into foster mothers. (Photo by John L. Hoogland.)

problem until about 1984, when I noticed that juveniles from early-emerging litters sometimes seek out a mother whose young have just emerged, and then spend the night in the same burrow with the foster mother and her juveniles (fig. 9.2). Sometimes juveniles spend the night with mothers whose juveniles have not yet appeared aboveground! Why would juveniles act in this way, unless searching for milk from foster mothers?

Despite the extensive aboveground intermingling of young from different litters, recently emerged prairie dog littermates usually spend the night together in the same burrow—i.e., *entire litters* usually spend the night in the same burrow with other *entire litters*. How do mothers respond to all this mingling? If her own juveniles remain in the home nursery burrow following the invasion by young from other litters, the mother continues to spend the night there also. When her juveniles move themselves into another burrow with other juveniles, the mother follows them and spends the night with them there. When the mother herself moves her juveniles into a new burrow containing other juveniles, she spends the

Fig. 9.2. Circumstantial evidence for communal nursing. *(a)* The maximum litter size observed at the study colony is six. The seven juveniles shown here implicate the mixing of at least two litters and probable communal nursing. (Photo by Wendy Shattil/Bob Rozinski, copyright 1992.) *(b)* Juvenile from HBSX litter (in middle) interacts with two juveniles from TSX litter at burrow entrance-C1. Juveniles from two litters that interact aboveground usually spend the night together and probably obtain milk from both their own and foster mothers. (Photo by John L. Hoogland.)

night there also. Mothers thus consistently spend the night with their own recently emerged offspring—with or without other mothers and with or without foster offspring. Consequently, communal nursing probably only occurs when the foster mother also suckles her own offspring.

The observations that suggest communal nursing might have alternative explanations. For example, older juveniles might join litters of pre-emergent or just-emergent juveniles in order to reduce predation on themselves (see below), with no interest in milk from foster mothers. Perhaps the gain in body mass by emergent juveniles during inclement weather results from eating plants that the mother has taken underground. Two lines of evidence support this latter possibility. First, most plants that mothers take underground are dry and presumably used for nesting material. However, mothers sometimes take fresh, green plants underground just before or just after their offspring first appear aboveground. Second, fecal pellets of just-emerged juveniles commonly indicate a diet that includes grasses and other plants rather than milk only.

Despite the plausible alternatives, I could not shake the possibility of communal nursing. Does communal suckling of the offspring of close kin occur in the same colony where the killing of the offspring of close kin also occurs? This mesmerizing question deserved an answer.

Frequency of Communal Nursing

To investigate communal nursing, I inject lactating females with radionuclides, and then examine juvenile scat (fecal) or blood samples for radionuclide transmitted through the milk of a foster mother (see chap. 4). Blood samples of 14% of the juveniles sampled in 1986 (7/49) showed evidence of communal nursing. The results implicate six foster mothers, six litters, and four coteries. In 35% of sampled litters (6/17), at least one juvenile nursed from a foster mother.

For two reasons, I hypothesized that the 1986 estimate of communal nursing was too low. First, in May and June 1986 I sometimes collected blood from a foster offspring as long as 2 weeks after injecting the foster mother with radionuclide. However, blood samples from the mothers themselves sometimes failed to show radionuclide as soon as 5 days after injection. I did not recognize this problem, of course, until after I had collected all the 1986 blood samples and had sent them to Boston University for analysis (chap. 4). Second, a few scat samples fortuitously collected in 1986 indicated that radionuclide is more easily detected in scats than in blood samples.

I again investigated communal nursing in 1987, with two important changes in procedure. First, I concentrated on scats rather than blood samples. The hunch that radionuclide would show up better in scats than in blood samples was correct (fig. 9.3). Second, I collected all samples from juveniles suspected to be foster offspring within 3 days after the injection of foster mothers.

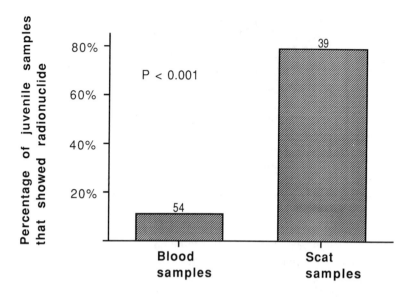

Fig. 9.3. Probability of detecting radionuclide in juvenile scat and blood samples. The number above each bar indicates the number of samples. The *P*-value is from the 2 × 2 chi-square test. For all these sampled juveniles, behavioral evidence indicated communal nursing from a foster mother injected with radionuclide.

Scats show that 68% of juveniles (25/37) received radionuclide from a foster mother in 1987 (table 9.1). These results implicate fourteen litters, thirteen foster mothers, and eight coteries. In 88% of the litters sampled (14/16), at least one juvenile showed evidence of communal nursing.

Recently emerged juveniles do not usually venture outside the home coterie territory (King 1955; see also chap. 7). Consequently, communal nursing can only occur in coterie territories that produce at least two emergent litters. The frequencies of 68% and 88% for communal nursing came from coterie territories with two or more emergent litters. However, only 70% of litters (256/367) emerge in coterie territories with at least one other emergent litter. More accurate estimates of the frequency of communal nursing are therefore 48% (68% × 70%) and 62% (88% × 70%). These revised frequencies correctly assume that quick mixing of young from different litters and communal nursing are practically automatic when two or more litters emerge in the same coterie territory.

Each litter usually showed radionuclide from only one foster mother. However, juveniles from one litter (HRSX litter in table 9.1) showed radionuclide from two foster mothers.

Table 9.1 demonstrates that most juveniles are not weaned at first emergence from the natal burrow. I documented the same thing anecdotally in 1987 without using radionuclides. On 29 May, the juveniles of female-50 first emerged. On 30 May, an invading male killed two of female-50's

Table 9.1. Communal Nursing in 1987

Litter designation	Number of juveniles in this litter	Number of juveniles with scats examined for radionuclide	Number of juveniles showing radionuclide from true mother only	Number of juveniles showing radionuclide from foster mother only	Number of juveniles showing radionuclide from both true and foster mother
TSX	4	3			3
WA3X	2	2			2
HBBX	4	2			2
RSX	5	2	1		1
RABX	4	3			2
5X	4	2	1		1
5strX	4	1			1
5SBSX	2	2			2
7X	4	2		1	1
HRSX[a]	5	4		4	
WA2X	4	4	2		2
6X[a]	4	1		1	
3SBSX	4	3	1		1
HX	4	1			1
BB8X	3	1			
WARSX	4	4			
Totals	61	37	5	6	19

Note: All data are from juveniles that had already emerged from the natal burrow. Of the sampled juveniles, 68% showed evidence of communal nursing (25/37). At least one juvenile communally nursed in 88% of the sampled litters (14/16). The communal nursing involved 25 foster offspring and 13 foster mothers from 8 coteries. Communal nursing also occurred at a lower frequency in 1986 (see text).

[a] I did not inject the mothers of these litters with radionuclide.

juveniles and brought them aboveground. Dissection showed that the stomachs of both juveniles were full of *milk only* with no herbaceous material.

As expected, most juveniles sampled in 1987 also received milk from their own mothers (table 9.1). Juveniles from only two litters that spent the night with injected foster mothers failed to show radionuclide from the foster mothers. However, juveniles from both these litters also failed to show radionuclide from their own injected mothers. Perhaps weaning for these litters was complete upon first juvenile emergence.

Radionuclide could possibly transfer from one injected prairie dog to another by means other than nursing. For example, transfer could occur during oral kissing and licking, anal sniffing and licking, or ingestion of urine and feces. I have investigated the possible transfer of radionuclide by means other than nursing in two ways. First, I looked for, but failed to find, radionuclide in forty-one adults and yearlings of both sexes that regularly interacted with, and spent at least one night in the same burrow with, injected mothers. Second, I injected seven males and three nonlactating females that regularly interacted with, and spent the night in the same burrow with, recently emerged juveniles. Radionuclide never transferred from any of the males or nonlactating females to any of the sampled sixty-eight juveniles with which they interacted. The only logical conclusion is that the transfer of radionuclide from foster mothers to foster offspring results from communal nursing.

The procedure with radionuclides can verify that communal nursing *has occurred,* but cannot specify *how much milk* foster offspring have obtained from foster mothers. The flushing of radionuclides from an animal's body varies with both the rate of metabolism for each radionuclide and individual metabolic differences (Tamarin, Sheridan, and Levy 1983; Morimoto, Tamarin, and Levy 1985). Consequently, experiments for detecting *quantitative differences* in the amount of milk transferred via communal nursing will be difficult.

Is Communal Nursing Merely an Unnatural Response to Livetrapping?

To save her offspring from capture in a livetrap, a prairie dog mother sometimes transfers the offspring from the home nursery burrow to another burrow (chap. 4). If the new burrow contains another mother's offspring, then mingling of the young from different litters continues indefinitely, with consequent communal nursing. Does this mean that communal nursing is merely an unnatural response to livetrapping, and therefore of no biological significance? Though livetrapping is directly responsible for a few cases of communal nursing, the answer to this important question is negative for at least three reasons. First, mixing of two litters occurs most commonly after I have captured all juveniles of both litters and have removed the livetraps at both home nursery burrows. Second, mixing of two litters sometimes occurs before I set livetraps at either litter's home nursery burrow. Finally, at colonies where I do not livetrap, I commonly see six or seven recently emerged juveniles on the same burrow mound (see fig. 9.2). Because litter size ranges from one through six with a mode of three (chap. 16), most groups of six recently emerged juveniles at the same mound, and *all* groups of seven, must include young from at least two litters. As further indication of amalgamation, such groups commonly contain two, three, or four same-sized juveniles (presumably members of one litter) that are noticeably larger than the other juveniles (presumably members of the other litter).

How Costly Is Communal Nursing?

Communal nursing means lost milk that otherwise could go to offspring. I therefore assume that communal nursing is costly to both foster mothers and their own offspring. I also assume that foster offspring benefit from the additional milk obtained through communal nursing. I have not measured either the cost of communal nursing to foster mothers and their own offspring or its benefit to foster offspring.

Recall that communal nursing occurs only after first juvenile emergences—i.e., after the period of approximately 6 weeks during which pre-emergent juveniles suckle exclusively from their own mothers. Consequently, the physiological and energetic cost of communal nursing to foster mothers is probably small compared with the cost of producing milk exclusively for their own pre-emergent offspring.

Are Foster Mothers Willing Participants in Communal Nursing?

For animals such as house mice and dwarf mongooses, foster mothers sometimes dispense milk willingly to foster offspring (Rood 1980b; Creel et al. 1991; Manning, Wakeland, and Potts 1992). However, communal nursing in other animals, such as northern elephant seals, results when juveniles surreptitiously "steal" milk from unwilling foster mothers (Le Boeuf and Briggs 1977; Reiter, Pankin, and Le Boeuf 1981). Prairie dog females commonly transfer their own just-emerged offspring into a burrow containing just-emerged juveniles from another litter (chap. 5)—and then evidently suckle both their own and foster offspring. Further, mothers do not reject a foster juvenile that wanders near or into the home nursery burrow containing her own offspring. Thus, prairie dog foster mothers seem to be willing participants in communal nursing.

Genetic Relationship of Foster Mother to Foster Offspring

Barring the extraordinary transfer of juveniles to another coterie territory (chaps. 6 and 14), females suckle only foster offspring living in the home coterie territory. Because females within the same coterie are always close kin, foster mothers are always genetically related to their foster offspring (table 9.2).

Like house mouse foster mothers (Manning, Wakeland, and Potts 1992), prairie dog foster mothers seem just as likely to suckle foster nondescendant

Table 9.2. Genetic Relationship of Foster Mothers to Mothers of Foster Offspring

Relationship	Frequency
Mother	6
Daughter	1
Full sister	12
Half sister	3
Full aunt	2
Half aunt	2
Half niece	2
Full first cousin	2
Full second cousin	2
Total	32

Note: Included here are seven cases of communal nursing observed in 1986 (see text). Note the similarity of this table to table 7.1, which shows the genetic relationship of infanticidal mothers to the mothers of victimized juveniles.

juvenile kin as their own offspring when both are present in the same burrow at night. However, this conclusion must remain tentative in view of my small sample sizes and my inability to measure the volume of milk dispensed.

Do Infanticidal Females Become Foster Mothers?

Variation in the behavior of individuals toward kin is commonplace among social species (Hamilton 1964, 1972; Sherman 1980a; Armitage and Johns 1982; Emlen 1991). However, variation of the magnitude that occurs among prairie dogs—from infanticide to communal nursing—is more unusual.

Do the same mothers kill and communally nurse in the same year? Before using radionuclides I documented that certain infanticidal mothers spend the night in the same burrow with other females' emergent juveniles. This indicates that some killers later become foster mothers. Curiously, however, none of the foster mothers in 1986 or 1987 was a known killer. More data are necessary to determine whether the same female sometimes engages in both infanticide and communal nursing in the same or different years.

Possible Payoffs from Communal Nursing

Why do prairie dog foster mothers so commonly suckle foster offspring? In proximate terms, communal nursing might result simply because mothers cannot discriminate between their own and others' emergent juveniles. Before juveniles appear aboveground, mothers probably can easily discriminate between their own home nursery burrows containing their own offspring—as targets for nursing—and other nursery burrows containing the offspring of other females—as targets for infanticide (chap. 7). Following first juvenile emergences, however, mothers might find discrimination between their own and others' offspring too difficult or too costly, so that infanticide ceases and communal nursing commences. If nursing of emergent juveniles is not physiologically very costly (see above), for example, then why should mothers bother to discriminate between their own and others' offspring? Prairie dog females also seem unable to discriminate between their own offspring and other kin in other contexts (chaps. 7, 8, and 10).

At least three possible ultimate explanations for communal nursing among prairie dogs come to mind (see also Wilkinson 1992a). These possibilities, discussed below, are not mutually exclusive.

Decreased Predation on Multi-Litter Groupings

Many of the benefits of infanticide by lactating females (chap. 7) are unavailable or unimportant following first emergences of juveniles from their natal burrows. However, the emergent juveniles of close kin might be useful to mothers in another way, which might ultimately explain the evolution of communal nursing. Recently emerged prairie dog juveniles are especially susceptible to predation (chaps. 5 and 8). By mixing with young from other litters and thereby forming large multi-litter groupings, young might reduce predation on themselves through increased awareness of predators, "selfish herd effects," or "protection by dilution" (Hamilton 1971; Vine 1971; McKaye and McKaye 1977; Williams 1994; chap. 5). By suckling the juveniles of other females, a mother increases the probability that these juveniles will cluster around her own offspring. Thus, prairie dog mothers might willingly pay the cost of communal nursing in order to obtain the benefits of multi-litter groupings for their own offspring. In this scenario, communal nursing is a selfish behavior by which mothers attempt to increase the survivorship of their own offspring by using others' offspring.

Multi-litter groupings are larger and more likely to form when numerous litters emerge in the same coterie territory. If multi-litter groupings are important, then juvenile survivorship probably should vary directly with the number of emergent juveniles within a coterie territory. Figure 9.4 offers no support for this hypothesis. Perhaps the benefit of multi-litter groupings is only important during the first month or two after juvenile emergences, and is later offset by increased competition.

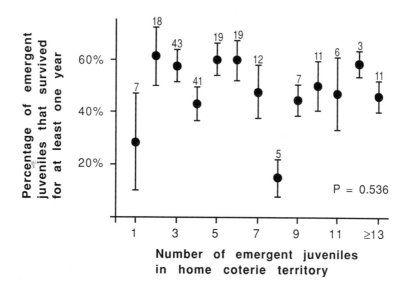

Fig. 9.4. Juvenile survivorship versus the number of emergent juveniles in the home coterie territory. The number above each SE line indicates the number of coterie territories examined. The *P*-value is from the Kruskal-Wallis analysis of variance.

Elevated Inclusive Fitness via Nondescendant Kin

An individual's inclusive fitness (Hamilton 1964) is the sum of both personal reproductive success and the reproductive success of kin (see also Maynard Smith 1964; West-Eberhard 1975; Grafen 1982; Brown 1987; chap. 1). An individual sometimes might contribute more copies of its alleles to future generations—i.e., increase its inclusive fitness—by helping nondescendant kin rather than offspring.

Because foster offspring are always from the home coterie territory, beneficiaries of communal nursing are always the offspring of close kin (see table 9.2). Mothers sometimes might increase their inclusive fitness more by suckling hungry offspring of their sisters (i.e., their own nieces and nephews) than by suckling their own well-fed offspring. Elevated inclusive fitness resulting from the communal nursing of nondescendant kin might be especially important when the mother disappears shortly after her offspring first emerge—as occurs for 2% of emergent litters (9/367) at the study colony.

Reproductive Value of Juveniles

Reproductive value—an individual's expected lifetime reproductive output (Fisher 1958; Emlen 1970; Pianka and Parker 1975; Rubenstein 1982; Zammuto 1987)—also might help explain communal nursing in prairie dogs. The probability that an *emergent juvenile* will survive to reproduce is approximately 35% (chap. 16). However, the probability that a neonate will live long enough to emerge from the natal burrow is only about 66%; this 66% results because 34% of litters suffer infanticide before first emergence (chap. 7). The probability that a *neonate* will survive to reproduce is therefore approximately 23% (35% × 66%). Perhaps this difference of 12% (35% − 23%) related to reproductive value of emergent juveniles and neonates is sufficient to cause mothers to switch from infanticide to communal nursing. Specifically, perhaps natural selection favors mothers who *discriminate against* the pre-emergent offspring of close kin via infanticide when juvenile reproductive value is minimal and personal gain through killing is high. Conversely, perhaps natural selection favors mothers who *help* the emergent offspring of close kin via communal nursing when juvenile reproductive value is higher and personal gain through killing is lower.

One glaring problem with this explanation is that infanticide by lactating females is the major cause of mortality for pre-emergent juveniles (chap. 7). However, even though the reproductive value of pre-emergent juveniles would be higher without infanticide, it always would be lower than the reproductive value of emergent juveniles.

I cannot satisfactorily explain the co-existence at the study colony of communal nursing and infanticide by lactating females. With so many unanswered questions, why haven't I further investigated communal nursing since 1987? Two compelling reasons, neither related to the high financial cost of radionuclides, have dissuaded me. First, despite all the standard precautions, and even though I have detected no evidence for such, I am concerned that radionuclides might either reduce prairie dog survivorship or damage gametes. Second, confirmation of communal nursing requires a second disruptive livetrapping and handling of foster offspring. This second capture involves surrounding nursery burrows with livetraps for a day or more, during which time no aboveground foraging can occur.

Does Communal Nursing Occur in Other Species of Squirrels?

Mixing of juveniles from different litters shortly after first emergences from the natal burrow is not unique to prairie dogs. Rather, such inter-litter mingling is practically universal among various species of chip-munks, ground squirrels, and marmots (chap. 5). Further, arctic ground squirrel mothers (Holmes and Sherman 1982; McLean 1982) and Gunnison's prairie dog mothers (my own unpublished data) sometimes transfer *pre-emergent* offspring into a nursery burrow with other pre-emergent juve-niles. Still further, pairs of mothers sometimes give birth in the same nursery burrow and rear their offspring together there until first emergence; this occurs for yellow-bellied marmots (Armitage 1984, 1989), Richardson's ground squirrels (L. S. Davis, pers. comm.), Gunnison's prairie dogs (Rayor 1988; my own unpublished data), and white-tailed prairie dogs (my own unpublished data). Mothers might conceivably channel milk to only their own offspring in all these cases, but this seems unlikely. Rather, I hypoth-esize that communal nursing occurs not only among black-tailed prairie dogs, but among most species of chipmunks, ground squirrels, and mar-mots as well.

Summary

1. Communal nursing occurs when mothers suckle the offspring of other females. Prairie dogs nurse underground, thereby precluding behavioral observations of communal nursing. I investigate the possibility of communal nursing among prairie dogs by injecting lactating mothers with radionuclides.

2. Of 37 sampled prairie dog juveniles, 25 (68%) received milk from 13 foster mothers (in 8 coteries) via communal nursing. At least one juvenile received milk from a foster mother in 88% of sampled litters.

3. Prairie dog mothers seem to be willing participants in communal nursing.

4. Both killing and communal nursing of nondescendant juvenile kin occur at the study colony. Some females might engage only in

infanticide and others only in communal nursing. Perhaps certain females do both.

5. In proximate terms, communal nursing might result if prairie dog mothers are unable to discriminate between their own and others' emergent juveniles.

6. In ultimate terms, communal nursing might result because it promotes the formation of large multi-litter groupings in which a foster mother's own offspring are safer from predation.

7. Beneficiaries of communal nursing are the offspring of close kin. Thus, elevated inclusive fitness might be another ultimate explanation for communal nursing among prairie dogs.

8. Communal nursing occurs not only among prairie dogs, but perhaps also among most species of chipmunks, ground squirrels, and marmots.

10 Kin Recognition, Social Learning, and Eusociality

Factors That Affect Alloparenting

Individuals of solitary species usually have few opportunities to promote the survivorship and reproduction of nondescendant kin such as siblings, cousins, and nieces and nephews. But such opportunities for *alloparenting* abound for individuals within colonial, philopatric species such as Florida scrub jays, gray-crowned babblers, spotted hyenas, hanuman langurs, and prairie dogs (Kruuk 1972; Hrdy and Hrdy 1976; Woolfenden and Fitzpatrick 1984; Brown 1987).

When the recipient's benefit varies directly with the donor's investment, then individuals should help only their closest kin and should ignore more distant kin (Altmann 1979; Dawkins 1979; Weigel 1981). However, benefits to close kin commonly do not vary directly with investment. Rather, they usually reach a point of diminishing return, after which natural selection will favor individuals that start helping more distant kin. For example, a female mammal probably would increase her inclusive fitness more by providing milk to a starving juvenile full first cousin (for which the coefficient of genetic relatedness, r, = .1250) than to a well-fed juvenile full niece or full nephew (r = .2500). Factors other than kinship and need also influence alloparenting. For example, reciprocity, competition, reproductive value, and the beneficiary's efficiency at using assistance might be important for some animals under certain conditions (Alexander 1974; West-Eberhard 1975; Schulman and Rubenstein 1983; Emlen and Wrege 1988, 1989; Mumme, Koenig, and Ratnieks 1989). These other factors lead to some exceptions (Rabenold 1985; Payne, Payne, and Rowley 1985), but helping nonetheless should usually vary directly with kinship, as it does for animals such as Australian bell miners, pied kingfishers, Galápagos mockingbirds, and Japanese macaques (Kurland 1977; Clarke 1984; Reyer 1984; Curry 1988).

Prairie dogs favor kin over nonkin when giving antipredator calls (chap. 8) and during communal nursing (chap. 9). Do they show similar nepotism in behavioral interactions, as do female yellow-bellied marmots and female

Richardson's, Belding's, and arctic ground squirrels (Michener 1973; Sherman 1980a, 1981a, 1991; McLean 1982; Armitage 1984, 1987b, 1991)? An affirmative answer emerges in this chapter from analyses of 9,555 interactions involving 100 dyads of copulating males and 11,948 interactions involving 182 dyads of females that reared emergent juveniles (see chap. 4 for a discussion of methods). Curiously, however, neither male nor female breeding prairie dogs seem to discriminate between close and more distant kin in behavioral interactions.

Definitions

Kin recognition, kin discrimination, and *kin identification* are synonymous terms for differential treatment of conspecifics on the basis of kinship (Holmes and Sherman 1982, 1983; Waldman, Frumhoff, and Sherman 1988; Reeve 1989; Grafen 1990; Holmes 1990).

Nepotism is the preferential treatment of kin (Alexander 1974; Sherman 1980b), and therefore is a form of kin recognition. Nepotism occurs, for example, when individuals fight with nonkin and cooperate with kin at higher frequencies than expected by chance alone.

Nepotism in Behavioral Interactions

Hostile interactions such as fights, chases, and territorial disputes among prairie dogs are numerous, involve losses of time and energy, and sometimes lead to injury or death (chap. 5). Consequently, interacting more amicably with kin than with nonkin—e.g., by fighting and chasing less and by kissing and allogrooming more—might be an important expression of nepotism among prairie dogs (fig. 10.1).

Unlike females from different coteries, females living in the same coterie are invariably close kin (chaps. 6 and 14). If nepotism is important, then breeding females should interact more amicably with breeding females from the home coterie than with breeding females from other coteries. Figure 10.2a supports this prediction.

Coteries sometimes contain two or more sexually mature males. Like the breeding males of multi-male African lion prides (Bygott, Bertram, and Hanby 1979; Packer and Pusey 1982), the breeding males of multi-male coteries are often close kin (father and son or full brothers, for example; see chap. 6). If nepotism is important, then breeding males should interact more amicably with breeding male kin from the home coterie than with unrelated breeding males from either the home or foreign coteries. Figure 10.2b supports this prediction.

Genetically unrelated breeding males of the *same* multi-male coterie do not interact significantly more amicably than unrelated breeding males from *different* coteries (fig. 10.2b). Nepotism among breeding males thus seems to result primarily from kinship and direct social learning (see below) rather than from merely living together in the same coterie territory.

Fig. 10.1. Amicable interactions involving prairie dogs of the same coterie. *(a)* Three individuals engage in oral sniffing and kissing. *(b)* One prairie dog searches for fleas, lice, and ticks as it allogrooms another. (Photos courtesy of Wind Cave National Park.)

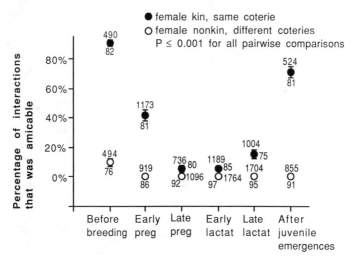

a) female-female nepotism versus competition

b) male-male nepotism versus competition

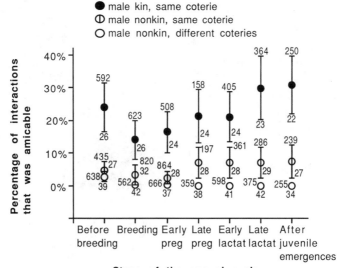

◄ **Fig. 10.2.** Nepotism versus competition for breeding males and breeding females. *(a)* Nepotism versus competition for breeding females. All females included in this graph reared a litter to first juvenile emergence. Nepotism among breeding female kin of the same coterie varies with the stage of the annual cycle ($P < .001$, Kruskal-Wallis analysis of variance), and is minimal when competition is maximal during the stages of late pregnancy and early lactation. *P*-values are from the Mann-Whitney *U* test. Breeding females interact more amicably with kin of the home coterie than with nonkin from other coteries at all stages of the annual cycle. *(b)* Nepotism versus competition for breeding males. All males included in this graph copulated at least once during the breeding season. Nepotism among breeding male kin ($r \geq .0625$) of the same coterie varies with the stage of the annual cycle ($P < .001$, Kruskal-Wallis analysis of variance), and is minimal when competition is maximal during the breeding season. Males interact more amicably with kin of the home coterie than with nonkin ($r < .0625$) from either the home coterie or other coteries at all stages of the annual cycle ($P \leq .079$ for each stage, Mann-Whitney *U* test). Regarding amicability, interactions involving nonkin from the home coterie and nonkin from other coteries are equivalent ($P \geq .085$ for all stages of the annual cycle, Mann-Whitney *U* test). For these graphs, the number above each SE line indicates the number of observed interactions, and the number below each SE line indicates the number of observed dyads.

A similar comparison is not possible for females, for whom kinship and common membership in the same coterie are practically inseparable—so that interactions involving female nonkin from the same coterie almost never occur.

The more than 20,000 interactions summarized in this chapter involve breeding adults of the same sex only, and constitute only a small subset of the interactions observed from 1975 through 1988. Behavioral interactions are common for other social animals, such as acorn woodpeckers, yellow-bellied marmots, and chimpanzees (Armitage 1986; Goodall 1986; Koenig and Mumme 1987), but only rarely at such a high frequency.

Nepotism versus Competition

Nepotism should vary inversely with competition (Hamilton 1964; Alexander 1974). Numerous studies have demonstrated nepotism under conditions of reduced competition (West-Eberhard 1975), and a few others have demonstrated an apparent lack of nepotism under conditions of extreme competition for animals such as black eagles, great egrets, and uterine pronghorn antelopes (O'Gara 1969; Gargett 1978; Mock 1984b, 1985). Rare, however, are studies of marked individuals that track changes in nepotism with changes in competition.

For males of mammalian species in general (Darwin 1871; Trivers 1972; Emlen and Oring 1977; Clutton-Brock 1988b) and for prairie dog males in particular, the major source of competition is estrous females. Competition among breeding males therefore should be most extreme, and nepotism should be least apparent, during the breeding season of February and March when females come into estrus. Conversely, competition among breeding males should taper off, and nepotism should become more evident, after the conclusion of the breeding season. Figure 10.2b supports this prediction.

Although coterie territories usually contain scores of burrows (chap. 6), only a few of these burrows are suitable for rearing juveniles. Further, lactating females regularly try to kill the unweaned offspring of other lactating females of the home coterie (chap. 7). Competition among breeding females therefore should be most extreme—and nepotism should be minimal—during the stages of late pregnancy (when competition for nursery burrows peaks) and early lactation (when infanticide is most likely). Conversely, competition among breeding females should be least extreme, and nepotism most evident, before the breeding season and after first juvenile emergences. Figure 10.2a supports this prediction.

Competition reduces nepotism but does not eliminate it. Even when competition is maximal during the breeding season, males still interact more amicably with kin than with nonkin (fig. 10.2b). Similarly, when competition is maximal during the stages of late pregnancy and early lactation, females still interact more amicably with kin than with nonkin (fig. 10.2a).

Changes in nepotism are sometimes striking. For example, a female usually interacts amicably with female kin of the home coterie until the day after copulation—when all interactions abruptly become hostile (chap. 11). Such hostility usually persists until the first appearance of the female's offspring aboveground—when interactions abruptly become amicable again. Similarly, in a multi-male coterie containing a father and his breeding son, the two males consistently and frequently interacted hostilely during the 1983 breeding season. On the first day after the final copulation in the home coterie territory, however, the father and son suddenly began to interact amicably. Two breeding half brothers in another multi-male coterie in 1987 showed almost precisely the same pattern (see also chap. 6).

The nepotism that is so prominent in intrasexual, intracoterie behavioral interactions following first juvenile emergences always continues until the end of my field season in June. Such conspicuous nepotism probably persists until February of the next breeding season (my own unpublished, sporadic observations from July through January; see also King 1955). Because it only depicts interactions from February through June, figure 10.2 thus underestimates the importance of nepotism in behavioral interactions throughout the year.

Do Prairie Dogs Have Dominance Hierarchies?

One individual is dominant to another when it consistently wins aggressive encounters and has first access to valuable resources such as food and mates (Hausfater 1975; Seyfarth 1976; de Waal 1982; Cowlishaw and

Dunbar 1991). Dominance commonly varies directly with body mass, and often leads to a stable *dominance hierarchy*. For example, a stable dominance hierarchy results if animal A is heavier than and dominant to animals B, C, and D; B is heavier than and dominant to C and D; and C is heavier than and dominant to D (Walters and Seyfarth 1987).

Dominance can occur between members of the same or the opposite sex, but behavioral ecologists usually focus on intrasexual dominance hierarchies. Conspicuous dominance hierarchies with numerous aggressive interactions occur among males for animals such as boat-tailed grackles, mountain sheep, rhesus macaques, and chimpanzees (Geist 1971; Drickamer and Vessey 1973; Bygott 1979; Nishida 1979; Post 1992). Dominance hierarchies are usually more subtle among females, occurring for animals such as red deer, hanuman langurs, savannah baboons, and vervet monkeys (Hrdy and Hrdy 1976; Walters 1980; Clutton-Brock, Guinness, and Albon 1982; Horrocks and Hunte 1983).

Do prairie dogs within a coterie have dominance hierarchies? For males, the answer is affirmative. Specifically, reproductive males—i.e., heavy resident males that have copulated in the current reproductive season or heavy invaders that are likely to copulate in the next breeding season— regularly initiate, and win, aggressive encounters with lighter, nonreproductive males of the home coterie throughout the year. When a coterie contains two breeding males, the heavier one usually dominates the other. When both breeding males of a multi-male coterie are about the same size, however, neither dominates the other. Among nonreproductive yearling males of the same coterie, interactions are almost always amicable, with no evidence of dominance.

Female prairie dogs within a coterie also have a dominance hierarchy. For example, heavy females consistently copulate earlier than lighter females and thereby gain a reproductive advantage (chap. 13). Further, heavy pregnant and lactating females consistently dominate lighter nonreproductive females in behavioral interactions from February (the breeding season) through May (first juvenile emergences). However, a dominance hierarchy is either absent or subtle among nonreproductive females from February through May, and among all females from first juvenile emergences until the following breeding season (see also above and Hoogland 1986).

Do Males Discriminate between Their Own and Other Males' Offspring?

Because of cuckoldry (chap. 12), juveniles in one-male social groups sometimes are not the offspring of the resident breeding male. In theory, cuckolded males perhaps should be able to discriminate between their own and other males' juveniles living in the same territory. In practice, however, evidence for such paternal discrimination under natural conditions is almost nonexistent for animals in general (Bertram 1976; Holmes 1986a,b; Burke et al. 1989; Alexander 1990a, 1991; Sherman 1991) and prairie dogs in particular. However, prairie dog males resemble males of some other animals, such as white-footed and house mice, arctic ground squirrels, and hanuman langurs (Hrdy 1977a,b; McLean 1983; Wolff and Cicirello 1989; Perrigo, Bryant, and vom Saal 1990), in making a simple distinction between (1) juveniles in areas where they copulated—their own potential offspring— as targets for paternal care and (2) juveniles in areas where they did not copulate—other males' offspring—as targets for infanticide (see also chap. 7).

The system just described means that prairie dog males sometimes provide paternal care—through antipredator calling, allogrooming, territorial defense, and protection from infanticide—to other males' offspring. For example, a cuckolded breeding male of a one-male coterie (chap. 12) cares for both his own and other males' offspring. And both breeding males of a multi-male coterie provide paternal care to all the offspring—their own and the other male's—in the home coterie territory (chaps. 6 and 13). Prairie dog males would presumably gain by being able to recognize their own offspring more precisely, so why haven't they evolved a better mechanism for doing so? One deterrent to such a mechanism is that the cost to a cuckolded male of mistakenly discriminating against his own offspring (by infanticide, for example) would usually far outweigh the cost of caring for other males' offspring (Hrdy 1979; Jeppsson 1986).

Perhaps prairie dog males resemble dunnock males in having a conflict of interest with females and offspring regarding paternal recognition (Davies et al. 1992; Davies 1992; see also Beecher 1988). For example, a juvenile in a multi-male coterie that conceals its paternity receives paternal care from both males. Both the juvenile and its mother gain from such concealment, but the male that did not sire the juvenile loses. Perhaps the evolutionary resolution to this intersexual conflict of interest is the male's unsophisticated ability to make the simple distinction between juveniles in coterie territories where he has copulated and juveniles in coterie territories where he has not.

Do Prairie Dogs Interact More Amicably with Close Kin Than with More Distant Kin?

Prairie dogs discriminate between kin and nonkin during behavioral interactions (see fig. 10.2). Do they go one step further and discriminate between close kin and more distant kin, thereby showing *differential nepotism* or *discriminative nepotism* (Alexander 1979, 1990a; see also Hamilton 1975 and Crozier 1987)? Evidently not. Figure 10.3a shows that amicability of interactions among breeding females does not vary systematically with kinship at any stage of the annual cycle. Thus, prairie dog females show *nondiscriminative nepotism* (Alexander 1979), interacting

Fig. 10.3. Nepotism versus the coefficient of genetic relatedness *(r)* for breeding females and males. *(a)* Nepotism versus kinship for breeding females at different stages of the annual cycle. All females included in this graph reared a litter to first juvenile emergence. *P*-values are from the Kruskal-Wallis analysis of variance. Breeding females do not consistently interact more amicably with female close kin than with more distant kin. *(b)* Nepotism versus kinship for breeding males at different stages of the annual cycle. All males included in this graph copulated at least once during the breeding season. Breeding males interact with distant kin (.0025 > *r* ≥ .0625) as though they are unrelated at all stages of the annual cycle. Further, breeding males do not consistently interact more amicably with fathers, sons, and full brothers (*r* = .5000) than with half brothers (*r* = .2500) (*P* ≥ .293 for all stages of the annual cycle, Mann-Whitney *U* test). For these graphs, the numbers above each SE line indicate the number of interactions and the number of dyads observed.

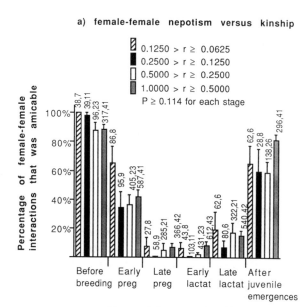

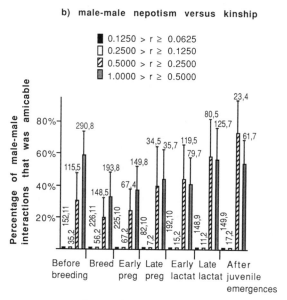

just as amicably with more distant kin, such as female full and half first cousins, as with daughters and full sisters.

Patterns of nepotism versus kinship are different for males (fig. 10.3b). Breeding males in the same coterie territory interact amicably only with close kin—sons, fathers, and full and half brothers ($r \geq .2500$)—*whom they have learned to recognize via direct social learning* (see below). Interactions with more distant kin ($.2500 > r > 0$) are consistently hostile and resemble interactions with nonkin. Among those dyads showing amicability, closer kin (fathers and sons, $N = 4$ dyads, and full brothers, $N = 4$ dyads) do not systematically interact more amicably than more distant kin (half brothers, $N = 5$ dyads) at any stage of the annual cycle.

Nepotism versus Kinship in Other Contexts

Prairie dogs do not discriminate between close and distant kin in behavioral interactions. Do they show such discrimination in other contexts? Apparently not. For example, individuals with only distant kin within earshot are just as likely to give antipredator calls as are individuals with closer kin nearby (chap. 8). Also, prairie dog females seem just as likely to band with distant kin as with closer kin in the fission of large coteries (chap. 6). Further, infanticidal mothers are just as likely to kill the offspring of close kin as the offspring of more distant kin (chap. 7). Finally, mothers do not preferentially suckle the offspring of close kin when presented with a choice of foster offspring (chap. 9).

I do not conclude here or elsewhere that prairie dogs *cannot* discriminate among various classes of kin, but only that such discriminative nepotism is not evident from behavioral observations under natural conditions.

Kin Recognition and Direct Social Learning

Behavioral ecologists universally agree that kinship is paramount in the evolution of social systems, but they disagree about the mechanisms by which individuals recognize kin. For example, Dawkins (1982), Holmes (1986a,b, 1988; Holmes and Sherman 1982, 1983), Sherman (1991; Lacy and Sherman 1983; Sherman and Holmes 1985), Hepper (1986), and Hamilton (1987) argue that individuals sometimes use their own phenotypes as reference and thereby can recognize kin with whom they have not previously associated. Animals that might show such kin recognition via self-referential matching of phenotypes include honeybees (Getz and Smith 1983, 1986; Evers and Seeley 1986; Visscher 1986), sweat bees (Greenberg 1979; Buckle and Greenberg 1981), paper wasps (Pfennig, Reeve, and Shellman 1983; Pfennig et al. 1983), white-footed and house mice (Grau 1982; Kareem and Barnard 1982; Manning, Wakeland, and Potts 1992) and arctic, Richardson's, and Belding's ground squirrels (Davis 1982b; Holmes and Sherman 1982, 1983; Holmes 1986a,b; Schwagmeyer 1988a). However, Alexander (1990a, 1991) argues that none of these studies unambiguously rules out social learning as the explanation for the observed results.

Social learning means that an individual "evolves to learn who its actual associates are and to remember them, and that the learning evolves because associates in a particular stage and circumstance have during evolution represented kin of the kind appropriate to whatever is learned or done as a result of the learning" (Alexander 1991, 388; see also Bekoff 1978, 1981). Social learning can be either direct or mediated (Alexander 1979, 1990a, 1991; Sherman and Holmes 1985). In *direct social learning,* individuals learn to recognize kin via direct behavioral interactions with those kin. Animals that unambiguously show the importance of direct social learning for kin recognition include spiny mice (Porter, Wyrick, and Pankey 1978; Porter, Tepper, and White 1981), gray-tailed voles (Boyd and Blaustein 1985), thirteen-lined ground squirrels (Holmes 1984b), and humans (Alexander 1979, 1990a). In conjunction with possible self-referential matching of phenotypes for kin recognition, direct social learning is also important for Richardson's, Belding's, and arctic ground squirrels (Sheppard and Yoshida 1971; Michener 1974; Davis 1982b; Holmes and Sherman 1982, 1983; Holmes 1986a,b). In *mediated social learning,* individuals learn to recognize unfamiliar kin because of the presence of a third conspecific who is genetically related to both and familiar with both via direct social learning. Mediated social learning is difficult to document, with equivocal examples coming from animals such as house mice, Belding's ground squirrels, and rhesus macaques (Labov 1980; Berenstain, Rodman, and Smith 1981; Sherman 1980a; Alexander 1991).

Prairie dogs discriminate between kin and nonkin in numerous contexts (see above and chaps. 8, 9, and 14). Five lines of evidence summarized here indicate that such kin recognition results *primarily from direct social learning within the home coterie territory* rather than from self-referential matching of phenotypes. However, I emphasize that I have not performed the careful experiments that would be necessary to exclude the possible importance of self-referential matching of phenotypes to kin recognition among prairie dogs.

Experiments Involving the Transfer of Juveniles

Perhaps the best evidence of the importance of direct social learning to kin recognition among prairie dogs comes from a series of transfer experiments. Specifically, I remove single juveniles (*foster juveniles*) from their own litters and place them in different recipient litters. Recipient litters are always in a different, distant coterie territory, and usually in a different ward (subcolony; see chap. 2) as well. Adults and yearlings within the recipient coterie territory accept these foster juveniles if they have recently first emerged from their natal burrows. However, coterie members reject introduced foster juveniles that have been aboveground for a month or more (table 10.1). Thus, recognition of kin evidently depends on familiarity with juveniles during their first month aboveground (i.e., direct social learning) rather than on self-referential matching of phenotypes.

Interesting, indeed, would be experiments that remove juveniles from the natal coterie territory upon their first emergence, retain them in another coterie territory for a month or so, and then reintroduce them into the natal coterie territory. If direct social learning during the first weeks aboveground is critical, as suggested here, then coterie members should reject the reintroduced juvenile kin.

Why the change in behavior of parents toward juveniles that have been aboveground for about a month (table 10.1)? For the first month or so following first emergence, prairie dog juveniles stay in the central portion of the home coterie territory. Thereafter, however, juveniles begin to approach the territory boundary and to wander into adjacent coterie territories (see also King 1955). This wandering coincides precisely with the time when prairie dogs begin to discriminate between juvenile members

Table 10.1. Acceptance or Rejection of Juvenile Transfers at Different Stages

Approximate age of juvenile transfers	Approximate age of juveniles in recipient (foster) coterie territory	Number of transfers	Number of definite acceptances	Number of possible rejections	Number of definite rejections
At first emergence	Several days before first emergence	15	12	3	0
At first emergence	At first emergence	16	15	1	0
1 month after first emergence	1 month after first emergence	22	11	0	11
2 months after first emergence	2 months after first emergence	15	1	0	14
5 months after first emergence	5 months after first emergence	6	1	0	5

Note: I transferred single juveniles into distant coterie territories that usually were in a different ward. Scorings are as follows: Acceptance if the juvenile transfer was still in the recipient coterie territory for at least 9 days following the transfer; definite rejection if the transfer disappeared within 9 days; and possible rejection if the transfer was still alive but in a territory other than the recipient coterie territory at the end of 9 days. Young juveniles are more likely than older juveniles to be accepted into foster coterie territories ($P < .001$, chi-square analysis, df = 4; for this analysis, I have ignored possible rejections and have considered only definite acceptances and definite rejections).

of the home coterie and juveniles of other coteries. Prairie dogs thus have an unusual system of kin recognition. Parents do not seem to discriminate between their own and others' recently emerged juveniles within the home coterie territory, even though mixing of juveniles from different litters is immediate, extensive, and potentially costly (chaps. 5 and 9). However, just when juveniles from other coteries start to invade the home coterie territory, adults and yearlings begin to discriminate between resident, juvenile kin and invading, unrelated (or only distantly related) juveniles. The result is that prairie dogs discriminate only between juveniles born in the home coterie territory (i.e., kin at some level) and juveniles born in other coterie territories (i.e., nonkin). Because prairie dogs discriminate only between kin and nonkin among emergent juveniles, should we be surprised that they discriminate only between kin and nonkin among yearlings and adults as well?

Lack of Nepotism among Paternal Half Sisters Living in Adjacent Coterie Territories

Breeding males that sire daughters in one coterie territory sometimes transfer to an adjacent coterie territory and sire daughters there as well (chaps. 14 and 16). If self-referential matching of phenotypes occurs, then paternal half sisters living in adjacent coterie territories perhaps should recognize each other and interact amicably. If direct social learning of others' phenotypes is crucial, however, then (unrecognized) paternal half sisters in adjacent coterie territories should interact aggressively because they were separated during the critical learning period. Behavioral obser-vations once again indicate the greater importance of direct social learning. Specifically, none of the twenty pairs of paternal half sisters in adjacent coterie territories have shown any evidence of kin discrimination. Rather, paternal half sisters living in different coterie territories always interact aggressively, as though genetically unrelated.

Extreme Inbreeding versus Common Rearing

Despite several mechanisms for avoiding extreme inbreeding, sexually active close kin of the opposite sex sometimes end up together in the same coterie territory (chap. 14). When such potential mates have *not* lived together in the same coterie territory when one or both first appeared aboveground as a juvenile, they routinely copulate. When they *have* lived together for one or the other's first emergence, however, they avoid copulation. This pattern is consistent with the notion that prairie dogs require direct social learning of kin as juveniles for later avoidance of extreme inbreeding. If self-referential matching of phenotypes occurs, on the other hand, then avoidance of inbreeding should be possible without shared rearing. Prairie dogs thus resemble humans (Westermarck 1921, 1934a,b; Wolf 1966, 1968, 1970; Shepher 1978, 1983; Alexander 1979,

1990a) in evidently requiring direct social learning for the avoidance of extreme inbreeding.

Infanticide by Invading Young Males

If self-referential matching of phenotypes or mediated social learning occurs among prairie dogs, then a young male that invades a coterie territory dominated by his father probably should recognize and interact amicably with his juvenile kin (i.e., his paternal half siblings) there. If direct social learning is critical, however, then invading young males probably should interact aggressively with their (unrecognizable) paternal half siblings. The immediate, predictable killing of paternal half siblings by invading young males (chap. 7) indicates the greater importance of direct social learning.

If a young male invades a new coterie territory containing a genetically unrelated breeding male before the first emergences of juveniles there, then opportunities exist for direct social learning upon the juvenile emergences— so that the invader might learn to regard, erroneously, the emergent, unrelated juveniles as his kin. Interestingly, however, males that invade before first juvenile emergences are infanticidal, killing the juvenile nonkin either before or after their first emergence (chap. 7). Invading males evidently do not learn to regard juveniles in the new breeding coterie territory as kin unless they have copulated, and thus possibly sired offspring, there.

Failure of Cuckolded Males to Recognize Offspring

If self-referential matching of phenotypes occurs, then cuckolded prairie dog males perhaps should be able to recognize, and preferentially care for, their own offspring. As noted above, however, such recognition evidently does not occur—presumably because direct social learning is more important than self-referential matching of phenotypes for kin recognition among prairie dogs.

Why Don't Prairie Dogs Discriminate between Close Kin and More Distant Kin?

Throughout this book I commonly say for the sake of abbreviation and convenience that prairie dogs discriminate between kin and nonkin. More precisely, I should say that prairie dogs discriminate between individuals of the home coterie with whom they have associated shortly after one or the other's first emergence from the natal burrow, and all other individuals. The justification for the abbreviation, of course, is that the former individuals are almost invariably kin, while the latter individuals are either nonkin or distant kin (chaps. 14 and 16). Nepotism and kin discrimination within coteries thus seem to depend entirely on direct social learning.

The prairie dog mechanism for learning to recognize kin has a serious potential flaw. Specifically, juveniles from one coterie territory could transfer to another territory shortly after first emergence—i.e., during the critical period of direct social learning—and gain lifetime acceptance there by nonkin. Such deceptions sometimes occur, but are exceedingly rare (chap. 14).

Individuals might recognize different individuals but still be unable to discriminate among different classes of kin. For example, individuals might recognize and interact amicably with certain other individuals—large, dominant ones, perhaps—regardless of kinship. I have not investigated this possibility for prairie dogs.

The nondiscriminatory aspect of kin recognition among prairie dogs seems puzzling. Juveniles from different litters of the same coterie territory get thoroughly mixed up shortly after first emergences from their natal burrows (chaps. 5 and 9). Consequently, the costs to a juvenile of assessing its precise kinship to a nonlittermate juvenile of the natal coterie territory might exceed the possible benefits. If so, then differential nepotism among nonlittermate juveniles of the home coterie territory will not evolve. However, prairie dog mothers keep their litters isolated in a separate home nursery burrow for approximately 6 weeks after parturition, before first juvenile emergences. Surely this prolonged association is sufficient for mothers to learn to recognize their offspring and for offspring to learn to recognize their mother and littermate siblings, who usually will be full siblings due to the rarity of multiple paternity (chap. 12). So why don't prairie dogs show discriminative nepotism and distinguish between at least two categories of kin: mothers, offspring, and littermate siblings ($r \geq .5000$) versus other, more distant kin of the home coterie ($.5000 > r > 0$)?

In one-male coterie territories, the resident breeding male usually sires all litters born there (chap. 12). Consequently, all nonlittermate juveniles in one-male coteries—and many nonlittermate juveniles in multi-male coteries as well (chap. 12)—are usually paternal half siblings. Further, breeding females in a coterie often are full sisters or mothers and daughters (chaps. 6, 14, and 16), so that nonlittermate juveniles in the same coterie are commonly either full first cousins or half aunt-half niece as well via their mothers. Consequently, nonlittermate juveniles in the same coterie sometimes share a coefficient of genetic relatedness as high as $.3750$ ($.2500$ via the common father $+ .1250$ via the genetically related mothers)—which does not greatly differ from the coefficient of $.5000$ between mothers and offspring and between full siblings. Might this factor explain why natural selection does not seem to have favored discriminatory nepotism among prairie dogs? Evidently not. Figure 10.4 shows great variation in the kinship among members of the same home coterie, with only a small percentage having a coefficient of genetic relatedness equal to $.3750$. So why not natural selection for prairie dogs that interact more amicably with (easily learned?) mothers, offspring, and full siblings than with other, more distant kin of the home coterie? The lack of at least two levels of nepotism within the home coterie ($r \geq .5000$ versus $.5000 > r > 0$) remains puzzling.

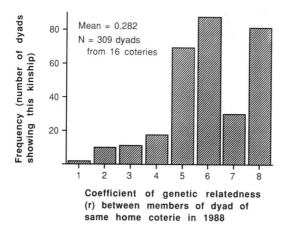

a) kinships among members
of same home coterie

1: 0.0156 ≥ r ≥ 0.0000
2: 0.0313 > r ≥ 0.0156
3: 0.0625 > r ≥ 0.0313
4: 0.1250 > r ≥ 0.0625
5: 0.2500 > r ≥ 0.1250
6: 0.3750 > r ≥ 0.2500
7: 0.5000 > r ≥ 0.3750
8: 1.0000 > r ≥ 0.5000

Mean = 0.282
N = 309 dyads
from 16 coteries

Frequency (number of dyads showing this kinship)

Coefficient of genetic relatedness
(r) between members of dyad of
same home coterie in 1988

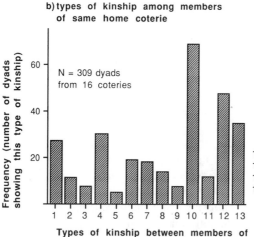

b) types of kinship among members
of same home coterie

N = 309 dyads
from 16 coteries

Frequency (number of dyads showing this type of kinship)

Types of kinship between members of
dyad of same home coterie in 1988

1: more distant kin
2: full first cousins once removed
3: half first cousins
4: full first cousins
5: full great aunt-full great niece
   or full great nephew
6: half uncle-half niece
   or half nephew
7: half aunt-half niece
   or half nephew
8: full aunt-full niece
   or full nephew
9: grandmother-grandoffspring
10: paternal half siblings
11: maternal half siblings
12: full siblings
13: mother-offspring

Fig. 10.4. Kinships within the home coterie. *(a)* Coefficient of genetic relatedness *(r)* between members of dyads consisting of coterie members in 1988. *(b)* Types of kinship between members of dyads consisting of coterie members in 1988. When two prairie dogs have more than one common ancestor, I depict the closer kinship in *(b)*. For example, if two prairie dogs have the same father and are half first cousins via another common ancestor, then I depict them in *(b)* as paternal half siblings; for *(a)*, I have computed a cumulative coefficient of genetic relatedness by adding coefficients from all common ancestors. For "more distant kin," *r* < .0625. For both graphs, dyads include yearling males and both adult and yearling females within the home coterie. Dyads do not include breeding males, which come from other coteries and are unrelated or only distantly related to members of their breeding coteries (until they sire offspring there). Including dyads with breeding males obviously would lower the mean kinship values.

Cooperative Breeding and Eusociality

Cooperative breeding—also known as communal breeding—occurs when breeding or nonbreeding individuals help conspecifics rear offspring, as for animals such as groove-billed anis, dwarf and banded mongooses, chimpanzees, and silverbacked and golden jackals (Brown 1978; Goodall 1986; Moehlman 1983, 1986; Rood 1986; Emlen 1991). A helper—also known as a worker, alloparent, or "auntie"—within a cooperatively breeding species is "an individual that performs parent-like behavior toward young that are not genetically its own offspring" (Brown 1987). Helping behaviors include nestbuilding, feeding of juveniles or mothers, allogrooming, antipredator calls, harassment of predators, incubation, territorial defense, guarding juveniles while the mother is away, and communal nursing (Brown 1978; Malcolm and Marten 1982; Michener and Murie 1983; Woodroffe 1993). The number and frequency of helping behaviors necessary for classification of a species as cooperatively breeding is somewhat arbitrary (Brown 1978; Hoogland 1983a).

Despite intense competition within coteries, prairie dogs are legitimate cooperative breeders (but see Michener and Murie 1983 versus Hoogland 1983a). Specifically, individuals—males and females, yearlings and adults, breeders and nonbreeders—help parents of the home coterie via scanning for predators, antipredator calling, mobbing of small predators, allogrooming, and defense of the home territory. Lactating females also help via the suckling of foster offspring.

Eusociality is a specialized type of cooperative breeding found in certain insects (Wilson 1971; Aoki 1982; Ito 1989; Crespi 1992; Kent and Simpson 1992) and the naked mole rat (Jarvis 1981; Lacey and Sherman 1991). Eusociality has three prerequisites: (1) overlapping generations, (2) production of offspring by only one or a few individuals within the group, and (3) temporarily or permanently sterile helpers (Michener 1969; Wilson 1975; Andersson 1984b; Alexander, Noonan, and Crespi 1991). Many animals satisfy the first two prerequisites. The third is plainly the most problematic in any attempt to designate a species as eusocial (Lacey and Sherman 1991; Sherman et al. 1994).

Obligate, or *physiological,* sterility means that an individual cannot produce offspring under any circumstances. *Sociological,* or *psychological,* sterility results when physiologically competent individuals temporarily or permanently do not produce offspring for some reason. Absolute physiological sterility is rare, but sociological sterility is common among social animals. If sociological sterility satisfies the third prerequisite for eusociality, then eusociality is commonplace (Alexander, Noonan, and Crespi 1991; Lacey and Sherman 1991).

Presence or absence of *evolutionary design* (Williams 1966a, 1992) perhaps dichotomizes sterility in a more meaningful way. Workers within colonies of mound-building termites and fungus ants, for example, show unmistakable morphological and behavioral evidence of design for sterility, with only a minute probability of personal reproduction (Wilson 1971; Hölldobler and Wilson 1991). By contrast, helpers of cooperatively breeding animals such as splendid fairy-wrens, Florida scrub jays, stripe-backed wrens, and dwarf mongooses show little evidence of design for sterility and quickly reproduce when given the opportunity (Woolfenden and Fitzpatrick 1984; Rood 1986; Rabenold 1990; Rowley and Russell 1990; Creel and Creel 1991). If unambiguous evolutionary design for sterility is necessary to satisfy the third prerequisite of eusociality, then eusociality probably occurs only among certain social insects.

Of the three prerequisites for eusociality, prairie dogs easily satisfy the first two. First, nonbreeding male and female prairie dogs live with their parents and invariably help rear nondescendant juvenile kin within the natal coterie territory (chaps. 14 and 16). Second, in 41% of coteries (109/265), only one female rears emergent juveniles. In another 20% of coteries (52/265), only two females rear emergent juveniles (fig. 10.5). Regarding the third prerequisite, sociological sterility is common among prairie dog females: each year about half of the adult females help without rearing their own litters (chap. 7), and more than 50% of females do nothing but help for their entire lives (chap. 16). However, prairie dogs show little evolutionary design for sterility. For example, almost all unsuccessful adult females and many unsuccessful yearling females copulate, give birth, and

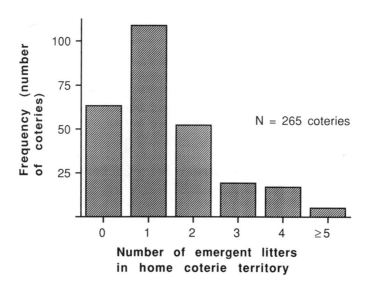

Fig. 10.5. Number of emergent litters per coterie territory. Notice here that 61% of coteries (161/265) produced only one or two emergent litters.

try to rear offspring in the years when they help (chaps. 7, 11, and 16). Helping is thus secondary to personal reproduction—helpers are simply making the best of a bad deal. Further, most surviving males and females who help in one year rear their own offspring in later years (chap. 16). Prairie dogs are unequivocally cooperative breeders, but to lump them with eusocial species such as fungus ants and mound-building termites seems inappropriate.

Summary

1. Hostile prairie dog interactions include fights, chases, and territorial disputes. Amicable prairie dog interactions include allogrooming, kissing, playing, and anal sniffing.

2. When dealing with other breeding individuals of the same sex, breeding male and female prairie dogs interact more amicably with kin than with nonkin.

3. Nepotism in male-male and female-female interactions involving breeding prairie dogs varies inversely with competition for both sexes. Specifically, same-sex nepotism is minimal when the major sources of competition—estrous females for breeding males, nursery burrows and possible benefits from infanticide for breeding females—are maximal.

4. Nepotism in behavioral interactions among reproductively successful females involves not only mothers and daughters and full and half sisters, but also extends to more distant kin such as half aunts, half nieces, and full and half first cousins. Interestingly, however, breeding females do not interact more amicably with breeding female close kin than with more distant breeding female kin within the home coterie territory. Nepotism among breeding females is thus nondiscriminatory.

5. Nepotism in behavioral interactions among copulating males occurs between fathers and sons and between full and half brothers, but does not extend to more distant kin such as full and half first cousins ($r < .2500$). Further, breeding males do not interact more amicably with breeding fathers, sons, and full brothers ($r = .5000$) than with breeding half brothers ($r = .2500$).

6. Patterns of antipredator calling, communal nursing, and infanticide also imply nondiscriminatory nepotism for male and female prairie dogs.

7. Nepotism in same-sex dyads of breeding kin is only evident when members of the dyad have lived together during one or the other's first juvenile emergence. This suggests a critical period for direct social learning of 3 to 4 weeks after first emergence. Close kin

reared apart—paternal half sisters sired in adjacent coterie territories by the same male, for example—show no evidence of nepotism.

8. Prairie dogs are cooperative breeders with extensive overlap of generations. Further, in 61% of coteries, only one or two females produce emergent juveniles, with the aid of helpers. These trends suggest eusociality. However, prairie dogs show no evolutionary design for sterility. For example, unsuccessful adult females who help almost always copulate, give birth, and try to rear their own offspring. Categorization of prairie dogs as eusocial thus seems inappropriate.

11 Behavioral Observations of Estrus and Copulations

Especially for males, colonies sometimes offer superb opportunities for reproductive success. Documenting male and female reproductive success is therefore a natural focus of my research. What a disappointment to learn that black-tailed prairie dogs copulate underground! How might I overcome this monumental obstacle and figure out the black-tail mating system?

Luckily for me, seven diagnostic aboveground behaviors couple with estrus and underground copulations of prairie dog females. Consequently, field assistants and I are able to document estrus and copulation(s) for over 90% of the females at the study colony each year ($N = 770$ detected copulations by 557 females from 1978 through 1988).

The first part of this chapter reports the discovery that copulations occur underground. The second part describes the seven diagnostic behaviors associated with underground copulations, and the third part documents their accuracy for pinpointing estrus and copulation.

Discovery That Copulations Occur Underground

On 11 March 1978, I had already been at Wind Cave National Park for almost a month in my first attempt to observe black-tail copulations. By then the breeding season should have been more than half over, according to earlier reports (King 1955; Pfeiffer 1972). Yet I had not yet seen a single aboveground copulation! Late in the day, however, female-62 was constantly fighting and chasing with the single breeding male, male-17, in her coterie. Further, the pair remained aboveground long after all other colony residents had submerged for the night. But they never copulated aboveground.

On 12 March 1978 I watched female-62 closely. Male-17 no longer showed any interest in her, and female-62's behavior was radically different. She began acting aggressively toward male-17 and toward the other adult female in her home coterie, and she began to collect mouthfuls of dry grass for an underground nest. Female-62 was acting maternally! Begrudgingly, I conceded that black-tails must copulate underground. Discouragement followed. How was I going to decipher the black-tail mating system if I could not see copulations? Before throwing in the towel, I decided to focus on females that acted the way female-62 did on 11 March 1978. Perhaps I would be able to identify some diagnostic signs associated with underground copulations.

My hunch was correct. Over the next 2 weeks and in later years I discovered seven diagnostic behaviors that signal underground copulations: the underground consortship itself, attention directed toward an estrous female by the breeding male, self-licking of genitals, nestbuilding by the breeding male, the mating call, late final submergence of the estrous female, and unusual behaviors of the resident breeding male or estrous female.

Except for certain animals such hanuman langurs, vervet monkeys, pygmy chimpanzees, and humans, mammalian females usually copulate only during a brief period called *estrus* or *heat* (Hrdy 1977b; Alexander and Noonan 1979; Thompson-Handler, Malenky, and Badrian 1984; Andelman 1987). Usually commencing just before fertilization is possible, estrus typically starts shortly before, and ends shortly after, ovulation (Butler 1974; Beach 1976).

Copulation is the coupling of male and female genitalia, and *insemination* is the deposition of sperm into the female reproductive tract (Eberhard 1985). Copulation does not always involve insemination, and insemination does not always lead to fertilization (Dewsbury 1984; Eberhard 1985). A *breeding individual* is one that copulates—or that is sexually mature and capable of copulating (see below)—in the year of investigation.

Results described in this chapter for black-tailed prairie dogs might be useful for other sciurid species that usually copulate underground, such as Alaska and black-capped marmots and Uinta, Columbian, California, arctic, rock, and Richardson's ground squirrels (Fitch 1948; Kapitonov 1960; Rausch and Rausch 1971; Slade and Balph 1974; Murie and McLean 1980; Michener 1985; Ortega 1990). For example, Sherman (1989) uses these same methods to document underground copulations of Idaho ground squirrels. And I have been using them since 1989 to document underground copulations of Gunnison's prairie dogs.

Diagnostic Behaviors Associated with Underground Copulations

The Underground Consortship

My first objective was to determine how often a female and a breeding male submerge together into the same burrow after first emerging in the morning. To do this, I make a *missing male list* (MML) every 20 minutes. Longer intervals would mean that I am not checking individual males often enough, and shorter intervals would leave too little time for watching other behaviors. The objective is to locate every breeding male at the 20-minute mark. If all males are foraging aboveground, I assume that an underground copulation cannot be occurring. If a breeding male is missing, I then search for all breeding females in his coterie territory. If a female is also missing, I suspect an underground copulation. Between MMLs I focus on the breeding males. I watch burrow entrances carefully when a male and a female are missing in the same MML to see if they emerge together.

My general impression before MMLs was that prairie dogs of both sexes commonly enter and exit burrows in February and March. If so, then tracking of individuals would be a nightmare. Unable to think of a better alternative, I gave MMLs a try. I immediately realized that my pre-MML impression was dead wrong. Specifically, individuals almost never submerge into a burrow after waking up except during inclement weather, when a predator charges too close, when taking nest material underground, or when retiring for the night. The co-submergence of a male and female— here termed an *underground consortship*—is even rarer, unless the female shows one or more of the signs of estrus discussed below. Tracking underground consortships thus provides a method for detecting prairie dog copulations.

For approximately 50% of underground consortships, I see both the submergence and the emergence of the copulating pair and thus know the exact duration of the consortship. For the other 50% of consortships, I see either the submergence or the emergence of the pair, but not both. For these latter cases, my frequent scannings allow me to accurately estimate within 3 or 4 minutes the duration of the underground consortship.

At the start of each breeding season, I assume that any male who is at least 2 years old is capable of copulating, and I therefore include all adult males in MMLs. I strongly suspect that certain adult males with neither descended testes nor a pigmented scrotum are incapable of copulation (chap. 4), but I include them in MMLs anyway. Yearling males occasionally show evidence of sexual maturity either from behavioral observations or by having a pigmented scrotum with descended testes. I include these yearling males in MMLs, of course.

Estrous females usually have numerous underground consortships (fig. 11.1a). For example, female-70 kept me busy in 1979 when she had thirty-nine separate underground consortships with three different males! The time underground for a consorting pair ranges from 15 seconds—by convention, this is the shortest time that I record—to the entire day (see below). The mean ± SD length (minutes) of an underground consortship is 22.2 ± 38.0 ($N = 445$ estrous females, with a single mean used for each estrous female's set of consortships; I have excluded all-day consortships for the calculation of this mean).

a) number of underground consortships

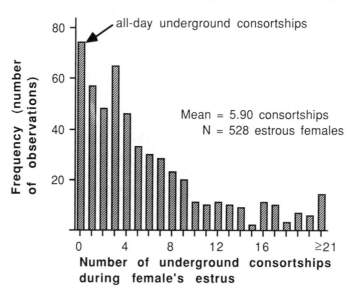

all-day underground consortships

Mean = 5.90 consortships
N = 528 estrous females

Number of underground consortships
during female's estrus

b) number of burrow entrances used
for underground consortships

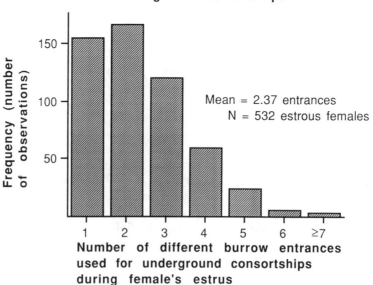

Mean = 2.37 entrances
N = 532 estrous females

Number of different burrow entrances
used for underground consortships
during female's estrus

◀ **Fig. 11.1.** Number of underground consortships and number of burrow entrances used by estrous females. *(a)* Number of underground consortships during a female's estrus. When a female stays underground all day with a breeding male (all-day consortship; see text), I score her number of underground consortships as 0—so that all-day consortships are easily separable from estrous periods that include only one underground consortship but which show diagnostic aboveground behaviors. *(b)* Number of different burrow entrances used for underground consortships during a female's estrus. When the same burrow has multiple entrances, I score each entrance separately.

Usually the breeding male and female are alone during a consortship, but occasionally other coterie members join them underground. Sometimes the consorting male and female seem unfazed by visitors, but other times they make deliberate attempts to avoid visitors and to escape, unnoticed and alone, into a burrow.

Most estrous females restrict their underground consortships to only a few burrow entrances (fig. 11.1b), but one female used nine different entrances. Not surprisingly, the number of burrow entrances used varies directly with the number of underground consortships ($P < .001$, Spearman rank correlation test).

The first underground consortship sometimes occurs within minutes after a female first appears aboveground in the morning. More commonly, however, the first and later underground consortships occur in late morning or afternoon (fig. 11.2). Afternoon copulations are also the rule for Belding's and Idaho ground squirrels (Hanken and Sherman 1981; Sherman 1989), and also for white-tailed and Gunnison's prairie dogs (my own unpublished data). Estrous prairie dog females are sexually receptive for one day only.

Usually the male aggressively chases the estrous female into a burrow and then follows her down for the underground consortship. Sometimes, however, the estrous female solicits the male by ambling up to him, presenting her rear end for sniffing, then trotting off into a burrow with the male following. Rarely, (<1% of consortships) the male precedes the female underground.

Prior to insemination, a breeding male initiates and dominates most behavioral interactions with the estrous female. If the female copulates with only one male, the usual sequence goes something like this: The breeding male's dominance continues until a certain underground consortship, when insemination presumably occurs. I call this the *critical underground consortship*—hereafter abbreviated CUC. After the CUC, the estrous female's behavior toward the male suddenly and dramatically changes. She no longer allows anal sniffing, and usually initiates a fight when the male comes too close. The copulating male's behavior also changes after the CUC, from sexual interest (sniffing and short underground consortships) to *guarding.* Guarding males remain close at the female's side, ready to chase away other breeding males from the home

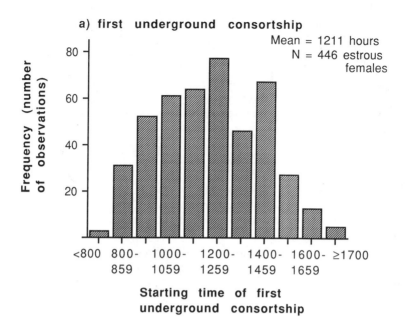

a) first underground consortship

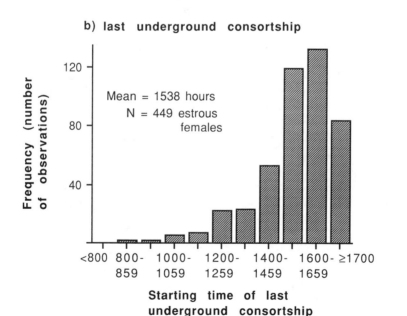

b) last underground consortship

c) critical underground consortship

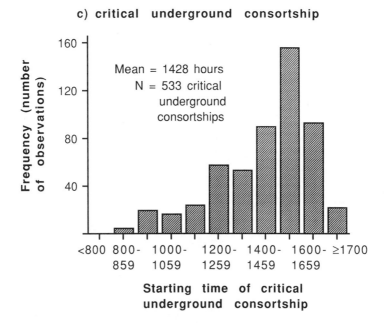

◀ ▲ **Fig. 11.2.** Time of day for *(a)* first underground consortship, *(b)* last underground consortship, and *(c)* critical underground consortship (CUC), when insemination occurs. Each estrous female can have only one first and only one last underground consortship, but she can have two or three critical underground consortships if she receives sperm from two or three different males.

or adjacent coteries (fig. 11.3a). Sometimes a guarding male chases the estrous female into a burrow and coerces her to remain there by perching on the burrow mound (fig. 11.3b). Like guarding in other animals, such as mountain cavies, wild guinea pigs, and Idaho ground squirrels (Rood 1972; Sherman 1989), guarding by prairie dog males thus deters copulations with other males.

Guarding is difficult to quantify, but I nonetheless have uncovered three factors that affect its expression. First, when the CUC occurs *late* in the day (e.g., after about 1500), the copulating prairie dog male usually guards the estrous female until the end of the day and then submerges with her into the same burrow for the night. When the CUC occurs *early* in the day (e.g., before about 1200), however, the male sometimes abandons guarding later in the day—thus giving the female an easy opportunity to copulate with a second male. Second, a breeding male shortens his guarding of one estrous female after copulating with her when a second female in the home coterie territory is in estrus at the same time. Such shortening makes it easier for the male to copulate with the second female as well, before she can be monopolized by some other male. Guarding is thus a

Fig. 11.3. Guarding of estrous female by breeding male. After inseminating a female, a breeding male tries to prevent copulations with other males. *(a)* One way to guard is to keep other males away. Here male-07 has a territorial dispute with male-24; the female watches from burrow entrance-20. *(b)* Another way to guard is to sequester the estrous female in a burrow. Here male-05 uses his body to block the exit of a female from burrow entrance-40. (Photos by John L. Hoogland.)

flexible male response that is sensitive to, and secondary to, the opportunity for copulations with additional females. Third, when a prairie dog female copulates with only one male, that male's confidence of paternity for the resulting litter is 100%. But sometimes a female copulates with two, three, or even four males (chap. 12), so that confidence of paternity for each copulating male is lower than 100%. For each male that copulates with a female, the confidence of paternity probably varies inversely with the total number of males that copulate with that female. For example, the first male's confidence of paternity drops from 100% to perhaps 50% if the female copulates with a second male. But the first and second male's confidence of paternity might drop from 50% to 33% if the female copulates with a third male. Consequently, the first male has proportionately more to lose, genetically, than the second and third males if the female copulates with an additional male. Probably for this reason, males that copulate first predictably guard females longer and more assiduously than do males that copulate second or third. Perhaps because of this better guarding, first-copulating males are more likely than second- and third-copulating males to sire offspring (chap. 13).

Besides the associated changes in male and female behavior, the CUC is unique in two other ways. First, the CUC is usually either the ultimate or penultimate underground consortship of the day for the estrous female. Of 394 estrous females (all-day consortships again excluded), for example, the CUC was the last one for 58% (229) and the next-to-the-last one for 23% (90). Second, the CUC is longer than the preceding consortships. Whereas the mean ± SD time (minutes) for all consortships is 22.2 ± 38.0, as noted above, the mean ± SD time for CUCs is 42.0 ± 67.3 ($P < .001$, Mann-Whitney U test) (fig. 11.4). Approximately 60% of CUCs last 20 minutes or more, and 5% last for more than 200 minutes.

The changes in behavior following the CUC affect only the male and female that have just copulated. Breeding males are always interested in estrous females with whom they have not yet copulated, and mated females still in estrus often accept—and sometimes solicit—the advances of such males. When a female copulates with only one male, she has only one CUC. When she copulates with two or three males, however, then she has two or three CUCs—one with each breeding male.

The first male to inseminate a female usually has several short underground consortships with her before the CUC. For example, one first male in 1981 had thirty-five underground consortships before his final CUC! Not so for the second and third males that copulate, who frequently inseminate during the first underground consortship. Consequently, like the number of copulations for first-copulating wild guinea pig males (Rood 1972), the number of underground consortships is higher for first-copulating prairie dog males than for later-copulating males (fig. 11.5).

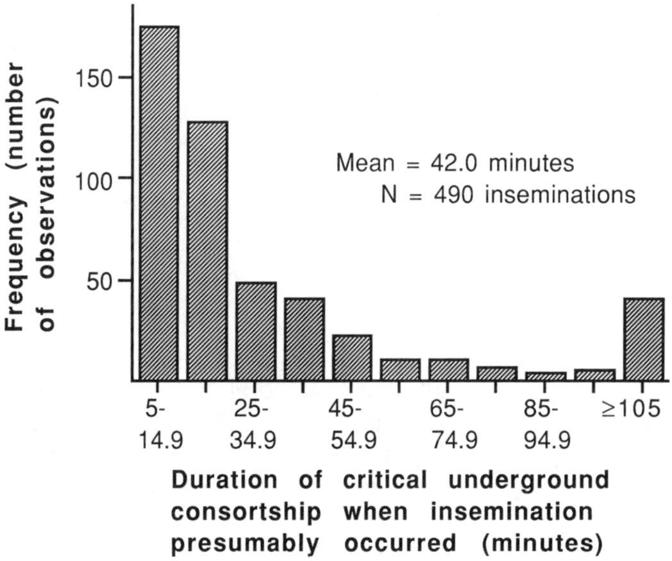

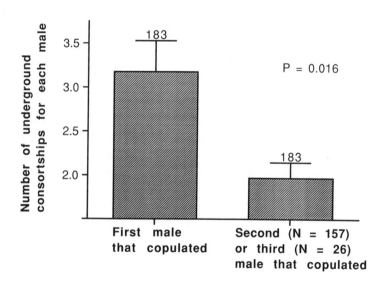

Fig. 11.4. Duration of critical underground consortship (CUC), when insemination occurs. When a female copulates with two different males, I have used times for the CUC with each male. This graph excludes data from all-day underground consortships.

Fig. 11.5. Number of underground consortships per male for the first, second, and third males to copulate with females that copulate with more than one male. The number above each SE line indicates the number of estrous females. The *P*-value is from the Wilcoxon matched-pairs signed-ranks test.

The copulatory sequences of some animals, such as Norway rats, golden hamsters, Mongolian gerbils, wild guinea pigs, and perhaps pygmy chimpanzees, include early intromissions without ejaculation followed by later intromissions with ejaculation (Beach and Jordon 1956; Dewsbury 1972, 1975, 1984; Rood 1972; Kano 1992). Curiously, the copulatory sequences of other animals, such as hispid cotton rats and oldfield, white-footed, and cactus mice, involve early intromissions with ejaculation followed by later intromissions without ejaculation (Dewsbury 1975, 1979; Dewsbury and Estep 1975). For prairie dogs, I surmise that the CUC is the only one that involves the transfer of sperm to the estrous female. The previous, shorter consortships probably involve mounting, intromission, and pelvic thrusting but no ejaculation. However, because of the difficulty of livetrapping estrous females (see below), the solid evidence for this argument is weak and comes from only two females, as described below:

1. I captured female-71 at approximately 1100 on the day of her estrus (28 February 1984), after she had already had one underground consortship with the resident breeding male, male-37. After I released her, female-71 had four other underground consortships with male-37 before the CUC. The CUC, when insemination presumably occurred, lasted from 1537 to 1549. A vaginal lavage (see below) from female-71 at 1100 on 28 February 1984 did *not* show any sperm. However, a vaginal lavage from 1020 on the next day (29 February 1984) *did* show sperm.

2. I captured female-R62 at approximately 1020 on the day of her estrus (17 March 1984), after she already had consorted underground twice with male-42, the breeding male of her home coterie. After I released her, female-R62 had one more underground consortship with male-42 before the CUC. The CUC lasted from 1214 to 1227. A vaginal lavage from female-R62 at 1020 on 17 March 1984 (at which time her vulva was open) did *not* show sperm. However, the vaginal lavage only 4 hours later (at 1420 on 17 March 1984) *did* show sperm.

Early (or late) intromissions without ejaculation sometimes increase the probability of successful fertilization by later (or earlier) intromissions with ejaculation (Wilson, Adler, and Le Bouef 1965; Adler 1969; Matthews and Adler 1978; Dewsbury 1978, 1982a; Eberhard 1985). This higher probability of fertilization might result because nonejaculatory intromissions sometimes (1) open the female's closed vulva before the actual transmission of sperm (see below), (2) help the male attain sufficient sexual stimulation for ejaculation (Beach 1956), (3) initiate neuroendocrine reflexes in the female necessary for ovulation and the initiation of pregnancy (Dewsbury and Estep 1975; van Tienhoven 1983; Huck, Lisk, and Thierung 1986; Ginsberg and Huck 1989), or (4) increase the rate of uterine contractions and hence facilitate the transfer of sperm from the vagina to ovulated eggs (Eberhard 1985).

Perhaps early underground consortships involve transfer of sperm that is not readily detectable in a vaginal lavage because the cumulative volume of sperm after the first few consortships is too low (Dewsbury 1984; Sherman 1989). In view of the numerous questions that remain, ultimate explanations for the high frequency of prairie dog underground consortships per estrus remain elusive. In any event, for whatever reason, the estrous female's interest in the male changes dramatically after her ultimate or penultimate underground consortship (i.e, the CUC) with him, as does his interest in her.

Insemination does not necessarily require a long underground consortship. The longest underground consortship was only 5 minutes for two estrous females, but each weaned a litter. I score a male as copulating with (inseminating) an estrous female if he is in the same burrow with her for 5 minutes or more. I score all underground consortships that last less than 5 minutes (but not less than 15 seconds; see above), but these shorter consortships probably do not involve transfer of sperm.

After copulating with one male, an estrous female sometimes submerges for the night with a different breeding male with whom she has not previously consorted. Obvious sexual interest from the male usually precedes this final submergence, so that the only logical step is to score a copulation. Rarely, an estrous female submerges for the night into a burrow containing a breeding male with whom she has not yet copulated ($N < 30$ observations) without any aboveground preliminaries, sometimes after the male has been underground for more than 30 minutes. Unusual behaviors associated with some of these late consortships—switching of burrows during the night, for example—indicate probable copulation. With or without prior aboveground sexual interest, I therefore score an insemination whenever an estrous female spends all or part of the night with a breeding male with whom she has not previously consorted.

During the breeding season, the resident breeding male is usually the first in his coterie to emerge each morning and the last to submerge at night. Further, he initiates more than 50% of the fights, chases, and anal sniffings that occur in his coterie territory in February and March. Occasionally, however, a breeding male avoids all aboveground behavioral interactions and remains underground with a female for an entire day during the breeding season. Usually the pair is alone, but sometimes other coterie members are with them for all or part of the day. These all-day consortships are so unusual that I hypothesized that they *must* involve estrus and copulation. Six of the seven lines of evidence discussed in the second part of this chapter confirm this hypothesis. Further, females that consort underground all day with a breeding male do not consort on any subsequent day.

Of 546 estrous females, 41 (8%) copulated while staying underground all day with a breeding male. I observed at least one all-day consortship in every year except 1978, and in each of 3 years I observed eight of them.

Prairie dogs have two other copulatory sequences that resemble all-day consortships. Sometimes a breeding male and an estrous female submerge together into the same burrow early in the day—occasionally as much as 4 or 5 hours before other members of the home coterie retire for the night—and never reappear aboveground for the rest of the day. Other times a breeding male and estrous female remain underground for almost the entire day, appearing aboveground for the first time only when almost all other prairie dogs in the colony have already submerged for the night.

Like females of other squirrels, such as Richardson's ground squirrels and Asian chipmunks (Michener 1985; Blake and Gillett 1988), prairie dog females sometimes come into estrus on two separate occasions during the same breeding season ($N = 19$ females). One of these nineteen females came into estrus on 3 separate days in 1985. The second estrus is usually about 2 weeks after the first one (fig. 11.6). Regarding the diagnostic behaviors of underground consortships, first versus second periods of estrus show no consistent differences.

True estrus involves ovulation. When coupled with copulation and insemination, true estrus frequently leads to fertilization and pregnancy (Bronson 1989). At some point after true estrus and fertilization, pregnant water voles and house mice and pregnant females of primate species such

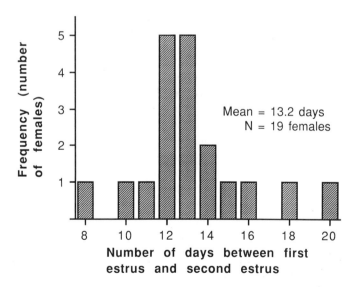

Fig. 11.6. Number of days between first estrus and second estrus for those females that come into estrus more than once during a single breeding season.

as hanuman langurs and red colobus monkeys sometimes show *pseudo-estrus* (Hrdy 1977b, 1979; vom Saal 1985; Jeppsson 1986; Hrdy and Whitten 1987; Elwood 1991, 1992). Pseudo-estrous females copulate, but pseudo-estrus does not involve ovulation and therefore does not lead to fertilization and pregnancy. Rather, pseudo-estrus probably functions to reduce the probability of infanticide by male invaders via confusing the issue of paternity: the new male might not kill offspring if "tricked" into thinking that they are his own (Hrdy 1977b, Hausfater 1984; but see Sommer 1987; Struhsaker and Leland 1985; see also chap. 10). Might the second estrus of certain prairie dog females be pseudo-estrus? Probably not. The timing of parturition and of first juvenile emergence both show that the second estrus of prairie dog females is real. Specifically, for all ten females with double estrus that later gave birth, parturition was always 34 or 35 days (the usual length of gestation; see chap. 16) after the second rather than the first estrus. Similarly, for all seven females with double estrus that later produced emergent juveniles, the first emergence was always approximately 76 days (the usual length of both gestation and lactation) after the second rather than the first estrus.

Why does first estrus sometimes fail to yield pregnancy? My small sample size of nineteen double-estrous prairie dog females precludes any rigorous conclusions, but I have identified three factors that might contribute to failed conception in the first estrus. First, three of the nineteen double-estrous females were yearlings, and three others were adults that copulated with a yearling male in the first estrus. Yearlings of both sexes are less successful at reproduction than older prairie dogs (chaps. 13 and 16). Second, eleven of the nineteen double-estrous females copulated with a different male or set of males during the second estrus. Shortly after copulating with one male, a female might find a more suitable male and might abort pregnancy and come into second estrus to take advantage of the new male. The more suitable male might be one who has recently invaded or who might invade later. By copulating with him, a female reduces the probability of later infanticide by the invading male (chap. 7). Finally, two of the nineteen double-estrous females were the first in the colony to copulate during their first estrus, and four others first copulated within the first 4 days of the breeding season. Perhaps the offspring of females that copulate too early would first emerge from the natal burrow when vegetation necessary for juvenile growth is still too sparse. If so, then aborted pregnancy and second estrus might serve to improve reproductive timing for females who copulate too early (chap. 13).

Attention Directed toward an Estrous Female by the Breeding Male

As in other rodents, such as mountain cavies, Olympic marmots, and Belding's ground squirrels (Rood 1972; Barash 1973; Sherman 1976), frequent anal sniffing of a particular female by a breeding prairie dog male indicates that she will come into estrus later in the same day (fig. 11.7a). On the other hand, frequent fights and chases associated with guarding an estrous female (see above) usually mean that she has already copulated earlier in the same day. Females in heat thus receive disproportionate male attention that facilitates my detection of estrus and copulation (fig. 11.8).

Fig. 11.7. Aboveground behaviors that indicate underground copulations. *(a)* Before copulating underground with her, male-08 sniffs the vulva of estrous female-RR7 (ring-around-the-rear-7). *(b)* After copulating underground, male-08 licks his penis at burrow entrance-A6. *(c)* Before copulating underground with female-R62 (rear legs + 62), male-8 collects nest material and takes it into burrow entrance-69. *(d)* After copulating underground with her, male-7 gives a 5-minute mating call as estrous female-H3 (black head + three stripes) peeks out from burrow entrance-40. (Photos by John L. Hoogland.)

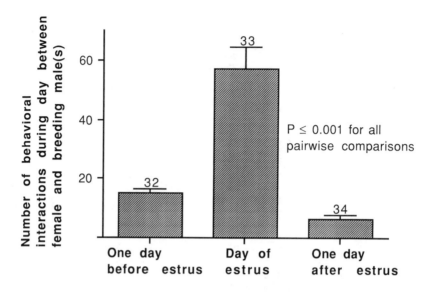

Fig. 11.8. Behavioral interactions between breeding male(s) and female before, during, and after estrus. The number above each SE line indicates the number of females observed. *P*-values are from the Wilcoxon matched-pairs signed-ranks test.

Male attention to an estrous female is sometimes dramatic. For example, female-82 in 1979 interacted with breeding males only 11 times on the day before estrus and only 22 times on the day after estrus, but 177 times on the day of estrus. Similarly, female-70 in 1979 interacted with breeding males only 38 times on the day before estrus and only 8 times on the day after estrus, but 124 times on the day of estrus.

Sometimes a female seems ready to come into estrus, but then delays until the next day—usually in deference to a larger female of the home coterie who is in estrus or pre-estrus (chap. 13). Early in the day before the delay is certain, breeding males frequently interact with such females and sometimes even give mating calls—as though the males cannot discriminate between the females that will come into full estrus later in the same day and the females that will delay estrus until the next day. This early-day attention to pre-estrous females that later delay estrus probably explains why males generally interact with females more on the day before estrus than on the day after (fig. 11.8).

Figure 11.8 indicates that breeding males recognize a female's estrus and discriminate between females that have and have not copulated. Patterns of *gallivanting* (Barash 1981, 1989)—temporary invasions by breeding males into adjacent coterie territories, presumably in search of estrous females—also indicate such recognition and discrimination. Specifically, gallivanting usually does not begin until all eligible females in a breeding male's home coterie territory have come into estrus and copulated.

Self-Licking of Genitals

Like Richardson's and thirteen-lined ground squirrels and tassel-eared, fox, gray, red, and Douglas's tree squirrels (Smith 1968; Horwich 1972; Farentinos 1974; McCloskey and Shaw 1977; Davis 1982a; Schwagmeyer and Parker 1987), prairie dogs commonly lick their genitals after copulating (fig. 11.7b). Specifically, within minutes after emergence from an underground consortship—and especially after the CUC, when insemination presumably occurs—the male sometimes licks his penis and the female licks her vulva. Reaching the genitals for self-licking is difficult for prairie dogs, and they often fall over in the process. Genital licking is therefore easy to detect. The breeding male licks his penis at least once aboveground for 47% of estrous females with whom he consorts (255/539). The estrous female licks her vulva at least once at a frequency of 28% (153/539).

Is self-licking of the genitals specific to copulations and therefore diagnostic of them, or does it commonly occur at other times as well? Table 11.1 documents the coupling of genital self-licking with copulation.

Males and females might lick their genitals before resurfacing after a copulation. For obvious reasons I am unable to investigate this possibility. I have, however, made the qualitative observation that genital licking is more likely after a short underground consortship—when individuals have little time for genital licking before resurfacing—than after a longer underground consortship.

Table 11.1. Does Self-Licking of Genitals Correlate with Copulation?

	On days during the 1986 breeding season when individuals did not copulate	On day(s) during the 1986 breeding season when individuals copulated
Observed (expected) number of times that female licked her own vulva ($N = 43$ different females)	12 (39.6)	29 (1.4)
Observed (expected) number of times that male licked his own penis ($N = 14$ different males)	8 (34.1)	37 (10.9)

Note: In 1986 I recorded self-licking of the genitals for 29 days, from 26 February (first copulation) through 26 March (last copulation). If self-licking of the vulva is independent of copulation, then it should have been 28 times more common for the days when estrus and copulation did not occur than on the single day for each female when estrus and copulation did occur. One male in 1986 copulated on 7 different days, so I used this maximum number to calculate the expected number of self-lickings of the penis. If self-licking of the penis is independent of copulation, then it should have occurred $22/29 \times 45$ (observed number of penile lickings) = 34.1 times during the days when males did not copulate and only $7/29 \times 45 = 10.9$ times during the days when males did copulate. For both sexes, self-licking of the genitals is more likely on the day of copulation ($P < .001$ for both, 2×2 chi-square test).

Why do prairie dogs lick their genitals after copulating? Three possibilities come to mind. First, the licking might thwart certain genital infections or sexually transmitted diseases (Hart, Korinek, and Brennan 1987; Hart 1990; Read 1990). Second, like gray and fox squirrel females (Koprowski 1992), prairie dog females might lick the vulva in an attempt to remove either sperm or the copulatory plug that forms shortly after copulation (see below). Finally, genital licking simply might be a response to pain or irritation associated with copulation.

Nestbuilding by the Breeding Male

During the breeding season, adults and yearlings of both sexes sometimes take a mouthful of nest material underground when they submerge for the night. Adult females and yearlings of both sexes occasionally take nest material underground in the morning or early afternoon during the breeding season as well. However, breeding males during the breeding season almost never take nest material underground in the morning or early afternoon—unless a female is in estrus. Specifically, a breeding male takes nest material underground at least once shortly before the CUC for 15% of estrous females with whom he consorts (81/541) (fig. 11.9). Nestbuilding by a breeding prairie dog male on a morning or afternoon during the breeding

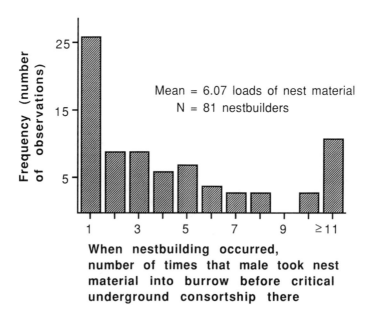

Fig. 11.9. Number of mouthfuls of nest material that male takes into burrow before critical underground consortship there. This graph includes data only from those males that provisioned with nest material at least once.

season is thus a useful indicator of an imminent copulation (see fig 11.7c). Rarely (for <1% of estrous females), and inexplicably, the male takes nest material underground *after* the CUC.

Most provisioning males take only one or two mouthfuls of nest material into a burrow before copulating there. At the other extreme, male-04 took forty-seven mouthfuls underground before copulating with female-H4 on 25 February 1981!

Why do males sometimes initiate underground nests just before copulation? Two possibilities come to mind. First, perhaps the nest material facilitates copulation; for example, it might function to keep the copulating pair off the cold ground. The second, more likely, hypothesis concerns the elaborate underground nest that a female builds in the nursery burrow where she attempts to rear her offspring (see below). Perhaps a male is more likely to induce copulation if he initiates the female's nest. If so, then the male's nest material might be either a nuptial offering or paternal investment (Thornhill and Alcock 1983). Consistent with this hypothesis, 56% of females (147/261) rear their litters to first emergence in a nursery burrow where they consorted at least once during estrus.

The Mating Call

Like males of other sciurids such as Richardson's and Belding's ground squirrels, tassel-eared and Douglas's tree squirrels, and white-tailed and Gunnison's prairie dogs (Farentinos 1972, 1974; Davis 1982a; Koford 1982; Leger, Berney-Key, and Sherman 1984; my own unpublished data), male black-tailed prairie dogs sometimes give a unique call shortly before or after copulating (see fig. 11.7d). For obvious reasons, I have named this vocalization the *mating call.* Except when copulations occur aboveground, the mating call is the single best confirmation that a female is in estrus.

To human observers, mating calls sound similar to antipredator calls. However, mating calls contain fewer barks per minute than antipredator calls, and are softer—i.e., have a lower intensity (Grady and Hoogland 1986). Prairie dogs clearly distinguish between the two calls: nearby individuals run to a burrow mound in response to an antipredator call, but they often do not even look up for a mating call.

Usually the copulating male starts to give the mating call just after sniffing an estrous female or just after she follows him aboveground after an underground consortship. These observations suggest that males direct their calls to the estrous females. However, the male sometimes emerges from an underground consortship and starts calling as much as 10 to 15 minutes before the female resurfaces—which suggests that the intended listeners might be other males or nonestrous females.

At least one mating call resounds for 57% of estrous females (308/542) (fig. 11.10). By contrast, mating calls unrelated to estrus are rare ($N = 30$ calling males detected from 1978 through 1988). In one sense these thirty exceptions further demonstrate the link between estrus and the mating call: 13% (4/30) involved females that had been in estrus on the previous day, and 60% (18/30) involved females that came into estrus 1 ($N = 14$) or 2 ($N = 4$) days later.

As noted above, females sometimes seem ready to come into estrus on one day, but then defer to another estrous female of the home coterie and delay their own estrus until the following day. Many of the mating calls that occur on the day before estrus are in response to such females, at a point early in the day when delay of estrus until the next day probably is not yet inevitable.

In every aspect except its tight association with estrus, the mating call shows phenomenal variation. Consider the following, for example:

1. Some males always call in response to an estrous female, some never call, and others call for certain females but not for others (fig. 11.11).

2. Forty-three percent of estrous females (234/542) never elicit a single mating call (see fig. 11.10). At the other extreme, yearling female-R57 set the record by eliciting thirty-seven mating calls when she came into estrus on 12 March 1987.

3. Some mating calls last only a few seconds and contain fewer than five individual barks. Others persist for more than 60 consecutive

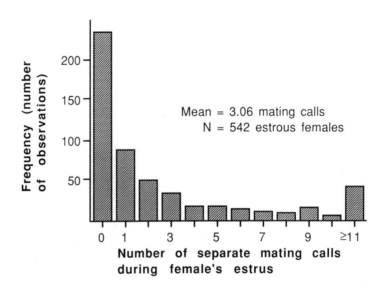

Fig. 11.10. Number of mating calls during female's estrus. I score a mating call by the same male as discrete when it is separated from his other mating calls by 60 seconds or more.

minutes and contain thousands of barks. Similarly, the *cumulative* calling time of all mating calls in response to a single estrous female ranges from less than 2 *seconds* to more than 2 *hours*.

4. In some cases the male calls before his CUC with the estrous female, in other cases after, and in still other cases he calls both before and after the CUC.

5. The same male sometimes gives frequent, long mating calls in response to certain estrous females but only one or a few short calls in response to other estrous females.

6. Certain females elicit mating calls while in estrus in one year but not in other years.

Males seeking to copulate must compete with other males. Often the mating call seems to be the first signal to nearby competitors that a female is in estrus. To outweigh the cost of broadcasting estrus to competing males, the mating call's benefit should be substantial and easy to identify. Not so. I considered five possible payoffs, as discussed below.

The first possible payoff is that the mating call reduces female aggression and increases sexual receptivity (Smith 1968; Nyby and Whitney 1978; Barfield et al. 1979). If so, then males should call before, but not

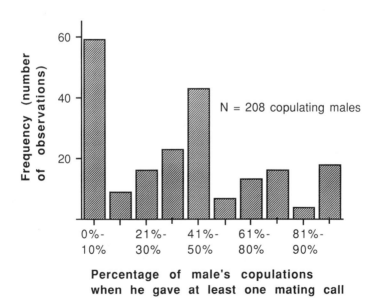

Percentage of male's copulations
when he gave at least one mating call

Fig. 11.11. Percentage of male's copulations when he gives at least one mating call. The mean ± SD number of copulations for each male shown here is 3.71 ± 1.98 (range = 1 to 11). The four most common percentages are 0% (*N* = 59 copulating males), 50% (*N* = 41), 33% (*N* = 17), and 100% (*N* = 17).

after, the CUC. As noted above, many males call both before and after the CUC, and many others call only after the CUC. Thus, the mating call probably does not function to increase female sexual receptivity.

The second possible payoff is that the prairie dog mating call, like roaring in red deer (McComb 1987), induces ovulation. The call might induce ovulation in the estrous female herself or in other females that will come into estrus later. Perhaps calling to pre-estrous females promotes reproductive synchrony among females within the same coterie (chap. 13). Researchers have discovered some of the physiological details of prairie dog reproduction, but a possible link between the mating call and the induction of ovulation remains unknown (Anthony 1953, 1955; Anthony and Foreman 1951; Foreman 1962, 1967, 1974, 1981; Foreman and Williams 1967; Foreman and Garris 1984).

The third possible payoff from the mating call concerns intrasexual competition and female choice. Perhaps the mating call announces a male's competitive status, good health, and freedom from parasites, and thereby renders him more attractive to estrous females and less vulnerable to invasions and takeovers by other males (Hamilton 1990; Berger and Cunningham 1991; Møller 1991c). Three predictions follow from this hypothesis:

1. Because they compete better than smaller males (chap. 13), large, successful males should be more likely to give mating calls. Figure 11.12 supports this prediction.

2. As noted above, the first male to copulate with a female should be more interested than later-copulating males in preventing her from copulating with additional males. First-copulating males therefore should call more often than second- and third-copulating males. Figure 11.13a supports this prediction.

3. Females should be less likely to copulate with a second male when the first male gives the mating call. Figure 11.13b provides support, albeit weak, for this prediction.

The fourth and fifth possible payoffs from the mating call are similar, again involving female choice (Leger, Berney-Key, and Sherman 1984; Møller 1991c). Fourth, the mating call probably attracts the attention of unmated females. Perhaps these females are more likely to copulate with the calling male when they later came into estrus. Finally, for animals such as black grouse, sage grouse, and fallow deer (Clutton-Brock, Hiraiwa-Hasegawa, and Robertson 1989; Hoglund, Alatalo, and Lundberg 1990; Gibson, Bradbury, and Vehrencamp 1991; Gibson and Hoglund 1992; Pruett-Jones 1992), unmated females sometimes copy the mate choice of earlier-copulating females. Perhaps the mating call facilitates such copying by pinpointing the copulating male. If either the fourth or fifth possibility applies—or if the call functions to induce ovulation among females that

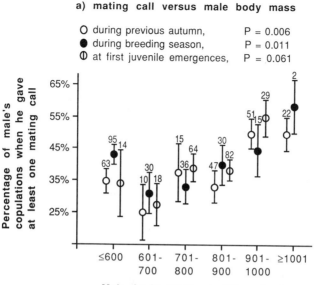

a) mating call versus male body mass

O during previous autumn,   P = 0.006
● during breeding season,   P = 0.011
◑ at first juvenile emergences, P = 0.061

Male body mass at different stages
of the annual cycle (grams)

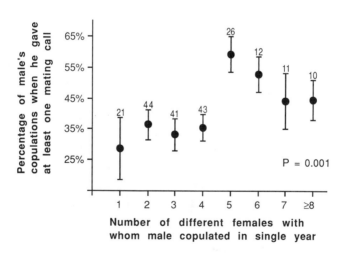

b) mating call versus male copulatory success

P = 0.001

Number of different females with
whom male copulated in single year

Fig. 11.12. Probability of giving a mating call versus male body mass and male copulatory success. *(a)* Probability of giving a mating call versus male body mass at different stages of the annual cycle. This graph does not depict data from one noncalling breeding male whose body mass at first juvenile emergences was 1,010 grams, but I have included him in statistical analyses. *(b)* Probability of giving a mating call versus male copulatory success. For these graphs, the number above each SE line indicates the number of males, and *P*-values are from the Spearman rank correlation test.

a) mating call versus male copulatory order

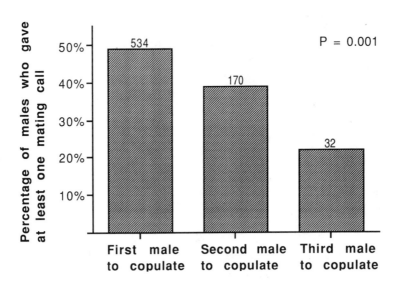

b) mating call versus second copulation

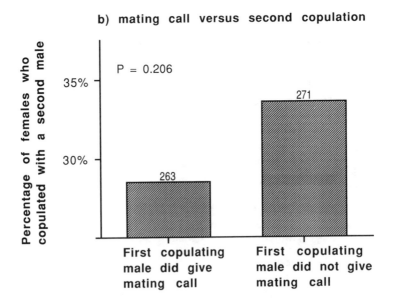

◀ **Fig. 11.13.** *(a)* Probability of giving a mating call versus male copulatory order. The number above each bar indicates the number of copulating males. The *P*-value is from the 3 × 2 chi-square analysis. *P*-values from the 2 × 2 pairwise chi-square tests are as follows: first male versus second male, $P = .018$; first versus third, $P = .003$; second versus third, $P = .067$. This graph includes data not only from estrous females that copulated with two or more males, but also from estrous females that copulated with only one male. *(b)* Success of mating call by the first-copulating male at deterring copulation with a second male. The number above each bar indicates the number of estrous females. The *P*-value is from the 2 × 2 chi-square test.

have not yet come into estrus (see above)—then mating calls should be more common early in the breeding season than later, because the number of unmated females declines with time. Figure 11.14 provides no support for this hypothesis.

Using data through 1983 only, Mark Grady and I (1986) reported an unexpected result: females that elicit at least one mating call during estrus are *less* likely to rear emergent juveniles than are noneliciting females. The statistical significance of this negative association has disappeared with the inclusion of additional data from 1984 through 1988, but the perplexing trend remains (fig. 11.15).

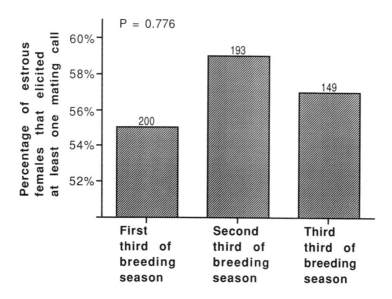

Fig. 11.14. Mating calls versus stage of the breeding season. The number above each bar indicates the number of estrous females. The *P*-value is from the 3 × 2 chi-square test. All pairwise comparisons are also insignificant ($P > .400$ for all three, 2 × 2 chi-square test).

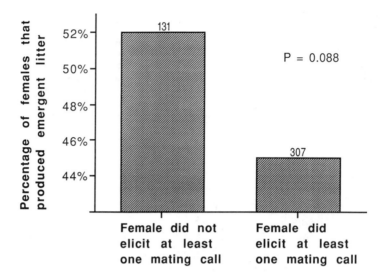

Fig. 11.15. Estrous females that elicit mating calls are less likely to produce emergent juveniles. The number above each bar indicates the number of estrous females. The *P*-value is from the 2 × 2 chi-square test.

Unique calls by sexually receptive females might incite male-male competition and thus facilitate female choice in some animals, such as red jungle fowl (Montgomerie and Thornhill 1989), chaffinches (Sheldon 1994), northern elephant seals (Cox and Le Boeuf 1977), chimpanzees and pygmy chimpanzees (Goodall 1986; Hauser 1990; Kano 1992), gray squirrels (Taylor 1966), and Asian, Merriam's, and California chipmunks (Callahan 1981; Blake and Gillett 1988; Blake 1992). I listen carefully each year, but I have not heard estrous prairie dog females making unique calls before or after underground consortships. However, females do give a soft, repetitious, unique vocalization during those rare copulations that occur aboveground (see below). Perhaps females give the same vocalization when copulating underground, and perhaps the call incites competition among breeding males. The low intensity of the vocalization, coupled with the muffling of the call by the burrow during an underground copulation, has precluded my investigation of this intriguing possibliity.

Late Final Submergence of the Estrous Female

Sixty-eight percent of estrous females (364/534) remain aboveground long after all yearlings and nonestrous adult females in the colony have submerged for the night. This trend is especially evident when I consider only members of the same home coterie. Specifically, all the yearlings and adult females in a coterie usually submerge for the night within 5 to 10 minutes of one another in February and March when no female is in estrus. However, an estrous female sometimes remains aboveground for as much as 60 to 90 minutes after the yearlings and nonestrous adult females of her home coterie have disappeared for the night. Commonly the resident breeding male guards the estrous female late into the evening if he has copulated with her. The two then submerge together for the night, or he submerges shortly after her. Sometimes, however, the breeding male submerges for the night *before* the estrous female (see below).

An estrous female might delay final submergence for the night to compensate for foraging time lost during underground consortships. A more likely explanation is that she stays aboveground late to increase the probability of copulating with an additional male. For example, female-RAB copulated with the single breeding male in her home coterie, male-19, early in the day on 20 March 1985. Male-19 guarded female-RAB for most of the day after copulating, but then abruptly abandoned his guarding and submerged for the night into burrow entrance-12 at 1726, when female-RAB was one of the few prairie dogs still aboveground at the study colony. The breeding male of the adjacent coterie, male-24, evidently was aware that female-RAB was in estrus and also stayed aboveground late. At 1733 female-RAB began to solicit male-24. The pair submerged at 1736 into burrow entrance-A5 (in female-RAB's home coterie territory) and remained together—and presumably copulated—until at least 1850, when darkness precluded further observations. Female-RAB had the opportunity to copulate with a second male only because she stayed aboveground so late. Curiously, male-24 and female-RAB, like certain other pairs that copulate at the end of the day, switched burrows sometime during the night after my departure.

Unusual Behaviors of the Resident Breeding Male or Estrous Female

By practically living with them for 5 months of each year, I become intimately familiar with the habits of every prairie dog at the study colony. For example, certain individuals regularly first appear aboveground early in the day, while others predictably first appear late. When the first emergence for a breeding male or an unmated female is unusual for any reason—e.g., late when usually early or early when usually late—such deviation often indicates estrus and copulation. For example, male-36 was always one of the first prairie dogs to appear aboveground at the study colony in February 1982. However, male-36 and four of the five adult females in his coterie were still underground at 1030 on 21 February 1982, when all other colony residents were foraging aboveground. I became suspicious that at least one of the females was in estrus. Male-36 finally first surfaced at 1130. As soon as female-WA0 first emerged 1 minute later, male-36 initiated a series of 16 interactions with her (kisses, anal sniffs, runaways, and chases). He then initiated a 7-minute mating call. At 1138, male-36 and female-WA0 submerged for a 73-minute underground consortship, after which male-36 gave several other mating calls. Later in the day female-WA0 copulated with the second and third breeding males in her multi-male home coterie.

Unusual deviations in the behavior of specific prairie dogs are difficult to quantify, but they alert me to at least 10% of the copulations that follow.

Evidence for the Accuracy of Behavioral Observations of Estrus and Copulations

Because prairie dogs copulate underground, critics legitimately question the accuracy of my behavioral observations of estrus and copulation. I therefore have looked carefully for independent corroborating evidence, seven lines of which I describe below.

Date of Underground Consortship versus Date of First Juvenile Emergence

If underground consortships involve copulations, then females that consort underground early in the breeding season should rear their young to first emergence sooner than females that consort later. Data from 11 consecutive years (1978 through 1988) support this prediction ($P < .001$ for all years, Spearman rank correlation test). Figure 11.16a depicts representative data from 1981.

Date of Underground Consortship versus Date of Parturition

If copulations occur during underground consortships, then females that consort underground early in the breeding season should give birth earlier than females that consort later. Data from all years when I recorded both copulations and parturitions (1981 through 1988) support this prediction ($P < .001$ for all years, Spearman rank correlation test). Figure 11.16b depicts representative data from 1981.

The mean ± SD length of gestation is 34.6 ± 0.73 days (range = 33 to 38), and the mean ± SD length of lactation is 41.3 ± 2.46 days (range = 37 to 51) (chap. 16). Because gestation is less variable than lactation, figure 11.16b is better evidence for the accuracy of the behavioral observations than is figure 11.16a.

Onset of Maternal Behaviors

At some point pregnant prairie dog females start to act maternally. As for Belding's, Uinta, round-tailed, and Columbian ground squirrels (Dunford 1977c; Sherman 1980a; Festa-Bianchet and Boag 1982; Balph 1984), three maternal behaviors are especially obvious among pregnant and lactating prairie dog females (see also King 1955). First, the female spends every night alone in the same home nursery burrow (or the *prospective* home nursery burrow, if she is still pregnant). Second, she chases all conspecifics

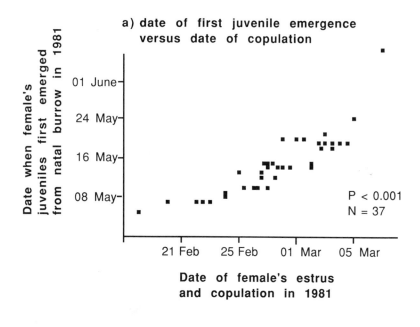

a) date of first juvenile emergence
versus date of copulation

P < 0.001
N = 37

Date of female's estrus
and copulation in 1981

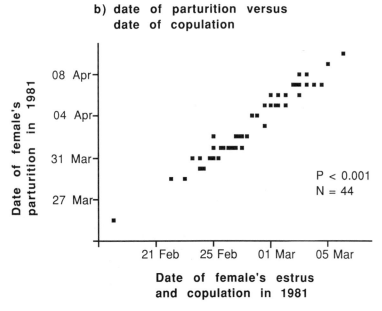

b) date of parturition versus
date of copulation

P < 0.001
N = 44

Date of female's estrus
and copulation in 1981

Fig. 11.16. Dates of first juvenile emergence and of parturition versus date of copulation. *(a)* Date of first juvenile emergence versus date of copulation in 1981. *(b)* Date of parturition versus date of copulation in 1981. *P*-values for both graphs are from the Spearman rank correlation test. Mainly because of infanticide, many females that give birth are unable to rear their offspring to first emergence.

away from her nursery burrow during the day. Third, she takes mouthfuls of dry grass into the home nursery burrow frequently (fig. 11.17)—as opposed to the sporadic nestbuilding that some females show during the breeding season (see above).

Pregnant and lactating females vary in the intensity of maternal behaviors. For example, certain females aggressively defend a large territory around the home nursery burrow, while other females casually defend only a small surrounding territory. Further, certain females take more than 200 mouthfuls of dry grass into the home nursery burrow over the course of pregnancy and lactation. On some mornings these females devote more than 60 consecutive minutes to nestbuilding, with each "round trip"—i.e., the appearance aboveground, the collection of dry grass, the submergence into the home nursery burrow with the mouthful of grass, and the reappearance aboveground—taking about 3 or 4 minutes. By contrast, other females take fewer than 50 mouthfuls of dry grass into the home nursery burrow during pregnancy and lactation, and usually devote only a few minutes at a time to this task.

If underground consortships involve copulations, then maternal behaviors should begin after, and not before, the series of underground consortships that includes the CUC. This prediction is true for all 264 females whose estrus and copulation(s) I observed and who eventually produced emergent

Fig 11.17. Nestbuilding by pregnant female-4stripe, who is about to take this mouthful of dry grass into burrow entrance-07. Aggressive defense of, and serious nestbuilding in, a prospective nursery burrow usually begins on the day after copulation. (Photo by John L. Hoogland.)

juveniles. The prediction is also true for the more than 200 females who gave birth to juveniles that did not survive long enough to emerge from the natal burrow.

Variation in the onset of maternal behaviors is phenomenal. At one extreme, territorial defense of the prospective nursery burrow and nest-building begin as soon as 15 minutes after the CUC. At the other extreme, some mothers delay maternal behaviors until the day before parturition! Most commonly, females initiate both defense of a prospective nursery burrow and serious nestbuilding on the first day after copulation. Spending the night alone in the prospective nursery burrow usually begins several days later.

Aboveground Copulations

Rarely, and inexplicably, black-tailed prairie dogs copulate aboveground: the male mounts the female from the rear and immediately begins pelvic thrusting. Like Belding's, Richardson's, Columbian, and thirteen-lined ground squirrels that copulate aboveground (McCarley 1966; Wistrand 1974; Sherman and Morton 1979; Davis 1982a; Schwagmeyer 1984), both the male and female prairie dog lie on their sides during an aboveground copulation. While copulating aboveground, prairie dog females give a soft, unique vocalization. This call might attract the attention of other breeding males, and thus incite male-male competition among potential suitors (see above).

Like female Richardson's ground squirrels that copulate aboveground (Davis 1984a), female prairie dogs that copulate aboveground sometimes try to bite the throat or cheeks of the copulating male. Perhaps this ag-gression helps explain why breeding males have more facial scars than breeding females at the conclusion of the breeding season (see fig. 5.5).

If underground consortships involve copulations, then the diagnostic features of these underground consortships also should be evident in aboveground copulations. Table 11.2 supports this prediction for the 2% of estrous females (9/546) that copulated aboveground. All nine females that copulated aboveground also had at least one underground consortship, all nine delayed final submergence until late in the day, six elicited at least one mating call, and six self-licked the vulva. Further, six of the males that copulated aboveground with these nine estrous females self-licked the penis.

One of the cases in table 11.2 is especially instructive. Female-WA3 had three short aboveground copulations with male-3 before one long, final aboveground copulation with him. The early, short aboveground copula-tions were probably equivalent to the several short underground consortships during a typical female's estrus. The long, final aboveground copulation was probably equivalent to a typical CUC, when insemination occurs. Three other cases in table 11.2 involved one last, longer aboveground

Table 11.2. Diagnostic Behaviors of Underground Copulations Also Observed with Aboveground Copulations

Date	Estrous female	Number of aboveground copulations	Number of underground consortships before or after the aboveground copulation(s)	Duration times for aboveground copulations (mins), listed in order of occurrence	Diagnostic behaviors observed[a]
31 Mar 1978	Un=FR	2	8	1.0, 15.5	LP, MC, LFS
14 Mar 1979	3str	7	7	1.0, 0.3, 1.0, 1.0, 1.5, 1.0, 0.5	LP, LV, MC, LFS
15 Mar 1980	R60	1	1	10.0	LV, LFS
02 Mar 1981	R51	3	5	3.0, 2.0, 10.0	LP, LV, MC, LFS
04 Mar 1981	75	3	8	2.0, 0.5, 0.3	MC, LFS
03 Mar 1983	WA3	4	7	2.0, 3.0, 0.5, 7.0	LP, LV, LFS
04 Mar 1984	WA8	7	23	0.2, 0.1, 1.9, 0.1, 1.1, 1.5, 0.7	LP, LFS
18 Mar 1985	BB8	1	9	2.0	LV, MC, LFS
03 Mar 1986	R70	1	8	0.2	LP, LV, MC, LFS

[a]LP, self-licking of penis; LV, self-licking of vulva; MC, mating call; LFS, late final submergence of estrous female

copulation ($\geq$7 minutes) that was probably equivalent to the CUC of most estrous females. The other five females that copulated aboveground evidently received sperm during one of the underground consortships rather than during one of the aboveground copulations.

Vulvar Examinations Before and After Copulation

Especially during the breeding season, livetrapping is potentially disruptive (chap. 4). What will happen, for example, if a female comes into estrus while the resident breeding male of her coterie is in a livetrap? On the other hand, livetrapping combined with an examination of female condition might confirm or refute behavioral observations of estrus and copulation. Could I livetrap and somehow keep disruption to a minimum? My original plan was to concentrate on individuals that are especially fond of oats and livetraps, and to limit livetrapping to days when these individuals copulate. How frustrating to learn that trap-happy females are almost impossible to capture when in estrus! And trap-happy breeding males are equally uncooperative when a female of the home coterie territory is in estrus. Consequently, I capture few individuals on the day of copulation. Most data are therefore from individuals captured on the day before and the day after copulation.

Just before the onset of the breeding season, females have a swollen vulva that appears to be sealed shut by a thin layer of skin. After the breeding season, however, their vulvas are open and less swollen (fig. 11.18) (see also King 1955). Might vulvar condition therefore be useful for pinpointing estrus and copulation, as it is for Richardson's and thirteen-lined ground squirrels (Foster 1934; Michener 1980b, 1984b; Schwagmeyer and Brown 1983)? To test this hypothesis, I regularly livetrapped females and recorded vulvar condition. If the vulva does not open until copulation, then each female should have a closed vulva before her series of underground consortships and an open vulva afterwards.

A closed vulva is unequivocal proof that a female has not yet copulated (fig. 11.19). An open vulva usually—but not always—means that the female has copulated. I have not been able to figure out why 22% of females (11/49) have an open vulva before copulation.

Despite their lack of cooperation, I somehow captured eight females on the day of estrus shortly after the CUC (fig. 11.19). Three of these eight females had a conspicuous, white, rubbery plug—here called a copulatory plug (Asdell 1964; Voss 1979; Murie and McLean 1980; Michener 1984b; Koprowski 1992)—inside the vulva. As it might for wild guinea pig and chimpanzee females (Rood 1972; Goodall 1986), the copulatory plug might provide nutrients to the prairie dog female so that she can better rear her offspring (Thornhill and Alcock 1983). If so, this form of paternal care might explain why females often self-lick the vulva after the CUC (see

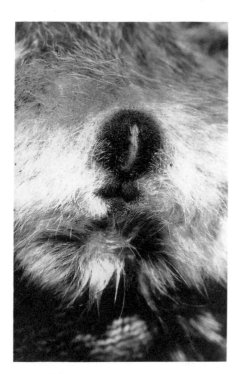 

Fig. 11.18. Confirmation of underground copulation from vulvar examination. *(a)* On the morning of the day when she later comes into estrus and consorts underground with a breeding male, a female's vulva is swollen and sealed shut. *(b)* Early the next morning, the female's vulva is conspicuously open. (Photos by John L. Hoogland.)

table 11.1). Such licking might in turn explain why 63% of females (5/8) do not have a copulatory plug when captured sometime after the CUC on the day of estrus. Self-licking of the vulva also might explain why— as for gray and fox squirrels (Koprowski 1992)—plugs are always absent among prairie dog females captured 1 day ($N = 62$) or 2 days ($N = 5$) after estrus. The copulatory plug might function in at least two other ways, on which I have no information: to reduce the probability of insemination by a second male (Rood 1972; Ehrlich and Ehrlich 1978; Hartung and Dewsbury 1978; Voss 1979; Eberhard 1985), or to facilitate retention and transport of sperm within the female reproductive tract (Voss 1979; Brock Fenton 1984; Dewsbury 1988).

Though I have looked for signs such as a wet crotch, I have found no way to identify, from appearance alone, prairie dog males that have recently copulated.

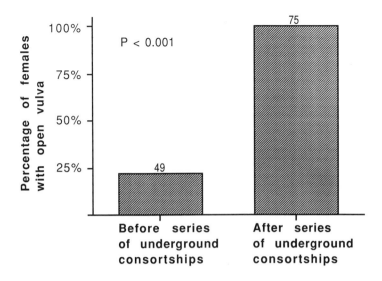

Fig. 11.19. Percentage of females with an open vulva before and after the series of underground consortships. Before the series of underground consortships, I have data from 2 days before estrus ($N = 4$ females), 1 day before estrus ($N = 18$), and the day of estrus ($N = 27$, all trapped before the first underground consortship). After the series of underground consortships, I have data from the day of estrus ($N = 8$ females, all trapped after the CUC), 1 day after estrus ($N = 62$), and 2 days after estrus ($N = 5$). The number above each bar indicates the number of females examined. The P-value is from the 2×2 chi-square test.

Vaginal Lavages Before and After Copulation

One obvious way to verify copulation is to find sperm in the vagina. When I inspect females for an open vulva shortly after presumed copulation (see fig. 11.18), I also take a vaginal lavage and look for sperm. Specifically, I inject a small amount of distilled water into a female's open vagina with an eyedropper, withdraw the water after 2 to 3 seconds, and then make two air-dried slides from the eyedropper's contents. When possible, I also collect vaginal lavages from females that have open vulvas but have not yet copulated.

I was expecting prairie dog semen to be milky. Curiously, however, examination of three estrous females captured shortly after (<120 minutes) the CUC suggests that the semen is *clear* rather than milky.

If underground consortships signal estrus and copulation and the CUC involves insemination, then vaginal lavages taken before a female's CUC should not show sperm, while lavages taken after the CUC should show sperm. Figure 11.20 supports this prediction.

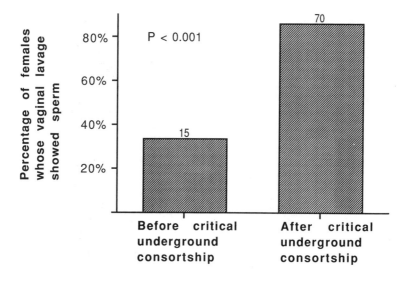

Fig. 11.20. Percentage of females whose vaginal lavage showed sperm before and after the CUC. From each lavage I made two air-dried slides, and scored insemination if one or both slides showed sperm. Matthew Keller and U. William Huck of Princeton University scored all slides blindly—i.e., without any information about when sampled females presumably copulated. I collected precopulatory slides from females with open vaginas on the day before ($N = 3$) or the day of copulation ($N = 12$; all slides prepared before the CUC). I collected postcopulatory slides on the day of ($N = 8$, all trapped after the CUC) or the day after ($N = 62$) copulation. The number above each bar indicates the number of females sampled. The P-value is from the 2×2 chi-square test. See text regarding the exceptions.

But wait, 33% of vaginal lavages taken before the female's CUC (5/15) show sperm (fig. 11.20)! How could that happen? I cannot obtain a lavage from most unmated females because their vulvas are sealed shut (see fig. 11.18). With fifteen unmated females, however, I was able to gently force out a white substance from a vulva that was just beginning to open (i.e., the female could not have previously copulated). Perhaps this white substance, which is probably a vaginal lubricant that differs from clear semen, contains cells that sometimes resemble sperm. In support of this hypothesis, 100% of the anomalous precopulatory lavages (5/5) show putative sperm in only *one* of two prepared slides. By contrast, only 11% of postcopulatory lavages (8/70) show a discrepancy in the scoring of the two slides from each female ($P = .032$, 2×2 chi-square test).

Blood Samples

Behavioral observations indicate that 365 females copulated with only one male in 1978 through 1988 (chap. 12). Of these, 170 females reared a litter to first emergence. If the behavioral observations are accurate, then paternities determined from electrophoresis (Hoogland and Foltz 1982) should be consistent with those single paternities inferred from the observations. Such consistency occurs for 99% of the litters (168/170). Both of the inconsistencies involve females that copulated during cold, wretched weather—i.e., when behavioral observations of estrous females are especially difficult (see below).

Multiple paternity occurs for animals such as mallards, indigo buntings, dwarf mongooses, and Belding's, thirteen-lined, and Idaho ground squirrels when two or more males sire the offspring in a single clutch or litter (Hanken and Sherman 1981; Evarts and Williams 1987; Westneat 1987; Foltz and Schwagmeyer 1989; Sherman 1989; Keane et al. 1994). If behavioral observations of underground consortships are accurate, then multiple paternity should occur only when an estrous female consorts underground with more than male. In support of this hypothesis, all thirteen unequivocal cases of multiple paternity (chap. 12) involve females that consorted with more than one male.

Inclement Weather: The Worst Enemy of Behavioral Observations

To this point I have summarized data that support the accuracy of my behavioral observations of underground consortships. If detecting copulations is so easy and accurate, why don't I obtain data for *every* prairie dog female that comes into estrus each year? I probably would, except for my worst enemy: inclement weather.

The weather at Wind Cave National Park in February and March, when the prairie dogs copulate, is usually sunny and mild. Daily high temperatures usually are between 5° and 10°C, and sometimes between 15° and 20°C (see also King 1955). Occasionally, however, the weather at Wind Cave National Park turns sour in February and March. On cold days (about 0°C or less) and during and just after heavy snowfall, the prairie dogs first appear aboveground late, submerge for the night early, and submerge frequently for short periods—presumably to warm up—between first appearance and final submergence. Naturally, these complications greatly hinder my behavioral observations of estrus and copulations. Further, because prairie dogs sometimes do not emerge at all for the first day or so after heavy snowfall, all-day consortships are difficult to identify in inclement weather.

From vulvar examinations and behavioral observations, I usually can pinpoint within a day or two when a female will come into estrus. If inclement weather strikes on a day when a female would probably come into estrus, she commonly delays estrus for 1 or 2 days until the return of better weather. If the severe weather continues for more than about 3 or 4 consecutive days, however, then the female usually comes into estrus on the 3rd or 4th day. Thus, within limits, females are more likely to come into estrus on warm, sunny days. Consequently, inaccuracies in my behavioral observations of estrus and copulations are usually rare unless inclement weather persists for more than a day or two during the breeding season.

The effect of inclement weather on the thoroughness of my behavioral observations of estrus and copulation is sometimes dramatic. In 1981, when the weather was consistently warm and sunny during the entire breeding season, field assistants and I documented copulations for 97% of the females that came into estrus (69/71). By contrast, in 1987, when the weather was consistently cold and wet, we documented copulations for only 86% of the females that came into estrus (43/50). The mean ± SD percentage of females whose estrus and copulation(s) we observe each year is 92.1% ± 6.95%.

Why Do Black-Tailed Prairie Dogs Copulate Underground?

The probability of predation is usually highest for individuals of solitary or weakly colonial species. On the other hand, male-male competition for females and interference with copulations is usually most pronounced for individuals of highly colonial species (chap. 5). In the most common type of interference, one male attacks another male that is vulnerable because he is preoccupied with copulation. Suppose that underground copulations reduce not only the probability of predation during copulation, but also male-male competition for estrous females and interference with copulations. If the risk of predation is the primary factor determining the site of copulation, then underground copulations should be more common among solitary and weakly colonial species. If male-male competition for females and interference with copulations are the primary factors, however, then underground copulations should be more common among highly colonial species (Davis 1982a; Møller and Birkhead 1989; Schwagmeyer 1990).

Unlike black-tailed prairie dogs (which live in large colonies of high density), white-tailed prairie dogs (which live in smaller colonies of lower density; see chap. 5) copulate aboveground (my own unpublished observations; see also Erpino 1968). This difference suggests that, as for mammals in general (Møller and Birkhead 1989), male-male competition for females and interference with copulations have been more important than predation in the evolution of the copulatory site for white-tailed and black-tailed prairie dogs.

Colony sizes and colony densities of Gunnison's prairie dogs are usually intermediate between those of white-tailed and black-tailed prairie dogs (Fitzgerald and Lechleitner 1974; Rayor 1985b, 1988; my own unpublished data). Perhaps because male-male competition for estrous females and interference with copulations are more important than the risk of predation in determining the site of their copulations, gunnisons resemble black-tails and copulate underground.

Summary

1. Black-tailed prairie dogs copulate underground. Behaviors that indicate an underground copulation include (1) frequent co-submergence of a breeding male and an estrous female into the same burrow during daylight hours, (2) unusually high frequency of interactions between the estrous female and breeding male(s), (3) self-licking of the genitals, (4) taking of nest material underground by the breeding male, (5) a unique male mating call, (6) late final submergence at the end of the day by the estrous female, and (7) other actions that deviate from the breeding male's or estrous female's usual pattern.

2. Females that consort underground early in the breeding season give birth and rear juveniles to first emergence sooner than females that consort later. Further, maternal behaviors such as nestbuilding and defense of a home nursery burrow do not commence until after a female's series of underground consortships.

3. Aboveground copulations show the same behaviors that are characteristic of underground copulations.

4. A female's vulva is predictably swollen and closed before her series of underground consortships, but open afterward. Further, vaginal lavages show sperm after, but not before, a female's series of underground consortships.

5. Electrophoretic analyses of blood samples confirm paternities inferred from behavioral observations of estrus and copulations.

6. Black-tailed prairie dog pairs probably copulate underground to avoid both male-male competition for females and interference with copulations from other males.

12 Annual and Lifetime Reproductive Success

Ways to Determine Maternity and Paternity in Natural Populations

Despite some notable exceptions among cooperatively breeding species such as groove-billed anis, acorn woodpeckers, and pukekos (Vehrencamp 1977, 1978; Koenig and Mumme 1987; Craig 1980; Craig and Jamieson 1985) and among polyandrous species such as American jacanas, ostriches, and greater rheas (Jenni and Collier 1972; Bertram 1978, 1979, 1993; Bruning 1974), maternity within natural populations is usually easy for behavioral ecologists to establish. Maternity is also easy to establish for prairie dogs, because each mother isolates her offspring in a separate home nursery burrow from parturition until first juvenile emergence (chaps. 4, 9, and 16). Paternity within natural populations, on the other hand, is consistently elusive (see examples in Clutton-Brock 1988a and Newton 1989b; Sutherland 1989). Consequently, accurate estimates of male reproductive success are rare.

Biochemical techniques such as electrophoresis (Selander et al. 1971; Harris and Hopkinson 1976) and DNA fingerprinting (Burke and Bruford 1987; Burke 1989) have helped resolve paternity for some species, such as stripe-backed wrens, lesser snow geese, dunnocks, yellow-bellied marmots, and Belding's ground squirrels (Schwartz and Armitage 1980, 1981; Hanken and Sherman 1981; Quinn et al. 1987; Rabenold et al. 1990; Davies et al. 1992). However, these techniques are only reliable when combined with detailed information on social organization or male copulatory success. Consequently, sample sizes for estimating male reproductive success from short-term studies of only 1 or 2 years are usually small.

Starch-gel electrophoresis became popular among behavioral ecologists in the late 1960s and early 1970s, but DNA fingerprinting did not emerge until the mid-1980s. Mainly for this reason, my resolution of prairie dog paternities depends totally on the former procedure.

Since discovering how to detect prairie dog copulations in 1978 (chap. 11), I have recorded 770 copulations. These copulations involve 557 periods

Fig. 12.1. Blood samples from a juvenile prairie dog. To confirm paternities inferred from behavioral observations, I collect several capillary tubes of blood from all juveniles, mothers, and breeding males each year. Label shows juvenile marker (mostly obscured by full capillary tubes), eartags, and date. (Photo by John L. Hoogland.)

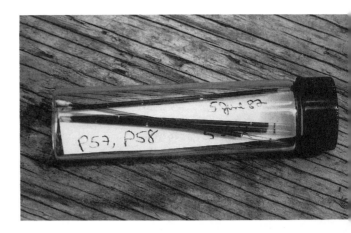

of estrus of 220 different females, and 132 different males (chap. 4). I have also collected blood samples for electrophoretic analyses from 898 emergent juveniles that resulted from these copulations (fig. 12.1). These large sample sizes provide a unique opportunity for investigating annual and lifetime reproductive success of male and female prairie dogs.

Assignment of Paternity

Table 12.1 (see also chap. 4) shows the raw data available for estimating male reproductive success. Of 294 emergent litters, behavioral observations of the mother's estrus and copulation(s) are available for 87% (257), blood samples are available for 99% (291), and both behavioral observations and blood samples are available for 86% (254). For each of the three litters for which I was unable to collect blood samples, I observed the mother's estrus and copulation(s). Consequently, I have at least one estimate of paternity (behavioral observations or blood samples) for 100% of the 294 litters used for estimating male reproductive success in 1978 through 1988.

Table 12.2 summarizes the accuracy of paternal assignments. I consider paternity to be *unambiguous* when electrophoretic analyses of polymorphic blood proteins (chap. 4) confirm behavioral observations of estrus and copulation(s). For example, if a female copulates with only one male and the genotypes of that female's emergent juveniles are compatible with the genotype of the putative father, then paternity is unambiguous. Paternity is *less certain* when I am unable to collect blood samples from the emergent juveniles for some reason, or when I do not see the mother's copulation(s) (see also chap. 4).

Paternity is unambiguous for 72% of litters that emerged at the study colony in 1978 through 1988 (216/301). More specifically, paternity is unambiguous for 77% of the juveniles that emerged from their natal burrows

Table 12.1. Raw Data for Estimating Male Reproductive Success

Type of data	Sample size
Number of estrous females observed	557
Number of observed copulations by the 557 estrous females	770
Number of emergent litters produced by the 557 estrous females	294
Number of emergent litters for which blood samples are available for most or all juveniles	291/294 = 99%
Number of emergent litters for which behavioral observations of mother's copulation(s) are available	257/294 = 87%
Number of emergent litters for which both observations of mother's copulation(s) and blood samples from most or all juveniles are available	254/294 = 86%
Number of emergent litters for which either observations of mother's copulation(s) or blood samples from most or all juveniles are available	294/294 = 100%
Number of juveniles in the 294 emergent litters	915
Number of juveniles for which blood samples are available	898/915 = 98%

Note: I collected all data at the study colony from 1978 through 1988. Because certain data are missing for some of the 557 estrous females, sample sizes in the text sometimes differ from those shown here.

in these 11 years (733/958) (table 12.2). When paternity is less certain, I assign paternity to the most likely breeding male—e.g., to the single breeding male of a one-male coterie, to the male with the highest "likelihood of paternity" (Foltz and Hoogland 1981; Hoogland and Foltz 1982; Foltz and Schwagmeyer 1989) when the female copulates with two males, and so on (see chap. 4 and table 12.2).

Despite the logic used to assign paternity to the 23% of juveniles whose paternity is less certain (225/958; see table 12.2), the precise accuracy of these assignments remains unknown. However, the probability of detecting offspring sired via either multiple paternity, cuckoldry, or missed copulations is high for prairie dogs (see below and Hoogland and Foltz 1982). I therefore estimate that my paternal assignments are probably accurate for over 95% of emergent juveniles.

Ways to Estimate Reproductive Success

Depending on the biology of the organism, researchers estimate annual reproductive success (ARS) and lifetime reproductive success (LRS) in different ways (Howard 1979, 1983). The best estimates, of course, rely on tracking reproductive units (eggs, juveniles, or yearlings) for as long as possible. Ultimately, one would like to count the number of reproductive offspring, reproductive grandoffspring, reproductive great grandoffspring, and so on, produced by different individuals (Alexander 1974; West-

Eberhard 1975). More realistically, investigators are lucky if they can count offspring up to the termination of parental care (Williams 1975; Howard 1979, 1983; Grafen 1982; Clutton-Brock 1988b; McCleery and Perrins 1988).

I have three estimates of ARS and LRS for prairie dogs: (*a*) the number of observed copulations, (*b*) the number of juveniles that emerge from the natal burrow, and (*c*) the number of emergent juveniles that survive for at least one year (i.e., the number of yearlings). Copulations occur in February and March (chap. 11), juveniles first emerge from the natal burrows about 11 weeks later in May and June, and scoring of yearlings occurs 11 months later in the following April. A yearling is more likely than an emergent juvenile, and an emergent juvenile is more likely than a copulation, to eventually yield a reproductively successful offspring. Thus, in terms of accuracy, $c > b$ as an estimate of ARS (and of LRS; see below), $b > a$, and $c > a$. I do not see prairie dog juveniles until they first emerge from the natal burrow, and thus cannot count younger juveniles (e.g., neonates) for estimates of reproductive success.

Male and female prairie dogs sometimes disperse away from the home colony—and thus are not easily distinguishable from individuals that die—as soon as 12 months after their first emergence from the natal burrow (chaps. 14 and 16). Consequently, estimates of reproductive success based on offspring that have been coming aboveground for more than about 11 months are unreliable for prairie dogs.

For my analyses of reproductive success, I consider only prairie dogs that copulated at least once during the breeding season (for ARS) or at least once during their lifetimes (for LRS). Below I discuss the effects of this procedure on my estimates of ARS and LRS (see also chap. 4).

Annual Reproductive Success

A female prairie dog evidently can obtain enough sperm to fertilize all her ovulated eggs from a single insemination. Consequently, females that copulate with a single male usually should rear as many offspring as females that copulate with two or more males (but see below). The same logic does not apply to males. Because each insemination could mean the siring of some or all offspring in an additional litter, male ARS probably should vary directly with the number of different sexual partners.

Even though it might not accurately predict ARS, the number of different sexual partners for estrous females in a single breeding season is of interest for other reasons. Figure 12.2a shows that 67% of estrous females (365/542) copulate with a single male. Other females copulate with either two or three males, but female-RR4 set the record in 1986 by consorting underground with four different breeding males. The mean ± SD number of different males with whom estrous females copulate in a single year is 1.39 ± 0.61.

Table 12.2. Accuracy of Paternal Assignments

Evidence of paternity	Number of emergent litters	Number of juveniles
Paternity is unambiguous		
Mother copulated with a single male, and single paternity confirmed by blood samples	168	535
Mother copulated with two or more males, but blood samples unequivocally showed that only one copulating male sired all juveniles	35	92
Mother copulated with two or more males, and blood samples showed unequivocal multiple paternity	13	45[a]
Paternity is less certain		
Mother copulated with a single male; I have assigned paternity to the copulating male, but confirming blood samples were unavailable	2	3
Mother appeared to copulate with a single male, but blood samples showed that she evidently copulated with at least one other breeding male that had highest likelihood of paternity for entire litter and to whom I have assigned single paternity	2	6
Mother copulated with two or more males, and I have assigned paternity to the one copulating male that unequivocally sired at least one juvenile and had highest likelihood of paternity for entire litter	38	139[b]
Mother copulated with three males; I have assigned single paternity to the first male that copulated, but confirming blood samples were unavailable	1	3
Mother copulated with two or more males, and I have assigned paternity to the one copulating male that had the highest likelihood of paternity for entire litter	5	17
Mother's copulation(s) not seen; I have assigned paternity to single breeding male of home one-male coterie because blood samples were consistent with this male	15	51
Mother's copulation(s) not seen; I have assigned single paternity to one breeding male of home multi-male coterie because blood samples excluded all other breeding males of home multi-male coterie	12	32

Mother's copulations(s) not seen; I have assigned single paternity to the one breeding male of home multi-male coterie that unequivocally sired at least one juvenile within litter	6	19
Mother's copulation(s) not seen; I have assigned single paternity to the one breeding male of home multi-male coterie that had highest likelihood of paternity for entire litter	2	6
Mother's copulation(s) not seen, but blood samples showed unequivocal multiple paternity involving two breeding males of home multi-male coterie; I have assigned paternity of each juvenile to the appropriate sire	2	10
Totals	301	958[c]

Note: Sample sizes differ from those in Table I2.1 because I have omitted certain paternal assignments in my estimates of annual or lifetime male reproductive success (e.g., when males were breeding adults of unknown age at the study colony in 1978) but have used them for other analyses (e.g., for estimating the frequency of cuckoldry). For more details, see text and chapter 4.

[a] Of these 45 juveniles, I can unambiguously assign paternity for 38. For the other 7 juveniles, I have assigned paternity to the copulating male with the highest likelihood of paternity.

[b] Of these 139 juveniles, I can unambiguously assign paternity for 68. For each of the other 71 juveniles, I have assigned paternity to the one breeding male who unequivocally sired at least one other juvenile of the same litter.

[c] Paternity is unambiguous for a minimum of 733 of the 958 juveniles that emerged from their natal burrows from 1978 through 1988 (77%). This total of 733 juveniles comes from the addition of the following numbers from this table: 535 + 92 + 38 (see note a) + 68 (see note b). Probably over 95% of the assignments are accurate (see text).

a) ARS measured by sexual partners

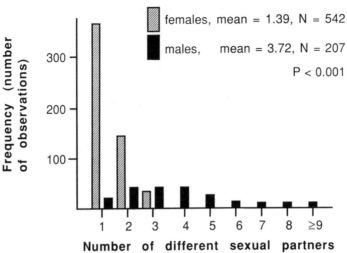

females, mean = 1.39, N = 542

males,   mean = 3.72, N = 207

P < 0.001

Number of different sexual partners with whom individual copulated in single year

b) ARS measured by emergent juveniles

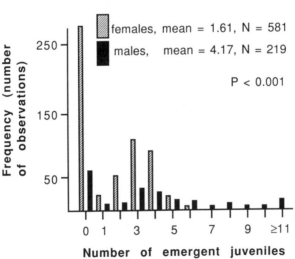

females, mean = 1.61, N = 581

males,   mean = 4.17, N = 219

P < 0.001

Number of emergent juveniles produced in single year

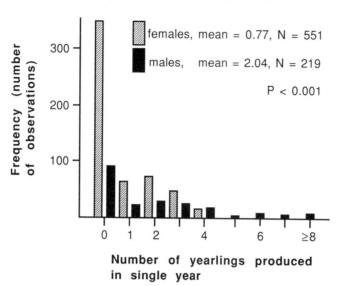

c) ARS measured by yearlings

females, mean = 0.77, N = 551

males,   mean = 2.04, N = 219

P < 0.001

Frequency (number of observations)

Number of yearlings produced in single year

◀▲ **Fig. 12.2.** Annual reproductive success (ARS) for males and females, measured by *(a)* number of different sexual partners, *(b)* number of emergent juveniles, and *(c)* number of emergent juveniles that survive for at least one year (yearlings). This graph excludes data from individuals that did not copulate at least once during the breeding season. *P*-values for all three graphs are from the Mann-Whitney *U* test.

Table 12.3 shows the *identity* of males with whom estrous females copulate. Eighty-four percent (457/542) of females copulate exclusively with the resident breeding male(s) of the home coterie; 11% (62/542) copulate with the resident breeding male and with one or more males from

Table 12.3. Number of Sexual Partners for Females of One-Male Coteries and Females of Multi-Male Coteries

	One male from the home coterie	One male from outside the home coterie	Two or more males, all from the home coterie	Two or more males, from both inside and outside the home coterie	Two or more males, all from outside the home coterie
Females in one-male coteries	256	18	—	41	3
Females in multi-male coteries	88	2	113	21	0

other coteries as well. Only 4% (23/542) copulate exclusively with one or more males from other coteries (see also below).

Females in multi-male coteries are more likely to copulate with a second male than are females in one-male coteries (fig. 12.3). However, copulation with additional males evidently does not enhance female ARS (fig. 12.4).

What might a female of any species gain by copulating with a second male? Possible benefits include increased probability of fertilization, greater genetic diversity among her offspring, additional nuptial offerings (e.g., more food from courtship feedings), and more paternal care for her offspring (Taub 1980; Schwagmeyer 1984; Huck et al. 1989; Westneat, Sherman, and Morton 1990; Birkhead and Møller 1992, 1993). As for dunnocks, vervet monkeys, and hanuman langurs (Hrdy 1977b; Andelman 1987; Davies 1992), one of these benefits seems especially likely for prairie dogs: promotion of paternal care. Prairie dog males seem only to make a simple distinction between (1) juveniles in coterie territories where they copulated—their own potential offspring—as targets for paternal care and (2) juveniles in coterie territories where they did not copulate—other males' offspring—as targets for infanticide (chaps. 7 and 10). If so, then copulating with both breeding males of a multi-male coterie might be adaptive because it increases paternal care and reduces the probability of later infanticide of the female's litter by the noncopulating male. Perhaps a single copulation by a breeding male of a multi-male coterie is sufficient to deter his later killing of *any* juveniles later born in the home coterie territory, including those of females with whom he did not copulate.

These arguments pertaining to male tolerance of juveniles and paternal care might explain an otherwise puzzling observation. In certain multi-male coteries, one breeding male is dominant to the other(s) (chap. 6). After copulating first with a female, the dominant male sometimes makes little effort to guard her from additional copulations with the subordinate male. Is the dominant male satisfied with first-male advantage (chap. 13), and willing to allow copulation by the subordinate male to deter later infanticide by him? Specifically, does the dominant male gain more by siring three of four offspring that might survive than by siring all of four offspring that the noncopulating subordinate male will later kill? More research is necessary to investigate further the relationship between copulations, confidence of paternity, kin recognition, and male-perpetrated infanticide among prairie dogs (see also chaps. 7 and 10).

Figures 12.2b and c show female ARS estimated from emergent offspring and yearlings. Mean ± SD values are 1.61 ± 1.74 and 0.77 ± 1.17, respectively. The same female set the record in both categories: female-4str produced six emergent offspring in 1982, and all six survived to be yearlings.

Figure 12.2a shows male ARS estimated from copulations. The mean ± SD number of different sexual partners for males that copulate at least

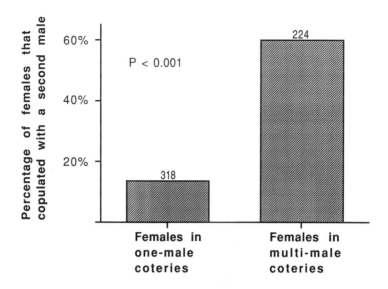

Fig. 12.3. Probability of copulating with a second male for females in one-male and multi-male coteries. The number above each bar indicates the number of estrous females observed. The *P*-value is from the 2 × 2 chi-square test.

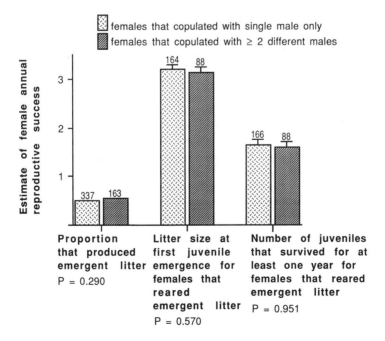

Fig. 12.4. Annual reproductive success (ARS) for females that copulate with one male versus females that copulate with two or more different males. The number above each bar indicates the number of estrous females observed. *P*-values are from either the 2 by 2 chi-square test or the Mann-Whitney *U* test.

once is 3.72 ± 1.98. Male-3 set the record in 1985 when he copulated with eleven different females.

Figures 12.2b and c show male ARS estimated from emergent offspring and yearlings. Mean ± SD values are 4.17 ± 4.22 and 2.04 ± 2.48, respectively. One record belongs to male-0, who sired twenty-one emergent juveniles in 1987. Male-15 set the other record when twelve of his 1985 emergent juveniles survived for at least 1 year.

As expected for a polygynous species (Trivers 1972; Alexander et al. 1979; Clutton-Brock, Guinness, and Albon 1982), variance in ARS among prairie dogs is greater for males than for females (fig. 12.2).

Lifetime Reproductive Success

Figure 12.5 shows estimates of female LRS. The mean ± SD number of lifetime sexual partners for females is 3.53 ± 2.43; female-6str set the record by copulating with twelve different males over her lifetime. For lifetime production of emergent juveniles, the mean ± SD is 4.25 ± 3.85, and female-WA2 set the record with eighteen. No female at the study colony has ever produced more than five litters of emergent juveniles (mean ± SD = 1.35 ± 1.13). The mean ± SD number of yearlings reared over a female's lifetime is 2.14 ± 2.28, with the record of twelve going to female-70.

Figure 12.5 also shows estimates of male LRS. Means ± SD for number of different sexual partners, emergent juveniles, and yearlings are 6.17 ± 5.06, 7.06 ± 7.67, and 3.45 ± 4.17, respectively. One male, male-15, holds

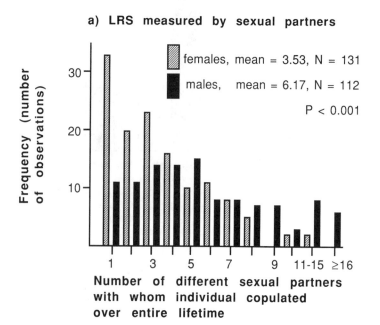

a) LRS measured by sexual partners

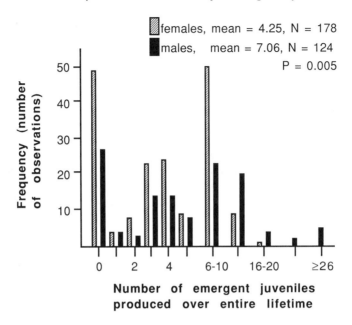

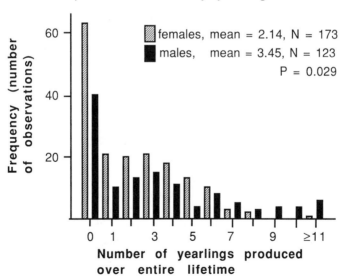

◀ ▲ **Fig. 12.5.** Lifetime reproductive success (LRS) for males and females measured by *(a)* number of different sexual partners, *(b)* number of emergent juveniles, and *(c)* number of emergent juveniles that survive for at least one year (yearlings). This graph excludes data from individuals that did not copulate at least once in their lifetimes. *P*-values for all three graphs are from the Mann-Whitney *U* test.

the record in all three lifetime categories with thirty-four different sexual partners, forty-five emergent juveniles, and twenty-four yearlings!

A polygynous mating system, by definition, is one in which variance in LRS is greater for males than for females (Trivers 1972; Alexander et al. 1979). For prairie dogs this is true for lifetime estimates of copulations, emergent juveniles, and yearlings (fig. 12.5). Thus, prairie dogs are unequivocally polygynous.

Interestingly, but as expected (Clutton-Brock, Guinness, and Albon 1982; Hrdy and Williams 1983; see also examples in Clutton-Brock 1988a and Newton 1989b), the difference in variance in LRS of male and female prairie dogs (fig. 12.5) is not as striking as an examination of male and female variance in ARS might predict (see fig. 12.2). The reason is simple: the long-lived prairie dog females (chap. 16) have time to "catch up" with the high reproductive success realized in only a few years by the shorter-lived males.

What about Prairie Dogs That Never Copulate?

In all discussion to this point, I have ignored prairie dogs that do not copulate at least once during the breeding season (for ARS) or during their lifetimes (for LRS). The majority of these noncopulating individuals are juveniles that die before becoming yearlings; most of the others are sexually immature yearlings that do not survive to become adults. Might the inclusion of noncopulating prairie dogs disproportionately increase female variance in ARS and LRS, and thus nullify the conclusion that prairie dogs are polygynous?

Of 523 females reared to first emergence (chap. 16), 239 died before becoming yearlings; 41 survived to become yearlings (all sexually immature), but died or dispersed before becoming adults; and another 2 survived only long enough to become 2-year-olds, but did not copulate as either yearlings or 2-year-olds. No female survived through the third breeding season without copulating at least once. Thus, I have excluded 282 females (239 + 41 + 2), all of which did not copulate, from my analyses of female ARS and LRS.

Of 587 males reared to first emergence, 312 died before becoming yearlings; 91 survived to become yearlings (all sexually immature), but died or dispersed before becoming adults; 26 survived only long enough to become 2-year-olds, but did not copulate as either yearlings or 2-year-olds; and 3 others survived only long enough to become 3-year-olds without ever copulating. Thus, I have excluded 432 males (312 + 91 + 26 + 3), all of which did not copulate, from my analyses of male ARS and LRS.

These data show that female prairie dogs survive better than males, and that males are more likely than females to delay the age of first reproduction (see also chap. 16). Consequently, the inclusion of prairie dogs that never copulate would disproportionately increase *male* rather than female variance in both ARS and LRS. The conclusion that prairie dogs are polygynous is therefore secure.

Multiple Paternity

Multiple paternity occurs when two or more males each sire at least one offspring of a single female's litter (chap. 11). Thirty-three percent of estrous females (177/542) copulate with two or more males (see fig. 12.2a). Of these multiply copulating females, 51% (91/177) eventually rear juveniles to first emergence. Nine percent (8/91) of these emergent litters contain a single juvenile, and thus cannot show multiple paternity. Thirty-three percent of the remaining litters with two or more emergent juveniles (27/83) unequivocally show no multiple paternity, and 16% (13/83) show unambiguous multiple paternity. For the other 52% of the litters with two or more emergent juveniles (43/83), I cannot rule out multiple paternity because I cannot unambiguously assign one or more juveniles to any of the copulating males. Perhaps the most useful data are from the 40 litters of multiply copulating females (27 + 13) that I can unambiguously score. Of these, 32.5% (13/40) show multiple paternity, while 67.5% (27/40) do not.

Besides examining the 91 litters of females that copulated with two or more males, I also have looked for, but have failed to find, evidence for multiple paternity in the 168 litters of females that appeared to copulate with only a single male. The minimal frequency of multiple paternity is therefore 5% (13/[91 + 168]). As noted above, I cannot rule out multiple paternity for 43 litters of females that copulated with more than one male. If 32.5% (see above) of these 43 litters involve (undetected) multiple paternity, then the real frequency of multiple paternity among prairie dog litters might be as high as 10%: (13 + [.325 × 43])/(91 + 168).

Like African lion, yellow-bellied marmot, and Idaho ground squirrel females (Schwartz and Armitage 1980, 1981; Packer and Pusey 1983; Sherman 1989; Packer et al. 1991), estrous prairie dog females usually copulate with a single male. Surely this is the main reason that multiple paternity in these species is rarer than in species such as Belding's and thirteen-lined ground squirrels, in which females usually copulate with two or more males (Hanken and Sherman 1981; Foltz and Schwagmeyer 1989; Schwagmeyer and Foltz 1990). Other factors that might reduce multiple paternity or its detection among prairie dogs include (1) small litter size (mean = 3.08; see chap. 16) and small number of polymorphic loci ($N = 7$; see chap. 4) available for electrophoresis (McCracken and Bradbury 1977, 1981); (2) the small number of different males (usually 2; see fig. 12.2a) that inseminate multiply copulating females (Hanken and Sherman 1981; Schwagmeyer and Brown 1983; Schwagmeyer 1984, 1986); (3)

electrophoretic similarity of the copulating males, because breeding males of multi-male coteries are commonly close kin (chap. 6); and (4) long delays between successive copulations, sometimes involving several hours (Parker 1970; Dewsbury and Baumgardner 1981; Smith 1984; Schwagmeyer and Foltz 1990; Møller 1991b).

Paternity in Multi-Male Coteries

Although most coteries contain a single breeding male, 27% of coteries (74/273) contain two or more (chap. 6). I have attempted to determine whether the resident breeding males within multi-male coteries share copulations and the siring of litters, or whether one male usually monopolizes both. Regarding copulations, 50% of the females in multi-male coteries (113/224) copulate with more than one of the resident breeding males (see fig. 12.3). Thus, one male does not routinely monopolize copulations in multi-male coteries.

Despite failing to monopolize copulations, dominant prairie dog males in multi-male coteries, like dominant males in multi-male groups of golden lion tamarins (Baker, Dietz, and Kleiman 1993), might monopolize the siring of offspring. For example, dominant prairie dog males might copulate exclusively with heavy, middle-aged females, which are most likely to wean offspring (chap. 13). Or they might maximize their chances of siring offspring by copulating first with each estrous female (see above). To investigate the siring of offspring in multi-male coteries, I have examined paternity in the 34 multi-male coteries that produced two or more emergent litters. In 26% of these coteries (9/34), one male sired all the litters. In 21% (7/34), one male sired one or more offspring in all the litters, but a second male sired at least one offspring in one or more litters via multiple paternity. In the other 53% of coteries (18/34), at least two males sired entire litters. The obvious conclusion is that one male does not routinely monopolize the siring of litters in multi-male coteries.

Females in one-male coteries usually copulate exclusively with the resident breeding male (see table 12.3). Consequently, all the nonlittermate juveniles within the same one-male coterie in any single year are usually half siblings (same father, different mothers). In addition, of course, these half siblings have common ancestors via their mothers, which are always close kin (chaps. 6, 10, and 14). In multi-male coteries, however, nonlittermate juveniles within the same coterie commonly are *not* paternal half siblings due to the shared paternity among the breeding males. Does this difference in kinship between same-year, nonlittermate juveniles of one-male and multi-male coteries have any relevance to kin recognition among prairie dogs? Probably not, because kin recognition depends primarily on direct social learning shortly after first juvenile emergences rather than on coefficients of genetic relatedness (chap. 10).

Cuckoldry

Prairie dog females usually copulate only with the breeding male(s) resident in the home coterie territory (see table 12.3). Sometimes, however, estrous females copulate with a temporary invader, or leave the home coterie territory and copulate with a male from an adjacent coterie territory (see also chap. 6). Four percent of estrous females (23/542) copulate exclusively with males from outside coteries. Another 11% (62/542) copulate with outside males before or after copulating with the male(s) of the home coterie. Thus, 16% of estrous prairie dog females (85/542) copulate at least once with a male from an outside coterie.

When extracoterie copulations yield offspring, the result is *cuckoldry* of the resident breeding male—i.e., the siring of offspring in his coterie territory by a male from an outside coterie. Eight percent of emergent prairie dog litters (25/316) show unequivocal evidence of cuckoldry. Six of the twenty-five affected litters also show multiple paternity, with the resident breeding male siring some of the juveniles and the outside male siring the rest. Cuckoldry is common for some harem-polygynous animals, such as red-winged blackbirds and greater spearnose bats (Bray, Kennelly, and Guarino 1975; McCracken and Bradbury 1977, 1981; Gibbs et al. 1990), but rare for other species such as African lions and yellow-bellied marmots (Schwartz and Armitage 1980, 1981; Packer et al. 1991). Cuckolded prairie dog males evidently cannot discriminate between their own and other males' offspring (chap. 10).

Whether or not they also copulate with outside males, copulating with the resident breeding male(s) is evidently important to female prairie dogs. Specifically, 96% of estrous females (519/542) copulate with the breeding male(s) of the home coterie. Amazingly, reasonable explanations exist for all 4% of the females (23/542) that copulated exclusively with outside males. In eleven of the twenty-three cases, the only resident adult male was apparently sexually inactive, as indicated by his having no descended testes, no pigmented scrotum, and no observed copulations (chaps. 4 and 7). In seven of the cases, the female copulated with a male that invaded the home coterie territory and was temporarily resident during the breeding season. Each of these invaders dominated the resident breeding male and acted as though he intended to remain in the invaded territory following the conclusion of breeding season. By copulating with them, females reduce the probability of later infanticide by males that invade during the breeding season (chap. 7). In the five remaining cases, the resident breeding male was either the female's father ($N = 4$) or her half brother ($N = 1$). Exclusive copulation with a male from an outside coterie in these cases was a way of avoiding extreme inbreeding (chap. 14).

Females that copulate exclusively with males from outside the home coterie are less likely to rear a litter to first emergence (fig. 12.6). Why

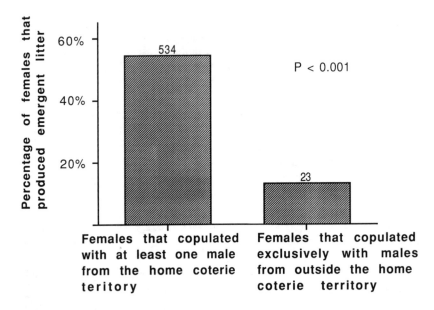

Fig. 12.6. Females that copulate exclusively with males from outside the home coterie are less likely to produce emergent juveniles. The number above each bar indicates the number of estrous females observed. The *P*-value is from the 2×2 chi-square test.

might such females incur this cost? One reason is that cuckolded males or sexually inactive adult males of the home coterie territory sometimes kill the offspring sired by outside males (chap. 7). Another reason is that the circumstances that induce females to copulate with outside males are perhaps the same circumstances that lead to poor female reproduction. Specifically, either the absence of a sexually active male in the home coterie territory or the presence of a breeding male that cannot appropriately protect the home coterie territory from invading males is probably incompatible with the rearing of juveniles to first emergence.

Evidence of Female Choice

Despite heated controversy about its nature and extent, biologists generally agree that at least some genetic variation must prevail among the breeding males of all sexual species (Hamilton and Zuk 1982; Read 1987, 1991; Pomiankowski 1988, 1989; Maynard Smith 1978, 1991; Thornhill and Sauer 1992; Norris 1993). Female choice, the nonrandom choice of sexual partners by females, should therefore be universal (Cox and Le Boeuf 1977; Borgia 1987; Kirkpatrick 1987; Hill 1991; Kirkpatrick and Ryan 1991). Variation in male ability to help rear offspring further promotes female choice for animals that exhibit paternal care, such as over 90% of avian species, and mammals such as raccoon dogs, owl monkeys, prairie voles, and prairie dogs (Lack 1968; Thomas and Birney 1979; Getz, Carter, and Gavish 1981; Wright 1984; Yamamoto 1987; chap. 6).

Female prairie dogs do not copulate randomly with any breeding male in the general vicinity (see table 12.3). Female choice must therefore operate. I have identified at least two forms of female choice, one obvious and the other more subtle. First, females frequently refuse to copulate with sexually active male close kin in the home coterie territory (chap. 14). Instead, such discriminating females outbreed with a genetically unrelated male from either the home coterie territory (when the home coterie is multi-male) or an adjacent coterie territory. Second, females usually copulate exclusively with the resident breeding male(s) in the home coterie territory. In one sense, this pattern might suggest the *absence* of female choice. However, resident breeding males frequently face challenges from possible invaders. Females rarely participate directly in these challenges, but often encourage them with their "defense barks" (chap. 6). When a female copulates with the resident breeding male(s), then, she is choosing the male that has repeatedly demonstrated his prowess at repelling possible invaders. This second form of female choice, though more subtle and passive than the first form (Alexander 1975; Cox and Le Boeuf 1977), has probably been equally important in the evolution of the prairie dog mating system.

Do the Different Estimates of ARS and LRS Correlate for Females?

Despite some intriguing exceptions (Madsen at al. 1992), female ARS for most animals does not vary directly with the number of different sexual partners (see above). The same is true for prairie dogs (fig. 12.7a). On the other hand, females that rear numerous juveniles to first emergence should rear more yearlings than females that rear only a few juveniles to first emergence. Figure 12.7b supports this prediction.

Unlike females of animals such as red-winged blackbirds, northern fulmars, spotted sandpipers, and rhinolophid and vespertilionid bats which can store sperm for long periods (Racey 1973, 1975, 1979; Bray, Kennelly, and Guarino 1975; Hatch 1983; Shugart 1988; Oring et al. 1992), female prairie dogs evidently cannot. Thus, a female must copulate with at least one male each breeding season in order to conceive and rear offspring. Long-lived females therefore copulate more times and have more opportunities to rear offspring over their lifetimes than do shorter-lived females. The number of different sexual partners over a female's *lifetime* should therefore correlate with estimates of female LRS based on emergent juveniles and yearlings—even though comparable correlations do not occur for female ARS. Figure 12.8a supports this prediction. Also, as expected, female LRS estimated from yearlings correlates positively with female LRS estimated from emergent juveniles (fig. 12.8b).

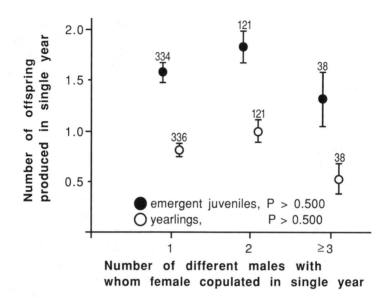

a) female reproductive success in single year
versus female copulatory success in single year

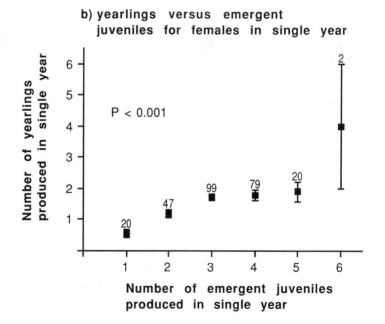

b) yearlings versus emergent
juveniles for females in single year

◄ **Fig. 12.7.** Correlations among the different estimates of female annual reproductive success. *(a)* Female reproductive success in single year versus female copulatory success in single year. The number above each SE line indicates the number of estrous females observed. This graph excludes data from females that did not come into estrus and copulate. *P*-values are from the Spearman rank correlation test. *(b)* Number of yearlings produced by females in single year versus number of emergent juveniles produced by these females in single year. The number above each SE line indicates the number of reproductively successful females. The *P*-value is from the Spearman rank correlation test. This graph excludes data from adult females that did not produce at least one emergent juvenile for the year; when I include data from such females, the positive relationship is still significant (*P* < .001, Spearman rank correlation test).

Do the Different Estimates of ARS and LRS Correlate for Males?

For animals such as satin bowerbirds, black grouse, hammer-headed bats, and vervet monkeys (Bradbury 1977; Borgia 1985; Cheney et al. 1988; Kruijt and de Vos 1988), investigators count copulations by different males, and from these counts infer male ARS and male LRS. But do copulations accurately predict male reproductive success? And does the number of juveniles sired by males correlate with later estimates of reproductive success? Mainly because of the difficulty of assigning paternity, the answers to these questions remain elusive (Howard 1979, 1983; see chapters in Clutton-Brock 1988a and Newton 1989b).

For male prairie dogs, ARS and LRS estimated from copulations correlate positively with ARS and LRS estimated from both the number of emergent offspring sired and the number of yearlings sired (figs. 12.9a and 12.10a). Thus, as for male red deer (Pemberton et al. 1992), copulatory success is a good predictor of ARS and LRS for male prairie dogs. Further, male ARS and LRS estimated from yearlings vary directly with male ARS and LRS estimated from emergent offspring (figs. 12.9b and 12.10b).

Despite the correlations in figures 12.7 through 12.10, trying to infer reproductive success from copulatory success for any *single* individual is risky. For example, female-6str set the record by copulating with twelve different males over her lifetime. However, female-6str reared only one litter of two juveniles to first emergence, and none of these juveniles survived to be a yearling. For a male example, consider male-02. In 1988 he copulated with ten different females—only one short of the single-season record of eleven—but did not sire a single emergent juvenile (or yearling) that year. Over his lifetime male-02 copulated with fourteen different females—well above the mean number of 6.17 (see fig. 12.5a)—but he never sired a single emergent juvenile. Male-02's complete reproductive failure did not result from sterility, because most of his sexual partners gave birth to litters before losing them to infanticide.

a) female reproductive success over entire lifetime versus female copulatory success over entire lifetime

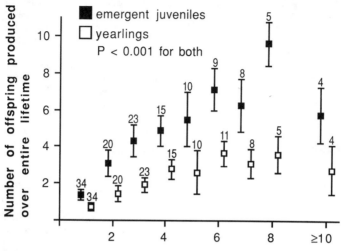

b) yearlings versus emergent juveniles for females over entire lifetime

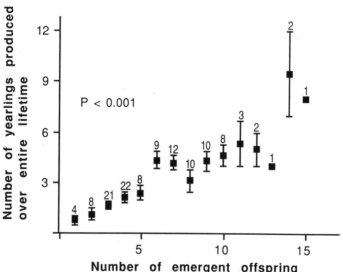

◄ **Fig. 12.8.** Correlations among the different estimates of female lifetime reproductive success. *(a)* Female reproductive success over entire lifetime versus female copulatory success over entire lifetime. The number above each SE line indicates the number of females for which I could record all copulations over their entire lifetimes. This graph excludes data from females that did not come into estrus and copulate at least once in their lifetimes. *P*-values are from the Spearman rank correlation test. *(b)* Number of yearlings produced by females over entire lifetime versus number of emergent juveniles produced by these females over entire lifetime. The number above each SE line indicates the number of reproductively successful females. The *P*-value is from the Spearman rank correlation test. This graph excludes data from females that did not produce at least one emergent juvenile in their lifetimes; when I include data from such females, the positive relationship is still significant (*P* < .001, Spearman rank correlation test).

Spearman correlation coefficients for male ARS estimated from copulations versus male ARS estimated from emergent juveniles and versus male ARS estimated from yearlings are 0.486 and 0.340, respectively. Spearman correlation coefficients for male LRS estimated from copulations versus male LRS estimated from emergent juveniles and versus male LRS estimated from yearlings are 0.664 and 0.535, respectively. Copulatory success thus explains from 12% to 44% of the variance in male ARS and male LRS. Why doesn't male copulatory success more accurately predict male reproductive success? At least five factors reduce the correlations in figures 12.9 and 12.10, as explained below.

1. Like females of other animals, such as Florida scrub jays, red deer, dwarf mongooses, and African lions (Clutton-Brock, Guinness, and Albon 1982; Rood 1980b, 1990; Woolfenden and Fitzpatrick 1984; Packer et al. 1988; Creel et al. 1992), female prairie dogs vary greatly in their ability to rear offspring (see figs. 12.2 and 12.5). Consequently, copulating with a few competent females might yield more offspring than copulating with numerous females of lower competence.

2. Like ejaculates of other animals, such as red flour beetles, domestic chickens, house mice, Norway rats, and domestic cattle (Edwards 1955; Adler and Zoloth 1970; Sharma and Hays 1975; Ginsberg and Huck 1989), prairie dog ejaculates probably vary in volume and capacity to fertilize. Copulations of some males are therefore more likely than copulations of other males to impregnate.

3. For the 33% of females that copulate with two males, siring of offspring can occur in three ways: the first male sires all the offspring, the second male sires all the offspring, or both males

a) male reproductive success in single year versus male copulatory success in single year

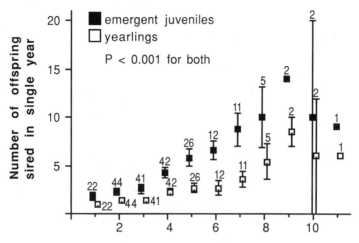

b) yearlings versus emergent juveniles for males in single year

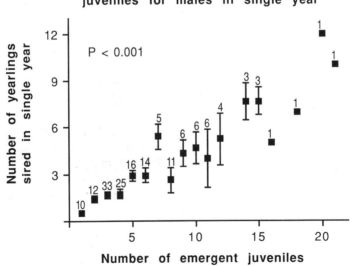

◄ **Fig. 12.9.** Correlations among the different estimates of male annual reproductive success. *(a)* Male reproductive success in single year versus male copulatory success in single year. The number above each SE line indicates the number of males for which I could record all copulations in a single year. This graph excludes data from males that did not copulate at least once during the breeding season. *P*-values are from the Spearman rank correlation test. *(b)* Number of yearlings sired by males in single year versus number of emergent juveniles sired by these males in single year. The number above each SE line indicates the number of males for which I could accurately record siring of offspring in a single year. The *P*-value is from the Spearman rank correlation test. This graph excludes data from adult males that did not sire at least one emergent juvenile for the year; when I include data from such males, the positive relationship is still significant (*P* < .001, Spearman rank correlation test).

sire at least one offspring (i.e., multiple paternity). The probability that a male's copulation will impregnate is thus lowered, due to sperm competition, when the female copulates with a second male.

4. Chance probably accounts for some of the discrepancy between male copulatory success and male reproductive success. For example, certain males breed in a year of little precipitation when female condition and reproduction—and hence male reproductive success—are poor. Other, luckier males breed in a year of copious precipitation when female condition and reproduction—and hence male reproductive success—are better.

5. Because large coteries contain more females, male copulatory success is usually higher within large coteries. However, infanticide is also more common within large coteries, affecting almost half of all litters born (chap. 7). Consequently, the high copulatory success of males in large coteries commonly does not translate into high production of emergent juveniles and yearlings.

The answer to the question posed at the beginning of this section is thus *yes* and *no. Yes,* because the correlations between male copulatory success and male reproductive success are statistically significant. And *no,* because the numerous exceptions make it difficult to infer reproductive success from copulatory success for any particular male.

Infanticide partially or totally eliminates 39% of prairie dogs litters (chap. 7). Such infanticide is probably more responsible than any other factor for lowering the correlation between male copulatory success and male reproductive success for prairie dogs. Although infanticide occurs in hundreds of other animals, its frequency is usually much lower (chap. 7). Consequently, male copulatory success might predict male reproductive success more accurately for other animals than for prairie dogs.

a) male reproductive success over entire lifetime
   versus male copulatory success over entire lifetime

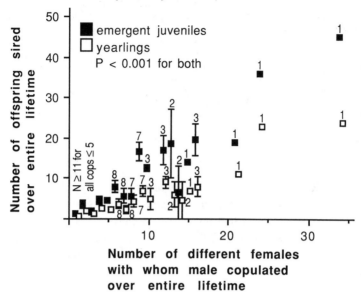

Number of different females
with whom male copulated
over entire lifetime

b) yearlings versus emergent juveniles
   for males over entire lifetime

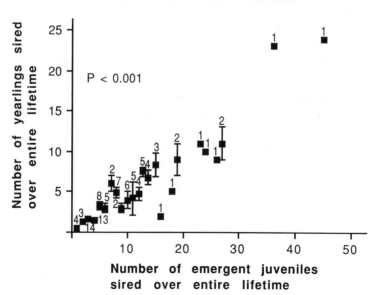

Number of emergent juveniles
sired over entire lifetime

◀ **Fig. 12.10.** Correlations among different estimates of male lifetime reproductive success. *(a)* Male reproductive success over entire lifetime versus male copulatory success over entire lifetime. The number above each SE line indicates the number of males for which I could accurately record siring of offspring over their entire lifetimes. This graph excludes data from males that did not copulate at least once in their lifetimes. *P*-values are from the Spearman rank correlation test. *(b)* Number of yearlings sired by males over entire lifetime versus number of emergent juveniles sired by these males over entire lifetime. The number above each SE line indicates the number of males for which I could accurately record siring of offspring over their entire lifetimes. The *P*-value is from the Spearman rank correlation test. This graph excludes data from males that did not sire at least one offspring in their lifetimes; when I include data from such males, the positive relationship is still significant (*P* < .001, Spearman rank correlation test).

Summary

1. Behavioral observations of the mother's estrus and copulation are available for 87% of the litters that emerged at the study colony in 1978 through 1988. Blood samples for electrophoresis are available for most or all juveniles from 99% of these litters.

2. The minimal estimate of accuracy of paternal assignments is 77%. Probably over 95% of assignments are accurate.

3. Sixty-seven percent of estrous females copulate with a single male. Females in multi-male coteries are more likely than females in one-male coteries to copulate with a second male.

4. The number of emergent juveniles produced in one year by females that copulate ranges from 0 to 6, with a mean ± SD of 1.61 ± 1.74. The number of emergent offspring sired by breeding males in one year ranges from 0 to 21, with a mean ± SD of 2.31 ± 2.89.

5. The number of emergent juveniles produced by females over their entire lifetimes ranges from 0 to 18, with a mean ± SD of 4.28 ± 3.85. The number of emergent juveniles sired by males over their entire lifetimes ranges from 0 to 45, with a mean ± SD of 7.05 ± 7.68.

6. Variance in lifetime reproductive success is greater for males than for females. The prairie dog mating system is therefore polygynous.

7. The minimal frequency of multiple paternity among prairie dogs is 5%.

8. Cuckoldry of the resident breeding male occurs when a male from an outside coterie sires offspring in the home coterie territory. Eight percent of litters show unequivocal evidence of cuckoldry.

9. Different measures of male annual and lifetime reproductive success correlate with one another. For example, males that copulate frequently sire more emergent juveniles and yearlings than do males that copulate only once.

13 Factors That Affect Annual and Lifetime Reproductive Success

How was male-15 able to sire forty-five emergent juveniles over his life-time when most males sire no juveniles at all (chap. 12)? And how was female-4str able to wean six juveniles when the usual litter size at first emergence is only three or four (chap. 16)? In this chapter I investigate ten factors that affect the annual and lifetime reproductive success (ARS and LRS) of prairie dogs.

Any factor that affects ARS also affects LRS, and vice versa. For simplicity, however, I usually investigate the effect of a particular factor on either ARS alone or LRS alone.

Age versus ARS

Almost all alleles affect more than one aspect of the phenotype (Williams 1957). If an allele produces effects both early and late in life, then the early effects will be more important because they have a greater impact on fitness. Natural selection might therefore favor alleles with early, ben-eficial effects even when their later effects are highly deleterious. The consequence will be senescence, the decline in survivorship and fecundity associated with advancing age (Williams 1957; Hamilton 1966; Preston 1972; Caswell 1982; Alexander 1987; Rose 1984, 1991; Partridge and Barton 1993). In general, both age-specific survivorship and ARS should increase up to a certain age, after which they should steadily decline—as one or both do for animals such as arctic terns, collared flycatchers, raccoon dogs, ringed seals, and Uinta and Belding's ground squirrels (Coulson and Horobin 1976; Helle 1980; Sherman and Morton 1984; Sauer and Slade 1987; Gustafsson and Part 1990; Helle and Kauhala 1993).

Because they have demonstrated their ability to survive over time, old individuals might be more attractive to potential mates than are younger individuals (Howard 1983; Manning 1985; Møller 1985). Older individuals also might be better parents because of their cumulative parental experi-ence (Orians 1969b; Searcy 1978; Rowley 1977; Woolfenden and Fitzpatrick

1984). Perhaps increased attractiveness and cumulative parental experience sometimes offset the decline in ARS otherwise expected for older individuals.

Prairie dog survivorship varies curvilinearly with age for both sexes, but especially for females. Consequently, middle-aged individuals survive better than older and younger individuals (fig. 13.1). In ultimate terms, the trends in figure 13.1 probably result from the greater importance of, and stronger natural selection for, survivorship in early and mid-life than in later life. In proximate terms, the trends might result from similar age-related trends in body mass (chap. 16).

I have investigated the effect of senescence on ARS by investigating age versus the probability of copulation, versus the production of emergent juveniles, and versus the production of yearlings. Small sample sizes of older individuals render all conclusions tentative, but figure 13.2 suggests the expected curvilinear relationship between age and probability of copulation for both males and females.

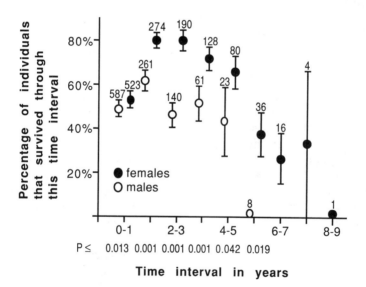

Fig. 13.1. Age-specific survivorship of male and female prairie dogs. The number above each SE line indicates the number of individuals alive at the beginning of each interval. *P*-values compare male versus female survivorship for each interval, and are from the 2 × 2 chi-square test for the first five intervals and from the Fisher exact probability test for the sixth interval; no male has survived into the seventh and later intervals. For both sexes, the probability of survivorship varies across different intervals ($P \leq .008$ for each sex, Kruskal-Wallis analysis of variance).

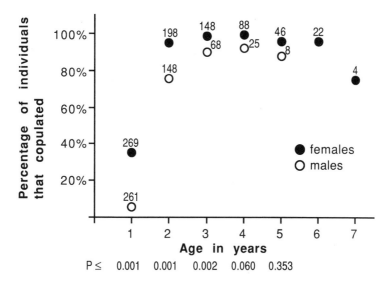

Fig. 13.2. Probability of copulation versus age. The number above each circle indicates the number of individuals. *P*-values compare male versus female probability for each age, and are from the 2 × 2 chi-square test; no male has survived to be 6 years old or older.

I have examined the number of emergent juveniles produced by individuals in a single year versus age in two ways. First, I have used data only from individuals that produced at least one emergent juvenile (fig. 13.3a). With these data, prairie dog females show a slight curvilinear trend with age. Males show an unexpected result: the number of emergent juveniles produced in a single season increases directly with age.

Second, I have included data from known-aged individuals that failed to produce emergent juveniles in a particular year for any reason—e.g., failure to copulate, abortion, or juveniles lost to infanticide. With these additional data, the curvilinear relationship between female age and the number of emergent juveniles is striking (fig. 13.3b). And once again the number of emergent juveniles varies directly with male age.

Production of yearlings is a better indicator of reproductive success than is production of emergent juveniles (chap. 12). The production of yearlings versus age suggests a curvilinear trend for both sexes, especially when I include data from individuals that failed to produce any emergent juveniles (fig. 13.4).

Menopause is the permanent cessation of ovulation among older females (Hogden et al. 1977; Gould, Flint, and Graham 1981; Hrdy 1981a; Hrdy and Whitten 1987). By channeling all their remaining investment into extant, older offspring, menopausal females might rear more grandoffspring

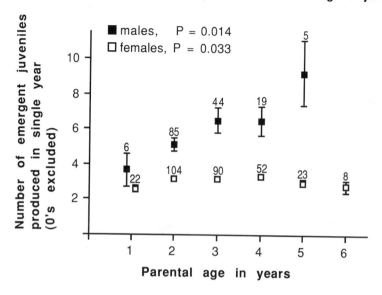

a) production of emergent juveniles for those
individuals who produced ≥1 emergent juvenile

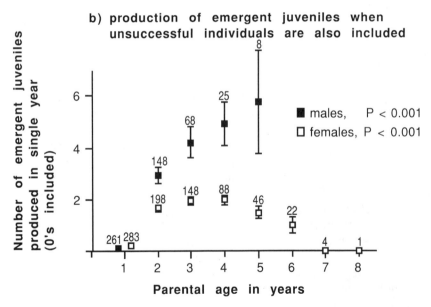

b) production of emergent juveniles when
unsuccessful individuals are also included

Fig. 13.3. Production of offspring versus parental age. *(a)* Number of emergent juveniles produced in a single year versus parental age when I exclude data from males and females that failed to produce emergent juveniles in a particular year. *(b)* Number of emergent juveniles produced in a single year versus parental age when I include data from males and females that failed to produce emergent juveniles in a particular year. For these graphs, the number above each SE line indicates the number of individuals in each age class, and *P*-values are from the Kruskal-Wallis analysis of variance.

a) production of yearlings for those individuals who produced ≥1 emergent juvenile

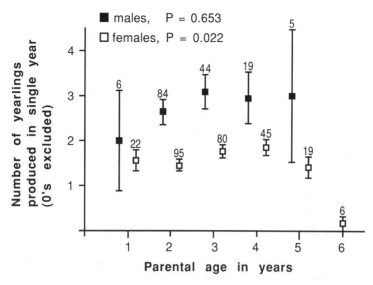

b) production of yearlings when individuals who did not produce ≥1 emergent juvenile are also included

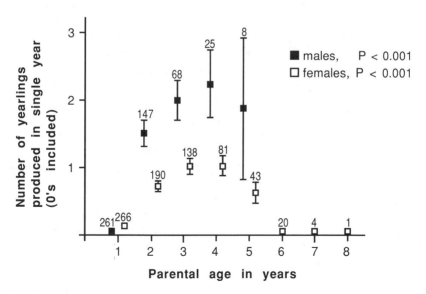

Fig. 13.4. Production of yearlings versus parental age. *(a)* Number of yearlings produced in a single year versus parental age when I exclude data from males and females that failed to produce emergent juveniles in a particular year. *(b)* Number of yearlings produced in a single year versus parental age when I include data from males and females that failed to produce emergent juveniles in a particular year. For these graphs, the number above each SE line indicates the number of individuals in each age class, and *P*-values are from the Kruskal-Wallis analysis of variance.

than do other females that ignore older offspring and continue with attempts to reproduce until death (Williams 1957; Alexander 1974, 1990b; Dawkins 1976; Mayer 1982; Lancaster and King 1985). Menopause starts sooner (relative to maximal longevity) and lasts longer for humans than for any other animal (Lancaster and King 1985; Alexander 1990b), but shorter forms of menopause also might occur for African elephants (Douglas-Hamilton and Douglas-Hamilton 1975), false killer whales (Marsh and Kasuya 1986), short-finned pilot whales (Kasuya and Marsh 1984), and nonhuman primates such as gray-cheeked mangabeys, chimpanzees, and toque and rhesus macaques (Dittus 1975; Hogden et al. 1977; Waser 1978; Graham, Kling, and Steiner 1979; Gould, Flint, and Graham 1981). Menopause is not evident among prairie dog females. For example, 95% of 6-year-old females come into estrus and copulate (21/22), as do 75% of 7-year-old females (3/4) (see fig. 13.2).

Why does the number of emergent juveniles vary directly with paternal age (fig. 13.3) while the number of yearlings versus paternal age is more curvilinear, as expected (fig. 13.4)? Specifically, why do 3- and 4-year-old males end up with more surviving yearlings per year even though 5-year-old males sire more emergent juveniles per year? Two possible explanations come to mind. First, the number of 5-year-old males that sire offspring is small. Observed discrepancies might therefore be spurious. Second, juvenile survivorship is higher when the resident breeding male remains in the same coterie territory until the next year (see below). However, 5-year-old males are less likely than 3- and 4-year-old males to survive until the next year (see fig. 13.1). The improved survivorship of middle-aged males allows them to provide more cumulative paternal care, so that they end up with more surviving yearlings.

In some animals that show senescence, such as California gulls, collared flycatchers, and red deer, natural selection seems to favor increased reproductive effort for those individuals that reach maximal longevity (Pugesek 1981, 1983; Part, Gustafsson, and Moreno 1992; Clutton-Brock 1984). The result is "terminal reproductive effort," which is higher than any previous effort (Fisher 1958; Williams 1966a,b; Stearns 1976). Terminal reproductive effort is not obvious among prairie dog females. For example, 6- and 7-year-old females do not have larger litters or rear more yearlings than do younger females (figs. 13.3 and 13.4). Nor is terminal reproductive effort obvious among prairie dog males (fig. 13.4). However, terminal reproductive effort could nonetheless occur among prairie dogs in subtle ways that are practically immune to detection by behavioral ecologists (Clutton-Brock 1984; Partridge and Harvey 1988; Part, Gustafsson, and Moreno 1992).

Order of Copulations versus Male ARS

When a female copulates with two or more males, the siring of the resulting offspring might be related to the order of copulations (Dewsbury 1982a,

1984; Smith 1984; Ginsberg and Huck 1989; Birkhead and Hunter 1990). For some animals, such as European rabbits, house mice, and Belding's and thirteen-lined ground squirrels, the first male to copulate usually sires most of the offspring (Dziuk 1965; Hanken and Sherman 1981; Dewsbury 1984; Huck, Quinn, and Lisk 1985; Foltz and Schwagmeyer 1989). For other animals, such as northern fulmars, prairie voles, and Idaho ground squirrels, the last male to copulate usually sires most of the offspring (Oglesby, Lanier, and Dewsbury 1981; Dewsbury and Baumgardner 1981; Sherman 1989; Hunter, Burke, and Watts 1992). For still other animals, such as domestic pigs, Norway rats, and deer mice, siring and copulatory order seem unrelated (Sumption and Adams 1961; Lanier, Estep, and Dewsbury 1979; Dewsbury and Hartung 1980; Dewsbury 1985).

For prairie dogs, I have data from 87 litters produced by females that copulated with more than one male and for which I determined the order of copulations. In 47% of these litters (41/87), the copulating males are too similar electrophoretically to allow assignment of paternity for each juvenile—often because the males are close kin such as father and son or full brothers (chaps. 6 and 11). For the remaining litters, the first male to copulate is more likely than later males to sire offspring (fig. 13.5). This first-male advantage is consistent with the finding that first-copulating males guard estrous females longer and more diligently after copulation than do later-copulating males (chap. 11).

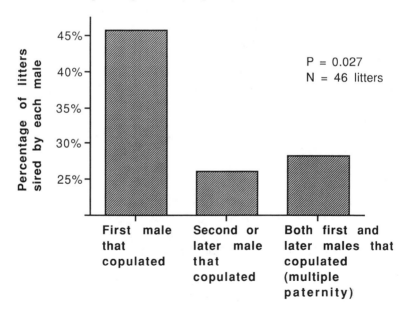

Fig. 13.5. Paternity versus order of copulations when females copulate with more than one male. The first male to copulate is more likely than later males to sire the resulting litter. The P-value is from the 2×2 chi-square test that ignores the 13 litters showing multiple paternity.

Immediately following the copulation of his "mate" with another male, a male dramatically increases the frequency of his copulations with her for animals such as mallards, rooks, mountain sheep, and rhesus and pigtailed macaques (Goodwin 1955; Barash 1977b; Busse and Estep 1984; Estep et al. 1986; Hogg 1988). Such "retaliatory copulations" probably reduce the risk of cuckoldry resulting from sperm competition (McKinney and Stolen 1982; Møller and Birkhead 1989, 1991; see below). I observed no retaliatory copulations by male prairie dogs. Rather, as for mountain cavy males (Rood 1972), a prairie dog male's sexual interest in an estrous female abruptly ceases following his insemination of her, at which point guarding usually commences (chap. 11). Further, unlike the situation in yellow-toothed cavies and wild guinea pigs (Rood 1972), sexual interest by a copulating prairie dog male does not return in those cases when the female later copulates with a second male.

Litter Size and Juvenile Body Mass at First Emergence versus ARS

The volume of maternal milk available for each juvenile is probably easily adequate when a litter contains only one juvenile. However, a mother's milk might be limiting when litter size is five or six (Kenagy et al. 1990). Probably as a consequence, mean juvenile body mass at first emergence varies inversely with litter size at first emergence for prairie dogs (fig. 13.6), as it also does for Richardson's ground squirrels (Michener 1989a). Despite this inverse relationship, the cumulative body mass of all prairie dog juveniles within a litter at first emergence varies *directly* with litter size (fig. 13.6).

The percentage of juveniles in a litter that survives for at least 1 year varies directly with mean juvenile body mass at first emergence (fig. 13.7a). An examination of juvenile body masses for survivors and nonsurvivors conveys a similar message. Specifically, juveniles that survive for at least 1 year average 15 grams heavier at first emergence than shorter-lived juveniles (fig. 13.7b). Further, for those juveniles that survive until early autumn, October body mass varies directly with body mass at first emergence (fig. 13.7c).

In view of these relationships between litter size and juvenile body mass and between juvenile survivorship and juvenile body mass, the inverse relationship between the percentage of juveniles that survive for at least one year and litter size is inevitable (fig. 13.8).

Depending on the steepness of the decline in juvenile survivorship with litter size, females that wean large litters might rear more or fewer offspring through the first year than females with smaller litters. For prairie dogs the decline is slight. As a result, females with large litters rear more yearlings than females with smaller litters (fig. 13.8).

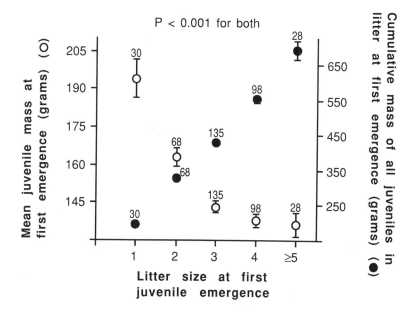

Fig. 13.6. Mean juvenile body mass and cumulative body mass of all juveniles in litter versus litter size at first juvenile emergence. The number above each SE line indicates the number of litters. *P*-values are from the Spearman rank correlation test. For the analysis with mean juvenile body mass, I have used a single mean juvenile body mass for each litter.

Lack (1947, 1954a,b) hypothesized that clutch (or litter) size reflects the maximum number of nestlings for which parents can find food. If clutch size is heritable, then the most productive clutch size also will be the most common one. Some animals, such as starlings, common and alpine swifts, and white-footed mice, support Lack's hypothesis (Lack 1968; Fleming and Rauscher 1978). However, other animals, such as northern gannets, kittiwakes, glaucous-winged gulls, and common muskrats, do not support it (Coulson and Porter 1985; Boutin, Moses, and Caley 1988; Ydenberg and Bertram 1989; Godfray, Partridge, and Harvey 1991; Lessels 1991). Figure 13.8 suggests that prairie dogs contradict Lack's hypothesis. Specifically, large litters at first juvenile emergence (4, 5, and 6) yield more yearlings than does the most common litter size of 3 (1.84 ± 1.49, $N = 101$ versus 1.73 ± 1.08, $N = 99$). The contradiction is weak, however, because the difference here is not significant ($P = .722$, Mann-Whitney U test).

Since its original formulation, two important modifications to Lack's hypothesis have emerged. First, numerous authors have argued that clutch

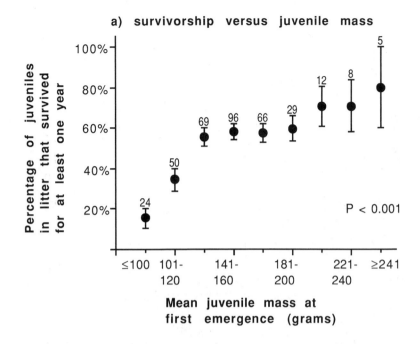

a) **survivorship versus juvenile mass**

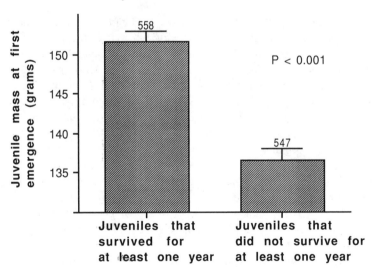

b) **body masses of juvenile survivors and juvenile nonsurvivors**

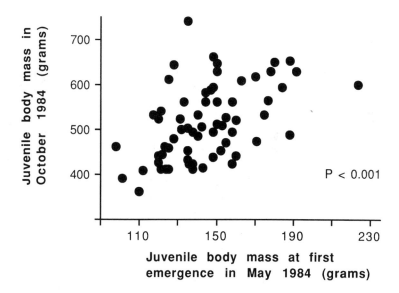

◀ ▲ Fig. 13.7. Juvenile survivorship versus juvenile body mass. *(a)* Survivorship in the first year versus juvenile body mass at first emergence. The number above each SE line indicates the number of litters. The *P*-value is from the Spearman rank correlation test. For this analysis I have used a single mean juvenile body mass for each litter. *(b)* Body mass of juveniles that did and did not survive for at least 1 year. The number above each SE line indicates the number of juveniles weighed. The *P*-value is from the Mann-Whitney *U* test. *(c)* Juvenile body mass in October 1984 versus body mass from the same prairie dogs at first emergence in May 1984. The *P*-value is from the Spearman rank correlation test.

size primarily reflects maternal condition and competence at rearing offspring rather than availability of food. If so, then experienced, middle-aged parents in good condition should lay more eggs or start larger litters than should inexperienced, older or younger parents in poor condition—as they do for animals such as great tits, kittiwakes, and Columbian ground squirrels (Perrins and Moss 1975; Coulson and Porter 1985; Murie and Dobson 1987; Festa-Bianchet and King 1991). Second, G. Hogstedt has argued that parents with good territories should produce larger clutches than parents with poorer territories, as they do for animals such as black-billed magpies (Hogstedt 1980). Because I did not attempt to rank the quality of coterie territories, I am unable to investigate Hogstedt's modification for prairie dogs. I have, however, uncovered two supporting lines of evidence regarding maternal condition and competence. First, as noted above, middle-aged prairie dog females rear more emergent juveniles and yearlings than do

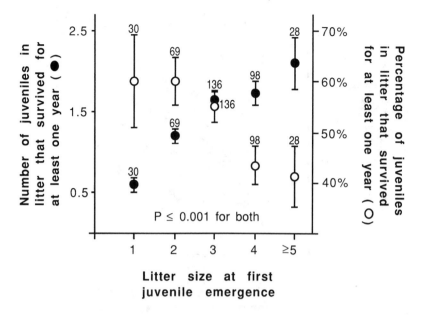

Fig. 13.8. Number and percentage of juveniles in litter that survive for at least 1 year versus litter size at first juvenile emergence. The number above each SE line indicates the number of litters. *P*-values are from the Spearman rank correlation test.

younger and older females (see figs. 13.3 and 13.4). Second, as noted below, heavy females are more likely to produce emergent juveniles and have larger litters than lighter females.

Parental Body Mass and Dominance versus ARS

Body mass is important for survival and reproduction for animals in general (Cheeseman et al. 1987; Gittleman and Thompson 1988; Clutton-Brock, Albon, and Guinness 1989; Glazier 1990; Campbell and Slade 1993; Madsen et al. 1993) and for sciurids such as hoary marmots and Columbian, Uinta, Richardson's, and Belding's ground squirrels in particular (Murie and Dobson 1987; Sauer and Slade 1987; Barash 1989; Michener 1989a; Trombulak 1991). I predicted that the same would be true for prairie dogs. Because body mass and dominance vary directly with each other for prairie dogs (chap. 10), I made no attempt to distinguish between their effects on reproductive success.

I weigh adult and yearling prairie dogs at three times each year: in autumn (October and November), prior to the following breeding season; in winter (February and March), during or just before the breeding season; and in spring (May and June), when juveniles are first emerging from their natal burrows (figs. 13.9 and 13.10). For adults and yearlings of both sexes, the body masses of the same individuals at different times positively correlate ($P < .001$ and $N \geq 57$ for all pairwise comparisons, Spearman rank correlation test). Figure 13.11 depicts representative data for 1985 adults and 1984 yearlings.

Body mass positively affects reproduction of prairie dog females in several related ways. Both as yearlings and as adults, heavy females are more likely than lighter females to copulate (fig. 13.12) and to produce emergent juveniles (fig. 13.13). Among those females that produce emergent juveniles, heavy females rear larger litters than lighter females (fig. 13.14a). The differences in figures 13.12–13.14 result in part because light females are more likely than heavier females to lose their litters to infanticide (chap. 7).

Fig. 13.9. Determining body mass. *(a)* My son (Mark Hoogland) and I use a spring balance to measure the body mass of an adult or yearling prairie dog held within a conical canvas bag. (Photo by Terry Moore.) *(b)* Before obtaining juvenile body mass, I put the juvenile in a plastic sandwich bag. (Photo by Judy G. Hoogland.)

Fig. 13.10. Extremes of body mass. *(a)* At the end of the summer, adult males such as this one might have a body mass as high as 1,400 grams. (Photo courtesy of Wind Cave National Park.) *(b)* At the end of lactation, emaciated mothers such as female-4stripe shown here might have a body mass as low as 500 grams. At first emergence, juveniles such as these 4strx offspring might have a body mass as low as 60 grams or as high as 288 grams. Lower juvenile body mass is more common in large litters. (Photo by John L. Hoogland.)

a) correlations of body masses for adults

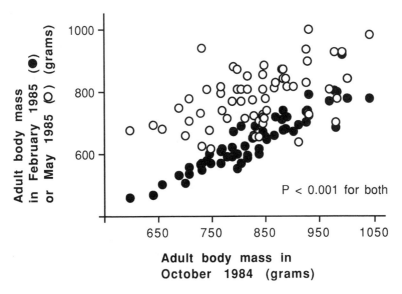

b) correlations of body masses for yearlings

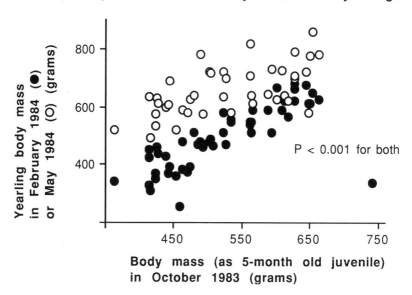

Fig. 13.11. Correlations of body masses of the same individuals at different times. *(a)* Adult body masses in February and May 1985 versus body masses of the same individuals in October 1984. *(b)* Yearling body masses in February and May 1984 versus body masses of the same individuals in October 1983 (when they were 5-month-old juveniles). *P*-values for these graphs are from the Spearman rank correlation test.

Fig. 13.12. Probability of copulation versus body mass at different stages of the annual cycle for *(a)* yearling females and *(b)* adult females. For these graphs, the number above each SE line indicates the number of females weighed, and *P*-values are from the Mann-Whitney *U* test.

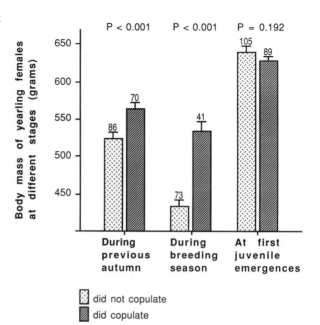

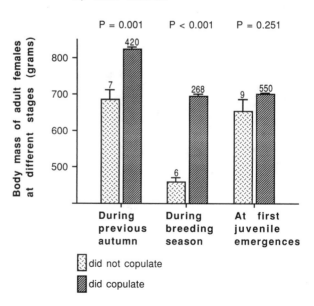

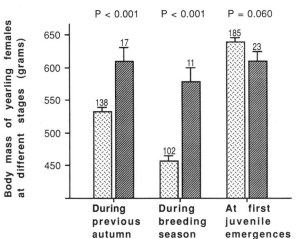

a) yearling females

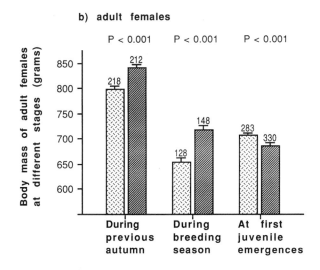

b) adult females

Fig. 13.13. Probability of producing emergent juveniles versus body mass at different stages of the annual cycle for *(a)* yearling females and *(b)* adult females. For these graphs, the number above each SE line indicates the number of females weighed, and *P*-values are from the Mann-Whitney *U* test.

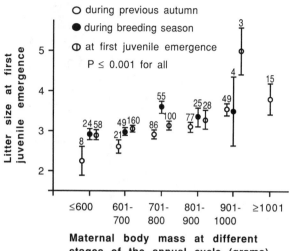

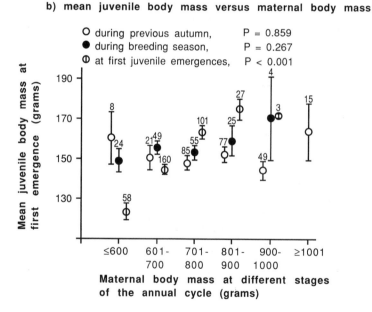

Fig. 13.14. Litter size and mean juvenile body mass versus maternal body mass. *(a)* Litter size at first juvenile emergence versus maternal body mass at different stages of the annual cycle. *(b)* Mean juvenile body mass at first emergence versus maternal body mass at different stages of the annual cycle. For this analysis I have used a single mean juvenile body mass for each litter. These graphs include data only from females that produced at least one emergent juvenile. The number above each SE line indicates the number of mothers weighed, and *P*-values are from the Spearman rank correlation test.

A mother's body mass when her juveniles first emerge is especially good at predicting reproductive success. Besides the relationships shown in figures 13.12–13.14a, maternal body mass at first emergence also varies directly with mean juvenile body mass at first emergence (fig 13.14b) and with the number and percentage of juveniles in the litter that survive for at least 1 year ($P \leq .001$ for both, Spearman rank correlation test).

Body mass also positively affects male reproductive success in several related ways. Both as yearlings and as adults, heavy males are more likely than lighter males to copulate (fig. 13.15) and to sire emergent juveniles (fig. 13.16). Among those males that copulate, heavy males copulate with more estrous females and sire more emergent juveniles than do lighter males (fig. 13.17).

Fully expecting that heavy individuals would survive better, I also have investigated survivorship until the next year versus winter, spring, and autumn body masses. The results are surprising. For adult males, survivorship seems unrelated to body mass ($P \geq .183$, Mann-Whitney U test, for comparisons of winter, spring, and autumn body masses of survivors and nonsurvivors). For adult females, only autumn body mass affects survivorship until the next year (829 ± 106 grams, $N = 285$ survivors versus 807 ± 96.4 grams, $N = 168$ nonsurvivors; $P = .022$, Mann-Whitney U test). Yearling males that are heavier in February and March, and yearlings of both sexes that are heavier in May and June, are *less* likely to be at the study colony in the following year ($P \leq .031$ for all three comparisons, Mann-Whitney U test). This latter perplexing pattern might result if heavier yearlings are more likely to disperse away from the study colony. Mainly because the identification and tracking of dispersers are so difficult (chap. 16), I am unable to investigate this hypothesis.

Weather and Precipitation versus ARS

The reproductive success of male and female prairie dogs varies directly with body mass (see above). Body mass and other estimates of physical and physiological condition probably vary directly with the quality and quantity of vegetation available for food. Finally, the quality and quantity of vegetation within prairie dog colonies probably depend largely on the amount of precipitation. Consequently, male and female reproductive success should correlate positively—albeit weakly, perhaps, because of the indirect connection—with the amount of precipitation. I did not investigate this possibility, but Knowles (1987) has observed that prairie dog litter sizes positively correlate with precipitation in the previous summer (Knowles 1987).

Survivorship of juveniles in their first year is lower when winters are harsh for animals such as Belding's ground squirrels and yellow-bellied, hoary, and Olympic marmots (Armitage and Downhower 1974; Morton and Sherman 1978; Barash 1989). The same is probably true for prairie dogs, but I did not pursue this qualitative impression further.

Fig. 13.15. Probability of copulation versus body mass at different stages of the annual cycle for *(a)* yearling males and *(b)* adult males. For these graphs, the number above each SE line indicates the number of males weighed, and *P*-values are from the Mann-Whitney *U* test.

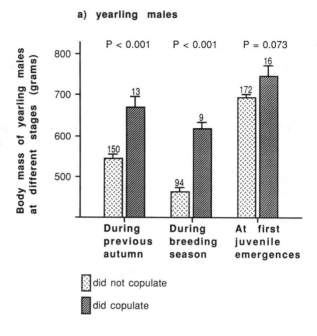

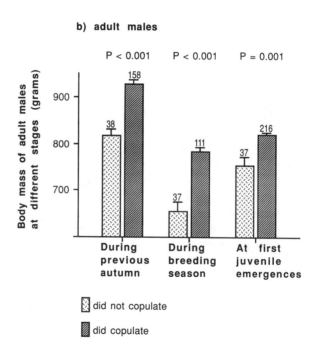

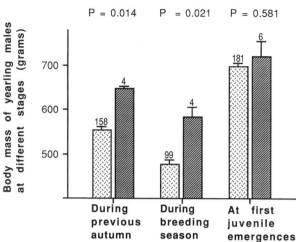

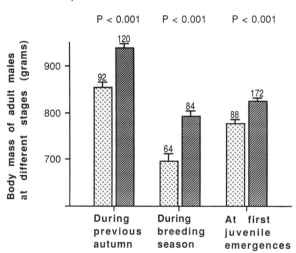

Fig. 13.16. Probability of siring emergent juveniles versus body mass at different stages of the annual cycle for *(a)* yearling males and *(b)* adult males. For these graphs, the number above each SE line indicates the number of males weighed, and *P*-values are from the Mann-Whitney *U* test.

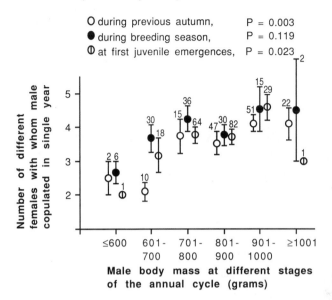

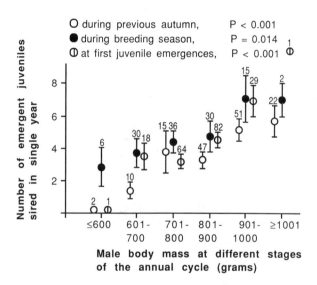

Fig. 13.17. Male copulatory success and male reproductive success versus male body mass. *(a)* Number of different females with which male copulates in a single year versus male body mass at different stages of the annual cycle. *(b)* Number of emergent offspring sired in a single year versus male body mass at different stages of the annual cycle. For these graphs, the number above each SE line indicates the number of males weighed, and *P*-values are from the Spearman rank correlation test.

Costs Associated with Previous Reproduction versus ARS

Successful reproduction in one year—here defined as the production of at least one emergent juvenile—frequently reduces the probability or magnitude of successful reproduction in the following year (Williams 1966a,b; Reznick 1985; Nur 1988; Gustafsson and Sutherland 1988; Linden and Møller 1989; Stearns 1992; but see Charnov 1993). As outlined below, I have investigated four possible costs of reproduction for prairie dogs.

Probability of Survivorship until the Next Year for Successful and Unsuccessful Individuals

One common cost of successful reproduction in one year is lower survivorship until the next year. Animals that incur this cost include blue tits, glaucous-winged gulls, red deer, Eurasian badgers, and hoary marmots (Reid 1987; Nur 1984, 1988; Cheeseman et al. 1987; Barash 1989; Clutton-Brock, Albon, and Guinness 1989). Prairie dogs evidently do not pay this cost (fig. 13.18a), and thus resemble northern elephant seals and Richardson's and Columbian ground squirrels (Murie and Dobson 1987; Le Boeuf, Condit, and Reiter 1989; Michener and Locklear 1990; Hare and Murie 1992).

Probability of Successful Reproduction in the Next Year for Successful and Unsuccessful Individuals

Successful reproduction in one year sometimes inhibits successful reproduction in the following year for animals such as yellow-bellied, hoary, and Olympic marmots (Johns and Armitage 1979; Barash 1973, 1989). I have investigated this possibility for prairie dogs, with surprising results. Like Eurasian badger females (Kruuk and Parish 1987; Kruuk 1989), successful prairie dogs of both sexes that survive until the next year are *more* likely than unsuccessful individuals to be successful in the following year as well (fig. 13.18b; see also below).

Number of Emergent Juveniles Produced in the Next Year for Successful and Unsuccessful Individuals

Successful breeding in one year reduces clutch size in the following year for animals such as rooks and blue tits (Roskaft and Slagsvold 1985; Williams 1966b; Nur 1984, 1988; Reznick 1985). Similarly, successful breeding in one year might reduce male ability to sire offspring in the following year. Like successful Richardson's and Columbian ground squirrels (Murie and Dobson 1987; Michener and Locklear 1990; Hare and Murie 1992), successful prairie dogs that survive until the next year evidently do not incur this cost (fig. 13.18c).

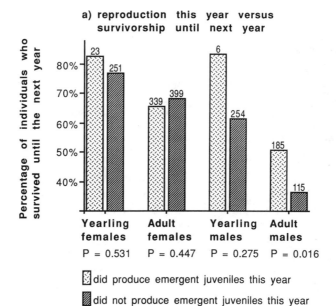

a) reproduction this year versus survivorship until next year

Percentage of individuals who survived until the next year

	Yearling females	Adult females	Yearling males	Adult males
	P = 0.531	P = 0.447	P = 0.275	P = 0.016

▨ did produce emergent juveniles this year

▨ did not produce emergent juveniles this year

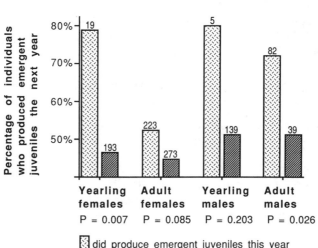

b) reproduction this year versus reproduction next year for individuals who survive

Percentage of individuals who produced emergent juveniles the next year

	Yearling females	Adult females	Yearling males	Adult males
	P = 0.007	P = 0.085	P = 0.203	P = 0.026

▨ did produce emergent juveniles this year

▨ did not produce emergent juveniles this year

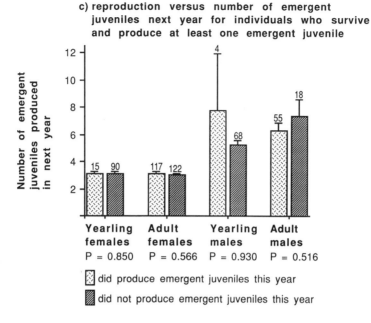

c) reproduction versus number of emergent juveniles next year for individuals who survive and produce at least one emergent juvenile

Yearling females P = 0.850 Adult females P = 0.566 Yearling males P = 0.930 Adult males P = 0.516

did produce emergent juveniles this year

did not produce emergent juveniles this year

◀ ▲ **Fig. 13.18.** Do prairie dogs incur costs of reproduction? *(a)* Probability of producing emergent juveniles in one year versus probability of survivorship until the next year. *P*-values are from the 2 × 2 chi-square test. Curiously, successful individuals are usually *more* likely than unsuccessful individuals to be at the study colony in the following year. *(b)* Probability of producing emergent juveniles in one year versus probability of producing emergent juveniles in the next year. This graph includes only individuals that survived until the next year. *P*-values are from the 2 × 2 chi-square test. Unexpectedly, successful individuals are consistently *more* likely than unsuccessful individuals to produce emergent juveniles in the following year as well. *(c)* Does production of emergent juveniles in one year affect the number of emergent juveniles produced in the next year? This graph includes only individuals that survived until the next year and which produced at least one emergent juvenile in the next year. *P*-values are from the Mann-Whitney *U* test. For all these graphs, the number above each bar or SE line indicates the number of individuals tracked for 2 consecutive years.

Body Masses at Different Stages of the Annual Cycle in the Next Year for Successful and Unsuccessful Individuals

Because reproduction requires time, energy, and resources, successful individuals commonly lose body mass during the reproductive period— except during actual pregnancy, when female body mass usually increases. Animals that incur this cost include Eurasian badgers, woodchucks, and hoary and Olympic marmots (Cheeseman et al. 1987; Barash 1989; Gittleman and Thompson 1988). Curiously, successful prairie dogs usually gain body mass during the reproductive period of February through May (see figs.

13.12 and 13.13 for females, figs. 13.15 and 13.16 for males). However, successful prairie dogs gain body mass less rapidly than do unsuccessful individuals. For example, successful yearling males are significantly heavier than unsuccessful yearling males before the onset of the breeding season, and both successful and unsuccessful yearling males gain body mass during the periods of gestation and lactation. However, although successful yearling males are still heavier than unsuccessful yearling males by the time of first juvenile emergences, the statistical significance of this advantage has disappeared (figs. 13.15a and 13.16a). Like successful Eurasian badger, Columbian ground squirrel, and yellow-bellied and hoary marmot females (Andersen, Armitage, and Hoffmann 1976; Cheeseman et al. 1987; Murie and Dobson 1987; Barash 1989; Armitage and Salsbury 1992), successful prairie dog females are *heavier* than unsuccessful females before the onset of the breeding season, but are *lighter* at first juvenile emergences (see fig. 13.13). Presumably a consequence of lactation (Millar 1977; Gittleman and Thompson 1988; Mendl 1988; Clutton-Brock, Albon, and Guinness 1989), this lower body mass of successful females persists through autumn and into the next breeding season (fig. 13.19).

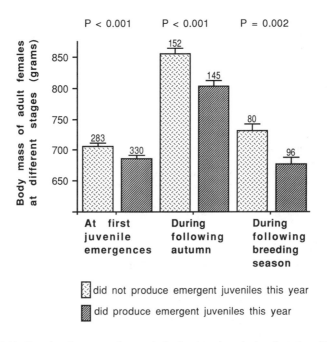

Fig. 13.19. Females do not easily regain body mass lost during lactation. Notice that successful females not only have lower body mass when their juveniles first emerge, but also in the following October and February. The number above each SE line indicates the number of females weighed. *P*-values are from the Mann-Whitney *U* test.

Heavy females reproduce more successfully than lighter females (see figs. 13.12 and 13.13), and successful females do not easily regain weight lost during lactation (fig. 13.19). However, successful females are *more* likely than unsuccessful individuals to be successful in the following year as well (fig. 13.18b). Are these results inconsistent and incompatible? Perhaps not, if parental experience is important to prairie dogs, as it probably is to birds such as brown pelicans, glaucous-winged gulls, white-winged choughs, and Florida scrub jays (Orians 1969a; Rowley 1977; Searcy 1978; Woolfenden and Fitzpatrick 1984). Specifically, perhaps the maternal experience of weaning a litter offsets the lower body mass in the following year for successful prairie dog females.

The unexpected take-home message of this section is clear: evidence that reproduction is costly to prairie dogs is slim. Losses in female body mass due to lactation are probably offset by gains in maternal experience.

Reproductive Synchrony versus ARS

Reproductive synchrony is the breeding of conspecifics in the same general area at the same general time (Darling 1938; Ims 1990a,b). Like coloniality, reproductive synchrony promotes "selfish herd effects" (Hamilton 1971; Parrish 1989; chap. 5). Specifically, the probability that any particular juvenile will be a predator's victim varies inversely with reproductive synchrony for animals such as black-headed gulls, lesser snow geese, caribou, and wildebeest (Kruuk 1964; Patterson 1965; Bergerud 1974; Estes 1976; Findlay and Cooke 1982a,b; Gochfield 1980). Reproductive synchrony among prairie dogs is evident at three levels: latitude, colony, and coterie.

Reproductive Synchrony versus Latitude

Trivial, perhaps, is the observation that prairie dogs in southern latitudes breed earlier than prairie dogs in more northern latitudes. For example, autopsies have shown that prairie dogs usually copulate in January in Oklahoma, in late February in Colorado, in late February through March in South Dakota, and in late March and early April in Montana (Anthony and Foreman 1951; King 1955; Tileston and Lechleitner 1966; Pfeiffer 1972; Knowles 1987; see also chap. 11). Dates of first juvenile emergences also indicate that southern prairie dogs breed earlier. Juveniles usually first appear aboveground in late April and early May in Oklahoma and Texas, in mid- and late May in Colorado and South Dakota, and in late May and June in North Dakota and Montana (Anthony and Foreman 1951; Tileston and Lechleitner 1966; Stockrahm and Seabloom 1988; Knowles 1987; Loughry 1987b; Garrett and Franklin 1988).

Reproductive Synchrony within Colonies

In 1979, dates of first juvenile emergence were available from three colonies within Wind Cave National Park (Hoogland 1981a; Garrett, Hoogland,

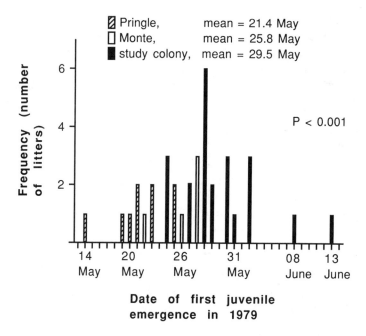

Fig. 13.20. Dates of first juvenile emergence at three sympatric colonies at Wind Cave National Park in 1979. The Pringle colony is approximately 1 kilometer distant from the study colony, and the Monte colony (Garrett, Hoogland, and Franklin 1982; Garrett and Franklin 1988) is approximately 10 kilometers away. The *P*-value is from the Kruskal-Wallis analysis of variance. Two of the three pairwise comparisons (Mann-Whitney *U* test) are also significant (*P* = .018 for Monte versus Pringle, *P* = .085 for Monte versus the study colony, and *P* < .001 for Pringle versus the study colony).

and Franklin 1982). Despite this small sample size, intracolonial synchronization of first juvenile emergences is nonetheless evident (fig. 13.20).

Reproductive Synchrony within Coteries

To promote "selfish herd effects" (Hamilton 1971) even more within colonies, natural selection might sometimes favor individuals that maximize nearest-neighbor reproductive synchrony. Thus, in addition to general reproductive synchrony within colonies, local synchronization sometimes results within intracolonial subgroups of animals such as tricolored blackbirds, pinyon jays, Franklin's gulls, and African lions (Payne 1969; Balda and Bateman 1972; Burger 1974; Bertram 1975; Packer and Pusey 1983). Prairie dogs also show such localized synchronization. Specifically, intracoterie synchrony of estrus and copulation at the study colony was significant ($P \le .055$, Kruskal-Wallis analysis of variance) in 7 of 11 years. Figure 13.21 depicts representative data from 1986.

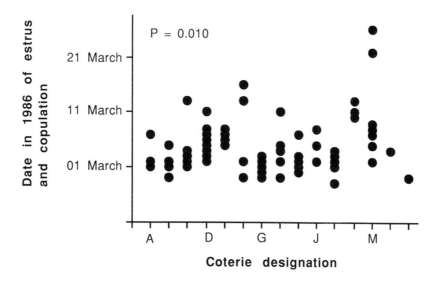

Fig. 13.21. Within-coterie synchrony of estrus and copulation in 1986. The *P*-value is from the Kruskal-Wallis analysis of variance.

At one extreme, all females within the same coterie territory could come into estrus and copulate on the same day. This pattern does sometimes occur, but only rarely. Rather, females of the same coterie deliberately seem to "spread out" their reproductive synchronization. In a coterie of four females, for example, the females typically come into estrus on four consecutive days. However, short skips of 1 or 2 days between estrous periods of different females of the same coterie also occur (fig. 13.21).

When two females of the same coterie are both ready to come into estrus on the same day, the smaller female sometimes defers to the larger by delaying her estrus until the following day (chap. 11). Why do smaller females defer, and thereby reduce reproductive synchronization? As noted in chapter 12, copulation with the resident breeding male of the home coterie territory is important to estrous females. However, the estrus of one female in the home coterie territory reduces another female's opportunities to copulate with the resident breeding male—because he is engrossed with courtship of, long underground copulations with, and guarding of the first female (chaps. 11 and 12). When a female comes into estrus by herself, she is certain to receive more attention from the resident breeding male. Further, suppose that temporary sperm depletion occurs for prairie dog males, as it does for males of animals such as smooth newts, spoonbills, house mice, and domestic goats and sheep (Halliday 1976; Dewsbury 1982b; Aguilera 1989; Birkhead and Møller 1992). If so, then sole estrus might increase the probability that each prairie dog female obtains sufficient sperm from the resident breeding male for fertilization.

By what mechanism do females within a coterie achieve reproductive synchrony without all coming into estrus on the same day? I found no answer to this intriguing question. Surely the frequent anal sniffing that occurs among pre-estrous and estrous females of the same coterie (chap. 10) is somehow involved.

The length of both gestation and, especially, lactation varies among prairie dog females (chap. 16). However, unlike female American bison (Berger 1992), female prairie dogs evidently do not lengthen or shorten the period of either gestation or lactation to improve reproductive synchrony. The synchrony of parturitions and first juvenile emergences within coteries and colonies is thus an inevitable consequence of the synchrony of estrous cycles and copulations.

Reproductive synchrony can be either *fortuitous* or an *evolved function* (Williams 1966a). When fortuitous, the synchrony results because individuals respond independently to the same environmental cues (day length, for example). When reproductive synchrony is an evolved function, however, then individuals monitor, and deliberately synchronize with, the reproduction of nearby conspecifics. Reproductive synchrony versus latitude among prairie dogs is almost surely fortuitous. On the other hand, reproductive synchrony within colonies, and especially reproductive synchrony within coteries, are probably evolved functions.

Does Reproductive Synchrony Enhance Reproductive Success?

To investigate the effect of intracolonial reproductive synchrony on annual reproductive success, I consider dates of copulation as *synchronous* if they occur within one standard deviation (SD) of the mean date for the study colony for that year (Emlen and Demong 1975; Brown and Brown 1987). *Early* copulations occur one or more SD before the mean date, and *late* copulations occur one or more SD after the mean date. Very early and very late copulations—two or more SD before or after the mean date, for example (see Brown and Brown 1987)—are too rare for meaningful statistical analyses.

Dates of copulations and first juvenile emergences (chap. 16) show significant annual variation. When a mild winter follows a summer of abundant precipitation, for example, the prairie dogs copulate earlier than in colder, drier years (Knowles 1987). Scoring copulations as early, synchronous, or late *within* years means that I can pool data *across* years for statistical analyses (Brown and Brown 1987).

Contrary to my prediction, reproductive synchrony does not promote reproductive success. Instead, early females produce more emergent and yearling offspring than synchronous females, which do better than late females ($P < .001$, Kruskal-Wallis analysis of variance). This trend does not result because of differences in litter size or juvenile survivorship. Rather, the trend results because of differences in the probability of rearing a litter to first emergence (fig. 13.22).

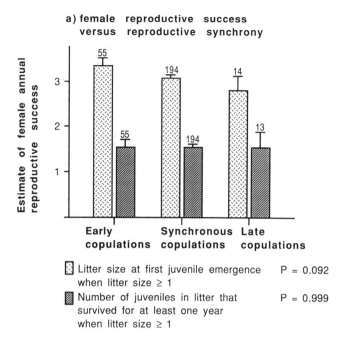

a) female reproductive success
versus reproductive synchrony

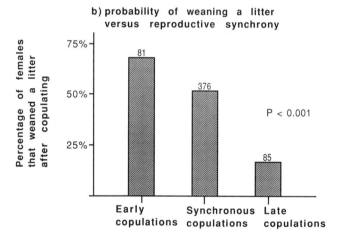

b) probability of weaning a litter
versus reproductive synchrony

Fig. 13.22. Female annual reproductive success versus intracolonial synchrony of copulations. *(a)* Litter size and production of yearlings for those females that produced emergent juveniles. The number above each SE line indicates the number of litters. *P*-values are from the Kruskal-Wallis analysis of variance. Of the pairwise comparisons, only litter sizes of early versus synchronous copulations are significantly different (*P* = .042, Mann-Whitney *U* test). *(b)* Probability of weaning a litter versus intracolonial synchrony of estrus and copulation. The number above each bar indicates the number of estrous females. The *P*-value value is from the 3 × 2 chi-square test. All pairwise comparisons are also significant (*P* ≤ .008 for all three, 2 × 2 chi-square test). Synchronous females are those that come into estrus and copulate within 1 SD of the mean date of copulation for the study colony; early females copulate ≥ 1 SD before the mean date; and late females copulate ≥ 1 SD after the mean date.

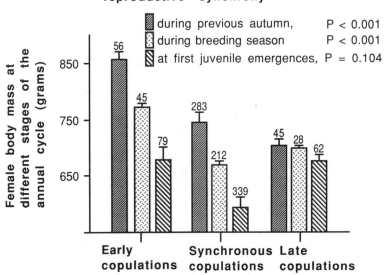

a) female body mass versus reproductive synchrony

b) probability of copulation by yearling female versus reproductive synchrony

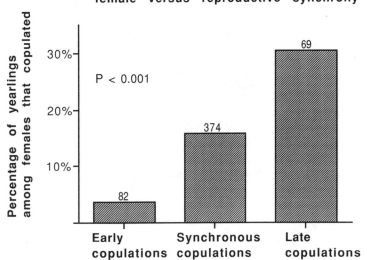

Why do early copulations lead to higher female ARS than later copulations? Heavy prairie dog females reproduce better than lighter females (see above). In proximate terms, then, the seasonal decline in ARS might result if heavy prairie dog females, like heavy European sparrowhawk and red deer females (Mitchell and Lincoln 1973; Newton and Marquiss 1984), copulate earlier than lighter females. Figure 13.23a supports this prediction.

Yearling females are lighter than adults (chap. 16; see also figs. 13.12 and 13.13). Do the trends in figures 13.22 and 13.23a result because prairie dog yearling females, like Belding's, California, round-tailed, and thirteen-lined ground squirrel yearling females (Fitch 1948; McCarley 1966; Dunford 1975; Morton and Gallup 1975; Sherman and Morton 1984), reproduce later than adult females? The answer here is yes and no: yes, because yearling females do copulate later than adult females (fig. 13.23b); but no, because the significant seasonal declines in reproductive success and body mass are still significant when I ignore yearling females and examine adult females only.

In ultimate terms, figure 13.22 is difficult to interpret. Why don't synchronous females benefit more from "selfish herd" effects (Hamilton 1971) and thereby reproduce better than both early and late females? If this were the case, then heavy females would prefer to breed synchronously rather than early. Early breeding might promote reproductive success more than synchronous breeding within colonies for at least two reasons. First, even though prairie dog colonies contain hundreds of burrows, only a few are suitable for rearing offspring. Competition among breeding females for the best nursery burrows is intense (chaps. 3, 7, and 10). Females usually begin to defend a prospective nursery burrow on the day after copulation (chap. 11). Females that copulate early thus have an easier opportunity to obtain a suitable nursery burrow. Females that copulate late, by contrast, quickly learn that the best nursery burrows are no longer available. Second,

◀ **Fig. 13.23.** Maternal body mass and age versus intracolonial synchrony of estrus and copulation. *(a)* Maternal body mass at different stages of the annual cycle versus intracolonial synchrony of estrus and copulation. *P*-values are from the Kruskal-Wallis analysis of variance. All pairwise comparisons are also significant for maternal body masses in both the previous autumn and the breeding season ($P <$ .001 for all six, Mann-Whitney U test). Regarding maternal body masses at first juvenile emergence, $P = .956$ for early versus synchronous, $P = .123$ for early versus late, and $P = .032$ for synchronous versus late (Mann-Whitney U test). *(b)* Percentage of yearlings among females that copulate versus intracolonial reproductive synchrony. The *P*-value is from the 3×2 chi-square test. All pairwise comparisons are also significant ($P \leq .004$ for all three, 2×2 chi-square test). For these graphs, synchronous females are those that copulate within 1 SD of the mean date of copulation for the study colony; early females copulate ≥ 1 SD before the mean date; and late females copulate ≥ 1 SD after the mean date. For these graphs, the number above each bar indicates the number of estrous females.

Fig. 13.24. ▶
Female annual reproductive success and age versus intracoterie synchrony of estrus
and copulation. *(a)* Probability of weaning a litter versus intracoterie synchrony of
estrus and copulation. The *P*-value is from the 3×2 chi-square test. Two of the
three pairwise comparisons (2×2 chi-square test) are also significant ($P = .079$ for
early versus synchronous, $P < .001$ for early versus late, and $P < .001$ for
synchronous versus late). *(b)* Percentage of yearling females among females that
copulate versus intracoterie synchrony of estrus and copulation. The *P*-value is from
the 3×2 chi-square test. Two of the three pairwise comparisons (2×2 chi-square
test) are also significant ($P = .565$ for early versus synchronous, $P = .032$ for early
versus late, and $P < .001$ for synchronous versus late). These two graphs include
data only from coteries where three or more females came into estrus. Early and
late females are those that come into estrus and copulate 4 or more days earlier or
later than more synchronous females within the same home coterie. For both graphs,
the number above each bar indicates the number of estrous females.

lactating mothers regularly kill the neonates of other mothers, but pregnant
females only rarely kill (chap. 7). Early females give birth when most other
females are still pregnant, so that their young are safe when most vulnerable to infanticide. The young of synchronous and late females, by contrast, are in danger as soon as they are born.

Does ARS also vary with the timing of copulation within the home
coterie? To find out, I have examined coteries with three or more females
that come into estrus. I consider a copulation as *early* or *late* if it occurs
4 or more days earlier or later than the other, more synchronous copulations
within the same coterie. Despite small sample sizes, intracoterie patterns
of female ARS versus timing of copulation are similar to patterns for the
study colony as a whole. Specifically, females that copulate early within
the home coterie are more likely to wean a litter than are synchronous and
later females (fig. 13.24a); the percentage of yearlings among copulating
females within the same coterie is lowest for early females (fig. 13.24b);
and females that copulate early within the home coterie are heavier than
synchronous and late females (e.g., $P = .004$ for body masses in autumn
prior to breeding season; $N = 139$, Kruskal-Wallis analysis of variance).
The advantages of early breeding within the home coterie are probably
the same as those for early breeding within the colony as a whole: better
access to suitable nursery burrows, and reduced vulnerability of neonatal
offspring to infanticide.

Coterie Size versus ARS

Large coteries contain more adult and yearling females than smaller coteries
(chap. 6). Predictably, therefore, large coteries are more productive than
smaller ones in terms of the number of estrous females, the probability
of producing at least one emergent litter, the number of emergent litters,
the number of emergent juveniles, and the number of juveniles that survive
for at least 1 year (fig. 13.25).

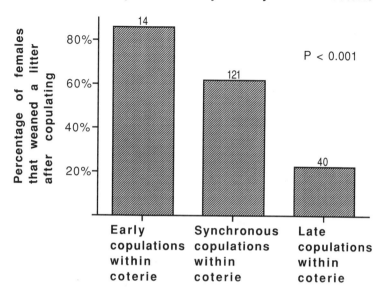

a) probability of weaning a litter versus reproductive synchrony within coterie

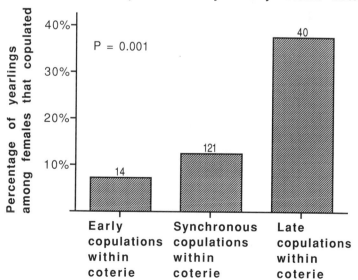

b) probability of copulation by yearling female versus reproductive synchrony within coterie

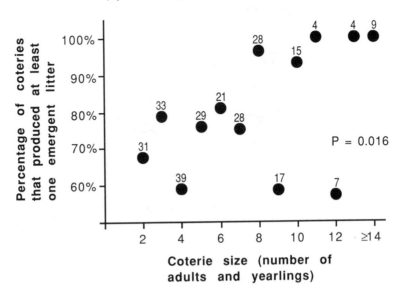

a) probability of at least one litter

b) number of estrous females and litters

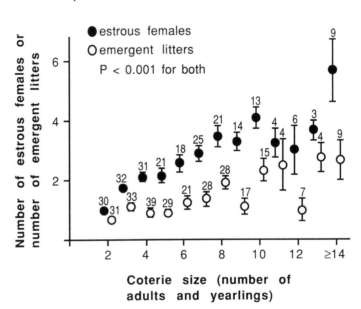

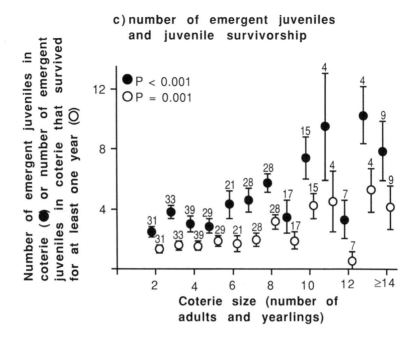

◄▲ Fig. 13.25. Number of estrous females, litters, emergent juveniles, and yearlings versus coterie size. *(a)* Coterie's probability of producing at least one litter of emergent juveniles versus coterie size. *(b)* Coterie's number of estrous females and coterie's number of emergent litters versus coterie size. *(c)* Coterie's number of juveniles at first emergence and coterie's number of juveniles that survive for at least 1 year versus coterie size. For all these graphs, the number above each dot or SE line indicates the number of coteries, and *P*-values are from the Spearman rank correlation test.

More interesting than the trends shown in figure 13.25, perhaps, are the effects of coterie size on individual, *per capita* reproduction. Is a prairie dog female more likely to rear juveniles in a larger group? As for some other cooperatively breeding animals, such as Florida scrub jays, acorn woodpeckers, and dwarf mongooses (Rood 1980b; Woolfenden and Fitzpatrick 1984; Koenig and Mumme 1987), the answer here is negative. Rather, three lines of evidence indicate that females in large coteries reproduce *less* successfully than females in smaller coteries. First, adult females in large coteries are less likely to wean a litter ($P = .086$, Spearman rank correlation test). Second, estrus and copulation among yearling prairie dog females are never common (chaps. 13 and 14), but are rarer within large coteries ($P = .017$, Spearman rank correlation test). Third, litter size at first juvenile emergence varies inversely with coterie size (fig. 13.26). Despite this latter trend, however, the number of yearlings reared per litter does not vary similarly (fig. 13.26).

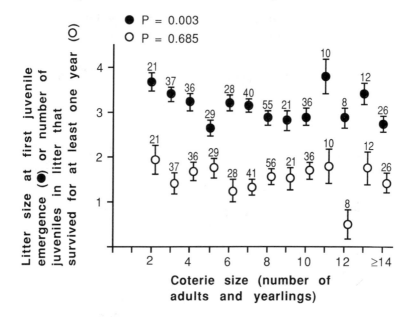

Fig. 13.26. Litter size at first juvenile emergence and number of juveniles in litter that survive for at least 1 year versus coterie size. The number above each SE line indicates the number of coteries. *P*-values are from the Spearman rank correlation test.

Most of the observed trends between female ARS and coterie size are weak. I therefore regard as tentative the conclusion that female ARS varies inversely with coterie size. However, the data in figure 13.26 do allow a related conclusion that is more robust: females in large coteries do not obviously reproduce and survive better than females in smaller coteries.

ARS is not the only component of fitness within cooperatively breeding animals. Thus, even though female per capita reproduction might appear inferior in larger groups, survivorship there might be better, as it is for acorn woodpeckers, Florida scrub jays, and dwarf mongooses (Woolfenden and Fitzpatrick 1984; Koenig and Mumme 1987; Rood 1990). If so, then female LRS might be higher in larger groups despite the opposite trend in female ARS. These arguments evidently do not apply to prairie dogs. Specifically, survivorship of adult and yearling females from one year to the next does not vary systematically with coterie size (fig. 13.27). Juvenile survivorship also does not vary systematically with coterie size (fig. 13.27).

Why might females in smaller coteries reproduce better than females in large coteries? Two possibilities come to mind. First, females in smaller coteries have access to more territory per individual and more burrows per individual (chap. 6). Second, females in smaller coteries live with and compete with fewer female kin (chaps. 6 and 7).

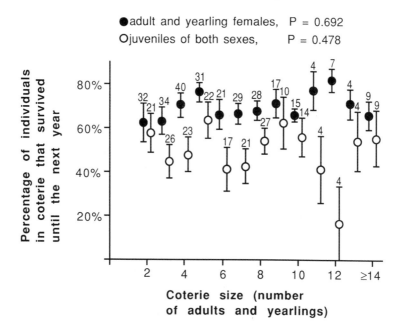

Fig. 13.27. Survivorship of adult and yearling females and of male and female juveniles versus coterie size. The number above each SE line indicates the number of coteries. *P*-values are from the Spearman rank correlation test.

So why do so many females live in large coteries (chap. 6)? Does elevated inclusive fitness via helping nondescendant kin (Hamilton 1964; Maynard Smith 1965; Brown 1987) provide the answer here, as it might for animals such as pied kingfishers, Australian bell miners, and European and white-fronted bee-eaters (Reyer 1984; Clarke 1984; Brown 1987; Emlen and Wrege 1989)? Suppose, for example, that litter size correlates positively with coterie size. If so, then nonreproductive females in a large coterie might contribute more copies of their own alleles to future generations by helping to rear the offspring of close kin than by trying to rear their own offspring in a smaller coterie. Note, however, that ARS of successful females does not correlate positively with coterie size (figs. 13.26 and 13.27). Elevated inclusive fitness via nondescendant kin in this context is thus an implausible explanation for the prevalence of large coteries.

Might a shortage of suitable habitat offer a second possible explanation for the high percentage of females in large coteries? Like females of other cooperatively breeding animals, such as superb blue fairy-wrens, acorn woodpeckers, Hall's and gray-crowned babblers, and red foxes (Brown and Balda 1977; Macdonald 1979; Brown et al. 1983; Nias 1984; Emlen 1991; Koenig et al. 1992), perhaps prairie dog females commonly have no safe place to go outside the home territory. As argued in chapter 5, prairie dog coloniality is probably an evolutionary response to predation rather than to a shortage of suitable habitat. Although suitable habitat away from colony sites seems available, colonization of such habitat—involving excavation of burrows and clipping of tall vegetation (King 1955; Costello 1970)—entails considerable danger. Consequently, leaving the safety of the home coterie territory to colonize a new area might be almost suicidal for a mother and her daughter. Stay-at-home females in large coteries might experience lower reproduction and survivorship than females in smaller coteries, but the former probably do better than if they attempted dispersal. In other words, perhaps females in large coteries are simply trying to make the best of a bad situation. One prediction that follows from these arguments is that females in large coteries should band together and evict females from smaller coteries whenever possible. Surprisingly, cooperative takeovers of this sort are exceedingly rare ($N = 3$ at the study colony in 1976 through 1988; see chap. 6).

A third possible explanation for the prevalence of large coteries concerns extinctions. Because of either the death of all coterie members or eviction by prairie dogs from another coterie, coteries sometimes go extinct. Could membership in a large coterie provide insurance against extinction? I have pursued this possibility in two ways. First, I have investigated whether extinctions occur very often. Specifically, I have investigated how often a group of female kin and their offspring (i.e., a coterie) go extinct. Data are available for 44 groups (each scored one time only for extinction, regardless of longevity before extinction). Extinctions—scored when all females within a coterie disappear—occurred for 57% of the female groups observed at the study colony (25/44) from 1976 through 1988. Extinctions are thus common, so that insurance against them might be important. Second, I have examined the probability of extinction versus coterie size. Specifically, I have compared extinction with the number of adult females in the home coterie, with the number of both adult and yearling females in the home coterie, and with coterie size (the number of adults and yearlings of both sexes in the home coterie) (fig. 13.28). By all three comparisons, small groups are more prone than larger groups to extinction. Thus, despite their lower ARS, but because of their greater matrilineal longevity, females in large coteries might contribute as many or more copies of their alleles to future generations as females in smaller coteries. More data are necessary for a better understanding of the differences in ARS and LRS between females of small and large coteries (see also Hoogland 1981b, 1983a).

How does male ARS vary with coterie size? The number of estrous females, the probability of producing at least one emergent litter, the number of emergent litters, the number of emergent juveniles, and the number of juveniles that survive for at least 1 year all increase directly with coterie size (see fig. 13.25). Because the typical coterie territory

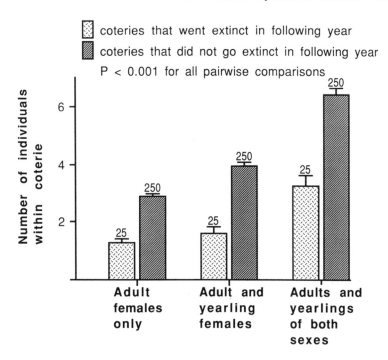

Fig. 13.28. Extinction versus coterie size. The number above each SE line indicates the number of coteries. The *P*-value for each pairwise comparison is from the Mann-Whitney *U* test. I score an extinction when all females living in a coterie disappear from the home coterie territory.

contains a single breeding male that sires most of the offspring born there (chaps. 6 and 12), these trends suggest that male ARS should increase directly with harem (coterie) size, as it does for other harem-polygynous animals such as yellow-bellied marmots, African lions, red deer, and northern elephant seals (Downhower and Armitage 1971; Armitage 1986; Clutton-Brock, Albon, and Guinness 1988; Le Boeuf and Reiter 1988; Packer et al. 1988, 1991). However, recall that large coteries are more likely to have a second or third resident breeding male (chap. 6). The sharing of paternity among the breeding males of large, multi-male coteries (chap. 12) might mean that males who monopolize smaller coteries actually fare better. With these considerations in mind, I have investigated male reproductive success versus coterie size.

A typical large coterie contains yearlings of both sexes, most of whom do not successfully breed. The number of females, especially adult females, within the home coterie therefore might be more important than coterie size per se to breeding males. I therefore have compared male reproductive success with three indices of coterie size: the number of adults and yearlings of both sexes (i.e., the usual measure of coterie size), the number of adult females only, and the number of both adult and yearling females living in the home coterie. My three estimates of male ARS (see chap. 12) are the number of different females with which a male copulates in a single year, the number of offspring at first emergence, and the number of offspring that survive for at least 1 year.

By all three indices of coterie size, males in large coteries copulate with more females than do males in smaller coteries (fig. 13.29). These trends suggest that male ARS varies directly with coterie size. However, females in large coteries, which are usually multi-male (chap. 6), are more likely to copulate with a second male than are females in smaller, one-male or half-male coteries (chap. 12). Consequently, copulations in smaller coteries are better than copulations in large coteries from a male's perspective—i.e., are more likely to yield offspring. The correlations between the number of paternal offspring and the three indices of coterie size are all positive (fig. 13.30). These trends again suggest that male ARS varies directly with coterie size. However, only some of these positive correlations are statistically significant. In summary, then, males in large coteries sire more emergent juveniles and yearlings than males in smaller coteries—but not by much.

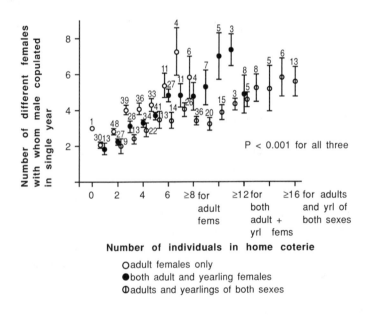

Fig. 13.29. Number of different females with which male copulates in a single year versus coterie size. The number above each SE line indicates the number of coteries. *P*-values are from the Spearman rank correlation test.

Coterie density varies directly with coterie size (chap. 6). I have not attempted to separate these related variables. However, I recognize that coterie density might be just as important as coterie size to the reproductive success of male and female prairie dogs.

Type of Coterie versus ARS

Neither the probability of estrus and copulation nor the probability of producing emergent juveniles varies among half-male, one-male, and multi-male coteries for either adult or yearling females ($P \geq .239$ for all, Kruskal-Wallis analysis of variance). Litter size at first emergence also does not vary with the type of coterie (fig. 13.31). However, the number of juveniles per litter that survive for at least 1 year does vary, almost significantly, with the type of coterie—with females in multi-male coteries doing best and females in half-male coteries doing worst (fig. 13.31). Differences in paternal care might account for this variation in the rearing of yearlings, for two reasons. First, breeding males interact amicably with and protect all juveniles that emerge in the home coterie territory—both their own and those sired by other males (chaps. 6, 8 and 10). Consequently, paternal care is probably most copious in multi-male coteries, less copious in one-male coteries, and least copious in half-male coteries. The second reason concerns mortality. When the single male in a half-male or one-male coterie dies or disperses, then paternal care in that coterie ceases. However, the second male of a multi-male coterie still provides paternal care when the first male disappears. The probability that a breeding male will remain and provide extended paternal care is thus higher in multi-male coteries (fig. 13.32).

Males sometimes dominate two separate groups of females, each of which is called a half-male coterie (chap. 6). Males in multi-male coteries, on the other hand, share females of only one group with another male. I therefore predicted that male ARS would be highest for males that dominate two half-male coteries, intermediate in one-male coteries, and lowest in multi-male coteries. Figure 13.33 partially supports this prediction: male ARS is highest for males that dominate two half-male coteries, but estimates of male ARS in one-male and multi-male coteries are approximately equal.

Like males and females of other animals, such as red-winged black-birds, dunnocks, and yellow-belled marmots (Orians 1969b, 1980; Downhower and Armitage 1971; Holm 1973; Davies 1985), male and female prairie dogs probably have a conflict of interest regarding the optimal social setting for maximal ARS. Females probably reproduce best in multi-male coteries (fig. 13.31), but males fare best when they can monopolize two separate half-male coteries (fig. 13.33). Perhaps the prevalence of one-male coteries, where both sexes experience intermediate reproductive success, is the evolutionary resolution to the conflicting interests of males and females.

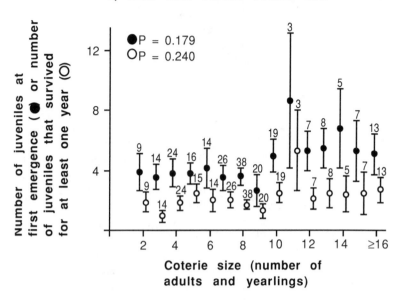

a) male ARS versus coterie size

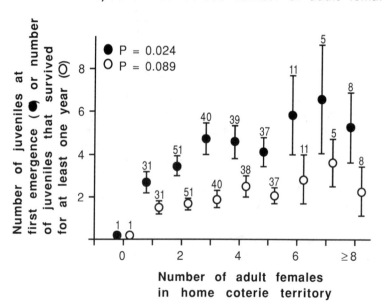

b) male ARS versus number of adult females

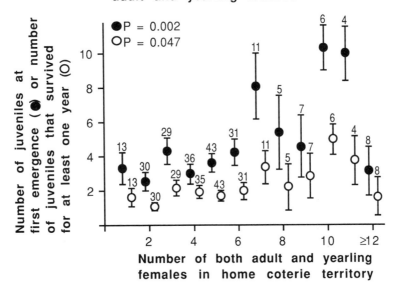

◀ ▲ **Fig. 13.30.** Male annual reproductive success versus *(a)* coterie size, *(b)* the number of adult females in the home coterie territory, and *(c)* the number of both adult and yearling females in the home coterie. For all these graphs, the number above each SE line indicates the number of coteries, and *P*-values are from the Spearman rank correlation test.

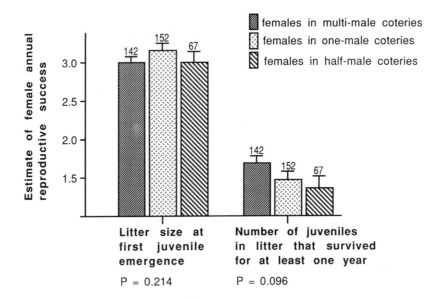

Fig. 13.31. Female annual reproductive success in multi-male, one-male, and half-male coteries. The number above each SE line indicates the number of coteries. *P*-values for both three-way comparisons are from the Kruskal-Wallis analysis of variance. All two-way comparisons are insignificant ($P \geq .096$ for all, Mann-Whitney U test) except for the number of yearlings per litter for half-male versus multi-male coteries ($P = .046$, Mann-Whitney U test). Notice, however, that females in multi-male coteries rear the most yearlings, even though they have the smallest litter size at first juvenile emergence.

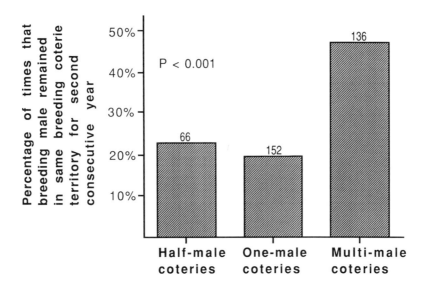

Fig. 13.32. Breeding male's length of residency versus type of coterie. I score extended residency in multi-male coteries whenever at least one of the breeding males remains for a second consecutive year. The number above each bar indicates the number of coteries. The *P*-value is from the 3 × 2 chi-square test. Both pairwise comparisons with multi-male coteries are also significant (*P* ≤ .001 for both, 2 × 2 chi-square test). The comparison of half-male coteries versus one-male coteries is not significant (*P* = .616, 2 × 2 chi-square test).

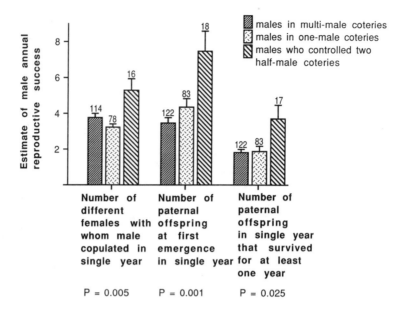

Fig. 13.33. Male annual reproductive success in multi-male, one-male, and half-male coteries. The number above each SE line indicates the number of coteries. *P*-values for all three-way comparisons are from the Kruskal-Wallis analysis of variance. All two-way comparisons with half-male coteries are significant (*P* ≤ .018 for all six, Mann-Whitney *U* test), but two-way comparisons between one-male and multi-male coteries are not significant (*P* ≥ .084 for all three, Mann-Whitney *U* test).

Longevity versus LRS

A long-lived individual has more opportunities to rear offspring than does an individual that dies after a single reproductive season. Longevity thus has a major influence on lifetime reproductive success for animals such as lesser snow geese, splendid fairy-wrens, northern fulmars, African lions, and vervet monkeys (Cheney et al. 1988; Cooke and Rockwell 1988; Ollason and Dunnet 1988; Packer et al. 1988; Rowley and Russell 1990). The same is true for prairie dogs. Specifically, long-lived individuals of both sexes copulate more often, produce more emergent juveniles, and produce more yearlings than do shorter-lived individuals (fig. 13.34). Indeed, longevity promotes LRS among male and female prairie dogs more than any other factor.

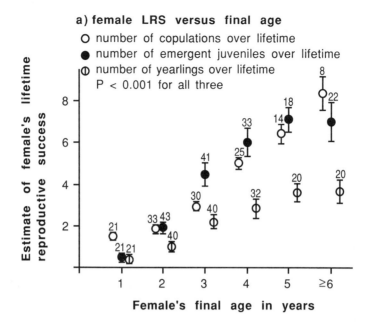

a) female LRS versus final age
○ number of copulations over lifetime
● number of emergent juveniles over lifetime
① number of yearlings over lifetime
P < 0.001 for all three

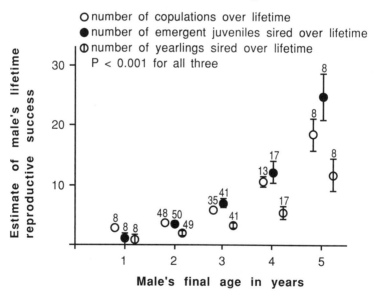

b) male LRS versus final age

○ number of copulations over lifetime
● number of emergent juveniles sired over lifetime
① number of yearlings sired over lifetime
P < 0.001 for all three

Fig. 13.34. Lifetime reproductive success versus longevity for *(a)* females and *(b)* males. For these graphs, the number above each SE line indicates the number of individuals for each final age, and *P*-values are from the Spearman rank correlation test.

Summary

1. Both males and females show evidence of senescence. Specifically, both survivorship and annual reproductive success (ARS) vary curvilinearly with age for both sexes.

2. When a female copulates with two or more males, the first male to copulate sires more offspring than later males.

3. Juvenile body mass and juvenile survivorship both vary inversely with litter size. Despite these trends, however, female ARS varies directly with litter size.

4. Heavy individuals of both sexes are more likely to copulate and rear offspring than are lighter individuals. Further, among those males and females that successfully breed, heavy individuals produce more offspring than lighter individuals.

5. Litter size correlates positively with precipitation in the previous summer.

6. Curiously, reproductive costs seem negligible for prairie dogs.

7. Reproductive synchrony is evident within large geographical areas, within colonies, and even within coteries. Within colonies and coteries, early breeders are more successful than synchronous and late breeders.

8. Female ARS correlates negatively, but male ARS correlates positively, with coterie size.

9. For females, ARS is highest in multi-male coteries. For males, on the other hand, ARS is highest for those individuals that dominate two half-male coteries.

10. Longevity promotes LRS among male and female prairie dogs more than any other factor.

14   Levels of Inbreeding

The avoidance of inbreeding is probably easy for animals that live solitarily and disperse widely, such as pottos, western tarsiers, and orangutans (Charles-Dominique 1977; Niemitz 1984; Bearder 1987; Rodman and Mitani 1987). But avoidance might be more difficult for animals that live in isolated colonies and are more philopatric, such as American pikas, prairie dogs, and yellow-bellied, Olympic, and hoary marmots (Armitage 1984; Smith 1987; Barash 1989).

The first section of this chapter outlines the advantages and disadvantages of inbreeding for animals in general. The next section describes four mechanisms by which prairie dogs avoid extreme inbreeding, all discovered early in my research. The third section documents a later discovery: despite the avoidance of extreme inbreeding, moderate inbreeding (with first and second cousins, for example) is common within prairie dog colonies. The fourth section evaluates two costs and two benefits of inbreeding and outbreeding among prairie dogs.

Costs and Benefits of Inbreeding and Outbreeding

Inbreeding and outbreeding each involve certain costs and benefits. By reducing heterozygosity and the impact of recombination, for example, extreme inbreeding dilutes the benefits of sexual reproduction that promote resistance to diseases, parasites, and environmental changes (Williams 1975, 1988; Stearns 1987; Michod and Levin 1988; Seger and Hamilton 1988; Charlesworth 1989; Clayton 1991). For animals that usually outbreed, extreme inbreeding also increases the probability of exposing deleterious recessive alleles (Li 1955; Fisher 1965; Crow and Kimura 1970; Ford 1971; Falconer 1981). Extreme outbreeding, on the other hand, tends to diminish genetic adaptation to local environments and to disrupt coadapted gene complexes (Dobzhansky 1951; Shields 1982; Partridge 1983; Waser 1993). Further, individuals that disperse long distances in search of unrelated mates lose time and energy, are more susceptible to predation, and incur other risks associated with entering unfamiliar territories (Wilson 1963; Ghiselin 1969; Alexander 1977). To balance the costs and benefits of inbreeding and outbreeding, natural selection probably should favor individuals that avoid the extremes by copulating with moderately close kin such as first and second cousins (Alexander 1977, 1979; Bateson 1978, 1980, 1983; Shields 1982, 1983, 1993; Partridge 1983; Keane 1990a,b).

Animals such as Florida scrub jays, acorn woodpeckers, and Darwin's medium ground finches usually copulate with members of their own local population—that is, they do not maximally outbreed with members of other populations—while also avoiding inbreeding with close kin (Woolfenden and Fitzpatrick 1984; Koenig and Mumme 1987; Gibbs and Grant 1989). However, mainly because of the difficulties of assigning paternities and tracking genealogies over an extended period of time, precise quantification of inbreeding-outbreeding under natural conditions has been elusive.

What, exactly, do the terms *inbreeding* and *outbreeding* mean? The terms are indefinite, and mean different things to different investigators (Alexander 1977, 1979; Shields 1982; Bateson 1983; van den Berghe 1983; Partridge 1983). Here I define *extreme inbreeding* as copulation involving two individuals whose coefficient of genetic relatedness, r, is equal to or greater than .2500; *moderate inbreeding* as copulation involving two individuals whose r is less than .2500 but equal to or greater than .0078; and *outbreeding* as copulation involving two individuals whose r is less than .0078 (table 14.1). *Natal dispersal* is the permanent emigration of young individuals from the area of parturition or hatching, and *breeding dispersal* is the emigration of a sexually mature individual from the area where it copulated (Greenwood 1980; Holekamp 1984a). The *natal coterie territory* is the territory where a prairie dog is born, and the *breeding coterie territory* is the territory where a prairie dog copulates. For females, but not males (see below), the natal coterie territory and the breeding coterie territory are usually identical. An *immigrant* is a prairie dog born at a different colony that disperses into the study colony.

I have used conventional analysis of pedigrees (Crow and Kimura 1970; Falconer 1981; Shields 1982) to calculate the coefficient of genetic relatedness for the male and female of a copulating pair, who frequently have more than one common ancestor. As noted in chapter 4, coefficients are theoretical, for alleles identical by descent, and thus do not reflect the actual genetic similarity between two individuals. Coefficients are available for 770 copulations by 557 estrous females (chaps. 11 and 12). The mean ± SD number of known generations per pedigree is 3.96 ± 1.33 (range = 1 to 6). The mean ± SD number of different copulating males per estrous female is 1.38 ± .60 (range = 1 to 4; see chap. 12). When r is greater than 0, r ranges from .0020 to .5039. Thirty percent (234/770) of copulations involve inbreeding at some level (i.e., $r \geq .0078$), and 35% of estrous females (194/557) copulate with at least one male kin (i.e., $r \geq .0078$).

Table 14.1. Classification of Inbreeding and Outbreeding

Level of inbreeding	Coefficient of genetic relatedness (r) for copulatory pair	Observed pairings
Extreme inbreeding	$r \geq .2500$	Father-daughter; full siblings; grandmother-grandson; half siblings; full aunt-full nephew; full uncle-full niece
Moderate inbreeding	$.2500 > r \geq .0078$	Half uncle-half niece; half aunt-half nephew; half great uncle-half great niece; half great aunt-half great nephew; full and half first cousins; full and half first cousins once removed; full and half first cousins twice removed; full and half second cousins; full and half second cousins once removed; full third cousins
Outbreeding	$.0078 > r \geq 0$	Half second cousins twice removed; half third cousins; full and half third cousins once removed; full and half fourth cousins; no known kinship

Note: I have listed only *observed* types of inbreeding and outbreeding. I have not observed certain possibilities, such as mother-son or grandfather-granddaughter pairings (see table 14.6).

Four Mechanisms for Avoiding Extreme Inbreeding

Mechanism 1: Male-Biased Natal Dispersal

As for mammals in general (Greenwood 1980; Dobson 1982; Cockburn, Scott, and Scotts 1985; Pusey 1987) and probably all species of marmots and ground squirrels in particular (Armitage 1984; Holekamp 1984a,b; Barash 1989; Holekamp and Sherman 1989), natal dispersal among prairie dogs is male-biased. Of 239 females first marked as juveniles that survived for at least 1 year, only 11 (5%) moved from the natal coterie territory to another coterie territory within the study colony (fig. 14.1a). Ten of these dispersing females (91%) were victims of extraordinary circumstances (table 14.2). Thus, most prairie dog females are markedly philopatric and live their entire lives within the natal coterie territory (fig. 14.1b).

By contrast, most prairie dog males disperse away from the natal coterie territory as yearlings (fig. 14.1a)—i.e., well before reaching sexual maturity at the usual age of about 21 months following first emergence from the natal burrow (chap. 16). Of 312 males first marked as juveniles that survived for at least 1 year, not a single one was still in the natal coterie territory by April of the fourth year (fig. 14.1b). Like long-distance male dispersals to other colonies (chap. 16), short-distance male dispersals within the study colony occur most often in May and June, approximately 12 or

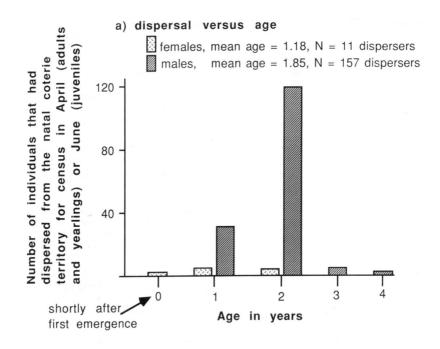

a) dispersal versus age

🔲 females, mean age = 1.18, N = 11 dispersers
🔳 males,   mean age = 1.85, N = 157 dispersers

Number of individuals that had dispersed from the natal coterie territory for census in April (adults and yearlings) or June (juveniles)

shortly after first emergence

Age in years

b) philopatry versus age

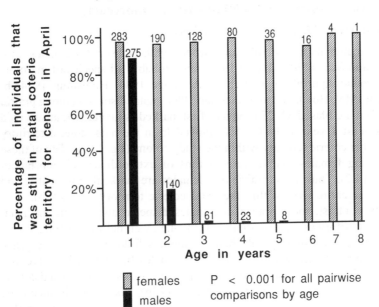

Percentage of individuals that was still in natal coterie territory for census in April

Age in years

🔲 females   P < 0.001 for all pairwise
⬛ males   comparisons by age

◀ **Fig. 14.1.** Dispersal and philopatry versus age. *(a)* Dispersal versus age for males and females. This graph includes only individuals that dispersed from the natal coterie territory to another coterie territory within the study colony—i.e., I exclude individuals that disappeared and thereby might have dispersed to another colony. *(b)* Percentage of males and females that are still in the natal coterie territory at different ages. The number above each bar indicates the number of individuals alive and still living at the study colony. For ages 1 through 4, P-values are from the 2 × 2 chi-square test; for age 5, the P-value is from the Fisher exact probability test. No male has survived beyond 5 years.

Table 14.2. Unusual Circumstances Surrounding the Dispersal of Females ($N = 11$) from the Natal Coterie Territory

Year of birth	Age at dispersal (years)	Female that dispersed	Unusual circumstances surrounding dispersal
1976	2	Female-58	Evicted by invading females from another coterie
1976	2	Female-RR8	Same as for female-58, who was female-RR8's full sister
1979	0	Female-5str	Shortly after she first emerged from the natal burrow, fem-5str and her mother were evicted by an invading female immigrant
1980	2	Female-62	None—dispersal seemed unforced and self-motivated
1985	1	Female-R65	Evicted by older female kin of the natal coterie shortly after copulating as a yearling
1985	0	Female-R63	Was part of a half-male coterie; dispersed shortly after weaning into adjacent half-male coterie territory that contained several paternal half siblings
1986	1	Female-H5	Was part of a half-male coterie; dispersed into adjacent half-male coterie territory that contained several paternal half siblings
1986	2	Female-BB3	Was probably sexually immature as a 2-year old; evicted by the breeding male and her older female kin of the natal coterie
1987	1	Female-64	All female-64's female kin disappeared when she was a yearling; evicted by invading females from an adjacent coterie
1988	0 or 1	Female-R71	Born in a peripheral coterie territory containing only one adult (her mother); abandoned by mother shortly after weaning; dispersed to new coterie territory sometime between July and April of first year
1988	0 or 1	Female-R57	Same as for female-R71, who was female-R57's full sister

Note: All dispersals were from the natal coterie territory to another coterie territory within the study colony. In the first few months after first emergence from the natal burrow, I consider the juvenile's age in years to be 0.

13 months after the disperser's first emergence from the natal burrow (Knowles 1985; Garrett and Franklin 1988).

Sexually asymmetrical natal dispersal among prairie dogs precludes many types of extreme inbreeding. Specifically, females have little opportunity to copulate with any of the following: sons, full and half brothers, grandsons, full uncles, and full nephews.

I have implied that male-biased natal dispersal among prairie dogs functions to deter extreme inbreeding, but other functions are also possible (Greenwood 1980, 1983; Moore 1984; Moore and Ali 1984; Brody and Armitage 1985). The exceptions to the rule of male-biased dispersal tend to support the implied function. For example, as figure 14.1 shows, most males remain in the natal coterie territory through April of their first year and then disperse sometime before reaching sexual maturity as 2-year-olds. Male dispersal before April of the first year correlates with sexual maturity—and consequently the likelihood of extreme inbreeding—in the first year (fig. 14.2). Further, two of the three sexually mature yearling males that did not disperse in the first year had good reason to stay home. The

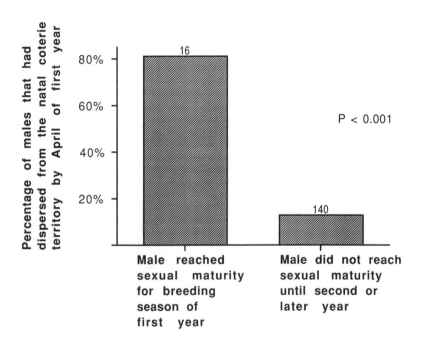

Fig. 14.2. Timing of dispersal versus timing of sexual maturity for males. This graph includes only males that either did not disperse or dispersed from the natal coterie territory to another coterie territory within the study colony—i.e., I exclude males that disappeared and thereby might have dispersed to another colony. The number above each bar indicates the number of observed males. The P-value is from the 2 × 2 chi-square test.

first male's close female kin had all disappeared, and unrelated (or only distantly related) females from an adjacent coterie territory moved into his natal coterie territory. The second male associated exclusively with an unrelated female immigrant who had usurped a section of his natal coterie territory from his female kin. The philopatry of the third sexually mature yearling male remains anomalous. Finally, those rare males that remain in the natal coterie territory for a second or third year (fig. 14.1b) have not yet attained sexual maturity for some reason—so that extreme inbreeding cannot occur.

Mechanism 2: Older Males Disperse Away from Sexually Mature Daughters

Males frequently live for as long as 4 or 5 years, and females usually first copulate when 2 years old (chap. 16). Consequently, an older male might co-exist in a breeding coterie territory with his sexually mature daughters. If the avoidance of extreme inbreeding is important, then male prairie dogs should not remain in the same breeding coterie territory for more than 2 consecutive years. Figure 14.3 supports this prediction of male-biased

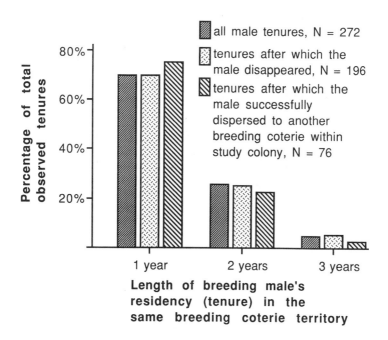

Fig. 14.3. Length of breeding male's residency (tenure) in the same breeding coterie territory. None of the differences among the different types of tenures is statistically significant ($P = .865$ for the 3×3 chi-square tests, $P \geq .400$ for all pairwise tests). Males only rarely remain in the same breeding coterie for a third consecutive year, so that opportunities for father-daughter inbreeding are rare.

breeding dispersal, which is also evident for animals such as hanuman langurs, savannah baboons, and Belding's, arctic, and Richardson's ground squirrels (Altmann and Altmann 1970; Hrdy 1977b; Michener and Michener 1977; McLean 1983; Sherman and Morton 1984).

Short male tenures commonly result from death rather than dispersal (fig. 14.3). However, figure 14.3 also depicts data from long-lived males who could have remained in the same breeding coterie territory for a third consecutive year. As expected, 97% of these long-lived males (74/76) remained in the same breeding coterie territory for only 1 or 2 years before leaving their daughters and moving to a new coterie territory.

Once again the exceptions are instructive. Consider those few males that remain in the same breeding coterie territory for 3 consecutive years, for example. Such males usually have not sired any surviving daughters in the first year, so that father-daughter inbreeding in the third year is impossible (fig. 14.4). The implication is that breeding dispersal by male prairie dogs functions primarily to deter father-daughter inbreeding.

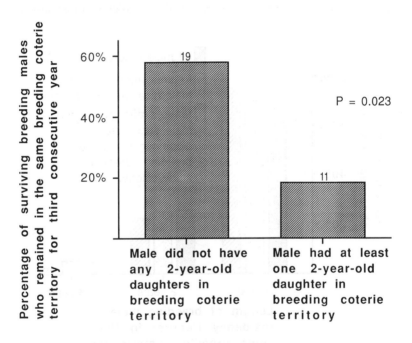

Fig. 14.4. Dispersal of older males versus the likelihood of father-daughter inbreeding. I consider father-daughter inbreeding likely when a breeding male has at least one 2-year-old daughter in his breeding coterie during his third year of residency. The number above each bar indicates the number of observed males. This graph includes only males that were still in the study colony after 2 consecutive years in the same breeding territory—i.e., excluded are males that disappeared and thereby might have died or might have dispersed to another colony. The P-value is from the Fisher exact probability test.

Mechanism 3: A Yearling Female Is Less Likely to Come into Estrus When Her Father Is Still in Her Natal Coterie Territory

Especially when heavy and in good condition, prairie dog females sometimes advance the initial estrus and copulate in their first year (chap. 16). If the avoidance of extreme inbreeding is important, perhaps yearling prairie dog females, like young females of other rodents such as white-footed mice and yellow-bellied and hoary marmots (Armitage 1984; Barash 1989; Wolff 1992), should only come into estrus when the father is gone from the natal territory. Whereas 41% of yearling females (80/193) come into estrus and copulate when the father has disappeared from the natal coterie territory, only 33% (17/51) copulate when the father is still present. Although in the predicted direction, this difference is not significant (*P* = .292, 2 × 2 chi-square test).

When I first investigated yearling estrus versus the presence of the father in the natal coterie territory (Hoogland 1982a), the negative association was statistically significant. Why the discrepancy between the earlier results and the later results based on a larger sample size? Once again the exceptions are revealing. Nine of the 17 (53%) yearling females that copulated in the presence of the father lived in multi-male coteries that contained a second, unrelated (or only distantly related) breeding male. Avoidance of inbreeding with the father was therefore easy (see below).

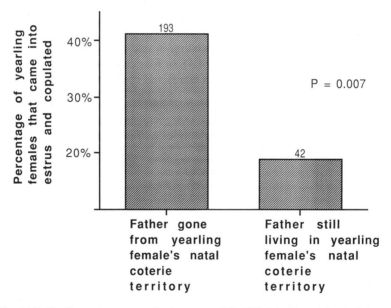

Fig. 14.5. Yearling estrus versus the presence of the father in the natal coterie territory. The number above each bar indicates the number of yearling females. The *P*-value is from the 2 × 2 chi-square test. Excluded here are data from yearlings that lived in multi-male coteries that contained a second unrelated breeding male besides the father (see text).

When I delete these nine cases, the negative association between yearling estrus and the presence of the father is once again statistically significant (fig. 14.5).

Mechanism 4: Behavioral Avoidance of Extreme Inbreeding

The first three mechanisms for avoiding extreme inbreeding work well for prairie dogs, but they are not flawless. Sometimes, for example, males reach sexual maturity as yearlings before dispersing from the natal coterie territory (see fig. 14.2). Other times yearling females come into estrus when the father is still in the natal coterie territory (fig. 14.5). In one unusual case, a male moved away from his natal coterie territory when he reached sexual maturity in his first year, then returned to the natal coterie territory when he was a sexually active 2-year-old.

What happens when sexually mature close kin of the opposite sex end up in the same coterie territory? Like acorn woodpeckers, chimpanzees, and rhesus and Japanese macaques in similar circumstances (Sade 1968; Koenig and Pitelka 1979; Pusey 1980; Takahata 1982; Goodall 1986), the prairie dog kin often do not copulate (tables 14.3–14.5). Depending on the type of coterie (multi-male or one-male), avoidance is of two general types.

In multi-male coteries, the female avoids her male kin during her estrus and copulates exclusively with the unrelated (or distantly related) male instead (table 14.3). This sort of avoidance might seem trivial, until one remembers that females in multi-male coteries usually copulate with both resident breeding males (chap. 12).

The avoidance of extreme inbreeding in one-male coteries ($N = 5$) is more spectacular (tables 14.4 and 14.5). In four cases, a female rigorously avoided her close male kin while in estrus and copulated exclusively with

Table 14.3. Probability of Copulating with a Second Male within the Home Multi-Male Coterie versus the Probability of Extreme Inbreeding

	Estrous female copulated with only one of the breeding males	Estrous female copulated with two or more of the breeding males
One of the breeding males in multi-male coterie was close kin ($r \geq .2500$)	11	0
None of the breeding males in multi-male coterie was close kin ($r < .2500$)	80	122

Note: When faced with the likely possibility of extreme inbreeding, females are more likely to copulate with only a single breeding male within the home multi-male coterie ($P < .001$, 2×2 chi-square test). In all 11 cases of single copulation when extreme inbreeding was likely, the female avoided her male kin and copulated exclusively with the unrelated (or distantly related) male of the home coterie ($P < .001$, sign test; see table 14.5).

Table 14.4. Probability of Exclusive Copulation with Males Outside the Home One-Male Coterie versus the Probability of Extreme Inbreeding

	Estrous female copulated with single breeding male in home coterie	Estrous female copulated exclusively with breeding male from outside the home coterie
Single breeding male in home coterie was close kin ($r \geq .2500$)	0	4[a]
Single breeding male in home coterie was not close kin ($r < .2500$)	297	17

Note: When faced with the likely possibility of extreme inbreeding, females are more likely to avoid the single breeding male relative in the home one-male coterie and to copulate exclusively with an unrelated (or only distantly related) male from an outside coterie ($P < .001$, Fisher exact probability test).

[a] A fifth 2-year-old female lived in a one-male coterie whose only breeding male was her full brother. This female (female-WA7) came into estrus but did not copulate with her brother or with any other male (see table 14.5).

an unrelated male from an adjacent coterie (table 14.4). One of these estrous females left the home coterie territory in search of unrelated males. The other three copulated with unrelated males that temporarily invaded the home coterie territory on the day of estrus (table 14.4; see also chaps. 6 and 12). In the fifth case, female-WA7 came into estrus and seemed to solicit her sexually mature full brother. At the end of the day, however, she had not copulated with him or with any other male. Female-WA7 was one of only five females (out of the 557 observed) that came into estrus and did not copulate.

Despite the four mechanisms described here, extreme inbreeding nonetheless sometimes occurs. Specifically, 5% of copulations (36/770) involve close kin ($r \geq .2500$) (fig. 14.6). However, coupled with these 36 copulations are three intriguing lines of evidence which indicate that extreme inbreeding is the last resort for estrous females. First, behavioral observations indicate the lengths to which females sometimes go in their attempts to avoid extreme inbreeding. For example, females R70 and R78 were yearling full sisters whose father was still in their natal coterie territory. Both females came into estrus on the same day in 1986, when they repeatedly left the home coterie territory in search of other males. Mainly because of resistance from females in other coterie territories (chaps. 6 and 10), neither female was able to copulate with an unrelated outside male. Each ended up copulating at the end of the day with her father. Second, females that copulate with a closely related male are more likely to copulate with a second (unrelated) male as well (fig. 14.7). Copulation with a second male means that the unrelated male rather than

Table 14.5. Avoidance of Extreme Inbreeding when Two Sexually Mature Close Kin of the Opposite Sex Live in the Same Coterie Territory

Type of extreme inbreeding that was likely	Type of coterie	Number of cases	Outcome
Mother-son	Multi-male	3	In all three cases, the mother avoided her son while in estrus and copulated exclusively with another breeding male within the home coterie territory.
Father-daughter	One-male	3	In all three cases, the daughter avoided her father while in estrus and copulated exclusively with another breeding male from another coterie. In one case the daughter left the home coterie territory in search of a male, and in the other two cases an unrelated male temporarily invaded the daughter's home coterie territory.
Father-daughter	Multi-male	5	In all five cases, the daughter avoided her father while in estrus and copulated exclusively with another breeding male within the home coterie territory. One of the daughters also copulated with a second male from an adjacent coterie territory.
Full siblings	One-male	1	The female (female-WA7) seemed to solicit her full brother, but did not copulate with him or with any other male.
Full siblings	Multi-male	2	In both of these cases, the female avoided her full brother while in estrus and copulated exclusively with another breeding male within the home coterie territory.
Half siblings	One-male	1	The female avoided her half brother while in estrus and copulated exclusively with a male from an adjacent coterie territory who temporarily invaded the home coterie territory on the day of her estrus.
Half siblings	Multi-male	1	The female avoided her half brother while in estrus and copulated exclusively with another breeding male within the home coterie territory.

the related male might sire any offspring that result (chap. 12). Third, females are more likely to avoid copulating with male close kin *with whom they have continuously associated since first juvenile emergence* (fig. 14.8). Most cases of extreme inbreeding result after members of the related pair have lived in different coterie territories since one or the other first emerged from the natal burrow—so that identification of the potential mate as close kin is probably difficult (chap. 10). Below I discuss further the significance

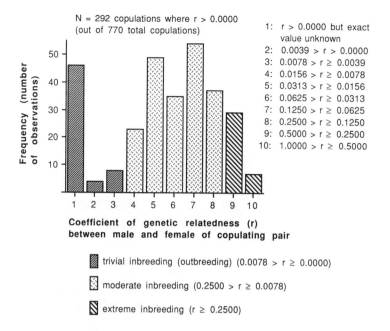

Fig. 14.6. Frequencies of different levels of observed inbreeding. I determine maternal and sibling genetic relationships from the marking of entire litters associated with single mothers. I determine paternal genetic relationships from detailed behavioral observations of copulations in combination with electrophoretic analyses of blood samples (see chaps. 11 and 12). Not included here are data from 478 copulations involving males and females of no known kinship.

of familiarity and direct social learning to the avoidance of extreme inbreeding (see also Bischof 1975; Wilson 1978; Alexander 1979, 1990a, 1991; van den Berghe 1983; Berger and Cunningham 1987; chap. 10).

I imply here that *female* prairie dogs are primarily responsible for the avoidance of extreme inbreeding via behavioral mechanisms. This implication is probably correct—consider the attempts to outbreed by females R70 and R78, for example—but three lines of evidence indicate *male* concern and responsibility as well. First, like vervet monkey males (Cheney et al. 1988), prairie dog males commonly show only minimal interest in their estrous female kin—that is, they are *easy* for the female kin to avoid. Second, in the case described above for female-WA7, it seemed that the sexually mature full brother refused to copulate with his estrous full sister, rather than vice versa. Finally, and outlandishly, the resident breeding male of a one-male coterie sometimes deliberately reduces his defense of the home coterie territory during the few hours when one of his female kin is in estrus. Consequently, an unrelated male can easily invade and copulate (table 14.5).

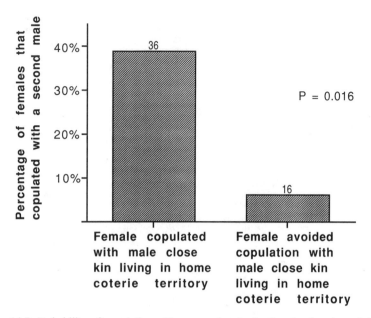

Fig. 14.7. Probability of copulating with a second male for females that do and do not copulate with male close kin ($r \geq .2500$) living in the home coterie territory. The number above each bar indicates the number of estrous females. The P-value is from the 2×2 chi-square test. This difference does not result simply because females that copulate with close kin are more likely to live in multi-male coteries (where copulation with a second male is more likely; see chapter 12). Specifically, only 42% of females that copulate with close kin (15/36) live in multi-male coteries; the other 58% (21/36) live in one-male coteries.

If prairie dogs avoid extreme inbreeding, then the frequency of heterozygotes should be higher than expected under conditions of random mating and Hardy-Weinberg equilibrium (Li 1955; Crow and Kimura 1970; Falconer 1981). Electrophoretic analyses of polymorphic blood proteins support this prediction (Foltz and Hoogland 1983).

Each of the four mechanisms described in this chapter probably has evolved primarily to avoid extreme inbreeding. However, perhaps male dispersal patterns (mechanisms 1 and 2) are secondary consequences of female choice (mechanisms 3 and 4) (Maynard Smith 1978; Pusey and Packer 1987a; Keane 1990a). Why should a male remain in a coterie territory if his female kin there are unlikely to mate with him?

Single mechanisms that deter inbreeding might evolve primarily in another context, so that outbreeding is secondary and fortuitous (Lidicker 1975; Shields 1982, 1987; Dobson and Jones 1985; Pusey 1987). Dispersal by young males might function primarily to avoid future competition with older males, for example, with outbreeding being merely an incidental

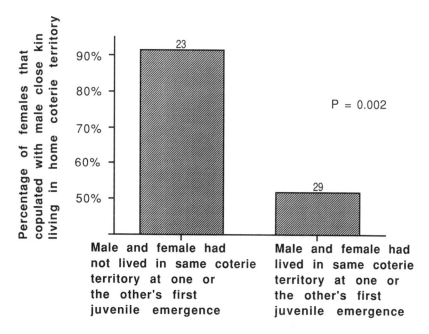

Fig. 14.8. Probability of copulating with male close kin ($r \geq .2500$) for females living with sexually mature male close kin in the same coterie territory versus whether the male and female lived together in the same coterie territory at one or the other's first juvenile emergence. The number above each bar indicates the number of estrous females. The *P*-value is from the 2 × 2 chi-square test. Direct social learning at first juvenile emergence evidently is important for the avoidance of extreme inbreeding among prairie dogs.

consequence (Greenwood 1980, 1983; Moore 1984; Moore and Ali 1984; Brody and Armitage 1985). However, prairie dogs have four different mechanisms for separating breeding kin of the opposite sex. For prairie dogs, at least, the urgency and primary importance of outbreeding are unambiguous.

The Regular Occurrence of Moderate Inbreeding

After learning that prairie dogs systematically avoid *extreme* inbreeding, I wondered whether they also avoid less extreme inbreeding with more distant kin. As time passed and the prairie dog pedigrees became more complete, I was in a unique position to investigate this important question.

Figure 14.6 supports the earlier argument that prairie dogs avoid extreme inbreeding: only 5% of copulations (36/770) involve close kin ($r \geq .2500$) ($P < .010$ for 2 × 2 chi-square analysis that compares observed number of extreme inbreedings verses number expected if copulations are random with respect to r). However, figure 14.6 also shows that prairie dogs resemble animals such as great tits, Darwin's medium ground finches, and humans (Alexander 1977, 1979; van Noordwijk and Scharloo 1981; van den Berghe 1983; Gibbs and Grant 1989; Bixler 1992) by regularly practicing less extreme, *moderate* inbreeding with kin such as full and half first and second cousins.

Known pedigrees for each individual were short in the early years of my research, sometimes extending back only one generation. Pedigrees were longer in later years, sometimes going back as far as six generations. Figure 14.6 includes data from both early and later years, and therefore underestimates the frequency of various levels of inbreeding among prairie dogs. Many of the cases I have scored as "$r = 0$" (no known kinship; see below), for example, are from early years and probably involve undetected moderate inbreeding. In 1988, when genealogies were most complete, every one of the 44 estrous females copulated with at least one male with whom she shared at least one known common ancestor. Of the 69 copulations by these 44 estrous females, 8 (12%) involve pairs with no known common ancestry, 8 (12%) involve low-level inbreeding (essentially outbreeding, when $.0078 > r > 0$), 47 (68%) involve moderate inbreeding, and 6 (9%) involve extreme inbreeding.

A copulating pair frequently has more than one common ancestor. For example, female-72 and male-6 in 1987 were half second cousins once removed via one common ancestor, full third cousins once removed via another pair of common ancestors, and half third cousins via still another common ancestor. Table 14.6 shows the observed kinships between the male and female of copulating pairs. A single copulation can account for several entries in table 14.6. For example, the single copulation involving female-72 and male-6 in 1987 accounted for three separate entries. By contrast, figure 14.6 depicts a single cumulative coefficient of genetic relatedness for each copulating pair.

Figure 14.6 shows a high frequency of moderate inbreeding. However, estrous females might consistently and actively solicit the males with whom the coefficient of genetic relatedness is lowest. In other words, prairie dogs might *try* to avoid moderate as well as extreme inbreeding whenever possible. For example, individuals might systematically solicit immigrants, who are presumably more distantly related than individuals born and reared at the study colony. Alternatively, individuals might try to *promote* moderate inbreeding by consistently choosing moderately close kin as mates ($.2500 > r \geq .0078$). To investigate possible preference for, or avoidance of, moderate inbreeding among prairie dogs, I would have liked to compare the coefficient of genetic relatedness for all observed copulating pairs ($N = 770$) and all possible copulatory pairings ($N = 13,847$) for 1978 through 1988. However, the herculean task of computing so many coefficients has deterred me. I therefore have chosen a more

Table 14.6. Types of Observed Inbreeding ($N = 679$)

Type of inbreeding (genetic relationship of prairie dog to its sexual partner	Observed number of pairings
Father-daughter	6
Mother-son	0
Full siblings[a]	1
Half siblings[a]	13
Grandfather-granddaughter	0
Grandmother-grandson	2
Full uncle-full niece	2
Half uncle-half niece	23
Full great uncle-full great niece	0
Half great uncle-half great niece	4
Full aunt-full nephew	2
Half aunt-half nephew	13
Full great aunt-full great nephew	0
Half great aunt-half great nephew	1
Full first cousins	13
Half first cousins	41
Full first cousins once removed	22
Half first cousins once removed	53
Full first cousins twice removed	3
Half first cousins twice removed	14
Full second cousins	29
Half second cousins	68
Full second cousins once removed	29
Half second cousins once removed	65
Full second cousins twice removed	0
Half second cousins twice removed	11
Full third cousins	7
Half third cousins	31
Full third cousins once removed	8
Half third cousins once removed	28
Full third cousins twice removed	0
Half third cousins twice removed	0
Full fourth cousins	1
Half fourth cousins	9
Full fourth cousins once removed	0
Half fourth cousins once removed	0
Kinship at unknown level[b]	180

Note: A copulating pair often has more than one common ancestor, all of which I show in this table. When a pair has more than one common ancestor, I add all the relevant coefficients of genetic relatedness and use the single cumulative coefficient for analyses such as those for inbreeding depression (table 14.8). The mean number of single or paired common ancestors per inbreeding is 679 (the number of entries in this table) / 292 (the number of copulations from fig. 14.6 for which $r > 0$) = 2.33.

[a]Full siblings have two common parents, whereas half siblings have only one common parent.

[b]Females living together in the same coterie territory when I initiated research in 1975 were almost certainly genetic relatives (fig. 14.1), but I do not know the exact level of kinship. These females and their offspring account for most of the 180 cases of "kinship at unknown level" in this table. For all these cases $r < .2500$, and for most cases, $r \le .0625$.

manageable data set and have analyzed copulations for 1988 only. Specifically, I have compared the values of r for the 69 observed copulations and the 44 (number of estrous females) × 17 (number of sexually active males) = 748 possible copulatory pairings. Table 14.7 shows a close agreement between the observed and expected frequencies if choice of mates is independent of r. Further, estrous females in 1988 did not preferentially choose immigrant males ($P = .380$, 2 × 2 chi-square test). Thus, prairie dogs resemble other animals, such as Japanese macaques (Takahata 1982), that neither avoid nor promote moderate inbreeding. Moderate inbreeding is nonetheless common simply because moderately close kin ($.2500 > r \geq .0078$) as potential mates are so common.

The most common type of extreme inbreeding involves half siblings ($N = 13$), but six cases resulted when fathers copulated with their daughters (table 14.6). Most cases of moderate inbreeding result from movements of male kin into the female's home coterie territory. Matings involving full first cousins result, for example, in the following way: female-A's full brother disperses into a breeding coterie territory and sires a son there; the son then disperses back into female-A's coterie territory and copulates with female-A's philopatric daughters.

Table 14.7. Observed versus Expected Frequencies of Inbreeding in 1988

Coefficient of genetic relatedness (r) between male and female of copulating pair	Observed number of pairings	Expected number of pairings
$r \geq .2500$[a]	6	6
$.2500 > r \geq .1250$	4	5
$.1250 > r \geq .0625$	18	10
$.0625 > r \geq .0313$	12	12
$.0313 > r \geq .0156$	10	11
$.0156 > r \geq .0078$	3	7
$.0078 > r \geq .0000$	8	8
No known kinship ("$r = 0$")	8	10
Totals	69	69

Note: For the 44 estrous females and 17 sexually active males in 1988 (18 coteries), I have computed the 44 × 17 = 748 coefficients of genetic relatedness for all possible copulatory pairings. I then have used these coefficients to calculate the expected value for each type of inbreeding if choice of mates is unrelated to r. For example, 18% of the possible pairings (131/748) include a male and female of .0625 $> r \geq .0313$. The expected number of copulations for which $.0625 > r \geq .0313$ is therefore 18% × 69 = 12. Observed values do not differ from expected values, indicating that choice of mates is independent of r ($P = .227$, chi-square goodness-of-fit test, df = 7).

[a]Five of the six cases of extreme inbreeding ($r \geq .2500$) involve a pair of 2-year-old full brothers who moved into a breeding coterie containing females sired by their father. The males had not associated with the females at first juvenile emergence, and probably did not recognize them as their half sisters (see fig. 14.8). The six cases of extreme inbreeding in 1988 might suggest that prairie dogs do not avoid copulations when $r \geq .2500$. When I combine data from all years, however, the avoidance of extreme inbreeding is statistically significant ($P < .010$, 2 × 2 chi-square test that compared observed versus expected number of extreme inbreedings).

Individuals of both sexes usually remain in the natal coterie territory for at least the first 11 months after first juvenile emergence from the natal burrow (see fig. 14.1). Consequently, familiarity and direct social learning probably facilitate recognition of close kin such as parents, offspring, and full and half siblings as members of the same home (natal or breeding) coterie territory. However, the recognition of kin born in different coterie territories would be difficult. Such recognition perhaps would require self-referential matching of phenotypes without opportunities for direct social learning (Holmes and Sherman 1982, 1983; Holmes 1986a, 1988; Sherman 1991). Recognition of unfamiliar kin born in different areas is rare among animals (Alexander 1990a, 1991), and almost certainly does not occur among prairie dogs (chap. 10).

In proximate terms, then, moderate inbreeding probably results because prairie dogs can easily learn to recognize and avoid close kin (as members of the home coterie), but cannot easily recognize and avoid more distant kin from outside coteries (chap. 10). In ultimate terms, moderate inbreeding probably results from the natural selection of individuals that compromise between the costs and benefits of inbreeding and outbreeding (Alexander 1977; Shields 1982; Bateson 1983; Partridge 1983; Keane 1990a,b).

Measuring Costs and Benefits of Inbreeding and Outbreeding

Measuring levels of inbreeding under natural conditions is difficult, but measuring possible costs and benefits of inbreeding and outbreeding under natural conditions is even more difficult. As discussed below, I have been able to examine two possible costs (inbreeding depression and lost mating opportunities) and two possible benefits (overdominance and ease of finding mates via inbreeding). Unfortunately, I have not been able to investigate whether outbreeding among prairie dogs promotes increased resistance to environmental change, diseases, and parasites.

Inbreeding Depression

Inbreeding depression is the reduction in fitness of inbred offspring. Biologists have generally assumed that inbreeding depression results primarily from the increased probability of exposing deleterious recessive alleles that accompanies inbreeding (Crow and Kimura 1970; Falconer 1981; Bateson 1978, 1983; Greenwood, Harvey, and Perrins 1978; Shields 1982). However, inbreeding depression also might result from other, related disadvantages of inbreeding—such as the lower resistance to diseases, parasites, and environmental changes that follows from reductions in both heterozygosity and recombination (Williams 1978, 1987; Alexander 1977, 1979; Stearns 1987; Seger and Hamilton 1988). Perhaps the notion of "inbreeding depression" should encompass *all maladaptive effects* that result directly from inbreeding. If so, then natural selection should favor outbreeding so that individuals can avoid inbreeding depression.

Inbreeding depression occurs in wild plants such as Nelson's larkspur (Price and Waser 1979), in humans (Adams and Neel 1967; Cavalli-Sforza 1977; Stine 1977; Lindelius 1980; Bittles 1983; but see Darlington 1960 and Shields 1993), and in captive and domestic populations of animals such as Burchell's zebras, caribou, brown-headed spider monkeys, and chimpanzees (Seal 1978; Connor and Belluchi 1979; Warwick and Legates 1979; Ralls, Brugger, and Ballou 1979; Ralls, Ballou, and Templeton 1988; Lacy, Petric, and Warneke 1993). However, despite relevant research with animals such as splendid fairy-wrens, pukekos, dwarf mongooses, yellow-bellied marmots, and savannah baboons (Rowley, Russell, and Brooker 1986; Rood 1987; Bulger and Hamilton 1988; Craig and Jamieson 1988; K. B. Armitage, cited in Smith 1993), evidence of inbreeding depression from natural populations of nonhuman animals is almost nonexistent. One exception is the great tit, for which investigators have inferred paternity from pairing patterns (Bulmer 1973; Greenwood, Harvey, and Perrins 1978; van Noordwijk and Scharloo 1981). This exception is dubious for statistical reasons (Shields 1993). It is also questionable because recent research with electrophoresis and DNA fingerprinting has shown that the paired males of animals such as lesser snow geese, white-crowned sparrows, cliff swallows, and splendid fairy-wrens commonly do not sire the offspring in their nests (Quinn et al. 1987; Sherman and Morton 1988; Brown and Brown 1988a; Rowley, Russell, and Brooker 1993; Russell and Rowley 1993). As with prairie dogs (see above), siring by a paired great tit male might be especially unlikely when the members of the pair are close kin.

Inbreeding depression evidently does not occur among wild prairie dogs (table 14.8, for which I have confirmed all paternities via electrophoresis of polymorphic blood proteins; see chap. 4). Any pairwise or multivariate analysis fails to show a significant depression for any of five estimates of reproductive success ($P > .100$ for all comparisons). Inbreeding depression is even absent in comparisons involving immigrants, the most distantly related of all possible mates ($P > .100$ for all pairwise comparisons).

The sample sizes in table 14.8 are among the largest ever reported for a natural population. However, inbreeding depression might still occur among prairie dogs in some fashion that I cannot easily detect, for at least three reasons. First, the severity of inbreeding depression usually varies directly with the intensity of inbreeding (Crow and Kimura 1970; Falconer 1981; Ralls, Ballou, and Templeton 1988). Perhaps serious, detectable depression occurs only in the most extreme cases of inbreeding ($r \geq .5000$, for which sample sizes are small because of avoidance) but does not occur at lower levels of inbreeding ($.5000 > r \geq .0078$, for which sample sizes are much larger). Second, shooting and poisoning have probably reduced prairie dog numbers by over 90% during the last century (Clark 1979;

Table 14.8. Reproductive Success of Inbred and Outbred Litters

	Estimate of Reproductive Success				
Coefficient of genetic relatedness (r) between parents	Probability of producing emergent litter	Litter size at first juvenile emergence	Juvenile mass at first juvenile emergence[a]	Number of emergent young that survived for at least 1 year	Proportion of emergent young that survived for at least 1 year
1 > r ≥ .5000	.500 (6)	3.00 ± 1.73 (3)	148 ± 27.5 (4)	1.33 ± 1.16 (3)	0.67 ± 0.58 (3)
.5000 > r ≥ .2500	.615 (26)	3.25 ± 0.97 (12)	151 ± 20.5 (12)	1.78 ± 1.39 (9)	0.48 ± 0.38 (9)
.2500 > r ≥ .1250	.484 (31)	3.11 ± 1.05 (9)	143 ± 31.5 (9)	1.78 ± 1.20 (9)	0.61 ± 0.33 (9)
.1250 > r ≥ .0625	.460 (50)	3.35 ± 1.11 (17)	154 ± 25.9 (17)	2.00 ± 0.97 (16)	0.64 ± 0.32 (16)
.0625 > r ≥ .0313	.533 (30)	3.08 ± 1.12 (13)	153 ± 19.7 (13)	0.57 ± 0.79 (7)	0.24 ± 0.38 (7)
.0313 > r ≥ .0156	.559 (34)	3.11 ± 0.83 (18)	149 ± 21.7 (18)	1.41 ± 1.06 (17)	0.47 ± 0.36 (17)
.0156 > r ≥ .0078	.500 (16)	3.78 ± 0.44 (9)	160 ± 20.4 (9)	1.86 ± 1.21 (7)	0.49 ± 0.31 (7)
.0078 > r ≥ .0039	.500 (4)	— (0)	— (0)	— (0)	— (0)
.0039 > r ≥ .0010	.000 (1)	— (0)	— (0)	— (0)	— (0)
r > 0 but exact value of r unknown	.368 (38)	2.75 ± 1.18 (16)	167 ± 40.2 (17)	1.88 ± 1.22 (17)	0.69 ± 0.36 (17)
No known kinship, but copulation did not involve immigrant ("r = 0")[b]	.510 (253)	3.16 ± 1.08 (147)	152 ± 33.4 (148)	1.53 ± 1.30 (146)	0.49 ± 0.38 (146)
Copulation with immigrant ("r = 0")[c]	.484 (64)	3.00 ± 1.15 (33)	151 ± 41.4 (32)	1.86 ± 1.46 (29)	0.62 ± 0.43 (29)

Notes: Numbers are means ± one standard deviation. I assign paternity from behavioral observations of estrus and copulation in combination with electrophoretic analyses of blood proteins (chaps. 11 and 12). I exclude those cases in which the copulating female disappears before first juvenile emergences ($N = 4$). Sample sizes in parentheses indicate either the number of females that copulated (for the probability of producing an emergent litter) or the number of litters that emerged from the natal burrow (for the other four measures of reproductive success). All pairwise and multivariate analyses are statistically insignificant ($P > .050$ for all). Thus, prairie dogs under natural conditions do not seem to experience inbreeding depression.

[a] For juvenile mass at first emergence, I use a single mean juvenile mass for the entire litter for all statistical analyses.

[b] In cases of no known kinship ("r = 0") that do not involve an immigrant, I can always trace genealogies back at least one full generation.

[c] The 64 copulations with immigrants involve 3 different female immigrants and 15 different male immigrants.

Halpin 1987). Perhaps populations have lost most deleterious recessive alleles while passing through this genetic and population bottleneck, when inbreeding at times has perhaps been unavoidable (Shields 1982; Templeton 1987; Daley 1992)—so that residual inbreeding depression due to deleterious recessive alleles is not easily detectable. Finally, the selective disadvantage of extreme inbreeding in prairie dogs might be as low as 1% or 2%. This disadvantage would be sufficient to lead to the avoidance of extreme inbreeding (Fisher 1965; Falconer 1981), but would require huge sample sizes for detection under natural conditions.

Lost Mating Opportunities

As noted above, prairie dog females sometimes refuse to copulate with sexually mature male close kin in the home coterie territory (tables 14.3–14.5). Such discriminating females sometimes are unable to copulate with unrelated males from other coterie territories, and pay the cost of avoiding extreme inbreeding by losing an entire breeding season. For example, female-R63 refused to copulate with the only breeding male in her home coterie territory, her father, when she was in estrus in 1986. Female-R63 was unable to solicit a male from outside the home coterie territory, and therefore did not copulate in 1986. As noted above, failure to copulate occurs at a frequency of only 1% among estrous females (5/557).

Overdominance

For a variety of reasons, heterozygosity at one or more loci sometimes increases survivorship and reproduction for animals such as peppered moths, tiger salamanders, white-tailed deer, and humans (Ford 1965, 1971; Pierce and Mitton 1982; Cothran et al. 1983; Mitton and Grant 1984; Mitton 1993). When such overdominance (heterosis, or heterozygote superiority) occurs, natural selection will favor outbreeding over inbreeding because the former is more likely to produce heterozygotes (Fisher 1965; Falconer 1981). Electrophoretic data from polymorphic blood proteins indicate that neither maternal nor juvenile heterozygosity affects survivorship or reproductive success among prairie dogs (Foltz, Hoogland, and Koscielny 1988). The possibility remains, however, that overdominance occurs at other loci hidden to electrophoresis.

Ease of Finding Mates

When a prairie dog male disperses, his new coterie territory is commonly adjacent to his former territory, or more distant but still within the boundaries of the home colony. Rarely, the new coterie territory is in a new colony as far away as several kilometers (chap. 16). Like dispersing yellow-bellied marmot males (Van Vuren 1990; Van Vuren and Armitage 1994), prairie dog males that attempt to move between colonies—away from both burrows and vigilant, antipredator-calling conspecifics—are more susceptible to predation than are males that disperse locally within the safety of the home colony (Garrett and Franklin 1988; see also chaps. 5 and 16). Thus, locally dispersing males that moderately inbreed find mates more easily and safely than do males that risk long-distance dispersal to find mates for outbreeding; consequently, the former usually outreproduce the latter.

The study colony is small relative to most prairie dog colonies (chap. 4). Outbreeding (i.e., r of copulating pair < .0078) by males born at the study colony might sometimes require hazardous, long-distance movement to another colony. By contrast, males of larger colonies can always outbreed more easily and safely by taking over distant coteries that are still within the confines of the home colony. If prairie dog males are reluctant to initiate risky dispersal to other colonies, then extreme and moderate inbreeding might be more common at the study colony than at larger colonies. For animals in general and prairie dogs in particular, additional studies are imperative for a better understanding of the levels of inbreeding under natural conditions.

Summary

1. The primary advantage of outbreeding is probably increased resistance to environmental change, diseases, and parasites. The primary advantage of inbreeding is probably greater ease and safety in finding mates. To compromise between the costs and benefits of inbreeding and outbreeding, natural selection probably favors individuals that moderately inbreed.

2. Prairie dogs avoid extreme inbreeding ($r \geq .2500$) by four mechanisms. (1) Natal dispersal is male-biased. (2) An adult male usually disperses from his breeding coterie territory before his daughters reach sexual maturity. (3) A female is less likely to come into estrus as a yearling when her father is still living with her in her natal coterie territory. (4) When the first three mechanisms fail and sexually mature close kin of the opposite sex end up in the same coterie territory, the female often refuses to copulate with her male relative.

3. Females that copulate with male close kin are more likely than other females to copulate with a second (unrelated) male as well.

4. Extreme inbreeding is more likely when the female and her male kin have lived in different coterie territories since one or the other first emerged from the natal burrow.

5. Although they avoid *extreme* inbreeding, prairie dogs regularly engage in *moderate* inbreeding ($.2500 > r \geq .0078$) with kin such as full and half first and second cousins.

6. An examination of five measures of reproductive success fails to reveal any evidence for inbreeding depression among wild prairie dogs.

15   Do Mothers Manipulate the Sex Ratio of Their Litters?

Fisher's Theory of Juvenile Sex Ratios

The *sex ratio* is the ratio of males to females in a population (Fisher 1930, 1958; Trivers and Willard 1973; Charnov 1982; Trivers 1985; Frank 1990). The *primary sex ratio* is the sex ratio of all fertilized eggs. For convenience, however, researchers often use this term for the sex ratio of the youngest juveniles that they can easily observe and sex—e.g., at hatching or at birth (Trivers 1985).

Among animals in general (Darwin 1859, 1871; Williams 1979; but see Bull and Charnov 1988) and among sciurids such as yellow-bellied marmots and round-tailed, Richardson's, and Belding's ground squirrels in particular (Dunford 1977a; Schmutz, Boag, and Schmutz 1979; Sherman and Morton 1984; Armitage 1987a; Michener 1980a, 1989b), parents usually produce approximately equal numbers of male and female offspring. The reason for this ubiquitous equality puzzled biologists for a long time until R. A. Fisher (1930, 1958) pointed out that the sex ratio of the *population* affects *individual* reproductive success. When males are rare, for example, then each male will be more valuable. Parents that produce male-biased litters when males are rare will therefore leave more grandoffspring than parents that produce female-biased litters. Natural selection for production of the rarer sex will continue until equilibrium is reached, at which point each sex will be equally valuable.

One sex is sometimes more expensive to rear than the other. For great-tailed grackles, red deer, northern fur seals, California sea lions, and African elephants, for example, males are more expensive to rear than females (Clutton-Brock, Albon, and Guinness 1981; Clutton-Brock, Guinness, and Albon 1982; Costa and Gentry 1986; Lee and Moss 1986; Oftedal, Iverson, and Bonness 1987; Teather and Weatherhead 1988). Producing the more expensive sex is disadvantageous, and natural selection will favor parents that produce the cheaper sex. However, every offspring in a sexual species has exactly one father and one mother. Consequently, each sex, taken collectively, will always produce the same average number of offspring as the other. Fisher (1930, 1958) recognized this problem, and theorized that *parents should invest equally in both sexes until the termination of parental care* (see also Shaw 1958; Maynard Smith 1978; Myers 1978; Williams 1979; Slagsvold 1990). If one sex is cheaper to rear, then parents should produce more of that sex so that the total investment for each sex is equal. If the sexes are equally expensive to rear, then parents should produce equal numbers of males and females. Fisher's theory holds for monogamous, polygynous, and polyandrous mating systems.

One important assumption of Fisher's theory is that reproductive success varies linearly with parental investment in each sex (Charnov 1982). But what if the number of grandoffspring varies directly with parental invest-ment in sons but increases at a diminishing rate—i.e., approaches an asymptote—with additional parental investment in daughters? Under these circumstances, natural selection probably will favor parents that invest more in sons than in daughters. Frequency-dependent selection will still operate, but the total expected investment will be greater for males (Charnov 1982; Frank 1986, 1987b, 1990).

Fisher's (1930) theory predicts that *parents as a collective unit* should invest approximately equally in male and female offspring. However, natural selection might nonetheless favor *individual parents* that specialize in the production of only one sex (Trivers and Willard 1973; Alexander 1974; Maynard Smith 1978; Williams 1979; Clutton-Brock and Iason 1986).

In this chapter I first discuss parental investment and the sex ratio of prairie dog litters at first emergence. I then examine five factors that might affect the sex ratio of litters produced by particular parents.

For 97% of the emergent litters at the study colony in 1975 through 1988 (349/361), I have captured all the juveniles ($N = 1,110$ juveniles) and have determined the sex ratio of each litter at first emergence. For the other 12 emergent litters, one or more juveniles disappeared or mixed with juveniles from another litter before marking so that I could not determine the sex ratio.

Adaptive variation of the sex ratio of litters is easier and more likely when litter (or clutch) size is only one or two, as it is for animals such as black-footed albatrosses, northern elephant seals, red deer, and humans (Klomp 1970; Williams 1979; Clutton-Brock and Iason 1986; Le Boeuf, Condit, and Reiter 1989). For prairie dogs, however, the most common litter size at first emergence is three or four. Consequently, prairie dogs are probably less likely than other, less fecund animals to show adaptive variation of the sex ratio of litters.

Sex Ratio of Litters at First Emergence versus Parental Investment

The first stage at which I can measure the sex ratio for each litter is first emergence from the natal burrow, approximately 6 weeks after parturition.

Because the resorption of embryos (chap. 16) and mortality of pre-emergent juveniles (chap. 7) both occur, the sex ratio of litters at first emergence is not equivalent to the sex ratio of litters at either fertilization or birth. Nor is it equivalent to the sex ratio of litters at the termination of parental care, because parental investment continues after first emergence (see below). Further, all nursing and other forms of maternal care of pre-emergent juveniles occur underground. I am therefore unable to investigate whether mothers invest more in one sex prior to first emergence. With these shortcomings in mind, I have investigated whether parents adaptively vary the sex ratio of litters at first emergence.

Of 1,100 juveniles that emerged at the study colony from 1975 through 1988, 587 (53%) were males and 523 (47%) were females. These numbers, like those from other prairie dog colonies (King 1955; Tileston and Lechleitner 1966; Garrett and Franklin 1988; Halpin 1987), do not differ significantly from the expected values of 555 for each sex if the overall sex ratio of juveniles at first emergence were even ($P = .174$, 2×2 chi-square goodness-of-fit test).

Unlike every other variable that I have examined (chap. 16), the sex ratio of litters at first juvenile emergence shows no significant annual variation (fig. 15.1).

Prairie dog males average about 6 grams heavier than females at first juvenile emergence (fig. 15.2). Data from only those litters with at least

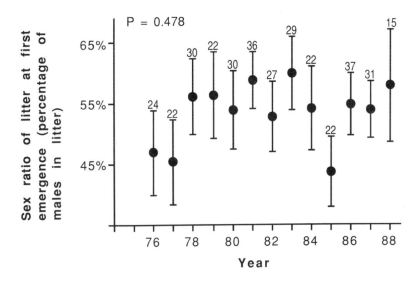

Fig. 15.1. Annual variation in the sex ratio of litters at first emergence. The number above each SE line indicates the number of emergent litters each year. The *P*-value is from the Kruskal-Wallis analysis of variance.

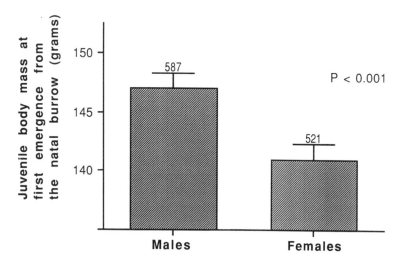

Fig. 15.2. Mean juvenile body mass at first emergence from the natal burrow for males and females. The number above each bar indicates the number of juveniles weighed. The *P*-value is from the Mann-Whitney *U* test.

one juvenile of each sex also demonstrate a male advantage. Specifically, mean male body mass is greater than mean female body mass in 72% of two-sex litters (164/228) ($P < .001$, Wilcoxon matched-pairs signed-ranks test).

The higher frequency and larger size of male juveniles at first emergence suggest that prairie dog mothers invest more in males than in females. But this would be a risky conclusion, for at least three reasons. First, heavier juvenile body mass in one sex can occur without differential parental investment if males and females allocate food differently to growth and development, as they do for animals such as yellow-headed blackbirds, European sparrowhawks, golden eagles, and northern elephant seals (Newton and Marquiss 1979; Richter 1983; Collopy 1986; Kretzmann, Costa, and Le Boeuf 1993). Second, as noted above, I am unable to investigate any possible sexual bias in juvenile mortality between parturition and first juvenile emergence. Perhaps pre-emergent juvenile mortality due to disease, genetic defects, or selective removal by the mother (chap. 7) is consistently higher for females. If so, then parental investment in females might equal or exceed parental investment in males, even though males are heavier and more numerous at first juvenile emergence. Finally, unlike dispersing males, prairie dog females usually remain in the natal coterie territory for life (chaps. 6 and 14). Consequently, parents might invest in females for a longer time—that is, the termination of parental care might be later for females than for males (see also below). If so, then parental investment in females might equal or exceed parental investment in males.

When parents manipulate the sex ratio, significant deviations from the expected sex ratios in litters of various sizes usually occur (Williams 1979; but see Frank 1990). For example, suppose that the overall sex ratio of prairie dog juveniles at first emergence is even. Without adaptive manipulation, a sample of 100 litters of size 2 should show 25 litters with 2 males, 50 litters with 1 male and 1 female, and 25 litters with 2 females. Higher than expected numbers of all-male or all-female litters would indicate natural selection on the sex ratio. Table 15.1 shows the frequencies of sex ratios at first juvenile emergence of prairie dog litters of different sizes. Observed and expected sex ratios agree closely for all litter sizes, and thus suggest that prairie dog mothers do not adaptively vary the sex ratio of litters at first emergence.

One type of natural selection on the sex ratio might balance another type of natural selection (Williams 1979). For example, natural selection for heavy females in a polygynous species to produce male-biased litters might offset natural selection for light females to produce female-biased litters (Trivers and Willard 1973). If so, then observed frequencies of litters with each sex ratio might be equivalent to expected frequencies despite frequent parental manipulation of the sex ratio. Thus, despite the implication of table 15.1, prairie dog mothers commonly might adaptively vary

Table 15.1. Sex Ratio at First Juvenile Emergence versus Litter Size

Litter size at first juvenile emergence	Number of litters of this size	Observed number of litters with the following number of male juveniles (expected number)						
		0	1	2	3	4	5	6
1	30	12 (14)	18 (16)					
2	68	15 (15)	35 (34)	18 (19)				
3	128	17 (13)	40 (45)	48 (51)	23 (19)			
4	95	5 (5)	16 (21)	41 (35)	27 (27)	6 (7)		
5	26	2 (1)	2 (3)	8 (8)	9 (9)	5 (5)	0 (1)	
6	2	0 (0)	0 (0)	0 (0)	2 (1)	0 (1)	0 (0)	0 (0)

Note: Of the 1,110 emergent juveniles captured and sexed at the study colony from 1975 through 1988, 52.9% (587) were males. I have used this percentage to compute the expected frequencies of litters with different sex ratios. For example, the expected number of litters of size 1 with a male is $0.529 \times 30 = 16$. For each litter size, the observed distribution of litters with different sex ratios does not differ from the expected distribution ($P > .100$ for all, chi-square goodness-of-fit test).

the sex ratio of litters at first emergence. In the sections that follow, I investigate this possibility further.

Sex Ratio of Litters at First Emergence versus Sex Ratio of Adults and Yearlings

Members of one sex among older (i.e., nonjuvenile) individuals in the population are sometimes rare—i.e., less frequent than expected under conditions of equilibrium. When such imbalance occurs for animals such as southern green stinkbugs, guppies, iridens trout, and exculenta frogs (Werren and Charnov 1978; McLain and Marsh 1990), then frequency-dependent natural selection favors parents that produce more of the rarer sex (Fisher 1930, 1958; Maynard Smith 1978; Charnov 1982; Frank 1990).

Do prairie dog parents vary the sex ratio of litters at first emergence in response to the sex ratio among adults and yearlings? To find out, I have examined the sex ratio of litters at first emergence each year versus the absolute number of adult and yearling males in the study colony in May (fig. 15.3a) and versus the percentage of males among adult and yearling residents in May (fig. 15.3b). The prediction, of course, is that the percentage of males in emergent litters should vary negatively with both the absolute number of adult and yearling males at the study colony and the percentage of males among adult and yearling residents. Curiously, both correlations in figure 15.3 are *positive rather than the expected negative.* Specifically, mothers produce more male juveniles in those years when adult and yearling males are most common!

The sex ratio of litters at first emergence also correlates positively with the number of adult and yearling males within the home *coterie* in May (fig. 15.4). Perhaps mothers use the number of adult and yearling males within the home coterie as an indicator of the number of males within the whole colony.

Two of the correlations between juvenile and adult-yearling sex ratios are almost statistically significant—and all three are positive rather than negative (figs. 15.3 and 15.4). Thus, prairie dogs offer no support for Fisher's (1930, 1958) theory of adaptive variation of the sex ratio of juveniles in response to the sex ratio of older individuals.

Sex Ratio of Litters at First Emergence versus Maternal Age, Rank, and Body Mass

For animals such as red and white-tailed deer, meadow voles, yellow-bellied marmots, and Japanese macaques, natural selection sometimes favors older mothers that produce intralitter sex ratios different from those of younger mothers (Clutton-Brock, Guinness, and Albon 1982; Noyes 1982; Verme 1983; Armitage 1987a). For prairie dogs, the percentage of males in a litter is lowest for the oldest (6-year-old) and youngest (1-year-old) mothers, but this trend is not significant (fig. 15.5). Also statistically

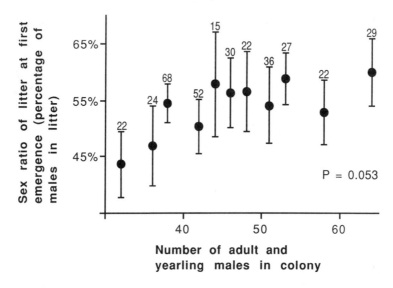

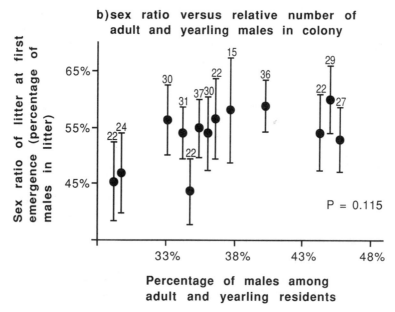

Fig. 15.3. Sex ratio of litters at first emergence versus *(a)* the absolute number of, and *(b)* the relative number of, adult and yearling males living at the study colony when juveniles start emerging from their natal burrows in May. For both graphs, the number above each SE line indicates the number of emergent litters, and *P*-values are from the Spearman rank correlation test. Unexpectedly, both correlations are positive rather than negative.

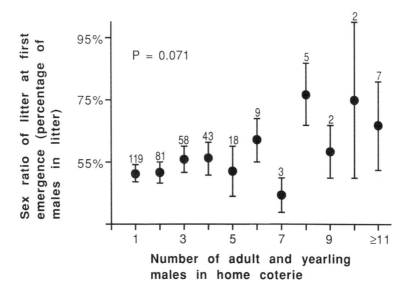

Fig. 15.4. Sex ratio of litters at first emergence versus the number of adult and yearling males in the home coterie at first juvenile emergence. The number above each SE line indicates the number of litters. The *P*-value is from the Spearman rank correlation test. Curiously, this correlation is positive rather than negative.

insignificant is the relationship between the sex ratio of litters at first emergence and age of the *father* (fig. 15.5).

For animals such as red deer, savannah baboons, and rhesus and bonnet macaques, dominant females are sometimes more—or less—likely to produce males than are subordinate females (Silk 1983; Simpson and Simpson 1982; Clutton-Brock, Albon, and Guinness 1984; Altmann, Hausfater, and Altmann 1988). I did not directly investigate the sex ratio of prairie dog litters at first emergence versus female dominance. However, I did investigate the possible influence of female body mass (see below), which directly affects female dominance (chap. 10).

In polygynous species, variance in reproductive success is greater for males than for females. Consequently, the most successful males in polygynous species produce more offspring than the most successful females—but more males than females produce no offspring at all (Trivers 1972; Alexander et al. 1979; Clutton-Brock, Guinness, and Albon 1982). Trying to produce a successful son in a polygynous species is therefore more chancy than trying to produce a successful daughter. Because they can provide more resources to their offspring, which are therefore more likely to survive and reproduce, heavy females in good condition should be more likely than lighter females to take the greater gamble of rearing sons (Alexander et al. 1979; Clutton-Brock, Albon, and Guinness 1981,

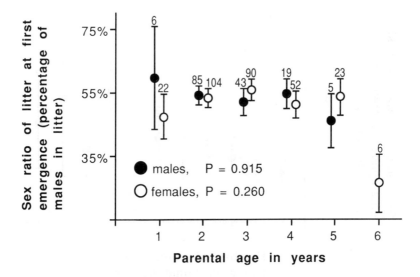

Fig. 15.5. Sex ratio of litters at first emergence versus parental age in years. The number above each SE line indicates the number of litters. *P*-values are from the Kruskal-Wallis analysis of variance.

1984; Clutton-Brock and Iason 1986; Clark, Bone, and Galef 1990; Clark, Waddingham, and Galef 1991). Such male-biasing of litters by heavy mothers occurs for animals such as red deer, American bison, humpback whales, common opossums, and black spider monkeys (Clutton-Brock, Albon, and Guinness 1984; Rutberg 1986; Austad and Sunquist 1986; McFarland-Symington 1987; Kojola and Eloranta 1989; Wiley and Clapham 1993).

For animals in general and for prairie dogs in particular, "condition" is difficult to quantify. Like previous investigators (see examples in Clutton-Brock 1988a), I use body mass as a measure of condition (chap. 13). Because prairie dogs are highly polygynous, and because body mass is so important to female reproduction, I predicted that heavy females would produce litters more male-biased than those of lighter females. Curiously, figure 15.6 provides no support for this prediction.

Figure 15.6 combines data on the sex ratios of emergent litters of all sizes. Might such pooling of data obscure adaptive patterns for specific litter sizes? Evidently not. Maternal body mass does not vary significantly with the sex ratio of litters at first emergence for any litter size ($P \geq .165$ for all comparisons, Kruskal-Wallis analysis of variance). Figure 15.7 depicts data for the most common litter size of three.

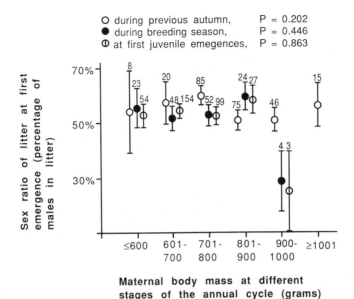

Fig. 15.6. Sex ratio of litters at first emergence versus maternal body mass at different stages of the annual cycle. The number above each SE line indicates the number of litters. *P*-values are for Spearman rank correlation coefficients, all negative.

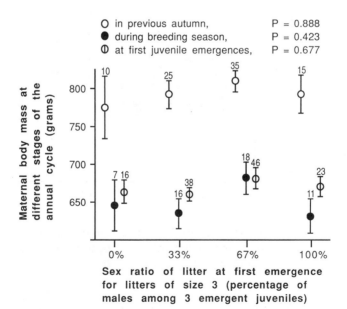

Fig. 15.7. Maternal body mass at different stages of the annual cycle versus sex ratio of litter at first emergence for litters of size 3. The number above each SE line indicates the number of litters. *P*-values are from the Kruskal-Wallis analysis of variance.

Sex Ratio of Litters at First Emergence versus Paternal Reproductive Success

Suppose that male reproductive success is heritable, so that sons of highly polygynous males are more likely than other sons to be highly polygynous themselves. If so, then females that copulate with highly polygynous males will leave more grandoffspring—because of their successful sons—than will less discriminating females (Trivers 1972; Alexander 1974; Weather-head and Robertson 1979; Burley 1981, 1986; Curtsinger and Heisler 1988). Further, females that copulate with highly polygynous males should produce male-biased litters—to capitalize on the production of successful sons—while females that copulate with less successful males should produce female-biased litters (Alexander 1974; Hartung 1976; Weatherhead and Robertson 1979). Despite this logic, significant correlations between the intralitter sex ratio and paternal reproductive success remain elusive, with possible exceptions coming only from humans (Dickemann 1979, 1981; Clutton-Brock and Iason 1986).

The sex ratio of prairie dog litters at first emergence does not vary with paternal copulatory success or paternal siring success in a single year (fig.

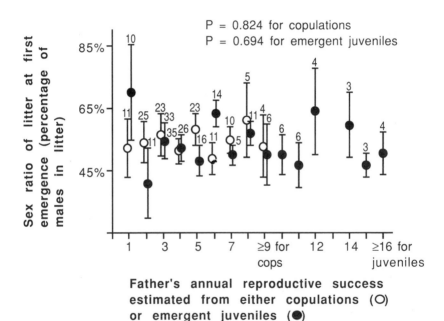

Father's annual reproductive success estimated from either copulations (O) or emergent juveniles (●)

Fig. 15.8. Sex ratio of litters at first emergence versus father's annual reproductive success, estimated from both copulations and the number of emergent juveniles sired. The number above each SE line indicates the number of litters. *P*-values are from the Kruskal-Wallis analysis of variance.

15.8). Similarly, the sex ratio of litters at first emergence does not vary with lifetime estimates of either paternal copulatory success or paternal siring success ($P \geq .908$ for both, Kruskal-Wallis analysis of variance).

Sex Ratio of Litters at First Emergence versus Local Mate Competition

Fisher's (1930, 1958) theory of adaptive variation of the juvenile sex ratio has a hidden assumption: competition for mates must be randomly distributed throughout the population. If not, then local mate competition—the nonrandom distribution of competition for mates—will occur, and parental investment in the two sexes should not necessarily be equal (Hamilton 1967, 1979; Werren 1980, 1983; Frank 1990). For example, suppose that females mate only with their brothers, as they commonly do for animals such as scolytid bark beetles, agaontid fig wasps, Nasonia wasps, and scelionid wasps (Hamilton 1967, 1979; Beaver 1977; Werren 1980, 1983; Waage 1982). If so, and if a single male can inseminate numerous females, then litters with only one or two males will yield more grandoffspring than litters with a more balanced sex ratio. Natural selection will therefore favor mothers that somehow skew litters in favor of females (Hamilton 1967; Alexander and Sherman 1977; Maynard Smith 1978; Yamaguchi 1985).

Close male kin, such as a father and son or full brothers, frequently compete for sexual rights to the same estrous prairie dog female (chaps. 11, 12, and 14), as do more distant male kin (chap. 14). Further, transfer of prairie dogs between colonies is uncommon (chaps. 14 and 16). Thus, competition for estrous females is not randomly distributed among the males of the numerous prairie dog colonies at Wind Cave National Park. Consequently, the sex ratio of litters at first emergence should perhaps be female-biased. Contrary to this prediction, as noted above, the sex ratio of litters at first emergence is consistently *male-biased*. The local mate competition that occurs within prairie dog colonies evidently does not affect the sex ratio of litters at first emergence.

Sex Ratio of Litters at First Emergence versus Local Resource Competition and Local Resource Enhancement

Local mate competition is a specific case of local resource competition, the nonrandom distribution of competition for resources. Consequently, competition among same-sex kin for resources other than mates also can lead to a biased juvenile sex ratio for animals such as thick-tailed bushbabies, vervet monkeys, savannah baboons, and rhesus macaques (A. B. Clark 1978; Johnson 1988; van Schaik and Hrdy 1991; see also Gowaty 1993). Specifically, natural selection might sometimes favor females that produce an intralitter sex ratio biased against the competing sex.

Conversely, *cooperation* among close kin of the same sex might lead to a biased juvenile sex ratio via local resource enhancement, the nonrandom distribution of cooperation. Specifically, in some animals, such as African wild dogs and red-cockaded woodpeckers, natural selection might sometimes favor females that produce an intralitter sex ratio biased in favor of the cooperating sex (Malcolm and Marten 1982; Gowaty and Lennartz 1985). Such cooperating offspring "pay back" some of the parental effort invested in them, and are thus cheaper to rear (Trivers and Hare 1976; A. B. Clark 1978; Emlen, Emlen, and Levin 1986; Frank 1987a; Lessels and Avery 1987).

Prairie dog males usually remain in the natal coterie territory for only about 1 year after first emergence, but females usually remain there for life. Females cooperate with their yearling and adult daughters and other close female kin of the home coterie via antipredator calls, allogrooming, defense of the home coterie territory, and cooperative excavation and maintenance of burrows. Indeed, maternal investment in daughters might continue until the death of either mother or daughter! Because of this longterm cooperation, natural selection might favor females that produce *female-biased* litters in response to local resource enhancement. However, females also compete with female kin of the home coterie for nursery burrows and other resources during the periods of pregnancy and lactation. In the most extreme form of competition, mothers kill the offspring of female close kin (chap. 7). In view of this longterm competition, natural selection might favor females that produce *male-biased* litters in response to local resource competition. With these arguments in mind, I have looked for maternal manipulation of the sex ratio of litters at first emergence in response to either local resource enhancement or local resource competition.

The slight male bias in the sex ratio of litters at first emergence suggests that local resource competition might be more important than local resource enhancement among prairie dog females. However, as noted above, this male bias (53% versus 47%) is statistically insignificant.

Large litters probably would promote both cooperation and competition among mothers and daughters. If either local resource enhancement or local resource competition is important to prairie dogs, then the sex ratio of litters at first emergence should perhaps vary with litter size, as it does for animals such as domestic cattle, meadow voles, white-tailed deer, and humans (James 1975; Skjervold and James 1979; Verme 1983; McGinley 1984; McShea and Madison 1986). Curiously, the percentage of males within a prairie dog litter does not vary systematically with litter size at first emergence (fig. 15.9).

Prairie dog females cooperate and compete not only with their mothers, sisters, and daughters, but with other female (and male) kin within the

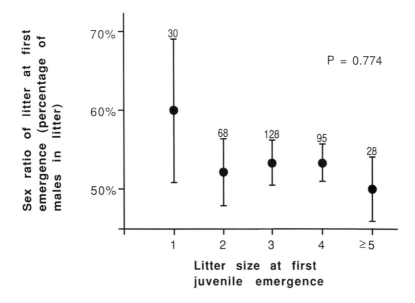

Fig. 15.9. Sex ratio of litters at first emergence versus litter size at first juvenile emergence. The number above each SE line indicates the number of litters. The *P*-value is from the Kruskal-Wallis analysis of variance.

home coterie as well. Perhaps mothers manipulate the sex ratio of litters at first emergence more in response to cooperation and competition with *any female kin* than in response to cooperation and competition with daughters only. To investigate this possibility, I have examined the sex ratio of litters at first emergence versus the number of adult and yearling females within the home coterie and versus the number of females in the home coterie that produce emergent juveniles. Neither analysis shows any systematic variation. The sex ratio of litters at first emergence also does not vary with coterie size (fig. 15.10).

With so little evidence for adaptive variation of the sex ratio of prairie dog litters at first emergence from the natal burrow, why have I bothered to devote a chapter to this topic? Data that support certain theories about juvenile sex ratios are perhaps more interesting, but nonsupporting data—especially when sample sizes are as large as they are for prairie dogs—are nonetheless important. The data from prairie dogs do not negate the theories about juvenile sex ratios, but perhaps call into question the generality and feasibility of these theories for animals living under natural conditions.

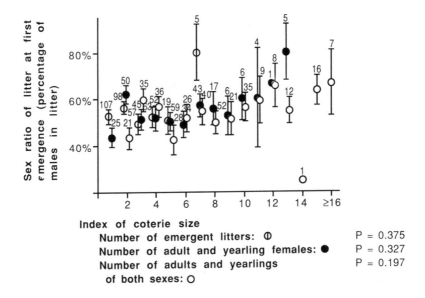

Fig. 15.10. Sex ratio of litters at first emergence versus the number of emergent litters within the home coterie, the number of adult and yearling females within the home coterie, and the number of adults and yearlings of both sexes within the home coterie (i.e., coterie size). The number above each SE line indicates the number of litters. *P*-values are from the Kruskal-Wallis analysis of variance.

Summary

1. At first juvenile emergence, males are both heavier and more numerous than females. However, this asymmetry does not necessarily mean that prairie dog parents invest more in sons than in daughters, for at least three reasons: (*a*) pre-emergent sons might emphasize allocation of parental resources to body mass, while pre-emergent daughters might allocate resources differently; (*b*) mortality prior to first emergence might be female-biased; (*c*) the termination of parental care might be later for daughters than for sons.

2. Contrary to prediction, prairie dog mothers produce male-biased litters in those years when adult and yearling males are most common within the home colony.

3. The sex ratio of litters at first emergence does not vary with either maternal or paternal age.

4. The sex ratio of litters at first emergence does not vary with maternal body mass—even though maternal body mass promotes female reproductive success and even though the prairie dog mating system is polygynous.

5. The sex ratio of litters at first emergence does not correlate with either annual or lifetime paternal reproductive success.

6. Close male kin frequently compete for sexual rights to the same estrous female, as do more distant male kin. However, this local mate competition among males does not lead to a female-biased sex ratio of litters at first emergence.

7. Prairie dog females both compete with and cooperate with close female kin for their entire lives. However, neither local resource competition nor local resource enhancement seems to affect the sex ratio of litters at first emergence.

16 Demography and Population Dynamics

With only a few exceptions, such as northern and southern flying squirrels (Muul 1968, 1969; Dolan and Carter 1977; Sonenshine et al. 1979; Wells-Gosling 1985; Stapp and Mautz 1991), squirrels are diurnal and easy to livetrap. Consequently, squirrels such as eastern chipmunks, gray squirrels, yellow-bellied and hoary marmots, and Richardson's and Uinta ground squirrels are common subjects for studies of demography and population dynamics (Tryon and Snyder 1973; Armitage and Downhower 1974; Slade and Balph 1974; Thompson 1978; Barash 1989; Michener 1989b).

Neither demography nor population dynamics has ever been a primary emphasis of my prairie dog research. However, my investigations of issues such as nepotism versus kinship and competition (chap. 10), annual and lifetime reproductive success (chap. 12), and levels of inbreeding (chap. 14) require the eartagging and dye-marking of *every* resident at the study colony each year (1975–1989). The thoroughness of this longterm marking program has allowed me to collect copious information on demography and population dynamics, which I describe in this chapter (see also chaps. 6 and 14).

Variations in Colony Size and Colony Composition

In May and June of each year, I mark all colony residents for a complete census (table 16.1). Colony size—the number of adults and yearlings living at the colony—in May ranges from 92 to 143 (fig. 16.1). The number of emergent juveniles each year ranges from 41 to 133 (fig. 16.1).

Undeveloped methods of observation and livetrapping marred my first year at the study colony (1975). I therefore have ignored most 1975 data. One thing about 1975, though, has always perplexed me. Adults and yearlings in the spring of that year numbered 216, and they produced only 4 emergent juveniles! At no later date has colony size ever approached 216, and never again have so few juveniles survived until first emergence. My naive, disruptive trapping methods in 1975 were probably primarily responsible for the poor reproduction that year, but severe crowding also might have played a part.

Table 16.1. Number of Adults, Yearlings, and Juveniles at the Study Colony in May in Different Years

Time of census	Number of adult males	Number of adult females	Number of yearling males	Number of yearling females	Number of male emergent juveniles[a]	Number of female emergent juveniles[a]
May 76	35	85	0[b]	1[b]	37	42
May 77	26	72	16	29	28	34
May 78	27	70	19	23	57	41
May 79	31	70	16	12	32	26
May 80	27	59	15	12	43	39
May 81	20	52	33	26	67	52
May 82	31	48	26	21	49	38
May 83	38	53	23	25	55	38
May 84	26	55	35	21	36	30
May 85	19	43	13	17	31	43
May 86	20	45	18	25	70	63
May 87	15	38	23	35	58	56
May 88	21	47	23	25	24	17
May 89	29	61	11	10	51	57

[a]In addition to the juveniles counted here, 17 emergent juveniles disappeared before I could capture them (1 in 1977 and in 1985, 2 in 1982, 4 in 1978 and in 1987, and 5 in 1983). The juvenile counts for each year include all the emergent juveniles captured in that year, even though a few juveniles from early-emerging litters sometimes disappear before I capture all the juveniles from late-emerging litters.

[b]The small number of yearlings in 1976 resulted because the study colony produced only four emergent juveniles in 1975, my first year of research there.

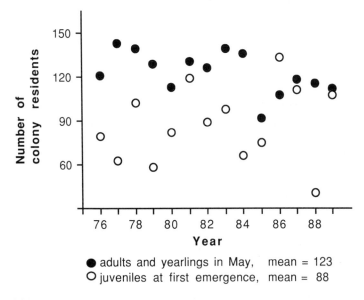

● adults and yearlings in May,   mean = 123
○ juveniles at first emergence,   mean = 88

Fig. 16.1. Annual variation in the number of adult, yearling, and juvenile residents at the study colony. The number of emergent juveniles does not significantly correlate with the number of adults and yearlings in May ($P = .439$, Spearman rank correlation test).

When food and other resources are limiting, juvenile production usually varies inversely with population size (Slobodkin 1961; Williams 1966a; Krebs 1978; Ricklefs 1973; Futuyma 1979). Unlike Eurasian badgers (Cheeseman et al. 1987), prairie dogs at the study colony do not show this trend (fig. 16.1).

Annual Variation in Demographic Measures

Significant annual variation occurs not only in colony size and in the number of emergent juveniles, but also in the date of copulation ($P < .001$, Kruskal-Wallis analysis of variance); the date of first juvenile emergence (fig. 16.2a); litter size at first juvenile emergence (fig. 16.2b); the percentage of juveniles in a litter that survive for at least 1 year ($P = .004$, Kruskal-Wallis analysis of variance); the number of juveniles per litter that survive for at least 1 year ($P = .014$, Kruskal-Wallis analysis of variance); and juvenile body mass at first emergence ($P < .001$, Kruskal-Wallis analysis of variance). One gets the impression that *every* demographic variable shows significant annual variation. I found only one exception: the sex ratio of litters at first emergence (chap. 15).

I have not probed the possible causes of annual variation in demographic measures. Meteorological factors such as mean daily temperature, precipitation, and duration of snow cover are obvious candidates (Knowles 1987; see also chaps. 7 and 11).

Disappearance versus Dispersal and Mortality

Discriminating between animals that disappear because of long-distance dispersal and animals that disappear because of mortality is usually difficult (Caughley 1966, 1977; Pfeifer 1982; Sherman and Morton 1984). I have this problem with most of the more than 1,200 marked prairie dogs that disappeared from the study colony from 1975 through 1989. In the 22 cases of predation that field assistants and I observed (chap. 5), I am certain that the disappearing animals died rather than dispersed. I also verified death for the 30 or so prairie dogs whose carcasses I found aboveground. I am confident, but not certain, that mortality accounted for the disappearances of approximately 20 other prairie dogs. Each of these 20 showed a gradual or abrupt decline in health followed by sudden disappearance; I observed 2 or 3 submerge for the night into a particular burrow and then never reappear.

I have verified long-distance dispersal from the study colony for only 2 prairie dogs. In June 1980, I observed one marked yearling male living at the Pringle colony, 1 kilometer from the study colony. In April 1988, James G. Daley livetrapped an eartagged male at the Sanctuary colony, 2 kilometers away; this male was 2 years old at the time of capture, but disappeared from the study colony in June 1987 while still a yearling.

a) annual variation in date of first juvenile emergence

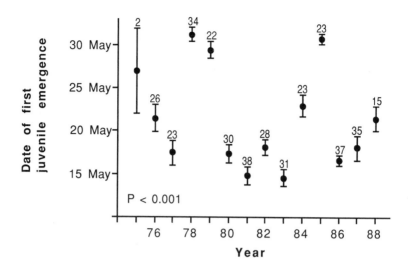

b) annual variation in litter size

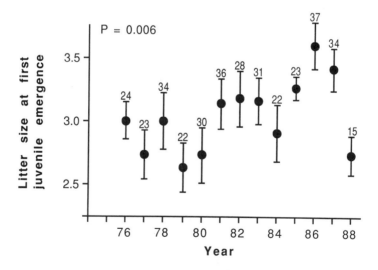

Fig. 16.2. Annual variation in *(a)* date of first juvenile emergence and *(b)* litter size at first juvenile emergence. For both graphs, the number above each SE line indicates the number of emergent litters each year, and *P*-values are from the Kruskal-Wallis analysis of variance.

Despite my ignorance of the reasons for disappearance, I have discovered a surprising pattern in the *timing* of disappearance. Food for the prairie dogs is most scarce during the winter months (King 1955; Koford 1958; Tileston and Lechleitner 1966; Smith 1967). I therefore hypothesized that disappearance would be greatest during the winter months, as it is for other sciurids such as yellow-bellied marmots and Uinta, Columbian, and Belding's ground squirrels (Slade and Balph 1974; Armitage and Downhower 1974; Boag and Murie 1981; Sherman and Morton 1984; Young 1990). Oddly, adult and yearling prairie dogs disappear more often during the shorter, warmer interval of maximal availability of food (i.e., June through September) than during the colder, longer interval of minimal availability of food (i.e., November through April) (table 16.2). Juvenile prairie dogs disappear over five times more often during the warmer months of maximal availability of food (table 16.3)!

Factors other than the weather and availability of food obviously influence the disappearances of prairie dogs. For the older individuals (adults and yearlings), long-distance dispersal might account for much of the higher rate of disappearance in the warmer months of maximal food availability (see below). Long-distance dispersal cannot account for the higher rate of disappearance of juveniles in warmer months, however, because prairie dogs do not disperse as juveniles (see below and chap. 14). Some of the juvenile disappearances in June result when males invade new coterie territories and kill recently emerged juveniles there (chap. 7). Do infanticidal males continue to invade in July through September and thereby account for most of the juvenile disappearances during that period? Thus far I have been unable to investigate this intriguing possibility because I end my field season each year in June.

In a study that focused on intercolonial dispersal of radio-collared prairie dogs, Garrett and Franklin (1988; see also Knowles 1985; Cincotta, Uresk, and Hansen 1987) made eight interesting discoveries (fig. 16.3). First, intercolonial dispersers sometimes travel as far as 5 kilometers. Second, like yellow-bellied marmot dispersers (Van Vuren 1990; Van Vuren and Armitage 1994), prairie dogs that attempt intercolonial dispersal are more vulnerable to predation than are individuals that remain in the safety of the home colony. Third, individuals that disperse from the home colony almost always move into an established colony rather than attempting to initiate a new colony. Fourth, and unexpectedly, females are almost as likely as males to move between colonies (see below). Fifth, most male intercolonial dispersers and almost half of female intercolonial dispersers are yearlings. Because intercolonial dispersal by juveniles does not occur, the other dispersers are necessarily adults. Sixth, movement between colonies of adults and yearlings is most common in the month or so after the first emergences of juveniles from the natal burrow. Seventh, contrary to popular

Table 16.2. Disappearance of Adult and Yearling Prairie Dogs in June through September versus Disappearance in November through April

Year	Number of adults and yearlings in May	Number (percentage) of adults and yearlings that disappeared between June and following September		Number (percentage) of adults and yearlings that disappeared between November and following April	
1978	139	27	(19%)	11	(8%)
1979	129	5	(4%)	38	(29%)
1980	113	17	(15%)	24	(21%)
1981	131	29	(22%)	23	(18%)
1982	126	23	(18%)	11	(9%)
1983	139	43	(31%)	15	(11%)
1984	137	42	(31%)	33	(24%)
1985	92	16	(17%)	11	(12%)
Totals	1006	202	(20%)	166	(17%)

Note: Adults and yearlings are more likely to disappear during the 4 warm months when food is abundant than during the 6 colder months when food is more scarce. However, this difference is not significant ($P = .430$ for Mann-Whitney U test that compares percentages). I base the results shown here on censuses made in May and October of each year. Data are missing for certain years (1975 through 1977 and 1986 through 1988) because I do not always mark colony residents in October. The 1978 fall census is from November rather than October, and the 1979 fall census is from September rather than October.

Table 16.3. Disappearance of Juvenile Prairie Dogs in June through September versus Disappearance in November through April

Year	Number of juveniles in May	Number (percentage) of juveniles that disappeared between June and following September		Number (percentage) of juveniles that disappeared between November and following April	
1978	102	69	(68%)	5	(5%)
1979	58	28	(48%)	3	(5%)
1980	82	22	(27%)	1	(1%)
1981	119	66	(55%)	7	(6%)
1982	89	34	(38%)	7	(8%)
1983	98	32	(33%)	10	(10%)
1984	66	23	(35%)	12	(18%)
1985	75	23	(31%)	9	(12%)
Totals	689	297	(43%)	54	(8%)

Note: Juveniles are more likely to disappear during the 4 warm months when food is abundant than during the 6 colder months when food is more scarce ($P = .001$ for Mann-Whitney U test that compares percentages). I base the results shown here on censuses made in May and October of each year. Data are missing for certain years (1975 through 1977 and 1986 through 1988) because I do not always mark colony residents in October. The 1978 fall census is from November rather than October, and the 1979 fall census is from September rather than October.

Fig. 16.3. Prairie dog with radio-collar. Radio-collaring has demonstrated that prairie dogs sometimes disperse as far as 5 kilometers. (Photo courtesy of Monte G. Garrett.)

opinion and a few anecdotal reports (summarized in Costello 1970), prairie dogs disperse singly, not in groups. Finally, of the females that disperse to another colony as adults, some have not given birth in the year of dispersal (no visible teats); others have given birth but have lost their offspring before weaning (long, dry, flat teats); and still others evidently have reared juveniles to first emergence (long, turgid teats).

Immigration

From 1975 through 1989, 28 males and 21 females immigrated into the study colony from some other colony and remained there long enough for me to mark them. Each immigrant arrived alone. All but 1 of these 49 immigrants arrived sometime between mid-May and the end of September, and 59% (29/49) arrived between 13 May and 17 June. A few other prairie dogs immigrated and departed again too quickly for capture and marking ($N < 10$, probably) during my 5 months of research each year (February through June). Other temporary immigrants might have visited in my absence.

Of male immigrants, 59% (16/27) copulate at least once and 48% (13/27) sire at least one emergent juvenile. The 28th male immigrant arrived in the spring of 1989, so I have not obtained any information on his copulatory and siring success in later years. Of female immigrants, 24% (5/21) rear at least one litter to first emergence. Most of the reproductively unsuccessful immigrants disappear from the study colony shortly after their arrival and never return.

Male prairie dogs resort to either long-distance dispersal to new colonies (mostly as yearlings, rarely as adults) or short-distance dispersal within the home colony (either as yearlings or as adults). However, female prairie dogs disperse only over long distances to other colonies (as either yearlings or adults). Curiously, short-distance dispersal of females within the home colony almost never occurs (see above and chap. 14).

Coterie members resist attempted invasions by all conspecifics, including immigrants. Resident females show aggression toward, and bark defensively at, any male that tries to invade. However, successful repulsion of male invaders is ultimately the responsibility of the resident breeding prairie dog male(s), as it is for other harem-polygynous animals such as wild horses, African lions, and northern elephant seals (Schaller 1972; Le Boeuf 1974; Berger 1986). Similarly, even though the resident breeding male usually interacts aggressively with a female invader, successful defense against her invasion depends ultimately on the efforts of the resident adult and yearling females (chap. 6).

Often I first recognize an immigrant as an unmarked prairie dog being chased out of one coterie territory, then out of another, then out of another, and so on. Sometimes the unmarked invader eventually makes its way into a coterie territory, but on other occasions it disappears—presumably in search of another colony with better possibilities for invasion.

All thirteen male immigrants that have sired offspring at the study colony have succeeded by the same general route: by taking over an occupied coterie territory and breeding there. The five female immigrants that have produced emergent offspring have succeeded by two routes. Three have pinched off small parts of coterie territories containing several adult females, and have reared offspring there with only their mates. The other two female immigrants have invaded coterie territories containing only a single female, have permanently evicted the single female and taken over the entire territory, and then have settled down to breed there with only their mates. The latter strategy has been more successful (table 16.4). Notice that female immigrants always start out alone or with only a mate: they never are able to insinuate themselves among the adult and yearling females of established coteries.

One immigrant's behavior defies explanation. On 24 May 1979 I eartagged and dye-marked a female immigrant (female-CB) who disappeared almost immediately. I did not see female-CB again during the remaining 4 weeks of the 1979 field season. When I returned in September

Table 16.4. Lifetime Reproductive Success versus Pattern of Invasion for Female Immigrants

Pattern of invasion	Number of immigrant females that used this pattern	Cumulative number of emergent juveniles reared by each female over her lifetime	Cumulative number of yearlings reared by each female over her lifetime	Cumulative number of 2-year-olds reared by each female over her lifetime
Pinched off small part of coterie territory containing several adult females	3	4, 8, 3 (4 litters)	2, 0, 0	0, 0, 0
Took over entire coterie territory after evicting resident adult female there	2	6, 7 (2 litters for each female)	4, 7	4, 6
Significance of this difference[a]		$P = .564$	$P = .076$	$P = .053$

[a]P-values are from the Mann-Whitney U test.

of 1979, however, female-CB had returned! She was living in an area approximately 250 meters from the area where I first captured her.

Litter Size and Juvenile Body Mass at First Emergence

Litter size at first juvenile emergence ranges from 1 to 6, with a mean ± SD of 3.08 ± 1.06 (figs. 16.4a and 16.5). As noted elsewhere (chaps. 4 and 13), I have obtained no information about litter size at birth or at any other stage prior to first juvenile emergence. Anecdotal information on litter size at birth—which ranges from 1 to 8—comes from laboratory studies (Wade 1928; Anthony and Foreman 1951; Foreman 1962) and necropsies of pregnant and lactating females (Tileston and Lechleitner 1966; Knowles 1987).

Juvenile body mass at first emergence ranges from 60 to 288 grams, with a mean ± SD of 144 ± 31.7 (fig. 16.4b).

Conception, Abortion, Gestation, Parturition, and Lactation

The period of gestation is the number of days between copulation and parturition, and the period of lactation is the number of days between parturition and weaning. Determination of either period requires knowing the date of parturition. I identify parturition among prairie dogs in three ways, the first two of which also apply to Belding's and Richardson's

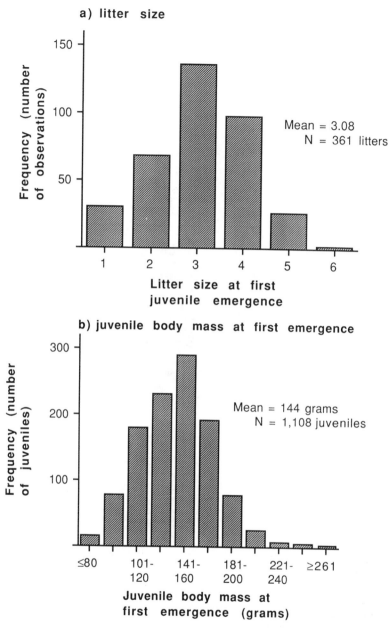

Fig. 16.4. Litter size and juvenile body mass at first juvenile emergence. *(a)* Litter size at first juvenile emergence. Besides the 361 litters shown here, 6 other litters emerged at the study colony for which I could not determine exact litter size because of either mixing of unmarked juveniles from two litters before first emergence of one of them (*N* = 4 litters) or killing of some emergent juveniles within a litter by an invading male before I could get an accurate count (*N* = 2 litters). *(b)* Juvenile body mass at first emergence. Besides the 1,108 emergent juveniles depicted here, 17 other emergent juveniles disappeared before I could livetrap them; I failed to weigh 2 other emergent juveniles.

Fig. 16.5. Variation in litter size at first juvenile emergence. *(a)* Minimal litter size of 1. (Photo courtesy of Wind Cave National Park.) *(b)* Maximal litter size of 6. The mean litter size is 3.08, and the modal litter size is 3. (Photo by John L. Hoogland.)

ground squirrels (Sherman 1976; Michener 1985). First, approximately 5 weeks after copulation, each female shows a white vagina with no visible blood for 1 or more days. She then abruptly shows a distinctly pink or red vagina, usually coupled with bloodstains on the surrounding fur (fig. 16.6). I infer parturition on the first day that the vagina is pink rather than white. Second, on the same day that the vagina is first pink, body mass suddenly drops about 60 grams (fig. 16.7). Third, a dramatic behavioral change also accompanies the first appearance of the pink vagina and the precipitous drop in body mass. Pregnant females usually emerge early in the morning, spend the entire day foraging aboveground, and are among the last to submerge for the night. On the first day of the pink vagina, however, the female is usually one of the last to appear aboveground in the morning, sometimes first emerging as much as 4 hours after all the other prairie dogs. Some females do not first emerge until late afternoon on the first day of the pink vagina, and a few females ($N = 4$ from 1981 through 1988) *never* appear aboveground on the presumed day of parturition. Further, the female usually makes one or more long visits to the home nursery burrow, often for as long as 3–4 hours, on the first day of

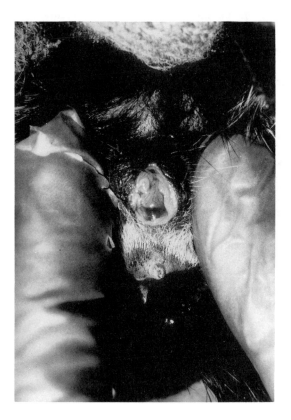

Fig. 16.6. Verification of parturition. Before she gives birth, a female's vagina is white. On the morning of parturition, however, the vagina is pink or red, and sometimes exudes fresh blood, as shown here. In addition, on the day of parturition, a mother's body mass usually drops about 60 grams and she spends inordinate lengths of time underground in her home nursery burrow. (Photo by John L. Hoogland.)

the pink vagina, and she is one of the first to submerge for the night. These striking changes in behavior are presumably indicative of parturition and maternal care (especially nursing) of neonates. The altered behaviors usually continue for 2 weeks or so, after which most mothers resume the routine typical of pregnant females. Only during inclement weather, when prairie dogs emerge late and often go underground to dry off or warm up (chaps. 3 and 11), are the changes in behavior associated with parturition difficult to identify.

The pink vagina coupled with loss in body mass has pinpointed parturition for 45 females (fig. 16.7). However, this method requires livetrapping and is therefore disruptive and time-consuming. The late first emergence and long underground visits have provided a simple, yet still accurate, alternative method for identifying parturition—and hence determining length of gestation when the date of copulation is also known—for 180 additional females.

The most common period of gestation is 34 or 35 days (fig. 16.8a). This period is longer than previous estimates, all flawed because the researchers did not know the date of copulation (Anthony and Foreman 1951; Tileston and Lechleitner 1966; Costello 1970; Burt and Grossenheider 1976; Chace 1976; Nowak and Paradiso 1983). At birth, juveniles are

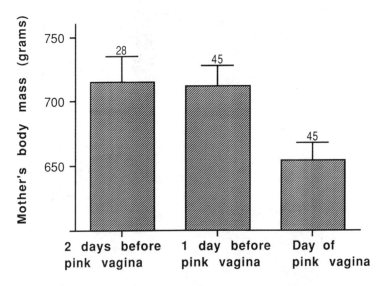

Fig. 16.7. Maternal body mass just before, and on the first day of, the pink vagina. Of the 45 females, 44 (98%) lost body mass between the last day that the vagina was white and the first day that it was pink ($P < .001$, Wilcoxon matched-pairs signed-ranks test). However, the difference between maternal body mass one versus two days before the first appearance of the pink vagina is not significant ($P = .255$, Wilcoxon matched-pairs signed-ranks test; for this analysis, I have used data from only the 28 females for which both body masses are available).

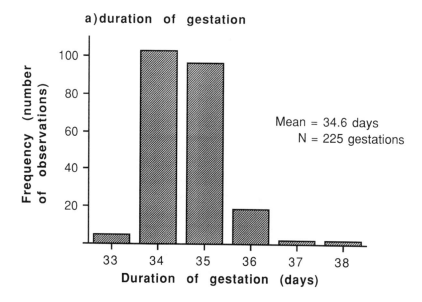

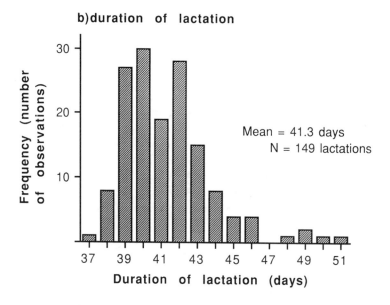

Fig. 16.8. Duration of gestation and lactation. *(a)* Duration of gestation. I estimate the duration of gestation by counting the number of days between copulation and parturition, as determined by either the first appearance of a pink vagina, a precipitous loss in maternal body mass (fig. 16.7), or the first exceedingly late first maternal appearance aboveground in the morning. *(b)* Duration of lactation. I estimate the duration of lactation by counting the number of days between parturition and first juvenile emergence. Using similar but less accurate methods, King (1955) and Knowles (1987) estimated the average length of prairie dog lactation to be 45 and 44 days, respectively.

about 70 millimeters long, weigh about 15 grams, are blind, and have no fur (see fig. 7.5). Fur appears about 3 weeks after parturition, and the eyes open about 2 weeks later (Johnson 1927).

For some animals such as mountain cavies, parturition almost always occurs in the morning (Rood 1972). For other animals such as Richardson's ground squirrels, however, parturition commonly occurs in late afternoon or early evening as well (Michener 1985). I assign parturition to a prairie dog female on the morning of the first day when I observe either the pink vagina coupled with a precipitous loss in body mass or the delayed first emergence in the morning coupled with long daytime periods (>60 minutes) spent in the home nursery burrow. The freshness of the blood in most vaginal examinations indicates that parturition really does occur on the assigned morning. However, parturition occasionally might occur in the late afternoon or evening of the day before I detect the diagnostic signs. For example, females typically retire for the night into the home nursery burrow unusually early in the afternoon of the day before the assigned parturition—perhaps to give birth that night, or perhaps to prepare for parturition on the following morning.

Not every prairie dog female that copulates gives birth. Failure to give birth could result either from failure to conceive or from abortion of all embryos (with or without resorption) after conception (Anthony and Foreman 1951; Knowles 1987). I found only one way to verify failure to give birth: no pink vagina, no sudden loss in body mass, and no radical changes in time spent aboveground approximately 5 weeks after copulation. Most females that fail to give birth have vaginas sealed shut by a thin layer of skin, but others have open, whitish vaginas that never turn pink. Of the copulating females that I could unambiguously score, 82% (248/301) gave birth while 18% (53/301) did not. The probability of giving birth after copulation is higher for adults than for yearlings (fig. 16.9).

I have found no accurate way to discriminate between failure to conceive and abortion of all embryos sometime after conception. Both probably occur. For example, the second estrus of a few females in the same breeding season (chap. 11) is almost certainly a response to failed conception. On the other hand, abortion of all embryos probably explains why certain nonparous females have enlarged teats shortly after they should have given birth.

Like long-tailed marmot females (Davidov et al. 1978), pregnant prairie dog females sometimes resorb certain implanted embryos and later give birth to the others (Anthony and Foreman 1951; Tileston and Lechleitner 1966; Foreman 1962; Knowles 1987). I have obtained no information—which usually requires killing of examined females—on such selective resorption.

Pre-emergent prairie dog juveniles depend primarily on their mother's milk for nourishment, but sometimes eat plants brought underground by

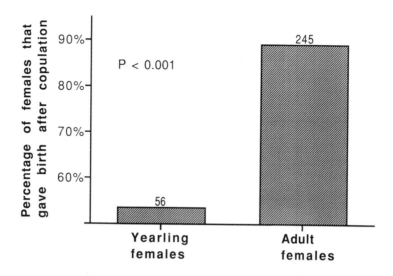

Fig. 16.9. Probability of parturition for adult and yearling females that copulate. The *P*-value is from the 2 × 2 chi-square test.

the mother. Conversely, emergent juveniles depend primarily on their own foraging for nourishment, but sometimes receive additional nourishment from nursing (chap. 9). To complicate matters further, nursing occurs underground. With these complications in mind, and cognizant of the difficulty of trying to specify the exact day of weaning, I estimate the period of lactation by counting the number of days between parturition and first juvenile emergence. Lactation usually lasts for about 41 days (fig. 16.8b).

For humans and some domestic animals such as goats, pigs, cattle, and sheep (Clegg 1959; Dziuk 1977), the length of gestation varies inversely with litter size. For prairie dogs, curiously, and also for Richardson's ground squirrels (Michener 1985), the length of gestation is unaffected by litter size (fig. 16.10). However, figure 16.10 plots gestation versus litter size *at first juvenile emergence*. A better plot would be gestation versus litter size *at birth*. Mainly because of infanticide, prairie dog litter size at first emergence is often lower than litter size at birth (chap. 7). If information on litter size at birth becomes available, perhaps prairie dogs will show the expected inverse relationship between length of gestation and litter size.

Weaning might occur primarily because a female's offspring have received enough milk and are ready and large enough to obtain all their nourishment from their own foraging. If so, then females with small litters

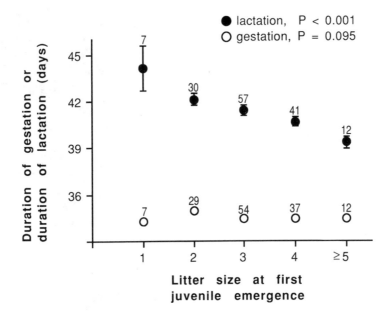

Fig. 16.10. Duration of gestation and duration of lactation versus litter size at first juvenile emergence. The number above each SE line indicates the number of litters. *P*-values are from the Spearman rank correlation test.

presumably provide more milk per juvenile and are better able to accelerate weaning than are females with larger litters. The length of lactation should therefore vary *directly* with litter size. On the other hand, weaning might occur primarily because a mother has exhausted all her personal resources for producing milk, such as internal fat reserves and food in the defended territory around the home nursery burrow—even though her offspring might not be ready or large enough to obtain all their own nourishment. If so, then females with large litters presumably run out of resources faster than females with smaller litters. The length of lactation in this latter scenario should vary *inversely* with litter size. Another possibility is that weaning occurs primarily when a female has exhausted her personal resources, but females appropriately adjust litter size relative to personal resources (see below)—so that the length of lactation does not vary with litter size, as is the case for animals such as Richardson's and cascade golden-mantled ground squirrels (Michener 1985; Kenagy et al. 1990). With these arguments in mind, I have examined litter size at first juvenile emergence versus length of lactation. Figure 16.10 shows a significant inverse relationship. These results, along with the smaller juvenile size in larger litters (chap. 13), indicate that weaning in prairie dogs results primarily from exhaustion of maternal resources.

Survivorship, Fecundity, and Life Tables

Life tables, which summarize data on survivorship and fecundity, are of two general types (Caughley 1966, 1977; Krebs 1978; Zammuto and Sherman 1986). A *time-specific* life table—also called a static, stationary, current, or vertical life table—requires determination of the age structure of a population at a single point in time. A *cohort-specific* life table—also called a generation, composite, or horizontal life table—requires the tracking of an entire cohort (group of individuals born at approximately the same time) over time. Cohort-specific life tables involve fewer assumptions and are more accurate than time-specific life tables, but they also require more time and effort.

Life tables of both types involve numerous related symbols and conventions (Deevey 1947; Caughley 1966; Krebs 1978). The letter x indicates the age of the individuals at the beginning of a certain time period; lx indicates the proportion of the original number of individuals that is still alive at the beginning of interval (or age) x; dx indicates the number of individuals that die during the interval of x to $x + 1$; qx indicates the rate of mortality during the interval of x to $x + 1$; mx indicates the proportion of individuals that produce offspring at age x times the mean number of offspring when production occurs; $lxmx$ is the product of lx and mx and indicates the relative proportion of offspring contributed by each age class; Ro is the sum of the $lxmx$ values for all ages and indicates whether the population is declining ($Ro < 1.0$) or increasing ($Ro > 1.0$) in size.

Two aspects of the prairie dog life tables require clarification. First, although I can accurately count the number of juveniles that first emerge from the natal burrow, I cannot determine litter size at birth (see above). Therefore, the starting point for each cohort of juveniles is first emergence rather than birth. Second, whereas mx data usually consider female offspring only (Deevey 1947; Caughley 1966), the prairie dog mx data include both male and female offspring. Otherwise, I would bias the life tables against individuals producing male-skewed sex ratios (chap. 15). With this latter convention, mx of 2.0 (rather than the usual 1.0 when one counts only daughters) indicates individual replacement in a single year, and Ro of 2.0 (rather than the usual 1.0) indicates stable population size.

I started eartagging all emergent juveniles in 1975, and immigration is rare (see above). Consequently, I have known the exact ages of almost all prairie dogs at the study colony in all years except the first few (when original residents present in 1975 were still alive). For any year from about 1979 through 1989, then, I can construct a time-specific life table that includes all residents at the study colony. Tables 16.5 and 16.6 show representative time-specific life tables for males and females living at the study colony in 1986.

For all years except the last few—when prairie dogs were at the study colony who survived beyond the termination of my research in 1989— I can construct a cohort-specific life table that includes all residents at the

Table 16.5. Time-Specific Life Table for Male Prairie Dogs at the Study Colony in 1986

Age (years)	n_x	d_x	l_x	q_x	m_x[a]	l_xm_x
0[b]	70	52	1.000	0.743	0.000	0.000
1	18	9	0.257	0.500	0.000	0.000
2	9	1	0.129	0.111	2.333	0.301
3	8	7	0.114	0.875	9.250	1.055
4	1	0	0.014	0.000	15.000	0.210
5	2	2	0.029	1.000	11.500	0.334
≥ 6	0	—	0.000	—	—	—

Ro (offspring of both sexes) = Σl_xm_x = 1.900

[a]Includes both male and female offspring.

[b]Because I cannot capture juveniles until they appear aboveground, the starting point for this life table is first juvenile emergence rather than birth.

Table 16.6. Time-Specific Life Table for Female Prairie Dogs at the Study Colony in 1986

Age (years)	n_x	d_x	l_x	q_x	m_x[a]	l_xm_x
0[b]	63	38	1.000	0.603	0.000	0.000
1	25	11	0.397	0.440	0.320	0.127
2	14	2	0.222	0.143	2.929	0.650
3	12	0	0.190	0.000	2.667	0.507
4	12	8	0.190	0.667	3.083	0.586
5	4	1	0.063	0.250	3.250	0.205
6	3	3	0.048	1.000	0.667	0.032
7	0	—	0.000	—	—	—
8	0	—	0.000	—	—	—
≥9	0	—	0.000	—	—	—

Ro (offspring of both sexes) = Σl_xm_x = 2.107

[a]Includes both male and female offspring.

[b]Because I cannot capture juveniles until they appear aboveground, the starting point for this life table is first juvenile emergence rather than birth.

study colony. Tables 16.7 and 16.8 show representative cohort-specific life tables for males and females born at the study colony in 1981.

I have combined the information from the cohort-specific life table for each year to construct *cumulative* cohort-specific life tables for males and females (tables 16.9 and 16.10). Because they include data from 14 cohorts and 15 years rather than from a single year or from a single cohort, tables 16.9 and 16.10 are the best and most representative life tables for the prairie dogs at the study colony. Consistent with the observation that the number of residents at the study colony is somewhat constant (see fig. 16.1), Ro in the cumulative cohort-specific life table is approximately 2.0 for both sexes.

Table 16.7. Cohort-Specific Life Table for Male Prairie Dogs that First Emerged at the Study Colony in 1981

Age (years)	nx	dx	lx	qx	mx[a]	$lxmx$
0[b]	67	41	1.000	0.612	0.000	0.000
1	26	5	0.388	0.192	0.000	0.000
2	21	12	0.313	0.571	1.857	0.581
3	9	7	0.134	0.778	2.000	0.268
4	2	0	0.030	0.000	7.500	0.225
5	2	2	0.030	1.000	11.500	0.345
≥6	0	—	0.000	—	—	—

Ro (offspring of both sexes) = $\Sigma lxmx$ = 1.419

[a]Includes both male and female offspring.

[b]Because I cannot capture juveniles until they appear aboveground, the starting point for this life table is first juvenile emergence rather than birth.

Table 16.8. Cohort-Specific Life Table for Female Prairie Dogs that First Emerged at the Study Colony in 1981

Age (years)	nx	dx	lx	qx	mx[a]	$lxmx$
0[b]	52	31	1.000	0.596	0.000	0.000
1	21	2	0.404	0.095	0.143	0.058
2	19	5	0.365	0.263	1.632	0.596
3	14	7	0.269	0.500	1.143	0.307
4	7	3	0.135	0.429	1.429	0.193
5	4	2	0.077	0.500	3.250	0.250
6	2	1	0.038	0.500	2.500	0.095
7	1	0	0.019	0.000	0.000	0.000
8	1	1	0.019	1.000	0.000	0.000
≥9	0	—	0.000	—	—	—

Ro (offspring of both sexes) = $\Sigma lxmx$ = 1.499

[a]Includes both male and female offspring.

[b]Because I cannot capture juveniles until they appear aboveground, the starting point for this life table is first juvenile emergence rather than birth.

Survivorship from one year to the next varies curvilinearly with age for both sexes. As for Eurasian badgers and Belding's ground squirrels (Sherman and Morton 1984; Cheeseman et al. 1987), annual survivorship at each age is always higher for prairie dog females than for males (chap. 13). The oldest age recorded for males is 5 years ($N = 8$; table 16.9). Four females lived to be 7 years old. The record for prairie dog longevity under natural conditions belongs solely to female-6stripe, who, like a female held in captivity by Young (1944; see also King 1955 and Costello 1970), lived to be 8 years old (table 16.10).

Table 16.9. Cumulative Cohort-Specific Life Table for Male Prairie Dogs that First Emerged at the Study Colony from 1975 through 1988

Age (years)	nx	dx	lx	qx	mx[a]	$lxmx$
0[b]	587	312	1.000	0.532	0.000	0.000
1	261	101	0.468	0.387	0.084	0.039
2	140	74	0.287	0.529	2.926	0.840
3	61	35	0.135	0.574	4.206	0.568
4	23	15	0.058	0.652	4.920	0.285
5	8	8	0.020	1.000	5.750	0.115
≥6	0	—	0.000	—	—	—

Ro (offspring of both sexes) = $\Sigma lxmx$ = 1.847

Note: In this cumulative cohort-specific life table, which uses data from 14 consecutive years, nx and dx data are incompatible across years because certain emergent individuals can be used for analyses of survivorship in some years but not others. For example, data are available for 14 years for survivorship during the first year (age 0 to age 1). However, data are only available for 13 years for survivorship during the second year (age 1 to age 2) because the final census in 1989 could not reveal survivorship during the second year for the 1988 emergent juveniles. Similarly, data are only available for 12 years for survivorship during the third year, 11 years for survivorship during the fourth year, and so on.

[a] Includes both male and female offspring.

[b] Because I cannot capture juveniles until they appear aboveground, the starting point for this life table is first juvenile emergence rather than birth.

Table 16.10. Cumulative Cohort-Specific Life Table for Female Prairie Dogs that First Emerged at the Study Colony from 1975 through 1988

Age (years)	nx	dx	lx	qx	mx[a]	$lxmx$
0[b]	523	239	1.000	0.457	0.000	0.000
1	274	61	0.543	0.223	0.230	0.125
2	190	44	0.422	0.232	1.657	0.699
3	128	39	0.324	0.305	1.939	0.628
4	80	33	0.225	0.413	1.966	0.442
5	36	20	0.132	0.556	1.478	0.195
6	16	12	0.059	0.750	1.000	0.059
7	4	3	0.015	0.750	0.000	0.000
8	1	1	0.004	1.000	0.000	0.000
≥9	0	—	0.000	—	—	—

Ro (offspring of both sexes) = $\Sigma lxmx$ = 2.148

Note: The note to table 16.9 also applies to this table.

[a] Includes both male and female offspring.

[b] Because I cannot capture juveniles until they appear aboveground, the starting point for this life table is first juvenile emergence rather than birth.

Age of Sexual Maturity

For both sexes, the most common age of sexual maturity, as measured by the age of first copulation, is 2 years (chap. 13; see also King 1955; Koford 1958; Tileston and Lechleitner 1966; Garrett, Hoogland, and Franklin 1982; Halpin 1987; Knowles 1987; Stockrahm and Seabloom 1988). More precisely, individuals usually first copulate in the second February or March following birth, approximately 21 months following their first emergence from the natal burrow.

Some individuals first copulate as yearlings, with the probability being higher for females than for males (35% versus 6%; see chap. 13). The probability of a yearling's producing emergent juveniles—low for both sexes—is also higher for females (fig. 16.11a). Conversely, some individuals delay sexual maturation until the third year. Again a sexual asymmetry prevails, with males being more likely than females to delay (fig. 16.11b). Further, no females, but three males, did not reach sexual maturity until the fourth year.

Sexual Dimorphism in Body Mass

Sexual dimorphism in body mass, with males being larger, is common among polygynous animals in general (Jarman 1974; Clutton-Brock, Harvey, and Rudder 1977; Alexander et al. 1979; Payne 1984) and among sciurids, such as Belding's, arctic, and Richardson's ground squirrels and hoary, yellow-bellied, and Olympic marmots, in particular (Morton and Sherman 1978; Armitage 1981; McLean and Towns 1981; Michener 1984a,c; Barash 1989). Consistent with their polygynous mating system (chaps. 11 and 12), prairie dogs also show male-biased sexual dimorphism in body mass at all ages (fig. 16.12; see also Bakko, Porter, and Wunder 1988). During the first year of life, sexual dimorphism is slight but significant at first juvenile emergence and in October and November, trivial in February and March, and pronounced and significant in May and June. Among adults, males average about 10% to 15% heavier than females throughout most of the year. In late pregnancy, however, adult females commonly weigh more than adult males (my own unpublished data; see also Knowles 1987).

For both sexes, but especially for females, notice that autumn, winter, and spring body masses vary *directly* with age up to a certain middle age, and then vary *inversely* with age for later ages (fig. 16.12). This curvilinear relationship between age and body mass might help to explain a similar curvilinear relationship between age and annual reproductive success (chap. 13).

Sexual dimorphism in body mass is statistically significant, but extensive intersexual overlap nonetheless occurs. Consequently, I cannot use relative body mass to sex unmarked individuals from a distance. Unfortunately, I have detected no other intersexual differences—in color or morphology, for example—that would allow sexing from a distance.

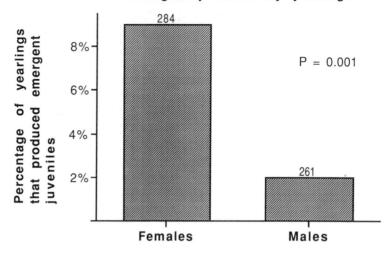

a) sexual asymmetry in production
   of emergent juveniles by yearlings

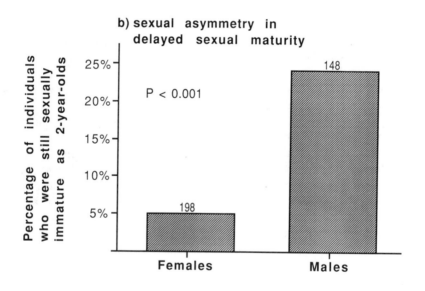

b) sexual asymmetry in
   delayed sexual maturity

◀ **Fig. 16.11.** Sexual asymmetry in *(a)* production of emergent juveniles by yearlings and *(b)* delayed sexual maturity. For both graphs, the number above each bar indicates the number of individuals observed, and *P*-values are from the 2 × 2 chi-square test. I determine sexual maturity either from an examination of external genitalia or from observation of one or more copulations.

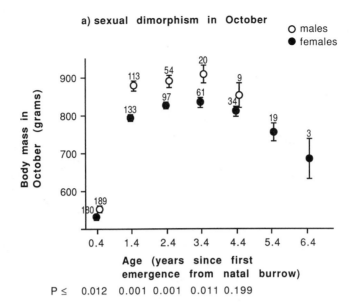

a) sexual dimorphism in October

○ males
● females

Body mass in October (grams)

Age (years since first emergence from natal burrow)

P ≤   0.012   0.001 0.001   0.011 0.199

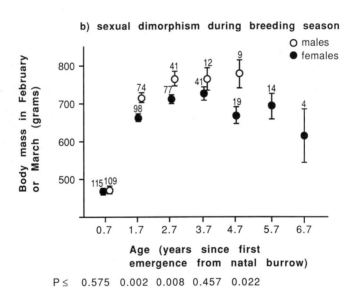

b) sexual dimorphism during breeding season

○ males
● females

Body mass in February or March (grams)

Age (years since first emergence from natal burrow)

P ≤   0.575   0.002 0.008   0.457 0.022

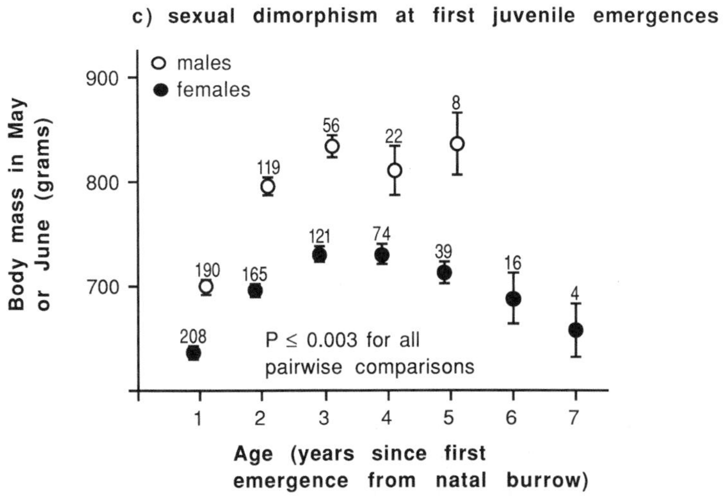

c) sexual dimorphism at first juvenile emergences

◀ ▲ **Fig. 16.12.** Sexual dimorphism in body mass at different ages. *(a)* In October, 4 months before the breeding season. *(b)* During the breeding season of February and March. *(c)* At first juvenile emergences in May and June. For all these graphs, the number above each SE line indicates the number of individuals weighed, and *P*-values comparing male and female masses are from the Mann-Whitney *U* test.

Summary

1. The number of adults and yearlings at the study colony in May of each year ranges from 92 to 143.

2. Significant annual variation is evident for all the following: colony size, the number of emergent juveniles, litter size at first juvenile emergence, the number and percentage of juveniles in a litter that survive for at least 1 year, juvenile body mass at first emergence, and the date of first juvenile emergence.

3. From 1975 through 1989, 28 males and 21 females immigrated into the study colony.

4. Mortality during the first year after emergence from the natal burrow is approximately 50% for both sexes. Females that survive the first year sometimes live as long as 8 years, but males never live longer than 5 years.

5. The first age of sexual maturity is usually 2 years for both sexes. However, 35% of females and 6% of males first copulate as yearlings.

6. At all ages, male prairie dogs are 5% to 15% heavier than females. Because of the extensive intersexual overlap, however, I cannot use relative body mass to sex unmarked individuals from a distance.

17 Behavioral Ecology of Prairie Dogs

Not surprisingly, 16 years and 73,210 person-hours of research have yielded copious information about behavioral ecology in general and black-tailed prairie dogs in particular. More prolific than the questions *answered,* however, are the questions *raised* by my research. In this final chapter I evaluate my most important conclusions and explore some of the vexing questions that remain.

Some animals live in colonies because of an extreme shortage of suitable habitat, others to obtain more food, and still others to avoid predators. Notice that these three factors are ecological rather than genetic. Thus, prairie dogs and other animals do not live in large colonies *in order* to maximize nepotism toward nondescendant kin. Such nepotism, when it occurs, is a secondary consequence of coloniality imposed by ecological constraints (Alexander 1974; Hoogland and Sherman 1976; Koenig and Pitelka 1981; Emlen 1991).

Even though the costs of grouping are high for prairie dogs, all individuals live in colonies. Why don't some prairie dogs live solitarily when costs are so high? At least three factors are relevant here. First, catastrophic crashes in colony size due to disease or ectoparasitism are easily observable for animals as conspicuous as prairie dogs. Such crashes therefore might appear to be more common and costly for prairie dogs than for other, more cryptic animals (Lechleitner et al. 1968; Miles, Wilcomb, and Irons 1952). Second, observed costs are sometimes unnatural. For example, bubonic plague was first introduced into North America—via fleas on animals unloaded from European ships—only a few hundred years ago. Consequently, prairie dogs have had little time to evolve adequate resistance, so that bubonic plague quickly obliterates entire colonies. Finally, even though costs of coloniality sometimes eliminate so many prairie dogs, the high rate of predation on solitary individuals might eliminate even *more* individuals. If costs within colonies eliminate 50% of residents, for example, natural selection will nonetheless favor coloniality if predation on solitary prairie dogs kills 55%.

Coloniality might sometimes involve more than one advantage. Besides increased protection from predators, for example, prairie dog colonies also offer both improved thermoregulation via communal usage of burrows and better selection of foodplant species via "farming." When multiple advantages result, one is usually the ultimate, primary reason for coloniality. The others are secondary benefits that probably cannot arise unless coloniality has already evolved in response to the ultimate, primary benefit. Without the ultimate advantage, secondary advantages probably cannot outweigh the costs of coloniality in most cases. In the absence of increased protection from predators, for example, improved thermoregulation and "farming" probably could not maintain prairie dog coloniality.

Secondary benefits of coloniality sometimes seem unrelated to primary benefits—farming versus reduced predation within prairie dog colonies, for example. But other times the relationship is obvious. For example, prairie dogs in colonies detect predators more quickly than do solitary individuals. Consequently, individuals in colonies can spend less time scanning for predators and more time feeding. Decreased individual alertness is thus a secondary benefit of coloniality that results directly from the primary benefit of increased awareness of predators. With the passage of time, a secondary benefit might become more important than the benefit ultimately responsible for the evolution of coloniality. If so, the secondary benefit assumes primary responsibility for the maintenance of coloniality.

Behaviors that are feasible and lucrative for certain individuals within colonies are devastating for others. Consider infanticide within prairie dog colonies, for example. Should we consider such a phenomenon a cost or a benefit of coloniality? Calling infanticide a cost seems more reasonable for at least two reasons. First, costs to the victim usually exceed benefits to the perpetrator. Specifically, the loss of a litter has a dramatic effect on the victimized mother's annual and lifetime reproductive success. By contrast, increased reproductive success for infanticidal individuals, however logical, has proved difficult to demonstrate. Second, victims of infanticide are usually more numerous than perpetrators. Specifically, a few lactating prairie dog females within each colony specialize in infanticide each year, and these specialists account for the demise of numerous litters.

Some animals have more choice than others regarding the size of the colony in which they live. Female prairie dogs, for example, usually spend their entire lives in the natal coterie territory of their natal colony, regardless of that colony's size. Those rare prairie dog females that do attempt long-distance dispersal usually settle in the first colony they encounter, when they are lucky enough to escape predation while looking for a new home. Thus, most prairie dog females are "stuck" with the colony size into which they are born. By contrast, animals such as cliff swallows typically visit several colony sites each year before settling down, and commonly change colony site and colony size from one year to the next (Brown 1992;

Brown and Brown, in press). Cliff swallows are obviously more suitable than prairie dogs for an investigation of "optimal" colony size.

Infanticide is one of the most intriguing, controversial, and misunderstood issues in behavioral and evolutionary ecology. Perhaps the major problem in trying to understand infanticide is that the critical evidence is often fragmentary and circumstantial. One reason for poor data is that infanticide can occur instantly with little warning, so that confirmation by human observers is exceedingly difficult (Michener 1982; Boggess 1984; Hrdy 1984). Marauding prairie dog females sometimes spend as little as 7 minutes underground while killing juveniles, for example, and only rarely signal their intention to commit infanticide (e.g., by repeated attempts to invade a particular nursery burrow).

Another reason for poor data on infanticide is that killing sometimes requires surreptitious behaviors that defy detection not only by the defending parents, but also by human observers. Impressive, indeed, are the furtive behaviors used by certain marauding prairie dog females to gain access to other females' nursery burrows.

Males most commonly perpetrate infanticide in many species, such as African lions, hanuman langurs, mountain gorillas, and red howler monkeys (Crockett and Sekulic 1984; Fossey 1984; Packer and Pusey 1984; Vogel and Loch 1984). However, females are the main perpetrators in other species, such as acorn woodpeckers, African wild dogs, Eurasian badgers, dwarf mongooses, and California ground squirrels (Frame et al. 1979; Rood 1980b; Mumme, Koenig, and Pitelka 1983; Trulio et al. 1986; Woodroffe 1993). Both sexes are commonly infanticidal in still other species, such as white-footed mice, Belding's ground squirrels, and prairie dogs (Sherman 1981b; Wolff and Cicirello 1989). Why such sexual asymmetry in the execution of infanticide? Of numerous possibilities, three factors are probably especially important. The first factor concerns the mating system and the timing of male dispersal. African lions, hanuman langurs, mountain gorillas, red howler monkeys, and prairie dogs usually live in stable groups consisting of one or two males and their harem of several females. Further, males of these species typically disperse into new territories when conditions promote infanticide: specifically, when juveniles of their new territories are young, genetically unrelated to the invader, and vulnerable to infanticide. By contrast, acorn woodpeckers, African wild dogs, Eurasian badgers, dwarf mongooses, and California ground squirrels do not live in stable one-male harems. Further, males of these species usually disperse when juveniles are older and harder to kill. The second factor concerns the speed with which a female comes into estrus following the death of her unweaned offspring. When a female African lion, hanuman langur, mountain gorilla, or red howler monkey loses her unweaned offspring for any reason, she soon comes into estrus and thereby conceives again more quickly than do females that retain their offspring and continue lactation. By killing juveniles in their new harems, male African lions, hanuman langurs, mountain gorillas, and red howler monkeys are thus able to copulate and sire offspring more quickly than are noninfanticidal male invaders. However, this payoff is not readily available to male Belding's ground squirrels, California ground squirrels, or prairie dogs, because the females of these species come into estrus only once each year during a short breeding season. The third factor affecting sexual asymmetry in the execution of infanticide—and the one most difficult to measure—is female-female competition. When female-female competition is weak, the benefits of infanticide to marauding females are slight. In a coterie of prairie dogs packed into a small home territory, however, female-female competition for resources such as food, nursery burrows, and mates is intense—so that infanticide might be more advantageous. Infanticide among prairie dogs not only provides important sustenance via cannibalism, but also removes future competitors of the marauders and their offspring.

I estimate that infanticide partially or totally eliminates 39% of all litters at my prairie dog study colony in Wind Cave National Park. Might this estimated frequency be seriously flawed or unnatural? I carefully look for, and usually find, other signs of infanticide when a trespassing prairie dog enters a mother's nursery burrow. For example, careful licking of the front claws and rubbing of the face in the dirt are behaviors that are unique to maraudings. The sudden cessation of lactation following the marauding of a mother's nursery burrow is another reliable indicator of infanticide. Further, my excavation of one nursery burrow provides direct proof of infanticide, as do several aboveground killings that I have observed. Thus, my estimated frequency of 39% for infanticide at the study colony is probably accurate.

But is the estimated frequency of 39% for infanticide at the study colony *natural* and *representative*? That's a tougher question. Monte G. Garrett observed one unambiguous case of aboveground infanticide at Wind Cave National Park's Monte colony, and I observed several presumed cases as well as one unambiguous case (verified by excavation) at the Pringle colony. However, though it occurs there, I have no information about the *frequency* of infanticide at the Monte and Pringle colonies, or at any other colony except the study colony. Consequently, I do not know if my estimate of 39% accurately reflects the frequency of infanticide at prairie dog colonies other than the study colony. I assume such accurate reflection in the discussion that follows, but emphasize that attempts to document the frequency of infanticide at other colonies would be eminently worthwhile.

Infanticide occurs in hundreds of species from all taxonomic groups, but the frequency of affected litters is usually 10% or less (Hrdy 1979; Sherman 1981b; Hrdy and Hausfater 1984). Why is infanticide so common and the major source of juvenile mortality within prairie dog colonies?

Recall that the increased probability of infanticide is a cost of coloniality, and that prairie dogs are among the most colonial of animals. Because of the intense competition for resources that occurs within colonies, the potential advantages of infanticide are probably more important for prairie dogs than for other, less colonial animals.

The current rarity of black-footed ferrets also might partially explain the prevalence of infanticide in today's prairie dog colonies. If black-footed ferrets invaded colonies in early spring before first juvenile emergences, they would presumably prey on unweaned juveniles. This predation would eliminate some target litters for marauding females, so that the frequency of infanticide would necessarily decrease.

I am not suggesting here that infanticide within prairie dog colonies is a maladaptive response to the unnatural absence of black-footed ferrets. The complex behaviors associated with marauding and the potential benefits to perpetrators, in particular, indicate that infanticide is an adaptation resulting directly from natural selection. Black-footed ferrets would affect the *frequency* of infanticide within prairie dog colonies, but not its ultimate expression. More specifically, the absence of black-footed ferrets promotes, but does not ultimately cause, infanticide within prairie dog colonies. Similarly, the clearing of forests leads to unnaturally high population densities of hanuman langurs in certain areas. Such high density promotes, but does not cause, infanticide by invading males (Sugiyama 1984; Hrdy 1984; but see Curtin and Dolhinow 1978, 1979; Boggess 1979, 1984).

Why don't other predators move into the niche left vacant by the disappearance of black-footed ferrets? For example, why don't burrow-entering predators such as long-tailed weasels, American badgers, rattlesnakes, and bull snakes capitalize on the pre-emergent litters that black-footed ferrets otherwise might take in March and April? Of these possible alternative predators, I have never seen a long-tailed weasel at my study colony; I have never seen reamings of prairie dog burrows by American badgers in March and April, perhaps because the ground usually is still frozen; and I have never seen rattlesnakes or bull snakes until May or later. In geographic areas other than Wind Cave National Park, perhaps predators do invade the niche left vacant by the black-footed ferret. If so, then the frequency of infanticide in these areas should be lower than the 39% at my study colony.

Infanticide among prairie dogs is striking for several reasons, but its most sensational aspect is the connection with kinship. For most animals, the most common victims of infanticide are nonkin or distant kin (Hrdy 1979; Sherman 1981b; Hrdy and Hausfater 1984). Amazingly, however, lactating prairie dog females regularly kill the offspring of close kin such as mothers, daughters, and full sisters. Why are female prairie dogs so unusual regarding infanticide and kinship? Once again extreme competition is probably relevant. Specifically, competition among animals as densely colonial as prairie dogs might coerce individuals to find novel means for survival and reproductive success. The rigid social organization within prairie dog colonies is also relevant. Because all coterie members defend the home coterie territory, mothers cannot easily invade an adjacent territory to kill and cannibalize juvenile nonkin there. Within the home coterie territory, however, a marauding female need only elude a single mother's defense of her home nursery burrow to find victims. This difference in *accessibility* probably explains why marauders regularly kill the offspring of kin within the home coterie territory rather than the offspring of nonkin in adjacent coterie territories.

On the other hand, perhaps prairie dogs are not so unusual regarding infanticide and kinship. Infanticide by lactating females is so subtle that I did not even suspect it for the first 7 years of my research. Could it be that kin-directed infanticide is equally common, but equally subtle, for other animals whose social systems are similar to that of prairie dogs? Only careful, longterm studies can answer this important question.

Like prairie dogs, all other ground-dwelling squirrels have distinct antipredator calls. For species such as Sonoma and eastern chipmunks and round-tailed and Belding's ground squirrels, calling individuals almost always have offspring within earshot (Dunford 1977b; Sherman 1977; Smith 1978; Yahner 1978; Shields 1980). Prairie dogs too call when offspring are nearby. However, *nonparental* prairie dogs also give the antipredator call when nondescendant kin such as siblings, nieces, nephews, and cousins are within earshot. The prairie dog's antipredator call is thus a clear example of natural selection for preferential treatment of nondescendant kin.

Hoary marmots and Uinta, Richardson's, and Belding's ground squirrels usually give one antipredator call in response to terrestrial predators and another distinct call in response to avian predators (Balph and Balph 1966; Taulman 1977; Davis 1984a; Sherman 1985). In contrast, prairie dogs have only one distinct antipredator call. However, by varying the number of chirks per minute, individuals can call at different rates. As first suggested by King (1955), perhaps future research will show that the rate of antipredator calling by prairie dogs communicates explicit, detailed information about each approaching predator.

Like Uinta, Columbian, Richardson's, and Idaho ground squirrels and Olympic and hoary marmots (Slade and Balph 1974; Murie and McLean 1980; Michener 1985; Barash 1989; Sherman 1989), prairie dogs have the exasperating habit of performing many of their important behaviors underground. Copulations, infanticides, and communal nursings among prairie dogs, for example, almost always occur within burrows. Consequently, my information on these behaviors has come from inference rather than direct observation. By using fiber optics or underground one-way glass windows, perhaps future investigators will be able to view copulations, infanticides, and communal nursings directly. If so, answers to numerous critical questions are certain to emerge.

Elaborate theories predict that females should vary the sex ratio of their litters in response to factors such as sex ratio among breeding adults, local resource competition, local resource enhancement, local mate competition, maternal age and rank, and paternal reproductive success (Fisher 1958; Hamilton 1967; Trivers and Willard 1973; Charnov 1982; Frank 1987b, 1990). Supportive empirical data come from numerous invertebrates (Hamilton 1967; Werren and Charnov 1978; Werren 1980, 1983; Waage 1982; McLain and Marsh 1990). Curiously, however, unequivocal evidence that mothers adaptively vary the sex ratio of their offspring is rare for birds and mammals (Williams 1979; Clutton-Brock 1986; Clutton-Brock and Iason 1986; Frank 1990). Prairie dogs also show no evidence for adaptive variation of the sex ratio at first juvenile emergence—even for those comparisons involving middle-aged, heavy mothers versus older and younger, lighter mothers. For myriad possible reasons (Williams 1979; Clutton-Brock and Iason 1986; Frank 1990), perhaps sex ratio is one of those problems for which birds and mammals cannot easily evolve a solution that theoretical biologists might regard as adaptive (Davies 1992; Williams 1992).

Kin recognition is another controversial issue among behavioral ecologists. Do individuals sometimes use their own phenotypes as a reference and thereby recognize kin with whom they have never previously associated (Dawkins 1982; Holmes and Sherman 1982, 1983; Sherman 1991; Hamilton 1987)? Or does kin recognition almost always require direct or mediated social learning (Alexander 1990a, 1991)? Prairie dogs show no evidence whatsoever for self-referential matching of phenotypes, even though such matching probably would be useful in numerous circumstances. Rather, all kin recognition among prairie dogs seems to require direct social learning within the home coterie territory. This social learning occurs during a critical period of about 1 month following a juvenile's first emergence from the natal burrow.

In ultimate terms, natural selection probably should favor individuals that compromise the costs and benefits of inbreeding and outbreeding, so that some intermediate level of inbreeding-outbreeding results (Alexander 1977; Bateson 1978, 1983; Shields 1982, 1993; Partridge 1983; Waser 1993). Qualitative support for this notion of moderate inbreeding comes from longterm research on animals such as Florida scrub jays, acorn woodpeckers, and Darwin's medium ground finches. Individuals of these species usually copulate with members of the same local population, but avoid copulations with close kin (Woolfenden and Fitzpatrick 1984; Koenig and Mumme 1987; Gibbs and Grant 1989). Do individuals also avoid copulations with more distant kin such as first and second cousins? Mainly because of the difficulties of assigning paternity, the answer to this question for these and other animals remains elusive. However, an answer is now available for prairie dogs, mainly because I am able to assign paternity for 95% of juveniles at my study colony each year. Like other animals, prairie dogs copulate with members of the same local population and avoid extreme inbreeding. However, prairie dogs regularly engage in moderate inbreeding with more distant kin such as half uncles and half nephews, half aunts and half nieces, and full and half first and second cousins.

In proximate terms, kin recognition dependent on direct social learning is pivotal in molding the levels of inbreeding among prairie dogs. Specifically, individuals learn to recognize as kin those individuals born in the home coterie territory, and avoid copulating with them. However, individuals regard individuals born in other coterie territories as nonkin and will readily copulate with them. This system efficiently avoids extreme inbreeding, because individuals born in the home coterie territory are invariably close kin and individuals born in other coterie territories are usually nonkin. Occasionally, however, extreme inbreeding results because individuals born in other coterie territories are (unrecognizable) paternal half siblings. And moderate inbreeding routinely results because individuals born in other coterie territories are commonly more distant kin such as full and half first and second cousins.

Kin recognition might evolve primarily in one context and then be secondarily available for the evaluation of potential mates. For example, kin recognition might evolve so that individuals are less likely to harm close kin during competition for food and nesting sites, and then be secondarily available for the evaluation of the kinship of potential mates. Alternatively, kin recognition might evolve primarily as a mechanism for evaluating mates' kinship. Either way, limits on kin recognition—the importance of direct social learning and the rarity of self-referential matching of phenotypes among prairie dogs, for example—will put limits on the choice of mates with respect to kinship.

Fascinating indeed would be the discovery that mothers of any species regularly kill the offspring of close kin. Also fascinating would be the discovery that mothers of any species commonly suckle the offspring of close kin. The coexistence of both killing and communal nursing of nondescendant juvenile kin within the same prairie dog colony staggers the imagination! Why the switch from infanticide to communal nursing over a short period of several weeks? In proximate terms, the answer probably centers on kin recognition. Before juveniles appear aboveground, mothers probably can easily discriminate between their own home nursery burrows containing their own offspring—as targets for nursing—and other nursery burrows containing the offspring of other females—as targets for infanticide. Following first juvenile emergences and the extensive mixing of young from different litters that quickly occurs, however, mothers might find discrimination between their own and others' offspring too difficult or too costly—so that infanticide ceases and communal nursing commences. In ultimate terms, many of the benefits of infanticide by lactating females—such as increased sustenance resulting from cannibalism—are unavailable or unimportant following first emergences of juveniles from their natal burrows. However, by suckling the juveniles of other females, a mother increases the probability that those juveniles will cluster around her own offspring. The large multi-litter groupings that result might reduce predation on the foster mother's own offspring via "selfish herd effects" or "protection by dilution" (Hamilton 1971; Vine 1971; McKaye and McKaye 1977). In this scenario, prairie dog mothers selfishly use the juveniles of close kin as sustenance via cannibalism when the killers' own offspring are small. Later, prairie dog foster mothers selfishly manipulate the juveniles of close kin via communal nursing in order to improve the survivorship of their own offspring.

Direct fitness is an estimate of reproductive success based on the number of one's own offspring, and indirect fitness is an estimate of reproductive success based on the number of offspring produced by genetic relatives. Nepotism directed toward nondescendant kin is so prominent for some animals, such as Australian bell miners, pied kingfishers, Galápagos mockingbirds, and white-fronted bee-eaters (Clark 1984; Reyer 1984; Curry 1988; Emlen and Wrege 1988, 1989), that indirect fitness seems to be almost as important as direct fitness for the inclusive fitness of individuals. Regarding their antipredator calling, prairie dogs give the same impression, because individuals with only nondescendant kin within earshot are just as likely to give antipredator calls as are individuals with nearby offspring. However, close inspection of prairie dogs and other animals usually shows that direct fitness contributes more than indirect fitness to the inclusive fitness of most individuals—i.e, natural selection is usually more intense for the direct production of offspring than for helping close kin to produce offspring (Hamilton 1964; Alexander 1974; Rubenstein and Wrangham 1980; Armitage 1987b, 1988, 1991). Regarding infanticide, for example, notice that marauding prairie dog mothers almost always spare their own offspring, but regularly kill the offspring of close kin such as daughters and full sisters. Further, even though prairie dog mothers commonly suckle the offspring of close kin, such communal nursing does not commence until a mother has exclusively suckled her own offspring for at least 5 weeks—i.e., mothers always give much more milk to their own offspring than to foster offspring.

Black-tailed prairie dogs were my faithful research animals for 16 consecutive years. With so many good memories, such detailed genealogies, and so many remaining questions, the thought of leaving them was sometimes unbearable. On the other hand, I constantly wondered about the generality of my conclusions. Cognizant of the importance of comparative data from closely related species (Darwin 1859; Lack 1968; Jarman 1974; Ridley 1983; Harvey and Pagel 1991), I decided in 1989 to terminate my research with black-tailed prairie dogs and to initiate research with Gunnison's prairie dogs. More recently I have initiated additional research with Utah prairie dogs as well. While sharing certain common features, the different species of prairie dogs show puzzling differences (see table 2.2). More comparative research with these marvelous animals is certain to increase our understanding of natural selection and the evolution of social behavior.

Appendix A

Common and Scientific Names of Organisms Mentioned in This Book

Appendix A. Common and Scientific Names of Organisms Mentioned in This Book

Plants

Wheatgrass	*Agropyron* spp.
Wild onion	*Allium* spp.
Pigweed or amaranth	*Amaranthus retroflexus*
Ragweed	*Ambrosia* spp.
Threeawn or wiregrass	*Aristida* spp.
Sagebrush or sage or sagewort	*Artemisia* spp.
Aster	*Aster* spp.
Milkvetch	*Astragalus* spp.
Saltbrush	*Atriplex* spp.
Grama	*Bouteloua* spp.
Brome	*Bromus* spp.
Buffalo grass	*Buchloe dactyloides*
Sedge	*Carex* spp.
Mat sandbur	*Cenchrus pauciflorus*
Lambsquarters	*Chenopodium album*
Rabbitbrush	*Chrysothamnus* spp.
Thistle	*Cirsium* spp.
Glorybind or bindweed	*Convolvulus* spp.
Horseweed	*Conyza ramosissima*
Cryptantha	*Cryptantha* spp.
Nelson's larkspur	*Delphinium nelsoni*
Inland saltgrass	*Distichlis stricta*
Prairie dog weed or fetid marigold	*Dyssodia (Boebera) papposa*
Spurge	*Euphorbia* spp.
Winterfat	*Eurotia lanata*
Fescue	*Festuca* spp.
Fluffweed	*Filago* spp.
False pennyroyal	*Hedeoma hispida*
Foxtail	*Hordeum* spp.
Summer cypress	*Kochia scoparia*
Stickseed or stickweed	*Lappula* spp.
Pepperweed	*Lepidium* spp.
Biscuitroot or lomatium	*Lomatium* spp.
Skeleton weed or skeleton plant	*Lygodesmia* spp.
Prickly pear cactus	*Opuntia* spp.
Ricegrass	*Oryzopsis* spp.

Bubonic plague or sylvatic plague or plague	*Pastuerella (Yersinia) pestis*
Phlox	*Phlox* spp.
Plantain	*Plantago* spp.
Knotweed	*Polygonum* spp.
Scurfpea	*Psoralea* spp.
Russian thistle	*Salsola kali*
Tumblegrass	*Schedonnardus* spp.
Black nightshade	*Solanum nigrum*
Spiny buffalobur nightshade	*Solanum rostratum*
Cutleaf nightshade	*Solanum triflorum*
Scarlet globemallow	*Sphaeralcea coccinea*
Dropseed or sand dropseed	*Sporobolus cryptandrus*
Needle-and-thread	*Stipa comata*
Snowberry	*Symphoricarpos occidentalis*
Mullein	*Verbascum thapsus*
Verbena	*Verbena* spp.
Cocklebur	*Xanthium* spp.
Sorrel	*Xanthoxalis* spp.
Deathcamus	*Zygadenus* spp.

Animals

Internal parasites
    Spiny-headed worms   class Acanthocephala
    Tapeworms   class Cestoda
    Roundworms   class Nematoda
    Protozoans   phylum Protozoa

Arachnids (Arachnida)
    Ticks and mites   Order Acarina
    Pseudoscorpions   Order Chelonethida
    Black widow spider   *Latrodectus mactans*

Insects (Insecta)
    Lice or sucking lice   Order Anoplura
    Fleas   Order Siphonaptera
    Short-horned grasshoppers   Family Acrididae
    Agaontid fig wasps   Family Agaontidae
    Robber flies   Family Asilidae
    Bluebottle flies   Family Calliphoridae
    Ground beetles   Family Carabidae
    Cutworms   Family Noctuidae
    Dung beetles   Family Scarabaeidae
    Scelionid wasps   Family Scelionidae
    Scolytid bark beetles   Family Scolytidae
    Darkling beetles   Family Tenebrionidae
    Honeybee   *Apis mellifera*
    Fungus ant   *Atta* spp.
    Peppered moth   *Biston betularia*
    Bombardier beetle   *Brachinus* spp.
    Cave cricket or camel cricket   *Ceuthophilus* spp.
    Monarch butterfly   *Danaus plexippus*
    Sweat bee   *Lasioglossum zephyrum*
    Mound-building termite   *Macrotermes* spp.
    Nasonia wasp   *Nasonia vitripennis*
    Southern green stinkbug   *Nezara viridula*
    Swallow bug   *Oeciacus vicarius*

Harvester ant	*Pogonomyrmex occidentalis*
Paper wasp	*Polistes fuscatus*
Red flour beetle	*Tribolium castaneum*

Fishes (Osteichthyes)
| Guppy | *Lebistes reticulatus* |
| Iridens trout | *Salmo iridens* |

Amphibians (Amphibia)
Tiger salamander	*Ambystoma tigrinum*
Toads	*Bufo* spp.
Plains spadefoot toad	*Scaphiopus bombifrons*
Exculenta frog	*Rana exculenta*
Smooth newt	*Triturus vulgaris*

Reptiles (Reptilia)
Rattlesnake	*Crotalus* spp.
Prairie rattlesnake	*Crotalus viridis*
Western hognose snake	*Heterodon nasicus*
Lesser earless lizard	*Holbrookia maculata*
Texas horned lizard	*Phrynosoma cornutum*
Bull snake	*Pituophys melanoleucus*
Western box turtle or ornate box turtle	*Terrapene ornata*
Lined snake	*Tropidoclonion lineatum*
Adder	*Vipera berus*

Birds (Aves)
Accipiter hawk	*Accipiter* spp.
Cooper's hawk	*Accipiter cooperii*
Northern goshawk	*Accipiter gentilis*
European sparrowhawk	*Accipiter nisus*
Sharp-shinned hawk	*Accipiter striatus*
Spotted sandpiper	*Actitis macularia*
Red-winged blackbird	*Agelaius phoeniceus*
Tricolored blackbird	*Agelaius tricolor*
Mallard	*Anas platyrhynchos*
Goose	*Anser* spp. or *Branta* spp.
Lesser snow goose	*Anser caerulescens*
Sprague's pipit	*Anthus spragueii*
Florida scrub jay	*Aphelocoma coerulescens*
Mexican jay	*Aphelocoma ultramarina*
Common swift	*Apus apus*
Alpine swift	*Apus melba*
Golden eagle	*Aquila chrysaetos*
Black eagle	*Aquila verreauxi*
Gray heron	*Ardea cinerea*
Canada goose	*Branta canadensis*
Cattle egret	*Bubulcus ibis*
Buteo hawk	*Buteo* spp.
Red-tailed hawk	*Buteo jamaicensis*
Rough-legged hawk	*Buteo lagopus*
Ferruginous hawk	*Buteo regalis*
Swainson's hawk	*Buteo swainsoni*
Lark bunting	*Calamospiza malanocorys*
Lapland longspur	*Calcarius lapponicus*
Western sandpiper	*Calidris mauri*
Stripe-backed wren	*Campylorhynchus nuchalis*
Great egret	*Casmerodius albus*

Sage grouse	*Centrocercus urophasianus*
Pied kingfisher	*Ceryle rudis*
Northern harrier or marsh hawk	*Circus cyaneus*
Bobwhite	*Colinus virginianus*
Wood pigeon	*Columba palumbus*
White-winged chough	*Corcorax malanorhamphus*
Rook	*Corvus frugilegus*
Groove-billed ani	*Crotophaga sulcirostris*
Wandering albatross	*Diomedea exulans*
Black-footed albatross	*Diomedea nigripes*
Horned lark	*Eremophila alpestris*
Crested penguin	*Eudyptes* spp.
Mountain plover	*Eupoda montana*
Prairie falcon	*Falco mexicanus*
Peregrine falcon	*Falco peregrinus*
American kestrel or sparrow hawk	*Falco sparverius*
Collared flycatcher	*Ficedula albicollis*
Little blue heron	*Florida caerulea*
Chaffinch	*Fringilla coelebs*
Northern fulmar or fulmar	*Fulmarus glacialis*
Domestic chicken	*Gallus domesticus*
Red jungle fowl	*Gallus gallus spadiceus*
Darwin's medium ground finch	*Geospiza fortis*
Pinyon jay	*Gymnorhinus cyanocephalus*
Bald eagle	*Haliaeetus leucocephalus*
Cliff swallow	*Hirundo (Petrochelidon) pyrrhonota*
Barn swallow	*Hirundo rustica*
American jacana	*Jacana spinosa*
Willow ptarmigan	*Lagopus lagopus*
Herring gull	*Larus argentatus*
Laughing gull	*Larus atricilla*
California gull	*Larus californicus*
Common gull	*Larus canus*
Ring-billed gull	*Larus delawarensis*
Glaucous-winged gull	*Larus glaucescens*
Franklin's gull	*Larus pipixcan*
Black-headed gull	*Larus ridibundus*
Superb blue fairy-wren	*Malurus cyaneus*
Splendid fairy-wren	*Malurus splendens*
Australian bell miner	*Manorina melanophrys*
Acorn woodpecker	*Melanerpes formicivorus*
European bee-eater	*Merops apiaster*
White-fronted bee-eater	*Merops bullockoides*
Galápagos mockingbird	*Nesomimus parvulus*
Osprey	*Pandion haliaetus*
Harris's hawk	*Parabuteo unicinctus*
Blue tit	*Parus caeruleus*
Great tit	*Parus major*
House sparrow	*Passer domesticus*
Indigo bunting	*Passerina cyanea*
Sharp-tailed grouse	*Pedioecetes phasianellus*
Brown pelican	*Pelecanus occidentalis*
Shag	*Phalacrocorax aristotelis*
Black-billed magpie or American magpie	*Pica pica*
Red-cockaded woodpecker	*Picoides borealis*
Spoonbill	*Platalea leucorodia*
Hall's babbler	*Pomatostomus halli*
Gray-crowned babbler	*Pomatostomus temporalis*

Pukeko	*Porphyrio porphyrio melanotus*
Purple martin	*Progne subis*
Dunnock	*Prunella modularis*
Satin bowerbird	*Ptilonorhynchus violaceus*
Adélie penguin	*Pygoscelis adeliae*
Quelea	*Quelea quelea*
Boat-tailed grackle	*Quiscalus major*
Great-tailed grackle	*Quiscalus mexicanus*
Greater rhea	*Rhea americana*
McCown's longspur	*Rhynchophanes mccownii*
Bank swallow	*Riparia riparia*
Kittiwake	*Rissa tridactyla*
Mountain bluebird	*Siala currucoides*
Common eider	*Somateria mollissima*
Burrowing owl	*Speotyto cunicularia*
Crested tern	*Sterna bergii*
Sooty tern	*Sterna fuscata*
Common tern	*Sterna hirundo*
Royal tern	*Sterna maxima*
Arctic tern	*Sterna paradisaea*
Sandwich tern	*Sterna sandvicensis*
Laughing dove	*Streptopelia senegalensis*
Ostrich	*Struthio camelus*
Western meadowlark	*Sturnella neglecta*
Starling	*Sturnus vulgaris*
Northern gannet or gannet	*Sula (Morus) bassana*
Peruvian gannet	*Sula (Morus) variegata*
Ancient murrelet	*Synthliboramphus antiquus*
Tree swallow	*Tachycineta (Iridoprocne) bicolor*
Shelduck	*Tadorna tadorna*
Black grouse	*Tetrao tetrix*
House wren	*Troglodytes aedon*
Black-lored babbler	*Turdoides malanops*
Arabian babbler	*Turdoides squamiceps*
American robin	*Turdus migratorius*
Missel thrush	*Turdus viscivorus*
Common murre or common guillemot	*Uria aalge*
Thick-billed murre	*Uria lomvia*
Yellow-headed blackbird	*Xanthocephalus xanthocephalus*
Mourning dove	*Zenaidura macroura*
White-crowned sparrow	*Zonotrichia leucophrys*

Mammals (Mammalia)
  Whales and porpoises (Cetacea)

Short-finned pilot whale	*Globicephala macrorhynchus*
Humpback whale	*Megaptera novaeangliae*
Killer whale	*Orcinus orca*
False killer whale	*Pseudorca crassidens*

  Even-toed ungulates (Artiodactyla)

Pronghorn antelope or pronghorn	*Antilocapra americana*
American bison or American buffalo	*Bos bison*
Domestic cow	*Bos taurus*
Domestic goat or milch goat	*Capra hircus*
Red deer or wapiti or elk	*Cervus elaphus*
Wildebeest	*Connochaetes taurinus*
Fallow deer	*Dama dama*
Grant's gazelle	*Gazella granti*

Thomson's gazelle	*Gazella thomsonii*
Mule deer	*Odocoileus hemionus*
White-tailed deer	*Odocoileus virginianus*
Domestic sheep	*Ovis aries*
Mountain sheep or bighorn sheep	*Ovis canadensis*
Caribou	*Rangifer tarandus*
Domestic pig	*Sus scrofa*
Collared peccary	*Tayassu tajacu*

Odd-toed ungulates (Perissodactyla)

Burchell's zebra	*Equus burchelli*
Wild, feral, or domestic horse	*Equus caballus*

Carnivores (Carnivora)

Galápagos fur seal	*Arctocephalus galapagoensis*
Northern fur seal	*Callorhinus ursinus*
Golden jackal	*Canis aureus*
Domestic dog	*Canis familiaris*
Coyote	*Canis latrans*
Gray wolf or wolf	*Canis lupus*
Silverbacked jackal	*Canis mesomelas*
Spotted hyena	*Crocuta crocuta*
Mountain lion or cougar or puma	*Felis concolor*
Dwarf mongoose	*Helogale parvula*
Brown hyena	*Hyaena brunnea*
African wild dog	*Lycaon pictus*
Bobcat	*Lynx (Felis) rufus*
Eurasian badger or European badger	*Meles meles*
Northern elephant seal	*Mirounga angustirostris*
Southern elephant seal	*Mirounga leonina*
Banded mongoose	*Mungos mungo*
Long-tailed weasel	*Mustela frenata*
Black-footed ferret	*Mustela nigripes*
Mink	*Mustela vison*
White-nosed coati or coati	*Nasua narica*
Raccoon dog	*Nyctereutes procyonoides*
Southern sea lion	*Otaria byronia*
African lion or lion	*Panthera leo*
Baikal seal	*Phoca sibirica*
Harbor seal or common seal	*Phoca vitulina*
Ringed seal	*Pusa hispida*
Meerkat	*Suricata suricatta*
American badger or badger	*Taxidea taxus*
Common gray fox	*Urocyon cinereoargenteus*
Grizzly bear or brown bear	*Ursus arctos*
Swift or kit fox	*Vulpes velox*
Red fox	*Vulpes vulpes*
California sea lion	*Zalophus californianus*
Galápagos sea lion	*Zalophus californianus wollebaeki*

Bats (Chiroptera)

Rhinolophid bats	Family Rhinolophidae
Vespertilionid bats	Family Vespertilionidae
Common vampire bat	*Desmodus rotundus*
Hammer-headed bat	*Hypsignathus monstrosus*
Evening bat	*Nycticeius humeralis*
Greater spearnose bat	*Phyllostomus hastatus*
Townsend's big-eared bat	*Plecotus townsendii*
Mexican free-tailed bat	*Tadarida brasiliensis mexicana*

Marsupials (Marsupialia)
    Kangaroos   Family Macropodidae
    Common opossum   *Didelphis marsupialis*
    Virginia opossum   *Didelphis virginiana*

Insectivores (Insectivora)
    Moles   Family Talpidae

Rabbits, hares, and pikas (Lagomorpha)
    White-tailed jackrabbit   *Lepus townsendi*
    American pika   *Ochotona princeps*
    European rabbit   *Oryctolagus cuniculus*
    Desert or plains cottontail   *Sylvilagus auduboni*

Elephants (Proboscidea)
    African elephant   *Loxodonta africana*

Hyraxes (Hyracoidea)
    Bush hyrax   *Heterohyrax brucei*
    Rock hyrax   *Procavia johnstoni*

Rodents (Rodentia)
    Pocket gophers   Family Geomyidae
    Spiny mouse   *Acomys cahirinus*
    Water vole   *Arvicola terrestris*
    Malaysian tree squirrel #1   *Callosciurus caniceps*
    Malaysian tree squirrel #2   *Callosciurus nigrovittatus*
    Malaysian tree squirrel #3   *Callosciurus notatus*
    Wild guinea pig   *Cavia aperea*
    Vole   *Clethrionomys* spp. or *Microtus* spp.
    Prairie dog[a]   *Cynomys* spp. or *Cynomys ludovicianus*
    Gunnison's prairie dog   *Cynomys gunnisoni*
    White-tailed prairie dog   *Cynomys leucurus*
    Black-tailed prairie dog   *Cynomys ludovicianus*
    Mexican prairie dog   *Cynomys mexicanus*
    Utah prairie dog   *Cynomys parvidens*
    Collared lemming   *Dicrostonyx groenlandicus*
    Yellow-toothed cavy   *Galea musteloides*
    Flying squirrel   *Glaucomys* spp.
    Northern flying squirrel   *Glaucomys sabrinus*
    Southern flying squirrel   *Glaucomys volans*
    Naked mole rat   *Heterocephalus glaber*
    Marmots   *Marmota* spp.
    Bobak marmot or steppe marmot   *Marmota bobak*
    Alaska or arctic or Brower's marmot   *Marmota broweri*
    Hoary marmot   *Marmota caligata*
    Black-capped marmot or
        Kamchatka marmot   *Marmota camtschatica*
    Long-tailed marmot or red marmot   *Marmota caudata*
    Yellow-bellied marmot   *Marmota flaviventris*
    Alpine marmot   *Marmota marmota*
    Woodchuck or groundhog   *Marmota monax*
    Olympic marmot   *Marmota olympus*
    Mongolian gerbil   *Meriones unguiculatus*
    Golden hamster   *Mesocricetus auratus*
    Mountain cavy   *Microcavia australis*
    Gray-tailed vole   *Microtus canicaudus*
    Prairie vole   *Microtus ochrogaster*
    Meadow vole   *Microtus pennsylvanicus*

House mouse	*Mus musculus*
Common muskrat	*Ondatra zibethicus*
Northern grasshopper mouse	*Onychomys leucogaster*
Pocket mouse	*Perognathus* spp.
California mouse	*Peromyscus californicus*
Cactus mouse	*Peromyscus eremicus*
White-footed mouse	*Peromyscus leucopus*
Deer mouse	*Peromyscus maniculatus*
Oldfield mouse	*Peromyscus polionotus*
Norway rat	*Rattus norvegicus*
Tree squirrels	*Sciurus* spp. and *Tamiasciurus* spp.
Tassel-eared or Abert's squirrel	*Sciuris aberti*
Gray squirrel or eastern gray squirrel	*Sciurus carolinensis*
Fox squirrel or eastern fox squirrel	*Sciurus niger*
Hispid cotton rat	*Sigmodon hispidus*
Ground squirrel	*Spermophilus* spp.
Uinta ground squirrel	*Spermophilus armatus*
California ground squirrel	*Spermophilus beecheyi*
Belding's ground squirrel	*Spermophilus beldingi*
Idaho ground squirrel	*Spermophilus brunneus*
Columbian ground squirrel	*Spermophilus columbianus*
Wyoming ground squirrel	*Spermophilus elegans*
Arctic ground squirrel	*Spermophilus parryii*
Richardson's ground squirrel	*Spermophilus richardsonii*
Cascade golden-mantled ground squirrel	*Spermophilus saturatus*
Round-tailed ground squirrel	*Spermophilus tereticaudus*
Thirteen-lined ground squirrel	*Spermophilus tridecemlineatus*
Rock squirrel	*Spermophilus variegatus*
Chipmunk	*Tamias (Eutamias)* spp.
California chipmunk	*Tamias obscurus*
Asian chipmunk	*Tamias sibiricus*
Sonoma chipmunk	*Tamias (Eutamias) sonomae*
Eastern chipmunk	*Tamias striatus*
Douglas's squirrel	*Tamiasciurus douglasii*
Red squirrel	*Tamiasciurus hudsonicus*

Primates

Mantled howler monkey	*Alouatta palliata*
Red howler monkey	*Alouatta seniculus*
Owl monkey or night monkey	*Aotus trivirgatus*
Brown-headed spider monkey	*Ateles fusciceps robrustrus*
Black spider monkey	*Ateles paniscus*
Gray-cheeked mangabey	*Cercocebus albigena*
Vervet monkey or vervet	*Cercopithecus aethiops*
Red-tailed monkey	*Cercopithecus ascanius*
Red colobus monkey	*Colobus badius*
Thick-tailed bushbaby or thick-tailed galago	*Galago crassicaudatus*
Mountain gorilla	*Gorilla gorilla beringei*
Human	*Homo sapiens*
Golden lion tamarin	*Leontopithecus rosalia*
Macaque	*Macaca* spp.
Stump-tailed macaque	*Macaca arctoides*
Long-tailed macaque	*Macaca fascicularis*
Japanese macaque or Japanese monkey	*Macaca fuscata*
Rhesus macaque or rhesus monkey	*Macaca mulatta*
Pigtailed macaque	*Macaca nemestrina*
Bonnet macaque	*Macaca radiata*

Toque macaque	*Macaca sinica*
Pygmy chimpanzee or bonobo	*Pan paniscus*
Chimpanzee	*Pan troglodytes*
Baboon	*Papio* spp.
Savannah, yellow, olive, or chacma baboon	*Papio cynocephalus*
Potto	*Perodicticus potto*
Orangutan	*Pongo pygmaeus*
Silvered-leaf monkey	*Presbytis cristata*
Hanuman langur or gray langur	*Presbytis entellus*
Purple-faced langur	*Presbytis senex*
Western tarsier	*Tarsius bancanus*
Gelada baboon	*Theropithecus gelada*

Note: Sources for common and scientific names include field guides such as Palmer and Fowler 1975, Stebbins 1985, and Peterson 1990. Sources also include myriad scientific reports such as King 1955, Schaller 1972, Fagerstone 1982, Nowak and Paradiso 1983; Hausfater and Hrdy 1984, McLain and Marsh 1990, and Jones et al. 1992.

[a]Prairie dogs are squirrels of the genus *Cynomys,* of which there are five species. Usually in this book I refer to black-tailed prairie dogs simply as prairie dogs.

Appendix B

Descriptions of Infanticides by Marauding Females

Appendix B. Descriptions of Infanticides by Marauding Females

Date	Killer and her age (years)	Killer's condition[a]	Victimized mother and her age (years)	Genetic relationship of killer to victimized mother	Age of killer's juveniles at time of kill (days)[b]	Age of victims at time of kill (days)[b]	Litter size at first emergence for victimized litter	Killer showed BF or DF	Killer showed RFD	Killer showed LFC
04 Apr 81	RB3 (2)	lac	H0 (5)	Daughter	3	4	0	Yes	No	No
04 Apr 81	76 (2)	lac	RB3 (2)	Full sister	5	3	0	Yes	No	No
05 Apr 81	RS (3)	lac	RC (3)	Full sister	4	3	0	Yes	Yes	Yes
05 Apr 81	RSBB (4)	preg	55 (1)	Mother	—	0	0	No	Yes	Yes
15 Apr 81	R71 (1)	LL	RR5 (5)	Full niece	19	13	0	No	Yes	No
20 Apr 81	RS (3)	lac	WA (≥7)	Daughter	—	12	0	Yes	No	Yes
23 Apr 81	R71 (1)	LL	BB6 (2)	Full 1st cousin	19	21	0	No	Yes	Yes
24 Apr 81	RR6 (4)	lac	RSBS (2)	Mother	23	13	1	No	Yes	Yes
25 Apr 81	H-1 (3)	lac	88 (1)	Half sister	8	20	0	No	No	No
15 Apr 82	RC (4)	lac	RS (4)	Full sister	?	9	0	No	No	No
15 Apr 82	H-1 (4)	lac	88 (2)	Half sister	9	14	0	Yes	No	Yes
15 Apr 82	RR5 (6)	lac	BB6 (3)	Mother	11	12	0	Yes	Yes	No
17 Apr 82	RR5 (6)	lac	2RSA (2)	Mother	17	15	0	No	Yes	Yes
21 Apr 82	H4 (3)	lac	BB6 (3)	Full sister	?	18	0	No	Yes	Yes
23 Apr 82	RSBS (3)	lac	RR6 (5)	Daughter	18	?	0	No	Yes	Yes
24 Apr 82	RR5 (6)	lac	H4 (3)	Mother	20	20	3	Yes	No	Yes
24 Apr 82	H4 (3)	lac	RR5 (6)	Half sister	—	18	2	No	No	No
01 May 82	BB6 (3)	LL	2RSA (2)	Mother	28	29	0	No	Yes	No
02 May 82	H6 (3)	lac	80 (2)	Mother	8	32	2	No	No	Yes
07 Apr 83	H4 (4)	lac	2RSA (3)	Half sister	7	10	0	No	No	No
08 Apr 83	92 (1)	lac	H6 (4)	Daughter	10	11	0	No	Yes	No
09 Apr 83	H4 (4)	lac	RR5 (7)	Daughter	—	1	0	No	No	Yes
09 Apr 83	H6 (4)	LL	92 (1)	Mother	8	8	3	No	No	No
27 Apr 83	92 (1)	lac	80 (3)	Half sister	26	30	2	Yes	No	No
09 Apr 84	55 (4)	lac	81 (4)	No kinship	5	1	0	Yes	No	No

Date				Relationship						
12 Apr 84	BB6 (5)	lac	WA4 (1)	Mother	4	9	0	No	No	No
13 Apr 84	RR0 (4)	lac	55 (4)	Full sister	5	9	0	Yes	No	Yes
16 Apr 84	92 (2)	lac	RSBB (2)	Full sister	14	12	0	Yes	Yes	No
17 Apr 84	H4 (5)	lac	85 (1)	Mother	10	6	0	No	No	Yes
19 Apr 84	55 (4)	LL	6str (3)	Half sister	—	10	0	No	No	Yes
19 Apr 84	2RSA (4)	lac	WA4 (1)	Half aunt	15	16	0	No	Yes	No
21 Apr 84	H4 (5)	lac	2RSA (4)	Half sister	14	17	2	Yes	No	Yes
03 May 84	81 (4)	LL	70 (1)	Mother	—	23	3	Yes	No	Yes
06 May 84	84 (5)	lac	WABS (2)	Full sister	31	31	3	No	No	No
07 May 84	H4 (2)	lac	BB6 (5)	Full sister	30	29	2	No	Yes	Yes
07 May 84	92 (2)	lac	5SBS (2)	Half sister	35	34	0	Yes	No	No
09 May 84	92 (2)	lac	H4 (5)	Full niece	37	32	1	Yes	Yes	Yes
11 May 84	RAB (3)	lac	BB2 (4)	Half sister	33	41	0	Yes	Yes	Yes
15 May 84	52 (4)	lac	H-2 (2)	No kinship	28^d	32	0	Yes	Yes	Yes
30 May 84	H3 (2)	post	56 (1)	Full aunt	47^d	40	4	No	Yes	No
06 Jun 84	BSBB (2)	post	CR (3)	No kinship	57^d	65^d	0	Yes	No	Yes
13 Apr 85	H4 (6)	lac	WA4 (2)	Full aunt	2	6	0	Yes	No	Yes
14 Apr 85	FR (2)	lac	H4 (6)	Daughter	2	3	0	Yes	Yes	Yes
27 Apr 85	85 (2)	lac	FR (2)	Full sister	11	15	0	Yes	Yes	Yes
19 May 85	92 (3)	lac	5SBS (3)	Half sister	21	29	4	No	Yes	Yes
08 Apr 86	RAC (5)	lac	AB (2)	Full sister	5	3	0	Yes	No	Yes
15 Apr 86	6str (4)	lac	RAC (2)	Half great aunt	9	12	0	Yes	Yes	Yes
16 Apr 86	RB3 (4)	lac	68 (6)	Daughter	10	5	0	No	No	Yes
20 Apr 86	FR (3)	lac	62 (6)	Half 1st cousin once removed	14	6	0	No	No	Yes
25 Apr 86	2RSB (2)	lac	5SBS (4)	Half niece	16	19	0	No	No	No
02 May 86	2RSB (2)	lac	R96 (1)	Half sister	23	20	0	No	No	Yes
06 May 86	72 (2)	lac	F (2)	Half sister	25	26	2	Yes	Yes	Yes
31 Mar 87	66 (2)	lac	HBS (4)	Full niece	7	1	0	Yes	No	No
05 Apr 87	66 (2)	lac	75 (4)	Daughter	12	11	2	No	No	No
27 Apr 87	BB8 (5)	lac	H-3 (2)	Mother	23	15	0	No	Yes	Yes
12 May 87	RAB (2)	lac	FR (4)	Full niece	38	37	4	No	No	No
31 May 87	AB (3)	post	RAC (3)	Full sister	48^d	35	1	No	No	No
07 Apr 88	FR (5)	preg	5str (3)	Full aunt	—	3	0	No	No	Yes

Continued

Appendix B. Descriptions of Infanticides by Marauding Females (Concluded)

Date	Killer and her age (years)	Killer's condition[a]	Victimized mother and her age (years)	Genetic relationship of killer to victimized mother	Age of killer's juveniles at time of kill (days)[b]	Age of victims at time of kill (days)[b]	Litter size at first emergence for victimized litter	Killer showed BF or DF	Killer showed RFD	Killer showed LFC
15 Apr 88	75 (5)	lac	66 (3)	Mother	7	3	0	Yes	No	Yes
30 Apr 88	5str (3)	LL	FR (5)	Full niece	—	12	0	No	Yes	No
30 Apr 88	FR (5)	lac	RAB (3)	Full aunt	12	25	0	No	Yes	Yes
10 May 88	2RSB (4)	LL	65 (3)	Half sister	—	28	0	No	Yes	Yes
12 May 88	H0 (2)	lac	76 (2)	Half sister	31	31	0	No	Yes	Yes
16 May 88	HWA (2)	lac	RS (2)	Full sister	39	39	0	?	Yes	?
25 May 88	HRS (3)	NL	RR6 (2)	Full sister	—	50[d]	3	?	?	?

Note: Each prairie dog female in this table has a unique identification mark, but the same female might be a killer or victim more than once in the same or different years. Three mothers (BB6 in 1982, 2RSA in 1982, and WA4 in 1984) had their litters marauded on two separate occasions in the same year: the first marauder evidently eliminated only some of the juveniles; the second marauder then killed the juveniles spared by the first marauder. Four mothers (81 in 1984, H4 in 1984, 62 in 1986, and RR6 in 1988) lost litters to a marauder from a different coterie; all other killings involved marauders from the home coterie.

[a] Preg, pregnant; lac, lactating; LL, loss of killer's own litter before killing; post, killer's juveniles had already appeared aboveground at time of killing; NL, failure of killer to give birth in year of killing.

[b] Number of days since birth.

[c] BF, bloody face; DF, dirty face; RFD, rubbing of face in the dirt; LFC, licking of front claws.

[d] At the time of killing, these juveniles had already first emerged from their natal burrow.

Bibliography

Abramson, M. 1979. Vigilance as a factor influencing flock formation among curlews *Numenius arquata*. *Ibis* 121:213–216.

Adams, M. S., and J. V. Neel. 1967. Children of incest. *Pediatrics* 40:55–62.

Adler, N. T. 1969. Effects of the male's copulatory behavior on successful pregnancy of the female rat. *Journal of Comparative and Physiological Psychology* 6:613–622.

Adler, N. T., and S. R. Zoloth. 1970. Copulatory behavior can inhibit pregnancy in female rats. *Science* 168:1480–1482.

Agnew, W., D. W. Uresk, and R. M. Hansen. 1986. Flora and fauna associated with prairie dog colonies and adjacent ungrazed mixed-grass prairie in western South Dakota. *Journal of Range Management* 39:135–139.

Agoramoorthy, G., S. M. Mohnot, V. Sommer, and A. Srivastava. 1988. Abortions in free ranging hanuman langurs *(Presbytis entellus)*—a male induced strategy? *Human Evolution* 3:297–308.

Agren, G. 1990. Sperm competition, pregnancy initiation and litter size: Influence of the amount of copulatory behavior in Mongolian gerbils, *Meriones unguiculatus. Animal Behaviour* 40:417–427.

Aguilera, E. 1989. Sperm competition and copulation intervals of the white spoonbill *(Platalea leucorodia,* Aves: Threskiornithidae). *Ethology* 82:230–237.

Ahnlund, H. 1980. Sexual maturity and breeding season of the badger, *Meles meles* in Sweden. *Journal of Zoology* (London) 190:77–95.

Alcorn, J. R. 1940. Life history notes on the piute ground squirrel. *Journal of Mammalogy* 21:160–170.

Aldous, C. M. 1941. Report of a wholesale die-off of young herring gulls at Hogback Island, Moosehead Lake, Maine. *Bird Banding* 12:30–32.

Alerstam, T., and G. Hogstedt. 1984. How important is clutch size dependent adult mortality? *Oikos* 43:253–254.

Alexander, R. D. 1971. The search for an evolutionary philosophy of man. *Proceedings of the Royal Society, Victoria* 84:99–120.

Alexander, R. D. 1974. The evolution of social behavior. *Annual Review of Ecology and Systematics* 5:325–383.

Alexander, R. D. 1975. Natural selection and specialized chorusing behavior in acoustical insects. Pages 35–77 in D. Pimental, ed., *Insects, Science, and Society*. New York: Academic Press.

Alexander, R. D. 1977. Natural selection and the analysis of human sociality. Pages 283–337 in C. E. Goulden, ed., *The Changing Scenes in the Natural Sciences, 1776–1976*. Philadelphia: Academy of Natural Sciences.

Alexander, R. D. 1979. *Darwinism and Human Affairs*. Seattle: University of Washington Press.

Alexander, R. D. 1987. *The Biology of Moral Systems*. New York: Aldine de Gruyter.

Alexander, R. D. 1990a. Epigenetic rules and Darwinian algorithms: The adaptive study of learning and development. *Ethology and Sociobiology* ll:241–303.

Alexander, R. D. 1990b. *How Did Humans Evolve? Reflections on the Uniquely Unique Species*. Special Publication no. 1., Museum of Zoology, The University of Michigan. Ann Arbor, Mich.

Alexander, R. D. 1991. Social learning and kin recognition: An addendum and reply to Sherman. *Ethology and Sociobiology* 12:387–399.

Alexander, R. D., J. L. Hoogland, R. D. Howard, K. M. Noonan, and P. W. Sherman. 1979. Sexual dimorphisms and breeding systems in pinnipeds, ungulates, primates, and humans. Pages 402–435 in N. A. Chagnon and W. G. Irons, eds., *Evolutionary Biology and Human Social Behavior: An Anthropological Perspective*. North Scituate, Mass.: Duxbury Press.

Alexander, R. D., and K. M. Noonan. 1979. Concealment of ovulation, parental care, and human social evolution. Pages 436–453 in N. A. Chagnon and W. Irons, eds., *Evolutionary Biology and Human Social Behavior: An Anthropological Perspective*. North Scituate, Mass.: Duxbury Press.

Alexander, R. D., K. M. Noonan, and B. J. Crespi. 1991. The Evolution of eusociality. Pages 3–44 in P. W. Sherman, J. U. M. Jarvis, and R. D. Alexander, eds., *The Biology of the Naked Mole Rat*. Princeton, N.J.: Princeton University Press.

Alexander, R. D., and P. W. Sherman. 1977. Local mate competition and parental investment in social insects. *Science* 196:494–500.

Allan, P. F., and B. Osborn. 1954. Tall grass defeats prairie dogs. *Soil Conservation* 20:103–105.

Allee, W. C., A. E. Emerson, O. Park, T. Park, and K. P. Schmidt. 1949. *Principles of Animal Ecology*. Philadelphia: W. B. Saunders.

Allen, D. 1967. *The Life of Prairies and Plains*. New York: McGraw-Hill.

Altmann, J., S. A. Altmann, and G. Hausfater. 1978. Primate infant's effects on mother's future reproduction. *Science* 201:1028–1030.

Altmann, J., G. Hausfater, and S. A. Altmann. 1988. Determinants of reproductive success in savannah baboons, *Papio cynocephalus*. Pages 403–418 in T. H. Clutton-Brock, ed., *Reproductive Success: Studies of Individual Variation in Contrasting Breeding Systems*. Chicago: University of Chicago Press.

Altmann, S. A. 1979. Altruistic behaviour: The fallacy of kin deployment. *Animal Behaviour* 27:958–962.

Altmann, S. A., and J. Altmann. 1970. *Baboon Ecology, African Field Research.* Chicago: University of Chicago Press.

Andelman, S. J. 1987. Evolution of concealed ovulation in vervet monkeys *(Cercopithecus aethiops). American Naturalist* 129:785–799.

Andersen, D. C., K. B. Armitage, and R. S. Hoffmann. 1976. Socioecology of marmots: Female reproductive strategies. *Ecology* 57:552–560.

Anderson, J. L., and R. Boonstra. 1979. Some aspects of reproduction in the vole *Microtus townsendii. Canadian Journal of Zoology* 57:18–24.

Anderson, P. K. 1989. *Dispersal in Rodents: A Resident Fitness Hypothesis.* American Society of Mammalogists Special Publication no. 9.

Anderson, S., and D. Inkley, eds. 1985. *Black-footed Ferret Workshop Proceedings.* Cheyenne, Wyo.: Wyoming Game and Fish Publications.

Andersson, M. 1976. Predation and kleptoparasitism by skuas in a Shetland seabird colony. *Ibis* 118:208–217.

Andersson, M. 1984a. Brood parasitism within species. Pages 195–228 in C. J. Barnard, ed., *Producers and Scroungers: Strategies of Exploitation and Parasitism.* London: Croom Helm.

Andersson, M. 1984b. The evolution of eusociality. *Annual Review of Ecology and Systematics* 15:165–189.

Anthony, A. 1953. Seasonal reproductive cycle in the normal and experimentally treated male prairie dog, *Cynomys ludovicianus. Journal of Morphology* 93:331–370.

Anthony, A. 1955. Behavior patterns in a laboratory colony of prairie dogs, *Cynomys ludovicianus. Journal of Mammalogy* 36:69–78.

Anthony, A., and D. Foreman. 1951. Observations on the reproductive cycle of the black-tailed prairie dog *(Cynomys ludovicianus). Physiological Zoology* 24:242–248.

Aoki, S. 1982. Soldiers and altruistic dispersal in aphids. Pages 154–158 in M. D. Breed, C. D. Michener, and H. E. Evans, eds., *The Biology of Social Insects.* Boulder, Colo.: Westview Press.

Arcese, P. 1989. Intrasexual competition, mating system and natal dispersal in song sparrows. *Animal Behaviour* 38:958–979.

Archer, J. 1970. Effects of population density on behaviour of rodents. Pages 169–210 in J. H. Crook, ed., *Social Behaviour in Birds and Mammals.* London: Academic Press.

Armitage, K. B. 1962. Social behaviour of a colony of the yellow-bellied marmot *(Marmota flaviventris). Animal Behaviour* 10:319–331.

Armitage, K. B. 1974. Male behaviour and territoriality in the yellow-bellied marmot. *Journal of Zoology* (London) 172:233–265.

Armitage, K. B. 1975. Social behavior and population dynamics of marmots. *Oikos* 26:341–354.

Armitage, K. B. 1977. Social variety in the yellow-bellied marmot: A population-behavioural system. *Animal Behaviour* 25:585–593.

Armitage, K. B. 1981. Sociality as a life-history tactic of ground squirrels. *Oecologia* 48:36–49.

Armitage, K. B. 1982. Marmots and coyotes: Behavior of prey and predator. *Journal of Mammalogy* 63:503–505.

Armitage, K. B. 1984. Recruitment in yellow-bellied marmot populations: Kinship, philopatry, and individual variability. Pages 377–403 in J. O. Murie and G. R. Michener, eds., *The Biology of Ground-Dwelling Squirrels.* Lincoln, Nebr.: University of Nebraska Press.

Armitage, K. B. 1986. Marmot polygyny revisited: Determinants of male and female reproductive strategies. Pages 303–331 in D. I. Rubenstein and R. W. Wrangham, eds., *Ecological Aspects of Social Evolution.* Princeton, N.J.: Princeton University Press.

Armitage, K. B. 1987a. Do female yellow-bellied marmots adjust the sex ratios of their offspring? *American Naturalist* 129:501–519.

Armitage, K. B. 1987b. Social dynamics of mammals: Reproductive success, kinship, and individual fitness. *Trends in Ecology and Evolution* 2:279–284.

Armitage, K. B. 1988. Resources and social organization of ground-dwelling squirrels. Pages 131–155 in C. N. Slobodchikoff, ed., *The Ecology of Social Behavior.* New York: Academic Press.

Armitage, K. B. 1989. The function of kin discrimination. *Ethology, Ecology, and Evolution* 1:111–121.

Armitage, K. B. 1991. Social and population dynamics of yellow-bellied marmots: Results from long-term research. *Annual Review of Ecology and Systematics* 22:379–407.

Armitage, K. B., and J. F. Downhower. 1970. Interment behavior in the yellow-bellied marmot *(Marmota flaviventris). Journal of Mammalogy* 51:177–178.

Armitage, K. B., and J. F. Downhower. 1974. Demography of yellow-bellied marmot populations. *Ecology* 55:1233–1245.

Armitage, K. B., J. F. Downhower, and G. E. Svendsen. 1976. Seasonal changes in weights of marmots. *American Midland Naturalist* 96:36–51.

Armitage, K. B., and D. W. Johns. 1982. Kinship, reproductive strategies and social dynamics of yellow-bellied marmots. *Behavioral Ecology and Sociobiology* ll:55–63.

Armitage, K. B., D. Johns, and D. C. Andersen. 1979. Cannibalism among yellow-bellied marmots. *Journal of Mammalogy* 60:205–207.

Armitage, K. B., and C. M. Salsbury. 1992. Factors affecting oxygen consumption in wild-caught yellow-bellied marmots *(Marmota flaviventris). Comparative Biochemical Physiology* 103A:729–737.

Arnold, W. 1988. Social thermoregulation during hibernation in alpine marmots *(Marmota marmota). Journal of Comparative Physiology* B 158:151–156.

Arnold, W. 1990a. The evolution of marmot sociality. I. Why to disperse late? *Behavioral Ecology and Sociobiology* 27:229–237.

Arnold, W. 1990b. The evolution of marmot sociality. II. Costs and benefits of joint hibernation. *Behavioral Ecology and Sociobiology* 27:239–246.

Arnold, W., G. Heldmaier, S. Ortmann, H. Pohl, T. Ruf, and S. Steinlechner. 1991. Ambient temperatures in hibernacula and their energetic consequences for alpine marmots *(Marmota marmota). Journal of Thermal Biology* 16:223–226.

Asdell, S. A. 1964. *Patterns of Mammalian Reproduction.* Ithaca, N.Y.: Cornell University Press.

Ashmole, P. 1963a. The biology of the wideawake or sooty tern *Sterna fuscata* on Ascension Island. *Ibis* 103b:297–364.

Ashmole, P. 1963b. The regulation of numbers of tropical oceanic birds. *Ibis* 103b:458–473.

Askenmo, C. 1979. Reproductive effort and return rate of male pied flycatchers. *American Naturalist* 114:748–753.

Austad, S. N., and M. E. Sunquist. 1986. Sex-ratio manipulation in the common opossum. *Nature* 324:58–60.

Axelrod, R., and W. D. Hamilton. 1981. The evolution of cooperation. *Science* 211:1390–1396.

Bachman, G. C. 1993. The effect of body condition on the trade-off between vigilance and foraging in Belding's ground squirrels. *Animal Behaviour* 46:233–244.

Bailey, V. 1893. *The Ground Squirrels or Spermophiles of the Mississippi Valley.* United States Department of Agriculture, Bulletin of the Division of Ornithology and Mammalogy, no. 4. Washington, D.C.

Bailey, V. 1905. *A Biological Survey of Texas.* United States Department of Agriculture, North American Fauna, no. 25. Washington, D.C.

Baker, A. J., J. M. Dietz, and D. G. Kleiman. 1993. Behavioral evidence for monopolization of paternity in multi-male groups of golden lion tamarins. *Animal Behaviour* 46:1091–1103.

Bakken, A. 1959. Behaviour of gray squirrels. Pages 393–407 in V. Flyger, ed., *Symposium on the Gray Squirrel.* Maryland Department of Research and Education, no. 162. Maryland Game and Inland Fish Commission.

Bakko, E. B. 1977. Field water balance performance in prairie dogs *(Cynomys leucurus* and *C. ludovicianus). Comparative Biochemical Physiology* 56:443–451.

Bakko, E. B., and L. N. Brown. 1967. Breeding biology of the white-tailed prairie dog, *Cynomys leucurus,* in Wyoming. *Journal of Mammalogy* 48:100–112.

Bakko, E. B., W. P. Porter, and B. A. Wunder. 1988. Body temperature patterns in black-tailed prairie dogs in the field. *Canadian Journal of Zoology* 66:1783–1789.

Balcombe, J. P. 1990. Vocal recognition of pups by mother Mexican free-tailed bats, *Tadarida brasiliensis mexicana. Animal Behaviour* 39:960–966.

Balcombe, J. P., and G. F. McCracken. 1992. Vocal recognition in Mexican free-tailed bats: Do pups recognize mothers? *Animal Behaviour* 43:79–87.

Balda, R. P., and G. C. Bateman. 1972. The breeding biology of the Pinon Jay. *Living Bird* 11:5–42.

Baldellou, M., and P. Henzi. 1992. Vigilance, predator detection and the presence of supernumerary males in vervet monkey troops. *Animal Behaviour* 43:451–461.

Balfour, D. 1983. Infanticide in the Columbian ground squirrel, *Spermophilus columbianus. Animal Behaviour* 31:949–950.

Ballou, J. D. 1989. Inbreeding and outbreeding depression in the captive propagation of black-footed ferrets. Pages 49–68 in U. S. Seal, E. T. Thorne, M. A. Bogan, and S. H. Anderson, eds., *Conservation Biology and the Black-footed Ferret.* New Haven, Conn.: Yale University Press.

Balph, D. F. 1984. Spatial and social behavior in a population of Uinta ground squirrels: Interrelations with climate and annual cycle. Pages 336–352 in J. O. Murie and G. R. Michener, eds., *The Biology of Ground-Dwelling Squirrels.* Lincoln, Nebr.: University of Nebraska Press.

Balph, D., and D. Balph. 1966. Sound communication of Uinta ground squirrels. *Journal of Mammalogy* 47:440–450.

Barash, D. P. 1973. The social biology of the Olympic marmot. *Animal Behaviour Monographs* 6:173–242.

Barash, D. P. 1974. The social behavior of the hoary marmot *(Marmota caligata). Animal Behaviour* 22:256–261.

Barash, D. P. 1975. Marmot alarm-calling and the question of altruistic behavior. *American Midland Naturalist* 94:468–470.

Barash, D. P. 1976. Social behaviour and individual differences in free-living alpine marmots *(Marmota marmota). Animal Behaviour* 24:27–35.

Barash, D. P. 1977a. *Sociobiology and Behavior.* New York: Elsevier.

Barash, D. P. 1977b. Sociobiology of rape in mallards *(Anas platyrhyncos):* Responses of the mated male. *Science* 197:788–789.

Barash, D. P. 1981. Mate guarding and gallivanting by male hoary marmots *(Marmota caligata). Behavioral Ecology and Sociobiology* 9:187–193.

Barash, D. P. 1989. *Marmots: Social Behavior and Ecology.* Stanford, Calif.: Stanford University Press.

Barfield, R. H., P. Auerbach, L. A. Geyer, and T. K. McIntosh. 1979. Ultrasonic vocalizations in rat sexual behavior. *American Zoologist* 19:469–480.

Barkalow, F. S., R. B. Hamilton, and R. F. Soots. 1970. The vital statistics of an unexploited gray squirrel population. *Journal of Wildlife Management* 34:489–500.

Barkalow, F. S., and R. F. Soots. 1975. Life span and reproductive longevity of the gray squirrel, *Sciurus c. carolinensis* Gmelin. *Journal of Mammalogy* 56:522–524.

Barnes, A. M. 1982. Surveillance and control of bubonic plague in the United States. *Symposia of the Zoological Society of London* 50:237–270.

Barnes, A. M. 1993. A review of plague and its relevance to prairie dog populations and the black-footed ferret. Pages 28–37 in J. L. Oldemeyer, D. E. Biggins, B. J. Miller, and R. Crete, eds., *Proceedings of the Symposium on the Management of Prairie Dog Complexes for the Reintroduction of Black-Footed Ferrets.* United States Fish and Wildlife Services, Biological Report no. 93. Washington, D.C.

Barnes, A. M., L. J. Ogden, and E. G. Campos. 1972. Control of the plague vector, *Opisocrostis hirsutis,* by treatment of prairie dog *(Cynomys ludovicianus)* burrows with 2% carbaryl dust. *Journal of Medical Entomology* 9:330–333.

Barrett, S. C. H., and D. Charlesworth. 1991. Effects of a change in the level of inbreeding on the genetic load. *Nature* 352:522–524.

Bart, J., and A. Tornes. 1989. Importance of monogamous male birds in determining reproductive success: Evidence for house wrens and a review of male-removal studies. *Behavioral Ecology and Sociobiology* 24:109–116.

Bartholomew, G. A. 1952. Reproductive and social behavior of the northern elephant seal. *University of California Publications in Zoology* 47:369–372.

Bartholomew, G. A. 1970. A model for the evolution of pinniped polygyny. *Evolution* 24:546–559.

Barton, R. 1985. Grooming site preferences in primates and their functional implications. *International Journal of Primatology* 6:519–531.

Bartos, L., and J. Madlafousek. 1994. Infanticide in a seasonal breeder: The case of red deer. *Animal Behaviour* 47:217–219.

Bateman, A. J. 1948. Intra-sexual selection in *Drosophila. Heredity* 2:349–368.

Bateson, P. 1978. Sexual imprinting and optimal outbreeding. *Nature* 273:659–660.

Bateson, P. 1980. Optimal outbreeding and the development of sexual preferences in Japanese quail. *Zeitschrift für Tierpsychologie* 53:231–244.

Bateson, P. 1983. Optimal outbreeding. Pages 257–277 in P. Bateson, ed., *Mate Choice*. Cambridge: Cambridge University Press.

Bayer, R. D. 1982. How important are bird colonies as information centers? *Auk* 99:31–40.

Bazin, R. C., and R. A. MacArthur. 1992. Thermal benefits of huddling in the muskrat *(Ondatra zibethicus). Journal of Mammalogy* 73:559–564.

Beach, F. A. 1956. Characteristics of masculine "sex drive." *Nebraska Symposium on Motivation* 4:1–32.

Beach, F. A. 1976. Sexual attractivity, proceptivity, and receptivity in female mammals. *Hormones and Behavior* 7:105–138.

Beach, F. A., and L. Jordan. 1956. Sexual exhaustion and recovery in the male rat. *Quarterly Journal of Experimental Psychology* 8:121–133.

Bearder, S. K. 1987. Lorises, bushbabies, and tarsiers: Diverse strategies in solitary foragers. Pages 11–24 in B. B. Smuts, D. L. Cheney, R. M. Seyfarth, R. W. Wrangham, and T. T. Struhsaker, eds., *Primate Societies*. Chicago: University of Chicago Press.

Beaver, R. A. 1977. Bark and ambrosia beetles in tropical forests. Pages 133–147 in *Proceedings of the Symposium of Forest Pests and Diseases in Southeast Asia. Biotropica* Special Publication, no. 2.

Bednarz, J. C. 1988. Cooperative hunting in Harris' hawk *(Parabuteo unicinctus). Science* 239:1525–1527.

Beecher, M. D. 1982. Signature systems and kin recognition. *American Zoologist* 22:477–490.

Beecher, M. D. 1988. Kin recognition in birds. *Behavioral Genetics* 18:465–482.

Beecher, M. D. 1990. The evolution of parent-offspring recognition in swallows. Pages 360–380 in D. A. Dewsbury, ed., *Contemporary Issues in Comparative Psychology*. Sunderland, Mass: Sinauer Associates.

Beecher, M. D., M. B. Medvin, P. K. Stoddard, and P. Loesche. 1986. Acoustic adaptations for parent-offspring recognition in swallows. *Experimental Biology* 45:179–183.

Beecher, M. D., P. K. Stoddard, and P. Loesche. 1985. Recognition of parent's voices by young cliff swallows. *Auk* 102:600–605.

Beer, C. G. 1970. Individual recognition of voice in the social behavior of birds. Pages 27–74 in D. S. Lehrman, R. A. Hinde, and E. Shaw, eds., *Advances in the Study of Behavior,* vol. 3. New York: Academic Press.

Bekoff, M. 1978. Social play: Structure, function, and the evolution of cooperative social behavior. Pages 367–383 in G. M. Burghardt and M. Bekoff, eds., *Development of Behavior: Comparative and Evolutionary Aspects.* New York: Garland Press.

Bekoff, M. 1981. Mammalian sibling interactions: Genes, facilitative environments, and the coefficient of familiarity. Pages 307–346 in D. J. Gubernick and P. H. Klopfer, eds., *Parental Care in Mammals.* New York: Plenum Press.

Bell, G. 1984. Measuring the cost of reproduction. I. The correlation structure of the life table of a rotifer. *Evolution* 38:300–313.

Bell, J. F., and C. Clifford. 1964. Effects of limb disability on lousiness of mice. II. Intersex grooming relationships. *Experimental Parasitology* 15:340–349.

Bell, W. B. 1920. Death to rodents. Pages 421–438 in *Yearbook of The United States Department of Agriculture* (1919). Washington, D.C.

Bennett, G. F. 1969. *Boophilus microplus* (Acarina: Ixodidae): Experimental infestations on cattle restrained from grooming. *Experimental Parasitology* 26:323–328.

Bennett, G. F. 1973. Some effects of *Cuterebra emasculator* Fitch (Diptera: Cuterebridae) on the blood and activity of its host, the eastern chipmunk. *Journal of Wildlife Diseases* 9:85–93.

Berenstain, L., P. S. Rodman, and D. G. Smith. 1981. Social relations between fathers and offspring in a captive group of rhesus monkeys *(Macaca mulatta). Animal Behaviour* 29:1057–1063.

Berger, J. 1978. Group size, foraging and antipredator ploys: An analysis of bighorn sheep decisions. *Behavioral Ecology and Sociobiology* 4:91–99.

Berger, J. 1983. Induced abortion and social factors in wild horses. *Nature* 303:59–61.

Berger, J. 1986. *Wild Horses of the Great Basin: Social Competition and Population Size.* Chicago: The University of Chicago Press.

Berger, J. 1992. Facilitation of reproductive synchrony by gestation adjustment in gregarious mammals: A new hypothesis. *Ecology* 73:323–329.

Berger, J., and C. Cunningham. 1987. Influence of familiarity on frequency of inbreeding in wild horses. *Evolution* 41:229–231.

Berger, J., and C. Cunningham. 1991. Bellows, copulations, and sexual selection in bison *(Bison bison). Behavioral Ecology* 2:1–6.

Bergerud, A. T. 1974. The role of environment in the aggregation, movement and disturbance behaviour of the caribou. Pages 552–584 in V. Geist and F. Walthers, eds., *The Behaviour of Ungulates and Its Relationship to Management.* Morges, Switzerland: IUCN.

Bertram, B. C. R. 1975. Social factors influencing reproduction in wild lions. *Journal of Zoology* 177:463–482.

Bertram, B. C. R. 1976. Kin selection in lions and in evolution. Pages 281–301 in P. P. G. Bateson and R. A. Hinde, eds., *Growing Points in Ethology.* Cambridge: Cambridge University Press.

Bertram, B. C. R. 1978. Living in groups: Predators and prey. Pages 64–96 in J. R. Krebs and N. B. Davies, eds., *Behavioural Ecology: An Evolutionary Approach.* 1st ed. Oxford: Blackwell Scientific Publications.

Bertram, B. C. R. 1979. Ostriches recognize their own eggs and discard others. *Nature* 279:233–234.

Bertram, B. C. R. 1980. Vigilance and group size in ostriches. *Animal Behaviour* 28:278–286.

Bertram, B. C. R. 1993. *The Ostrich Communal Nesting System.* Princeton, N.J.: Princeton University Press.

Betts, B. J. 1976. Behaviour in a population of Columbian ground squirrels, *Spermophilus columbianus columbianus. Animal Behaviour* 24:652–680.

Biggers, J. D., C. A. Flinn, and A. McLaren. 1962. Longterm reproductive performance of female mice. II. Variation of litter size with parity. *Journal of Reproduction and Fertility* 3:313–330.

Biggins, D., and M. H. Schroeder. 1988. Historical and present status of the black-footed ferret. Pages 93–97 in D. W. Uresk, G. L. Schenbeck, and R. Cefkin, technical coordinators, *Eighth Great Plains Wildlife Damage Control Workshop Proceedings.* General Technical Report RM-154. Fort Collins, Colo.

Birdsall, D. A., and D. Nash. 1973. Occurrence of successful multiple insemination of females in natural populations of deer mice *(Peromyscus maniculatus). Evolution* 27:106–110.

Birkhead, T. R. 1977. The effect of habitat and density on breeding success in common guillemots, *Uria aalge. Journal of Animal Ecology* 46:751–764.

Birkhead, T. R. 1978. Behavioural adaptations to high nesting density in the common guillemot *Uria aalge. Animal Behaviour* 26:321–331.

Birkhead, T. R., L. Atkin, and A. P. Møller. 1987. Copulation behaviour of birds. *Behaviour* 101:101–133.

Birkhead, T. R., and F. M. Hunter. 1990. Mechanisms of sperm competition. *Trends in Ecology and Evolution* 5:48–52.

Birkhead, T. R., and A. P. Møller. 1992. *Sperm Competition in Birds.* London: Academic Press.

Birkhead, T. R., and A. P. Møller. 1993. Why do male birds stop copulating while their partners are still fertile? *Animal Behaviour* 45:105–118.

Bischof, N. 1975. Comparative ethology of incest avoidance. In R. Fox, ed., *Biosocial Anthropology.* New York: John Wiley and Sons.

Bittles, A. H. 1979. Incest re-assessed. *Nature* 280:107.

Bittles, A. H. 1983. The intensity of human inbreeding depression. *Behavioral and Brain Sciences* 6:103–104.

Bixler, R. H. 1981. The incest controversy. *Psychological Reports* 48:531–536.

Bixler, R. H. 1992. Why littermates don't: The avoidance of inbreeding depression. *Annual Review of Sex Research* 3:291–328.

Black, C. C. 1963. A review of the North American Tertiary Sciuridae. *Museum of Comparative Zoology, Harvard University, Bulletin* 130:109–248.

Black, J. M., C. Carbone, R. L. Wells, and M. Owen. 1992. Foraging dynamics in goose flocks: The cost of living on the edge. *Animal Behaviour* 44:41–50.

Blake, B. H. 1992. Estrous calls in captive Asian chipmunks, *Tamias sibiricus. Journal of Mammalogy* 73:597–603.

Blake, B. H., and K. E. Gillett. 1988. Estrous cycle and related aspects of reproduction in captive Asian chipmunks, *Tamias sibiricus. Journal of Mammalogy* 69:598–603.

Blaustein, A. R., M. Bekoff, and T. J. Daniels. 1987a. Kin recognition in vertebrates (excluding primates): Empirical evidence. Pages 287–331 in D. J. C. Fletcher and C. D. Michener, eds., *Kin Recognition in Animals.* New York: John Wiley and Sons.

Blaustein, A. R., M. Bekoff, and T. J. Daniels. 1987b. Kin recognition in vertebrates (excluding primates): Mechanisms, functions, and future research. Pages 333–357 in D. J. C. Fletcher and C. D. Michener, eds., *Kin Recognition in Animals.* New York: John Wiley and Sons.

Blight, R. 1904. Truth about prairie dogs. *Current Literature* 37:75–76.

Blouin, S. F., and M. Blouin. 1988. Inbreeding avoidance behaviors. *Trends in Ecology and Evolution* 3:230–233.

Boag, D. A., and J. O. Murie. 1981. Population ecology of Columbian ground squirrels in southwestern Alberta. *Canadian Journal of Zoology* 59:2230–2240.

Boggess, J. E. 1979. Troop male membership changes and infant killing in langurs *(Presbytis entellus). Folia Primatologica* 32:65–107.

Boggess, J. E. 1984. Infant killing and male reproductive strategies in langurs *(Presbytis entellus).* Pages 283–310 in G. Hausfater and S. B. Hrdy, eds., *Infanticide: Comparative and Evolutionary Perspectives.* New York: Aldine.

Bollinger, E. K., S. J. Harper, J. M. Kramer, and G. W. Barrett. 1991. Avoidance of inbreeding in the meadow vole *(Microtus pennsylvanicus). Journal of Mammalogy* 72:419–421.

Bond, R. M. 1945. Range rodents and plant succession. *Transactions of the North American Wildlife Conference* 10:229–234.

Boness, D. J. 1990. Fostering behavior in Hawaiian monk seals: Is there a reproductive cost? *Behavioral Ecology and Sociobiology* 27:113–122.

Bonham, C. D., and A. Lerwick. 1976. Vegetation changes induced by prairie dogs on shortgrass range. *Journal of Range Management* 29:221–225.

Borgia, G. 1985. Bower quality, number of decorations and mating success of male satin bowerbirds *(Ptilonorynchus violaceus):* An experimental analysis. *Animal Behaviour* 33:266–271.

Borgia, G. 1987. A critical review of sexual selection models. Pages 55–66 in J. W. Bradbury and M. B. Anderson, eds., *Sexual Selection: Testing the Alternatives.* New York: John Wiley.

Boutin, S., R. A. Moses, and M. J. Caley. 1988. The relationship between juvenile survival and litter size in wild muskrats *(Ondatra zibethicus). Journal of Animal Ecology* 57:445–462.

Boyce, M. S. 1988. *Evolution of Life Histories of Mammals: Theory and Pattern.* New Haven, Conn.: Yale University Press.

Boyce, M. S., and C. M. Perrins. 1987. Optimizing great tit clutch size in a fluctuating environment. *Ecology* 68:142–153.

Boyd, S. K., and A. R. Blaustein. 1985. Familiarity and inbreeding avoidance in the gray-tailed vole *(Microtus canicaudus). Journal of Mammalogy* 66:348–352.

Bradbury, J. W. 1977. Lek mating behaviour in the hammer-headed bat. *Zeitschrift für Tierpsychologie* 45:225–255.

Bray, O. E., J. K. Kennelly, and J. L. Guarino. 1975. Fertility of eggs produced on territories of vasectomized red-winged blackbirds. *Wilson Bulletin* 87:187–195.

Breden, F., and G. Hausfater. 1990. Selection within and between social groups for infanticide. *American Naturalist* 136:673–688.

Brenneman, D. E., W. E. Connor, E. L. Forker, and L. DenBesten. 1972. The formation of abnormal bile and cholesterol gallstones from dietary cholesterol in the prairie dog. *Journal of Clinical Investigation* 51:1495–1503.

Brock Fenton, M. 1984. Sperm competition? The case of vespertilionid and rhonolophid [*sic*] bats. Pages 573–587 in R. L. Smith, ed., *Sperm Competition and the Evolution of Animal Mating Systems.* Orlando, Fla.: Academic Press.

Brody, A. K., and K. B. Armitage. 1985. The effects of adult removal on dispersal of yearling yellow-bellied marmots. *Canadian Journal of Zoology* 63:2560–2564.

Brody, A. K., and J. Melcher. 1985. Infanticide in yellow-bellied marmots. *Animal Behaviour* 33:673–674.

Bronson, F. H. 1979. The reproductive ecology of the house mouse. *Quarterly Review of Biology* 54:265–299.

Bronson, F. H. 1989. *Mammalian Reproductive Biology.* Chicago: University of Chicago Press.

Bronson, F. H., and A. Coquelin. 1980. The modulation of reproduction by priming pheromones in house mice: Speculations on adaptive function. Pages 243–265 in D. Muller-Schwarze and R. M. Silverstein, eds., *Chemical Signals: Vertebrates and Aquatic Invertebrates.* New York: Plenum Press.

Bronson, M. T. 1979. Altitudinal variation in the life history of the golden-mantled ground squirrel *(Spermophilus lateralis). Ecology* 60:272–279.

Brooker, M. G., I. Rowley, M. Adams, and P. R. Baverstock. 1990. Promiscuity: An inbreeding avoidance mechanism in a socially monogamous species. *Behavioral Ecology and Sociobiology* 26:191–199.

Broughton, G., A. Tseng, R. Fitzgibbons, S. Tyndall, G. Stanislav, and E. Rongone. 1991. The prevention of cholelithiasis with infused chenodeoxycholate in the prairie dog *(Cynomys ludovicianus)*. *Comparative Biochemical Physiology* 99A:609–613.

Brown, C. R. 1984. Laying eggs in a neighbor's nest: Benefit and cost of colonial nesting in swallows. *Science* 224:518–519.

Brown, C. R. 1985. The costs and benefits of coloniality in cliff swallows. Ph.D. dissertation, Princeton University, Princeton, N.J.

Brown, C. R. 1986. Cliff swallow colonies as information centers. *Science* 234:83–85.

Brown, C. R. 1988. Enhanced foraging efficiency through information centers: A benefit of coloniality in cliff swallows. *Ecology* 69:602–613.

Brown, C. R. 1992. Optimal colony size in cliff swallows. Pages 398–399 in J. W. Grier and T. Burk, eds. *Biology of Animal Behavior*. Saint Louis, Mo.: Mosby-Year Book.

Brown, C. R., and M. B. Brown. 1986. Ectoparasitism as a cost of coloniality in cliff swallows *(Hirundo pyrrhonota)*. *Ecology* 67:1206–1218.

Brown, C. R., and M. B. Brown. 1987. Group-living in cliff swallows as an advantage in avoiding predators. *Behavioral Ecology and Sociobiology* 21:97–107.

Brown, C. R., and M. B. Brown. 1988a. Genetic evidence of multiple parentage in broods of cliff swallows. *Behavioral Ecology and Sociobiology* 23:379–387.

Brown, C. R., and M. B. Brown. 1988b. A new form of reproductive parasitism in cliff swallows. *Nature* 331:66–68.

Brown, C. R., and M. B. Brown. 1989. Behavioural dynamics of intraspecific brood parasitism in colonial cliff swallows. *Animal Behaviour* 37:777–796.

Brown, C. R., and M. B. Brown. In press. *Coloniality in the Cliff Swallow: The Influence of Group Size on Social Behavior*.

Brown, C. R., M. B. Brown, and A. R. Ives. 1992. Nest placement relative to food and its influence on the evolution of avian coloniality. *American Naturalist* 139:205–217.

Brown, C. R., and J. L. Hoogland. 1986. Risk in mobbing for solitary and colonial swallows. *Animal Behaviour* 34:1319–1323.

Brown, C. R., B. J. Stutchbury, and P. D. Walsh. 1990. Choice of colony size in birds. *Trends in Ecology and Evolution* 5:398–403.

Brown, G. E., J. A. Brown, and A. M. Crosbie. 1993. Phenotype matching in juvenile rainbow trout. *Animal Behaviour* 46:1223–1225.

Brown, J. L. 1978. Avian communal breeding systems. *Annual Review of Ecology and Systematics* 9:123–155.

Brown, J. L. 1980. Fitness in complex avian social systems. Pages 115–128 in H. Markl, ed., *Evolution of Social Behavior: Hypotheses and Empirical Tests*. Dahlem Konferenzen. Weinheim: Verlag Chemie.

Brown, J. L. 1987. *Helping and Communal Breeding in Birds*. Princeton, N.J.: Princeton University Press.

Brown, J. L., and R. P. Balda. 1977. The relationship of habitat quality to group size in Hall's babbler *(Pomatostomus halli)*. *Condor* 79:312–320.

Brown, J. L., D. D. Dow, E. R. Brown, and S. D. Brown. 1983. Socioecology of the grey-crowned babbler: Population structure, unit size, and vegetation correlates. *Behavioral Ecology and Sociobiology* 13:115–124.

Brown, J. L., and G. H. Orians. 1970. Spacing patterns in mobile animals. *Annual Review of Ecology and Systematics* 1:239–262.

Bruce, H. M. 1959. An exteroceptive block to pregnancy in the mouse. *Nature* 184:105.

Bruce, H. M. 1960. A block to pregnancy in the house mouse caused by the proximity of strange males. *Journal of Reproduction and Fertility* 1:96–103.

Bruce, K. E., and D. Q. Estep. 1992. Interruption of and harassment during copulation by stumptail macaques, *Macaca arctoides*. *Animal Behaviour* 44:1029–1044.

Bruning, D. F. 1974. Social structure and reproductive behavior of the greater rhea. *Living Bird* 13:251–294.

Bryant, M. D. 1945. Phylogeny of nearctic Sciuridae. *American Midland Naturalist* 33:257–390.

Buckle, G. R., and L. Greenberg. 1981. Nestmate recognition in sweat bees *(Lasioglossum zephyrum):* Does an individual recognize its own odour or only odours of its nestmates? *Animal Behaviour* 29:802–809.

Buckley, P. A., and F. G. Buckley. 1972. Individual egg and chick recognition of adult royal terns *(Sterna maxima maxima)*. *Animal Behaviour* 20:457–462.

Bulger, J., and W. J. Hamilton. 1988. Inbreeding and reproductive success in a natural chacma baboon, *Papio cynocephalus ursinus,* population. *Animal Behaviour* 36:574–578.

Bull, J. J., and E. L. Charnov. 1988. How fundamental are Fisherian sex ratios? Pages 96–135 in P. H. Harvey and L. Partridge, eds., *Oxford Surveys in Evolutionary Biology,* vol. 5. New York: Oxford University Press.

Bulmer, M. G. 1973. Inbreeding in the great tit. *Heredity* 30:313–325.

Burger, J. 1974. Breeding adaptations of Franklin's gull *(Larus pipixcan)* to marsh habitat. *Animal Behaviour* 22:521–567.

Burger, J. 1984. *Pattern, Mechanism, and Adaptive Significance of Territoriality in Herring Gulls* (Larus argentatus). Ornithological Monographs, no. 34. Washington, D.C: American Ornithologists' Union.

Burger, J., and C. G. Beer. 1976. Territoriality in the laughing gull. *Behaviour* 55:301–320.

Burger, J., and M. Gochfeld. 1992. Effect of group size on vigilance while drinking in the coati, *Nasua narica* in Costa Rica. *Animal Behaviour* 44:1053–1057.

Burgerjon, J. J. 1964. Some census notes on a colony of South African cliff swallows *Petrochelidon spilodera* (Sundevall). *Ostrich* 35:77–85.

Burke, T. 1989. DNA fingerprinting and other methods for the study of mating success. *Trends in Ecology and Evolution* 4:139–144.

Burke, T., and M. W. Bruford. 1987. DNA fingerprinting in birds. *Nature* 327:149–152.

Burke, T., N. B. Davies, M. W. Bruford, and B. J. Hatchwell. 1989. Parental care and mating behavior of polyandrous dunnocks *Prunella modularis* related to paternity by DNA fingerprinting. *Nature* 338:249–251.

Burley, N. 1981. Sex-ratio manipulation and selection for attractiveness. *Science* 211:721–722.

Burley, N. 1986. Sex-ratio manipulation in color-banded populations of zebra finches. *Evolution* 40:1191–1206.

Burnett, W. L., and S. C. McCampbell. 1926. The Zuni prairie dog in Montezuma County, Colorado. *Colorado Agricultural College* 49:1–15.

Burns, J. R. 1968. The role of agonistic behavior in regulation of density in Uinta ground squirrels *(Citellus armatus).* Master's thesis, Utah State University, Logan, Utah.

Burt, W. H., and R. P. Grossenheider. 1976. *A Field Guide to the Mammals.* Boston: Houghton Mifflin.

Buscher, H. N., and J. D. Tyler. 1975. Parasites of vertebrates inhabiting prairie dog towns in Oklahoma. II. Helminths. *Proceedings of the Oklahoma Academy of Science* 55:108–111.

Busse, C. D., and D. Q. Estep. 1984. Sexual arousal in male pigtailed monkeys *(Macaca nemestrina):* Effects of serial matings by two males. *Journal of Comparative Psychology* 98:227–231.

Busse, C. D., and T. P. Gordon. 1983. Attacks on neonates by a male mangabey *(Cercocebus atys). American Journal of Primatology* 5:345–356.

Butler, H. 1974. Evolutionary trends in primate sex cycles. *Contributions to Primatology* 3:2–35.

Byers, J. A., J. D. Moodie, and N. Hall. 1994. Pronghorn females choose vigorous mates. *Animal Behaviour* 47:33–43.

Bygott, J. D. 1979. Agonistic behaviour, dominance, and social structure in wild chimpanzees of the Gombe National Park. Pages 404–427 in D. A. Hamburg and E. R. McCown, eds., *The Great Apes.* Menlo Park, Calif: Benjamin/Cummings.

Bygott, J. D., B. C. R. Bertram, and J. P. Hanby. 1979. Male lions in large coalitions gain reproductive advantages. *Nature* 282:839–841.

Cahalane, V. H. 1950. Badger-coyote "partnerships." *Journal of Mammalogy* 31:354–355.

Cahalane, V. H. 1954. Status of the black-footed ferret. *Journal of Mammalogy* 35:418–424.

Caley, M. J. 1987. Dispersal and inbreeding avoidance in muskrats. *Animal Behaviour* 35:1225–1233.

Calhoun, J. B. 1962. Population density and social pathology. *Scientific American* 206:139–148.

Callahan, J. R. 1981. Vocal solicitation and parental investment in female *Eutamias. American Naturalist* 118:872–875.

Calvert, W. H., L. E. Hedrick, and L. P. Brower. 1979. Mortality of the monarch butterfly *(Danaus plexippus* L.): Avian predation at five overwintering sites in Mexico. *Science* 204:847–851.

Camin, J. H., and W. W. Moss. 1970. Nest parasitism, productivity, and clutch size in purple martins. *Science* 168:1000–1002.

Campagna, C., C. Bisioli, F. Quintana, F. Perez, and A. Vila. 1992. Group breeding in sea lions: Pups survive better in colonies. *Animal Behaviour* 43:541–548.

Campagna, C., B. J. Le Boeuf, and H. Cappozzo. 1988. Pup abduction and infanticide in southern sea lions. *Behaviour* 107:44–60.

Campbell, T. M., and T. W. Clark. 1981. Colony characteristics and vertebrate associates of white-tailed and black-tailed prairie dogs in Wyoming. *American Midland Naturalist* 105:269–276.

Campbell, T. M., T. W. Clark, L. Richardson, S. C. Forrest, and B. R. Houston. 1987. Food habits of Wyoming black-footed ferrets. *American Midland Naturalist* 117:208–210.

Campbell, M. T., and N. A. Slade. 1993. Effect of mass on seasonal survivorship of northern cotton rats. *Journal of Mammalogy* 74:971–981.

Canals, M., M. Rosenmann, and F. Bozinovic. 1989. Energetics and geometry of huddling in small mammals. *Journal of Theoretical Biology* 141:181–189.

Caraco, T. 1979. Time budgeting and group size: A test of a theory. *Ecology* 60:618–627.

Caraco, T., and L. L. Wolf. 1975. Ecological determinants of group sizes of foraging lions. *American Naturalist* 109:343–352.

Carey, H. V., and P. Moore. 1986. Foraging and predation risk in yellow-bellied marmots *(Marmota flaviventris). American Midland Naturalist* 116:267–275.

Carl, E. A. 1971. Population control in arctic ground squirrels. *Ecology* 52:395–413.

Carlin, N. F., and B. Hölldobler. 1983. Nestmate and kin recognition in interspecific mixed colonies of ants. *Science* 222:1027–1029.

Casey, D. 1987. *The Friendly Prairie Dog.* New York: Dodd, Mead, and Company.

Casey, D. E., J. DuWaldt, and T. W. Clark. 1986. Annotated bibliography of the black-footed ferret. *Great Basin Naturalist Memoirs* 8:185–208.

Caswell, H. 1982. Optimal life histories and the age-specific costs of reproduction. *Journal of Theoretical Biology* 98:519–529.

Cates, E. C. 1927. Notes concerning a captive prairie-dog. *Journal of Mammalogy* 8:33–37.

Caughley, G. 1966. Mortality patterns in mammals. *Ecology* 47:906–918.

Caughley, G. 1977. *Analysis of Vertebrate Populations.* New York: John Wiley.

Cavalli-Sforza, L. L. 1977. *Elements of Human Genetics.* Elmsford, N.Y.: Benjamin.

Ceballos, G., and D. E. Wilson. 1985. *Cynomys mexicanus. Mammalian Species* 248:1–4.

Ceballos, G., E. Mellink, and L. Hanebury. 1993. Distribution and conservation status of prairie dogs *(Cynomys mexicanus* and *Cynomys ludovicianus)* in Mexico. *Biological Conservation* 63:105–112.

Chace, G. E. 1976. *Wonders of Prairie Dogs.* New York: Dodd, Mead, and Company.

Chadwick, D. H. 1993. The American prairie. *National Geographic* 184:90–119.

Chagnon, N. A. 1979. Mate competition, favoring close kin, and village fissioning among the Yanomamo Indians. Pages 86–131 in N. A. Chagnon and W. G. Irons, eds., *Evolutionary Biology and Human Social Behavior: An Anthropological Perspective.* North Scituate, Mass.: Duxbury Press.

Charles-Dominique, P. 1977. *Ecology and Behaviour of Nocturnal Prosimians.* London: Duckworth.

Charlesworth, B. 1977. Population genetics, demography and the sex ratio. Pages 345–363 in F. B. Christiansen and T. M. Fenchel, eds., *Measuring Selection in Natural Populations.* Berlin: Springer-Verlag.

Charlesworth, B. 1989. The evolution of sex and recombination. *Trends in Ecology and Evolution* 4:264–267.

Charnov, E. L. 1982. *The Theory of Sex Allocation.* Princeton, N.J.: Princeton University Press.

Charnov, E. L. 1993. *Life History Invariants: Some Explorations of Symmetry in Evolutionary Ecology.* Oxford: Oxford University Press.

Charnov, E. L., and J. R. Krebs. 1974. On clutch size and fitness. *Ibis* 116:217–219.

Charnov, E. L., and J. R. Krebs. 1975. The evolution of alarm calls: Altruism or manipulation? *American Naturalist* 109:107–112.

Chase, J. D., W. E. Howard, and J. T. Roseberry. 1982. Pocket gophers (Geomyidae). Pages 238–255 in J. A. Chapman and G. A. Feldhamer, eds., *Wild Mammals of North America.* Baltimore. Md.: Johns Hopkins University Press.

Cheeseman, C. L., J. W. Wilesmith, J. Ryan, and P. J. Mallinson. 1987. Badger population dynamics in a high density area. Pages 279–294 in S. Harris, ed., *Mammal Population Studies.* Oxford: Clarendon Press.

Cheney, D. L., and R. M. Seyfarth. 1981. Selective forces affecting the predator alarm calls of vervet monkeys. *Behaviour* 76:25–61.

Cheney, D. L., R. M. Seyfarth, S. J. Andelman, and P. C. Lee. 1988. Reproductive success in vervet monkeys. Pages 384–402 in T. H. Clutton-Brock, ed., *Reproductive Success: Studies of Individual Variation in Contrasting Breeding Systems.* Chicago: University of Chicago Press.

Cheng, T. C. 1974. *General Parasitology.* New York: Academic Press.

Chepko-Sade, B. D., and Z. T. Halpin, eds. 1987. *Mammalian Dispersal Patterns: The Effects of Social Structure on Population Genetics.* Chicago: University of Chicago Press.

Chesser, R. K. 1983. Genetic variability within and among populations of the black-tailed prairie dog. *Evolution* 37:320–331.

Chesser, R. K. 1991a. Gene diversity of female philopatry. *Genetics* 127:437–447.

Chesser, R. K. 1991b. Influence of gene flow and breeding tactics on gene diversity within populations. *Genetics* 129:573–583.

Chivers, D. J. 1969. On the daily behavior and spacing of howling monkey groups. *Folia Primatologica* 10:48–102.

Cicmanec, J. C., and A. K. Campbell. 1977. Breeding the owl monkey *(Aotus trivirgatus)* in a laboratory environment. *Laboratory Animal Science* 27:512–517.

Cid, M. S., J. K. Detling, A. D. Whicker, and M. A. Brizuela. 1991. Vegetational responses of a mixed-grass prairie site following exclusion of prairie dogs and bison. *Journal of Range Management* 44:100–105.

Cincotta, R. P., D. W. Uresk, and R. M. Hansen. 1987. Demography of black-tailed prairie dog populations reoccupying sites treated with rodenticide. *Great Basin Naturalist* 47:339–343.

Clark, A. B. 1978. Sex ratio and local resource competition in a prosimian primate. *Science* 201:163–165.

Clark, C. W., and M. Mangel. 1986. The evolutionary advantages of group foraging. *Theoretical Population Biology* 30:45–79.

Clark, G. M. 1959. Parasites of the gray squirrel. Pages 368–373 in V. Flyger, ed., *Symposium on the Gray Squirrel.* Maryland Department of Research and Education, no. 162. Maryland Game and Inland Fish Commission.

Clark, M. M., S. Bone, and B. G. Galef. 1990. Evidence of sex-biased maternal investment by Mongolian gerbils. *Animal Behaviour* 39:735–744.

Clark, M. M., C. L. Waddingham, and B. G. Galef. 1991. Further evidence of sex-biased maternal investment by Mongolian gerbil dams. *Animal Behaviour* 42:161–162.

Clark, T. W. 1968. *Ecological Roles of Prairie Dogs.* Laramie, Wyo.: Wyoming Range Management, no. 261.

Clark, T. W. 1971. Notes on White-tailed Prairie Dog *(Cynomys leucurus)* burrows. *Great Basin Naturalist* 31:115–124.

Clark, T. W. 1973. A field study of the ecology and ethology of the white-tailed prairie dog *(Cynomys leucurus):* With a model of *Cynomys* evolution. Ph.D. dissertation, University of Wisconsin, Madison, Wisc.

Clark, T. W. 1976. The black-footed ferret. *Oryx* 13:275–280.

Clark, T. W. 1977. *Ecology and Ethology of the White-tailed Prairie Dog (Cynomys leucurus).* Milwaukee: Publications in Biology and Geology, The Milwaukee Public Museum, no. 3.

Clark, T. W. 1978. Current status of the black-footed ferret in Wyoming. *Journal of Wildlife Management* 42:128–134.

Clark, T. W. 1979. The hard life of the prairie dog. *National Geographic* 156:270–281.

Clark, T. W. 1980. A listing of reports of black-footed ferrets in Wyoming (1851–1977). *Northwest Science* 54:47–54.

Clark, T. W. 1986. Some guidelines for management of the black-footed ferret. *Great Basin Naturalist Memoirs* 8:160–168.

Clark, T. W. 1989. *Conservation Biology of the Black-Footed Ferret,* Mustela nigripes. Special Scientific Report no. 3. Philadelphia: Wildlife Preservation Trust International.

Clark, T. W., and T. M. Campbell. 1981. Additional black-footed ferret *(Mustela nigripes)* reports in Wyoming. *Great Basin Naturalist* 41:360–361.

Clark, T. W., T. M. Campbell, M. H. Schroeder, and L. Richardson. 1984. *Handbook of Methods to Locate Black-Footed Ferrets.* Cheyenne, Wyo.: United States Department of Agriculture, Bureau of Land Management.

Clark, T. W., T. M. Campbell, D. G. Socha, and D. E. Casey. 1982. Prairie dog colony attributes and associated vertebrate species. *Great Basin Naturalist* 42:572–582.

Clark, T. W., S. C. Forrest, L. Richardson, D. E. Casey, and T. M. Campbell. 1986. Description and history of the Meeteetse black-footed ferret environment. *Great Basin Naturalist Memoirs* 8:72–84.

Clark, T. W., R. S. Hoffmann, and C. F. Nadler. 1971. *Cynomys leucurus. Mammalian Species* 7:1–4.

Clark, T. W., L. Richardson, D. Casey, T. M. Campbell, and S. C. Forrest. 1984. Seasonality of black-footed ferret diggings and prairie dog burrow plugging. *Journal of Wildlife Management* 48:1441–1444.

Clark, T. W., L. Richardson, S. C. Forrest, D. E. Casey, and T. M. Campbell. 1986. Descriptive ethology and activity patterns of black-footed ferrets. *Great Basin Naturalist Memoirs* 8:115–134.

Clarke, M. F. 1984. Co-operative breeding by the Australian bell miner *Manorina melanophrys:* A test of kin selection theory. *Behavioral Ecology and Sociobiology* 14:137–146.

Clayton, D. H. 1991. The influence of parasites on host sexual selection. *Parasitology Today* 7:329–334.

Clegg, M. T. 1959. Factors affecting gestation length and parturition. Pages 509–538 in H. H. Cole and P. T. Cupps, eds., *Reproduction in Domestic Animals.* 1st ed. London: Academic Press.

Clippinger, N. W. 1989. *Habitat Suitability Index Models: Black-Tailed Prairie Dog.* Biological Report 82 (10.156):1–21. Washington, D.C.: United States Department of the Interior, Fish and Wildlife Service, Research and Development.

Clutton-Brock, T. H. 1984. Reproductive effort and terminal investment in iteroparous animals. *American Naturalist* 123:212–229.

Clutton-Brock, T. H. 1986. Sex ratio variation in birds. *Ibis* 128:317–329.

Clutton-Brock, T. H., ed. 1988a. *Reproductive Success: Studies of Individual Variation in Contrasting Breeding Systems.* Chicago: University of Chicago Press.

Clutton-Brock, T. H. 1988b. Reproductive Success. Pages 472–485 in T. H. Clutton-Brock, ed., *Reproductive Success: Studies of Individual Variation in Contrasting Breeding Systems.* Chicago: University of Chicago Press.

Clutton-Brock, T. H. 1991. *The Evolution of Parental Care.* Princeton, N.J.: Princeton University Press.

Clutton-Brock, T. H., and S. D. Albon. 1979. The roaring of red deer and the evolution of honest advertisement. *Behaviour* 69:145–170.

Clutton-Brock, T. H., S. D. Albon, and F. E. Guinness. 1981. Parental investment in male and female offspring in polygynous mammals. *Nature* 289:487–489.

Clutton-Brock, T. H., S. D. Albon, and F. E. Guinness. 1983. The costs of reproduction to red deer hinds. *Journal of Animal Ecology* 52:367–383.

Clutton-Brock, T. H., S. D. Albon, and F. E. Guinness. 1984. Maternal dominance, breeding success and birth sex ratios in red deer. *Nature* 308:358–360.

Clutton-Brock, T. H., S. D. Albon, and F. E. Guinness. 1986. Great expectations: Maternal dominance sex ratios and offspring reproductive success in red deer. *Animal Behaviour* 34:460–471.

Clutton-Brock, T. H., S. D. Albon, and F. E. Guinness. 1987. Early development and population dynamics in red deer. I. Density-dependent effects on juvenile survival. *Journal of Animal Ecology* 56:53–67.

Clutton-Brock, T. H., S. D. Albon, and F. E. Guinness. 1988. Reproductive success in male and female red deer. Pages 325–343 in T. H. Clutton-Brock, ed., *Reproductive Success: Studies of Individual Variation in Contrasting Breeding Systems.* Chicago: University of Chicago Press.

Clutton-Brock, T. H., S. D. Albon, and F. E. Guinness. 1989. Fitness costs of gestation and lactation in wild mammals. *Nature* 337:260–262.

Clutton-Brock, T. H., F. E. Guinness, and S. D. Albon. 1982. *Red Deer: Behavior and Ecology of Two Sexes.* Chicago: University of Chicago Press.

Clutton-Brock, T. H., F. E. Guinness, and S. D. Albon. 1987. Interactions between population density and maternal characteristics affecting fecundity and juvenile survival in red deer. *Journal of Animal Ecology* 56:857–871.

Clutton-Brock, T. H., and P. H. Harvey. 1977a. Primate ecology and social organization. *Journal of Zoology* (London) 183:1–39.

Clutton-Brock, T. H., and P. H. Harvey. 1977b. Species differences in feeding and ranging behaviour of primates. Pages 557–584 in T. H. Clutton-Brock, ed., *Primate Ecology: Studies of Feeding and Ranging Behaviour in Lemurs, Monkeys, and Apes.* New York: Academic Press.

Clutton-Brock, T. H., P. H. Harvey, and B. Rudder. 1977. Sexual dimorphism, socionomic sex ratio and body weight in primates. *Nature* 269:797–799.

Clutton-Brock, T. H., M. Hiraiwa-Hasegawa, and A. Robertson. 1989. Mate choice on fallow deer leks. *Nature* 340:463–465.

Clutton-Brock, T. H., and G. R. Iason. 1986. Sex ratio variation in mammals. *Quarterly Review of Biology* 61:339–374.

Cockburn, A., P. Scott, and D. J. Scotts. 1985. Inbreeding avoidance and male-biased natal dispersal in *Antechinus* spp. (Marsupialia: Dasyuridae). *Animal Behaviour* 33:908–915.

Collier, G. D. 1975. *The Utah Prairie Dog: Abundance, Distribution, and Habitat Requirements.* Publication no. 75-10. Cedar City, Utah: State of Utah, Department of Natural Resources, Division of Wildlife Resources.

Collier, G. D., and J. J. Spillett. 1972a. Prairie dogs . . . a legend in danger. *Utah Science* 33:22–25.

Collier, G. D., and J. J. Spillett. 1972b. Status of the Utah prairie dog. *Proceedings of the Utah Academy of Sciences, Arts, and Letters* 49:27–39.

Collier, G. D., and J. J. Spillett. 1973. The Utah prairie dog—decline of a legend. *Utah Science* 34:83–87.

Collier, G. D., and J. J. Spillett. 1975. Factors influencing the distribution of the Utah prairie dog, *Cynomys parvidens* (Sciuridae). *Southwestern Naturalist* 20:151–158.

Collins, A. R., J. P. Workman, and D. W. Uresk. 1984. An economic analysis of black-tailed prairie dog [*Cynomys ludovicianus*] control. *Journal of Range Management* 37:358–361.

Collopy, M. W. 1986. Food consumption and growth energetics of nestling golden eagles. *Wilson Bulletin* 98:445–458.

Connor, J. L., and M. J. Belluchi. 1979. Natural selection resisting inbreeding depression in captive wild house mice *(Mus musculus)*. *Evolution* 33:929–940.

Conover, W. J. 1971. *Practical Nonparametric Statistics.* New York: John Wiley and Sons.

Cooke, F., and R. F. Rockwell. 1988. Reproductive success in a lesser snow goose population. Pages 237–250 in T. H. Clutton-Brock, ed., *Reproductive Success: Studies of Individual Variation in Contrasting Breeding Systems.* Chicago: University of Chicago Press.

Cooper, W. E., and L. J. Vitt. 1991. Influence of detectability and escape on natural selection of conspicuous autonomous defenses. *Canadian Journal of Zoology* 69:757–764.

Coppock, D. L., J. K. Detling, J. E. Ellis, and M. I. Dyer. 1983. Plant-herbivore interactions in a North American mixed-grass prairie. I. Effects of black-tailed prairie dogs on intraseasonal aboveground plant biomass and nutrient dynamics and plant species diversity. *Oecologia* 56:1–9.

Coppock, D. L., J. E. Ellis, J. K. Detling, and M. I. Dyer. 1983. Plant-herbivore interactions in a North American mixed-grass prairie. II. Responses of bison to modification of vegetation by prairie dogs. *Oecologia* 56:10–15.

Costa, D. P., and R. L. Gentry. 1986. Free ranging energetics of northern fur seals. Pages 79–101 in R. L. Gentry and G. L. Kooyman, eds., *Fur Seals: Maternal Strategies on Land and at Sea.* Princeton, N.J.: Princeton University Press.

Costello, D. F. 1970. *The World of the Prairie Dog.* Philadelphia: Lippincott.

Cothran, E. G., R. K. Chesser, M. H. Smith, and P. E. Johns. 1983. Influences of genetic variability and maternal factors on fetal growth in white-tailed deer. *Evolution* 37:282–291.

Cottam, C., and M. Caroline. 1965. The black-tailed prairie dog in Texas. *Texas Journal of Science* 17:294–302.

Couch, L. K. 1930. Notes on the yellow-bellied marmot. *Murrelet* 11:1–6.

Coues, E., and J. A. Allen. 1877. *Monographs of North American Rodentia.* United States Survey of the Territories, vol. 11. Washington, D.C.: Government Printing Office.

Coulson, J. C. 1966. The influence of the pair-bond and age on the breeding biology of the kittiwake gull *Rissa tridactyla. Journal of Animal Ecology* 35:269–279.

Coulson, J. C. 1968. Differences in the quality of birds nesting in the centre and on the edges of a colony. *Nature* 217:478–479.

Coulson, J. C., and F. Dixon. 1979. Colonial breeding in sea-birds. Pages 445–458 in G. Larwood and B. R. Rosen, eds., *Biology and Systematics of Colonial Organisms.* Systematics Association Special Volume, no. 11. London: Academic Press.

Coulson, J. C., and J. Horobin. 1976. The influence of age on the breeding biology and survival of the arctic tern *Sterna paradisaea. Journal of Zoology* 178:247–260.

Coulson, J. C., and J. M. Porter. 1985. Reproductive success of the kittiwake *Rissa tridactyla:* The roles of clutch size, chick grow rates and parental quality. *Ibis* 127:450–466.

Cowlishaw, G., and R. I. M. Dunbar. 1991. Dominance rank and mating success in male primates. *Animal Behaviour* 41:1045–1056.

Cox, C. R., and B. J. Le Boeuf. 1977. Female incitation of male competition: A mechanism in sexual selection. *American Naturalist* 111:317–335.

Cox, M. K., and W. L. Franklin. 1990. Premolar gap technique for aging live black-tailed prairie dogs. *Journal of Wildlife Management* 54:143–146.

Craig, J. L. 1980. Pair and group breeding behaviour of a communal gallinule, pukeko, *Porphyrio p. melanotus. Animal Behaviour* 28:593–603.

Craig, J. L., and I. G. Jamieson. 1985. The relationship between presumed gamete contribution and parental investment in a communally breeding bird. *Behavioral Ecology and Sociobiology* 17:207–211.

Craig, J. L., and I. G. Jamieson. 1988. Incestuous mating in a communal bird: A family affair. *American Naturalist* 131:58–70.

Creel, S. R., and N. M. Creel. 1991. Energetics, reproductive suppression and obligate communal breeding in carnivores. *Behavioral Ecology and Sociobiology* 28:263–270.

Creel, S. R., N. M. Creel, D. E. Wildt, and S. L. Monfort. 1992. Behavioural and endocrine mechanisms of reproductive suppression in Serengeti dwarf mongooses. *Animal Behaviour* 43:231–245.

Creel, S. R., S. L. Monfort, D. E. Wildt, and P. M. Waser. 1991. Spontaneous lactation is an adaptive result of pseudopregnancy. *Nature* 351:660–662.

Crespi, B. J. 1992. Eusociality in Australian gall thrips. *Nature* 359:724–726.

Crocker-Bedford, D. C., and J. J. Spillett. 1977. Home ranges of Utah prairie dogs. *Journal of Mammalogy* 58:672–673.

Crocker-Bedford, D. C., and J. J. Spillett. 1981. *Habitat Relationships of the Utah Prairie Dog.* Washington, D.C.: United States Government Publication 1981-0-677-202/4.

Crockett, C. M., and J. F. Eisenberg. 1987. Howlers: Variations in group size and demography. Pages 54–68 in B. B. Smuts, D. L. Cheney, R. M. Seyfarth, R. W. Wrangham, and T. T. Struhsaker, eds., *Primate Societies.* Chicago: The University of Chicago Press.

Crockett, C. M., and R. Sekulic. 1984. Infanticide in red howler monkeys *(Alouatta seniculus)*. Pages 173–191 in G. Hausfater and S. B. Hrdy, eds., *Infanticide: Comparative and Evolutionary Perspectives.* New York: Aldine.

Crook, J. H. 1960. Studies on the social behaviour of *Quelea q. quelea* in French West Africa. *Behaviour* 16:1–55.

Crook, J. H. 1964. The evolution of social organization and visual communication in the weaver birds (Ploceinae). *Behaviour Supplement* 10:1–178.

Crosby, L. A., and R. Graham. 1986. Population dynamics and expansion rates of black-tailed prairie dogs. Pages 112–115 in T. P. Salmon, ed., *Proceedings of the Twelfth Vertebrate Pest Conference.* University of California, Davis, Calif.

Crow, J., and M. Kimura. 1970. *An Introduction to Population Genetics Theory.* New York: Harper and Row.

Crozier, R. H. 1987. Genetic aspects of kin recognition: Concepts, models, and synthesis. Pages 55–73 in D. J. C. Fletcher and C. D. Michener, eds., *Kin Recognition in Animals.* New York: John Wiley and Sons.

Cullen, E. 1957. Adaptations in the kittiwake to cliff-nesting. *Ibis* 99:275–303.

Cullen, J. M. 1960. Some adaptations in the nesting behaviour of terns. Pages 153–157 in *Proceedings XII International Ornithological Congress,* Helsinki, 1958.

Cully, J. F. 1989. Plague in prairie dog ecosystems: Importance for black-footed ferret management. Pages 47–55 in T. W. Clark, D. Hinckley, and T. Rich, eds., *The Prairie Dog Ecosystem: Managing for Biological Diversity.* Wildlife Technical Bulletin no. 2. Billings, Mont.: Montana Bureau of Land Management.

Curio, E. 1983. Why do young birds reproduce less well? *Ibis* 125:400–403.

Curry, R. L. 1988. Influence of kinship on helping behavior in Galápagos mockingbirds. *Behavioral Ecology and Sociobiology* 22:141–152.

Curtin, R. A., and P. Dolhinow. 1978. Primate social behavior in a changing world. *American Scientist* 66:468–475.

Curtin, R. A., and P. Dolhinow. 1979. Infanticide among langurs: A solution to overcrowding? *Science Today* (New Delhi) 13:35–41.

Curtsinger, J. W., and I. L. Heisler. 1988. A diploid "sexy son" model. *American Naturalist* 132:437–453.

Cushing, F. H. 1931. *Zuni Folk Tales.* New York: Alfred A. Knopf.

Dale, H. F. 1947. Prairie dogs as pets. *Outdoor Nebraska* 24:22.

Daley, J. G. 1989. Relationships between population control and genetic variability in black-tailed prairie dogs. Master's thesis, Frostburg State University, Frostburg, Md.

Daley, J. G. 1992. Population reductions and genetic variability in black-tailed prairie dogs. *Journal of Wildlife Management* 56:212–220.

Dalquest, W. W. 1953. *Mammals of the Mexican State of San Luis Potosi.* Louisiana State University Studies, Biological Series 1.

Dalquest, W. W. 1967. Mammals of the Pleistocene Slaton local fauna of Texas. *Southwestern Naturalist* 12:1–30.

Dane, D. S. 1948. A disease of Manx shearwaters *(Puffinis puffinus)*. *Journal of Animal Ecology* 17:158–192.

Darling, F. F. 1937. *A Herd of Red Deer.* Oxford: Oxford University Press.

Darling, F. F. 1938. *Bird Flocks and the Breeding Cycle.* Cambridge: Cambridge University Press.

Darlington, C. D. 1960. Cousin marriage and the evolution of the breeding system in man. *Heredity* 14:297–332.

Darwin, C. R. 1859. *On the Origin of Species by Means of Natural Selection, or, the Preservation of Favoured Races in the Struggle for Life.* London: John Murray.

Darwin, C. R. 1871. *The Descent of Man and Selection in Relation to Sex.* London: John Murray.

Davidov, G. S., I. M. Neranov, G. P. Usachev, and E. P. Yakovlev. 1978. *Distribution and Ecology.* Moscow: Nauka.

Davies, N. B. 1985. Cooperation and conflict among dunnocks, *Prunella modularis,* in a variable mating system. *Animal Behaviour* 33:628–648.

Davies, N. B. 1992. *Dunnock Behaviour and Social Evolution.* Oxford: Oxford University Press.

Davies, N. B., B. J. Hatchwell, T. Robson, and T. Burke. 1992. Paternity and parental effort in dunnocks *Prunella modularis:* How good are male chick-feeding rules? *Animal Behaviour* 43:729–745.

Davies, S., and R. Carrick. 1962. On the ability of crested terns, *Sterna bergii,* to recognize their own young. *Australian Journal of Zoology* 10:171–177.

Davis, A. H. 1966. Winter activity of the black-tailed prairie dog in north-central Colorado. Master's thesis, Colorado State University, Fort Collins, Colo.

Davis, G. E. 1935. Tularemia. Susceptibility of the white-tailed prairie dog, *Cynomys leucurus* Merriam. *United States Public Health Report* 50:731–732.

Davis, J. W., and R. C. Anderson, eds. 1971. *Parasitic Diseases of Wild Animals.* Ames, Iowa: Iowa State University.

Davis, J. W. F. 1975. Age, egg-size, and breeding success in the herring gull, *Larus argentatus. Ibis* 117:460–472.

Davis, L. S. 1982a. Copulatory behaviour of Richardson's ground squirrels *(Spermophilus richardsonii)* in the wild. *Canadian Journal of Zoology* 60:2953–2955.

Davis, L. S. 1982b. Sibling recognition in Richardson's ground squirrels *Spermophilus richardsonii. Behavioral Ecology and Sociobiology* 11:65–70.

Davis, L. S. 1984a. Alarm calling in Richardson's ground squirrels *(Spermophilus richardsonii). Zeitschrift für Tierpsychologie* 66:152–164.

Davis, L. S. 1984b. Behavioral interactions of Richardson's ground squirrels: Asymmetries based on kinship. Pages 424–444 in J. O. Murie and G. R. Michener, eds., *The Biology of Ground-Dwelling Squirrels.* Lincoln, Nebr.: University of Nebraska Press.

Davis, L. S. 1984c. Kin selection and adult female Richardson's ground squirrels: A test. *Canadian Journal of Zoology* 62:2344–2348.

Davis, L. S., and J. O. Murie. 1985. Male territoriality and the mating system of Richardson's ground squirrels *(Spermophilus richardsonii)*. *Journal of Mammalogy* 66:268–279.

Davis, R. B., C. F. Herreid, and H. L. Short. 1962. Mexican free-tailed bats in Texas. *Ecological Monographs* 32:311–346.

Davis, R. O. 1986. Digital signal processing and the referents of animal acoustical communication. Ph.D. dissertation, University of California at Davis, Davis, Calif.

Dawkins, R. 1976. *The Selfish Gene.* New York: Oxford University Press.

Dawkins, R. 1979. Twelve misunderstandings of kin selection. *Zeitschrift für Tierpsychologie* 51:184–200.

Dawkins, R. 1982. *The Extended Phenotype.* San Francisco: W. H. Freeman.

Dawkins, R. 1986. *The Blind Watchmaker: Why the Evidence of Evolution Reveals a Universe Without Design.* New York: W. W. Norton.

Day, C. S., and B. G. Galef. 1977. Pup cannibalism: One aspect of maternal behavior in golden hamsters. *Journal of Comparative and Physiological Psychology* 91:1179–1189.

Deevey, E. S. 1947. Life tables for natural populations of animals. *Quarterly Review of Biology* 22:283–314.

Delcroix, I., J. P. Signoret, and R. Mauget. 1985. Communal rearing of the young within the social group of the European wild boar. *Annales de Zootechnie* 34:369.

DeSteven, D. 1980. Clutch size, breeding success, and parental survival in the tree swallow *(Iridoprocne bicolor)*. *Evolution* 34:278–291.

Devenport, J. A. 1989. Social influences on foraging in black-tailed prairie dogs. *Journal of Mammalogy* 70:166–168.

de Waal, F. B. M. 1982. *Chimpanzee Politics.* London: Allen and Unwin.

Dewsbury, D. A. 1972. Patterns of copulatory behavior in male mammals. *Quarterly Review of Biology* 47:1–33.

Dewsbury, D. A. 1975. Diversity and adaptation in rodent copulatory behavior. *Science* 190:947–954.

Dewsbury, D. A. 1978. The comparative method in studies of reproductive behavior. Pages 83–112 in T. E. McGill, D. A. Dewsbury, and B. D. Sachs, eds., *Sex and Behavior: Status and Prospectus.* New York: Plenum Press.

Dewsbury, D. A. 1979. Copulatory behavior of deer mice *(Peromyscus maniculatus):* I. Normative data, subspecific differences, and effects of cross-fostering. *Journal of Comparative Physiological Psychology* 93:151–160.

Dewsbury, D. A. 1982a. Dominance rank, copulatory behavior, and differential reproduction. *Quarterly Review of Biology* 57:135–159.

Dewsbury, D. A. 1982b. Ejaculate cost and male choice. *American Naturalist* 119:601–610.

Dewsbury, D. A. 1984. Sperm competition in muroid rodents. Pages 547–571 in R. L. Smith, ed., *Sperm Competition and the Evolution of Mating Systems.* Orlando, Fla.: Academic Press.

Dewsbury, D. A. 1985. Interactions between males and their sperm during multi-male copulatory episodes of deer mice *(Peromyscus maniculatus)*. *Animal Behaviour* 33:1266–1274.

Dewsbury, D. A. 1988. A test of the role of copulatory plugs in sperm competition in deer mice *(Peromyscus maniculatus)*. *Journal of Mammalogy* 69:854–857.

Dewsbury, D. A., and D. J. Baumgardner. 1981. Studies of sperm competition in two species of muroid rodents. *Behavioral Ecology and Sociobiology* 9:121–133.

Dewsbury, D. A., and D. Q. Estep. 1975. Pregnancy in cactus mice: Effects of prolonged copulation. *Science* 187:552–553.

Dewsbury, D. A., and T. G. Hartung. 1980. Copulatory behaviour and differential reproduction of laboratory rats in a two-male, one-female competitive situation. *Animal Behaviour* 28:95–102.

Diamond, M., and M. Mast. 1978. Crowding, reproduction, and maternal behavior in the golden hamster. *Behavioral Biology* 23:477–486.

Dickemann, M. 1975. Demographic consequences of infanticide in man. *Annual Review of Ecology and Systematics* 6:107–137.

Dickemann, M. 1979. The reproductive structure of stratified societies: A preliminary model. Pages 331–367 in N. A. Chagnon and W. Irons, eds., *Evolutionary Biology and Human Social Organization: An Anthropological Perspective*. North Scituate, Mass.: Duxbury Press.

Dickemann, M. 1981. Paternal confidence and dowry competition: A bicultural analysis of purdah. Pages 417–438 in R. D. Alexander and D. W. Tinkle, eds., *Natural Selection and Social Behavior*. New York: Chiron Press.

Dickerman, R. W. 1960. "Davian behavior complex" in ground squirrels. *Journal of Mammalogy* 41:403.

Dimond, S., and J. Lazarus. 1974. The problem of vigilance in animal life. *Brain, Behavior, and Evolution* 9:60–79.

Dittus, W. 1975. Population dynamics of the toque monkey *(Macaca sinica)*. Pages 125–152 in R. H. Tuttle, ed., *Socioecology and Psychology of Primates*. The Hague: Mouton.

Dobson, F. S. 1982. Competition for mates and predominant juvenile male dispersal in mammals. *Animal Behaviour* 30:1183–1192.

Dobson, F. S. 1990. Environmental influences on infanticide in Columbian ground squirrels. *Ethology* 84:3–14.

Dobson, F. S., and W. T. Jones. 1985. Multiple causes of dispersal. *American Naturalist* 126:855–858.

Dobson, F. S., and J. D. Kjelgaard. 1985. The influence of food resources on life history of Columbian ground squirrels. *Canadian Journal of Zoology* 63:2105–2109.

Dobzhansky, T. 1951. *Genetics and the Origin of Species*. New York: Columbia University Press.

Dolan, P. G., and D. C. Carter. 1977. *Glaucomys volans*. *Mammalian Species* 78:1–6.

Douglas-Hamilton, I., and O. Douglas-Hamilton. 1975. *Among the Elephants*. Glasgow: Collins.

Downhower, J. F., and K. B. Armitage. 1971. The yellow-bellied marmot and the evolution of polygamy. *American Naturalist* 105:355–370.

Downhower, J. F., and K. B. Armitage. 1981. Dispersal of yearling yellow-bellied marmots *(Marmota flaviventris). Animal Behaviour* 29:1064–1069.

Drearden, L. C. 1953. The gross anatomy of the viscera of the prairie dog. *Journal of Mammalogy* 34:15–26.

Drent, R., and P. Swierstra. 1977. Goose flocks and food finding: Field experiments with barnacle geese *(Branta leucopsis)* in winter. *Wildfowl* 28:15–20.

Drickamer, L. C. 1974. A ten-year summary of reproductive data for free-ranging *Macaca mulatta. Folia Primatologica* 21:61–80.

Drickamer, L. C., and S. Vessey. 1973. Group changing in free-ranging male rhesus monkeys. *Primates* 14:359–368.

Dublin, H. T. 1983. Cooperation and reproductive competition among female African elephants. Pages 291–313 in S. K. Wasser, ed., *Social Behavior of Female Vertebrates.* New York: Academic Press.

Dudley, R., and K. Milton. 1990. Parasite deterrence and the energetic costs of slapping in howler monkeys, *Alouatta palliata. Journal of Mammalogy* 71:463–465.

Duffy, D. C. 1983. The ecology of tick parasitism on densely nesting Peruvian seabirds. *Ecology* 64:110–119.

Dunbar, R. I. M. 1988. *Primate Social Systems.* London: Croom Helm.

Dunbar, R. I. M. 1991. Functional significance of social grooming in primates. *Folia Primatologica* 57:121–131.

Dunford, C. 1975. Density limitation and the social system of round-tailed ground squirrels. Ph.D. dissertation, University of Arizona, Tucson, Ariz.

Dunford, C. 1977a. Behavioral limitation of round-tailed ground squirrel density. *Ecology* 58:1254–1268.

Dunford, C. 1977b. Kin selection for ground squirrel alarm calls. *American Naturalist* 111:782–785.

Dunford, C. 1977c. Social system of round-tailed ground squirrels. *Animal Behaviour* 25:885–906.

Dziuk, P. J. 1965. Double mating of rabbits to determine capacitation time. *Journal of Reproduction and Fertility* 10:389–395.

Dziuk, P. J. 1977. Reproduction in pigs. Pages 455–474 in H. H. Cole and P. T. Cupps, eds. *Reproduction in Domestic Animals.* 3d ed. New York: Academic Press.

Eberhard, W. G. 1985. *Sexual Selection and Animal Genitalia.* Cambridge, Mass.: Harvard University Press.

Eberle, I. 1974. *Prairie Dogs in Prairie Dog Town.* New York: Thomas Y. Crowell.

Ecke, D. H., and C. W. Johnson. 1950. Sylvatic plague in Park County, Colorado. *Transactions of the North American Wildlife Conference* 15:191–196.

Ecke, D. H., and C. W. Johnson. 1952. Plague in Colorado. *United States Public Health Monograph* 6, Part I.

Edwards, R. G. 1955. Selective fertilization following the use of sperm mixtures in the mouse. *Nature* 175:215.

Edwards, R. L. 1946. Some notes on the life history of the Mexican ground squirrel in Texas. *Journal of Mammalogy* 27:105–115.

Ehrlich, A. H., and P. R. Ehrlich. 1978. Reproductive strategies in the butterflies. I. Mating frequency, plugging, and egg number. *Journal of the Kansas Entomological Society* 51:666–697.

Eickwort, K. R. 1973. Cannibalism and kin selection in *Labidomera clivicollis* (Coleoptera: Chrysomelidae). *American Naturalist* 107:452–453.

Eisenberg, J. F. 1966. The social organization of mammals. *Handbuch der Zoologie* 10:1–92.

Eisenberg, J. T. 1988. Reproduction in polyprotodont marsupials and similar-sized eutherians with a speculation concerning the evolution of litter size in mammals. Pages 291–310 in M. S. Boyce, ed., *Evolution of Life Histories in Mammals*. New Haven, Conn.: Yale University Press.

Elgar, M. A. 1989. Predator vigilance and group size in mammals and birds: A critical review of the empirical evidence. *Biological Review* 64:13–33.

Elgar, M. A., and B. J. Crespi. 1992. Ecology and evolution of cannibalism. Pages 299–322 in M. A. Elgar and B. J. Crespi, eds., *Cannibalism: Ecology and Evolution among Diverse Taxa*. New York: Oxford University Press.

Elgar, M. A., H. McKay, and P. Woon. 1986. Scanning, pecking and alarm flights in house sparrows. *Animal Behaviour* 34:1892–1894.

Elliot, M. W., P. K. Sehgal, and L. V. Chalifoux. 1976. Management and breeding of *Aotus trivirgatus*. *Laboratory Animal Science* 26:1037–1040.

Elliott, P. F. 1975. Longevity and the evolution of polygamy. *American Naturalist* 109:281–287.

Elwood, R. W. 1983. Paternal care in rodents. Pages 235–257 in R. W. Elwood, ed., *Parental Behaviour of Rodents*. New York: John Wiley.

Elwood, R. W. 1991. Parental states as mechanisms for kinship recognition and deception about relatedness. Pages 289–307 in P. Hepper, ed., *Kin Recognition*. Cambridge: Cambridge University Press.

Elwood, R. W. 1992. Pup-cannibalism in rodents: Causes and consequences. Pages 299–322 in M. A. Elgar and B. J. Crespi, eds., *Cannibalism: Ecology and Evolution among Diverse Taxa*. New York: Oxford University Press.

Elwood, R. W., and M. C. Ostermeyer. 1984a. Does copulation inhibit infanticide in male rodents? *Animal Behaviour* 32:293–294.

Elwood, R. W., and M. C. Ostermeyer. 1984b. Infanticide by male and female Mongolian gerbils: Ontogeny, causation, and function. Pages 367–386 in G. Hausfater and S. B. Hrdy, eds., *Infanticide: Comparative and Evolutionary Perspectives*. New York: Aldine.

Elwood, R. W., and M. C. Ostermeyer. 1984c. The effects of food deprivation, aggression, and isolation on infanticide in the male Mongolian gerbil. *Aggressive Behavior* 10:293–301.

Emlen, J. M. 1970. Age specificity and ecological theory. *Ecology* 51:588–601.

Emlen, S. T. 1982a. The evolution of helping. I. An ecological constraints model. *American Naturalist* 119:29–39.

Emlen, S. T. 1982b. The evolution of helping. II. The role of behavioral conflict. *American Naturalist* 119:40–53.

Emlen, S. T. 1991. Cooperative breeding in birds and mammals. Pages 301–337 in J. R. Krebs and N. B. Davies, eds., *Behavioural Ecology: An Evolutionary Approach.* 3d ed. Oxford: Blackwell Scientific Publications.

Emlen, S. T., and N. J. Demong. 1975. Adaptive significance of synchronized breeding in a colonial bird: A new hypothesis. *Science* 188:1029–1031.

Emlen, S. T., J. M. Emlen, and S. A. Levin. 1986. Sex-ratio selection in species with helpers-at-the-nest. *American Naturalist* 127:1–8.

Emlen, S. T., and L. W. Oring. 1977. Ecology, sexual selection, and the evolution of mating systems. *Science* 197:215–223.

Emlen, S. T., H. K. Reeve, P. W. Sherman, P. H. Wrege, F. L. W. Ratnieks, and J. Shellman-Reeve. 1991. Adaptive versus nonadaptive explanations of behavior: The case of alloparental helping. *American Naturalist* 138:259–270.

Emlen, S. T., and S. L. Vehrencamp. 1985. Cooperative breeding strategies among birds. Pages 359–374 in B. Hölldobler and M. Lindauer, eds., *Experimental Behavioral Ecology.* Stuttgart and New York: G. Fischer.

Emlen, S. T., and P. H. Wrege. 1986. Forced copulations and intra-specific parasitism: Two costs of social living in the white-fronted bee-eater. *Ethology* 71:2–29.

Emlen, S. T., and P. H. Wrege. 1988. The role of kinship in helping decisions among white-fronted bee-eaters. *Behavioral Ecology and Sociobiology* 23:305–315.

Emlen, S. T., and P. H. Wrege. 1989. A test of alternate hypotheses for helping behavior in white-fronted bee-eaters in Kenya. *Behavioral Ecology and Sociobiology* 25:303–319.

Emlen, S. T., and P. H. Wrege. 1992. Parent-offspring conflict and the recruitment of helpers among bee-eaters. *Nature* 356:331–333.

Endler, J. A., and A. M. Lyles. 1989. Bright ideas about parasites. *Trends in Ecology and Evolution* 4:246–248.

Erpino, M. J. 1968. Copulatory behavior in the white-tailed prairie dog. *American Midland Naturalist* 79:250–251.

Errington, P. L. 1963. *Muskrat Populations.* Ames, Iowa: Iowa State University Press.

Erwin, R. M. 1978. Coloniality in terns: The role of social feeding. *Condor* 80:211–215.

Erwin, R. M. 1979. Foraging and breeding adaptations to different food regimes in three seabirds: The common tern, *Sterna hirundo,* royal tern, *Sterna maxima,* and black skimmer, *Rynchops niger. Ecology* 58:389–397.

Erwin, W. 1971. The gross and histological anatomy of the perianal glands of the black-tailed prairie dog *(Cynomys ludovicianus).* Unpublished honors thesis, University of Northern Colorado, Greeley, Colo.

Eskey, C. R., and V. H. Haas. 1940. Plague in the western part of the United States. *United States Public Health Bulletin* 254:1–83.

Estep, D. Q., T. P. Gordon, M. E. Wilson, and M. L. Walker. 1986. Social stimulation and the resumption of copulation in rhesus *(Macaca mulatta)* and stumptail *(Macaca arctoides)* macaques. *International Journal of Primatology* 7:507–517.

Estes, R. D. 1966. Behaviour and life history of the wildebeest. *Nature* 212:999–1000.

Estes, R. D. 1976. The significance of breeding synchrony in the wildebeest. *East African Wildlife Journal* 14:135–152.

Evarts, S., and C. J. Williams. 1987. Multiple paternity in a wild population of mallards. *Auk* 104:597–602.

Evers, C. A., and T. D. Seeley. 1986. Kin discrimination and aggression in honey bee colonies with laying workers. *Animal Behaviour* 34:924–925.

Ewing, H. E., and I. Fox. 1943. *The Fleas of North America.* Miscellaneous Publication 500. Washington, D.C.: United States Department of Agriculture.

Fagerstone, K. A. 1982. A review of prairie dog diet and its variability among animals and colonies. Pages 178–184 in R. M. Timm and R. J. Johnson, eds., *Proceedings of the Fifth Great Plains Wildlife Damage Control Workshop.* Lincoln: Institute of Agriculture and Natural Resources, The University of Nebraska.

Fagerstone, K. A., H. P. Tietjen, and O. Williams. 1981. Seasonal variation in the diet of black-tailed prairie dogs. *Journal of Mammalogy* 62:820–824.

Falconer, D. S. 1981. *Introduction to Quantitative Genetics.* London: Longman.

Fanshawe, J. H., and C. D. Fitzgibbon. 1993. Factors influencing the hunting success of an African wild dog pack. *Animal Behaviour* 45:479–490.

Farentinos, R. C. 1972. Social dominance and mating activity in the tassel-eared squirrel *(Sciurus aberti ferreus). Animal Behaviour* 20:316–326.

Farentinos, R. C. 1974. Social communication of the tassel-eared squirrel *(Sciurus aberti):* A descriptive analysis. *Zeitschrift für Tierpsychologie* 34:441–458.

Farrell, R. K., and S. D. Johnson. 1973. Identification of laboratory animals: Freeze-marking. *Laboratory Animal Science* 23:107–110.

Feare, C. J. 1976. Desertion and abnormal development in a colony of sooty terns *Sterna fuscata* infested by virus-infected ticks. *Ibis* 118:112–115.

Feare, C. J., G. M. Dunnet, and I. J. Patterson. 1974. Ecological studies of the rook (*Corvus frugilegus* L.) in northeast Scotland: Food intake and feeding behaviour. *Journal of Applied Ecology* ll:867–896.

Ferrara, J. 1985. Prairie home companions. *National Wildlife* 23:48–53.

Ferron, J. 1984. Behavioral ontogeny analysis of sciurid rodents, with emphasis on the social behavior of ground squirrels. Pages 24–42 in J. O. Murie and G. R. Michener, eds., *The Biology of Ground-Dwelling Squirrels.* Lincoln, Nebr.: University of Nebraska Press.

Festa-Bianchet, M. 1988. Birthdate and survival in bighorn lambs *(Ovis canadensis). Journal of Zoology* (London) 214:653–661.

Festa-Bianchet, M., and D. A. Boag. 1982. Territoriality in adult female Columbian ground squirrels. *Canadian Journal of Zoology* 60:1060–1066.

Festa-Bianchet, M., and W. J. King. 1991. Effects of litter size and population dynamics on juvenile and maternal survival in Columbian ground squirrels. *Journal of Animal Ecology* 60:1077–1090.

Fiala, K. L. 1981. Reproductive cost and the sex ratio in red-winged blackbirds. Pages 198–214 in R. D. Alexander and D. W. Tinkle, eds., *Natural Selection and Social Behavior.* New York: Chiron Press.

Fiala, K. L., and J. D. Congdon. 1983. Energetic consequences of sexual size dimorphism in nestling red-winged blackbirds. *Ecology* 64:642–647.

Filipponi, A., and G. Petrelli. 1975. Laboratory studies on the autecology of three species of the glaber group (Acarina, Misostigmata). *Rivista di Parassitologia* 36:295–308.

Findlay, C. S., and F. Cooke. 1982a. Breeding synchrony in the lesser snow goose *(Anser caerulescens caerulescens).* I. Genetic and environmental components of hatch date variability and their effects on hatch synchrony. *Evolution* 36:342–351.

Findlay, C. S., and F. Cooke. 1982b. Breeding synchrony of the lesser snow goose *(Anser caerulescens caerulescens).* II. The adaptive value of reproductive synchrony. *Evolution* 36:786–799.

Fischer, H. 1982. War on the dog towns. *Defenders* 57:9–12.

Fisher, J. 1952. *The Fulmar.* London: Collins Press.

Fisher, R. A. 1930. *The Genetical Theory of Natural Selection.* 1st ed. Oxford: Oxford University Press.

Fisher, R. A. 1958. *The Genetical Theory of Natural Selection.* 2nd ed. New York: Dover.

Fisher, R. A. 1965. *The Theory of Inbreeding.* London: Oliver and Boyd.

Fitch, H. S. 1948. Ecology of the California ground squirrel on grazing lands. *American Midland Naturalist* 39:513–596.

Fitzgerald, G. J. 1992. Filial cannibalism in fishes: Why do parents eat their offspring? *Trends in Ecology and Evolution* 7:7–10.

Fitzgerald, G. J., and F. G. Whoriskey. 1992. Empirical studies of cannibalism in fish. Pages 238–255 in M. A. Elgar and B. J. Crespi, eds., *Cannibalism: Ecology and Evolution among Diverse Taxa.* New York: Oxford University Press.

Fitzgerald, J. P. 1970. The ecology of plague in prairie dogs and associated small mammals in South Park, Colorado. Ph.D. dissertation, Colorado State University, Fort Collins, Colo.

Fitzgerald, J. P. 1993. The ecology of plague in Gunnison's prairie dogs and suggestions for the recovery of black-footed ferrets. Pages 50–59 in J. L. Oldemeyer, D. E. Biggins, B. J. Miller, and R. Crete, eds., *Proceedings of the Symposium on the Management of Prairie Dog Complexes for the Reintroduction of Black-Footed Ferrets.* Washington, D.C.: United States Fish and Wildlife Services, Biological Report no. 93.

Fitzgerald, J. P., and R. R. Lechleitner. 1974. Observations on the biology of Gunnison's Prairie Dog in central Colorado. *American Midland Naturalist* 92:146–163.

Fitzgibbon, C. D. 1990. Mixed-species grouping in Thomson's and Grant's gazelles: The antipredator benefits. *Animal Behaviour* 39:l116–1126.

Flath, D. L. 1979. Mound characteristics of white-tailed prairie dog maternity burrows. *American Midland Naturalist* 102:395–398.

Fleming, T. H. 1970. Comparative biology of two temperate-tropical rodent counterparts. *American Midland Naturalist* 83:462–471. Fleming, T. H., and R. J. Rauscher. 1978. On the evolution of litter size in *Peromyscus leucopus*. *Evolution* 32:45–55.

Fletcher, D. J. C., and C. D. Michener. 1987. *Kin Recognition in Animals.* New York: John Wiley and Sons.

Fogden, S. C. L. 1971. Mother-young behaviour at grey seal breeding beaches. *Journal of Zoology* (London) 164:61–92.

Foltz, D. W., and J. L. Hoogland. 1981. Analysis of the mating system of the black-tailed prairie dog *(Cynomys ludovicianus)* by likelihood of paternity. *Journal of Mammalogy* 62:706–712.

Foltz, D. W., and J. L. Hoogland. 1983. Genetic evidence of outbreeding in the black-tailed prairie dog *(Cynomys ludovicianus)*. *Evolution* 37:273–281.

Foltz, D. W., J. L. Hoogland, and G. M. Koscielny. 1988. Effects of sex, litter size, and heterozygosity on juvenile weight in black-tailed prairie dogs *(Cynomys ludovicianus)*. *Journal of Mammalogy* 69:611–614.

Foltz, D. W., and P. L. Schwagmeyer. 1989. Sperm competition in the thirteen-lined ground squirrel: Differential fertilization success under field conditions. *American Naturalist* 133:257–265.

Ford, E. B. 1965. *Genetic Polymorphism.* Cambridge, Mass.: MIT Press.

Ford, E. B. 1971. *Ecological Genetics.* London: Chapman and Hall.

Foreman, D. 1962. The normal reproductive cycle of the female prairie dog and the effects of light. *Anatomical Record* 142:391–405.

Foreman, D. 1967. The effects of gonadotrophins in the metabolism of ovaries from prairie dogs *(Cynomys ludovicianus)*. *General and Comparative Endocrinology* 8:66–71.

Foreman, D. 1974. Structural and functional homologies of the accessory reproductive glands of two species of sciurids, *Cynomys ludovicianus* and *Citellus tridecemlineatus*. *Anatomical Record* 180:331–340.

Foreman, D. 1981. Follicular dynamics in a monestrous annually breeding mammal: Prairie dog *(Cynomys ludovicianus)*. Pages 245–251 in N. B. Schwartz and M. Hunzicker-Dunn, eds., *Dynamics of Ovarian Function.* New York: Raven Press.

Foreman, D., and D. Garris. 1984. Plasma progesterone levels and corpus luteum morphology in the female prairie dog *(Cynomys ludovicianus)*. *General and Comparative Endocrinology* 55:315–322.

Foreman, D., and D. Williams. 1967. The effects of gonadotrophic hormones on the oxygen consumption of testes from the prairie dog *(Cynomys lodovicianus)*. *General and Comparative Endocrinology* 9:287–294.

Forrest, S. C., D. E. Biggens, L. Richardson, T. W. Clark, T. M. Campbell, K. A. Fagerstone, and E. T. Thorne. 1988. Population attributes for the black-footed ferret *(Mustela nigripes)* at Meeteetse, Wyoming, 1981–1985. *Journal of Mammalogy* 62:261–273.

Fortenberry, D. K. 1972. *Characteristics of the Black-Footed Ferret.* United States Department of the Interior, Fish and Wildlife Service, Bureau of Sport Fisheries and Wildlife Resource Publication no. 109. Rapid City, S.D.

Fossey, D. 1984. Infanticide in mountain gorillas *(Gorilla gorilla beringei)* with comparative notes on chimpanzees. Pages 217–235 in G. Hausfater and S. B. Hrdy, eds., *Infanticide: Comparative and Evolutionary Perspectives.* New York: Aldine.

Foster, B. E. 1924. Provision of prairie-dog to escape drowning when town is submerged. *Journal of Mammalogy* 5:266–268.

Foster, M. 1934. The reproductive cycle in the female ground squirrel, *Citellus tridecemlineatus* (Mitchell). *American Journal of Anatomy* 54:487–511.

Foster, W. A., and H. E. Treherne. 1981. Evidence for the dilution effect in the selfish herd from fish predation on a marine insect. *Nature* 293:466–467.

Fowler, K., and L. Partridge. 1989. A cost of mating in female fruitflies. *Nature* 338:760–761.

Fox, K. A. 1991. Allonursing in *Peromyscus maniculatus.* Page 28 in W. D. Dawson and O. G. Ward, eds., *Peromyscus Newsletter* no. 12. Columbia, S.C.: *Peromyscus* Genetic Stock Center, University of South Carolina.

Fox, L. R. 1975. Cannibalism in natural populations. *Annual Review of Ecology and Systematics* 6:87–106.

Frame, L. H., J. R. Malcolm, G. W. Frame, and H. van Lawick. 1979. Social organization of African wild dogs *(Lycaon pictus)* on the Serengeti Plains, Tanzania 1967–1978. *Zeitschrift für Tierpsychologie* 50:225–249.

Frank, S. A. 1986. The genetic value of sons and daughters. *Heredity* 56:351–354.

Frank, S. A. 1987a. Demography and sex ratio in social spiders. *Evolution* 41:1267–1281.

Frank, S. A. 1987b. Individual and population sex allocation patterns. *Theoretical Population Biology* 31:47–74.

Frank, S. A. 1990. Sex allocation theory for birds and mammals. *Annual Review of Ecology and Systematics* 21:13–55.

Franklin, W. L., and A. a. El-Absy. 1985. Application of freeze marking to wildlife in the field: Prairie dogs. *Iowa State Journal of Research* 60:71–75.

Fraser, F. C., and C. J. Biddle. 1976. Estimating the risks for offspring of first cousin marriages. *American Journal of Human Genetics* 28:522–526.

Freed, L. A. 1987. Prospective infanticide and protection of genetic paternity in tropical house wrens. *American Naturalist* 130:948–954.

Freeland, W. J. 1976. Pathogens and the evolution of primate sociality. *Biotropica* 8:12–24.

Freeland, W. J. 1979. Primate social groups as biological islands. *Ecology* 60:240–242.

Fretwell, S. D., and H. L. Lucas. 1970. On territorial behaviour and other factors influencing habitat distribution in birds. *Acta Biotheoretica* 19:16–36.

Fuchs, S. 1981. Optimality of parental investment: The influence of nursing on reproductive success of mother and female young house mice. *Behavioral Ecology and Sociobiology* 10:39–51.

Futuyma, D. J. 1979. *Evolutionary Biology.* Sunderland, Mass.: Sinauer Associates.

Gadgil, M., and W. H. Bossert. 1970. Life historical consequences of natural selection. *American Naturalist* 104:1–24.

Galton, F. 1883. *Inquiries into Human Faculty and Its Development.* London: Macmillan.

Gandelman, R., and N. G. Simon. 1978. Spontaneous pup-killing in response to large litters. *Developmental Psychobiology* ll:235–241.

Gargett, V. 1978. Sibling aggression in the black eagle in the Matopos, Rhodesia. *Ostrich* 49:57–63.

Garrett, M. G. 1982. Dispersal of black-tailed prairie dogs *(Cynomys ludovicianus)* in Wind Cave National Park, South Dakota. Master's thesis, Iowa State University, Ames, Iowa.

Garrett, M. G., and W. L. Franklin. 1983. Diethylstilbestrol as a temporary chemosterilant to control black-tailed prairie dog populations. *Journal of Range Management* 36:753–756.

Garrett, M. G., and W. L. Franklin. 1988. Behavioral ecology of dispersal in the black-tailed prairie dog. *Journal of Mammalogy* 69:236–250.

Garrett, M. G., J. L. Hoogland, and W. L. Franklin. 1982. Demographic differences between an old and a new colony of black-tailed prairie dogs *(Cynomys ludovicianus). American Midland Naturalist* 108:51–59.

Garst, W. 1962. Technique for capturing young prairie dogs. *Journal of Wildlife Management* 26:108.

Gaston, A. J., L. N. De Forest, and D. G. Noble. 1993. Egg recognition and egg stealing in murres (*Uria* spp.). *Animal Behaviour* 45:30l–306.

Geist, V. 1971. *Mountain Sheep.* Chicago: University of Chicago Press.

Geodakian, V. A., V. I. Kosobutsky, and D. S. Bileva. 1967. The negative fee-dback [*sic*] regulation of sex ratio. *Genetika* 9:153–163.

Getz, L. L., C. S. Carter, and L. Gavish. 1981. The mating system of the prairie vole, *Microtus ochrogaster:* Field and laboratory evidence for pair bonding. *Behavioral Ecology and Sociobiology* 8:189–194.

Getz, W. M. 1991. The honey bee as a model kin recognition system. Pages 358–412 in P. G. Hepper, ed., *Kin Recognition.* Cambridge: Cambridge University Press.

Getz, W. M., and K. B. Smith. 1983. Genetic kin recognition: Honey bees discriminate between full and half sisters. *Nature* 302:147–148.

Getz, W. M., and K. B. Smith. 1986. Honey bee kin recognition: Learning self and nestmate phenotypes. *Animal Behaviour* 34:1617–1626.

Ghiselin, M. T. 1969. The evolution of hermaphroditism among animals. *Quarterly Review of Biology* 44:189–208.

Gibbs, H. L. 1988. Heritability and selection on clutch size in Darwin's medium ground finches *(Geospiza fortis). Evolution* 42:750–762.

Gibbs, H. L., and P. R. Grant. 1989. Inbreeding in Darwin's medium ground finches *(Geospiza fortis)*. *Evolution* 43:1273–1284.

Gibbs, H. L., P. J. Weatherhead, P. T. Boag, B. N. White, L. M. Tabak, and D. J. Hoysak. 1990. Realized reproductive success of polygynous red-winged blackbirds revealed by hypervariable DNA markers. *Science* 250:1394–1397.

Gibson, R. M., J. W. Bradbury, and S. L. Vehrencamp. 1991. Mate choice in lekking sage grouse revisited: The roles of vocal display, female site fidelity, and copying. *Behavioral Ecology* 2:165–180.

Gibson, R. M., and J. Hoglund. 1992. Copying and sexual selection. *Trends in Ecology and Evolution* 7:229–232.

Ginsberg, J. R., and U. W. Huck. 1989. Sperm competition in mammals. *Trends in Ecology and Evolution* 4:74–79.

Gittleman, J. L. 1985. Functions of communal care in mammals. Pages 187–205 in P. J. Greenwood, P. H. Harvey, and M. Slatkin, eds., *Evolution: Essays in Honour of John Maynard Smith.* Cambridge: Cambridge University Press.

Gittleman, J. L., and S. D. Thompson. 1988. Energy allocation in mammalian reproduction. *American Zoologist* 28:863–875.

Glazier, D. S. 1990. Reproductive efficiency and the timing of gestation and lactation in rodents. *American Naturalist* 135:269–277.

Gliddon, C. J., and P. H. Gouyon. 1989. The units of selection. *Trends in Ecology and Evolution* 4:204–208.

Gochfield, M. 1980. Mechanisms and adaptive value of reproductive synchrony in colonial seabirds. Pages 207–270 in J. Burger, B. L. Olla, and H. E. Winn, eds., *Behavior of Marine Animals.* Current Perspectives in Research. New York: Plenum Press.

Godfray, H. J. C., L. Partridge, and P. H. Harvey. 1991. Clutch size. *Annual Review of Ecology and Systematics* 22:409–429.

Gomendio, M., T. H. Clutton-Brock, S. D. Albon, F. E. Guinness, and M. J. Simpson. 1990. Mammalian sex ratios and variation in costs of rearing sons and daughters. *Nature* 343:261–263.

Goodall, J. 1977. Infant killing and cannibalism in free-living chimpanzees. *Folia Primatologica* 28:259–282.

Goodall, J. 1986. *The Chimpanzees of Gombe.* Cambridge, Mass.: Belknap Press.

Goodman, D. 1982. Optimal life histories, optimal notation, and the value of reproductive value. *American Naturalist* 119:803–823.

Goodwin, D. 1955. Some observations on the reproductive behaviour of rooks. *British Birds* 48:97–107.

Gorman, R. C. 1974. Baked prairie dog. Pages 102–103 in C. Counter and K. Tani, eds., *Palette in the Kitchen.* Santa Fe, N.M.: Sunstone Press.

Gosling, L. M. 1986. Selective abortion of entire litters in the coypu: Adaptive control of offspring production in relation to quality and sex. *American Naturalist* 127:772–795.

Gotmark, F., and M. Andersson. 1984. Colonial breeding reduces nest predation in the common gull *(Larus canus).* *Animal Behaviour* 32:485–492.

Gould, K. G., M. Flint, and C. Graham. 1981. Chimpanzee reproductive senescence: A possible model for evolution of menopause. *Maturitas* 3:157–166.

Gowaty, P. A. 1985. Multiple parentage and apparent monogamy in birds. Pages ll–21 in P. A. Gowaty and D. W. Mock, eds., *Avian Monogamy.* Ornithological Monographs 37. Washington, D.C.: American Ornithologists' Union.

Gowaty, P. A. 1993. Differential dispersal, local resource competition, and sex ratio variation in birds. *American Naturalist* 141:263–280.

Gowaty, P. A., and A. A. Karlin. 1984. Multiple maternity and paternity in single broods of apparently monogamous eastern bluebirds *(Sialia sialis). Behavioral Ecology and Sociobiology* 15:91–95.

Gowaty, P. A., and M. R. Lennartz. 1985. Sex ratios of nestling and fledgling red-cockaded woodpeckers *(Picoides borealis)* favor males. *American Naturalist* 126:347–353.

Grady, R. M., and J. L. Hoogland. 1986. Why do male black-tailed prairie dogs *(Cynomys ludovicianus)* give a mating call? *Animal Behaviour* 34:108–112.

Grafen, A. 1982. How not to measure inclusive fitness. *Nature* 298:425–426.

Grafen, A. 1990. Do animals really recognize kin? *Animal Behaviour* 39:42–54.

Graham, C. E., O. R. Kling, and R. A. Steiner. 1979. Reproductive senescence in female nonhuman primates. Pages 183–202 in D. M. Bowen, ed., *Aging in Nonhuman Primates.* New York: Van Nostrand Reinhold.

Grau, H. J. 1982. Kin recognition in white-footed deermice *(Peromyscus leucopus). Animal Behaviour* 30:497–505.

Green, D. G., and J. E. Dowling. 1975. Electrophysiological evidence for rod-like receptors in the gray squirrel, ground squirrel, and prairie dog retinas. *Journal of Comparative Neurology* 159:461–471.

Green, M. 1960. A Tertiary *Cynomys* from South Dakota. *Journal of Paleontology* 34:545–547.

Green, M. 1963. Some Late Pleistocene rodents from South Dakota. *Journal of Paleontology* 37:688–690.

Greenberg, L. 1979. Genetic component of bee odor in kin recognition. *Science* 206:1095–1097.

Greene, E. 1987. Individuals in an osprey colony discriminate between high and low quality information. *Nature* 329:329–241.

Greenwood, P. J. 1980. Mating systems, philopatry and dispersal in birds and mammals. *Animal Behaviour* 28:ll40–1162.

Greenwood, P. J. 1983. Mating systems and the evolutionary consequences of dispersal. Pages ll6–131 in I. R. Swingland and P. J. Greenwood, eds., *The Ecology of Animal Movement.* Oxford: Clarendon Press.

Greenwood, P. J., P. H. Harvey, and C. M. Perrins. 1978. Inbreeding and dispersal in the great tit. *Nature* 271:52–54.

Grossmann, J. 1987. A prairie dog companion. *Audubon* 89:52–67.

Gubernick, D. J., S. L. Wright, and R. E. Brown. 1993. The significance of father's presence for offspring survival in the monogamous California mouse, *Peromyscus californicus. Animal Behaviour* 46:539–546.

Guilford, T. 1990. The secrets of aposematism: Unlearned responses to specific colours and patterns. *Trends in Ecology and Evolution* 5:323.

Gunderson, H. L. 1978. Under and around a prairie dog town. *Natural History* 87:57–66.

Gurll, N., and L. DenBesten. 1978. Animal models of human cholesterol gallstone disease: A review. *Laboratory and Animal Science* 28:428–432.

Gustafsson, L. 1986. Lifetime reproductive success and heritability: Empirical support for Fisher's fundamental theorem. *American Naturalist* 128:761–764.

Gustafsson, L., and T. Part. 1990. Acceleration of senescence in the collared flycatcher *Ficedula albicollis* by reproductive costs. *Nature* 347:279–281.

Gustafsson, L., and W. J. Sutherland. 1988. The costs of reproduction in the collared flycatcher *Ficedula albicollis*. *Nature* 335:813–815.

Hafner, D. J. 1984. Evolutionary relationships of the Nearctic Sciuridae. Pages 3–23 in J. O. Murie and G. R. Michener, eds., *The Biology of Ground-Dwelling Squirrels*. Lincoln: University of Nebraska Press.

Hall, E. R. 1981. *The Mammals of North America*. New York: John Wiley and Sons.

Halliday, T. R. 1976. The libidinous newt: An analysis of variations in the sexual behavior of the male smooth newt, *Triturus vulgaris*. *Animal Behaviour* 24:398–414.

Halliday, T., and S. J. Arnold. 1987. Multiple mating by females: A perspective from quantitative genetics. *Animal Behaviour* 35:939–941.

Halloran, A. F. 1972. The black-tailed prairie dog: Yesterday and today. *Great Plains Journal* 11:138–144.

Halpin, Z. T. 1983. Naturally occurring encounters between black-tailed prairie dogs *(Cynomys ludovicianus)* and snakes. *American Midland Naturalist* 109:50–54.

Halpin, Z. T. 1987. Natal dispersal and the formation of new social groups in a newly established town of black-tailed prairie dogs *(Cynomys ludovicianus)*. Pages 104–118 in B. D. Chepko-Sade and Z. T. Halpin, eds., *Mammalian Dispersal Patterns: The Effects of Social Structure on Population Genetics*. Chicago: University of Chicago Press.

Hamilton, J. D., and E. W. Pfeiffer. 1977. Effects of cold exposure and dehydration on renal function in black-tailed prairie dogs. *Journal of Applied Physiological, Respiratory, and Environmental Exercise Physiology* 42:295–299.

Hamilton, W. D. 1964. The genetical evolution of social behavior. I and II. *Journal of Theoretical Biology* 7:1–52.

Hamilton, W. D. 1966. The moulding of senescence by natural selection. *Journal of Theoretical Biology* 12:12–45.

Hamilton, W. D. 1967. Extraordinary sex ratios. *Science* 156:477–488.

Hamilton, W. D. 1970. Ordering the phenomena of ecology. *Science* 167:1478–1480.

Hamilton, W. D. 1971. Geometry for the selfish herd. *Journal of Theoretical Biology* 31:295–311.

Hamilton, W. D. 1972. Altruism and related phenomena, mainly in social insects. *Annual Review of Ecology and Systematics* 3:193–232.

Hamilton, W. D. 1975. Innate social aptitudes of man: An approach from evolutionary genetics. Pages 135–155 in R. Fox, ed., *Biosocial Anthropology.* New York: John Wiley and Sons.

Hamilton, W. D. 1979. Wingless and fighting males in fig wasps and other insects. Pages 167–220 in M. S. Blum and N. A. Blum, eds., *Reproductive Competition and Selection in Insects.* New York: Academic Press.

Hamilton, W. D. 1987. Discriminating nepotism: Expectable, common, overlooked. Pages 417–437 in D. J. C. Fletcher and C. D. Michener, eds., *Kin Recognition in Animals.* New York: John Wiley and Sons.

Hamilton, W. D. 1990. Mate choice near and far. *American Zoologist* 30:341–352.

Hamilton, W. D., and M. Zuk. 1982. Heritable true fitness and bright birds: A role for parasites. *Science* 218:384–387.

Hanken, J., and P. W. Sherman. 1981. Multiple paternity in Belding's ground squirrel litters. *Science* 212:351–353.

Hansen, R. M., and I. K. Gold. 1977. Blacktail prairie dogs, desert cottontails, and cattle trophic relations on shortgrass range. *Journal of Range Management* 30:210–214.

Hare, J. F. 1991. Intraspecific killing of preweaned young in the Columbian ground squirrel, *Spermophilus columbianus. Canadian Journal of Zoology* 69:797–800.

Hare, J. F., and J. O. Murie. 1992. Manipulation of litter size reveals no cost of reproduction in Columbian ground squirrels. *Journal of Mammalogy* 73:449–454.

Harlow, H. J., and S. W. Buskirk. 1991. Comparative plasma and urine chemistry of fasting white-tailed prairie dogs *(Cynomys leucurus)* and American martens *(Martes americana):* Representative fat- and lean-bodied animals. *Physiological Zoology* 64:1262–1278.

Harlow, H. J., and G. E. Menkens. 1986. A comparison of hibernation in the black-tailed prairie dog, white-tailed prairie dog, and Wyoming ground squirrel. *Canadian Journal of Zoology* 64:793–796.

Harrington, F. H., L. D. Mech, and S. H. Fritts. 1983. Pack size and wolf pup survival: Their relationship under varying ecological conditions. *Behavioral Ecology and Sociobiology* 13:19–26.

Harris, H., and D. A. Hopkinson. 1976. *Handbook of Enzyme Electrophoresis in Human Genetics.* New York: American Elsevier.

Hart, B. L. 1990. Behavioral adaptations to pathogens and parasites. *Neuroscience and Biobehavioral Review* 14:273–294.

Hart, B. L., and L. A. Hart. 1992. Reciprocal allogrooming in impala, *Aepyceros malampus. Animal Behaviour* 44:1073–1083.

Hart, B. L., L. A. Hart, M. S. Mooring, and R. Olubayo. 1992. Biological basis of grooming behaviour in antelope: The body-size, vigilance and habitat principles. *Animal Behaviour* 44:615–631.

Hart, B. L., and C. M. Haugen. 1971. Prevention of genital grooming in mating behavior of male rats *(Rattus norvegicus). Animal Behaviour* 19:230–232.

Hart, B. L., E. Korinek, and P. Brennan. 1987. Postcopulatory genital grooming in male rats: Prevention of sexually transmitted infections. *Physiological Behavior* 41:321–325.

Hartung, J. 1976. On natural selection and the inheritance of wealth. *Current Anthropology* 17:607–622.

Hartung, T. G., and D. A. Dewsbury. 1978. A comparative analysis of copulatory plugs in muroid rodents and their relationship to copulatory behavior. *Journal of Mammalogy* 59:717–723.

Harvey, P. H., and P. J. Greenwood. 1978. Anti-predator defence strategies: Some evolutionary problems. Pages 129–151 in J. R. Krebs and N. B. Davies, eds., *Behavioural Ecology: An Evolutionary Approach.* lst ed. Oxford: Blackwell Scientific Publications.

Harvey, P. H., and R. M. May. 1989. Copulation dynamics: Out for the sperm count. *Nature* 337:508–509.

Harvey, P. H., and M. D. Pagel. 1991. *The Comparative Method in Evolutionary Biology.* Oxford: Oxford University Press.

Harwood, J., and A. Hall. 1990. Mass mortality in marine mammals: Its implications for population dynamics and genetics. *Trends in Ecology and Evolution* 5:254–257.

Hasenyager, R. N., T. Ball, and T. W. Clark. 1988. *Utah Prairie Dog Recovery Plan.* Denver, Colo.: United States Fish and Wildlife Service.

Hasler, J. F., and E. M. Banks. 1975. Reproductive performance and growth in captive collared lemmings *(Dicrostonyx groenlandicus). Canadian Journal of Zoology* 53:777–787.

Hatch, S. A. 1983. Mechanism and ecological significance of sperm storage in the northern fulmar with reference to its occurrence in other birds. *Auk* 100:593–600.

Hauser, M. D. 1990. Do chimpanzee copulatory calls incite male-male competition? *Animal Behaviour* 39:596–597.

Hausfater, G. 1975. Dominance and reproduction in baboons *(Papio cynocephalus):* A quantitative analysis. *Contributions to Primatology* 7:1–150.

Hausfater, G.. 1984. Infanticide in langurs: Strategies, counterstrategies, and parameter values. Pages 257–282 in G. Hausfater and S. B. Hrdy, eds., *Infanticide: Comparative and Evolutionary Perspectives.* New York: Aldine.

Hausfater, G., and S. B. Hrdy, eds. 1984. *Infanticide: Comparative and · Evolutionary Perspectives.* New York: Aldine.

Hayssen, V. 1984. Mammalian reproduction: Constraints on the evolution of infanticide. Pages 105–123 in G. Hausfater and S. B. Hrdy, eds., *Infanticide: Comparative and Evolutionary Perspectives.* New York: Aldine.

Heard, D. C. 1992. The effect of wolf predation and snow cover on musk-ox group size. *American Naturalist* 139:190–204.

Helle, E. 1980. Age structure and sex ratio of the ringed seal *Phoca (Pusa) hispida* Schreber population in the Bothnian Bay, northern Baltic Sea. *Zeitschrift Saugetierkunde* 45:310–317.

Helle, E., and K. Kauhala. 1993. Age structure, mortality, and sex ratio of the raccoon dog in Finland. *Journal of Mammalogy* 74:936–942.

Henderson, F. R., P. F. Springer, and R. Adrian. 1969. *The Black-Footed Ferret in South Dakota.* Technical Bulletin 4. Pierre, S.D.: South Dakota Department of Game, Fish, and Parks.

Hepper, P. G. 1986. Kin recognition: Functions and mechanisms. A review. *Biological Reviews* 61:63–93.

Hepper, P. G., ed. 1991. *Kin Recognition.* Cambridge: Cambridge University Press.

Hertwig, R. 1912. Ueber den derzeitigen stand des sexualproblems. *Biologisches Zentrablat* 21:1–146.

Hess, E. H. 1964. Imprinting in birds. *Science* 146:1128–1139.

Hess, E. H. 1973. *Imprinting.* New York: Van Nostrand Reinhold.

Hibbard, C. W. 1937. *Cynomys ludovicianus ludovicianus* from the Pleistocene of Kansas. *Journal of Mammalogy* 18:517–518.

Hibbard, C. W. 1942. Pleistocene mammals from Kansas. *State Geology Survey of Kansas Bulletin* 41:261–269.

Hibbard, C. W. 1956. Vertebrate fossils from the Meade formation of southwestern Kansas. *Papers of the Michigan Academy of Arts and Letters* 41:145–200.

Hill, G. E. 1991. Plumage coloration is a sexually selected indicator of male quality. *Nature* 350:337–339.

Hill, J. L. 1974. *Peromyscus:* Effect of early pairing on reproduction. *Science* 186:1042–1044.

Hillman, C. N. 1968. Field observations of black-footed ferrets in South Dakota. *Transactions of the North American Wildlife and Natural Resources Conference* 33:433–443.

Hillman, C. N. 1971. The black-footed ferret. *South Dakota Conservation Digest* 38:5–7.

Hillman, C. N., and T. W. Clark. 1980. *Mustela nigripes. Mammalian Species* 126:1–3.

Hillman, C. N., and R. L. Linder. 1973. The black-footed ferret. Pages 10–23 in R. L. Linder and C. N. Hillman, eds., *Proceedings of the Black-Footed Ferret and Prairie Dog Workshop.* Brookings, S.D.: South Dakota State University.

Hilton, D. J., and J. L. Mahrt. 1971. Ectoparasites from three species of *Spermophilus* (Rodentia: Sciuridae) in Alberta. *Canadian Journal of Zoology* 49:1501–1504.

Hiraiwa-Hasegawa, M. 1988. Adaptive significance of infanticide in primates. *Trends in Ecology and Evolution* 3:102–105.

Hiraiwa-Hasegawa, M. 1992. Cannibalism among non-human primates. Pages 323–338 in M. A. Elgar and B. J. Crespi, eds., *Cannibalism: Ecology and Evolution among Diverse Taxa.* New York: Oxford University Press.

Hirshfield, M. F., and D. W. Tinkle. 1975. Natural selection and the evolution of reproductive effort. *Proceedings of the Natural Academy of Science* 72:2227–2231.

Hirst, L. F. 1953. *The Conquest of Plague.* Oxford: Clarendon Press.

Hoeck, H. N. 1982. Population dynamics, dispersal and genetic isolation in two species of hyrax *(Heterohyrax brucei* and *Procavia johnstoni)* on habitat islands in the Serengeti. *Zeitschrift für Tierpsychologie* 59:177–210.

Hoeck, H. N. 1989. Demography and competition in hyrax. A 17 year study. *Oecologia* 89:353–360.

Hoelzer, G. A. 1989. The good parent process of sexual selection. *Animal Behaviour* 38:1067–1078.

Hofer, S., and P. Ingold. 1984. The whistles of the alpine marmot *(Marmota marmota):* Their structure and occurrence in the antipredator context. *Revue Suisse de Zoologie* 91:861–865.

Hogden, G. D., A. K. Goodman, A. O'Conner, and D. K. Johnson. 1977. Menopause in rhesus monkeys: Model for study of disorders in the human climacteric. *American Journal of Obstetrics and Gynecology* 127:581–584.

Hogg, J. T. 1988. Copulatory tactics in relation to sperm competition in Rocky Mountain bighorn sheep. *Behavioral Ecology and Sociobiology* 22:49–59.

Hoglund, J., R. V. Alatalo, and A. Lundberg. 1990. Copying the mate choice of others? Observations on female black grouse. *Behaviour* 114:221–231.

Hogstedt, G. 1980. Evolution of clutch size in birds: Adaptive variation in relation to territory quality. *Science* 210:1148–1150.

Holdenreid, R., F. C. Evans, and D. S. Longanecker. 1951. Host-parasite-disease relationships in a mammalian community in the central coast region of California. *Ecological Monographs* 21:1–18.

Holekamp, K. E. 1984a. Dispersal in ground-dwelling sciurids. Pages 297–320 in J. O. Murie and G. R. Michener, eds., *The Biology of Ground-Dwelling Squirrels.* Lincoln, Nebr.: University of Nebraska Press.

Holekamp, K. E. 1984b. Natal dispersal in Belding's ground squirrels *(Spermophilus beldingi). Behavioral Ecology and Sociobiology* 16:21–30.

Holekamp, K. E., and P. W. Sherman. 1989. Why male ground squirrels disperse. *American Scientist* 77:232–239.

Hölldobler, B., and E. O. Wilson. 1991. *The Ants.* Cambridge, Mass.: Harvard University Press.

Hollister, N. 1916. A systematic account of the prairie dogs. *North American Fauna* 40:1–37.

Holm, C. H. 1973. Breeding sex ratios, territoriality and reproductive success in the red-winged blackbird *(Agelaius phoeniceus). Ecology* 54:356–365.

Holmes, W. G. 1977. Cannibalism in the arctic ground squirrel *(Spermophilus parryii). Journal of Mammalogy* 58:437–438.

Holmes, W. G. 1984a. Ontogeny of dam-young recognition in captive Belding's ground squirrels. *Journal of Comparative Psychology* 98:246–256.

Holmes, W. G. 1984b. Sibling recognition in thirteen-lined ground squirrels: Effects of genetic relatedness, rearing association, and olfaction. *Behavioral Ecology and Sociobiology* 14:225–233.

Holmes, W. G. 1986a. Identification of paternal half siblings by captive Belding's ground squirrels. *Animal Behaviour* 34:321–327.

Holmes, W. G. 1986b. Kin recognition by phenotype matching in female Belding's ground squirrels. *Animal Behaviour* 34:38–47.

Holmes, W. G. 1988. Kinship and the development of social preferences. Pages 389–413 in E. M. Blass, ed., *Developmental Psychobiology and Behavioral Ecology.* New York: Plenum Press.

Holmes, W. G. 1990. Parent-offspring recognition in mammals: A proximate and ultimate perspective. Pages 441–460 in N. A. Krasnegor and R. S. Bridges, eds., *Mammalian Parenting.* New York: Oxford University Press.

Holmes, W. G., and P. W. Sherman. 1982. The ontogeny of kin recognition in two species of ground squirrels. *American Zoologist* 22:491–517.

Holmes, W. G., and P. W. Sherman. 1983. Kin recognition in animals. *American Scientist* 71:46–55.

Holzbach, R. T., C. Corbusier, M. Marsh, and K. Naito. 1976. The process of cholesterol cholelithiasis induced by diet in the prairie dog: A physicochemical characterization. *Journal of Laboratory and Clinical Medicine* 87:987–998.

Hoogland, J. L. 1977. The evolution of coloniality in white-tailed and black-tailed prairie dogs (Sciuridae: *Cynomys leucurus* and *C. ludovicianus*). Ph.D. dissertation, University of Michigan, Ann Arbor, Mich.

Hoogland, J. L. 1979a. Aggression, ectoparasitism, and other possible costs of prairie dog (Sciuridae: *Cynomys* spp.) coloniality. *Behaviour* 69:1–35.

Hoogland, J. L. 1979b. The effect of colony size on individual alertness of prairie dogs (Sciuridae: *Cynomys* spp.). *Animal Behaviour* 27:394–407.

Hoogland, J. L. 1981a. The evolution of coloniality in white-tailed and black-tailed prairie dogs (Sciuridae: *Cynomys leucurus* and *C. ludovicianus*). *Ecology* 62:252–272.

Hoogland, J. L. 1981b. Nepotism and cooperative breeding in the black-tailed prairie dog (Sciuridae: *Cynomys ludovicianus*). Pages 283–310 in R. D. Alexander and D. W. Tinkle, eds., *Natural Selection and Social Behavior.* New York: Chiron Press.

Hoogland, J. L. 1982a. Prairie dogs avoid extreme inbreeding. *Science* 215:1639–1641.

Hoogland, J. L. 1982b. Reply to a comment by Powell. *Ecology* 63:1968–1969.

Hoogland, J. L. 1983a. Black-tailed prairie dog coteries are cooperatively breeding units. *American Naturalist* 121:275–280.

Hoogland, J. L. 1983b. Nepotism and alarm calling in the black-tailed prairie dog *(Cynomys ludovicianus). Animal Behaviour* 31:472–479.

Hoogland, J. L. 1985. Infanticide in prairie dogs: Lactating females kill offspring of close kin. *Science* 230:1037–1040.

Hoogland, J. L. 1986. Nepotism in prairie dogs *(Cynomys ludovicianus)* varies with competition but not with kinship. *Animal Behaviour* 34:263–270.

Hoogland, J. L., D. K. Angell, J. G. Daley, and M. C. Radcliffe. 1988. Demography and population dynamics of prairie dogs. Pages 18–22 in D. W. Uresk, G. L. Schenbeck, and R. Cefkin, technical coordinators, *Eighth Great Plains Wildlife Damage Control Workshop Proceedings.*

United States Department of Agriculture, Forest Service, General Technical Report RM-154. Fort Collins, Colo.

Hoogland, J. L., and D. W. Foltz. 1982. Variance in male and female reproductive success in a harem-polygynous mammal, the black-tailed prairie dog (Sciuridae: *Cynomys ludovicianus*). *Behavioral Ecology and Sociobiology* 11:155–163.

Hoogland, J. L., and J. M. Hutter. 1987. Aging live prairie dogs from molar attrition. *Journal of Wildlife Management* 51:393–394.

Hoogland, J. L., and P. W. Sherman. 1976. Advantages and disadvantages of bank swallow *(Riparia riparia)* coloniality. *Ecological Monographs* 46:33–58.

Hoogland, J. L., R. H. Tamarin, and C. K. Levy. 1989. Communal nursing in prairie dogs. *Behavioral Ecology and Sociobiology* 24:91–95.

Horn, H. S. 1968. The adaptive significance of colonial nesting in the Brewer's blackbird *(Euphagus cyanocephalus)*. *Ecology* 49:682–694.

Horn, H. S., and D. I. Rubenstein. 1984. Behavioral adaptations and life history. Pages 279–298 in J. R. Krebs and N. B. Davies, eds., *Behavioural Ecology: An Evolutionary Approach*. 2d edition. Oxford: Blackwell Scientific Publications.

Horrocks, J., and W. Hunte. 1983. Maternal rank and offspring rank in vervet monkeys: An appraisal of the mechanisms of rank acquisition. *Animal Behaviour* 31:772–782.

Horwich, R. H. 1972. *The Ontogeny of Social Behavior in the Gray Squirrel (Sciurus carolinensis)*. Hamburg: Verlag Paul Parey.

Howard, R. D. 1979. Estimating reproductive success in natural populations. *American Naturalist* 114:221–231.

Howard, R. D. 1983. Sexual selection and variation in reproductive success in a long-lived organism. *American Naturalist* 122:301–325.

Howe, H. F. 1979. Evolutionary aspects of parental care in the common grackle, *Quiscalus quiscala* L. *Evolution* 33:41–51.

Hrdy, S. B. 1974. Male-male competition and infanticide among the langurs *(Presbytis entellus)* of Abu, Rajasthan. *Folia Primatologia* 22:19–58.

Hrdy, S. B. 1976. Care and exploitation of nonhuman primate infants by conspecifics other than the mother. *Advances in the Study of Behavior* 6:101–158.

Hrdy, S. B. 1977a. Infanticide as a primate reproductive strategy. *American Scientist* 65:40–49.

Hrdy, S. B. 1977b. *The Langurs of Abu: Female and Male Strategies of Reproduction*. Cambridge, Mass.: Harvard University Press.

Hrdy, S. B. 1979. Infanticide among animals: A review, classification, and examination of the implications for the reproductive strategies of females. *Ethology and Sociobiology* 1:13–40.

Hrdy, S. B. 1981a. "Nepotists" and "altruists": The behavior of old females among macaques and langur monkeys. Pages 59–76 in P. T. Amoss and S. Harrell, eds., *Other Ways of Growing Old*. Stanford, Calif.: Stanford University Press.

Hrdy, S. B. 1981b. *The Woman That Never Evolved*. Cambridge, Mass: Harvard University Press.

Hrdy, S. B. 1984. Assumptions and evidence regarding the sexual selection hypothesis: A reply to Boggess. Pages 315–319 in G. Hausfater and S. B. Hrdy, eds., *Infanticide: Comparative and Evolutionary Perspectives.* New York: Aldine.

Hrdy, S. B., and G. Hausfater. 1984. Comparative and evolutionary perspectives on infanticide: Introduction and overview. Pages xiii–xxxv in G. Hausfater and S. B. Hrdy, eds., *Infanticide: Comparative and Evolutionary Perspectives.* New York: Aldine.

Hrdy, S. B., and D. B. Hrdy. 1976. Hierarchical relations among female hanuman langurs (Primates: Colobinae, *Presbytis entellus*). *Science* 193:913–915.

Hrdy, S. B., and P. L. Whitten. 1987. Patterning of sexual activity. Pages 370–384 in B. B. Smuts, D. L. Cheney, R. M. Seyfarth, R. W. Wrangham, and T. T. Struhsaker, eds., *Primate Societies.* Chicago: University of Chicago Press.

Hrdy, S. B., and G. C. Williams. 1983. Behavioural biology and the double-standard. Pages 3–17 in S. K. Wasser, ed., *Social Behavior of Female Vertebrates.* New York: Academic Press.

Huck, U. W. 1984. Infanticide and the evolution of pregnancy block in rodents. Pages 349–365 in G. Hausfater and S. B. Hrdy, eds., *Infanticide: Comparative and Evolutionary Perspectives.* New York: Aldine.

Huck, U. W., R. D. Lisk, and C. L. Guyton. 1989. Multiple-male matings increase littering rates in golden hamsters mated late in the receptive period. *Animal Behaviour* 37:334–336.

Huck, U. W., R. D. Lisk, and C. Thierung. 1986. Stimulus requirements for pregnancy initiation in the golden hamster *(Mesocricetus auratus)* change with time of mating during the receptive period. *Journal of Reproduction and Fertility* 76:449–458.

Huck, U. W., R. P. Quinn, and R. D. Lisk. 1985. Determinants of mating success in the golden hamster *(Mesocricetus auratus)*. IV. Sperm competition. *Behavioral Ecology and Sociobiology* 17:239–252.

Huck, U. W., R. L. Soltis, and C. B. Coopersmith. 1982. Infanticide in male laboratory mice: Effects of social status, prior sexual experience, and basis for discrimination between related and unrelated young. *Animal Behaviour* 30:1158–1165.

Hunt, G. L., and M. W. Hunt. 1976. Gull chick survival: The significance of growth rates, timing of breeding, and territory size. *Ecology* 57:62–75.

Hunter, F. M., T. Burke, and S. E. Watts. 1992. Frequent copulation as a method of paternity assurance in the northern fulmar. *Animal Behaviour* 44:149–156.

Hurly, T. A. 1987. Male-biased adult sex ratios in a red squirrel population. *Canadian Journal of Zoology* 65:1284–1286.

Hussell, D. J. T. 1972. Factors affecting clutch size in arctic passerines. *Ecological Monographs* 42:317–364.

Ims, R. A. 1990a. The ecology and evolution of reproductive synchrony. *Trends in Ecology and Evolution* 5:135–140.

Ims, R. A. 1990b. On the adaptive value of reproductive synchrony as a predator-swamping strategy. *American Naturalist* 136:485–498.

Ito, Y. 1989. The evolutionary biology of sterile soldiers in aphids. *Trends in Ecology and Evolution* 4:69–73.

Ivins, B. L., and A. T. Smith. 1983. Responses of pikas (*Ochotona princeps,* Lagomorpha) to naturally occurring terrestrial predators. *Behavioral Ecology and Sociobiology* 13:277–285.

Jacobs, G. H. 1978. Spectral sensitivity and color vision in the ground dwelling sciurids. Results from golden-mantled ground squirrels and comparisons for 5 species. *Animal Behaviour* 26:409–421.

Jacobs, G. H., and R. L. Yolton. 1972. Some characteristics of the eye and the electroretinogram of the prairie dog. *Experimental Neurology* 37:538–549.

James, H. C. 1937. Sex ratios and the status of the male in Pseudococcinae (Hem. Coccidae). *Bulletin of Entomological Research* 28:429–461.

James, W. H. 1975. Sex ratio in twin births. *Annals of Human Biology* 2:365–378.

James, W. H. 1985. Sex ratio, dominance status and maternal hormone levels at the time of conception. *Journal of Theoretical Biology* 114:505–510.

Jameson, W. C. 1973. On the eradication of prairie dogs: A point of view. *Bios* 44:129–135.

Jarman, P. J. 1974. The social organization of antelope in relation to their ecology. *Behaviour* 48:215–267.

Jarvis, J. U. M. 1981. Eusociality in a mammal: Cooperative breeding in naked mole-rat colonies. *Science* 212:571–573.

Jarvis, J. U. M. 1991. Appendix: Methods for capturing, transporting, and maintaining naked mole-rats in captivity. Pages 467–483 in P. W. Sherman, J. U. M. Jarvis, and R. D. Alexander, eds., *The Biology of the Naked Mole Rat.* Princeton, N.J.: Princeton University Press.

Jarvis, J. U. M., and N. C. Bennett. 1991. Ecology and behavior of the family Bathyergidae. Pages 66–96 in P. W. Sherman, J. U. M. Jarvis, and R. D. Alexander, eds., *The Biology of the Naked Mole Rat.* Princeton, N.J.: Princeton University Press.

Jellison, W. L. 1939. Notes on the fleas of prairie dogs, with description of a new subspecies. *United States Public Health Reports* 54:840–844.

Jellison, W. L. 1945. Siphonaptera: The genus *Oropsylla* in North America (*Citellus, Callospermophilus, Cynomys,* and *Marmota* parasitized). *Journal of Parasitology* 31:83–97.

Jenni, D. A., and G. Collier. 1972. Polyandry in the American jacana *(Jacana spinosa). Auk* 89:743–765.

Jennings, A. R., and E. J. L. Soulsby. 1958. Disease in a colony of black-headed gulls *Larus ridibundus. Ibis* 100:305–312.

Jeppsson, B. 1986. Mating by pregnant water voles *(Arvicola terrestris):* A strategy to counter infanticide by males? *Behavioral Ecology and Sociobiology* 19:293–296.

Jillson, B. C. 1871. Habits of the prairie dog. *American Naturalist* 5:24–29.

Johns, D. W., and K. B. Armitage. 1979. Behavioral ecology of alpine yellow-bellied marmots. *Behavioral Ecology and Sociobiology* 5:133–157.

Johnson, C. N. 1988. Dispersal and the sex ratio at birth in primates. *Nature* 332:726–728.

Johnson, G. E. 1927. Observations on young prairie dogs *(Cynomys ludovicianus)* born in the laboratory. *Journal of Mammalogy* 8:110–115.

Johnson, M. L., and M. S. Gaines. 1990. Evolution of dispersal: Theoretical models and empirical tests using birds and mammals. *Annual Review of Ecology and Systematics* 21:449–480.

Jones, G. 1987. Colonization patterns in sand martins *Riparia riparia. Bird Study* 34:20–25.

Jones, I. L., J. B. Falls, and A. J. Gaston. 1987. Vocal recognition between parents and young of ancient murrelets, *Synthliboramphus antiquus* (Aves: Alcidae). *Animal Behaviour* 35:1405–1415.

Jones, J. K., R. S. Hoffmann, D. W. Rice, C. Jones, R. J. Baker, and M. D. Engstrom. 1992. *Revised Checklist of North American Mammals North of Mexico, 1991.* Occasional Papers of The Museum, Texas Tech University 146:1–23.

Jones, T. R. and R. K. Plakke. 1981. The histology and histochemistry of the perianal scent gland of the reproductively quiescent black-tailed prairie dog *(Cynomys ludovicianus). Journal of Mammalogy* 62:362–368.

Joste, N. E., W. D. Koenig, R. L. Mumme, and F. A. Pitelka. 1982. Intragroup dynamics of a cooperative breeder: An analysis of reproductive roles in the acorn woodpecker. *Behavioral Ecology and Sociobiology* 11:195–201.

Juelson, T. C. 1970. A study of the ecology and ethology of the rock squirrel, *Spermophilus variegatus* (Erxleben). Ph.D. dissertation, University of Utah, Salt Lake City.

Kano, T. 1992. *The Last Ape: Pygmy Chimpanzee Behavior and Ecology.* Translated by E. O. Vineberg. Stanford, Calif.: Stanford University Press.

Kapitonov, V. I. 1960. An essay on the biology of the black-capped marmot *(Marmota camtschatica* Pall). *Zoologichesky Zhurnal* 39:448–457.

Kareem, A. M., and C. J. Barnard. 1982. The importance of kinship and familiarity in social interactions between mice. *Animal Behaviour* 30:594–601.

Kartman, L., S. F. Quan, and R. R. Lechleitner. 1962. Die-off of a Gunnison's prairie dog colony in central Colorado. II. Retrospective determination of plague infection in flea vectors, rodents, and man. *Zoonoses Research* 1:201–224.

Kasuya, T., and H. Marsh. 1984. Life history and reproductive biology of the short-finned pilot whale, *Globicephala macrorhynchus,* off the Pacific coast of Japan. *Report of the International Whaling Commission,* Special Issue 6:259–310.

Kaufman, D. W., and G. A. Kaufman. 1987. Reproduction by *Peromyscus polionotus:* Number, size, and survival of offspring. *Journal of Mammalogy* 68:275–280.

Kaufmann, J. H. 1974. The ecology and evolution of social organization in the kangaroo family (Macropodidae). *American Zoologist* 14:51–62.

Keane, B. 1990a. Dispersal and inbreeding avoidance in the white-footed mouse, *Peromyscus leucopus. Animal Behaviour* 40:143–152.

Keane, B. 1990b. The effect of relatedness on reproductive success and mate choice in the white-footed mouse, *Peromyscus leucopus*. *Animal Behaviour* 39:264–273.

Keane, B., P. M. Waser, S. R. Creel, N. M. Creel, L. F. Elliott, and D. J. Minchella. 1994. Subordinate reproduction in dwarf mongooses. *Animal Behaviour* 47:65–75.

Kellogg, V. L., and G. F. Ferris. 1915. *The Anoplura and Mallophaga of North American Mammals*. Stanford University Publications, University Series, no. 19.

Kelso, L. H. 1939. *Food Habits of Prairie Dogs*. United States Department of Agriculture Circular 529:1–15. Washington, D.C.

Kenagy, G. J., D. Masman, S. M. Sharbaugh, and K. A. Nagy. 1990. Energy expenditure during lactation in relation to litter size in free-living golden-mantled ground squirrels. *Journal of Animal Ecology* 59:73–88.

Kennedy, C. R. 1975. *Ecological Animal Parasitology*. New York: John Wiley.

Kent, D. S., and J. A. Simpson. 1992. Eusociality in the beetle *Austroplatypus incompertus* (Coleoptera: Curculionidae). *Naturwissenschaften* 79:86–87.

Kenward, R. E. 1978. Hawks and doves: Factors affecting success and selection in goshawk attacks on woodpigeons. *Journal of Animal Ecology* 47:449–460.

Kerwin, L. 1972. Population size and productivity of the black-tailed prairie dog in Saskatchewan. *Blue Jay* 30:35–37.

Keyfitz, N. 1968. *Introduction to the Mathematics of Populations*. Reading, Mass.: Addison-Wesley.

Kildaw, S. D. 1991. Effects of predation risk and group size on the foraging behavior of black-tailed prairie dogs. Master's thesis, University of Alberta, Edmonton, Alberta.

King, J. A. 1955. *Social Behavior, Social Organization, and Population Dynamics in a Black-tailed Prairiedog Town in the Black Hills of South Dakota*. Contributions from the Laboratory of Vertebrate Biology, The University of Michigan, no. 67.

King, J. A. 1959. The social behavior of prairie dogs. *Scientific American* 201:128–140.

King, J. A. 1984. Historical ventilations on a prairie dog town. Pages 447–456 in J. O. Murie and G. R. Michener, eds., *The Biology of Ground-Dwelling Squirrels*. Lincoln, Nebr.: University of Nebraska Press.

King, K. A., D. R. Blankinship, and R. T. Paul. 1977. Ticks as a factor in the 1975 nesting failure of Texas brown pelicans. *Wilson Bulletin* 89:157–158.

King, W. J. 1989a. Kin-differential behavior of adult female Columbian ground squirrels. *Animal Behaviour* 38:354–356.

King, W. J. 1989b. Spacing of female kin in Columbian ground squirrels *(Spermophilus columbianus)*. *Canadian Journal of Zoology* 67:91–95.

King, W. J., M. Festa-Bianchet, and S. E. Hatfield. 1991. Determinants of reproductive success in female Columbian ground squirrels. *Oecologia* 86:528–534.

King, W. J., and J. O. Murie. 1985. Temporal overlap of female kin in Columbian ground squirrels *(Spermophilus columbianus)*. *Behavioral Ecology and Sociobiology* 16:337–341.

Kirkpatrick, M. 1987. Sexual selection by female choice in polygynous animals. *Annual Review of Ecology and Systematics* 18:43–70.

Kirkpatrick, M., and C. D. Jenkins. 1989. Genetic segregation and the maintenance of sexual reproduction. *Nature* 339:300–301.

Kirkpatrick, M., and M. J. Ryan. 1991. The evolution of mating preferences and the paradox of the lek. *Nature* 350:33–38.

Kivett, V. K. 1978. Integumentary glands of Columbian ground squirrels *(Spermophilus columbianus):* Sciuridae. *Canadian Journal of Zoology* 56:374–381.

Kivett, V. K., J. O. Murie, and A. L. Steiner. 1976. A comparative study of scent-gland location and related behavior in some northwestern Nearctic ground squirrel species (Sciuridae): An evolutionary approach. *Canadian Journal of Zoology* 54:1294–1306.

Klatt, L. E., and D. Hein. 1978. Vegetative differences among active and abandoned towns of black-tailed prairie dogs *(Cynomys ludovicianus)*. *Journal of Range Management* 31:315–317.

Kleiman, D. G. 1977. Monogamy in mammals. *Quarterly Review of Biology* 52:39–69.

Kleiman, D. G., and J. R. Malcolm. 1981. The evolution of male parental investment. Pages 347–387 in D. J. Gubernick and P. H. Klopfer, eds., *Parental Care in Mammals.* New York: Plenum.

Klomp, H. 1970. The determination of clutch-size in birds: A review. *Ardea* 58:1–124.

Knopf, F. L. 1979. Spatial and temporal aspects of colonial nesting in white pelicans. *Condor* 81:353–363.

Knowles, C. J. 1985. Observations on prairie dog dispersal in Montana. *Prairie Naturalist* 17:33–40.

Knowles, C. J. 1986a. Population recovery of black-tailed prairie dogs following control with zinc phosphide. *Journal of Range Management* 39:249–251.

Knowles, C. J. 1986b. Some relationships of black-tailed prairie dogs to livestock grazing. *Great Basin Naturalist* 46:198–203.

Knowles, C. J. 1987. Reproductive ecology of black-tailed prairie dogs in Montana. *Great Basin Naturalist* 47:202–206.

Ko, R. C. 1972a. Biology of *Ixodes cookei* Packard (Ixonidae) of groundhogs *(Marmota monax* Erxleben). *Canadian Journal of Zoology* 50:433–436.

Ko, R. C. 1972b. The transmission of *Ackertia marmotae* Webster (Nematoda: Onchocercidae) of groundhogs *(Marmota monax)* by *Ixodes cookei. Canadian Journal of Zoology* 50:437–450.

Koenig, W. D. 1981a. Reproductive success, group size, and the evolution of cooperative breeding in the acorn woodpecker. *American Naturalist* 117:421–443.

Koenig, W. D. 1981b. Space competition in the acorn woodpecker: Power struggles in a cooperative breeder. *Animal Behaviour* 29:396–409.

Koenig, W. D., and R. L. Mumme. 1987. *Population Ecology of the Cooperatively Breeding Acorn Woodpecker*. Princeton, N.J.: Princeton University Press.

Koenig, W. D., R. L. Mumme, and F. A. Pitelka. 1984. The breeding system of the acorn woodpecker in central coastal California. *Zeitschrift für Tierpsychologie* 65:289–308.

Koenig, W. D., and F. A. Pitelka. 1979. Relatedness and inbreeding avoidance: Counterploys in the communally nesting acorn woodpecker. *Science* 206:1103–1105.

Koenig, W. D., and F. A. Pitelka. 1981. Ecological factors and kin selection in the evolution of cooperative breeding in birds. Pages 261–280 in R. D. Alexander and D. W. Tinkle, eds., *Natural Selection and Social Behavior*. New York: Chiron Press.

Koenig, W. D., F. A. Pitelka, W. J. Carmen, R. L. Mumme, and M. T. Stanback. 1992. The evolution of delayed dispersal in cooperative breeders. *Quarterly Review of Biology* 67:lll–150.

Koeppl, J. W., R. S. Hoffmann, and C. F. Nadler. 1978. Pattern analysis of acoustical behavior in four species of ground squirrels. *Journal of Mammalogy* 59:677–696.

Koford, C. B. 1958. Prairie dogs, whitefaces, and blue grama. *Wildlife Monographs* 3:1–78.

Koford, R. R. 1982. Mating system of a territorial tree squirrel *(Tamiasciurus douglasii)* in California. *Journal of Mammalogy* 63:274–283.

Kojola, I., and E. Eloranta. 1989. Influences of maternal body weight, age, and parity on sex ratio in semidomesticated reindeer *(Rangifer t. tarandus)*. *Evolution* 43:1331–1336.

Koprowski, J. L. 1992. Removal of copulatory plugs by female tree squirrels. *Journal of Mammalogy* 73:572–576.

Krebs, C. J. 1978. *Ecology*. New York: Harper and Row.

Krebs, J. R. 1974. Colonial nesting and social feeding as strategies for exploiting food sources in the great blue heron *(Ardea herodias)*. *Behaviour* 51:99–131.

Krebs, J. R., and N. B. Davies. 1981. *An Introduction to Behavioural Ecology*. 1st ed. Oxford: Blackwell Scientific Publications.

Krebs, J. R., and N. B. Davies. 1993. *An Introduction to Behavioural Ecology*. 3d ed. Oxford: Blackwell Scientific Publications.

Kretzmann, M. B., D. P. Costa, and B. J. Le Boeuf. 1993. Maternal energy investment in elephant seal pups: Evidence for sexual equality? *American Naturalist* 141:466–480.

Krueger, K. 1986. Feeding relationships among bison, pronghorn, and prairie dogs: An experimental analysis. *Ecology* 67:760–770.

Kruijt, J. P. and G. J. de Vos. 1988. Individual variation in reproductive success in male black grouse, *Tetrao tetrix* L. Pages 279–290 in T. H. Clutton-Brock, ed., *Reproductive Success: Studies of Individual Variation in Contrasting Breeding Systems*. Chicago: University of Chicago Press.

Kruuk, H. 1964. Predators and anti-predator behaviour of the black-headed gull *(Larus ridibundus* L.). *Behaviour Supplement* 11:1–29.

Kruuk, H. 1972. *The Spotted Hyena.* Chicago: University of Chicago Press.

Kruuk, H. 1978. Spatial organization and territorial behaviour of the European badger *Meles meles. Journal of Zoology* (London) 184:1–19.

Kruuk, H. 1989. *The Social Badger: Ecology and Behaviour of a Group-Living Carnivore (Meles meles).* Oxford: Oxford University Press.

Kruuk, H., and T. Parish. 1982. Factors affecting population density, group size and territory size of the European badger, *Meles meles. Journal of Zoology* (London) 196:31–39.

Kruuk, H., and T. Parish. 1987. Changes in the size of groups and ranges of the European badger (*Meles meles* L.) in an area in Scotland. *Journal of Animal Ecology* 56:351–364.

Kunz, T. H. 1976. Observations on the winter ecology of the bat fly *Trichobius corynorhini* Cockerall (Diptera: Streblidae). *Journal of Medical Entomology* 12:631–636.

Kurland, J. A. 1977. Kin selection in the Japanese monkey. *Contributions to Primatology* 12:1–145.

Labov, J. B. 1980. Factors influencing infanticidal behavior in wild male house mice *(Mus musculus). Behavioral Ecology and Sociobiology* 6:297–303.

Labov, J. B. 1981a. Male social status, physiology, and ability to block pregnancy in female house mice *(Mus musculus). Behavioral Ecology and Sociobiology* 8:287–291.

Labov, J. B. 1981b. Pregnancy blocking in rodents: Adaptive advantages for females. *American Naturalist* 118:361–371.

Labov, J. B., U. W. Huck, R. W. Elwood, and R. J. Brooks. 1985. Current problems in the study of infanticidal behavior of rodents. *Quarterly Review of Biology* 60:1–20.

Lacey, E. A., and P. W. Sherman. 1991. Social organization of naked mole-rat colonies: Evidence for divisions of labor. Pages 275–336 in P. W. Sherman, J. U. M. Jarvis, and R. D. Alexander, eds., *The Biology of the Naked Mole Rat.* Princeton, N.J.: Princeton University Press.

Lack, D. 1947. The significance of clutch size. Parts 1 and 2. *Ibis* 89:302–352.

Lack, D. 1948a. Natural selection and family size in the starling. *Evolution* 2:95–110.

Lack, D. 1948b. The significance of litter size. *Journal of Animal Ecology* 17:45–50.

Lack, D. 1954a. The evolution of reproductive rates. Pages 143–156 in J. S. Huxley, A. C. Hardy, and E. B. Ford, eds., *Evolution as a Process.* London: Allen and Unwin.

Lack, D. 1954b. *The Natural Regulation of Animal Numbers.* Oxford: Clarendon Press.

Lack, D. 1968. *Ecological Adaptations for Breeding in Birds.* London: Methuen.

Lackey, J. A. 1976. Reproduction, growth, and development in the Yucatan deer mouse, *Peromyscus leucopus yucatanicus. Journal of Mammalogy* 59:69–83.

Lacy, R. C., A. Petric, and M. Warneke. 1993. Inbreeding and outbreeding in captive populations of wild animal species. Pages 352–374 in N. W. Thornhill, ed., *The Natural History of Inbreeding and Outbreeding: Theoretical and Empirical Perspectives.* Chicago: University of Chicago Press.

Lacy, R. C., and P. W. Sherman. 1983. Kin recognition by phenotype matching. *American Naturalist* 121:489–512.

Lancaster, J., and B. King. 1985. An evolutionary perspective on menopause. Pages 13–20 in J. K. Brown and V. Kerns, eds., *In Her Prime.* South Hadley, Mass.: Bergin and Garvey.

Lanier, D. L., D. Q. Estep, and D. A. Dewsbury. 1979. Role of prolonged copulatory behavior in facilitating reproductive success in a competitive mating situation in laboratory rats. *Journal of Comparative and Physiological Psychology* 93:781–792.

Lasley, J. F. 1978. *Genetics of Livestock Improvement.* Englewood Cliffs, N.J.: Prentice Hall.

Lawick, H. van. 1974. *Solo: The Story of an African Wild Dog.* London: Collins.

Lawick, H. van, and J. van Lawick-Goodall. 1971. *Innocent Killers.* Boston: Houghton Mifflin.

Lazarus, A. B., and F. P. Rowe. 1975. Freeze-marking rodents with a pressurized refrigerant. *Mammalian Review* 5:31–34.

Lazarus, J. 1978. Vigilance, flock size and domain of danger in the white-fronted goose. *Wildfowl* 29:135–145.

Lazarus, J. 1979. The early warning function of flocking in birds: An experimental study with captive quelea. *Animal Behaviour* 27:855–865.

Lazarus, J., and I. R. Inglis. 1978. The breeding behavior of the pink-footed goose: Parental care and vigilant behaviour during the fledging period. *Behaviour* 65:62–88.

Le Boeuf, B. J. 1972. Sexual behavior in the northern elephant seal, *Mirounga angustirostris. Behaviour* 41:1–26.

Le Boeuf, B. J. 1974. Male-male competition and reproductive success in elephant seals. *American Zoologist* 14:163–176.

Le Boeuf, B. J. 1981. The elephant seal. Pages 291–301 in P. Jewell, ed., *Problems in Management of Locally Abundant Wild Mammals.* New York: Academic Press.

Le Boeuf, B. J. 1986. Sexual strategies of seals and walruses. *New Scientist* 109:36–39.

Le Boeuf, B. J., and K. T. Briggs. 1977. The cost of living in a seal harem. *Mammalia* 41:168–195.

Le Boeuf, B. J., R. Condit, and J. Reiter. 1989. Parental investment and the secondary sex ratio in northern elephant seals. *Behavioral Ecology and Sociobiology* 25:109–117.

Le Boeuf, B. J., and R. S. Peterson. 1969. Social status and mating activity in elephant seals. *Science* 163:91–93.

Le Boeuf, B. J., and J. Reiter. 1988. Lifetime reproductive success in northern elephant seals. Pages 344–362 in T. H. Clutton-Brock, ed.,

Reproductive Success: Studies of Individual Variation in Contrasting Breeding Systems. Chicago: University of Chicago Press.

Le Boeuf, B. J., R. J. Whiting, and R. F. Gantt. 1972. Perinatal behavior of northern elephant seal females and their young. *Behaviour* 43:121–156.

Lechleitner, R. R. 1969. *Wild Mammals of Colorado.* Boulder, Colo.: Pruett.

Lechleitner, R. R., L. Kartman, M. I. Goldberg, and B. W. Hudson. 1968. An epizootic of plague in Gunnison's prairie dogs *(Cynomys gunnisoni)* in south-central Colorado. *Ecology* 49:734–743.

Lechleitner, R. R., J. V. Tileston, and L. Kartman. 1962. Die-off of a Gunnison's prairie dog colony in central Colorado. I. Ecological observations and description of the epizootic. *Zoonoses Research* 1:185–199.

Lee, P. C. 1987. Allomothering among African elephants. *Animal Behaviour* 35:278–291.

Lee, P. C., and C. J. Moss. 1986. Early maternal investment in male and female African elephant calves. *Behavioral Ecology and Sociobiology* 18:353–361.

Lee, S. P., M. C. Carey, and J. T. LaMont. 1981. Aspirin prevention of cholesterol gallstone formation in prairie dogs. *Science* 211:1429–1431.

Leger, D. W., S. D. Berney-Key, and P. W. Sherman. 1984. Vocalizations of Belding's ground squirrels *(Spermophilus beldingi). Animal Behaviour* 32:753–764.

Leger, D. W., and D. H. Owings. 1978. Responses to alarm calls by California ground squirrels: Effects of call structure and maternal status. *Behavioral Ecology and Sociobiology* 3:177–186.

Leger, D. W., D. H. Owings, and L. M. Boal. 1979. Contextual information and differential responses to alarm whistles in California ground squirrels. *Zeitschrift für Tierpsychologie* 49:142–155.

Leger, D. W., D. H. Owings, and D. L. Gelfand. 1980. Single-note vocalizations of California ground squirrels: Graded signals and situation-specificity of predator and socially evoked calls. *Zeitschrift für Tierpsychologie* 52:227–246.

Leigh, E. G. 1970. Sex ratio and differential mortality between the sexes. *American Naturalist* 104:205–210.

Leland, L., T. T. Struhsaker, and T. M. Butynski. 1984. Infanticide by adult males in three primates species of the Kibale Forest, Uganda: A test of hypotheses. Pages 151–172 in G. Hausfater and S. B. Hrdy, eds., *Infanticide: Comparative and Evolutionary Perspectives.* New York: Aldine.

Lessels, C. M. 1991. The evolution of life histories. Pages 32–68 in J. R. Krebs and N. B. Davies, eds., *Behavioral Ecology: An Evolutionary Approach.* 3rd ed. Oxford: Blackwell Scientific Publications.

Lessels, C. M., and M. I. Avery. 1987. Sex ratio selection in species with helpers at the nest: Some extensions of the repayment model. *American Naturalist* 129:610–620.

Levine, L. 1967. Sexual selection in mice. IV. Experimental demonstration of selective fertilization. *American Naturalist* 101:289–294.

Lewis, S. M., and S. N. Austad. 1990. Sources of intraspecific variation in sperm precedence in red flour beetles. *American Naturalist* 135:351–359.

Lewontin, R. C. 1970. The units of selection. *Annual Review of Ecology and Systematics* 1:1–18.

Lewontin, R. C. 1974. *The Genetical Basis of Evolutionary Change.* New York: Columbia University Press.

Li, C. C. 1955. *Population Genetics.* Chicago: University of Chicago Press.

Lidicker, W. Z. 1975. The role of dispersal in the demography of small mammals. Pages 103–128 in F. B. Golley, K. Petruscewicz, and C. Ryszkowski, eds., *Small Mammals: Their Productivity and Population Dynamics.* Cambridge: Cambridge University Press.

Lindelius, R. T. 1980. Effects of parental consanguinity on mortality and reproductive function. *Human Heredity* 30:185–191.

Linden, M., and A. P. Møller. 1989. Cost of reproduction and covariation of life history traits in birds. *Trends in Ecology and Evolution* 4:367–371.

Linder, R. L., and C. N. Hillman, eds. 1973. *Proceedings of the Black-Footed Ferret and Prairie Dog Workshop.* Brookings, S.D.: South Dakota State University.

Linsdale, J. M. 1946. *The California Ground Squirrel.* Berkeley, Calif.: University of California Press.

Lipetz, V. E., and M. Bekoff. 1982. Group size and vigilance in pronghorns. *Zeitschrift für Tierpsychologie* 58:203–216.

Longhurst, W. 1944. Observations on the ecology of the Gunnison prairie dog in Colorado. *Journal of Mammalogy* 25:24–36.

Lorenz, K. Z. 1970. *Studies on Animal and Human Behavior.* Vols. 1 and 2. Cambridge, Mass: Harvard University Press.

Lott, D. F. 1991. *Intraspecific Variation in the Social Systems of Wild Vertebrates.* Cambridge: Cambridge University Press.

Loughry, W. J. 1987a. Differences in experimental and natural encounters of black-tailed prairie dogs with snakes. *Animal Behaviour* 35:1568–1570.

Loughry, W. J. 1987b. The dynamics of snake harassment by black-tailed prairie dogs. *Behaviour* 103:27–48.

Loughry, W. J. 1988. Population differences in how black-tailed prairie dogs deal with snakes. *Behavioral Ecology and Sociobiology* 22:61–67.

Loughry, W. J. 1992. Ontogeny of time allocation in black-tailed prairie dogs. *Ethology* 90:206–224.

Loughry, W. J. 1993a. Determinants of time allocation by adult and yearling black-tailed prairie dogs. *Behaviour* 124:23–43.

Loughry, W. J. 1993b. Mechanisms of change in the ontogeny of black-tailed prairie dog time budgets. *Ethology* 95:54–64.

Lovaas, A. L. 1973. Prairie dogs and black-footed ferrets in National Parks. Pages 139–148 in R. L. Linder and C. N. Hillman, eds., *Proceedings of the Black-Footed Ferret and Prairie Dog Workshop.* Brookings, S.D.: South Dakota State University.

Low, B. S. 1978. Environmental uncertainty and the parental strategies of marsupials and placentals. *American Naturalist* 112:197–213.

Loye, J. E., and M. Zuk, eds. 1991. *Bird-Parasite Interactions: Ecology, Evolution, and Behaviour.* Oxford: Oxford University Press.

Lund, A., and R. V. Alatalo. 1992. *The Pied Flycatcher.* London: T. and A. D. Poyser.

Luo, J., and B. J. Fox. 1990. Life-table comparisons between two ground squirrels. *Journal of Mammalogy* 71:364–370.

Lups, P., and T. J. Roper. 1990. Cannibalism in a female badger *(Meles meles):* Infanticide or predation? *Journal of Zoology* (London) 221:314–315.

Lynch, M. 1991. The genetic interpretation of inbreeding depression and outbreeding depression. *Evolution* 45:622–629.

MacClintock, D. 1970. *Squirrels of North America.* New York: Van Nostrand Reinhold.

Macdonald, D. W. 1979. "Helpers" in fox society. *Nature* 282:69–71.

Macdonald, D. W. 1981. Dwindling resources and the social behavior of capybaras *(Hydrochoerus hydrochaeris)* (Mammalia). *Journal of Zoology* (London) 194:371–391.

Macdonald, D. W., and P. D. Moehlman. 1983. Cooperation, altruism, and restraint in the reproduction of carnivores. Pages 433–467 in P. P. G. Bateson and P. Klopfer, eds., *Perspectives in Ethology and Ontogeny,* vol. 5. New York: Plenum Press.

MacMahon, B. 1974. Infant mortality in the United States. Pages 189–209 in C. L. Erhardt and J. E. Berlin, eds., *Mortality and Morbidity in the United States.* Cambridge, Mass: Harvard University Press.

Madsen, T., and R. Shine. 1993. Temporal variability in sexual selection acting on reproductive tactics and body size in male snakes. *American Naturalist* 141:167–171.

Madsen, T., R. Shine, J. Loman, and T. Hakansson. 1992. Why do female adders copulate so frequently? *Nature* 355:440–441.

Madsen, T., R. Shine, J. Loman, and T. Hakansson. 1993. Determinants of mating success in male adders, *Vipera berus. Animal Behaviour* 45:491–499.

Madson, J. 1968. Dark days in dogtown. *Audubon* 70:32–43.

Maestripieri, D. 1993. Vigilance costs of allogrooming in macaque mothers. *American Naturalist* 141:744–753.

Malcolm, J. R., and K. Marten. 1982. Natural selection and the communal rearing of pups in African wild dogs *(Lycaon pictus). Behavioral Ecology and Sociobiology* 10:1–13.

Mallory, F. F., and R. J. Brooks. 1978. Infanticide and other reproductive strategies in the collared lemming, *Dicrostonyx groenlandicus. Nature* 273:144–146.

Mallory, F. F., and R. J. Brooks. 1980. Infanticide and pregnancy failure: Reproductive strategies in the female collared lemming *(Dicrostonyx groenlandicus). Biology of Reproduction* 22:192–196.

Manning, C. J., E. K. Wakeland, and W. K. Potts. 1992. Communal nesting patterns in mice implicate MHC genes in kin recognition. *Nature* 360:581–583.

Manning, J. T. 1985. Choosy females and correlates of male age. *Journal of Theoretical Biology* 116:349–354.

Marler, P. 1955. Characteristics of some animal calls. *Nature* 176:6–8.

Marler, P. 1957. Specific distinctiveness in the communication signals of birds. *Behaviour* ll:13–39.

Marler, P. 1959. Developments in the study of animal communication. Pages 150–206 in P. R. Bell, ed., *Darwin's Biological Work.* Cambridge: Cambridge University Press.

Marsh, H., and T. Kasuya. 1986. Evidence for reproductive senescence in female cetaceans. *Report of the International Whaling Commission,* Special Issue 8:57–74.

Martin, S. J., and M. H. Schroeder. 1978. *Black-Footed Ferret Surveys on Seven Coal Occurrence Areas in Southwestern and Southcentral Wyoming, June 8 to September 25, 1978: Final Report.* Denver, Colo.: United States Fish and Wildlife Service.

Martin, S. J., and M. H. Schroeder. 1980. *Black-Footed Ferret Surveys on Seven Coal Occurrence Areas in Wyoming, February–September, 1979: Final Report.* Cheyenne, Wyo.: Wyoming State Office, United States Bureau of Land Management.

Martin, S. J., M. H. Schroeder, and H. Tietjen. 1984. Burrow plugging by prairie dogs in response to Siberian polecats. *Great Basin Naturalist* 44:447–449.

Martinez, D. R., and E. Klinghammer. 1970. The behavior of the whale *Orcinus orca:* A review of the literature. *Zeitschrift für Tierpsychologie* 27:828–839.

Marzluff, J. M., and R. P. Balda. 1992. *The Pinyon Jay: Behavioral Ecology of a Colonial and Cooperative Corvid.* London: T. and A. D. Poyser.

Massey, A. 1977. Agonistic aids and kinship in a group of pigtail macaques. *Behavioral Ecology and Sociobiology* 2:31–40.

Matocha, K. 1977. The vocal repertoire of *Spermophilus tridecemlineatus. American Midland Naturalist* 98:482–487.

Matthews, M. K., and N. T. Adler. 1978. Systematic interrelationships of mating, vaginal plug position, and sperm transport in the rat. *Physiological Behavior* 20:303–309.

Mayer, P. J. 1982. Evolutionary advantage of the menopause. *Human Ecology* 10:477–493.

Mayer, W. V. 1953. A preliminary study of the barrow ground squirrel, *Citellus parryi barrowensis. Journal of Mammalogy* 34:334–345.

Maynard Smith, J. 1964. Group selection and kin selection. *Nature* 201:1145–1147.

Maynard Smith, J. 1965. The evolution of alarm calls. *American Naturalist* 99:59–63.

Maynard Smith, J. 1966. *The Theory of Evolution.* Baltimore, Md: Penguin Books.

Maynard Smith, J. 1978. *The Evolution of Sex.* London: Cambridge University Press.

Maynard Smith, J. 1979. Game theory and the evolution of behavior. *Proceedings of the Royal Society of London,* Series B, 205:475–488.

Maynard Smith, J. 1991. Theories of sexual selection. *Trends in Ecology and Evolution* 6:146–151.

Maynard Smith, J., and G. R. Price. 1973. The logic of animal conflict. *Nature* 246:15–18.

McCann, T. S. 1981. Aggression and sexual activity of male southern elephant seals, *Mirounga leonina*. *Journal of Zoology* (London) 195:295–310.

McCarley, H. 1966. Annual cycle, population dynamics and adaptive behavior of *Citellus tridecemlineatus*. *Journal of Mammalogy* 47:294–316.

McCarthy, M. M., and F. S. vom Saal. 1985. The influence of reproductive state on infanticide by wild female mice. *Physiology and Behavior* 35:843–849.

McCleery, R. H., and C. M. Perrins. 1988. Lifetime reproductive success of the great tit, *Parus major*. Pages 136–153 in T. H. Clutton-Brock, ed., *Reproductive Success: Studies of Individual Variation in Contrasting Breeding Systems*. Chicago: University of Chicago Press.

McCloskey, R. J., and K. C. Shaw. 1977. Copulatory behavior of the fox squirrel. *Journal of Mammalogy* 58:663–665.

McClure, P. A. 1987. The energetics of reproduction and life histories of cricetine rodents *(Neotoma floridana* and *Sigmodon hispidus)*. *Symposia of The Zoological Society of London* 57:241–258.

McComb, K. 1987. Roaring by red deer stags advances the date of oestrus in hinds. *Nature* 330:648–649.

McCracken, G. F. 1984. Communal nursing in Mexican free-tailed bat maternity colonies. *Science* 223:1090–1091.

McCracken, G. F. 1985. Locational memory and female-pup reunions in Mexican free-tailed bat maternity colonies. *Animal Behaviour* 45:811–813.

McCracken, G. F., and J. W. Bradbury. 1977. Paternity and genetic heterogeneity in the polygynous bat, *Phyllostomus hastatus*. *Science* 198:303–306.

McCracken, G. F., and J. W. Bradbury. 1981. Social organization and kinship in the polygynous bat *Phyllostomus hastatus*. *Behavioral Ecology and Sociobiology* 8:ll–34.

McCullough, D. R. 1969. *The Tule Elk: Its History and Ecology*. Berkeley, Calif.: University of California Press.

McFarland Symington, M. 1987. Sex ratio and maternal rank in wild spider monkeys: When daughters disperse. *Behavioral Ecology and Sociobiology* 20:421–425.

McGinley, M. A. 1984. The adaptive value of male-biased sex ratios among stressed animals. *American Naturalist* 124:597–599.

McGowan, K. J., and G. E. Woolfenden. 1989. A sentinel system in the Florida scrub jay. *Animal Behaviour* 37:1000–1006.

McKaye, K. R. 1981. Natural selection and the evolution of interspecific brood care in fishes. Pages 177–183 in R. D. Alexander and D. W. Tinkle, eds., *Natural Selection and Social Behavior*. New York: Chiron Press.

McKaye, K. R. 1985. Cichlid-catfish mutualistic defense of young in Lake Malawi, Africa. *Oecologia* 66:358–363.

McKaye, K. R., and N. M. McKaye. 1977. Communal care and kidnapping of young by parental cichlids. *Evolution* 31:674–681.

McKinney, F., K. M. Cheng, and D. J. Bruggers. 1984. Sperm competition in apparently monogamous birds. Pages 523–545 in R. L. Smith, ed., *Sperm Competition and the Evolution of Animal Mating Systems.* Orlando, Fla.: Academic Press.

McKinney, F., and P. Stolen. 1982. Extra-pair-bond courtship and forced copulation among captive green-winged teal *(Anas crecca carolinensis). Animal Behaviour* 30:461–474.

McKinney, T. D., and J. J. Christian. 1970. Incidence and effects of botfly parasitism in the eastern chipmunk. *Journal of Wildlife Diseases* 6:140–143.

McLain, D. K., and N. B. Marsh. 1990. Individual sex ratio adjustment in response to the operational sex ratio in the southern green stinkbug. *Evolution* 44:1018–1025.

McLean, I. G. 1982. The association of female kin in the Arctic ground squirrel *Spermophilus parryii. Behavioral Ecology and Sociobiology* 10:91–99.

McLean, I. G. 1983. Paternal behaviour and killing of young in arctic ground squirrels. *Animal Behaviour* 31:32–44.

McLean, I. G. 1984. Spacing behavior and aggression in female ground squirrels. Pages 321–335 in J. O. Murie and G. R. Michener, eds., *The Biology of Ground-Dwelling Squirrels.* Lincoln, Nebr.: University of Nebraska Press.

McLean, I. G., and A. J. Towns. 1981. Differences in weight changes and the annual cycle of male and female arctic ground squirrels. *Arctic* 34:249–254.

McNulty, F. 1971. *Must They Die? The Strange Case of the Prairie Dog and the Black-Footed Ferret.* Garden City, N.Y.: Doubleday.

McShea, W. J., and D. M. Madison. 1984. Communal nesting between reproductively active females in a spring population of *Microtus pennsylvanicus. Canadian Journal of Zoology* 62:344–346.

McShea, W. J., and D. M. Madison. 1986. Sex ratio shifts within litters of meadow voles. *Behavioral Ecology and Sociobiology* 18:431–436.

McShea, W. J., and D. M. Madison. 1989. Measurements of reproductive traits in a field population of meadow voles. *Journal of Mammalogy* 70:132–141.

Meanly, B. 1955. A nesting study of the little blue heron in eastern Arkansas. *Wilson Bulletin* 67:84–99.

Mech, L. D. 1970. *The Wolf: Ecology and Behavior of an Endangered Species.* New York: Natural History Press.

Melchior, H. R. 1971. Characteristics of arctic ground squirrel alarm calls. *Oecologia* 7:184–190.

Melchior, H. R., and F. A. Iwen. 1965. Trapping, restraining, and marking arctic ground squirrels for behavioral observations. *Journal of Wildlife Management* 29:671–678.

Mellink, E., and H. Madrigal. 1993. Ecology of Mexican prairie dogs, *Cynomys mexicanus,* in El Manantial, northeastern Mexico. *Journal of Mammalogy* 74:631–635.

Mendl, M. 1988. The effects of litter size variation on mother-offspring relationships and behavioural and physical development in several mammalian species (principally rodents). *Journal of Zoology* (London) 215:15–34.

Menkens, G. E., and S. H. Anderson. 1991. Population dynamics of white-tailed prairie dogs during an epizootic of sylvatic plague. *Journal of Mammalogy* 72:328–331.

Merriam, C. H. 1892. Description of a new prairie dog *(Cynomys mexicanus)* from Mexico. *Proceedings of the Biological Society of Washington* 7:157–158.

Merriam, C. H. 1902. The prairie dog of the great plains. Pages 257–270 in *Yearbook of United States Department of Agriculture* (1901). Washington, D.C.

Mesnick, S. L., and B. J. Le Boeuf. 1991. Sexual behavior of male northern elephant seals. II. Female response to potentially injurious encounters. *Behaviour* 117:262–280.

Michener, C. D. 1969. Comparative social behavior of bees. *Annual Review of Entomology* 14:299–342.

Michener, G. R. 1973. Field observations on the social relationships between adult female and juvenile Richardson's ground squirrels. *Canadian Journal of Zoology* 15:33–38.

Michener, G. R. 1974. Development of adult-young identification in Richardson's ground squirrels. *Developmental Psychobiology* 7:375–384.

Michener, G. R. 1977. Effect of climatic conditions on the annual activity and hibernation cycle of Richardson's ground squirrels and Columbian ground squirrels. *Canadian Journal of Zoology* 55:693–703.

Michener, G. R. 1979. Yearly variations in the population dynamics of Richardson's ground squirrels. *Canadian Field Naturalist* 93:363–370.

Michener, G. R. 1980a. Differential reproduction among female Richardson's ground squirrels and its relation to sex ratio. *Behavioral Ecology and Sociobiology* 7:173–178.

Michener, G. R. 1980b. Estrous and gestation periods in Richardson's ground squirrels. *Journal of Mammalogy* 61:531–534.

Michener, G. R. 1982. Infanticide in ground squirrels. *Animal Behaviour* 30:936–938.

Michener, G. R. 1983. Kin identification, matriarchies, and the evolution of sociality in ground-dwelling sciurids. Pages 528–572 in J. F. Eisenberg and D. G. Kleiman, eds., *Recent Advances in the Study of Mammalian Behavior*. American Society of Mammalogists Special Publication no. 7.

Michener, G. R. 1984a. Age, sex, and species differences in the annual cycles of ground-dwelling sciurids: Implications for sociality. Pages 81–107 in J. O. Murie and G. R. Michener, eds., *The Biology of Ground-Dwelling Squirrels*. Lincoln, Nebr.: University of Nebraska Press.

Michener, G. R. 1984b. Copulatory plugs in Richardson's ground squirrels. *Canadian Journal of Zoology* 62:267–270.

Michener, G. R. 1984c. Sexual differences in body weight patterns of Richardson's ground squirrels during the breeding season. *Journal of Mammalogy* 65:59–66.

Michener, G. R. 1985. Chronology of reproductive events for female Richardson's ground squirrels. *Journal of Mammalogy* 66:280–288.

Michener, G.R. 1989a. Reproductive effort during gestation and lactation by Richardson's ground squirrels. *Oecologia* 78:77–86.

Michener, G. R. 1989b. Sexual differences in interyear survival and life-span of Richardson's ground squirrels. *Canadian Journal of Zoology* 67:1827–1831.

Michener, G. R. 1990. Use of body mass and sex ratio to interpret the behavioral ecology of Richardson's ground squirrels. Pages 304–338 in M. Bekoff and D. Jamieson, eds., *Interpretation and Explanation in the Study of Animal Behavior,* vol. 2, *Explanation, Evolution, and Adaptation.* Boulder, Colo.: Westview Press.

Michener, G. R. 1993. Lethal myiasis of Richardson's ground squirrels by the sarcophagid fly *Neobellieria citellivora. Journal of Mammalogy* 74:148–155.

Michener, G. R., and L. Locklear. 1990. Differential costs of reproductive effort for male and female Richardson's ground squirrels. *Ecology* 71:855–868.

Michener, G. R., and D. R. Michener. 1977. Population structure and dispersal in Richardson's ground squirrels. *Ecology* 58:359–368.

Michener, G. R., and J. O. Murie. 1983. Black-tailed prairie dog coteries: Are they cooperatively breeding units? *American Naturalist* 121:266–274.

Michener, G. R., and D. H. Sheppard. 1972. Social behaviour between adult Richardson's ground squirrels *(Spermophilus richardsonii)* and their own and alien young. *Canadian Journal of Zoology* 50:1343–1349.

Michod, R. E., and B. R. Levin. 1988. Introduction. Pages 1–6 in R. E. Michod and B. R. Levin, eds., *The Evolution of Sex: An Examination of Current Ideas.* Sunderland, Mass.: Sinauer Associates.

Miles, V. I., M. J. Wilcomb, and J. V. Irons. 1952. Rodent plague in the Texas south plains 1947–49. *Public Health Monograph* 6, Part 2:39–53.

Millar, J. S. 1977. Adaptive features of mammalian reproduction. *Evolution* 31:370–386.

Millar, J. S., and R. M. Zammuto. 1983. Life histories of mammals: An analysis of life tables. *Ecology* 64:631–635.

Miller, D. E., and J. T. Emlen. 1975. Individual chick recognition and family integrity in the ring-billed gull. *Behaviour* 52:124–144.

Miller, E. H. 1975. Walrus ethology, 1: The social use of tusks and applications of multidimensional scaling. *Canadian Journal of Zoology* 53:590–613.

Miller, J. S. 1977. Adaptive features of mammalian reproduction. *Evolution* 31:370–386.

Milstein, P., S. Prestt, and A. A. Bell. 1970. The breeding cycle of the grey heron. *Ardea* 58:171–257.

Missakian, E. A. 1973. Genealogical mating activity in free-ranging groups of rhesus monkeys *(Macaca mulatta)* on Cayo Santiago. *Behaviour* 45:224–240.

Mitchell, B., and G. A. Lincoln. 1973. Conception dates in relation to age and condition in two populations of red deer in Scotland. *Journal of Zoology* (London) 171:141–152.

Mitton, J. B. 1993. Theory and data pertinent to the relationship between heterozygosity and fitness. Pages 17–41 in N. W. Thornhill, ed., *The Natural History of Inbreeding and Outbreeding: Theoretical and Empirical Perspectives.* Chicago: University of Chicago Press.

Mitton, J. B., and M. C. Grant. 1984. Associations among protein heterozygosity, growth rate, and developmental homeostasis. *Annual Review of Ecology and Systematics* 15:479–499.

Mock, D. W. 1984a. Infanticide, siblicide, and avian nestling mortality. Pages 3–30 in G. Hausfater and S. B. Hrdy, eds., *Infanticide: Comparative and Evolutionary Perspectives.* New York: Aldine.

Mock, D. W. 1984b. Siblicidal aggression and resource monopolization in birds. *Science* 225:731–733.

Mock, D. W. 1985. Siblicidal brood reduction: The prey-size hypothesis. *American Naturalist* 125:327–343.

Mock, D. W., and M. Fujioka. 1990. Monogamy and long-term pair bonding in vertebrates. *Trends in Ecology and Evolution* 5:39–43.

Moehlman, P. D. 1979. Jackal helpers and pup survival. *Nature* 277:382–383.

Moehlman, P. D. 1983. Socioecology of silver backed and golden jackals *(Canis mesomelas, Canis aureus).* Pages 423–453 in J. F. Eisenberg and D. G. Kleiman, eds., *Recent Advances in the Study of Mammalian Behavior.* American Society of Mammalogists Special Publication no. 7.

Moehlman, P. D. 1986. Ecology and cooperation in canids. Pages 64–86 in D. I. Rubenstein and R. W. Wrangham, eds., *Ecological Aspects of Social Evolution.* Princeton, N.J.: Princeton University Press.

Møller, A. P. 1985. Mixed reproductive strategy and mate guarding in a semi-colonial passerine, the swallow *Hirundo rustica. Behavioral Ecology and Sociobiology* 17:401–408.

Møller, A. P. 1989. Ejaculate quality, testis size and sperm production in mammals. *Functional Ecology* 3:91–96.

Møller, A. P. 1990. Effects of a haematophagous mite on the barn swallow *Hirundo rustica:* A test of the Hamilton and Zuk hypothesis. *Evolution* 44:771–784.

Møller, A. P. 1991a. The preening activity of swallows, *Hirundo rustica,* in relation to experimentally manipulated loads of haematophagous mites. *Animal Behaviour* 42:251–260.

Møller, A. P. 1991b. Sperm competition, sperm depletion, paternal care, and relative testis size in birds. *American Naturalist* 137:892–906.

Møller, A. P. 1991c. Why mated songbirds sing so much: Mate guarding and male announcement of mate fertility status. *American Naturalist* 138:994–1014.

Møller, A. P., and T. R. Birkhead. 1989. Copulation behavior in mammals: Evidence that sperm competition is widespread. *Biological Journal of the Linnean Society* 38:119–131.

Møller, A. P., and T. R. Birkhead. 1991. Frequent copulations and mate guarding as alternative paternity guards in birds: A comparative study. *Behaviour* 118:170–186.

Møller, A. P., and T. R. Birkhead. 1993. Cuckoldry and sociality: A comparative study of birds. *American Naturalist* 142:118–140.

Montgomerie, R., and R. Thornhill. 1989. Fertility advertisement in birds: A means of inciting male-male competition? *Ethology* 81:209–220.

Moore, J. 1984. Female transfer in primates. *International Journal of Primatology* 5:537–589.

Moore, J., and R. Ali. 1984. Are dispersal and inbreeding avoidance related? *Animal Behaviour* 32:94–112.

Moran, G. 1984. Vigilance behaviour and alarm calls in a captive group of meerkats, *Suricata suricatta*. *Zeitschrift für Tierpsychologie* 65:228–240.

Morgan, M. J., and J. G. J. Godin. 1985. Antipredator benefits of schooling behaviour in a cyprinodontid fish, the banded killifish *(Fundulus diaphanus)*. *Zeitschrift für Tierpsychologie* 70:236–246.

Mori, U., and R. I. M. Dunbar. 1985. Changes in the reproductive condition of female gelada baboons following the takeover of one-male units. *Zeitschrift für Tierpsychologie* 67:215–224.

Morimoto, D. C., R. H. Tamarin, and C. K. Levy. 1985. Whole-body biological elimination rates of gamma-emitting radionuclides in captive meadow voles, *Microtus pennsylvanicus*. *Health Physics* 49:1217–1228.

Morris, D. W. 1986. Proximate and ultimate controls on life-history variation: The evolution of litter size in white-footed mice *(Peromyscus leucopus)*. *Evolution* 40:169–181.

Morton, M. L., and J. S. Gallup. 1975. Reproductive cycle of the Belding ground squirrel *(Spermophilus beldingi beldingi):* Seasonal and age differences. *Great Basin Naturalist* 35:427–433.

Morton, M. L., and P. W. Sherman. 1978. Effects of a spring snowstorm on behavior, reproduction, and survival of Belding's ground squirrels. *Canadian Journal of Zoology* 56:2578–2590.

Mumme, R. L., W. D. Koenig, and F. A. Pitelka. 1983. Reproductive competition in the communal acorn woodpecker: Sisters destroy each other's eggs. *Nature* 306:583–584.

Mumme, R. L., W. D. Koenig, and F. L. W. Ratnieks. 1989. Helping behaviour, reproductive value, and the future component of indirect fitness. *Animal Behaviour* 38:331–343.

Munro, J., and J. Bedard. 1977. Gull predation and creching behaviour in the common eider. *Journal of Animal Ecology* 46:799–810.

Murie, J. O. 1973. Population characteristics and phenology of a Franklin ground squirrel *(Spermophilus franklinii)* colony in Alberta, Canada. *American Midland Naturalist* 90:334–340.

Murie, J. O. 1988. Multiple mating and paternity in Columbian ground squirrels. Abstract of paper presented at Behavioral Ecology Meeting, Vancouver.

Murie, J. O., and F. S. Dobson. 1987. The costs of reproduction in female Columbian ground squirrels. *Oecologia* 73:1–6.

Murie, J. O., and M. A. Harris. 1978. Territoriality and dominance in male Columbian ground squirrels *(Spermophilus columbianus)*. *Canadian Journal of Zoology* 56:2402–2412.

Murie, J. O., and M. A. Harris. 1988. Social interactions and dominance relationships between female and male Columbian ground squirrels. *Canadian Journal of Zoology* 66:1414–1420.

Murie, J. O., and I. G. McLean. 1980. Copulatory plugs in ground squirrels. *Journal of Mammalogy* 61:355–356.

Murie, J. O., and G. R. Michener, eds. 1984. *The Biology of Ground-Dwelling Squirrels.* Lincoln, Nebr.: University of Nebraska Press.

Murray, M. D. 1961. The ecology of the louse *Polyplax serrate* (Burm.) on the mouse *Mus musculus* L. *Australian Journal of Zoology* 9:1–13.

Murray, M. D. 1987. Effects of host grooming on louse populations. *Parasitology Today* 3:276–278.

Murton, R. K. 1968. Some predator-prey relationships in bird damage and population control. Pages 157–169 in R. K. Murton and E. N. Wright, eds., *The Problems of Birds as Pests.* New York: Academic Press.

Muul, I. 1968. *Behavioral and Physiological Influences on the Distribution of the Flying Squirrel,* Glaucomys volans. Miscellaneous Publications no. 134. Ann Arbor, Mich.: Museum of Zoology, The University of Michigan.

Muul, I. 1969. Mating behavior, gestation period and development of *Glaucomys sabrinus. Journal of Mammalogy* 50:121.

Myers, J. H. 1978. Sex ratio adjustment under food stress: Maximization of quality or numbers of offspring? *American Naturalist* 112:381–388.

Myers, K., and W. E. Poole. 1961. A study of the biology of the wild rabbit, *Oryctolagus cuniculus* (L.), in confined populations. II. The effects of season and population increase on behaviour. *Commonwealth Scientific and Industrial Research Organization Wildlife Research* 6:1–41.

Myers, P., and L. L. Masters. 1983. Reproduction by *Peromyscus maniculatus:* Size and compromise. *Journal of Mammalogy* 64:1–18.

Nadler, C. F., R. S. Hoffmann, and J. J. Pizzimenti. 1971. Chromosomes and serum proteins of prairie dogs and a model of *Cynomys* evolution. *Journal of Mammalogy* 52:545–555.

Neal, E. 1970. The banded mongoose, *Mungos mungo* Gmelin. *East African Wildlife Journal* 8:63–71.

Neal, E. G. 1986. *The Natural History of Badgers.* New York: Facts on File Publications.

Neill, S. R. Saint J., and J. M. Cullen. 1974. Experiments on whether schooling by their prey affects the hunting behavior of cephalopods and fish predators. *Journal of Zoology* (London) 172:549–569.

Nelson, J. B. 1978. *The Sulidae.* Oxford: Oxford University Press.

Newton, I. 1989a. Introduction. Pages 1–11 in I. Newton, ed., *Lifetime Reproduction in Birds.* New York: Academic Press.

Newton, I., ed. 1989b. *Lifetime Reproduction in Birds.* New York: Academic Press.

Newton, I., and M. Marquiss. 1979. Sex ratio among nestlings of the European sparrowhawk. *American Naturalist* 113:309–315.

Newton, I., and M. Marquiss. 1984. Seasonal trend in the breeding performance of sparrowhawks. *Journal of Animal Ecology* 53:809–829.

Nias, R. C. 1984. Territory quality and group size in the superb blue fairy-wren *Malurus cyaneus. Emu* 84:178–180.

Niemitz, C., ed. 1984. *Biology of Tarsiers.* Stuttgart: Fischer Verlag.

Nisbet, I. C. T. 1973. Courtship-feeding, egg-size and breeding success in common terns. *Nature* 241:141–142.

Nishida, T. 1979. The social structure of chimpanzees of the Mahale Mountains. Pages 72–121 in D. A. Hamburg and E. R. McCown, eds., *The Great Apes.* Menlo Park, Calif.: Benjamin/Cummings.

Nordyke, D., and L. Nordyke. 1964. The friendly nuisance. Pages 200–202 in *Marvels and Mysteries of Our Animal World.* Pleasantville, N.Y.: Reader's Digest Association.

Norris, J. J. 1950. *Effect of Rodents, Rabbits, and Cattle on Two Vegetation Types in Semi-desert Range Land.* Sante Fe, N.M.: New Mexico Agricultural Experiment Station Bulletin no. 353.

Norris, K. 1993. Heritable variation in a plumage indicator of viability in male great tits *Parus major. Nature* 362:537–539.

Novitski, E., and A. W. Kimball. 1958. Birth order, parental ages and sex of offspring. *American Journal of Human Genetics* 21:123–131.

Nowak, R. M., and J. L. Paradiso. 1983. *Walker's Mammals of the World.* 4th ed. Baltimore, Md.: Johns Hopkins University Press.

Noyes, D. H., and W. G. Holmes. 1979. Behavioral responses of free-living hoary marmots to a model golden eagle. *Journal of Mammalogy* 60:408–411.

Noyes, M. J. S. 1982. The association of maternal attributes with infant gender in a group of Japanese monkeys. *International Journal of Primatology* 3:320–327.

Nummelin, M. 1989. Cannibalism in waterstriders (Heteroptera: Gerridae): Is there kin recognition? *Oikos* 56:87–90.

Nur, N. 1984. The consequences of brood size for breeding blue tits. I. Adult survival, weight change and the cost of reproduction. *Journal of Animal Ecology* 53:479–496.

Nur, N. 1988. The cost of reproduction in birds: An examination of the evidence. *Ardea* 76:155–168.

Nyby, J., and G. Whitney. 1978. Ultrasonic communication of adult myomorph rodents. *Neuroscience and Biobehavioral Review* 2:1–14.

O'Brien, S. J., and J. F. Evermann. 1988. Interactive influence of infectious disease and genetic diversity in natural populations. *Trends in Ecology and Evolution* 3:254–259.

Oftedal, O. T., S. J. Iverson, and D. J. Bonness. 1987. Milk and energy intakes of suckling California sea lion *Zalophus californianus* pups in relation to sex, growth, and predicted maintenance requirements. *Physiological Zoology* 60:560–575.

O'Gara, B. W. 1969. Unique aspects of reproduction in the female pronghorn (*Antilocapra americana* Ord). American *Journal of Anatomy* 125:217–231.

Oglesby, J. M., D. L. Lanier, and D. A. Dewsbury. 1981. The role of prolonged copulatory behavior in facilitating reproductive success in male Syrian golden hamsters *(Mesocricetus auratus)* in a competitive mating situation. *Behavioral Ecology and Sociobiology* 8:47–54.

Oldemeyer, J. L., D. E. Biggins, B. J. Miller, and R. Crete, eds. 1993. *Proceedings of the Symposium on the Management of Prairie Dog Complexes for the Reintroduction of Black-Footed Ferrets.* Washington, D.C.: United States Fish and Wildlife Service, Biological Report no. 93.

Olendorff, R. R. 1976. The food habits of North American golden eagles. *American Midland Naturalist* 95:231–236.

Ollason, J. C., and G. M. Dunnet. 1988. Variation in breeding success in fulmars. Pages 263–278 in T. H. Clutton-Brock, ed., *Reproductive Success: Studies of Individual Variation in Contrasting Breeding Systems.* Chicago: University of Chicago Press.

Olsen, P. F. 1981. Sylvatic plague. Pages 232–243 in J. W. Davis, L. H. Karstadt, and D. O. Trainer, eds., *Infectious Diseases of Wild Animals.* Ames, Iowa: Iowa State University Press.

O'Meilia, M. E., F. L. Knopf, and J. C. Lewis. 1982. Some consequences of competition between prairie dogs *(Cynomys ludovicianus)* and beef cattle. *Journal of Range Management* 35:580–585.

Orians, G. H. 1969a. Age and hunting success in the brown pelican. *Animal Behaviour* 17:316–319.

Orians, G. H. 1969b. On the evolution of mating systems in birds and mammals. *American Naturalist* 103:589–603.

Orians, G. H. 1980. *Some Adaptations of Marsh-Nesting Blackbirds.* Princeton, N.J.: Princeton University Press.

Oring, L. W., R. C. Fleischer, J. M. Reed, and K. E. Marsden. 1992. Cuckoldry through stored sperm in the sequentially polyandrous spotted sandpiper. *Nature* 359:631–633.

Ortega, J. C. 1990. Reproductive biology of the rock squirrel *(Spermophilus variegatus)* in southeastern Arizona. *Journal of Mammalogy* 71:448–457.

Osborn, B. 1942. Prairie dogs in shinnery (Oak Scrub) savannah. *Ecology* 23:110–115.

Osborn, B., and P. F. Allan. 1949. Vegetation of an abandoned prairie dog town in tallgrass prairie. *Ecology* 30:322–332.

Ostfeld, R. S., M. C. Miller, and J. Schnurr. 1993. Ear tagging increases tick *(Ixodes dammini)* infestation rates of white-footed mice *(Peromyscus leucopus).* *Journal of Mammalogy* 74:651–655.

Owen, D. 1980. *Camouflage and Mimicry.* Chicago: University of Chicago Press.

Owens, N. W., and J. D. Goss-Custard. 1976. The adaptive significance of alarm calls given by shorebirds on their winter feeding grounds. *Evolution* 30:397–398.

Owings, D. H., M. Borchert, and R. Virginia. 1977. The behaviour of California ground squirrels. *Animal Behaviour* 25:221–230.

Owings, D. H., and D. F. Hennessy. 1984. The importance of variation in sciurid visual and vocal communication. Pages 169–200 in J. O. Murie and G. R. Michener, eds., *The Biology of Ground-Dwelling Squirrels.* Lincoln, Nebr.: University of Nebraska Press.

Owings, D. H., D. F. Hennessy, D. W. Leger, and A. B. Gladney. 1986. Different functions of "alarm" calling for different time scales: A preliminary report on ground squirrels. *Behaviour* 99:101–116.

Owings, D. H., and D. W. Leger. 1980. Chatter vocalizations of California ground squirrels: Predator- and social-role specificity. *Zeitschrift für Tierpsychologie* 54:163–184.

Owings, D. H., and W. J. Loughry. 1985. Variation in snake-elicited jump-yipping by black-tailed prairie dogs: Ontogeny and snake specificity. *Zeitschrift für Tierpsychologie* 70:177–200.

Owings, D. H., and S. C. Owings. 1979. Snake-directed behavior by black-tailed prairie dogs *(Cynomys ludovicianus). Zeitschrift für Tierpsychologie* 49:35–54.

Owings, D. H., and R. A. Virginia. 1978. Alarm calls of California ground squirrels *(Spermophilus beecheyi). Zeitschrift für Tierpsychologie* 46:58–70.

Packard, J. M., K. J. Babbitt, P. G. Hannon, and W. E. Grant. 1990. Infanticide in captive collared peccaries *(Tayassu tajuca). Zoo Biology* 9:49–53.

Packard, J. M., U. S. Seal, L. D. Mech, and E. D. Plotka. 1985. Causes of reproductive failure in two family groups of wolves *(Canis lupus). Zeitschrift für Tierpsychologie* 68:24–40.

Packer, C. 1986. The ecology of sociality in felids. Pages 429–451 in D. I. Rubenstein and R. W. Wrangham, eds., *Ecological Aspects of Social Evolution.* Princeton, N.J.: Princeton University Press.

Packer, C., D. A. Gilbert, A. E. Pusey, and S. J. O'Brien. 1991. A molecular genetic analysis of kinship and cooperation in African lions. *Nature* 351:562–565.

Packer, C., L. Herbst, A. E. Pusey, J. D. Bygott, J. P. Hanby, S. J. Cairns, and M. Borgerhoff Mulder. 1988. Reproductive success in lions. Pages 363–383 in T. H. Clutton-Brock, ed., *Reproductive Success: Studies of Individual Variation in Contrasting Breeding Systems.* Chicago: University of Chicago Press.

Packer, C., S. Lewis, and A. Pusey. 1992. A comparative analysis of non-offspring nursing. *Animal Behaviour* 43:265–281.

Packer, C., and A. E. Pusey. 1982. Cooperation and competition within coalitions of male lions: Kin selection or game theory? *Nature* 296:740–742.

Packer, C., and A. E. Pusey. 1983. Adaptation of female lions to infanticide by incoming males. *American Naturalist* 121:716–728.

Packer, C., and A. E. Pusey. 1984. Infanticide in carnivores. Pages 31–42 in G. Hausfater and S. B. Hrdy, eds., *Infanticide: Comparative and Evolutionary Perspectives.* New York: Aldine.

Packer, C., D. Scheel, and A. E. Pusey. 1990. Why lions form groups: Food is not enough. *American Naturalist* 136:1–19.

Palmer, E. L., and H. S. Fowler. 1975. *Fieldbook of Natural History.* New York: McGraw-Hill.

Parker, G. A. 1970. Sperm competition and its evolutionary significance in insects. *Biological Review* 45:525–567.

Parker, G. A. 1974. The reproductive behaviour and the nature of sexual selection in *Scatophaga stercoraria* L. (Diptera: Scatophagidae). IX. Spatial distribution of fertilization rates and evolution of male search strategy within the reproductive area. *Evolution* 28:93–108.

Parker, G. A., and W. J. Sutherland. 1986. Ideal free distributions when individuals differ in competitive ability: Phenotype-limited ideal free models. *Animal Behaviour* 34:1222–1242.

Parker, S. 1976. The precultural basis of the incest taboo. *American Anthropologist* 73:285–305.

Parrish, J. K. 1989. Re-examining the selfish herd: Are central fish safer? *Animal Behaviour* 38:1048–1053.

Parsons, J. 1971. Cannibalism in herring gulls. *British Birds* 64:528–537.

Parsons, J. 1975. Seasonal variation in the breeding success of the herring gull: An experimental approach to prefledging success. *Journal of Animal Ecology* 44:553–573.

Part, T., L. Gustafsson, and J. Moreno. 1992. "Terminal investment" and sexual conflict in the collared flycatcher *(Ficedula albicollis). American Naturalist* 140:868–882.

Partridge, L. 1983. Non-random mating and offspring fitness. Pages 227–255 in P. Bateson, ed., *Mate Choice.* Cambridge: Cambridge University Press.

Partridge, L. 1989. Lifetime reproductive success and life-history evolution. Pages 421–440 in I. Newton, ed., *Lifetime Reproduction in Birds.* New York: Academic Press.

Partridge, L., and N. H. Barton. 1993. Optimality, mutation and the evolution of ageing. *Nature* 362:305–311.

Partridge, L., and T. R. Halliday. 1984. Mating patterns and mate choice. Pages 222–250 in J. R. Krebs and N. B. Davies, eds., *Behavioural Ecology: An Evolutionary Approach.* 2d ed. Oxford: Blackwell Scientific Publications.

Partridge, L., and P. H. Harvey. 1988. The ecological context of life history evolution. *Science* 241:1449–1455.

Patterson, I. J. 1965. Timing and spacing of broods in the black-headed gull *Larus ridibundus. Ibis* 107:433–459.

Paunovich, R., and S. C. Forrest. 1987. Activity of a wild black footed ferret litter. *Prairie Naturalist* 19:159–162.

Payne, R. B. 1969. *Breeding Seasons and Reproductive Physiology of Tricolored Blackbirds and Redwing Blackbirds.* University of California Publications in Zoology, no. 90. Berkeley, Calif.

Payne, R. B. 1977. The ecology of brood parasitism in birds. *Annual Review of Ecology and Systematics* 8:1–28.

Payne, R. B. 1984. *Sexual Selection, Lek and Arena Behavior and Sexual Size Dimorphism in Birds.* Ornithological Monographs no. 33. Washington, D.C.: American Ornithologists' Union.

Payne, R. B., L. L. Payne, and I. Rowley. 1985. Splendid wren *Malurus splendens* response to cuckoos: An experimental test of social organization in a communal bird. *Behaviour* 94:108–127.

Pemberton, J. M., S. D. Albon, F. E. Guinness, T. H. Clutton-Brock, and G. A. Dover. 1992. Behavioral estimates of male mating success tested by DNA fingerprinting in a polygynous mammal. *Behavioral Ecology* 3:66–75.

Pereira, M. E. 1983. Abortion following the immigration of an adult male baboon *(Papio cynocephalus)*. *American Journal of Primatology* 4:93–98.

Pereira, M. E., and J. M. Macedonia. 1991. Ringtailed lemur anti-predator calls denote predator class, not response urgency. *Animal Behaviour* 41:543–544.

Perrigo, G. 1987. Breeding and feeding strategies in deer mice and house mice when females are challenged to work for their food. *Animal Behaviour* 35:1298–1316.

Perrigo, G., W. C. Bryant, and F. S. vom Saal. 1990. A unique neural timing system prevents male mice from harming their own offspring. *Animal Behaviour* 39:535–539.

Perrins, C. M., and T. R. Birkhead. 1983. *Avian Ecology.* Glasgow: Blackie Press.

Perrins, C. M., and D. Moss. 1975. Reproduction rates in the great tit. *Journal of Animal Ecology* 44:695–706.

Peterson, R. T. 1990. *A Field Guide to Western Birds.* Boston: Houghton Mifflin.

Petrie, M., and A. P. Møller. 1991. Laying eggs in others' nests: Intraspecific brood parasitism in birds. *Trends in Ecology and Evolution* 6:315–320.

Petzal, D. E. 1993. Doggin' it. *Field and Stream* 97:82–90.

Pfeifer, S. 1982. Disappearance and dispersal of *Spermophilus elegans* juveniles in relation to behavior. *Behavioral Ecology and Sociobiology* 10:237–243.

Pfeiffer, D. G. 1972. Effects of diethylstilbestrol on reproduction in the black-tailed prairie dog. Master's thesis, South Dakota State University, Brookings, S.D.

Pfeiffer, E. W., L. N. Reinking, and J. D. Hamilton. 1979. Some effects of food and water deprivation on metabolism in black-tailed prairie dogs *Cynomys ludovicianus. Comparative Biochemical Physiology* 63:19–22.

Pfennig, D. W., G. J. Gamboa, H. K. Reeve, J. Shellman Reeve, and I. D. Furgeson. 1983. The mechanism of nestmate discrimination in social wasps *(Polistes,* Hymenoptera: Vespidae). *Behavioral Ecology and Sociobiology* 13:299–305.

Pfennig, D. W., H. K. Reeve, and J. S. Shellman. 1983. Learned component of nestmate discrimination in workers of a social wasp, *Polistes fuscatus* (Hymenoptera: Vespidae). *Animal Behaviour* 31:412–416.

Pfennig, D. W., H. K. Reeve, and P. W. Sherman. 1993. Kin recognition and cannibalism in spadefoot toad tadpoles. *Animal Behavior* 46:87–94.

Phillips, W. W. A. 1924. Ectoparasites of the Ceylon bats. *Spolia Zeylanica, Bulletin National Museum of Ceylon* 13:65–70.

Pianka, E. R. 1976. Natural selection of optimal reproductive tactics. *American Zoologist* 16:775–784.

Pianka, E. R., and W. S. Parker. 1975. Age-specific reproductive tactics. *American Naturalist* 109:453–464.

Pienkowski, M. W., and P. R. Evans. 1982. Breeding behaviour, productivity and survival of colonial and non-colonial shelducks *(Tadorna tadorna)*. *Ornis Scandinavica* 13:101–116.

Pierce, B. A., and J. B. Mitton. 1982. Allozyme heterozygosity and growth in the tiger salamander, *Ambystoma tigrinum*. *Journal of Heredity* 73:250–253.

Pierotti, R. 1987. Behavioral consequences of habitat selection in the herring gull. *Studies in Avian Biology* 10:119–128.

Pierotti, R. 1991. Infanticide versus adoption: An intergenerational conflict. *American Naturalist* 138:1140–1158.

Pierotti, R., and E. C. Murphy. 1987. Intergenerational conflicts in gulls. *Animal Behaviour* 35:435–444.

Pizzimenti, J. J. 1975. *Evolution of the Prairie Dog Genus* Cynomys. Occasional Papers of the Museum of Natural History, The University of Kansas, no. 39. Lawrence, Kans.

Pizzimenti, J. J., and G. D. Collier. 1975. *Cynomys parvidens. Mammalian Species* 52:1–3.

Pizzimenti, J. J., and R. S. Hoffmann. 1973. *Cynomys gunnisoni. Mammalian Species* 25:1–4.

Pizzimenti, J. J., and L. R. McCleneghan. 1974. Reproduction, growth and development, and behavior in the Mexican prairie dog, *Cynomys mexicanus* (Merriam). *American Midland Naturalist* 92:130–145.

Pizzimenti, J. J., and C. F. Nadler. 1972. Chromosomes and serum proteins of the Utah prairie dog, *Cynomys parvidens* (Sciuridae). *Southwestern Naturalist* 17:279–286.

Player, R. L., and P. J. Urness. 1982. Habitat manipulation for Utah prairie dogs in Capitol Reef National Park. *Great Basin Naturalist* 43:517–523.

Polis, G. A. 1981. The evolution and dynamics of intraspecific predation. *Annual Review of Ecology and Systematics* 12:225–251.

Polis, G. A., C. A. Myers, and W. R. Hess. 1984. A survey of intraspecific predation within the class Mammalia. *Mammal Review* 14:187–198.

Pollitzer, R. 1951. Plague studies. 1. A summary of the history and a survey of the present distribution of the disease. *World Health Organization Bulletin* 4:475–533.

Pollitzer, R. 1952. Plague studies. 7. Insect vectors. *World Health Organization Bulletin* 7:231–342.

Pollitzer, R., and K. F. Meyer. 1961. The ecology of plague. Pages 433–501 in J. M. May, ed., *Studies of Disease Ecology*. New York: Hafner.

Pomiankowski, A. N. 1988. The evolution of female mate preferences for male genetic quality. Pages 136–184 in P. H. Harvey and L. Partridge, eds., *Oxford Surveys in Evolutionary Biology,* vol. 5. New York: Oxford University Press.

Pomiankowski, A. N. 1989. Choosing parasite-free mates. *Nature* 338:115–116.

Porter, R. H., M. Wyrick, and J. Pankey. 1978. Sibling recognition in spiny mice *(Acomys cahirinus). Behavioral Ecology and Sociobiology* 3:61–68.

Porter, R. H., V. J. Tepper, and D. M. White. 1981. Experimental influences on the development of huddling preferences and "sibling" recognition in spiny mice. *Developmental Psychology* 14:375–382.

Post, W. 1992. Dominance and mating success in male boat-tailed grackles. *Animal Behaviour* 44:917–929.

Potemkin, J. R. 1976. Aggression and territoriality in the Zuni prairie dog, *Cynomys gunnisoni zuniensis*. Abstract of paper presented at 56th Annual Meeting of the American Society of Mammalogists.

Powell, G. V. N. 1974. Experimental analysis of the social value of flocking by starlings *(Sturnus vulgaris)* in relation to predation and foraging. *Animal Behaviour* 22:501–505.

Powell, R. A. 1982. Prairie dog coloniality and black-footed ferrets. *Ecology* 63:1967–1968.

Preston, S. H. 1972. Interrelations between death rates and birth rates. *Theoretical Population Biology* 3:162–185.

Price, M. V., and N. M. Waser. 1979. Pollen dispersal and optimal outcrossing in *Delphinium nelsoni*. *Nature* 277:294–297.

Price, T., and L. Liou. 1989. Selection on clutch size in birds. *American Naturalist* 134:950–959.

Promislow, D. E. L. 1991. Senescence in natural populations of mammals: A comparative study. *Evolution* 45:1869–1887.

Pruett-Jones, S. 1992. Independent versus nonindependent mate choice: Do females copy each other? *American Naturalist* 140:1000–1009.

Pugesek, B. H. 1981. Increased reproductive effort with age in the California gull *(Larus californicus)*. *Science* 212:822–823.

Pugesek, B. H. 1983. The relationship between parental age and reproductive effort in the California gull *(Larus californicus)*. *Behavioral Ecology and Sociobiology* 13:161–171.

Pugh, S. R., and R. H. Tamarin. 1988. Inbreeding in a population of meadow voles, *Microtus pennsylvanicus*. *Canadian Journal of Zoology* 66:1831–1834.

Pulliam, H. R. 1973. On the advantages of flocking. *Journal of Theoretical Biology* 38:419–422.

Pulliam, H. R., and T. Caraco. 1984. Living in groups: Is there an optimal group size? Pages 122–147 in J. R. Krebs and N. B. Davies, eds., *Behavioural Ecology: An Evolutionary Approach*. 2d ed. Oxford: Blackwell Scientific Publications.

Pusey, A. E. 1980. Inbreeding avoidance in chimpanzees. *Animal Behavior* 28:543–552.

Pusey, A. E. 1987. Sex-biased dispersal and inbreeding avoidance in birds and mammals. *Trends in Ecology and Evolution* 2:295–299.

Pusey, A. E., and C. Packer. 1987a. Dispersal and philopatry. Pages 250–266 in B. B. Smuts, D. L. Cheney, R. M. Seyfarth, R. W. Wrangham, and T. T. Struhsaker, eds., *Primate Societies*. Chicago: University of Chicago Press.

Pusey, A. E., and C. Packer. 1987b. The evolution of sex-biased dispersal in lions. *Behaviour* 101:275–310.

Quanstrom, W. R. 1968. Some aspects of the ethoecology of Richardson's ground squirrel in eastern North Dakota. Ph.D. dissertation, University of Oklahoma, Norman, Okla.

Quinn, T. W., J. S. Quinn, F. Cooke, and B. N. White. 1987. DNA marker analysis detects multiple maternity and paternity in single broods of the lesser snow goose. *Nature* 326:392–395.

Rabenold, K. N. 1985. Cooperation in breeding by nonreproductive wrens: Kinship, reciprocity, and demography. *Behavioral Ecology and Sociobiology* 17:1–17.

Rabenold, K. N. 1990. *Campylorhynchus* wrens: The ecology of delayed dispersal and cooperation in the Venezuelan savanna. Pages 157–196 in P. B. Stacey and W. D. Koenig, eds., *Cooperative Breeding in Birds: Long-Term Studies of Ecology and Behavior.* Cambridge: Cambridge University Press.

Rabenold, P. P., K. N. Rabenold, W. H. Piper, J. Haydock, and S. W. Zack. 1990. Shared paternity revealed by genetic analysis in cooperatively breeding tropical wrens. *Nature* 348:538–540.

Racey, P. A. 1973. The viability of spermatozoa after prolonged storage by male and female European bats. *Periodical Biology* 75:201–205.

Racey, P. A. 1975. The prolonged survival of spermatozoa in bats. Pages 385–416 in J. G. Duckett and P. A. Racey, eds., *The Biology of the Male Gamete.* London: Academic Press.

Racey, P. A. 1979. The prolonged storage and survival of spermatozoa in Chiroptera. *Journal of Reproduction and Fertility* 56:403–416.

Racey, P. A., and D. M. Potts. 1970. Relationship between stored spermatozoa and the uterine epithelium in the pipistrelle bat *(Pipistrellus pipistrellus). Journal of Reproduction and Fertility* 22:57–63.

Radcliffe, M. C. 1992. Repopulation of black-tailed prairie dog *(Cynomys ludovicianus)* colonies after artificial reduction. Master's thesis, Frostburg State University, Frostburg, Md.

Ralls, K. 1976. Mammals in which females are larger than males. *Quarterly Review of Biology* 51:245–276.

Ralls, K. 1977. Sexual dimorphism in mammals: Avian models and unanswered questions. *American Naturalist* 111:917–938.

Ralls, K., J. D. Ballou, and A. R. Templeton. 1988. Estimates of lethal equivalents and the cost of inbreeding in mammals. *Conservation Biology* 2:185–193.

Ralls, K., K. Brugger, and J. Ballou. 1979. Inbreeding and juvenile mortality in small populations of ungulates. *Science* 206:1101–1103.

Ralls, K., P. H. Harvey, and A. M. Lyles. 1986. Inbreeding in natural populations of birds and mammals. Pages 35–56 in M. Soulé, ed., *Conservation Biology: The Science of Scarcity and Diversity.* Sunderland, Mass.: Sinauer Associates.

Ramsey, M. A., and I. Stirling. 1988. Reproductive biology and ecology of female polar bears *(Ursus maritimus). Journal of Zoology* (London) 214:601–634.

Randall, D. 1976a. Poison the damn prairie dogs. *Defenders* 51:381–383.

Randall, D. 1976b. Shoot the damn prairie dogs. *Defenders* 51:378–381.

Rasa, O. A. E. 1977. The ethology and sociology of the dwarf mongoose *(Helogale undulata rufula)*. *Zeitschrift für Tierpsychologie* 43:337–406.

Rasa, O. A. E. 1986. Coordinated vigilance in dwarf mongoose family groups: The "watchman's song" hypothesis and the costs of guarding. *Ethology* 71:340–344.

Rausch, R. L., and V. R. Rausch. 1971. The somatic chromosomes of some North American marmots (Sciuridae), with remarks on the relationships of *Marmota broweri* Hall and Gilmore. *Mammalia* 35:85–101.

Rayor, L. S. 1985a. Dynamics of a plague outbreak in Gunnison's prairie dog. *Journal of Mammalogy* 66:194–196.

Rayor, L. S. 1985b. Effects of habitat quality on growth, age of first reproduction, and dispersal in Gunnison's prairie dogs *(Cynomys gunnisoni)*. *Canadian Journal of Zoology* 63:2835–2840.

Rayor, L. S. 1988. Social organization and space-use in Gunnison's prairie dog. *Behavioral Ecology and Sociobiology* 22:69–78.

Rayor, L. S., A. K. Brody, and C. Gilbert. 1987. Hibernation in the Gunnison's prairie dog. *Journal of Mammalogy* 68:147–150.

Read, A. F. 1987. Comparative evidence supports the Hamilton and Zuk hypothesis on parasites and sexual selection. *Nature* 327:68–70.

Read, A. F. 1990. Parasites and the evolution of host sexual behaviour. Pages 117–157 in C. J. Barnard and J. M. Behnke, eds., *Parasitism and Host Behaviour*. London: Taylor and Francis.

Read, A. F. 1991. Passerine polygyny: A role for parasites? *American Naturalist* 138:434–459.

Read, A. F., and P. H. Harvey. 1989a. Genetic relatedness and the evolution of animal mating patterns. Pages 115–131 in C. G. N. Mascie-Taylor and A. J. Boyce, eds., *Human Mating Patterns*. Cambridge: Cambridge University Press.

Read, A. F., and P. H. Harvey. 1989b. Reassessment of comparative evidence for Hamilton and Zuk theory on the evolution of secondary sexual characters. *Nature* 339:618–620.

Reading, R. P., and T. W. Clark. 1990. *Black-Footed Ferret Annotated Bibliography, 1986–1990*. Montana Bureau of Land Management Technical Bulletin no.3. Billings, Mont.

Reena, M., and M. B. Ram. 1992. Rate of takeovers in groups of hanuman langurs *(Presbytis entellus)* at Jaipur. *Folia Primatologica* 58:61–71.

Reeve, H. K. 1989. The evolution of conspecific acceptance thresholds. *American Naturalist* 133:407–435.

Reeve, H. K., and P. W. Sherman. 1993. Adaptation and the goals of evolutionary research. *Quarterly Review of Biology* 68:1–32.

Reid, W. V. 1987. The cost of reproduction in the glaucous-winged gull. *Oecologia* 74:458–467.

Reiter, J., K. J. Panken, and B. J. Le Boeuf. 1981. Female competition and reproductive success in northern elephant seals. *Animal Behaviour* 29:670–687.

Reiter, J., N. L. Stinson, and B. J. Le Boeuf. 1978. Northern elephant seal development: The transition from weaning to nutritional independence. *Behavioral Ecology and Sociobiology* 3:337–367.

Remington, R. D., and M. A. Schork. 1970. *Statistics with Applications to the Biological and Health Sciences.* Englewood Cliffs, N.J.: Prentice-Hall.

Reyer, H. U. 1980. Flexible helper structure as an ecological adaptation in the pied kingfisher (*Ceryle rudis rudis* L.). *Behavioral Ecology and Sociobiology* 6:219–227.

Reyer, H. U. 1984. Investment and relatedness: A cost/benefit analysis of breeding and helping in the pied kingfisher *(Ceryle rudis). Animal Behaviour* 32:1163–1178.

Reznick, D. 1985. Costs of reproduction: An evaluation of the empirical evidence. *Oikos* 44:257–267.

Richardson, L. 1986. On the track of the last black-footed ferrets. *Natural History* 86:69–77.

Richardson, L., T. W. Clark, S. C. Forrest, and T. M. Campbell. 1987. Winter ecology of black-footed ferrets *(Mustela nigripes)* at Meeteetse, Wyoming. *American Midland Naturalist* 117:225–239.

Richter, W. 1983. Balanced sex ratios in dimorphic altricial birds: The contribution of sex-specific growth dynamics. *American Naturalist* 121:158–171.

Ricklefs, R. E. 1973. *Ecology.* Portland, Ore.: Chiron Press.

Ridley, M. 1983. *The Explanation of Organic Diversity: The Comparative Method and Adaptations for Mating.* Oxford: Oxford University Press.

Riedman, M. L. 1982. The evolution of alloparental care and adoption in mammals and birds. *Quarterly Review of Biology* 57:405–435.

Riedman, M. L., and B. J. Le Boeuf. 1982. Mother-pup separation and adoption in northern elephant seals. *Behavioral Ecology and Sociobiology* 11:203–215.

Robertson, R. J. 1973. Optimal niche space of the redwinged blackbird: Spatial and temporal patterns of nesting activity and success. *Ecology* 54:1085–1093.

Robinson, A. T., and C. N. Slobodchikoff. 1990. Intracolony dispersal in Gunnison's prairie dogs. Abstract of paper presented at American Society of Mammalogists 70th Annual Meeting.

Robinson, J. G., P. C. Wright, and W. G. Kinzey. 1987. Monogamous cebids and their relatives: Intergroup calls and spacing. Pages 44–53 in B. B. Smuts, D. L. Cheney, R. M. Seyfarth, R. W. Wrangham, and T. T. Struhsaker, eds., *Primate Societies.* Chicago: University of Chicago Press.

Robinson, S. K. 1985. Coloniality in the yellow-rumped cacique as a defense against nest predators. *Auk* 102:506–519.

Robinson, S. R. 1980. Antipredator behaviour and predator recognition in Belding's ground squirrels. *Animal Behaviour* 28:840–852.

Robinson, S. R. 1981. Alarm communication in Belding's ground squirrels. *Zeitschrift für Tierpsychologie* 56:150–178.

Rockwell, R. F., C. S. Findlay, and F. Cooke. 1987. Is there an optimal clutch size in snow geese? *American Naturalist* 130:839–863.

Rodman, P. S., and J. C. Mitani. 1987. Orangutans: Sexual dimorphism in a solitary species. Pages 146–164 in B. B. Smuts, D. L. Cheney, R. M. Seyfarth, R. W. Wrangham, and T. T. Struhsaker, eds., *Primate Societies*. Chicago: University of Chicago Press.

Rogers-Wydeven, P., and R. B. Dahlgren. 1982. A comparison of prairie dog stomach contents and feces using a microhistological technique. *Journal of Wildlife Management* 46:1104–1108.

Rohwer, F. C. 1992. The evolution of reproductive patterns in waterfowl. Pages 486–539 in B. D. J. Batt, A. D. Afton, M. G. Anderson, C. D. Ankney, D. H. Johnson, J. A. Kadlec, and G. L. Krapu, eds., *The Ecology and Management of Breeding Waterfowl*. Minneapolis, Minn.: University of Minnesota Press.

Rohwer, F. C., and S. Freeman. 1989. The distribution of conspecific nest parasitism in birds. *Canadian Journal of Zoology* 67:239–253.

Rohwer, S. 1978. Parent cannibalism of offspring and egg raiding as a courtship strategy. *American Naturalist* 112:429–440.

Ron, T., S. P. Henzi, and U. Motro. 1994. A new model of fission in primate troops. *Animal Behaviour* 47:223–226.

Rongstad, O. J. 1965. A life history study of thirteen-lined ground squirrels in southern Wisconsin. *Journal of Mammalogy* 46:76–87.

Rood, J. P. 1972. Ecological and behavioural comparisons of three genera of Argentine cavies. *Animal Behaviour Monographs* 5:1–83.

Rood, J. P. 1975. Population dynamics and food habits of the banded mongoose. *Journal of East African Wildlife* 13:89–111.

Rood, J. P. 1978. Dwarf mongoose helpers at the den. *Zeitschrift für Tierpsychologie* 48:277–287.

Rood, J. P. 1980a. Freeze marking mongooses. *Journal of Wildlife Management* 44:500–501.

Rood, J. P. 1980b. Mating relationships and breeding suppression in the dwarf mongoose. *Animal Behaviour* 28:143–150.

Rood, J. P. 1986. Ecology and social evolution in the mongooses. Pages 131–152 in D. I. Rubenstein and R. W. Wrangham, eds., *Ecological Aspects of Social Evolution*. Princeton, N.J.: Princeton University Press.

Rood, J. L. 1987. Migration and dispersal among dwarf mongooses. Pages 85–103 in B. D. Chepko-Sade and Z. T. Halpin, eds., *Mammalian Dispersal Patterns: The Effects of Social Structure on Population Genetics*. Chicago: University of Chicago Press.

Rood, J. P. 1990. Group size, survival, reproduction, and routes to breeding in dwarf mongooses. *Animal Behaviour* 39:566–572.

Roper, T. J. 1990. Responses of domestic chicks to artificially coloured insect prey: Effects of previous experience and background colour. *Animal Behaviour* 39:466–473.

Roper, T. J. 1992. The structure and function of badger setts. *Journal of Zoology* (London) 227:691–694.

Rose, M. 1984. The evolution of animal senescence. *Canadian Journal of Zoology* 62:1661–1667.

Rose, M. 1991. *Evolutionary Biology of Aging.* Oxford: Oxford University Press.

Rose, M., and B. Charlesworth. 1980. A test of evolutionary theories of senescence. *Nature* 287:141–142.

Roskaft, E., and T. Slagsvold. 1985. Differential mortality of male and female offspring in experimentally manipulated broods of the rook. *Journal of Animal Ecology* 54:261–266.

Roslyn, J. J., M. Z. Abedin, K. D. Saunders, J. A. Cates, S. D. Strichartz, M. Alperin, M. Fromm, and C. E. Palant. 1991. Uncoupled basal sodium absorption and chloride secretion in prairie dog *(Cynomys ludovicianus)* gallbladder. *Comparative Biochemical Physiology* 100A:335–341.

Rothschild, M., and T. Clay. 1957. *Fleas, Flukes, and Cuckoos.* New York: Macmillan.

Roughgarden, J. 1991. The evolution of sex. *American Naturalist* 138:934–953.

Rowley, I. 1977. Communal activities among white-winged choughs *Corcorax melanaorhamphus. Ibis* 120:1–20.

Rowley, I., and E. Russell. 1990. Splendid fairy-wrens: Demonstrating the importance of longevity. Pages 1–30 in P. B. Stacey and W. D. Koenig, eds., *Cooperative Breeding in Birds: Long-Term Studies of Ecology and Behavior.* Cambridge: Cambridge University Press.

Rowley, I., E. Russell, and M. Brooker. 1986. Inbreeding: Benefits may outweigh costs. *Animal Behaviour* 34:939–941.

Rowley, I., E. Russell, and M. Brooker. 1993. Inbreeding in birds. Pages 304–328 in N. W. Thornhill, ed., *The Natural History of Inbreeding and Outbreeding: Theoretical and Empirical Perspectives.* Chicago: University of Chicago Press.

Rubenstein, D. I. 1982. Reproductive value and behavioral strategies: Coming of age in monkeys and horses. Pages 469–487 in P. P. G. Bateson and P. H. Klopfer, eds., *Perspectives in Ethology,* vol. 5. New York: Plenum Press.

Rubenstein, D. I., and R. W. Wrangham. 1980. Why is altruism towards kin so rare? *Zeitschrift für Tierpsychologie* 54:381–387.

Rudran, R. 1973. Adult male replacement in one-male troops of purple-faced langurs *(Presbytis senex senex)* and its effect on population structure. *Folia Primatologica* 19:166–192.

Rusch, D. A., and W. G. Reeder. 1978. Population ecology of Alberta red squirrels. *Ecology* 59:400–420.

Russell, E. M., and I. Rowley. 1993. Philopatry or dispersal: Competition for territory vacancies in the splendid fairy-wren, *Malurus splendens. Animal Behaviour* 45:519–539.

Russell, J. K. 1981. Exclusion of adult male coatis from social groups: Protection from predation. *Journal of Mammalogy* 62:206–208.

Russell, J. K. 1983. Altruism in coati bands: Nepotism or reciprocity? Pages 263–290 in S. K. Wasser, ed., *Social Behavior of Female Vertebrates.* New York: Academic Press.

Rutberg, A. T. 1986. Lactation and fetal sex ratios in American bison. *American Naturalist* 127:89–94.

Saacke, R. G., W. E. Vinson, M. L. O'Connor, J. E. Chandler, J. Mullins, R. P. Amann, C. E. Marshall, R. A. Wallace, W. N. Vincel, and H. C. Kellgren. 1980. The relationship of semen quality and fertility: A heterospermic study. Pages 71–78 in *Proceedings VIII Technical Conference on Artificial Insemination and Reproduction.* Columbia, Mo.: National Association of Animal Breeders.

Sade, D. S. 1968. Inhibition of mother-son mating among free-ranging rhesus macaques. *Science and Psychoanalysis* 12:18–38.

Sargent, R. C. 1992. The ecology of filial cannibalism in fish: Theoretical perspectives. Pages 38–62 in M. Elgar and B. Crespi, eds., *Cannibalism: Ecology and Evolution among Diverse Taxa.* Oxford: Oxford University Press.

Sauer, J. R., and N. A. Slade. 1987. Uinta ground squirrel demography: Is body mass a better categorical variable than age? *Ecology* 68:642–650.

Schaffer, W. M. 1974. Selection of optimal life histories: The effects of age structure. *Ecology* 55:291–303.

Schaller, G. B. 1964. Breeding behavior of the white pelican at Yellowstone Lake, Wyoming. *Condor* 66:3–23.

Schaller, G. B. 1972. *The Serengeti Lion.* Chicago: University of Chicago Press.

Schaller, G. B. 1983. *Golden Shadows, Flying Hooves.* Chicago: University of Chicago Press.

Scheel, D. 1993. Watching for lions in the grass: The usefulness of scanning and its effects during hunts. *Animal Behaviour* 46:695–704.

Scheffer, T. H. 1937. Study of a small prairie-dog town. *Transactions of the Kansas Academy of Science* 40:391–395.

Scheffer, T. H. 1945. Historical encounter and accounts of the plains prairie dog. *Kansas History Quarterly* 13:527–537.

Scheffer, T. H. 1947. Ecological comparisons of the plains prairie dog and the Zuni species. *Transactions of the Kansas Academy of Science* 49:401–406.

Schleidt, W. M. 1973. Tonic communication: Continual effects of discrete signs in animal communication systems. *Journal of Theoretical Biology* 42:359–386.

Schmutz, S. M., D. A. Boag, and J. K. Schmutz. 1979. Causes of the unequal sex ratio in populations of adult Richardson's ground squirrels. *Canadian Journal of Zoology* 57:1849–1855.

Schoening, H. W., B. Schwartz, and A. W. Lindquist. 1956. How diseases and parasites are spread. Pages 40–45 in A. Stefferud, ed., *Animal Diseases.* United States Department of Agriculture Yearbook. Washington, D.C.

Schroeder, M. 1987. The black-footed ferret. Pages 446–455 in R. L. Silvestro, ed., *Audubon Wildlife Report, 1987.* New York: Academic Press.

Schuler, W., and E. Hesse. 1985. On the function of warning coloration: A black and yellow pattern inhibits prey-attack by naive domestic chicks. *Behavioral Ecology and Sociobiology* 16:249–255.

Schull, W. J., and J. V. Neel. 1965. *The Effects of Inbreeding on Japanese Children.* New York: Harper and Row.

Schull, W. J., and J. V. Neel. 1972. The effects of parental consanguinity and inbreeding in Hirado, Japan. V. Summary and interpretation. *American Journal of Human Genetics* 24:425–453.

Schulman, S. R., and D. I. Rubenstein. 1983. Kinship, need, and the distribution of altruism. *American Naturalist* 121:776–788.

Schwagmeyer, P. L. 1979. The Bruce effect: An evaluation of male/female advantages. *American Naturalist* 114:932–938.

Schwagmeyer, P. L. 1980. Alarm calling behavior of the thirteen-lined ground squirrel, *Spermophilus tridecemlineatus*. *Behavioral Ecology and Sociobiology* 7:195–200.

Schwagmeyer, P. L. 1984. Multiple mating and intersexual selection in thirteen-lined ground squirrels. Pages 275–293 in J. O. Murie and G. R. Michener, eds., *The Biology of Ground-Dwelling Squirrels*. Lincoln, Nebr.: University of Nebraska Press.

Schwagmeyer, P. L. 1986. Effects of multiple mating on reproduction in female thirteen-lined ground squirrels. *Animal Behaviour* 34:297–298.

Schwagmeyer, P. L. 1988a. Ground squirrel kin recognition abilities: Are there social and life-history correlates? *Behavior Genetics* 18:495–510.

Schwagmeyer, P. L. 1988b. Scramble-competition polygyny in an asocial mammal: Male mobility and mating success. *American Naturalist* 131:885–892.

Schwagmeyer, P. L. 1990. Ground squirrel reproductive behavior and mating competition: A comparative perspective. Pages 175–196 in D. A. Dewsbury, ed., *Contemporary Issues in Comparative Psychology*. Sunderland, Mass.: Sinauer Associates.

Schwagmeyer, P. L., and C. H. Brown. 1983. Factors affecting male-male competition in thirteen-lined ground squirrels. *Behavioral Ecology and Sociobiology* 13:1–6.

Schwagmeyer, P. L., and D. F. Foltz. 1990. Factors affecting the outcome of sperm competition in thirteen-lined ground squirrels. *Animal Behaviour* 39:156–162.

Schwagmeyer, P. L., and G. A. Parker. 1987. Queuing for mates in thirteen-lined ground squirrels. *Animal Behaviour* 35:1015–1025.

Schwagmeyer, P. L., and S. J. Wootner. 1985. Mating competition in an asocial ground squirrel, *Spermophilus tridecemlineatus*. *Behavioral Ecology and Sociobiology* 17:292–296.

Schwagmeyer, P. L., and S. J. Wootner. 1986. Scramble competition polygyny in thirteen-lined ground squirrels: The relative contributions of overt conflict and competitive mate searching. *Behavioral Ecology and Sociobiology* 19:359–364.

Schwartz, O. A., and K. B. Armitage. 1980. Genetic variation in social mammals: The marmot model. *Science* 207:665–667.

Schwartz, O. A., and K. B. Armitage. 1981. Social substructure and dispersion of genetic variation in the yellow-bellied marmot *(Marmota flaviventris)*. Pages 139–159 in M. H. Smith and J. Joule, eds., *Mammalian Population Genetics*. Athens, Ga.: University of Georgia Press.

Schwarz, M. P. 1988. Local resource enhancement and sex ratios in a primitively social bee. *Nature* 331:346–348.

Scott, J. D. 1977. *Little Dogs of the Prairie.* New York: G. P. Putnam's Sons.

Scott, J. P. 1958. *Animal Behavior.* Chicago: University of Chicago Press.

Scrimshaw, S. C. M. 1984. Infanticide in human populations: Societal and individual concerns. Pages 439–462 in G. Hausfater and S. B. Hrdy, eds., *Infanticide: Comparative and Evolutionary Perspectives.* New York: Aldine.

Seal, U. S. 1978. The Noah's ark problem: Multigeneration management of wild species in captivity. Pages 303–313 in S. A. Temple, ed., *Endangered Birds: Management Techniques for Preserving Threatened Species.* Madison, Wisc.: University of Wisconsin Press.

Seal, U. S., E. T. Thorne, M. A. Bogan, and S. H. Anderson, eds. 1989. *Conservation Biology and the Black-Footed Ferret.* New Haven, Conn.: Yale University Press.

Searcy, W. A. 1978. Foraging success in three age classes of glaucous winged gulls. *Auk* 95:586–588.

Seemanova, E. 1971. A study of children of incestuous matings. *Human Heredity* 21:108–128.

Seger, J., and W. D. Hamilton. 1988. Parasites and sex. Pages 176–193 in R. E. Michod and B. R. Levin, eds., *The Evolution of Sex: An Examination of Current Ideas.* Sunderland, Mass.: Sinauer Associates.

Sekulic, R. 1982. The function of howling in red howler monkeys *(Alouatta seniculus). Behaviour* 81:38–54.

Selander, R. K., M. H. Smith, S. Y. Yang, W. E. Johnson, and J. B. Gentry. 1971. Biochemical polymorphism and systematics in the genus *Peromyscus.* I. Variation in the old-field mouse *(Peromyscus polionotus). University of Texas Publication 7103, Studies in Genetics* 6:49–90.

Seton, E. T. 1926. The prairie dogs *(Cynomys ludovicianus)* at Washington Zoo. *Journal of Mammalogy* 7:229–230.

Seton, E. T. 1929. *Lives of Game Animals.* New York: Doubleday.

Seyfarth, R. M. 1976. Social relationships among adult female baboons. *Animal Behaviour* 24:917–938.

Seyfarth, R. M., D. L. Cheney, and P. Marler. 1980. Vervet monkey alarm calls: Semantic communication in a free-ranging primate. *Animal Behaviour* 28:1070–1094.

Shalaway, S., and C. N. Slobodchikoff. 1988. Seasonal changes in the diet of Gunnison's prairie dog. *Journal of Mammalogy* 69:835–841.

Sharma, O. P., and R. L. Hayes. 1975. Heterospermic insemination and its effect on the offspring ratio in rats. *Journal of Reproduction and Fertility* 45:533–535.

Shaw, R. F. 1958. The theoretical genetics of the sex ratio. *Genetics* 43:149–163.

Sheets, R. G., and R. L. Linder. 1969. Food habits of the black-footed ferret *(Mustela nigripes)* in South Dakota. *Proceedings of the South Dakota Academy of Science* 48:58–61.

Sheets, R. G., R. L. Linder, and R. B. Dahlgren. 1971. Burrow systems of prairie dogs in South Dakota. *Journal of Mammalogy* 52:451–453.

Sheets, R. G., R. L. Linder, and R. B. Dahlgren. 1972. Food habits of two litters of black-footed ferrets in South Dakota. *American Midland Naturalist* 87:249–251.

Sheldon, B. C. 1994. Sperm competition in the chaffinch: The role of the female. *Animal Behaviour* 47:163–173.

Shepher, J. 1978. Reflections on the origin of the human pair-bond. *Journal of Social and Biological Structures* 1:253–264.

Shepher, J. 1983. *Incest: A Biosocial View.* New York: Academic Press.

Sheppard, D. H., and S. M. Yoshida. 1971. Social behavior in captive Richardson's ground squirrels. *Journal of Mammalogy* 52:793–799.

Sheridan, M., and R. H. Tamarin. 1986. Kinships in a natural meadow vole population. *Behavioral Ecology and Sociobiology* 19:207–211.

Sherman, P. W. 1976. Natural selection among some group-living organisms. Ph.D. dissertation, University of Michigan, Ann Arbor, Mich.

Sherman, P. W. 1977. Nepotism and the evolution of alarm calls. *Science* 197:1246–1253.

Sherman, P. W. 1980a. The limits of ground squirrel nepotism. Pages 505–544 in G. W. Barlow and J. Silverberg, eds., *Sociobiology: Beyond Nature/Nurture?* Boulder, Colo.: Westview Press.

Sherman., P. W. 1980b. The meaning of nepotism. *American Naturalist* 116:604–606.

Sherman, P.W. 1981a. Kinship, demography, and Belding's ground squirrel nepotism. *Behavioral Ecology and Sociobiology* 8:251–259.

Sherman, P. W. 1981b. Reproductive competition and infanticide in Belding's ground squirrels and other animals. Pages 311–331 in R. D. Alexander and D. W. Tinkle, eds., *Natural Selection and Social Behavior.* New York: Chiron Press.

Sherman, P. W. 1982. Infanticide in ground squirrels. *Animal Behaviour* 30:938–939.

Sherman, P. W. 1985. Alarm calls of Belding's ground squirrels to aerial predators: Nepotism or self-preservation? *Behavioral Ecology and Sociobiology* 17:313–323.

Sherman, P. W. 1989. Mate guarding as paternity insurance in Idaho ground squirrels. *Nature* 338:418–420.

Sherman, P. W. 1991. Multiple mating and kin recognition by self-inspection. *Ethology and Sociobiology* 12:377–386.

Sherman, P. W., and W. G. Holmes. 1985. Kin recognition: Issues and evidence. Pages 437–460 in B. Hölldobler and M. Lindauer, eds., *Experimental Behavioral Ecology and Sociobiology.* Sunderland, Mass.: Sinauer Associates.

Sherman, P. W., J. U. M. Jarvis, and R. D. Alexander, eds. 1991. *The Biology of the Naked Mole-Rat.* Princeton, N.J.: Princeton University Press.

Sherman, P. W., E. A. Lacey, H. K. Reeve, and L. Keller. 1994. The eusociality continuum. *Behavioral Ecology and Sociobiology.* In press.

Sherman, P. W., and M. L. Morton. 1979. Four months of the ground squirrel. *Natural History* 88:50–57.

Sherman, P. W., and M. L. Morton. 1984. Demography of Belding's ground squirrels. *Ecology* 65:1617–1628.

Sherman, P. W., and M. L. Morton. 1988. Extra-pair fertilizations in mountain white-crowned sparrows. *Behavioral Ecology and Sociobiology* 22:413–420.

Sherman, P. W., and D. F. Westneat. 1988. Multiple mating and quantitative genetics. *Animal Behaviour* 36:1545–1547.

Shields, W. M. 1980. Ground squirrel alarm calls: Nepotism or parental care? *American Naturalist* 116:599–603.

Shields, W. M. 1982. *Philopatry, Inbreeding, and the Evolution of Sex.* Albany, N.Y.: State University of New York Press.

Shields, W. M. 1983. Optimal outbreeding and the evolution of philopatry. Pages 132–159 in I. R. Swingland and P. J. Greenwood, eds., *The Ecology of Animal Movement.* Oxford: Clarendon Press.

Shields, W. M. 1987. Dispersal in mating systems: Investigating their causal mechanisms. Pages 3–24 in B. D. Chepko-Sade and Z. T. Halpin, eds., *Mammalian Dispersal Pattens: The Effects of Social Structure and Population Genetics.* Chicago: University of Chicago Press.

Shields, W. M. 1993. The natural and unnatural history of inbreeding and outbreeding. Pages 143–169 in N. W. Thornhill, ed., *The Natural History of Inbreeding and Outbreeding: Theoretical and Empirical Perspectives.* Chicago: University of Chicago Press.

Shields, W. M., and J. R. Crook. 1987. Barn swallow coloniality: A net cost for group breeding in the Adirondacks? *Ecology* 68:1373–1386.

Shugart, G. W. 1988. Uterovaginal sperm-storage glands in sixteen species with comments on morphological differences. *Auk* 105:379–384.

Siegel, S. 1956. *Nonparametric Statistics for the Behavioral Sciences.* New York: McGraw-Hill.

Siegfried, W. R. 1972. Breeding success and reproductive output of the cattle egret. *Ostrich* 43:43–55.

Siegfried, W. R., and L. G. Underhill. 1975. Flocking as an anti-predator strategy in doves. *Animal Behaviour* 23:504–508.

Silk, J. B. 1983. Local resource competition and facultative adjustment of sex ratios in relation to competitive abilities. *American Naturalist* 121:56–66.

Sillén-Tullberg, B. 1990. Do predators avoid groups of aposematic prey? An experimental test. *Animal Behaviour* 40:856–860.

Silver, J. 1928. Badger activities in prairie-dog control. *Journal of Mammalogy* 9:63.

Simmons, R. 1990. Copulation patterns of African marsh harriers: Evaluating the paternity assurance hypothesis. *Animal Behaviour* 40:1151–1157.

Simms, B. T. 1956. Protection against transmissible diseases and parasites. Pages 54–60 in A. Stefferud, ed., *Animal Diseases.* United States Department of Agriculture Yearbook. Washington, D.C.

Simpson, M. J. A., and A. E. Simpson. 1982. Birth sex ratios and social rank in rhesus monkey mothers. *Nature* 300:440–441.

Skjervold, H., and J. W. James. 1979. Causes of variation in the sex ratio in dairy cattle. *Zeitschrift Tierz Zuechtungsbiologie* 95:293–305.

Slade, N. A., and D. F. Balph. 1974. Population ecology of Uinta ground squirrels. *Ecology* 55:989–1003.

Slagsvold, T. 1990. Fisher's sex ratio theory may explain hatching patterns in birds. *Evolution* 44:1009–1017.

Slagsvold, T., E. Roskaft, and S. Engen. 1986. Sex ratio, differential cost of rearing young, and differential mortality between the sexes during the period of parental care: Fisher's theory applied to birds. *Ornis Scandinavica* 17:117–225.

Sleggs, G. 1926. The adult anatomy of the anal glands of Richardson's ground squirrel, *Citellus richardsonii sabine. Anatomical Record* 32:1–43.

Slobodchikoff, C. N. 1984. Resources and the evolution of social behavior. Pages 227–251 in P. W. Price, C. N. Slobodchikoff, and W. S. Gaud, eds., *A New Ecology: Novel Approaches to Interactive Systems.* New York: John Wiley.

Slobodchikoff, C. N., and R. Coast. 1980. Dialects in the alarm calls of prairie dogs. *Behavioral Ecology and Sociobiology* 7:49–53.

Slobodchikoff, C. N., C. Fischer, and J. Shapiro. 1986. Predator-specific words in prairie dog alarm calls. *American Zoologist* 26:105A.

Slobodchikoff, C. N., J. Kiriazis, C. Fischer, and E. Creef. 1991. Semantic information distinguishing individual predators in the alarm calls of Gunnison's prairie dogs. *Animal Behaviour* 42:713–719.

Slobodchikoff, C. N., A. T. Robinson, and S. Travis. 1990. Variable social systems in Gunnison's prairie dogs. Abstract of paper presented at American Society of Mammalogists 70th Annual Meeting.

Slobodchikoff, C. N., and W. C. Schulz. 1988. Cooperation, aggression, and the evolution of social behavior. Pages 13–32 in C. N. Slobodchikoff, ed., *The Ecology of Social Behavior.* New York: Academic Press.

Slobodkin, L. B. 1961. *Growth and Regulation of Animal Populations.* New York: Holt, Rinehart, and Winston.

Smit, F. G. A. M. 1958. A preliminary note on the occurrence of *Pulex irritans* and *Pulex simulans* in North America. *Journal of Parasitology* 44:523–526.

Smith, A. T. 1987. Population structure of pikas: Dispersal versus philopatry. Pages 128–142 in B. D. Chepko-Sade and Z. T. Halpin, eds., *Mammalian Dispersal Pattens: The Effects of Social Structure and Population Genetics.* Chicago: University of Chicago Press.

Smith, A. T. 1993. The natural history of inbreeding and outbreeding in small mammals. Pages 329–351 in N. W. Thornhill, ed., *The Natural History of Inbreeding and Outbreeding: Theoretical and Empirical Perspectives.* Chicago: University of Chicago Press.

Smith, C. C. 1968. The adaptive nature of social organization in the genus of tree squirrels *Tamiasciurus. Ecological Monographs* 38:31–63.

Smith, D. H. 1977. Effects of experimental bot fly parasitism on gonad weights of *Peromyscus maniculatus. Journal of Mammalogy* 58:679–681.

Smith, H. J. 1980. Behavior of the coati *(Nasua narica)* in captivity. *Carnivore* 3:88–136.

Smith, J. N. M. 1981. Does high fecundity reduce survival in song sparrows? *Evolution* 35:1142–1148.

Smith, N. 1979. Life in a prairie dog town. *National Wildlife* 17:38–39.

Smith, R. E. 1967. *Natural History of the Prairie Dog in Kansas.*
Miscellaneous Publications of the Museum of Natural History, University
of Kansas, no. 49. Lawrence, Kans.

Smith, R. L., ed. 1984. *Sperm Competition and the Evolution of Animal
Mating Systems.* Orlando, Fla.: Academic Press.

Smith, S. F. 1978. Alarm calls, their origin and use in *Eutamias sonomae.*
Journal of Mammalogy 59:888–893.

Smith, W. J., S. L. Smith, E. C. Oppenheimer, and J. G. deVilla. 1977.
Vocalizations of the black-tailed prairie dog, *Cynomys ludovicianus.*
Animal Behavior 25:152–164.

Smith, W. J., S. L. Smith, E. L. Oppenheimer, J. G. deVilla, and F. A.
Ulmer. 1973. Behaviour of a captive population of black-tailed prairie
dogs: Annual cycle of social behaviour. *Behaviour* 46:189–220.

Smith, W. J., S. L. Smith, J. G. deVilla, and E. L. Oppenheimer. 1976. The
jump-yip display of the black-tailed prairie dog, *Cynomys ludovicianus.*
Animal Behaviour 24:609–621.

Smuts, B. B., D. L. Cheney, R. M. Seyfarth, R. W. Wrangham, and T. T.
Struhsaker, eds. 1987. *Primate Societies.* Chicago: University of Chicago
Press.

Smythe, N. 1970. On the existence of "pursuit invitation" signals in
mammals. *American Naturalist* 104:491–494.

Snapp, B. D. 1976. Colonial breeding in the barn swallow *(Hirundo rustica)*
and its adaptive significance. *Condor* 78:471–480.

Snell, G. P. 1985. Results of control of prairie dogs. *Rangelands* 7:30.

Snell, G. P., and B. D. Hlavachick. 1980. Control of prairie dogs—the easy
way. *Rangelands* 2:239–240.

Snow, B. K. 1963. The behavior of the shag. *British Birds* 56:164–186.

Snyder, R. L. 1960. Physiology and behavioral responses to an altered sex
ratio of adults in a population of woodchucks. Ph.D. dissertation, School
of Hygiene and Public Health, John Hopkins University, Baltimore, Md.

Snyder, R. L. 1962. Reproductive performance of a population of
woodchucks after a change in the sex ratio. *Ecology* 43:506–515.

Snyder, R. L. 1976. *The Biology of Population Growth.* London: Croom
Helm.

Sommer, V. 1987. Infanticide among free-ranging langurs *(Presbytis entellus)*
at Jodhpur (Rajasthan/India): Recent observations and a reconsideration
of hypotheses. *Primates* 28:163–197.

Sonenshine, D. E., D. M. Lauer, T. C. Walker, and B. L. Elisberg. 1979.
The ecology of *Glaucomys volans* (Linnaeus, 1758) in Virginia. *Acta
Theriologica* 24:363–377.

Soper, J. D. 1938. Discovery, habitat, and distribution of the black-tailed
prairie dog in western Canada. *Journal of Mammalogy* 19:290–300.

Soper, J. D. 1944. Further data on the black-tailed prairie dog in western
Canada. *Journal of Mammalogy* 25:47–48.

Southwick, C. H. 1955. Regulatory mechanisms of house mouse populations:
Social behavior affecting litter survival. *Ecology* 36:627–634.

Sparks, J. 1967. Allogrooming in primates. Pages 148–175 in D. Morris, ed., *Primate Ethology*. Chicago: Aldine Press.

Sperry, C. C. 1934. Winter food habits of coyotes: A report of progress, 1933. *Journal of Mammalogy* 15:286–290.

Spiro, M. E. 1958. *Children of the Kibbutz*. Cambridge, Mass.: Harvard University Press.

Squire, L. 1925. Cutie, a prairie pet. *Nature Magazine* 6:135–139.

Stacey, P. B., and W. D. Koenig, eds. 1990. *Cooperative Breeding in Birds: Longterm Studies of Ecology and Behavior*. Cambridge: Cambridge University Press.

Stacey, P. B., and J. D. Ligon. 1991. The benefits-of-philopatry hypothesis for the evolution of cooperative breeding: Variation in territory quality and group size effects. *American Naturalist* 137:831–846.

Stanback, M. T., and W. D. Koenig. 1992. Cannibalism in birds. Pages 277–298 in M. A. Elgar and B. J. Crespi, eds., *Cannibalism: Ecology and Evolution among Diverse Taxa*. New York: Oxford University Press.

Stapp, P., and W. M. Mautz. 1991. Breeding habits and postnatal growth of the southern flying squirrel *(Glaucomys volans)* in New Hampshire. *American Midland Naturalist* 126:203–208.

Stearns, S. C. 1976. Life-history tactics: A review of ideas. *Quarterly Review of Biology* 51:3–47.

Stearns, S. C. 1977. The evolution of life history traits: A critique of the theory and a review of the data. *Annual Review of Ecology and Systematics* 8:145–171.

Stearns, S. C.. 1987. Why sex evolved and the differences it makes. Pages 15–31 in S. C. Stearns, ed., *The Evolution of Sex and Its Consequences*. Boston: Birkhauser.

Stearns, S. C. 1992. *The Evolution of Life Histories*. Oxford: Oxford University Press.

Stebbins, R. C. 1985. *A Field Guide to Western Reptiles and Amphibians*. Boston: Houghton Mifflin.

Steiner, A. L. 1970a. Étude descriptive de quelques activités et comportements de base de *Spermophilus columbianus columbianus* (Ord.). I. Locomotion, soins du corps, alimentation, fouissage, curiosité et alarme, reproduction. *Revue Comparative Animal* 4:3–21.

Steiner, A. L. 1970b. Étude descriptive de quelques activités et comportements de base de *Spermophilus columbianus columbianus* (Ord.). II. Vie de groupe. *Revue Comparative Animal* 4:22–42.

Steiner, A. L. 1972. Mortality resulting from intraspecific fighting in some ground squirrel populations. *Journal of Mammalogy* 53:601–603.

Stewart, M. A., and F. C. Evans. 1941. A comparative study of rodent and burrow flea populations. *Proceedings of the Society of Experimental Biology and Medicine* 47:140–142.

Stine, G. J. 1977. *Biosocial Genetics*. New York: Macmillan.

Stirling, I. 1975. Adoptive suckling in pinnipeds. *Journal of the Australian Mammal Society* 1:389–391.

Stockard, A. H. 1929. Observations of reproduction in the white-tailed prairie dog *(Cynomys leucurus)*. *Journal of Mammalogy* 10:209–212.

Stockard, A. H. 1930. Observations on the seasonal activities of the white-tailed prairie dog, *Cynomys leucurus*. *Papers of the Michigan Academy of Science, Arts and Letters* 11:471–479.

Stockard, A. H. 1934. Studies of the female reproductive system of the prairie dog, *Cynomys leucurus*. I. Gross morphology. *Papers of the Michigan Academy of Science, Arts, and Letters* 20:725–735.

Stockard, A. H. 1936. Studies of the female reproductive system of the prairie dog, *Cynomys leucurus*. II. Normal cyclic phenomena of the ovarian follicles. *Papers of the Michigan Academy of Science, Arts, and Letters* 22:671–689.

Stockrahm, D. M. B. 1979. Comparison of population structures of black-tailed prairie dog, *Cynomys l. ludovicianus* (Ord), towns in southwestern North Dakota. Master's thesis, University of North Dakota, Grand Forks, N.D.

Stockrahm, D. M. B., and R. W. Seabloom. 1988. Comparative reproductive performance of black-tailed prairie dog populations in North Dakota. *Journal of Mammalogy* 69:160–164.

Stockrahm, D. M. B., and R. W. Seabloom. 1990. Tooth eruption in black-tailed prairie dogs from North Dakota. *Journal of Mammalogy* 71:105–108.

Storer, J. E. 1975. Pleistocene prairie dog in south-central Alberta. *Blue Jay* 33:247.

Stromberg, M. R. 1974. Group response in black-tailed prairie dogs to an avian predator. *Journal of Mammalogy* 55:850–851.

Stromberg, M. R. 1975. Habitat relationships of the black-tailed prairie dog *(Cynomys ludovicianus):* Vegetation, soils, comparative burrow structure and spatial pattern. Ph.D. dissertation, University of Wisconsin, Madison, Wisc.

Stromberg, M. R. 1978. Subsurface burrow connections and entrance spatial pattern of prairie dogs. *Southwestern Naturalist* 23:173–180.

Stromberg, M. R., R. L. Rayburn, and T. W. Clark. 1983. Black-footed ferret prey requirements: An energy balance estimate. *Journal of Wildlife Management* 47:67–73.

Struhsaker, T. T. 1977. Infanticide and social organization in the redtail monkey *(Cercopithecus ascanius schmidti)* in the Kibale forest. *Zeitschrift für Tierpsychologie* 45:75–84.

Struhsaker, T. T., and L. Leland. 1985. Infanticide in a patrilineal society of red colobus monkeys. *Zeitschrift für Tierpsychologie* 69:89–132.

Stutchbury, B. J. 1988. Evidence that bank swallow colonies do not function as information centers. *Condor* 90:953–955.

Stutchbury, B. J., and R. J. Robertson. 1988. Within season and age-related patterns of reproductive performance in female tree swallows *(Tachycineta bicolor)*. *Canadian Journal of Zoology* 66:827–834.

Sugiyama, Y. 1984. Proximate factors of infanticide among langurs at Dharwar: A reply to Boggess. Pages 311–314 in G. Hausfater and S. B. Hrdy, eds., *Infanticide: Comparative and Evolutionary Perspectives*. New York: Aldine.

Summers, C. A., and R. L. Linder. 1978. Food habits of the black-tailed prairie dog in western South Dakota. *Journal of Range Management* 31:134–136.

Sumption, L. J., and J. C. Adams. 1961. Multiple sire mating in swine. III. Factors influencing multiple paternity. *Journal of Heredity* 52:214–218.

Suomi, S. J. 1982. Sibling relationships in nonhuman primates. Pages 329–356 M. E. Lamb and B. Sutton-Smith, eds., *Sibling Relationships: Their Nature and Significance Across the Lifespan.* Hillsdale, N.J.: Lawrence Erlbaum Associates.

Sutherland, W. J. 1989. Breeding biology. *Trends in Ecology and Evolution* 4:218.

Svendsen, G. E. 1974. Behavioral and environmental factors in the spatial distribution and population dynamics of a yellow-bellied marmot population. *Ecology* 55:760–771.

Svendsen, G. E. 1976. Structure and location of burrows of yellow-bellied marmots. *Southwestern Naturalist* 20:487–494.

Swenk, M. H. 1915. The prairie dog and its control. Pages 3–38 in *Bulletin No. 154 of the Agricultural Experiment Station, University of Nebraska.* Lincoln, Nebr.

Takahata, Y. 1982. The socio-sexual behavior of Japanese monkeys. *Zeitschrift für Tierpsychologie* 59:89–108.

Tamarin, R. H., M. Sheridan, and C. K. Levy. 1983. Determining matrilineal kinship in natural populations of rodents using radionuclides. *Canadian Journal of Zoology* 61:271–274.

Tamura, N., and H. Yong. 1993. Vocalizations in response to predators in three species of Malaysian *Callosciurus* (Sciuridae). *Journal of Mammalogy* 74:703–714.

Tate, G. H. H. 1947. Albino prairie dog. *Journal of Mammalogy* 28:62.

Taub, D. M. 1980. Female choice and mating strategies among wild Barbary macaques (*Macaca sylvanus* L.). Pages 287–344 in D. Lindburg, ed., *The Macaques: Studies in Ecology, Behavior and Evolution.* New York: Van Nostrand-Reinhold.

Taulman, J. F. 1977. Vocalizations of the hoary marmot, *Marmota caligata. Journal of Mammalogy* 58:681–683.

Taylor, J. C. 1966. Home range and agonistic behaviour in the grey squirrel. *Symposia of the Zoological Society of London* 18: 229–335.

Taylor, P. D. 1981. Intra-sex and inter-sex sibling interactions as sex ratio determinants. *Nature* 291:64–66.

Taylor, P. D., and M. G. Bulmer. 1980. Local mate competition and the sex ratio. *Journal of Theoretical Biology* 86:249–263.

Taylor, R. H. 1962. The Adélie penguin *Pygoscelis adeliae* at Cape Royds. *Ibis* 104:176–204.

Taylor, W. P., and J. V. G. Loftfield. 1924. *Damage to Range Grasses by the Zuni Prairie Dog.* United States Department of Agriculture Bulletin No. 1227. Washington, D.C.

Teather, K. L., and P. J. Weatherhead. 1988. Sex-specific energy requirements of great-tailed grackle *(Quiscalus mexicanus)* nestlings. *Journal of Animal Ecology* 57:659–668.

Teather, K. L., and P. J. Weatherhead. 1989. Sex-specific mortality in nestling great-tailed grackles. *Ecology* 70:1485–1493.

Teitelbaum, M. S. 1972. Factors associated with the sex ratio in human populations. Pages 90–109 in G. A. Harrison and A. J. Boyce, eds., *The Structure of Human Populations.* Oxford: Oxford University Press.

Templeton, A. R. 1986. Coadaptation and outbreeding depression. Pages 19–34 in M. E. Soulé, ed., *Conservation Biology: The Science of Scarcity and Diversity.* Sunderland, Mass.: Sinauer Associates.

Templeton, A. R. 1987. Inferences on natural population structure from genetic studies on captive mammalian populations. Pages 257–272 in B. D. Chepko-Sade and Z. T. Halpin, eds., *Mammalian Dispersal Patterns: The Effects of Social Structure on Population Genetics.* Chicago: University of Chicago Press.

Templeton, A. R., H. Hemmer, G. Mace, U. S. Seal, W. M. Shields, and D. S. Woodruff. 1986. Local adaptation, coadaptation and population boundaries. *Zoo Biology* 5:115–125.

Tenaza, R. 1971. Behavior and nesting success relative to nest location in Adélie penguins *(Pygoscelis adeliae). Condor* 73:81–92.

Thomas, J. A., and E. C. Birney. 1979. Parental care and mating system of the prairie vole *Microtus ochrogaster. Behavioral Ecology and Sociobiology* 5:171–186.

Thomas, T. H., and M. L. Riedesel. 1975. Evidence of hibernation in the black-tailed prairie dog *Cynomys ludovicianus. Cryobiology* 12:559.

Thompson, D. C. 1977. Reproductive behavior of the gray squirrel. *Canadian Journal of Zoology* 55:1176–1184.

Thompson, D. C. 1978. Regulation of a northern grey squirrel *(Sciurus carolinensis)* population. *Ecology* 59:708–715.

Thompson-Handler, N., R. K. Malenky, and N. Badrian. 1984. Sexual behavior of *Pan paniscus* under natural conditions in the Lomako Forest, Equateur, Zaire. Pages 347–368 in R. L. Susman, ed., *The Pygmy Chimpanzee: Evolution, Biology, and Behavior.* New York: Plenum Press.

Thornhill, N. W, ed. 1993. *The Natural History of Inbreeding and Outbreeding: Theoretical and Empirical Perspectives.* Chicago: University of Chicago Press.

Thornhill, R., and J. Alcock. 1983. *The Evolution of Insect Mating Systems.* Cambridge, Mass.: Harvard University Press.

Thornhill, R., and P. Sauer. 1992. Genetic sire effects on the fighting ability of sons and daughters and mating success of sons in a scorpionfly. *Animal Behaviour* 43:255–264.

Tickell, W. L. N. 1968. Biology of the great albatrosses, *Diomedea exulans* and *Diomedea epomophora.* Pages 1–56 in O. L. Austin, ed., *Antarctic Bird Studies.* Antarctic Research Series, vol. 12. Washington, D.C.: American Geophysical Union of The National Academy of Sciences—National Research Council.

Tiger, L., and J. Shepfer. 1975. *Women in the Kibbutz.* Orlando, Fla: Harcourt Brace Jovanovich.

Tileston, J. V., and R. R. Lechleitner. 1966. Some comparisons of the black-tailed and white-tailed prairie dogs in north-central Colorado. *American Midland Naturalist* 75:292–316.

Tilman, D. 1982. *Resource Competition and Community Structure.* Princeton, N.J.: Princeton University Press.

Tinbergen, N. 1951. *The Study of Instinct.* Oxford: Oxford University Press.

Tinbergen, N. 1956. On the functions of territory in gulls. *Ibis* 98:401–411.

Tinbergen, N. 1960. *The Herring Gull's World.* Garden City, N.Y.: Anchor Books.

Tipton, V. J., and E. Mendez. 1968. New species of fleas (Siphonaptera) from Cerro Potisi, Mexico, with notes on ecology and host-parasite relationships. *Pacific Insects* 10:177–214.

Tooby, J., and L. Cosmides. 1990. On the universality of human nature and the uniqueness of the individual: The role of genetics and adaptation. *Journal of Personality* 58:17–67.

Torres, J. R. 1973. The future of the black-footed ferret in Colorado. Pages 27–33 in R. L. Linder and C. N. Hillman, eds., *Proceedings of the Black-Footed Ferret and Prairie Dog Workshop.* Brookings, S.D.: South Dakota State University.

Treisman, M. 1975a. Predation and the evolution of gregariousness. I. Models for concealment and evasion. *Animal Behaviour* 23:779–800.

Treisman, M. 1975b. Predation and the evolution of gregariousness. II. An economic model for predator-prey interaction. *Animal Behaviour* 23:801–825.

Trevino-Villarreal, J. 1990. *The Annual Cycle of the Mexican Prairie Dog (Cynomys mexicanus).* Occasional Papers of the Museum of Natural History, University of Kansas, no. 139.

Trillmich, F. 1981. Mutual mother-pup recognition in Galápagos fur seals and sea lions: Cues used and functional significance. *Behaviour* 78:21–42.

Trivers, R. L. 1971. The evolution of reciprocal altruism. *Quarterly Review of Biology* 46:35–57.

Trivers, R. L. 1972. Parental investment and sexual selection. Pages 136–179 in B. Campbell, ed., *Sexual Selection and the Descent of Man (1871–1971).* Chicago: Aldine Press.

Trivers, R. L. 1974. Parent-offspring conflict. *American Zoologist* 14:249–264.

Trivers, R. L. 1976. Sexual selection and resource-accruing abilities in *Anolis garmani. Evolution* 30:253–269.

Trivers, R. L. 1985. *Social Evolution.* Menlo Park, Calif.: Benjamin/ Cummins.

Trivers, R. L., and H. Hare. 1976. Haplodiploidy and the evolution of social insects. *Science* 191:249–263.

Trivers, R. L., and D. E. Willard. 1973. Natural selection of parental ability to vary the sex ratio of offspring. *Science* 179:90–92.

Trombulak, S. C. 1991. Maternal influence on juvenile growth rates in Belding's ground squirrel *(Spermophilus beldingi). Canadian Journal of Zoology* 69:2140–2145.

Trulio, L. A., W. J. Loughry, D. F. Hennessy, and D. H. Owings. 1986. Infanticide in California ground squirrels. *Animal Behaviour* 34:291–294.

Tryon, C. A., and D. P. Snyder. 1973. Biology of the eastern chipmunk, *Tamias striatus:* Life tables, age distributions, and trends in population numbers. *Journal of Mammalogy* 54:145–168.

Tulloch, D. G. 1979. The water buffalo, *Bubalus bubalis,* in Australia: Reproductive and parent-offspring behaviour. *Australian Wildlife Research* 6:265–287.

Turner, H. N., and C. H. Dolling. 1965. Vital statistics for an experimental flock of merino sheep. II. The influence of age on reproductive performance. *Australian Journal of Agricultural Research* 16:699–712.

Turner, L. W. 1973. Vocal and escape responses of *Spermophilus beldingi* to predators. *Journal of Mammalogy* 54:990–993.

Tyler, J. D. 1968. Distribution and vertebrate associates of the black-tailed prairie dog in Oklahoma. Ph.D. dissertation, University of Oklahoma, Norman, Okla.

Tyler, J. D. 1970. Vertebrates in a prairie dog town. *Proceedings of the Oklahoma Academy of Science* 50:110–113.

Tyler, J. D., and H. N. Buscher. 1975. Parasites of vertebrates inhabiting prairie dog towns in Oklahoma. I. Ectoparasites. *Proceedings of the Oklahoma Academy of Science* 55:166–168.

Ubelaker, J. E. 1970. Some observations of ecto- and endoparasites of Chiroptera. Pages 247–261 in B. H. Slaughter and D. W. Walton, eds., *About Bats: A Chiropteran Biology Symposium.* Dallas, Tex.: Southern Methodist University Press.

Ubico, S. R., G. O. Maupin, K. A. Fagerstone, and R. G. McLean. 1988. A plague epizootic in the white-tailed prairie dogs *(Cynomys leucurus)* of Meeteetse, Wyoming. *Journal of Wildlife Diseases* 24:399–406.

Uresk, D. W. 1984. Black-tailed prairie dog food habits and forage relationships in western South Dakota. *Journal of Range Management* 37:325–329.

Uresk, D. W. 1985. Effects of controlling black-tailed prairie dogs on plant production. *Journal of Range Management* 38:466–468.

Uresk, D. W., R. M. King, A. D. Apa, and R. L. Linder. 1986. Efficacy of zinc phosphide and strychnine for black-tailed prairie dog control. *Journal of Range Management* 39:298–299.

Uresk, D. W., J. G. MacCracken, and A. J. Bjugstad. 1982. Prairie dog density and cattle grazing relationships. Pages 199–201 in R. M. Timm and R. J. Johnson, eds., *Proceedings of the Fifth Great Plains Wildlife Damage Control Workshop.* Lincoln, Nebr.: Institute of Agriculture and Natural Resources, University of Nebraska.

Uresk, D. W., G. L. Schenbeck, and R. Cefkin, technical coordinators. 1988. *Eighth Great Plains Wildlife Damage Control Workshop Proceedings.* United States Department of Agriculture Forest Service, General Technical Report RM-154. Fort Collins, Colo.

van den Berghe, P. L. 1983. Human inbreeding avoidance: Culture in nature. *Behavioral and Brain Sciences* 6:91–123.

van Noordwijk, A. J., and W. Scharloo. 1981. Inbreeding in an island population of the great tit. *Evolution* 35:674–688.

van Schaik, C. P., and S. B. Hrdy. 1991. Intensity of local resource competition shapes the relationship between maternal rank and sex ratios at birth in cercopithecine primates. *American Naturalist* 138:1555–1562.

van Tienhoven, A. 1983. *Reproductive Physiology of Vertebrates.* Ithaca, N.Y.: Cornell University Press.

Van Vuren, D. 1990. Dispersal of yellow-bellied marmots. Ph.D. dissertation, University of Kansas, Lawrence, Kans.

Van Vuren, D., and K. B. Armitage. 1994. Survival of dispersing and philopatric yellow-bellied marmots: What is the cost of dispersal? *Oikos* 69: 179–181.

Veen, J. 1977. Functional and causal aspects of nest distribution in colonies of the sandwich tern (*Sterna s. sandvicensis* Lath.). *Behaviour Supplement* 20:1–193.

Vehrencamp, S. L. 1977. Relative fecundity and parental effort in communally nesting anis, *Crotophaga sulcirostris. Science* 197:403–405.

Vehrencamp, S. L. 1978. The adaptive significance of communal nesting in groove-billed anis *(Crotophaga sulcirostris). Behavioral Ecology and Sociobiology* 4:1–33.

Vehrencamp, S. L. 1979. The roles of individual, kin, and group selection in the evolution of sociality. Pages 351–394 in P. Marler and J. G. Vandenbergh, eds., *Social Behavior and Communication.* New York: Plenum Press.

Veiga, J. P. 1993. Prospective infanticide and ovulation retardation in free-living house sparrows. *Animal Behaviour* 45:43–46.

Verme, L. J. 1983. Sex ratio variation in *Odocoileus:* A critical review. *Journal of Wildlife Management* 47:573–582.

Vestal, B. M. 1991. Infanticide and cannibalism by male thirteen-lined ground squirrels. *Animal Behaviour* 41:1103–1104.

Vestal, B. M., and H. McCarley. 1984. Spatial and social relations of kin in thirteen-lined and other ground squirrels. Pages 404–423 in J. O. Murie and G. R. Michener, eds., *The Biology of Ground-Dwelling Squirrels.* Lincoln, Nebr.: University of Nebraska Press.

Vetterling, J. M. 1962. Endoparasites of the black-tailed prairie dog of northern Colorado. Master's thesis, Colorado State University, Fort Collins, Colo.

Vickery, W. L., and J. S. Millar. 1984. The energetics of huddling in endotherms. *Oikos* 43:88–93.

Vine, I. 1971. Risk of visual detection and pursuit by a predator and the selective advantage of flocking behaviour. *Journal of Theoretical Biology* 30:405–422.

Visscher, P. K. 1986. Kinship discrimination in queen rearing by honey bees *(Apis mellifera). Behavioral Ecology and Sociobiology* 18:453–460.

Vogel, C., and H. Loch. 1984. Reproductive parameters, adult-male replacements, and infanticide among free-ranging langurs *(Presbytis entellus)* at Jodhpur (Rajasthan), India. Pages 237–255 in G. Hausfater and S. B. Hrdy, eds., *Infanticide: Comparative and Evolutionary Perspectives.* New York: Aldine.

Vogel, S. 1989. *Life's Devices: The Physical World of Animals and Plants.* Princeton, N.J.: Princeton University Press.

Vogel, S., C. P. Ellington, and D. L. Kilgore. 1973. Wind-induced ventilation of the burrow of the prairie-dog, *Cynomys ludovicianus*. *Journal of Comparative Physiology* 85:1–15.

Volkmann-Rocco, B. 1972. The effect of delayed fertilization in some species of the genus *Tisbe* (Copepoda). *Biological Bulletin* 142:520–529.

vom Saal, F. S. 1984. Proximate and ultimate causes of infanticide and parental behavior in male house mice. Pages 401–424 in G. Hausfater and S. B. Hrdy, eds., *Infanticide: Comparative and Evolutionary Perspectives*. New York: Aldine.

vom Saal, F. S. 1985. Time-contingent change in infanticide and parental behavior induced by ejaculation in male mice. *Physiology and Behavior* 34:7–15.

Voss, R. 1979. *Male Accessory Glands and the Evolution of Copulatory Plugs in Rodents*. Occasional Papers of The Museum of Zoology, University of Michigan, no. 968. Ann Arbor, Mich.

Waage, J. K. 1982. Sib-mating and sex ratio strategies in scelionid wasps. *Ecological Entomology* 7:103–112.

Wade, O. 1928. Notes on the time of breeding and the number of young of *Cynomys ludovicianus*. *Journal of Mammalogy* 9:149.

Waldman, B., P. C. Frumhoff, and P. W. Sherman. 1988. Problems of kin recognition. *Trends in Ecology and Evolution* 3:8–13.

Walls, G. L. 1941. *The Vertebrate Visual System*. Bloomfield Hills, Mich.: Cranbrook Institute of Science.

Walls, G. L. 1942. *The Vertebrate Eye and Its Adaptive Radiation*. Bloomfield Hills, Mich.: Cranbrook Institute of Science.

Walters, J. R. 1980. Interventions and the development of dominance relationships in female baboons. *Folia Primatologica* 34:61–89.

Walters, J. R., and R. M. Seyfarth. 1987. Conflict and cooperation. Pages 306–317 in B. B. Smuts, D. L. Cheney, R. M. Seyfarth, R. W. Wrangham, and T. T. Struhsaker, eds., *Primate Societies*. Chicago: University of Chicago Press.

Waltz, E. C. 1982. Resource characteristics and the evolution of information centers. *American Naturalist* 119:73–90.

Waltz, E. C. 1987. A test of the information-centre hypothesis in two colonies of common terns, *Sterna hirundo*. *Animal Behaviour* 35:48–59.

Ward, P. 1965. Feeding ecology of the black-faced dioch *(Quelea quelea)* in Nigeria. *Ibis* 107:173–214.

Ward, P., and A. Zahavi. 1973. The importance of certain assemblages of birds as "information centers" for food-finding. *Ibis* 115:517–534.

Waring, G. H. 1966. Sounds and communications of the yellow-bellied marmot *(Marmota flaviventris)*. *Animal Behaviour* 14:177–183.

Waring, G. H. 1970. Sound communications of black-tailed, white-tailed, and Gunnison's prairie dogs. *American Midland Naturalist* 83:167–185.

Warwick, E. J., and J. E. Legates. 1979. *Breeding and Improvement of Farm Animals*. New York: McGraw-Hill.

Waser, N. M. 1993. Sex, mating systems, inbreeding, and outbreeding. Pages 1–13 in N. W. Thornhill, ed., *The Natural History of Inbreeding and Outbreeding: Theoretical and Empirical Perspectives*. Chicago: University of Chicago Press.

Waser, P. 1978. Postreproductive survival and behavior in free-ranging female mangabeys. *Folia Primatologica* 29:142–160.

Waser, P. M. 1985. Does competition drive dispersal? *Ecology* 66:1170–1175.

Wasser, S. K. 1983. Reproductive competition and cooperation among female yellow baboons. Pages 349–390 in S. K. Wasser, ed., *Social Behavior of Female Vertebrates.* New York: Academic Press.

Wasser, S. K., and D. P. Barash. 1983. Reproductive suppression among female mammals: Implications for biomedicine and sexual selection theory. *Quarterly Review of Biology* 58:513–538.

Waterman, J. M. 1984. Infanticide in the Columbian ground squirrel, *Spermophilus columbianus. Journal of Mammalogy* 65:137–138.

Watkins, L. C., and K. A. Shump. 1981. Roosting behavior in the evening bat, *Nycticeius humeralis. American Midland Naturalist* 105:258–268.

Watts, D. P. 1985. Relations between group size and composition and feeding competition in mountain gorilla groups. *Animal Behaviour* 33:72–85.

Watts, D. P. 1991. Harassment of immigrant female mountain gorillas by resident females. *Ethology* 89:135–153.

Weatherhead, P. J., and R. J. Robertson. 1979. Offspring quality and the polygyny threshold: "The sexy son hypothesis." *American Naturalist* 113:201–208.

Webster, A. B., R. G. Gartshore, and R. J. Brooks. 1981. Infanticide in the meadow vole, *Microtus pennsylvanicus:* Significance in relation to social system and population cycling. *Behavioral and Neural Biology* 31:342–347.

Wedel, W. R. 1961. *Prehistoric Man on the Great Plains.* Norman, Okla: University of Oklahoma Press.

Weigel, R. M. 1981. The distribution of altruism among kin: A mathematical model. *American Naturalist* 118:191–201.

Weinberg, D. 1986. Decline and fall of the black-footed ferret. *Natural History* 86:63–69.

Wells-Gosling, N. 1985. *Flying Squirrels: Gliders in the Dark.* Washington, D.C.: Smithsonian Institution Press.

Werren, J. H. 1980. Sex ratio adaptations to local mate competition in a parasitic wasp. *Science* 208:1157–1159.

Werren, J. H. 1983. Sex ratio evolution under local mate competition in a parasitic wasp. *Evolution* 37:116–124.

Werren, J. H., and E. L. Charnov. 1978. Facultative sex ratios and population dynamics. *Nature* 272:349–350.

West, R. W., and J. E. Dowling. 1975. Anatomical evidence for cone and rod-like receptors in the gray squirrel, ground squirrel, and prairie dog retinas. *Journal of Comparative Neurology* 159:439–459.

West, S. D., and H. T. Dublin. 1984. Behavioral strategies of small mammals under winter conditions. Pages 293–299 in J. F. Merritt, ed., *Winter Ecology of Small Mammals.* Special Publication of Carnegie Museum of Natural History, no. 10.

West-Eberhard, M. J. 1975. The evolution of social behavior by kin selection. *Quarterly Review of Biology* 50:1–33.

Westermarck, E. A. 1921. *The History of Human Marriage.* London: Macmillan.

Westermarck, E. A. 1934a. Recent theories on exogamy. *The Sociological Review* 26:22–40.

Westermarck, E. A. 1934b. *Three Essays on Sex and Marriage.* London: Macmillan.

Westneat, D. F. 1987. Extra-pair fertilizations in a predominantly monogamous bird: Genetic evidence. *Animal Behaviour* 35:877–886.

Westneat, D. F., P. W. Sherman, and M. L. Morton. 1990. The ecology and evolution of extra-pair copulations in birds. Pages 331–369 in D. M. Power, ed., *Current Ornithology,* vol. 7. New York: Plenum Press.

Whicker, A. D., and J. K. Detling. 1988. Ecological consequences of prairie dog disturbances. *BioScience* 38:778–785.

Whitaker, J. O., and L. L. Schmeltz. 1973. External parasites of the woodchuck, *Marmota monax,* in Indiana. *Entomology News* 84:69–72.

Whitaker, J. O., and N. Wilson. 1974. Most distribution lists of mites (Acari) of wild mammals of North America, north of Mexico. *American Midland Naturalist* 91:1–67.

Whitehead, L. C. 1927. Notes on prairie-dogs. *Journal of Mammalogy* 8:58.

Whitten, P. L. 1987. Infants and adult males. Pages 343–357 in B. B. Smuts, D. L. Cheney, R. M. Seyfarth, R. W. Wrangham, and T. T. Struhsaker, eds., *Primate Societies.* Chicago: University of Chicago Press.

Wickler, W. 1968. *Mimicry in Plants and Animals.* New York: McGraw-Hill.

Wickler, W. 1985. Coordination of vigilance in bird groups: The "watchman's song" hypothesis. *Zeitschrift für Tierpsychologie* 69:250–253.

Wiggett, D. R., and D. A. Boag. 1986. Establishing colonies of ground squirrels during the active season. *Wildlife Society Bulletin* 14:288–291.

Wilcomb, M. J. 1954. A study of prairie dog burrow systems and the ecology of their arthropod inhabitants in central Oklahoma. Ph.D. dissertation, University of Oklahoma, Norman, Okla.

Wilder, B. G. 1872. Note on the prairie dog. *American Naturalist* 6:46–47.

Wiley, D. N., and P. J. Clapham. 1993. Does maternal condition affect the sex ratio of offspring in humpback whales? *Animal Behaviour* 46:321–324.

Wilkinson, G. S. 1985. The social organization of the common vampire bat. I. Pattern and cause of association. *Behavioral Ecology and Sociobiology* 17:lll–121.

Wilkinson, G. S. 1986. Social grooming in the common vampire bat, *Desmodus rotundus. Animal Behaviour* 34:1880–1889.

Wilkinson, G. S. 1992a. Communal nursing in the evening bat, *Nycticeius humeralis. Behavioral Ecology and Sociobiology* 31:225–236.

Wilkinson, G. S. 1992b. Information transfer at evening bat colonies. *Animal Behaviour* 44:501–518.

Wilkinson, G. S., and A. E. M. Baker. 1988. Communal nesting among genetically similar house mice. *Ethology* 77:103–114.

Wilkinson, L. 1988. *Systat: The System for Statistics.* Evanston, Ill.: Systat, Inc.

Wilkinson, P. F., and C. C. Shank. 1976. Rutting-fight mortality among musk oxen on Banks Island, Northwest Territories, Canada. *Animal Behaviour* 24:756–758.

Williams, G. C. 1957. Pleiotropy, natural selection, and the evolution of senescence. *Evolution* 11:398–411.

Williams, G. C. 1966a. *Adaptation and Natural Selection.* Princeton, N.J.: Princeton University Press.

Williams, G. C. 1966b. Natural selection, the costs of reproduction, and a refinement of Lack's principle. *American Naturalist* 100:687–690.

Williams, G. C. 1975. *Sex and Evolution.* Princeton, N.J: Princeton University Press.

Williams, G. C. 1979. The question of adaptive sex ratio in outcrossed vertebrates. *Proceedings of the Royal Society of London* B 205:567–580.

Williams, G. C. 1988. Retrospect on sex and kindred topics. Pages 287–298 in R. E. Michod and B. R. Levin, eds., *The Evolution of Sex: An Examination of Current Ideas.* Sunderland, Mass.: Sinauer Associates.

Williams, G. C. 1992. *Natural Selection: Domains, Levels, and Challenges.* Oxford: Oxford University Press.

Williams, G. C., and R. M. Nesse. 1991. The dawn of Darwinian medicine. *Quarterly Review of Biology* 66:1–22.

Williams, S. L., and R. J. Baker. 1976. Vagility and local movement of pocket gophers (Geomyidae: Rodentia). *American Midland Naturalist* 96:303–316.

Williams, T. D. 1994. Adoption in a precocial species, the lesser snow goose: Intergenerational conflict, altruism or a mutually beneficial strategy? *Animal Behaviour* 47:101–107.

Wilson, E. O. 1963. Social modifications related to rareness in ant species. *Evolution* 17:249–253.

Wilson, E. O. 1971. *The Insect Societies.* Cambridge, Mass.: Harvard University Press.

Wilson, E. O. 1975. *Sociobiology: The New Synthesis.* Cambridge, Mass.: Harvard University Press.

Wilson, E. O. 1978. *On Human Nature.* Cambridge, Mass.: Harvard University Press.

Wilson, J. R., N. Adler, and B. Le Boeuf. 1965. The effects of intromission frequency on successful pregnancy in the female rat. *Proceedings of The National Academy of Sciences, U.S.A.,* 53:1392–1395.

Winkler, D. W., and G. S. Wilkinson. 1988. Parental effort in birds and mammals: Theory and measurement. Pages 185–214 in P. H. Harvey and L. Partridge, eds., *Oxford Surveys in Evolutionary Biology,* vol. 5. New York: Oxford University Press.

Wistrand, H. 1974. Individual, social, and seasonal behavior of the thirteen-lined ground squirrel *(Spermophilus tridecemlineatus). Journal of Mammalogy* 55:329–347.

Wittenberger, J. F. 1981. *Animal Social Behavior.* Boston: Duxbury Press.

Wittenberger, J. F., and G. L. Hunt. 1985. The adaptive significance of coloniality in birds. Pages 1–78 in D. S. Farner, J. R. King, and K. C. Parkes, eds., *Avian Biology.* New York: Academic Press.

Wittenberger, J. F., and R. L. Tilson. 1980. The evolution of monogamy: Hypotheses and evidence. *Annual Review of Ecology and Systematics* 11:197–232.

Wolf, A. P. 1966. Childhood association, sexual attraction, and the incest taboo: A Chinese case. *American Anthropologist* 68:883–898.

Wolf, A. P. 1968. Adopt a daughter-in-law, marry a sister: A Chinese solution to the problem of the incest taboo. *American Anthropologist* 70:864–874.

Wolf, A. P. 1970. Childhood association and sexual attraction: A further test of the Westermarck hypothesis. *American Anthropologist* 72:503–515.

Wolf, K. E. 1980. Social change and male reproductive strategy in silvered-leaf monkeys, *Presbytis cristata,* in Kuala Selangor, peninsular Malaysia. Paper presented at the 49th Annual Meeting of The Association of Physical Anthropologists, Niagara Falls, N.Y., 17–19 April 1980.

Wolfe, J. L. 1966. Agonistic behaviour and dominance relationships of the eastern chipmunk, *Tamias striatus. American Midland Naturalist* 76:190–200.

Wolff, J. O. 1992. Parents suppress reproduction and stimulate dispersal in opposite sex juvenile white-footed mice. *Nature* 359:409–411.

Wolff, J. O., and D. M. Cicirello. 1989. Field evidence for sexual selection and resource competition infanticide in white-footed mice. *Animal Behaviour* 38:637–642.

Wood, A. E. 1933. Pleistocene prairie-dog from Frederick, Oklahoma. *Journal of Mammalogy* 14:160.

Woodroffe, R. 1993. Alloparental behaviour in the European badger. *Animal Behaviour* 46:413–415.

Woolfenden, G. E., and J. W. Fitzpatrick. 1984. *The Florida Scrub Jay: Demography of a Cooperative-Breeding Bird.* Princeton, N.J.: Princeton University Press.

Wrege, P. H., and S. T. Emlen. 1987. Biochemical determination of paternal uncertainty in white-fronted bee-eaters. *Behavioral Ecology and Sociobiology* 20:153–160.

Wright, P. C. 1984. Biparental care in *Aotus trivirgatus* and *Callicebus moloch.* Pages 59–75 in M. F. Small, ed., *Female Primates: Studies by Women Primatologists.* New York: Alan R. Liss.

Wright-Smith, M. A. 1978. The ecology and social organization of *Cynomys parvidens* (Utah prairie dog) in south central Utah. Master's thesis, Indiana University, Bloomington, Ind.

Wynne-Edwards, V. C. 1962. *Animal Dispersion in Relation to Social Behaviour.* London: Oliver and Boyd.

Yahner, R. H. 1978. Seasonal rates of vocalizations in eastern chipmunks. *Ohio Journal of Science* 78:301–303.

Yamaguchi, Y. 1985. Sex ratios of an aphid subject to local mate competition with variable maternal control. *Nature* 318:460–462.

Yamamoto, I. 1987. Male parental care in the raccoon dog *Nyctereutes procyonoides* during the early rearing period. Pages 189–196 in Y. Ito, J. L. Brown, and J. Kikkawa, eds., *Animal Societies.* Tokyo: Japan Societies Scientific Press.

Yannone, V. D. 1973. The black-footed ferret in Montana. Pages 41–44 in R. L. Linder and C. N. Hillman, eds., *Proceedings of the Black-Footed Ferret and Prairie Dog Workshop.* Brookings, S.D.: South Dakota State University.

Yates, T. L., and R. J. Pedersen. 1982. Moles (Talpidae). Pages 37–51 in J. A. Chapman and G. A. Feldhamer, eds., *Wild Mammals of North America.* Baltimore, Md.: Johns Hopkins University Press. Ydenberg, R. C., and D. F. Bertram. 1989. Lack's clutch size hypothesis and brood enlargement studies on colonial seabirds. *Colonial Waterbirds* 12:134–137.

Yeaton, R. I. 1972. Social behavior and social organization in Richardson's ground squirrel *(Spermophilus richardsonii)* in Saskatchewan. *Journal of Mammalogy* 53:139–147.

Yom-Tov, Y. 1980. Intraspecific nest parasitism in birds. *Biological Review* 55:93–108.

Young, P. J. 1990. Hibernating patterns of free-ranging Columbian ground squirrels. *Oecologia* 83:504–511.

Young, S. D. 1944. Longevity and other data in a male and female prairie dog kept as pets. *Journal of Mammalogy* 25:317–319.

Zammuto, R. M. 1987. Life histories of mammals: Analyses among and within *Spermophilus columbianus* life tables. *Ecology* 68:1351–1363.

Zammuto, R. M., and P. W. Sherman. 1986. A comparison of time-specific and cohort-specific life tables for Belding's ground squirrels, *Spermophilus beldingi. Canadian Journal of Zoology* 64:602–605.

Zouros, E., and D. W. Foltz. 1987. The use of allelic isozyme variation for the study of heterosis. *Isozymes: Current Topics in Biological and Medical Research* 13:1–59.

Zuk, M., R. Thornhill, J. D. Ligon, K. Johnson, S. Austad, S. H. Ligon, N. W. Thornhill, and C. Costin. 1990. The role of male ornaments and courtship behavior in female choice of red jungle fowl. *American Naturalist* 136:459–473.

Index

Note: Except for common names of other organisms, entries refer to the black-tailed prairie dog. Scientific names for all organisms are in Appendix A.

abandonment, of litter by mother, 138, 151–153, fig. 7.10
  partial, selective, 153, 363
Abert's squirrel. *See* tassel-eared squirrel
abortion, 125, 151, 234, 289, 362, 390
aboveground
  carcasses, 35, 153, 157, 158, 378
  copulation, 246, 251–253, table 11.2
  infanticide, 134–135
  nursing, 188, fig. 9.1
accessibility
  of juveniles to infanticide, 140–142, 407
  of study colony to researchers, 42
accipiter hawk, 15. *See also following accipiter species:* Cooper's; European sparrowhawk; northern goshawk; sharp-shinned
accuracy, of behavioral observations of estrus and copulation, 248–257
acorn woodpecker, 77, 113, 149, 260, 323, 324, 325, 338, 346, 404–405, 408
adaptation, 149, 152–153, 268, 337, 361, 364, 365, 406
  defined, 2
adder, 113
Adélie penguin, 3, 74, 87
adoption, 146
adult, defined, 57
advantages. *See* benefits
African elephant, 187, 292, 360

African lion, 3, 5, 75, 108, 112, 121, 123, 153, 157, 158, 187, 202, 273, 275, 281, 314, 327, 334, 383, 404–405
African wild dog, 3, 4, 72, 127–128, 187, 372, 404–405
agaontid fig wasp, 371
age. *See also* aging
  vs. annual reproductive success, 287–292, figs. 13.1–13.4
  vs. antipredator calling, 179, fig. 8.11
  vs. body mass, 288, 298–305, 319–320, 397–401, fig. 16.12
  vs. copulation, 288–289, fig. 13.2
  determination of, 55, 56–57
  vs. dispersal, 263, 305, 339–344, 378–382, fig. 14.1a
  vs. first copulation, 156, 288–289, 342–343, 345, 397, figs. 13.2 and 14.2
  of infanticidal males, 156
  of juveniles victimized by infanticide, 139
  vs. litter size, 288–292, fig. 13.3
  of marauding females, 139
  from molar attrition, 56
  of mothers victimized by infanticide, 139
  of parents vs. sex ratio of juveniles at first emergence, 365–367, fig. 15.5
  vs. probability of parturition, 390, fig. 16.9
  vs. reproductive synchrony, 319, 320, 13.23b, 13.24b
  and senescence, 287–292, figs. 13.1–13.4
  vs. sexual maturation, 288–289, 397, fig. 13.2

vs. survivorship, 288, fig. 13.1
from tooth eruption and tooth wear,
    56
age-specific survivorship, 287–288, fig.
    13.1
aging, 55, 56–57. *See also* age
aggression
    costs of, 76–78, figs. 5.4 and 5.5
    intra- vs. intercoterie, 76
    measurement of, 60
    vs. ward size, 76–80, fig. 5.2
Alaska marmot, 34, 222
alarm
    visual, 63, 91–93, fig. 5.13
    vocal. *See* antipredator call
alarm bark. *See* antipredator call
alarm call. *See* antipredator call
alarm note. *See* antipredator call
albatross. *See following albatross
    species:* black-footed; wandering
albinism, 8
alertness. *See* vigilance
all clear call, 181–183, figs. 8.12 and
    8.13. *See also* jump-yip
all-day consortship. *See* underground
    consortship
allocation, of parental resources by
    juveniles, 360–365
allogrooming, 2, 4, 24, 61, 81–83, 97,
    115, 138, 193, 202, 217, figs. 5.8 and
    10.1
alloparenting, 115, 147, 201–202, 217–
    219
    defined, 201
    factors affecting, 201–202
alpine marmot, 26, 28, 34, 64, 166, 179
alpine swift, 295
amalgamation, of coteries. *See* fusion
amaranth. *See* pigweed
American badger, 14, 34, 35, 47, 69, 94,
    166, 169, 406, figs. 2.3b, 5.12, 8.4,
    table 2.3
    experiments with stuffed specimen,
        63–64, 89–93, 166, 170, 178, 183–
        184, figs. 5.12 and 8.4
    habituation to, 170, table 8.1
American bison, 14, 21, 22, 38, 57, 166,
    316, 368, fig. 4.2b, table 2.3
American buffalo. *See* American bison
American jacana, 260
American magpie. *See* black-billed
    magpie

American pika, 3, 5, 337
American robin, 166, table 2.3
amicability, of behavioral interactions, 2
    vs. kinship and competition, 111,
        202–210, 409, figs. 6.10 and 10.1–
        10.3
anal glands. *See* perianal scent glands
anal sniffing, 2, 60–61, 193, 225, 232,
    234–235, 247, fig. 11.7a
ancestor. *See* common ancestor
anesthesia, 52
ani. *See* groove-billed ani
annoyance, of predators caused by
    antipredator call, 92, 183
annual reproductive success (ARS), 260–
    286. *See also* lifetime reproductive
    success
    vs. age, 287–292, figs. 13.1–13.4
    correlation of different estimates,
        277–283, figs. 12.7 and 12.9
    vs. costs of reproduction, 309–313,
        figs. 13.18 and 13.19
    vs. coterie size, 283, 320–329, figs.
        13.25–13.30
    vs. dominance, 298–305
    of father, vs. sex ratio of juveniles,
        370–371, fig. 15.8
    of female marauders, 148–149, 157–
        158, table 7.3
    of females that copulate with a
        second male, 268, fig. 12.4
    of immigrants, 67, 383, table 16.4
    of infanticidal males, 157–158
    and heterozygosity, 358
    vs. juvenile body mass at first
        emergence, 294–298, fig. 13.7
    vs. litter size, 294–298, figs. 13.6 and
        13.8
    for males and females, 263–270, fig.
        12.2
    of marauders and nonmarauders,
        148–149, table 7.3
    and the mating call, 245, fig. 11.15
    methods of estimation, 65–67, 262–
        263, tables 12.1 and 12.2
    vs. order of copulations, 227–229,
        281–283, 292–294, fig. 13.5
    vs. parental body mass, 298–305,
        figs. 13.12–13.17
    vs. reproductive synchrony within
        colonies, 96, 316–320, fig. 13.22
    vs. reproductive synchrony within
        coteries, 320, fig. 13.24a

sexual asymmetry in, 4, 270, fig. 12.2
vs. type of coterie, 329–334, figs.
  13.31–13.33
vs. weather and precipitation, 305
annual variation. *See also* variation
  in annual reproductive success, 283
  in colony size and colony
    composition, 376–378, figs. 16.1
    and 16.2, table 16.1
  in coterie type, 108, fig. 6.8
  in demographic measures, 378, fig.
    15.1, fig. 16.2
  in frequency of infanticide, 160
  in litter size, 378, fig. 16.2
  in number of coteries at study colony,
    103, fig. 6.2a
  in sex ratio of juveniles at first
    emergence, 362, fig. 15.1
ant. *See following ant species:* fungus;
  harvester
antelope. *See* pronghorn antelope
antipredator call, 4, 5, 63–64, 91–93,
  115, 163–186, 217, 407
  and abdominal movements, 64, 166
  vs. aboveground presence of other
    coterie members, 183–185, fig.
    8.14c
  vs. age, 179, fig. 8.11
  vs. all clear call, 181–183, figs. 8.12
    and 8.13
  before and after first juvenile
    emergences, 175–176, table 8.2
  vs. changes in presence of nearby
    kin, 176–177, table 8.3
  and chatters, 166
  vs. colony size, 91–93, fig. 5.13
  conspicuousness of caller, 166, 171–
    172
  costs of giving, 163, 171–172
  vs. coterie size, 178–179, fig. 8.10
  description of, 163–169, figs. 8.2 and
    8.3
  for different predators, 6, 166–168,
    407
  vs. differential nepotism, 177–178,
    407, fig. 8.8
  vs. distance from predator, 169, figs.
    8.5 and 8.14a
  false vs. real, 166, 178
  frequency of, 164, 170–171, fig. 8.6
  individual variation in, 170–171, fig.
    8.6

for individuals in adjacent coteries,
  179–181
by individuals with no nearby kin,
  186, fig. 8.7
vs. jump-yip, 181–183, figs. 8.12 and
  8.13
by juveniles, 164–166
for kin in other coterie territories, 177
vs. kinship, 5, 163, 172–175, 176–
  178, 201, figs. 8.7–8.9
methods of investigation, 63–64, 170,
  fig. 8.4
and moving mouthparts, 64, 166
vs. nepotism, 5, 163, 172–175, 176–
  178
for nondescendant kin, 5, 163, 172–
  175, 176–178, 407, fig. 8.8
for offspring, 5, 163, 172–175, figs.
  8.8 and 8.9
in other coterie territories, 169, 179–
  181
other names for, 163–164
parasitism of, 181
vs. parental care, 172–175, 407, fig.
  8.8
and rate of calling, 166–168, 407
response of other prairie dogs to,
  168–169
in response to predators vs.
  nonpredators, 166
and selfish herd effects, 172, 183
vs. self-preservation, 183–186, fig.
  8.14
sexual asymmetry in, 170–171, 172,
  figs. 8.7 and 8.8
for snakes, 168
sonogram of, 164, fig. 8.1
submergence, in response to, 183, fig.
  8.14b
vs. susceptibility to predation, 171–
  172, 175–176
vs. urgency of attack, 166
various names for, 163–164
ventriloquism of, 172
vs. vulnerability of caller to
  predation, 171–172, 178
vs. vulnerability of listening juveniles
  to predation, 175–176, table 8.2
when others are also calling, 178
and whistles, 166
antisnake call, 168
Arabian babbler, 93

arctic ground squirrel, 126, 156, 166, 188, 199, 201–202, 208, 210, 211, 222, 344, 397
arctic marmot. *See* Alaska marmot
arctic tern, 287
Arctomys, 8
area
    of coterie territory, 1, 115, fig. 6.13a
    of study colony, 40, fig. 4.5
ARS. *See* annual reproductive success
Asian chipmunk, 233, 246
assistants. *See* field assistants
aster, table 2.3
asymmetry. *See* sexual asymmetry
Atricholaelaps, 62. *See also* tick
attention, to estrous female by males, 233–237, fig. 11.8
attractiveness
    of mates, 287–288
    of prairie dog colonies to predators, 75, 85–86
    of prairie dog colonies to ungulates and other animals, 21, table 2.3
auntie. *See* alloparenting
Australian bell miner, 201, 325, 410
autogrooming, 81–83, 97, fig. 5.8
avoidance, of extreme inbreeding, 5, 339–351, 408–409, figs. 14.1–14.8, tables 14.2–14.5
awareness, of prairie dogs against predators, 73–74, 89–93, 197, fig. 5.13

babbler. *See following babbler species:* Arabian; black-lored; gray-crowned; Hall's
baboon, 123. *See also following baboon species:* gelada; savannah
badger. *See* American badger. *See also* Eurasian badger
bag, for marking and handling, 49–52, fig. 4.10a
Baikal seal, 74
banded mongoose, 94, 217
bank swallow, 4, 74, 76, 84
bark. *See* antipredator call; defense bark; muffled bark
bark beetle. *See* scolytid bark beetle
barks. *See* antipredator call
barn swallow, 72, 80
bat. *See following bat species:* common vampire; evening; greater spearnose;

hammer-headed; Mexican free-tailed; rhinolophid; Townsend's; vespertilionid
bear. *See* grizzly bear
bee. *See following bee species:* honeybee; sweat
bee-eater. *See following bee-eater species:* European; white-fronted
beetle: *See following beetle species:* bombardier; darkling; dung; ground; red flour; scolytid bark
behavioral interactions
    amicable, 2, 60–62
    of estrus and copulation, 221–259
    with female before, during, and after estrus, 234–237, fig. 11.8
    hostile, 2, 60
behavioral observations, of estrus and copulations, 221–259. *See also* copulation, estrus
Belding's ground squirrel, 4, 28, 34, 64, 75, 87, 126, 128, 145, 146, 147, 150, 156, 158, 163, 164, 166, 168–169, 171, 172–173, 179, 186, 188, 201–202, 210, 211, 225, 234–235, 239, 248, 251, 257, 260, 273, 287, 293, 298, 305, 319, 344, 360, 380, 384–387, 395, 397, 404–405, 407
bell miner. *See* Australian bell miner
beneficiaries, of communal nursing, 187
benefits
    of coloniality, 4, 72–74, 87–96, 403
    of communal nursing, 196–199
    to female from copulation with second male, 268
    of inbreeding, 337–338, 358–359
    of infanticide, 145–149, 152–153, 157–158
    to male of copulating first, 292–294, fig. 13.5
    of mating call, 241–245, figs. 11.12–11.14
    of sexual reproduction, 337–338
Bernoulli's principle, and underground ventilation, 31
BF. *See* bloody face
bias. *See* sexual asymmetry
bighorn sheep. *See* mountain sheep
bindweed. *See* glorybind
birth. *See* parturition
biscuitroot, table 2.3
bison. *See* American bison

blackbird. *See following blackbird species:* red-winged; tricolored; yellow-headed
black eagle, 205
black grouse, 242, 279
black nightshade, 9, table 2.3
black spider monkey, 368
black widow spider, table 2.3
black-billed magpie, 297, table 2.3
black-capped marmot, 34, 222
black-footed albatross, 361
black-footed ferret, 14, 15, 22, 29, 35, 75, 94, 99, fig. 2.3d, table 2.3
    absence at study colony, 29, 69
    and evolution of coloniality, 97–99
    and frequency of infanticide, 406
black-headed gull, 4, 73, 75, 89, 313
black-lored babbler, 93
black-tail. *See* black-tailed prairie dog
black-tailed prairie dog, 8–24, 74, fig. 2.1b, table 2.2. *See also* prairie dog
block. *See* pregnancy block
blood. *See also* blood samples
    on face and claws, after infanticide, 126–130, 134–135
    removal of, by ectoparasites, 81
    near vulva, on day of parturition, 387, fig. 16.6
blood samples
    collection of, 52, 65, 261, fig. 12.1
    to determine paternity, 65–67, 256–257
    to investigate communal nursing, 65, 191, fig. 9.3
bloody face, after infanticide (BF), 126–130, 134–135
bluebird. *See* mountain bluebird
blue tit, 309
bluebottle fly, table 2.3
boat-tailed grackle, 207
bobak marmot, 166
bobcat, 14, 20, 35, 47, 69, 75, 94, 99, 166, fig. 2.3c, table 2.3
bobwhite, 3
body condition, 35, 49, 297, 305, 368. *See also* body mass
body mass
    of adults, 1, 8, 49, 298–305, 397–401, figs. 13.9a and 16.12
    vs. age, 288, 298–305, 319–320, 397–401, fig. 16.12
    vs. annual reproductive success for juveniles, 294–298, fig. 13.7

    vs. annual reproductive success for parents, 298–305, figs. 13.10–13.17
    correlations at different stages of annual cycle, 298–299, fig. 13.11
    vs. dispersal, 305
    vs. dominance, 207, 298, 367
    extremes, fig. 13.10
    of juveniles before first emergence, 47, 388–390
    of juveniles at first emergence, 294–298, 362–363, 384, figs. 13.7, 13.9, 15.2, and 16.4b
    of juveniles vs. litter size, 294, fig. 13.6
    of marauders and victimized mothers, 143–144, 299, fig. 7.9
    vs. mating call, 242, fig. 11.12a
    of mothers that abandon neonates, 151–152, table 7.10
    of mothers, vs. litter size and juvenile body mass, 299–305, fig. 13.14
    of mothers, vs. reproductive synchrony, 319, 320, fig. 13.23a
    of mothers, vs. sex ratio of juveniles at first emergence, 364–365, 367–369, figs. 15.6 and 15.7
    of pregnant females, 311–312, 397
    vs. probability of copulation and reproduction, 298–305, figs. 13.12–13.17
    reduction of, during reproduction, 311–312, fig. 13.19
    vs. reproduction in previous year, 311–313, fig. 13.19
    sexual asymmetry, among adults, 1, 397–401, fig. 16.12
    sexual asymmetry, among juveniles, 362–363, fig. 15.2
    of successful and unsuccessful individuals, 298–305, figs. 13.12–13.17
    vs. survivorship, 294–297, 305, fig. 13.7
body size, 49. *See also* body mass
body weight. *See* body mass
bombardier beetle, table 2.3
bonnet macaque, 367
bonobo. *See* pygmy chimpanzee
bottleneck, genetic and population, 357–358
boundary, of coterie territory, 115
bowerbird. *See* satin bowerbird
box turtle. *See* western box turtle

breeder. *See* breeding individual
breeding, cooperative. *See* cooperative
   breeding
breeding coterie territory, 343–344. *See
   also* coterie territory
   defined, 338
breeding dispersal, 343–344, figs. 14.3
   and 14.4
   defined, 338
breeding individual, defined, 67
breeding season, 205, 257, 263, 313
brome, table 2.3
brood parasitism. *See* intraspecific brood
   parasitism
Brower's marmot. *See* Alaska marmot
brown bear. *See* grizzly bear
brown-headed spider monkey, 356
brown hyena, 127–128
brown pelican, 74, 313
Bruce effect. *See* pregnancy block
bubonic plague, 74, 80, 402
buffalo. *See* American bison
buffalo grass, 14, table 2.3
bull snake, 14, 168, 406, table 2.3
bunting. *See following bunting species:*
   indigo; lark
Burchell's zebra, 356
burial. *See* interment
burrow entrance. *See* burrows, entrances
   of
burrow mound, 30–31, figs. 3.3 and 3.4
burrowing owl, 15, table 2.3
burrows, 26–36
   vs. colony size and colony density,
      36
   competition for, 35, 117, 119, 206,
      319–320, 372, 405
   per coterie territory, 1, 34
   defense of, 2, 34–35, 126, 134, 136–
      138, 151
   depth, 26, fig. 3.1
   deterioration of, 29 , 86
   diameter, 26
   dome crater, 30
   entrances, 26, 30, fig. 3.3
   excavation by humans, 28, fig. 3.1
   excavation by prairie dogs, 42, 326,
      372
   fecal pellets within, 28
   humidity within, 28
   latrine within, 28
   length, 26, fig. 3.1
   longevity, 29

   mortality within, 35, fig. 3.6
   mounds of, 30–31, figs. 3.3 and 3.4
   multiple entrances of, 28, fig. 3.1,
      fig. 3.2
   nest chambers within, 26, fig. 3.1
   number at study colony, 42, fig. 4.5
   number and density of, vs. colony
      size and colony density, 36, 96
   number and density of, vs. coterie
      size, 115–117, figs. 6.13a and 6.15
   nursery burrows, 2, 26, 35, 117, 119,
      126, 134, 136–138, 151, 196, 206,
      239, 319–320, 372, 405, 409–410,
      figs. 3.1 and 7.1
   plugging, 29
   for refuge, 26, 30, 168
   rim crater, 30, fig. 3.3, fig. 3.4
   sharing of, 34–35, 96
   for sleeping, 26, 30–33
   suitability, 26, 30
   switching of during night, 31–34, 247
   temperature within, 28
   toilet within, 28
   trails between, 26
   and underground ventilation, 5, 31,
      fig. 3.5
bush hyrax, 3
buteo hawk, 15. *See also following buteo
   species:* ferruginous; red-tailed; rough-
   legged; Swainson's

cactus. *See* prickly pear cactus
cactus mouse, 231
California chipmunk, 246
California ground squirrel, 63, 166, 168,
   176, 183, 186, 222, 319, 404–405
California gull, 292
California mouse, 115
California sea lion, 5, 360
camel cricket. *See* cave cricket
Canada goose, 3
cannibalism, 14, 126–128, 134, 135, 147,
   148, 151, 156, 158, 405, 410, figs. 5.4b
   and 7.5
cape hunting dog. *See* African wild dog
capillary tubes, for collecting blood
   samples, 52, 65
carcass, 35, 153, 157, 158, 378, figs. 3.6
   and 7.12
cardinal rule, of livetrapping, 47, fig. 4.9
caribou, 313, 356
cascade golden-mantled ground squirrel,
   392

cattle. *See* domestic cow
cattle egret, 3, 87
cave cricket, table 2.3
cavy. *See following cavy species:*
   mountain; yellow-toothed
center. *See* information center
center-edge differences, 96
chacma baboon. *See* savannah baboon
chaffinch, 172, 246
chain reaction, of jump-yips, 1, 181
chamber. *See* nest chamber
chance, and male reproductive success,
   283
chase, 2, 61, 119, 130, 136–138, 202,
   225–227, 232, 235, 247, 248–249, 383
   cooperative, to deter small predators,
      94–96
   defined, 60
   vs. ward size, 76–79, fig. 5.2
chasing, of small predators, 94, 115
chattering, of teeth, 2, 60, 63
chatters, of ground squirrels, 166
chimpanzee, 147, 158, 207, 217, 246,
   253, 292, 346, 356
chipmunk, 7, 199. *See also following*
   chipmunk species: eastern; Sonoma
chirk. *See* antipredator call
choice. *See* female choice
chough. *See* white-winged chough
chromosomes, number of, table 2.2
chuckle, 63
classification
   of different species of prairie dogs,
      7–13, table 2.1
   of types of inbreeding, 338, table
      14.1
cliff swallow, 3, 4, 73, 74, 80, 84, 96,
   356, 403
climate, at Wind Cave National Park, 13,
   107, 188, 257–258, 378, 380
clipping, of vegetation, 1, 9, 86, 88, 99,
   326, fig. 5.18, table 2.3
clutch size. *See* litter size
coadapted gene complexes, 337
coalition. *See* male coalition
coati. *See* white-nosed coati
cocklebur, table 2.3
coefficient of genetic relatedness, 61,
   274, 338, figs. 10.4 and 14.6. *See also*
   kinship
coexistence
   of prairie dogs and livestock, 21
   of infanticide and communal nursing,
      5–6, 188, 191, 198, 409

cohort-specific life table, 393–396, tables
   16.7–16.10
collared flycatcher, 287, 292
collared lemming, 158
collared peccary, 139
coloniality, 72–101, 402–404
   benefits of, 4, 72–74, 87–96, 403
   costs of, 3–4, 74–75, 76–87, 402
   defined, 3
   and farming, 88–89, 403
   forced, 72
   vs. increased attractiveness to
      predators, 75, 85–86
   vs. increased awareness of predators,
      73–74, 89–93, fig. 5.13
   vs. increased competition, 3, 75, 76–
      79, 406–407, fig. 5.2
   vs. increased conspicuousness, 75,
      85–86, fig. 5.11
   vs. increased ectoparasitism, 3, 74,
      80–83, figs. 5.6 and 5.7
   vs. increased incidence of disease, 3,
      74, 80
   and information centers, 72, 74
   levels of, 3
   and miscellaneous costs, 86–87
   and misdirected parental care, 3–4,
      83–85, fig. 5.9
   and mobbing, 73, 94–96
   multiple benefits of, 73–74, 403
   and optimal colony size, 75, 403–404
   primary benefits of, 403
   and protection by dilution, 73–74
   reasons for, 4, 87–96, 402–404
   vs. reduced predation, 73–74, 87–96
   secondary benefits of, 403
   and selfish herd effects, 73, 96, 99
   vs. shortage of suitable habitat, 72,
      87–88
   vs. social facilitation of foraging, 72–
      73, 88–89
   and social behavior, 4
   of white-tailed prairie dog, 96–99
colonization, 87–88, 380
colony. *See also* coloniality; colony size
   attractiveness to ungulates, 21
   composition, 376–378, figs. 16.1 and
      16.2, table 16.1
   density, 36.
   synonyms for, 13
colony size. *See also* ward size
   annual variation in, 376–378, figs.
      16.1 and 16.2, table 16.1

and antipredator calling, 91–93, fig.
5.13
vs. colony size of white-tailed prairie
dogs, 97
defined, 60
vs. ectoparasitism by fleas, 80–81,
fig. 5.6
vs. individual alertness, 93–94
vs. number and density of burrows,
36
optimal, 75, 403–404
ranking of, 60
relative to other colonies, 42, 70, 96
stability of, 376–378, 394, fig. 16.1
vs. vigilance, 93–94
color, of pelage, 1, 8
natural variation in, 52
Columbian ground squirrel, 60–61, 166,
183, 222, 248, 251, 297, 298, 309, 312,
380, 407
combing, for fleas, 62
common ancestor, 61, 338, 352, table
14.6
common eider, 7, 893
common gray fox, 14
common guillemot. See common murre
common gull, 73
common murre, 74, 83
common muskrat, 145, 295
common names, 37, Appendix A
for prairie dog, 8
common opossum, 368
common rearing. See direct social
learning
common seal. See harbor seal
common swift, 295
common tern, 73
common vampire bat, 4, 80, 81
communal nursing, 187–200, 217
aboveground vs. underground, 188,
fig. 9.1
beneficiaries of, 187
benefits of, 196–199, 410
caused by livetrapping, 194
and contamination of results, 193–
194
costs of, 84, 194–195
defined, 187
detection of radionuclides, 65, 191–
194
different types, 187–188
vs. direct and indirect fitness, 410
frequency of, 191–194

vs. inclement weather, 188–189
vs. inclusive fitness, 198
vs. infanticide, 5–6, 146, 196, 198,
409–410
vs. kin recognition, 196, 409–410
vs. kinship, 187, 195–196, 198, 201,
table 9.2
methods of investigation, 65, 191–
194
vs. mixing of juveniles from different
litters, 84–85, 188–191
vs. multi-litter groupings, 191, 196–
197, 409–410
in other species of squirrels, 199
vs. parent-offspring recognition, 84–
85, 196, 409–410
vs. reduced predation, 196–197, 409–
410
vs. reproductive value of juveniles,
198
vs. selfishness, of foster mother, 197,
409–410
verified by dissection, 192–193
vs. volume of milk, 194
vs. willing participation of foster
mothers, 195, 409–410
competence, maternal, 297
competition
and alloparenting, 201
vs. coloniality, 3, 75, 76–79, 406–
407, fig. 5.2
among female close kin, 371–373,
405, 409, figs. 15.9 and 15.10
incitation of, 246, 251, 277
vs. infanticide, 145–146, 206, 372
between juveniles and yearlings, 157
vs. kinship, 111, 202–210, figs. 6.10
and 10.1–10.3
among lactating females of same
coterie, 145–147, 206, 319–320,
324, 372, 405
among littermates for milk, 294, 391–
392
with livestock, 2, 20–21
local mate competition, 371
local resource competition, 371–373,
figs. 15.9 and 15.10
among males for estrous females,
205–206, 246, 251, 258–259, 277,
350–351, 371
vs. mating call, 242, figs. 11.12 and
11.13

vs. nepotism, 111, 202–210, figs.
6.10 and 10.1–10.3
for nursery burrows, 117, 119, 206,
319–320, 372, 405
between older and younger males,
350–351
removal of future competitors, 143,
145–147, 157, 405
vs. reproductive synchrony, 319
vs. ward size, 76–77, fig. 5.2
composition
of colony. *See* colony composition
of coterie, 1, 104–105, figs. 6.1 and
6.3
conception. 125, 151, 390
condition. *See* body condition;
reproductive condition
cones, in retina, 13
confidence of paternity, vs. infanticide
and paternal care, 156, 214, 268
conflict of interest, between males and
females
regarding coterie type and annual
reproductive success, 329
regarding paternal recognition of
offspring, 208
confusion, of predator caused by
antipredator call, 92, 183
consortship. *See also* underground
consortship
conspicuousness
of antipredator callers, 166, 171–172
of colonies to predators, 75, 85–86,
fig. 5.11
of foraging prairie dogs, 75, 85–86,
185
of prairie dogs that hear antipredator
call, 183, 185
of vocalizations, 75, 85–86, fig. 5.11
contagious vocalization. *See* jump-yip
contamination, of results with
radionuclides, 193–194
cooperation, 372–373. *See also*
antipredator calling; cooperative
breeding; kin recognition; nepotism
cooperative breeding, 217–219
cooperative chase, 94–96
Cooper's hawk, 15, 94–96, table 2.3
copulation. *See also* estrus; insemination
aboveground, 251–253, table 11.2
vs. age, 288–289, fig. 13.2
vs. all-day underground consortship,
232–233, fig. 11.1a

behavioral observations of, 221–259
benefit to female from copulation
with second male, 268
vs. body mass, 298–305, figs. 13.12–
13.17
vs. copulatory plug, 253–254
and critical underground consortship
(CUC), 225–232, 237, 238–239,
241–242, 250–251, 252–255, fig.
11.2
date of, vs. date of first juvenile
emergence, 248, fig. 11.16a
date of, vs. date of parturition, 248,
fig. 11.16b
defined, 222
to deter later infanticide, 234, 268
diagnostic aboveground behaviors of,
222–248
evidence of accuracy of behavioral
observations, 248–257
vs. guarding of estrous female, 225–
229, 235, 247, 268, 293, 294, 315,
fig. 11.13
vs. insemination, 6, 160, 222, 225,
229, 231–233, 237, 251, 254, 255,
263, 273, 294, 371
interference with, 86–87, 258–259
vs. intromission, 231–232
vs. late final submergence of estrous
female, 246–247
vs. male attention to estrous female,
233–237, fig. 11.8
with males from outside the home
coterie, 275–276, fig. 12.6
vs. mating call (MC), 6, 63, 222, 236,
239–246, 248, 251, figs. 11.10
through 11.15
and missing male list (MML), 222–
223
with more than one male, 229, 263–
268, figs. 12.2a, 12.3, and 14.7,
tables 12.3 and 14.3
in one-male vs. multi-male coteries,
268, fig. 12.3, table 12.3
order of, vs. paternity, 227–229, 281–
283, 292–294, fig. 13.5
retaliatory, 294
vs. self-licking of genitals, 237–238,
table 11.1
site of, 221–222, 258–259
timing of, 59, 205, 257, 313
underground, 258–259

vs. underground consortship (UC),
    221–234, figs. 11.1 through 11.5
unique vocalization during, 246, 251
unusual behaviors of individuals that
    copulate, 247–248
vs. vaginal lavage, 255–256, fig.
    11.20
vs. vulvar examination, 253–255,
    figs. 11.18 and 11.19
copulatory plug, 253–254
copulatory success. *See* annual
    reproductive success
copying, of female choice, 242
correlation
    of body mass, at different stages of
        annual cycle, 298–299, fig. 13.11
    of different estimates of male and
        female reproductive success, 277–
        285, figs. 12.7–12.10
costs
    of aggression, 77–78, figs. 5.4, and
        5.5
    of antipredator calls, 163, 171–172
    of auto- and allogrooming, 81, fig.
        5.8
    of coloniality, 3–4, 74–75, 76–87,
        402
    of communal nursing, 84, 194–195
    of ectoparasitism, 80–81, fig. 5.8
    of gestation and lactation, 152, 311–
        313
    of inbreeding, 5, 337–338, 355–358
    of infanticide, 140, 145
    of mating call, 241
    miscellaneous, 86–87
    of reproduction, 152, 309–313, figs.
        13.10, 13.18, and 13.19
co-submergence, of male and female. *See*
    underground consortship
coterie, 1, 14.
    composition of, 1, 104–105, figs. 6.1
        and 6.3
    defined, 102
    evolutionary reasons for, 123
    fission of, 121–122, table 6.1
    fusion of, 123
    half-male, 112–114, fig. 6.1
    longevity, 107, fig. 6.7
    multi-male, 108–112, fig. 6.1
    number of, at study colony, 103, fig.
        6.2
    one-male, 108–112, fig. 6.1

origin of members, 105, 339–343
parental care within, 115
productivity vs. presence of
    yearlings, 157, fig. 7.13
size. *See* coterie size
variations in coterie size, 105–107,
    figs. 6.5 and 6.6
coterie density, 117, 329.
coterie size
    vs. annual reproductive success, 283,
        320–329, figs. 13.25–13.30
    vs. antipredator calling, 178–179, fig.
        8.10
    vs. cooperative take-overs, 326
    vs. coterie composition, 108–110, fig.
        6.9
    vs. coterie density, 117, 329, fig.
        6.14b
    vs. coterie territory, 117–119, fig.
        6.14
    vs. coterie type, 112, fig. 6.11
    defined, 105, fig. 6.4
    and eviction, 326
    and extinctions, 107, 326, fig. 13.28
    vs. female reproductive success, 323–
        326, figs. 13.26–13.28
    vs. fission, 122, fig. 6.16
    and half-male coteries, 113–114, fig.
        6.12
    vs. infanticide, 140, 283, fig. 7.7
    vs. litter size, 323, fig. 13.26
    vs. male reproductive success, 326–
        329, figs. 13.29 and 13.30
    and multi-male coteries, 113–114,
        326–327, fig. 6.12
    vs. number and density of burrow
        entrances, figs. 6.13a and 6.15
    vs. production of emergent juveniles
        and yearlings, 320, fig. 13.25
    vs. sex ratio of juveniles at first
        emergence, 373, fig. 15.10
    vs. shortage of suitable habitat, 325–
        326
    vs. survivorship of adults and
        juveniles, 324, fig. 13.27
    variation in, 105–107, figs. 6.5 and
        6.6
    vs. weather, 107
coterie territory
    boundary, 115
    changes in, 117, 119
    constancy and longevity of, 117

vs. coterie density and coterie size, 117–119, fig. 6.14a
defense of, 115, 117, 119, 217, 347
map of, at study colony, fig. 4.5
number and density of burrow entrances within, 1, 34, 119, figs. 6.13b and 6.15
physical area, 1, 115, fig. 6.13a
variation in quality, 297
coterie type
vs. annual reproductive success, 329–334, figs. 13.31–13.33
annual variation, 108, fig. 6.8
vs. coterie size, 112, fig. 6.11
vs. female reproductive success, 329, figs. 13.31 and 13.32
half-male coterie, 1, 102, 112–114, fig. 6.1
vs. male reproductive success, 329, fig. 13.33
vs. male tenure and paternal care, 329, fig. 13.32
multi-male coterie, 1, 102, 109–112, fig. 6.1
one-male coterie, 1, 102, 108, fig. 6.1
cotton rat. See hispid cotton rat
cottontail. See desert cottontail
cougar. See mountain lion
cover. See protective cover
cow. See domestic cow
coyote, 14, 20, 35, 47, 64, 69, 75, 94, 99, 166, fig. 2.3a, table 2.3
crater. See dome crater; rim crater
crested penguin, 153
crested tern, 4, 83
cricket. See cave cricket
Cricket Graph, 67
critical period, for direct social learning, 210–215, 408
critical underground consortship (CUC), 225–232, 237, 238–239, 241–242, 250–251, 252–255
behavioral changes that follow, 225–230
defined, 225
duration of, 229, fig. 11.4
vs. guarding of estrous female, 227–229
number per estrous female, 227, 229
vs. time of day, 225, fig. 11.2c
cry. See jump-yip
cryptantha, table 2.3

cubicle, for marking and handling prairie dogs, 49, figs. 4.6 and 4.10c
CUC. See critical underground consortship
cuckoldry
as cost of coloniality, 5, 86–87, 294
defined, 275
vs. extreme inbreeding, 346–347, table 14.4
vs. female annual reproductive success, 275–276, fig. 12.6
vs. paternal recognition of offspring, 207–208, 214
curvilinear relationship, between age and reproductive success, 287–292, figs. 13.1–13.4
cutleaf nightshade, table 2.3
cutworm, 14, table 2.3
Cynomis, 8
Cynomomus, 8
Cynomys, 8
cypress. See summer cypress

daily routine, 57
darkling beetle, table 2.3
Darwin's medium ground finch, 338, 352, 408
date, of copulation, vs. dates of first juvenile emergence and parturition, 248, fig. 11.16
death. See mortality
deathcamus, table 2.3
deer. See following deer species: fallow; mule; red; white-tailed
deer mouse, 130, 158, 293, table 2.3
defense
of foraging area, by groups, 89
of home coterie territory, 115, 117, 119, 126, 217
of home nursery burrow, 2, 35, 126, 134, 136–138, 151, fig. 7.1
defense bark, 63, 119, 277
deference, of estrus. See delay, of estrus
degrees of freedom (df), 67–68
delay
of estrus, 236, 240, 257, 315
of sexual maturation, 397, fig. 16.11b
demography, 376–401. See also annual variation
abortion, 125, 151, 234, 289, 362, 390

body mass, 397–401, fig. 16.12. *See also* body mass

conception, 125, 151, 390

disappearance, dispersal, and mortality, 263, 305, 378–382

fecundity, 384, 393–396, figs. 16.4a and 16.5, tables 16.5–16.10

gestation, 152, 234, 248, 311–312, 316, 384–390, figs. 16.8a and 16.10

immigration, 70, 382–384

infanticide, 125–162

lactation, 152, 234, 248, 311–313, 316, 390–392, figs. 16.8b and 16.10

life tables, 393–396, tables 16.5–16.10

parturition. *See* parturition

vs. possible problems with study colony, 69

sexual asymmetry. *See* sexual asymmetry

sexual dimorphism, 1, 362–363, 397–401, figs. 15.2 and 16.12

survivorship. *See* survivorship and mortality

weaning, 88, 192–193, 390–392. *See also* lactation

density. *See also* colony density; ward density

of burrows, 36

of prairie dogs, 40, 97, 139–140, fig. 5.17

of predators at study colony, 69

dependence, of observations, 68

depletion, of sperm, 315

depression. *See* inbreeding depression

desert cottontail, table 2.3

design, evolutionary, 149, 217

deterrence, of predators, 94–96

df. *See* degrees of freedom

DF. *See* dirty face

diagnostic behaviors

of communal nursing, 188

of copulation, 222–248

of infanticide, 128–130

diet, 14

differential nepotism

and antipredator calling, 5, 177–178, 407, fig. 8.8

in behavioral interactions, 208–210, fig. 10.3

close kin vs. more distant kin, 214–216, 410

and communal nursing, 195–196, 410

and infanticide, 142–143, 410, fig. 7.8

dilution, protection by. *See* protection by dilution

dimorphism. *See* sexual dimorphism

direct fitness, 3, 146, 410

direct social learning, 6, 159, 201–220, 274, 408–409

and common rearing, 213–214

critical period of, 211–213, 408

by cuckolded males, 214

defined, 211

errors that result, 214–215

and infanticide, 214

and juvenile transfers, 211–213, table 10.1

and nepotism among paternal half sisters, 213

in prevention of extreme inbreeding, 213–214, 348, 355, 408–409, fig. 14.8

dirty face, after infanticide (DF), 126–130, 134–135

disadvantages. *See* costs

disappearance. *See also* dispersal

vs. dispersal and mortality, 263, 378–382.

discrimination. *See also* parent-offspring recognition

in communal nursing, by mothers, 195–196

between groups of females, by males, 156

between male and female pre-emergent juveniles, 147

between nursery burrows, by mothers, 196, 409–410

between own and other males' offspring, by males, 207–208, 214, 268

between territories, by males, 156, 208, 214, 268

discriminative nepotism. *See* differential nepotism

disease, 3, 74, 80–81, 138, 238

and mate choice, 337, 355

dispersal, 70. *See also* breeding dispersal and natal dispersal

vs. age, 263, 305, 339–344, 378–382, fig. 14.1a

away from study colony, verification of, 378

vs. body mass, 305
breeding, 343–344, figs. 14.3 and
    14.4
vs. disappearance and mortality, 263,
    378–382
distance traveled, 339, 358–359, 378,
    380, 403
in groups, 380–382
intercolonial, 263, 339, 358–359,
    378–384, 403
intracolonial, 339–344, 358–359, 383,
    fig. 14.1
by juveniles, 339–342, 380, fig. 14.1
local, 339–344, 358–359, 383, fig.
    14.1
long distance, 263, 339, 358–359,
    378–384, 403
natal, 339–343, figs. 14.1 and 14.2,
    table 14.2
of older males, 343–344, fig. 14.4
vs. reproductive condition, 382
sexual asymmetry in, 1, 105, 135,
    172, 363, 339–344, 380–383, fig.
    14.1
vs. sexual maturation, for males,
    342–343, fig. 14.2
vs. susceptibility to predation, 337,
    358–359, 380
timing of, 153, 263, 339, 355, 380–
    382, figs. 14.1 and 14.2
vs. weather and availability of food,
    380, tables 16.2 and 16.3
of young males, 339–343
disperser. See dispersal
dispute. See territorial dispute
disputing churr, 63
dissection, of marauder after infanticide,
    131, fig. 7.6
distraction, of predator caused by
    antipredator call, 92, 183
distribution, geographic, 12, fig. 2.2
disturbance
    from live-trapping, 47–48
    from presence of researchers in
        observation towers, 69
diurnality, 13
diversity, genetic. See genetic diversity
DNA fingerprinting, 260
dog. See following dog species: African
    wild; domestic; raccoon
dome crater, 30
domestic chicken, 281

domestic cow, 20–21, 38, 281, 372, 391
domestic dog, 8
domestic goat, 38, 315, 391
domestic horse, 20–21, 38. See also wild
    horse
domestic livestock, 2, 20–21, 38.
domestic pig, 293, 391
domestic sheep, 21, 38, 315, 391
dominance 5, 112–113, 153, 206–207,
    214, 215, 225, 268, 274–276, 298–305,
    329–334, 365–369. See also body mass
    vs. annual reproductive success, 207
    vs. body mass. 207, 298, 367
    of mother, vs. sex ratio of juveniles,
        367
dominance hierarchy, 206–207
dormancy, 18–19
double estrus, 233, 390, fig. 11.6
double marauding, 139
Douglas's squirrel, 237, 239
dove. See following dove species:
    laughing; mourning
dropseed, table 2.3
dung beetle, table 2.3
dunnock, 208, 260, 268, 329
dwarf mongoose, 93, 94, 127–128, 144,
    187, 195, 217, 218, 257, 281, 404–405,
    323, 324, 356
dyad, for behavioral interactions, 61–62
dye. See Nyanzol fur dye

eagle. See following eagle species:
    black; golden
ear. See pinna
earless lizard. See lesser earless lizard
eartagging, 44–45, 52, 376, figs. 4.10b
    and 4.13
ease, of finding mates, 358–359
eastern chipmunk, 81, 163, 176, 376,
    407
eastern fox squirrel. See fox squirrel
eastern gray squirrel. See gray squirrel
ectoparasites. See also ectoparasitism
    vs. auto- and allogrooming, 81–83,
        fig. 5.8
    vs. colony size, 80–83, fig. 5.6
    costs of, 80–83
    vs. fitness, 80–83
    methods of collection, 49, 62–63, fig.
        5.7
    species of, 62
    transmission of, 80–83

ectoparasitism, 3, 74, 80–83. *See also*
    ectoparasites
effort. *See* reproductive effort
egret. *See following egret species:* cattle;
    great
eider. *See* common eider
ejaculates, variation in, 281
ejaculation, 231–232. *See also*
    copulation; insemination
electrophoresis, to determine paternity,
    52, 65–67, 256–257, 260, tables 12.1
    and 12.2
elephant. *See* African elephant
elephant seal. *See following elephant
    seal species:* northern; southern
elk. *See* red deer; wapiti
embryo, resorption of, 151, 362, 390.
    See also abortion
emergence
    final, at end of day. *See* final
        submergence at end of day
    first, in morning. *See* first emergence
        in morning
    first juvenile. *See* first juvenile
        emergence
emigration, 87–88
endangered species of prairie dogs, 2, 20
endoparasites, 63
enhancement, local resource, 371–373,
    figs. 15.9 and 15.10
entrance. *See* burrow entrance
environmental change, and mate choice,
    337, 355
equilibrium
    Hardy-Weinberg, 350
    and juvenile sex ratios, 360–361
eradication, 2, 20–22
estrus. *See also* copulation
    behavioral observations of, 221–259
    vs. coterie size, 323
    vs. coterie type, 329
    defined, 222
    delayed, 236, 240, 257, 315
    detection by males, 234–237
    duration of, 225
    effect of weather on, 257–258
    length of, 222, 225
    once per year, 157, 225, 233–234,
        405
    probability of, vs. coterie size, 109,
        fig. 6.9a

vs. pseudo-estrus, 233–234
    second, 233, 390, fig. 11.6
    synchrony of, 313–320, fig. 13.21
    timing of, 205, 313
    and wandering by estrous female, 117
    of yearling females, 323, 345–346,
        fig. 14.5
Eurasian badger, 125, 128, 309, 311,
    312, 395, 404–405
European badger. *See* Eurasian badger
European bee-eater, 325
European rabbit, 139, 293
European sparrowhawk, 319, 363
eusociality, 217–219
evening bat, 73, 187
eviction
    from colony, 77
    and coterie size, 326
    of females from home coterie
        territory, 123, 136–137, 150, 326,
        383, table 14.2
    of males from home coterie territory,
        153
evolution, defined, 2
evolutionary design, 149, 217
excavation, of prairie dog burrows
    by humans, to verify infanticide, 28,
        130–134, 405, figs. 7.4–7.6
    by prairie dogs, 42, 326, 372, fig. 3.4
exculenta frog, 365
execution of infanticide, vs. prevention,
    149
exhaustion, of maternal resources, 391–
    392
expansion
    of colonies in general, 87–88
    of study colony, 42, 70
experience. *See* parental experience
extermination. *See* eradication
external genitalia, 49, figs. 4.11 and 4.12
extinction
    of coteries, vs. coterie size, 326, fig.
        13.28
    insurance against, 326
    of prairie dog species, 2, 20–22
extreme inbreeding, 347, 351, fig. 14.6.
    See also inbreeding
    avoidance of, 5, 339–351, 408–409,
        figs. 14.1–14.8, tables 14.2–14.5
    defined, 338
    vs. direct social learning, 346–349,
        355, fig. 14.8

vs. copulation with a second male,
346–347, fig. 14.7, table 14.3
vs. cuckoldry, 346–347, table 14.4

facial scars. *See* scars
falcon, 166. *See also following falcon
species:* peregrine; prairie
fallow deer, 242
fallow farming, 88
false antipredator calls, 166, 178
false killer whale, 292
false pennyroyal, table 2.3
familiarity. *See* direct social learning
farming, 88–89, 403
fecal pellets. *See also* feces
aboveground, 28
within burrows, 28
collection of, 65
for determining diet, 14
feces, 14, 193. *See also* fecal pellets
fecundity, 384, 393–396, figs. 16.4a and
16.5, tables 16.5–16.10
female choice, 242, 246, 276–277, 287–
288, 346–355
female-female competition. *See*
competition
female reproductive success. *See* annual
reproductive success; lifetime
reproductive success
feral horse. *See* wild horse
ferret. *See* black-footed ferret
ferruginous hawk, table 2.3
fertility. *See* fecundity
fertilization, 125, 151, 268, 315
fescue, table 2.3
fetid marigold. *See* prairie dog weed
fiber optics, to see into burrows, 407–
408
field assistants, 42–44, table 4.1
fig wasp. *See* agaontid fig wasp
fight, 2, 61, 128, 136–138, 202, 221,
225, 232, 235
defined, 60, fig. 5.1
vs. ward size, 76–79, fig. 5.2
final submergence at end of day, 57–60
of estrous female, 246–247
finch. *See* Darwin's medium ground
finch
fingerling eartag. *See* eartagging
fingerprint. *See* DNA fingerprinting
first emergence in morning, 57–60, fig.
4.16

first juvenile emergence
date of, vs. date of copulation, 248,
fig. 11.16
as point of reference for juvenile
body mass, juvenile sex ratios, life
tables, and litter size, 47, 263, 361–
362, 393
synchrony of, 316
vs. weaning, 188, 192–193, 390–392
fish, 158
fission, of coterie, 70, 121–122, table
6.1, fig. 6.16
vs. coterie size, 122, fig. 6.16
vs. kinship, 122, 210
fitness, 3, 146, 287, 410. *See also*
inclusive fitness
flannel, for counting fleas, 62–63
fleas, 402, table 2.3
vs. auto- and allogrooming, 75, 81–
83, fig. 5.8
vs. colony size, 80–83, fig. 5.6
costs of, 80–83
vs. fitness, 80–83
methods of collection, 49, 62–63, fig.
5.7
species of, 62
transmission of, 89–83
Florida scrub jay, 93, 113, 201, 218,
281, 313, 323, 324, 338, 408
flushing, of radionuclides from body,
194
fluffweed, table 2.3
fly. *See following fly species:* bluebottle;
robber
flycatcher. *See* collared flycatcher
flying squirrel, 7. *See also following
flying squirrel species:* northern;
southern
food. *See* diet
food-finding signals, 72–74
foot-thumping, during antisnake call, 168
foraging, social facilitation of. *See* social
facilitation of foraging
forced coloniality, 72
fossils, 7
foster juvenile, 211–213.
foster mother, 65, 187–200
defined, 187
as willing participant in communal
nursing, 195
foster offspring, 85, 187–200.
fox. *See following fox species:* common
gray; red

fox squirrel, 237, 238, 254
foxtail, table 2.3
Franklin's gull, 73, 314
freeze branding, 56
frequency
    of antipredator calls, 164, 170–171,
        fig. 8.6
    of communal nursing, 191–194, table
        9.1
    of different types of infanticide, 75,
        87, 136, 151, 155, 405–406, table
        7.2
    of different levels of inbreeding, 5,
        347–355, fig. 14.6, table 14.6
    of mating calls, 239–242, figs. 11.10
        and 11.11
frequency-dependent natural selection,
    360–361
frog. See exculenta frog
fulmar. See northern fulmar
fungus ant, 4, 217, 219
fur. See pelage
fur dye. See Nyanzol fur dye
fur seal. See following fur seal species:
    Galápagos; northern
fusion, of coteries, 123

Galápagos fur seal, 84
Galápagos mockingbird, 201, 410
Galápagos sea lion, 84
gall bladder, 23
gallivanting, 117, 236
gall stones, 23
gannet. See following gannet species:
    northern; Peruvian
gazelle. See following gazelle species:
    Grant's; Thomson's
gelada baboon, 158
genetic defects, 138, 363
genetic diversity, among offspring, 268
genetic relatedness. See kinship
genital licking. See self-licking, of
    genitals
genitalia, external, 49–52, figs. 4.11 and
    4.12
geographic range, 12, fig. 2.2
gerbil. See Mongolian gerbil
gestation
    vs. body mass, 311–312
    cost, 152
    length, 234, 248, 384–390, fig. 16.8a

vs. litter size, 391, fig. 16.10
vs. reproductive synchrony, 316
glaucous-winged gull, 145, 295, 309,
    313
globemallow. See scarlet globemallow
glorybind, table 2.3
goat. See domestic goat
golden eagle, 15, 69, 75, 94, 166, 363,
    fig. 2.4b, table 2.3
golden hamster, 130, 139, 153, 231
golden jackal, 217
golden lion tamarin, 274
golden-mantled ground squirrel. See
    cascade golden-mantled ground squirrel
goose, 93. See also following goose
    species: Canada; lesser snow
gopher. See pocket gopher
gorilla. See mountain gorilla
goshawk. See northern goshawk
grackle. See following grackle species:
    boat-tailed; great-tailed
grama, 14, table 2.3
Grant's gazelle, 81
grass. See following grass species:
    buffalo grass; inland saltgrass;
    ricegrass; tumble grass; wheatgrass;
    and wiregrass
grasshopper. See short-horned
    grasshopper
grasshopper mouse. See northern
    grasshopper mouse
gray fox. See common gray fox
gray heron, 5
gray langur. See hanuman langur
gray squirrel, 237, 238, 246, 254, 376
gray wolf, 187
gray-crowned babbler, 201, 325
gray-cheeked mangabey, 292
gray-tailed vole, 211
grazing. See overgrazing
great egret, 205
great tit, 297, 352, 356
greater rhea, 260
greater spearnose bat, 5, 275
great-tailed grackle, 360
green stinkbug. See southern green
    stinkbug
grizzly bear, 14
grooming, 24. See also autogrooming;
    allogrooming
groove-billed ani, 217, 260
ground beetle, 14, table 2.3

ground finch. *See* Darwin's medium
   ground finch
ground hog. *See* woodchuck
ground squirrel, 7, 8, 30, 83, 188, 199,
   339. *See also following ground squirrel
   species:* arctic; Belding's; California;
   cascade golden-mantled; Columbian;
   Idaho; Richardson's; rock; round-
   tailed; thirteen-lined; Uinta
group-defense, of foraging area, 89, 123
group-hunting, 72, 88
group-living, 3. *See also* coloniality
grouse. *See following grouse species:*
   black; sage; sharp-tailed
growl, 63
guarding, of estrous female by male,
   225–229, 235, 247, 268, 293, 294, 315,
   fig. 11.3
      vs. confidence of paternity, 227–229
      defined, 225–227
      flexibility of, 227–229
      vs. order of copulating males, 227–
      229, 293
guarding, of juveniles in mother's
   absence, 217
guinea pig. *See* wild guinea pig
gull. *See following gull species:* black-
   headed; California; common;
   Franklin's; glaucous-winged; herring;
   laughing
Gunnison's prairie dog, 8–24, 44, 74,
   166, 199, 222, 225, 239, 258–259, 411,
   table 2.2, fig. 2.2
guppy, 365

habitat
   shortage of, 87–88, 325–326
   unused, 72, 87–88
habituation, to stuffed American badger,
   170, table 8.1
half-male coterie
   vs. coterie size, 112, fig. 6.11
   defined, 102, 112, fig. 6.1
   vs. male and female annual
      reproductive success, 329–334, figs.
      13.31 and 13.32
   vs. number of breeding males in
      colony, 113–114, fig. 6.12
half siblings, and direct social learning,
   213, 409
Hall's babbler, 325

hammer-headed bat, 279
hamster. *See* golden hamster
handling, 49–56, fig. 4.10. *See also*
   marking
hanuman langur, 3, 5, 75, 108, 112, 139–
   140, 157, 158, 201, 207, 208, 222,
   233–234, 268, 344, 404–405, 406
harassment, of predators. *See* mobbing
harbor seal, 3, 74
Hardy-Weinberg equilibrium, 350
harem, 4. *See also* coterie
harem defense polygyny, 123
harrier. *See* northern harrier
Harris's hawk, 72
harvester ant, 22, table 2.3
hawk, 166. *See also following hawk
   species:* accipiter; buteo; Cooper's;
   European sparrowhawk; ferruginous;
   Harris's; northern goshawk; northern
   harrier; red-tailed; rough-legged; sharp-
   shinned; Swainson's
heat. *See* estrus
height
   of prairie dog, 1, 8
   of vegetation within colonies, 1, 9
helper. *See* alloparenting
herbivory, 14
heron. *See following heron species:* gray;
   little blue
herring gull, 5, 145, 157
heterosis, 358
heterozygosity, 337, 355
   vs. survivorship and reproductive
      success, 358
hibernation, 18–19, 23
hiding, from predators, 99
hierarchy, dominance. *See* dominance
   hierarchy
hispid cotton rat, 231
hoary marmot, 3, 4, 5, 29, 30, 34, 52,
   60–61, 64, 87, 108, 163, 166, 168, 172,
   174, 176, 179, 186, 298, 305, 309, 311,
   312, 337, 345, 376, 397, 407
hognose snake. *See* western hognose
   snake
honeybee, 4, 210
horned lark, table 2.3
horned lizard. *See* Texas horned lizard
horse. *See following horse species:*
   domestic; wild
horseweed, 14, table 2.3
hostility, of behavioral interactions, 2

house mouse, 81, 130, 139, 145, 153, 158, 187, 195, 208, 210, 211, 233–234, 281, 293, 315
house wren, 115
howler monkey. *See following howler monkey species:* mantled; red
human, 6, 14, 88, 153, 166, 211, 213, 222, 239, 292, 352, 356, 358, 361, 370, 372, 391, 404
humidity, within burrows, 28
humpback whale, 368
hunting, of prairie dogs. *See* shooting
hyena. *See following hyena species:* brown; spotted
hyrax. *See following hyrax species:* bush; rock

Idaho ground squirrel, 222, 225, 227, 257, 273, 293, 407
ideal free conditions, 75
identity, by descent, 61, 338
immigrant
    age of, 67, 380,
    in analyses of annual and lifetime reproductive success, 67
    annual reproductive success of, 67, 383, table 16.4
    defense against, 383
    defined, 338
    infanticide by, 150–151, 153–160
    and outbreeding, 352–354
    reproductive condition of, 382
    routes for reproductive success, 383, table 16.4
immigration, 382–384. *See also* immigrant
    into established coterie territory, 383
    vs. poisoning and shooting at nearby colonies, 70
imprinting, of prairie dogs to humans, 24
inactivity. *See* sexual inactivity, of adult males
inbreeding, 337–359, 408–409. *See also* extreme inbreeding
    avoidance of, 5, 339–351, 408–409, figs. 14.1–14.8
    benefits of, 337–338, 358–359
    vs. breeding dispersal, 338, 343–344, figs. 14.3 and 14.4
    classification of, 338, table 14.1
    vs. common rearing, 213–214, 348, 355, 408–409

costs of, 5, 337–338, 355–358
defined, 338
depression, 337, 355–358, table 14.8
vs. direct social learning, 213–214, 348, 355, 408–409
vs. dispersal, 339–344, 358–359, figs. 14.1–14.4
vs. ease of finding mates, 358–359
vs. estrus of yearling females, 345–346, fig. 14.5
extreme, 338, 347, 351, fig. 14.6
vs. familiarity, 213–214, 348, 355
vs. female choice, 277, 346–355
frequencies, observed vs. expected, 352–354, table 14.7
frequency of different levels, 347–355, fig. 14.6, table 14.6
vs. heterozygosity, 358
vs. inbreeding depression, 5, 337, 355–358, table 14.8
levels of, 351–355, fig. 14.6, table 14.6
vs. lost mating opportunities, 358
male vs. female responsibility, 349
mechanisms for avoidance, 339–351
moderate, 338, 351–355, 408–409
vs. natal dispersal, 338, 339–343, fig. 14.1
vs. overdominance, 358
vs. possible problems with study colony, 69–70
promotion of, 352–354
vs. self-referential matching of phenotypes, 213–214, 355, 408
vs. sexual reproduction, 337–338
trivial, fig. 14.6
incarceration, of lactating females to study infanticide, 131, 134
incitation, of male-male competition, 246, 251, 277
inclusive fitness
    close kin vs. more distant kin, 214–216
    and communal nursing, 198
    contributions of direct and indirect fitness, 3, 146, 410
    vs. coterie size, 325–326
    defined, 3
    and infanticide, 145
increased awareness, of predators, 73–74, 89–93, 197, fig. 5.13
independence, of observations, 68
induction, of ovulation, 242

Indians, 23
indigo bunting, 257
indirect fitness, 3, 146, 410
infanticide, 5, 75, 125–162, 403–407.
    See also marauder
    aboveground, 134–135
    vs. accessibility of juvenile victims,
        140–142, 407
    vs. age of infanticidal male, 156
    vs. age of perpetrators and victims,
        139, 156
    vs. annual reproductive success, 148–
        149, 157–158, 268, table 7.3
    annual variation in frequency, 160
    benefits of, 143, 145–149, 152–153,
        157–158, 405
    and bloody face (BF), 126–130, 134–
        135
    vs. body mass of females that
        abandon neonates, 151–152, fig.
        7.10
    vs. body masses of marauder and
        victimized mother, 143–144, 157,
        299, figs. 7.8 and 7.9
    vs. cannibalism, 126–128, 135, 147,
        148, 151, 158, 405, fig. 7.5
    characteristics of marauders and their
        victims, 139
    vs. communal nursing, 5–6, 146, 196,
        198
    vs. competition among females, 145–
        147, 405
    as cost of coloniality, 86–87, 125,
        403
    costs of, 140, 143, 145
    vs. coterie size, 140, 283, fig. 7.7
    critical evidence for, 130–135, 404
    cumulative frequency, 75, 87, 160,
        405–406, table 7.2
    vs. defensive prowess of victimized
        mother, 136–138, 143, fig. 7.8
    diagnostic behaviors of, 128–130
    direct evidence of, 130–135
    vs. direct and indirect fitness, 410
    and dirty face (DF), 126–130, 134–
        135
    documentation, 125–135
    double marauding, 139
    and excavations for verification, 130–
        134, figs. 7.4–7.6
    by female immigrants (Type II), 150–
        151

frequency, cumulative, 75, 87, 160,
    405–406, table 7.2
frequency, of different types, 136,
    151, 155, table 7.2
by invading males (Type IV), 153–
    160, figs. 7.11 and 7.12, table 7.4
vs. kin recognition, 145–146, 214,
    409–410
vs. kinship, 127, 135–136, 140–143,
    149, 159–160, 214, 406–407, fig.
    7.8, table 7.1
by lactating females (Type I), 125–
    149, fig. 7.3
and licking of front claws (LFC),
    126–130, 134–135, 405, fig. 7.2b
of marauder's litter while marauder is
    marauding, 140
vs. mating system, 404–405
by mothers that abandon their litters
    (Type III), 138, 151–153, 159
number of different killers and
    victimized litters, 139, 160, table
    7.2
vs. overcrowding, 139–140
partial-litter vs. whole-litter, 138–139
vs. possible problems with study
    colony, 69–70
prevention vs. execution, 149
vs. proximity of victimized mother's
    home burrow, 143, fig. 7.8
vs. rarity of black-footed ferret, 406
vs. removal of future competitors,
    143, 145–147, 157, 405
vs. reproductive synchrony, 319–320
response of victimized mother, 136–
    138
and rubbing of face in dirt (RFD),
    126–130, 134–135, 405, fig. 7.2a
selective, 153, 163
sex ratio of victims and survivors,
    146–147, 156–157
sexual asymmetry in execution of,
    404–405
by SIRAM (sexually inactive resident
    adult male), 160
subtleness of, 125–130, 149, 404, 407
vs. sustenance for infanticidal male,
    158, 405
vs. sustenance for marauding female,
    143, 147–148, 405, 410
vs. time until next estrus of
    victimized mother, 157, 405

vs. timing of male dispersal, 404–405
Type I (by lactating females), 125–149
Type II (by female immigrants), 150–151
Type III (involving abandonment of litter), 138, 151–153, 159, fig. 7.10
Type IV (by invading males), 153–160, 214, figs. 7.11 and 7.12, table 7.4
uniqueness, 5–6, 149, 406–407
variation in tendency to kill, 139, 152, 403
vulnerability of different mothers, 139, 144
vulnerability of juveniles, vs. reproductive synchrony, 319–320
information center, 72, 74
injuries. See also scars
  from copulation, 251
  from ectoparasites, 81
  from fights, 77–78, figs. 5.4 and 5.5
inland saltgrass, table 2.3
insect, 4, 14, 72, 158, 217–218. See also various insect species
insemination, 6, 160, 229, 231–233, 237, 251, 254, 255, 263, 273, 294, 371. See also copulation
  defined, 222
insurance, against extinction of coterie, 326
interference, with copulation, 86–87, 258–259
interment
  of black-footed ferrets and snakes, 94
  of other prairie dogs, 60
intersexual conflict of interest. See conflict of interest
intracolonial reproductive synchrony, 313–314, fig. 13.20
intracoterie reproductive synchrony, 314–316, fig. 13.21
intraspecific brood parasitism, 86–87
intromission, 231–232. See also copulation; insemination
invertebrate, 139–140, 408
investment. See parental investment
iridens trout, 365
isolated prairie dog, 88, 402
Ixodes kingi, 62. See also tick

jacana. See American jacana
jackal. See following jackal species: golden; silverbacked
jackrabbit. See white-tailed jackrabbit
Japanese macaque, 201, 346, 354, 365
Japanese monkey. See Japanese macaque
jay. See following jay species: Florida scrub; pinyon
jump-yip, 1, 24, 63, figs. 8.12, 8.13
  as an all clear signal, 181–183
  frequency vs. ward size, 85–86, fig. 5.11
  other names for, 85, 181
  in territorial interactions, 85–86, fig. 5.11
jungle fowl. See red jungle fowl
juvenile
  antipredator calling by, 164–166
  at birth, 388–390
  body mass, at first emergence, 188–191, 294–298, 362–363, 384, figs. 13.7, 13.9b, 15.2, and 16.4b
  defined, 57
  mixing of, after first emergences, 83–85, 188–191, 195, 213, 215, fig. 5.9
  survivorship of, vs. body mass of mother, 143–144, 157, 299, fig. 7.9
  survivorship of, vs. coterie size, 320–329, figs. 13.25 and 13.27
  survivorship of, vs. coterie type, 329–334, figs. 13.31 and 13.33
  survivorship of, vs. litter size and juvenile body mass, 294–298, figs. 13.6–13.8
  survivorship of, vs. parental age, 287–292, figs. 13.3 and 13.4
  survivorship of, vs. paternal care, 115, 292
  survivorship of, vs. reproductive synchrony, 316, fig. 13.22a
  survivorship of, vs. weather and precipitation, 305

Kamchatka marmot. See black-capped marmot
kangaroo, 99
karyotypes, 12
killer. See marauder
killer whale, 72
killing. See infanticide
kin discrimination. See kin recognition

kingfisher. *See* pied kingfisher
kin identification. *See* kin recognition
kin recognition, 6, 201–220, 408–410.
    See also direct social learning;
    discrimination; kinship; parent-
    offspring recognition
    vs. amicability of behavioral
        interactions, 111, 202–210, 409,
        figs. 6.10 and 10.1–10.3
    in communal nursing, 196, 409–410
    defined, 202
    vs. infanticide, 145–146, 214, 409–
        410
    in prevention of inbreeding, 213–214,
        348, 355, 408–409
kin selection. *See* inclusive fitness
kinship
    vs. antipredator calling, 2, 5, 142,
        163, 172–175, 176–178, 201, 210,
        figs. 8.7–8.9
    vs. behavioral interactions, 142, 201–
        210, figs. 10.1–10.3
    calculation of, 61
    close kin vs. more distant kin, 214–
        216
    vs. communal nursing, 142, 187,
        195–196, 198, 201, 210, table 9.2
    vs. competition, 111, 202–210, figs.
        6.10 and 10.1–10.3
    among females and yearlings of home
        coterie territory, 215, fig. 10.4
    vs. fissions of large coteries, 122,
        142, 210
    vs. infanticide, 127, 135–136, 140–
        143, 149, 159–160, 210, 214, 406–
        407, fig. 7.8, table 7.1
    between males of multi-male coterie,
        111–112
    between marauding female and
        mother of victims, 135, table 7.1
kiss, 2, 138, 193, 202, 247, fig. 10.1
    defined, 61
kittiwake, 3, 73, 87, 295, 297
knotweed, table 2.3

laboratory, and breeding of prairie dogs,
    24, 151, 153, 384
lactation. *See also* nursing
    vs. body mass, 311–312, fig. 13.10
    cost, 152, 311–313
    length, 234, 248, 390–392, fig. 16.8b
    vs. litter size, 391–392, fig. 16.10
    vs. reproductive synchrony, 316
lambsquarters, table 2.3
langur. *See following langur species:*
    hanuman; purple-faced
Lapland longspur, table 2.3
lark. *See following lark species:* horned;
    western meadowlark
lark bunting, table 2.3
larkspur. *See* Nelson's larkspur
late final submergence, of estrous
    female, 246–247
latitude, and reproductive synchrony,
    313
latrine, within burrow, 28
laughing dove, 4, 74
laughing gull, 5
lavage. *See* vaginal lavage
learning. *See* direct social learning;
    mediated social learning
lemming. *See* collared lemming
length
    of body, 1, 8
    of burrows, 26
    of tail, 8
Leptopsylla, 62. *See also* fleas
lesser earless lizard, table 2.3
lesser snow goose, 260, 313, 334, 356
Leucocrossuromys, 8
LFC. *See* licking, of front claws
lice, 62, 75, table 2.3
licking
    anal and oral, 193
    of front claws after infanticide (LFC),
        126–130, 134–135, 149, 156, 405,
        fig. 7.2b
    of genitals. *See* self-licking, of
        genitals
life tables, 393–396, tables 16.5–16.10
lifetime reproductive success (LRS),
    260–286. *See also* annual reproductive
    success
    correlation of different estimates,
        277–285, figs. 12.8 and 12.10
    vs. infanticide and coterie size, 283
    vs. longevity, 334, fig. 13.34
    for males and females, 270–272, fig.
        12.5
    methods of estimation, 65–67, 262–
        263, tables 12.1 and 12.2
    sexual asymmetry in, 270–272, fig.
        12.5

likelihood of paternity (LOP), 66–67, 262, table 12.2
lined snake, table 2.3
lion. *See* African lion
lion tamarin. *See* golden lion tamarin
litter size, at birth and before first juvenile emergence, 47, 384, 393
litter size, at first juvenile emergence
vs. age. 288–292, fig. 13.3
vs. annual reproductive success, 294–298, figs. 13.6 and 13.8
annual variation in, 378, fig. 16.2
vs. coterie size, 325, fig. 13.26
vs. gestation and lactation, 391–392, fig. 16.10
vs. juvenile body mass and juvenile survivorship, 294–298, fig. 13.6–13.8
vs. marauding, 128, 138–139, fig. 7.3
vs. parental body mass, 298–305, fig. 13.14a
after partial-litter infanticide, 138–139, fig. 7.3b
vs. reproduction in previous year, 309, fig. 13.18c
vs. sex ratio of juveniles at first emergence, 361, 364, 372, fig. 15.9, table 15.1
variation in, 378, 384, figs. 16.2b, 16.4a, 16.5
little blue heron, 5
livestock. *See* domestic livestock
livetrapping, 44–49, 253, figs. 4.7–4.9
bait used, 45
cardinal rule of, 47, fig. 4.9
description of traps, 45
disturbance from, 47–48, 69
ease at different times of year, 44
of every resident at study colony each year, 44–45, 376
mortality from, 48
as possible cause of communal nursing, 194
risks of, 48
surroundings, 45–47, fig. 4.8
trap-happy (oat-happy) individuals, 45, 253
trap-shy individuals, 48
livetraps, 45. *See also* livetrapping
for adults and juveniles, 45, figs. 4.7 and 4.8
marking of, and cardinal rule of livetrapping, 47, fig. 4.9

lizard. *See following lizard species:* lesser earless; Texas horned
local mate competition, 371
local resource competition, 371–373, figs. 15.9 and 15.10
local resource enhancement, 371–373, figs. 15.9 and 15.10
loci, polymorphic, 65
lomatium. *See* biscuitroot
longevity
of burrows, 29
of coteries, 107, fig. 6.7
of coterie territories, 117
vs. lifetime reproductive success, 334, fig. 13.34
of males, vs. inbreeding, 343
sexual asymmetry in, 1, 334, 395
longspur. *See following longspur species:* lapland; McCown's
long-tailed marmot, 34, 390
long-tailed weasel, 14, 94, 169, 406, table 2.3
LOP. *See* likelihood of paternity
lost mating opportunities, 358
louse. *See* lice
LRS. *See* lifetime reproductive success
lubricant. *See* vaginal lubricant
luck, and male reproductive success, 283

macaque, 123. *See also following macaque species:* bonnet; Japanese; pig-tailed; rhesus; stump-tailed; toque
MacDraw, 67
magpie. *See* black-billed magpie
Malaysian tree squirrel, three species of, 166, 168
male attention to estrous female, 233–237, fig. 11.8
male coalition, 108–112
male-male competition. *See* competition
male reproductive success. *See* annual reproductive success; lifetime reproductive success
male tenure, in coterie territory. *See* tenure
mallard, 24, 257, 294
Mamcynomiscus, 8
mangabey. *See* gray-cheeked mangabey
manipulation
of conspecifics, 73, 185, 410
of juvenile sex ratio, by mother, 360–375

mantled howler monkey, 4, 81
map
    of prairie dog colonies at Wind Cave
        National Park, fig. 4.3
    of study colony, fig. 4.5
marauder. *See also* infanticide
    annual reproductive success of, 148–
        149, table 7.3
    body mass of, 143–144, fig. 7.9
    characteristics of, 139
marigold. *See* prairie dog weed
marking, of burrow entrances, 57, figs.
    4.15 and 4.16
marking, of livetraps, 47, fig. 4.9
marking, of prairie dogs, 52–56
    canvas bag for, 49–52
    cubicle for, 49
    of every resident at study colony each
        year, 44–45, 376
    freeze-branding and tattooing, 56
    and molting, 56
    and Nyanzol fur dye, 52–54, figs.
        4.14 and 4.15
    permanent markers, 56
    system for, 54–55
    and vulnerability to predation, 56
marmot, 7, 8, 30, 83, 188, 199, 339. *See
    also following marmot species:* Alaska;
    alpine; black-capped; bobak; hoary;
    long-tailed; Olympic; woodchuck;
    yellow-bellied
marsh hawk. *See* northern harrier
mass. *See* body mass
matching. *See* self-referential matching
    of phenotypes
maternal behaviors, 126, 134, 147, 151,
    157
    intensity of, 250
    onset of, 248–251
maternal care, 87, 115, 157, 281, 296–
    297
    and antipredator calls, 172–175
maternal competence, 295–298
maternal reproductive success. *See*
    annual reproductive success; lifetime
    reproductive success
maternity, determination and assignment,
    59, 188, 195, 260
mating call (MC), 6, 63, 222, 236, 239–
    246, 248, 251, fig. 11.7d
    benefits of, 241–245, figs. 11.12
        through 11.14
    costs of, 241
    defined, 239, fig. 11.7d
    vs. deterrence of copulation with
        second male, 242, fig. 11.13b
    vs. estrus, 239–240
    to facilitate copying of female choice,
        242
    vs. female annual reproductive
        success, 245, fig. 11.15
    vs. female choice, 242–245
    frequency of, 239–240, fig. 11.10
    vs. induction of ovulation, 242
    intended listeners, 239
    vs. male body mass and male
        copulatory success, 242, fig. 11.12
    vs. male-male competition, 242
    for nonestrous females, 239–240
    number of, during female's estrus,
        240, fig. 11.10
    vs. order of copulating males, 242,
        fig. 11.13a
    payoffs from, 241–245, figs. 11.12
        through 11.14
    vs. promotion of reproductive
        synchrony, 242
    relative to critical underground
        consortship (CUC), 241–242
    similarity to antipredator call, 239
    vs. stage of breeding season, 243–
        245, fig. 11.14
    variation among males in tendency to
        give, 240–241, fig. 11.11
mating, random, 350, 371
mating season. *See* breeding season
mating system, 270, 272
    vs. infanticide, 404–405
mat sandbur, table 2.3
maturity. *See* sexual maturity
MC. *See* mating call
McCown's longspur, table 2.3
meadowlark. *See* western meadowlark
meadow vole, 365, 372
mechanisms, 6
    for avoidance of extreme inbreeding,
        5, 213, 337, 339–351, 408–409
    of kin recognition, 208, 210, 214, 409
    for reducing predation, 73
    for reproductive synchrony, 316
mechanism 1 (male-biased natal
    dispersal), 339–343, fig. 14.1
mechanism 2 (older males disperse away
    from daughters), 343–344, figs. 14.3
    and 14.4

mechanism 3 (yearling females defer estrus), 345–346, fig. 14.5

mechanism 4 (behavioral avoidance of inbreeding), 346–351, figs. 14.6–14.8, tables 14.3–14.5

mediated social learning, 211, 408

medium ground finch. See Darwin's medium ground finch

meerkat, 93

menopause, 289–292, fig. 13.2

methods, 42–70
  for aging, 56–57
  for assignment of paternity and determination of reproductive success, 65–67
  for comparisons with colony size and ward size, 60
  for counting of ectoparasites, 62–63
  daily routine, 57–60
  to determine amicability of behavioral interactions, 61–62
  for experiments with radionuclides, 65, 191–194
  for experiments with stuffed American badgers, 63–64, 170, fig. 8.4
  for handling, sexing, and eartagging, 49–52, figs. 4.10, 4.11, 4.12, and 4.13
  for livetrapping, 44–49, figs. 4.7, and 4.8, and 4.9
  for marking burrow entrances, 57, figs. 4.15b and 4.16
  for marking prairie dogs, 52–56, figs. 4.14 and 4.15
  for measurement of aggression, 60–61
  for monitoring field assistants, 42–44
  for statistical analyses, 67–68
  for studying antipredator calling, 63–64, 170, fig. 8.4
  time spent studying prairie dogs, 44, table 4.1

Mexican free-tailed bat, 74, 83, 84, 187

Mexican jay, 113

Mexican prairie dog, 8–24, 30, 44, table 2.2, fig. 2.2

milch goat. See domestic goat

milkvetch, table 2.3

miner. See Australian bell miner

missel thrush, 172

missing male list (MML), 222–223

mite, 22, table 2.3

mixing, of juveniles from different litters and communal nursing, 84–85, 188–191, 195, fig. 9.2
  as cost of coloniality, 83–85, 213, 215, figs. 5.9 and 9.2

MML. See missing male list

mobbing, of small predators, 73, 94–96, 217

mockingbird. See Galapágos mockingbird

moderate inbreeding, 351–355, 408–409, fig. 14.6
  defined, 338

molar attrition, to determine age, 56

mole, 13

mole rat. See naked mole rat

molting, 15, 18, 49, 56, fig. 2.5

monarch butterfly, 73

Monax, 8

Mongolian gerbil, 147, 231

mongoose. See following mongoose species: banded; dwarf

monkey. See following monkey species: black spider; brown-headed spider; Japanese; mantled howler; owl; red colobus; red howler; red-tailed; rhesus; silvered-leaf; vervet

monogamy, 361

Monte colony, 39, 126, 405, figs. 4.3 and 13.20

mortality. See also survivorship
  from bubonic plague, 74, 80, 402
  within burrows, 35
  vs. disappearance and dispersal, 263, 378–382
  from fighting, 77–78, fig. 5.4b
  of litters due to disease, genetic defects, and predation, 138
  of litters due to infanticide, 125–162
  from livetrapping, 48
  of males, vs. coterie type, 329
  sexual asymmetry in, 272, 287–288, 363, 393–396, fig. 13.1, tables 16.5–16.10

moth. See peppered moth

mound. See burrow mound

mound-building termite, 4, 217, 219

mountain bluebird, 166, table 2.3

mountain cavy, 227, 234–235, 294, 390

mountain gorilla, 157, 404–405

mountain lion, 14

mountain plover, table 2.3
mountain sheep, 207, 294
mourning dove, table 2.3
mouse, 131. *See also following mouse*
  species: cactus; California; deer; house;
  northern grasshopper; oldfield; pocket;
  spiny; white-footed
mouthparts, and movement during
  antipredator calling, 64, 166
muffled bark, 63
mule deer, 38, table 2.3
mullein, table 2.3
multi-litter groupings, and communal
  nursing, 191, 196–197, 410, fig. 9.4
multi-male coterie
  vs. coterie size, 112, 326–327, fig.
    6.11
  defined, 102, 108, fig. 6.1
  vs. kinship of males, 111–112, fig.
    6.10
  vs. male and female annual
    reproductive success, 112, 329–334,
    figs. 13.31 and 13.33
  vs. multiple paternity, 274
  vs. number of breeding males in
    colony, 113–114, fig. 6.12
  two types of, 109
multiple entrances, to burrow, 28, fig.
  3.1, fig. 3.2
multiple paternity, 66, 112, 257, 273–
  274
  defined, 257, 273
  reasons for interspecific variation,
    273–274
mummification, of underground
  carcasses, 35, fig. 3.6
murre. *See following murre species:*
  common; thick-billed
muskrat. *See* common muskrat

naked mole rat, 13, 49, 217
Nasonia wasp, 371
natal coterie territory, 339–343, fig. 14.1,
  table 14.2. *See also* coterie territory
  defined, 338
natal dispersal, 305, 339–342, fig. 14.1,
  table 14.2
  defined, 338
National Band and Tag eartags, 52
National livetraps, 45
natural conditions, 68

natural history, 13–20
natural selection, defined, 2
necropsy, 384. *See also* dissection
needle-and-thread, table 2.3
Nelson's larkspur, 356
neonates
  abandonment of, 151–153
  description of, 388–390
  maternal care of, 388–390
  reproductive value of, 198
  as victims of infanticide, 125–149,
    151–153, 155–156, 320, figs. 7.3,
    7.5, 7.10, and 7.11, table 7.2
nepotism
  vs. antipredator calls, 2, 5, 142, 163,
    172–175, 176–178, 201, 210, figs.
    8.7–8.9
  vs. behavioral interactions, 142, 201–
    210, figs. 10.1–10.3
  vs. competition, 111, 202–210, figs.
    6.10 and 10.1–10.3
  defined, 202
  differential. *See* differential nepotism
  discriminative vs. nondiscriminative,
    208, 410
  duration of, throughout year, 206
  vs. fissions of large coteries, 122,
    142, 210
  vs. kinship, 208–210, fig. 10.3
  between males of multi-male coterie,
    111–112
  as secondary consequence of
    coloniality, 402
  throughout the year, 206
nestbuilding, 1, 34, 115, 147, 151–152,
  191, 217, 221–222, 223
  by breeding male on day of
    copulation, 238–239, figs. 11.7c
    and 11.9
  by female shortly after copulation,
    250–251, fig. 11.17
nest chamber, 26, fig. 3.1
nest material, 26, 191. *See also*
  nestbuilding
  stealing of, 86–87
night monkey. *See* owl monkey
nightshade. *See following nightshade*
  species: black; cutleaf; spiny
  buffalobur
nondescendant kin. *See* kinship
nondiscriminative nepotism, 208
nonmaternally acting females, 151

northern elephant seal, 3, 5, 72, 74, 75, 83, 145, 187, 195, 246, 309, 327, 361, 363, 383
northern flying squirrel, 13, 376
northern fulmar, 277, 293, 334
northern fur seal, 360
northern gannet, 74, 295
northern goshawk, table 2.3
northern grasshopper mouse, table 2.3
northern harrier, 15, table 2.3
Norway rat, 139, 231, 281, 293
nuptial offering, 239, 253–254, 268
nursing, 115. See also lactation
    aboveground vs. underground, 188
    and competition for milk, 294
    duration of, 188, 387–388
    at night, 188
    and volume of milk dispensed, 194
nursery burrow, 2, 126, 134, 136–138, 151, 196, 372, 405, 409–410
    vs. burrow of copulation, 239
    competition for, and defense of, 35, 117, 119, 206, 319–320, fig. 7.1
    defined, 26
    diagram, fig. 3.1
    excavation of, 28, 130–134, 405, figs 7.4–7.6
Nyanzol fur dye, 52–54, figs. 4.14 and 4.15

obligate sterility, 217
observation towers, 46, 69, figs. 4.5 and 4.6
offering, nuptial. See nuptial offering
oldfield mouse, 231
olfaction, and recognition, 56
olive baboon. See savannah baboon
Olympic marmot, 26, 29, 30, 52, 60–61, 64, 87, 93, 108, 166, 168, 172, 176, 179, 188, 234–235, 305, 309, 311, 337, 397, 407
one-male coterie
    vs. coterie size, 112, fig. 6.11
    defined, 108, fig. 6.1
    vs. male and female annual reproductive success, 329–334, figs. 13.31 and 13.33
    vs. number of breeding males in colony, 113–114, fig. 6.12
onion. See wild onion
Opisocrostis, 62. See also fleas
opossum. See common opossum

orangutan, 337
order, of copulations
    vs. guarding, 228–229, 293
    vs. male annual reproductive success, 227–229, 281–283, 292–294, fig. 13.5
    vs. mating call, 242, fig. 11.13a
    vs. number of underground consortships, 229, fig. 11.5
ornate box turtle. See western box turtle
osprey, 73
ostrich, 93, 260
outbreeding, 337–359, 408–409. See also inbreeding
    defined, 338
overcrowding, vs. infanticide, 139–140
overdominance, vs. survivorship and reproductive success, 358
overgrazing, 21, 99
ovulation, induction of, 242
owl monkey, 115, 277

paleontology, 7
paper wasp, 210
parasites. See also ectoparasites; endoparasites
    and mate choice, 242, 337, 355
parasitism. See also intraspecific brood parasitism
    of antipredator calls, 181
parental care. See also maternal care; paternal care
    vs. antipredator calls, 5, 172–175
    within coteries, 115, 208
    vs. experience, 281, 313
    misdirection of, 3–4, 83–85, 87, fig. 5.9
    termination of, 263, 363
    variation in, 276, 281
parental experience, 281, 287–288, 313
parental investment, 239, 361–365
parent-offspring recognition. See also kin recognition; kinship
    and antipredator call, 5, 172–175, 407, fig. 8.8
    in behavioral interactions, 207–210
    and communal nursing, 84–85, 196
    and infanticide, 142–143, 146
    after mixing of juveniles from different litters, 84–85, 211–213, table 10.1
partial-litter infanticide, 138–139

parturition, 34, 35, 58, 59–60, 125, 138, 139, 144, 151, 156, 160, 188, 215, 234, 251, 260, 361, 363, 391
  date of, vs. date of copulation, 249, fig. 11.16
  detection of, 384–390
  in morning vs. afternoon, 390
  probability of, for adults vs. yearlings, 390, fig. 16.9
  synchrony of, 316
paternal care, 87, 115, 207–208, 253–254, 276–277. *See also* parental care
  vs. coterie type, 329
  vs. juvenile survivorship, 292, 329
  promotion of, vs. infanticide, 268
paternal half siblings, and direct social learning, 213, 409
paternal investment. *See* parental investment
paternal reproductive success. *See also* annual reproductive success; lifetime reproductive success
  vs. sex ratio of juveniles, 370–371, fig. 15.8
paternity
  confidence of, 156, 214, 268
  likelihood of (LOP), 66–67, 262, table 12.2
  determination and assignment, 65–67, 260–262, tables 12.1 and 12.2
  in multi-male coteries, 274
  multiple, 66, 273–274
  vs. order of copulations, 227–229, 281–283, 292–294, fig. 13.5
  unambiguous vs. less certain, 65–67, 261–262, table 12.2
payoffs. *See* benefits
peccary. *See* collared peccary
pedigrees
  calculation of, 61, 338
  length of, 338, 352
pelage, 1, 8, 15–18, 52, 390
pelican. *See* brown pelican
penguin. S*ee following penguin species:* Adélie; crested
penis, 49, figs. 4.11b and 4.12b
peppered moth, 358
pepperweed, table 2.3
peregrine falcon, 15, table 2.3
perianal scent glands, 2, 24, 60, fig. 4.17
periphery, and center-edge differences, 96
permanent marking, of individuals, 56

person-hours, of research, 44, 402, table 4.1
Peruvian gannet, 74
pets, 23–24, fig. 2.6
phenotypic matching. *See* self-referential matching of phenotypes
philopatry, 145, 156, 201, 337, 354, 363
  vs. age and sex, 339–345, fig. 14.1, table 14.2
phlox, table 2.3
physiological sterility, 217
pied kingfisher, 113, 201, 325, 410
pig. *See* domestic pig; wild guinea pig
pigeon. *See* wood pigeon
pigmented scrotum, 52, 160, 275, fig. 4.11
pigtailed macaque, 294
pigweed, 9, table 2.3
pika. *See* American pika
pilot whale. *See* short-finned pilot whale
pink vagina, on day of parturition, 384–390, figs. 16.6 and 16.7. *See also* vulva
pinna, 52
pinyon jay, 52, 314
pipit. *See* Sprague's pipit
plague, 74, 80, 402
plains cottontail. *See* desert cottontail
plains spadefoot toad, 128
plantain, table 2.3
play, 61, 115
pleiotropy, 287
plover. *See* mountain plover
plug. *See* copulatory plug
plugging, of burrows, 29
poaching, of prairie dogs. *See* shooting
pocket gopher, 13
pocket mouse, table 2.3
poisoning, of prairie dogs, 2, 37, 70, 356
polyandry, 361
polygyny, 361
  and annual lifetime reproductive success, 270
  defined, 272
  harem defense polygyny, 123
  and lifetime reproductive success, 272
  and sex ratio of juveniles at first emergence, 367–368, figs. 15.6 and 15.7
polymorphic loci, 65
population dynamics. *See* demography and annual variation

population size. *See also* colony size
for species, 2
population status, 2, 20
possum. *See* common opossum
potto, 337
prairie dog. *See also most other entries
in index and the following prairie dog
species:* black-tailed; Gunnison's;
Mexican; Utah; white-tailed
different species of, 8, fig. 2.1
and the ecosystem, 22
and gallstones, 23
as human food items, 23
isolated, 88, 402
and medicine, 23
other common names for, 8
and people, 20–24
as pets, 23–24
vs. ranchers, 2, 20–21
as rodents, 1, 7
as synonymous with black-tailed
prairie dog, 12, 37
prairie dog weed, 9, 14, table 2.3
prairie falcon, 15, 75, 166, fig. 2.4c
prairie rattlesnake, 14, 168
prairie vole, 277, 293, table 2.3
precipitation
vs. annual reproductive success, 305,
378
vs. litter size and coterie size, 107
predation, 14–15, 138, 196, 197
effect of dye markers on, 56
and colony size, 89
and communal nursing, 196–197
during dispersal, 337, 358–359, 380
and evolution of coloniality, 73–74,
87–99
as factor determining site of
copulation, 258–259
observations of, 89, tables 5.1 and 5.2
predators, 14–15, 75, 166, 168–169, 182,
fig. 2.3, fig. 2.4. *See also* accipiter
hawk; American badger; black-footed
ferret; bobcat; bull snake; buteo hawk;
common gray fox; Cooper's hawk;
coyote; golden eagle; grizzly bear;
human; long-tailed weasel; mountain
lion; northern harrier; peregrine falcon;
prairie falcon; prairie rattlesnake;
rattlesnake; red fox; red-tailed hawk;
snake
antipredator calls in response to, 163–
186

deterrence of, 94–96
observations of, tables 5.1 and 5.2
simulated, 63–64
pregnancy. *See* gestation
pregnancy block, 158–159
prickly pear cactus, 14, table 2.3
primary sex ratio, 360
primate, 99, 158, 233–234, 292. *See also
various species of monkeys and apes*
Pringle colony, 40, 59, 70, 130, 140,
405, figs. 4.3 and 13.20
pronghorn antelope, 21, 38, 57, 166, 205,
fig. 4.2a, table 2.3
prospective home nursery burrow, 248
protection, by dilution, 73–74, 197, 410
protective cover, 99
proteins. *See* serum proteins;
polymorphic loci
protozoan, 3, 63, table 2.3
pseudo-estrus, 233–234
pseudoscorpion, table 2.3
psychological sterility, 217
ptarmigan. *See* willow ptarmigan
pukeko, 260, 356
Pulex, 62. *See also* fleas
puma. *See* mountain lion
purple-faced langur, 157
purple martin, 74, 80
pygmy chimpanzee, 222, 231, 246

quelea, 73

r. See coefficient of genetic relatedness
rabbit. *See* European rabbit; white-tailed
jackrabbit
rabbitbrush, 14, table 2.3
raccoon dog, 277, 287
radio-collaring, to study dispersal, 380,
fig. 16.3
radionuclides, to study communal
nursing, 65, 191–194, 198–199, table
9.1
radio-telemetry. *See* radio-collaring
ragweed, table 2.3
rainfall. *See* precipitation
ranchers, 2, 20–21
random mating, 350, 371
range, 12, fig. 2.2
rank. *See* body condition; body mass;
dominance; and ranking

rank hierarchy. *See* dominance hierarchy

ranking, of colony and ward sizes, 60

raptor, 99. *See also various species of eagles, hawks, and owls*

rarity
of black-footed ferret, 20, 29, 97–99, 406
of prairie dogs, 2, 20

raspy purr, 63

rat. *See* hispid cotton rat; Norway rat

rattlesnake, 14, 406, fig. 2.4a, table 2.3. *See also* prairie rattlesnake

reciprocal altruism. *See* reciprocity

reciprocity, 201

recognition, parent-offspring. *See* parent-offspring recognition

red-cockaded woodpecker, 371

red colobus monkey, 160, 233–234

red deer, 4, 5, 73, 77, 157, 207, 242, 279, 281, 292, 309, 319, 327, 360, 361, 365, 367, 368. *See also* wapiti

red flour beetle, 281

red fox, 14, 325

red howler monkey, 4, 404–405

red jungle fowl, 246

red marmot. *See* long-tailed marmot

red squirrel, 237

red-tailed hawk, 15, 94–96, table 2.3

red-tailed monkey, 128

reduced predation, 89–99, 196–197

red vagina. *See* pink vagina

red-winged blackbird, 3, 5, 89, 275, 277, 329

relatedness. *See* kinship

reproduction
costs of, 309–313, figs. 13.18 and 13.19
when infanticide is so likely, 144
vs. reproduction in previous year, 309–313, figs. 13.18b and 13.18c
successful, defined, 309
vs. survivorship, 309, figs. 13.18a and 13.19

reproductive condition, 52, fig. 4.11

reproductive effort, terminal, 292, figs. 13.3 and 13.4

reproductive success. *See* annual reproductive success; lifetime reproductive success

reproductive synchrony
vs. age, 319, 320, figs. 13.23b and 13.24b

vs. annual reproductive success, 96, 313–320, figs. 13.20–13.24
within colonies, 96, 313–314, fig. 13.20
vs. competition for nursery burrows, 319
within coteries, 139, 314–316, fig. 13.21
defined, 316, 320
fortuitous vs. evolved, 316
vs. infanticide, 319–320
vs. latitude, 313
vs. maternal body mass, 319–320, fig. 13.23a
vs. mating call, 242
mechanisms of, 242, 316
reduction of, 315

reproductive value, 113, 179, 198, 201

resorption, of embryos, 151, 362, 390. *See also* abortion

retaliation, by mother victimized by infanticide, 136–138, 148

retaliatory copulations, 294

retina, 13

RFD. *See* rubbing of face in dirt

rhea. *See* greater rhea

rhesus macaque, 207, 211, 292, 294, 346, 367, 371

rhesus monkey. *See* rhesus macaque

rhinolophid bat, 277

ricegrass, table 2.3

Richardson's ground squirrel, 49, 60–61, 163, 166, 186, 188, 199, 201–202, 210, 211, 222, 233, 237, 239, 251, 253, 294, 298, 309, 344, 360, 376, 384–387, 390, 391, 392, 397, 407

rim crater, 30, 86, fig. 3.3, fig. 3.4

ringed seal, 287

risks. *See* costs

Ritchey cattle eartags, 57

robber fly, table 2.3

robin. *See* American robin

rock hyrax, 3

rock squirrel, 222

rods, in retina, 13

rook, 294, 309

rough-legged hawk, table 2.3

round-tailed ground squirrel, 126, 163, 164, 166, 172–173, 186, 248, 319, 360, 407

roundworm, 63, table 2.3

royal tern, 4, 83

rubbing of face in dirt, after infanticide (RFD), 126–130, 134–135, 405, fig. 7.2a
runaway
    defined, 60
    vs. ward size, 76–77, fig. 5.2
Russian thistle, table 2.3

sage. *See* sagebrush
sagebrush, 14, table 2.3
sage grouse, 242
sagewort. *See* sagebrush
salamander. *See* tiger salamander
saltbrush, table 2.3
saltgrass. *See* inland saltgrass
sample sizes, 67–68
Sanctuary colony, 40, 70, 378, fig. 4.3
sand dropseed. *See* dropseed
sandpiper. *See following sandpiper species:* spotted; western
sandwich tern, 74, 75
satin bowerbird, 279
savannah baboon, 122, 158, 207, 344, 356, 367, 371
scanning, for predators. *See* vigilance
scarlet globemallow, 9, 14, table 2.3
scars, 49, 77–78, 251, figs. 5.4 and 5.5. *See also* injuries
scat samples, 65, 191–194, fig. 9.3. *See also* fecal pellets
scelionid wasp, 371
scent glands. *See* perianal scent glands
sciurid, 13, 60, 80, 163, 166, 222, 239, 298, 360, 380, 397. *See also* squirrel
Sciuridae, 7
scolytid bark beetle, 371
scream, 63
scrotum, 160, 223, 275
    pigmented vs unpigmented, 52, fig. 4.11
scrub jay. *See* Florida scrub jay
scurfpea, table 2.3
seabirds, 72
seal. *See following seal species:* Baikal; Galápagos fur; harbor; northern elephant; northern fur; southern elephant
sea lion. *See following sea lion species:* California; Galápagos; southern
second estrus, 233–234, fig. 11.6
sedge, table 2.3

selective abandonment, of juveniles by mother, 153, 363
selfish herd effects
    vs. antipredator calling, 172, 178–179, 183
    vs. communal nursing, 197, 410
    vs. coloniality, 73, 96, 99
    vs. reproductive synchrony, 313–320
selfishness, and communal nursing, 197, 410
self-licking, of genitals, 222, 237–238, 251, 253–254, fig. 11.7b, table 11.1
self-preservation, and antipredator calls, 183–186, fig. 8.14
self-referential matching of phenotypes, 210–216, 355, 408
semen, 255–256. *See also* sperm
senescence, 287–288, figs. 13.1–13.4
sentinel, 93
serum proteins, 12
sex
    costs and benefits of, 337–338
    determination of. *See* sexing
    of victims of infanticide, 146–147, 156–157
sexing, 49–52, 397, figs. 4.11 and 4.12
sex ratio, of juveniles at first emergence
    vs. age, body mass, and rank of mother, 364–369, 408, figs. 15.5–15.7
    vs. age of father, 367, fig. 15.5
    and allocation of parental resources, 360–365
    annual variation in, 362, fig. 15.1
    vs. coterie size, 373, fig. 15.10
    defined, 360
    vs. female kin in home coterie, 373, fig. 15.10
    frequency-dependent, 360–361
    of juveniles before first juvenile emergence, 47
    of juveniles that survive infanticide, 146–147, 156–157
    lack of evidence for adaptive maternal adjustment, 6, 408
    vs. litter size, 361, 364, 372, fig. 15.9, table 15.1
    vs. local mate competition, 371, 408
    vs. local resource competition, 371–373, 408, figs. 15.9 and 15.10
    vs. local resource enhancement, 371–373, 408, figs. 15.9 and 15.10

vs. maternal dominance, 367, 408
observed vs. expected, 364, table
    15.1
overall, 362
vs. parental investment, 361–365
vs. paternal copulatory and siring
    success, 370–371, 408, fig. 15.8
primary, 360
and sex-biased juvenile mortality,
    363
vs. sex ratio of adults and yearlings
    in colony, 365, 408, fig. 15.3
vs. sex ratio of adults and yearlings
    in coterie, 365, fig. 15.4
and termination of parental care, 363
sexual asymmetry. *See also* sexual
    dimorphism
    in age of first copulation, 288–289,
        397, fig. 13.2
    in annual reproductive success, 263–
        270, fig. 12.2
    in antipredator calling, 170–171, 172,
        figs. 8.7 and 8.8
    in body mass of adults, 1, 397–401,
        fig. 16.12
    in body mass of juveniles, 362–363,
        fig. 15.2
    in breeding dispersal, 343–344, fig.
        14.4
    in delay of sexual maturation, 397,
        fig. 16.11b
    in dispersal, 1, 105, 135, 172, 363,
        339–344, 380–383, figs. 14.1–14.4,
        table 14.2
    in execution of infanticide, 404–405
    in lifetime reproductive success, 270–
        272, fig. 12.5
    in longevity, 1, 334, 395
    in mortality of pre-emergent
        juveniles, 363
    in natal dispersal, 339–343, fig. 14.1
    in probability of copulation, 288–289,
        fig. 13.2
    in production of emergent juveniles,
        397, fig. 16.11a
    in sexual maturation, 288–289, 397,
        fig. 13.2
    in survivorship, 272, 287–288, 363,
        393–396, fig. 13.1, tables 16.5–
        16.10
sexual bias. *See* sexual asymmetry

sexual dimorphism, in body mass
    of adults and yearlings, 1, 397–401,
        fig. 16.12
    of juveniles, 362–363, fig. 15.2
sexual inactivity, of adult males, 67, 108,
    112, 160, 275–276
sexual maturity
    age of first copulation, 288–289,
        342–343, 345, 397, figs. 13.2 and
        14.2
    delayed, 397, fig. 16.11b
    sexual asymmetry in, 288–289, 397,
        fig. 13.2
sexual reproduction, costs and benefits,
    337–338
sexuality. *See* sexual reproduction
sexually transmitted diseases, 238
sexy sons, 370
sharing, of burrows, 34–35, 96, 403
sharp-shinned hawk, table 2.3
sharp-tailed grouse, table 2.3
sheep. *See following sheep species:*
    domestic; mountain
shelduck, 75
shooting, of prairie dogs, 2, 20–21, 37,
    70, 356
shortage, of suitable habitat
    and coterie size, 325–326
    as factor promoting coloniality, 72,
        87–88
short-finned pilot whale, 292
short-horned grasshopper, 14, table 2.3
significance, levels of, 67–68
silverbacked jackal, 217
silvered-leaf monkey, 160
SIRAM (sexually inactive resident adult
    male), 160
sit-and-wait tactic, 69
size. *See* body mass; colony size; coterie
    size
skeleton weed, table 2.3
sleeping, 26, 30–33
smoke bombs, used in excavation, 131
smooth newt, 315
snake, 14, 29, 35, 94, 168, 182. *See also*
    following snake species: adder; bull
    snake; lined; prairie rattlesnake;
    rattlesnake; western hognose
    and antisnake call, 168
snarl, 63
sniffing, of perianal glands, 2, 60–61,
    193, 234–235, 247, fig. 11.7a

snowberry, table 2.3
snow goose. *See* lesser snow goose
social behavior, reasons for, 4
social facilitation of foraging, 72–73,
    88–89
social learning, 159, 211. *See also* direct
    social learning; mediated social
    learning
sociological sterility, 217
solicitation, of breeding male by estrous
    female, 225, 229, 247
solitary prairie dog, 88, 402
song. *See* jump-yip
song-bark. *See* jump-yip
sonogram
    of antipredator calls, 164, fig. 8.1
    of jump-yip (all clear or territorial)
        calls, 181, fig. 8.13
Sonoma chipmunk, 163, 176, 407
sooty tern, 3, 74, 145
sorrel, table 2.3
southern elephant seal, 3, 5, 74
southern flying squirrel, 13, 376
southern green stinkbug, 365
southern sea lion, 89
sparrow. *See* white-crowned sparrow
sparrowhawk. *See* European
    sparrowhawk
spearnose bat. *See* greater spearnose bat
sperm. *See also* semen
    depletion of, 315
    from vaginal lavage, 255–256, fig.
        11.20
Spermophilus, 8
spider monkey. *See following spider
    monkey species:* black; brown-headed
spiny mouse, 211
spiny buffalobur nightshade, table 2.3
spiny-headed worm, 63, table 2.3
splendid fairy-wren, 218, 334, 356
spoonbill, 315
spotted hyena, 3, 49, 72, 77, 123, 201
spotted sandpiper, 277
Sprague's pipit, table 2.3
spurge, table 2.3
squirrel, 7, 62, 77, 80, 125, 152, 376,
    table 2.1. *See also* sciurid *and the
    following:* chipmunk; flying squirrel;
    ground squirrel; marmot; prairie dog;
    tree squirrel
squit-tuck. *See* antipredator call
starling, 3, 73, 295
statistics, 67–68

stealing
    of milk from unwilling foster mother,
        195
    of nest material, 86–87
steppe marmot. *See* bobak marmot
sterility, 4, 217
stickseed, table 2.3
stickweed. *See* stickseed
stinkbug. *See* southern green stinkbug
stomach analysis, 14
stripe-backed wren, 218, 260
study colony
    accessibility of, 40, 42
    aerial photograph of, fig. 4.4a
    colony size and colony density, 40,
        70, 139–140, 359, 376–378, 394,
        fig. 16.1, table 16.1
    description, 40–42, figs. 4.4 and 4.5
    invisibility of, 42
    map of, fig. 4.5
    number of burrow entrances, 42
    observation towers, 42
    physical area, 40
    and possible overcrowding, 139–140
    possible problems with, 68–70
    shooting and poisoning, 2, 37, 70
    stable population size, 40, 70, 139–
        140, 359, 376–378, 394, fig. 16.1,
        table 16.1
study sites, 37–42
study ward, 40. *See also* study colony
stump-tailed macaque, 87
subcolony. *See* ward
submergence, into burrow
    vs. antipredator call and self-
        preservation, 183, fig. 8.14b
    after collecting nest material, 223,
        238–239, 250–251
    to cool off in hot weather, 13, 28
    for copulation, 13, 222–234
    final, at end of day. *See* final
        submergence at end of day
    in inclement weather, 13, 223, 257,
        388
    for infanticide, 13
    for nursing, 13, 188, 387–390
    in response to predators, 168, 223,
        figs. 5.16 and 8.3
    to warm up or dry off in cold
        weather, 28, 257, 388
successful reproduction, defined, 309
sucking lice. *See* lice
suckling. *See* nursing

summer cypress, table 2.3
superb blue fairy-wren, 325
surroundings, of livetraps, 45–47, fig. 4.8
survivorship. *See also* mortality
    of adults and juveniles, vs. coterie size, 324, fig. 13.27
    vs. age, 287–288, fig. 13.1
    vs. body mass, 294–297, 305, fig. 13.7
    vs. coterie type, 329–334, figs. 13.31–13.33
    vs. heterozygosity, 358
    of juveniles, vs. body mass of mother, 143–144, 157, 299, fig. 7.9
    of juveniles, vs. litter size and juvenile mass, 294–298, figs. 13.7 and 13.8
    of juveniles, vs. parental age, 287–292, figs. 13.3 and 13.4
    of juveniles, vs. paternal care, 115, 292
    of juveniles, vs. reproductive synchrony, 316, fig. 13.22a
    and life tables, 393–396, tables 16.5–16.10
    vs. reproduction in previous year, 309, fig. 13.18a
    sexual asymmetry in, 272, 287–288, 363, 393–396, fig. 13.1, tables 16.5–16.10
    vs. weather and precipitation, 305, 378, 380
susceptibility, to predation and infanticide. *See* vulnerability
sustenance, from cannibalism
    for infanticidal males, 158, 405
    for marauding females, 143, 147–148, 405, 410
Swainson's hawk, table 2.3
swallow. *See following swallow species:* bank; barn; cliff
sweat bee, 210
swift. *See following swift species:* alpine; common
swift fox, table 2.3
switching, of burrows during night, 31–34, 247
sylvatic plague, 74, 80, 402
synchrony
    of final submergence at end of day, 59, 246–247
    of first emergence in the morning, 58–59
    of reproduction. *See* reproductive synchrony
SYSTAT, 67

tail
    color, 8
    flaring of, 2, 60, fig. 5.3
    length, 8
tamarin. *See* golden lion tamarin
tapeworm, 63, table 2.3
tarsier. *See* western tarsier
tassel-eared squirrel, 237, 239
tattooing, 56
taxonomy, 7–13, table 2.1
teeth
    chattering of, 2, 60, 63
    for determination of age, 56
temperature
    within burrows, 28
    and diurnal submergence, 13
    daily, at Wind Cave National Park, 188, 257
tenure, of breeding male in coterie territory, 329, 343–344, fig. 14.3
terminal reproductive effort, 292, fig. 13.3 and 13.4
termination, of parental care, 263, 362–363
termite. *See* mound-building termite
tern. *See following tern species:* arctic; common; crested; royal; sandwich; sooty
territorial call, 85–86, fig. 5.11. *See also* jump-yip
territorial dispute, 2, 4, 61, 115, 119, 183, 202
    defined, 60, fig. 5.3
    duration of, 2, 77, fig. 5.3
    vs. ward size, 76–79, fig. 5.2
territoriality
    of coteries, 1, 119, 123
    of pregnant and lactating females, 2, 35, 126, 134, 136–138, 151, fig. 7.1
territory. *See* coterie territory
testes, 160, 223, 275
    descended vs. undescended (scrotal vs. nonscrotal), 52, fig. 4.11
Texas horned lizard, table 2.3
thermoregulation, 28, 34, 403
thick-billed murre, 83

thick-tailed bushbaby, 371

thick-tailed galago. *See* thick-tailed bushbaby

thirteen-lined ground squirrel, 28, 156, 163, 164, 166, 176, 211, 237, 251, 253, 257, 273, 293, 319, table 2.3

thistle, 14, table 2.3. *See also* Russian thistle

Thomson's gazelle, 4, 81

threeawn, 14, table 2.3

thrush. *See* missel thrush

tick, 62, 80–81, table 2.3

tic-uhl. *See* antipredator call

tiger salamander, 358, table 2.3

time, spent studying prairie dogs, 44, table 4.1

time-specific life table, 393–394, tables 16.5 and 16.6

timing
    of adult and juvenile disappearances, 378–382, tables 16.2 and 16.3
    of copulations vs. reproductive synchrony, 313–320
    of copulations vs. time of day, 225, fig. 11.2
    of dispersal, 153, 263, 339, 355, 380–382, 404–405, figs. 14.1 and 14.2
    of estrus, 205, 313
    of first, last, and critical underground consortships, 225, fig. 11.2

tit. *See following tit species:* blue; great

toad, table 2.3

toilet, within burrow, 28

Tomahawk livetraps, 45

tooth. *See* teeth

tooth chatter, 2, 60, 63

toque macaque, 292

tower. *See* observation tower

town, 13

Townsend's big-eared bat, 80

trails, between burrows, 26

transfer
    of juveniles by researcher, 211–213, table 10.1
    of juveniles by mother, 47, 83–85, 188–191, 194, 195, fig. 5.10

transmission, of diseases and ectoparasites, 80–82

tree squirrel, 7. *See also following tree squirrel species:* Douglas's; fox; gray; Malaysian #1; Malaysian #2; Malaysian #3; red; tassel-eared

tricolored blackbird, 89, 314

trout. *See* iridens trout

tumblegrass, table 2.3

turtle. *See* western box turtle

Type I infanticide (by lactating females), 125–149, fig. 7.3

Type II infanticide (by female immigrants), 150–151

Type III infanticide (by females that abandon their litters), 138, 151–153, 159

Type IV infanticide (by invading males), 153–160, 214, figs. 7.11 and 7.12, table 7.4

UC. *See* underground consortship

Uinta ground squirrel, 126, 166, 222, 248, 287, 298, 376, 380, 407

underground consortship (UC), 221–234
    all-day, 232–233, fig. 11.1a
    vs. critical underground consortship (CUC), 225
    defined, 223
    duration of, 223
    vs. insemination, 225–232
    number per estrus, 223, fig. 11.1a
    number of burrow entrances used, 225, fig. 11.1b
    number vs. order of copulating males, 229, fig. 11.5
    vs. time of day for first, last, and critical, 225, fig. 11.2
    ultimate, 229

underground ventilation, 5, 31, fig. 3.5

ungulate, 99. *See also various species of ungulates*

uniqueness
    of burrow entrances, 26, 30
    of critical underground consortship, 225–229
    of diagnostic behaviors associated with infanticide, 128–130, 149, 405
    of eartags and dye markings, 52–55, figs. 4.14–4.15
    of female vocalization during aboveground copulation, 246, 251
    of kin-directed infanticide, 149–150
    of mating call, 6, 239
    of opportunities in colonies for predatory specialists, 75
    of prairie dog social behavior, 5, 261, 351

of rim craters, 30
of vegetation within colonies, 9
unusual behaviors
    of individuals that copulate, 247–248
    of mother, on day of parturition, 387–388
unusual circumstances, that affect dispersal of females, table 14.2
unused suitable habitat, 87–88
urgency of attack, vs. antipredator calling, 166–168
urine, 193
Utah prairie dog, 8–24, 44, 74, 411, table 2.2, fig. 2.2

vagina, 390. *See also* vulva
    pink vs. white, 384–390, figs. 16.6 and 16.7
vaginal lavage, after copulation, 255–256, fig. 11.20
vaginal lubricant, 256
value. *See* reproductive value
vampire bat. *See* common vampire bat
variance. *See* sexual asymmetry
variation. *See also* annual variation; sexual asymmetry
    in antipredator calling, 170–171, figs. 8.1 and 8.6
    in colony size and colony composition, 376–378, fig. 16.1, table 16.1
    in coterie size, 1, 105–107, figs. 6.5 and 6.6
    in ejaculates, 281
    in jump-yip, 168, 182–183, fig. 8.13
    in litter size, 384, figs. 16.4a and 16.5
    in maternal behaviors, 250–251
    in mating call, 240–241, figs. 11.10 and 11.11
    in parental care, 276, 281
    in quality of coterie territories, 297
    in tendency to commit infanticide, 139, 152
    in vulnerability to infanticide, 139, 144
vegetation
    clipping, 1, 9, 86, 88, 99, fig. 5.18, table 2.3
    height within colonies, 1, 9
    uniqueness within colonies, 9

ventilation. *See* underground ventilation
ventriloquism, of antipredator call, 172
verbena, table 2.3
vervet monkey, 93, 207, 222, 268, 279, 334, 349, 371
vespertilionid bat, 277
victimized juveniles, characteristics of, 139
victimized mother
    body mass of, 143–144, fig. 7.9
    characteristics of, 139
vigilance, 403, fig. 4.16
    vs. auto- and allogrooming, 81
    and center-edge differences, 96
    vs. colony and ward size, 93–94, figs. 5.15 and 5.16
    decreased, as secondary benefit of coloniality, 403
    postures of, fig. 5.16
    and sentinels, 93
village, 13
visual alarm, 63, 91–93, figs. 5.13 and 5.14
visual conspicuousness, 75, 85–86, fig. 5.11
vocal alarm. *See* antipredator call
vocal conspicuousness, 75, 85–86
vocalizations, 63
    all clear call, 181–183, figs. 8.12 and 8.13. *See also* jump-yip
    antipredator call, 2, 5, 63
    chuckle, 63
    during copulation, 246, 251
    defense bark, 63
    disputing churr, 63
    growl, 63
    jump-yip, 1, 63
    mating call, 63, 239–246. *See also* mating call
    muffled bark, 63
    raspy purr, 63
    scream, 63
    snarl, 63
    for taxonomic identification, 12
    territorial call, 85–86, fig. 5.11. *See also* all clear call; jump-yip
    tooth chatter, 2, 60, 63
vole. *See following vole species:* gray-tailed; meadow; prairie; water
volume, of milk dispensed during nursing, 194

vulnerability
    of antipredator callers, 171–172
    of coterie territory to invasion by
        strange male, 113
    of dispersing individuals to predation,
        337, 358–359, 380
    of juveniles to infanticide, vs.
        reproductive synchrony, 319–320
    of juveniles to predation, 175–176
    of different mothers to infanticide,
        139, 144
vulva, 49, figs. 4.11a and 4.12a. *See also*
    pink vagina
    examination of, before and after
        copulation, 253–255, figs. 11.18
        and 11.19

wandering albatross, 5
wapiti, 38, 57, table 2.3. *See also* red
    deer
ward, 13, 76, 169, 211
ward density, 97, fig. 5.17b. *See also*
    ward size
ward size. *See also* colony size
    and antipredator callers, 89–92, fig.
        5.13
    vs. increased aggression, 75, 76–79,
        fig. 5.2
    vs. increased auto- and allogrooming,
        81–83, fig. 5.8
    vs. increased awareness of predators,
        89–94, fig. 5.13
    vs. increased visual conspicuousness,
        85–86
    vs. increased vocal conspicuousness,
        85–86, fig. 5.11
    vs. individual alertness, 93–94, fig.
        5.15
    ranking of, 60
    vs. vigilance, 93–94, fig. 5.15
    vs. visual alarmers, 89–92, figs. 5.13
        and 5.14
    vs. ward size of white-tailed prairie
        dogs, 97, fig. 5.17a
wariness. *See* vigilance
warning bark. *See* antipredator call
wasp. *See following wasp species:*
    agaontid fig; nasonia; paper;
    pteromalid; scelionid
water vole, 233–234

weaning, 88, 188, 192–193, 390–392.
    See also lactation
weasel. *See* long-tailed weasel
weather
    vs. annual reproductive success, 305,
        378, 380
    vs. communal nursing, 188–189
    effect on coterie size, 107
    effect on behavioral observations,
        257–258
    vs. onset of estrus, 257–258
    at Wind Cave National Park, 13, 107,
        188, 257–258, 305, 378, 380
wee-oo call. *See* jump-yip
weight. *See* body mass
Westermarck effect, 213–214
western box turtle, table 2.3
western hognose snake, table 2.3
western meadowlark, 166, table 2.3
western sandpiper, 115
western tarsier, 337
whale. *See following whale species:* false
    killer; humpback; killer; short-finned
    pilot
wheatgrass, 14, table 2.3
whistles, of ground squirrels, 166
white-crowned sparrow, 356
white-footed mouse, 52, 145, 147, 208,
    210, 231, 295, 345, 404–405
white-fronted bee-eater, 149, 325, 410
white-nosed coati, 93, 187
white-tail. *See* white-tailed prairie dog
white-tailed deer, 358, 365, 372
white-tailed jackrabbit, table 2.3
white-tailed prairie dog, 8–24, 44, 74,
    76, 166, 199, 225, 239, 258, table 2.2,
    figs. 2.lb, 2.2, and 4.10b
    benefits of coloniality, 96–97
    and black-footed ferrets, 97–99
    costs of coloniality, 96–97
    protective cover within colonies, 99
    ward size and ward density, 97, fig.
        5.17
white-winged chough, 313
whole-litter infanticide, vs. partial-litter
    infanticide, 138–139
wild dog. *See* African wild dog
wild guinea pig, 87, 227, 229, 231, 253,
    294
wild horse, 5, 108, 158, 383. *See also*
    domestic horse

wild onion, table 2.3
wild rodent plague, 74, 80, 402
wildebeest, 3, 313
willow ptarmigan, 115
Wind Cave National Park, 14, 15, 37–42,
    44, 68–70, 88, 126, 131, 134, 221, 313,
    371, 405–406, fig. 4.1
    density of predators, 69
    physical area, 69
    weather, 13, 107, 188, 257–258, 305,
        378, 380
winterfat, table 2.3
wiregrass. See threeawn
wolf. See gray wolf
woodchuck, 23, 81, 311
woodpecker. See following woodpecker
    species: acorn; red-cockaded
wood pigeon, 96
worker. See alloparenting
work schedule, 57
worm. See following worm species:
    cutworm; roundworm; spiny-headed
    worm; tapeworm
wounds. See injuries
wren. See following wren species: house;
    superb blue fairy-wren; splendid fairy-
    wren; stripe-backed

yearling
    defined, 57
    percentage that copulate, vs.
        reproductive synchrony, 319–320,
        figs. 13.23b and 13.24b
    probability of copulation, 223, 288,
        342–343, 345, 397, figs. 13.2 and
        14.2
    reproductive success, 287–292, 298–
        305, figs. 13.2–13.4, 13.12, 13.13,
        13.15, and 13.16
yellow baboon. See savannah baboon
yellow-bellied marmot, 5, 26, 28, 29, 30,
    58, 64, 69, 76, 93, 96, 108, 112, 166,
    199, 201–202, 260, 273, 275, 305, 309,
    312, 327, 329, 337, 345, 356, 358, 360,
    365, 376, 380, 397
yellow-headed blackbird, 363
yellow-toothed cavy, 87, 294
yelp. See jump-yip

zebra. See Burchell's zebra